Fishes

Fishes
An Introduction to Ichthyology
THIRD EDITION

Peter B. Moyle
Joseph J. Cech, Jr.

Department of Wildlife, Fish, and Conservation Biology
University of California, Davis

Prentice Hall, Upper Saddle River, New Jersey 07458

Library of Congress Cataloging-in-Publication Data
Moyle, Peter B.
  Fishes : an introduction to ichthyology / Peter B. Moyle, Joseph J. Cech, Jr. — 3rd ed.
  p. cm.
  Includes bibliographical references and index.
  ISBN 0–13–372996–6
  1. Fishes. 2. Ichthyology. I. Cech, Joseph J. II. Title.
QL615.M64   1996
597—dc20
                                                                    95–9637
                                                                       CIP

Senior editor: Sheri L. Snavely
Editorial/production service: Electronic Publishing Services Inc.
Manufacturing buyer: Trudy Pisciotti
Cover design: Bruce Kenselaar
Cover photograph: National Geographic Society

 © 1996, 1988, 1982 by Prentice-Hall, Inc.
Simon & Schuster/A Viacom Company
Upper Saddle River, New Jersey 07458

Printed in the United States of America

10 9 8 7 6 5 4 3

ISBN 0-13-372996-6

Prentice-Hall International [UK] Limited, *London*
Prentice-Hall of Australia, Pty. Limited, *Sydney*
Prentice-Hall Canada Inc., *Toronto*
Prentice Hall Hispanoamericana, S.A., *Mexico*
Prentice-Hall of India Private Limited, *New Delhi*
Prentice-Hall of Japan, Inc., *Tokyo*
Simon & Schuster Asia Pte. Ltd., *Singapore*
Editora Prentice-Hall do Brasil, Ltda., *Rio de Janeiro*

CONTENTS

22   Opahs, Squirrelfish, Dories, Pipefish, and Sculpins   298

23   Perciformes: Snooks to Snakeheads   314

24   Flounders, Puffers, and Molas   339

PART IV
Zoogeography   347

PART V
Ecology   383

PREFACE

The emphasis of ichthyology has traditionally been on the systematics, anatomy, and distribution of fishes. Most of the historically prominent names associated with the field have made their major contributions in these areas. Today, however, most people who study fish have interests that extend beyond the traditional areas. They study fish to find ways to improve fisheries or aquaculture, to determine the effects of human activities on aquatic environments, and to test ideas in rapidly developing fields such as ecology, physiology, behavior, and evolution. There are also growing numbers of sophisticated amateur ichthyologists who desire to increase their understanding of the fish they keep in aquaria or those they pursue with hook and line. Regardless of why fish are studied, those studying them still need the basic vocabulary and understanding of fish biology provided by the traditional areas of emphasis. The purpose of this book, therefore, is to provide that basic background but also to integrate it with recent developments in other areas and to provide some feeling for the excitement being engendered by recent research on fishes.

In large part this book is designed to serve as a text in classes on fish biology. The large number of chapters and the numerous cross references within chapters are meant to provide instructors of such courses with flexibility in assigning readings in the text. We have assumed that the book will be used in conjunction with a laboratory manual of fish anatomy (of which there are many), keys to fishes, and perhaps a collection of other readings (such as Love and Cailliet 1979). The students we had in mind while writing were junior- and senior-level university students. However, we also hope that this book will prove to be a useful and palatable summary of recent developments in ichthyology for individuals who have been away from the college classroom for some time or for anyone else who needs an introduction to the most numerous, diverse, and fascinating of all vertebrate groups.

This book would not have been possible without the encouragement and help of many people. Initial stimulation and support in fish biology in academia was provided by John B. Moyle, Evelyn W. Moyle, and James C. Underhill (to P.B.M.)

and by Donald E. Wohlschlog (to J.J.C.). Gary D. Grossman, Donald M. Baltz, and Robert A. Daniels were especially helpful in providing references, discussion, and criticisms of many of the first versions of these chapters. Numerous graduate and undergraduate students contributed valuable comments on various chapters and/or helped to keep our research programs going while we devoted time to writing. We benefited from discussions with Jeff Graham, Fred White, Hiram Li, Ken Gobalet, Dave Randall, Mikko Nikinmaa, George V. Lauder, Laurie Sanderson, and Serge Doroshov. The reviews of selected chapters in previous editions by Eugene Balon, Michael Bell, David Ehrenfeld, Dale Lott, John Radovich, Arnold Sillman, Randolph Smith, and Paul Webb are appreciated, as are comments by Bruce Herbold, Alfred Ebeling, Mark Hixon, and Frank J. Schwartz. We particularly appreciate B. Herbold's corrections of backward quotation marks and M. Hixon's pointing out that we forgot to mention the humuhumunukunukua-puaa. For this edition, we appreciate the many comments and criticisms by users of the book, but especially Brooks Burr, Barbara Block, Kurt Fausch, Ronald Frizsche, Malcolm Gordon, Paul James, Douglas Markle, John McEachran, Lawrence Page, Theodore Pietsch, Howard Reisman, Jerry J. Smith, Timothy Tricas, and Linda A. Ward. Comments by Ronald M. Yoshiyama substantially improved the ecology chapters. Sheri Snavely of Prentice-Hall provided encouragement despite our numerous delays and procrastinations. Leonard J. Compagno and Tim M. Berra kindly shared with us their photographs of curious fishes. Marjorie Kirkman and Brenda Nakamoto assisted us in many ways but especially by keeping the departmental office running efficiently, making it much easier to accomplish our regular duties while the book was in progress. Finally, we are exceedingly grateful to our wives, Marilyn Moyle and Mary Cech, for permitting our marriages to survive and even grow stronger during the many hours over the years we have worked on fish, and to our now-grown children, Petrea and Noah Moyle and Scott and Gregor Cech, for continuing to regard us with a bemused sense of tolerance.

The following reviewers were generous in their consideration of our manuscript: Brooks M. Burr, *Southern Illinois University*; Kurt D. Fausch, *Colorado State University*; Ronald A. Fritzsche, *Humboldt State University*; Malcolm S. Gordon, *University of California, Los Angeles*; Douglas F. Markle, *Oregon State University*; John D. McEachran, *Texas A & M University*; Douglas B. Noltie, *University of Missouri, Columbia*; Jerry J. Smith, *San Jose State University*; Theodore W. Pietsch, *University of Washington*; Howard M. Reisman, *Southampton College*; Timothy C. Tricas, *Florida Institute of Technology*. We want to thank them for their helpful suggestions.

Peter B. Moyle
Joseph J. Cech, Jr.

Fishes

PART I
INTRODUCTION

CHAPTER **1**

Introduction

MODERN FISHES

The fishes are the most numerous and diverse of the major vertebrate groups. They dominate the waters of the world through a marvelous variety of morphological, physiological, and behavioral adaptations. Their diversity is reflected in the large number of living species: Over 24,600 have been described so far, and the number may eventually increase to around 28,500 (Nelson 1994). Fish occupy an extraordinary array of habitats. They can be found thriving in vernal pools, intermittent streams, tiny desert springs, the vast reaches of the open oceans, deep oceanic trenches, cold mountain streams, saline coastal embayments, and so on through a nearly endless list of aquatic environments.

Modern fishes (and vertebrates in general) consist of three major lines that have been going their own evolutionary ways for at least 400 million years (Fig. 1.1). The line with the most ancestral[1] characteristics (Myxini) is that of the hagfishes (Myxiniformes, 40+ species), which arguably are not even vertebrates. They may represent, however, the line that did give rise to the vertebrates. The first unquestioned vertebrates are part of an evolutionary line (Cephalaspidomorpha) that is repre-

---

[1]The terms "ancestral" and "derived" are used throughout this book instead of the more traditional "primitive" and "advanced" to avoid connotations of "inferior" and "superior," respectively.

sented in the modern fauna by lampreys (Petromyzontiformes, 40+ species). Their heyday was 350 to 500 million years ago when the armored ostracoderms swam the seas. However, these jawless forms presumably did give rise to the jawed vertebrates (Gnathostomata), the line of vertebrates that dominates our planet today. The jawed fishes divided into three distinct lines early in their evolution: the now-extinct placoderms (Placodermi), the cartilaginous fishes (Chondrichthyes), and the bony fishes (Osteichthyes). The aberrant line of bony fishes that decided to leave the water and invade land became the modern tetrapods.

The cartilaginous fishes split into two distinct lines early in their history: the sharks and rays (Elasmobranchi), and the ratfishes and chimaeras (Holocephali). There are over 800 living species of sharks and rays and about 30 species of chimaeras and ratfishes. The bony fishes also split into a number of evolutionary lines early in their history, although the exact nature of these lines is being debated. The major lines of bony fishes represented in the modern fauna are the lungfishes (Dipnoi, 6 species); the coelacanths (Coelacanthiformes, 1 species); and the ray-finned fishes (Actinopterygii). Living ray-finned fishes represent two distinct lines. The Chondrostei (bichirs, sturgeons, and paddlefishes, 36 species) have many ancestral characteristics and are the specialized survivors of the earliest bony fish groups. The Neopterygii are the rest of the 22,000+ known species of modern bony fishes.

It might be expected that most of this diversity of fishes would be contained in the oceans, because salt water covers over 70% of the surface of the earth, while fresh water covers only about 1%. By volume, 97% of all water is in the oceans, and 0.0093% is in freshwater lakes and streams (the remainder is in ice, atmospheric water, etc.) (Horn 1972). Surprisingly, only 58% of modern fish species are marine, while 41% are freshwater inhabitants and 1% move on a regular basis between the two environments (Cohen 1970). The large number of species of freshwater fish is a reflection of the ease with which fish populations in landlocked waters become isolated from each other and thus have the opportunity to evolve into new species. The chances that populations will become isolated are increased by the fact that most freshwater fishes are incapable of entering salt water, even for brief periods of time.

While the freshwater habitat consists largely of thousands of distinct "islands" of water in a sea of land, most of the saltwater habitat consists of open ocean, which is rather unproductive and lighted only in the surface layer. Only 13% of all fish species are associated with the open ocean: 1% in the surface layer (epipelagic fishes); 5% in the unlighted sections of the water column (deepwater pelagic fishes); and 7% on the bottom (deepwater benthic fishes). A majority (78%) of marine fish species (making up 44% of all fishes) live in the narrow band of water less than 200 m deep along the margins of land masses. An additional factor affecting the number of fish species found in an area is the annual temperature regime. In both fresh and salt water, a majority of the species are found in warmer environments where annual temperature fluctuations are minimal.

Despite the diversity of fish habitats and the diversity of adaptations enabling fish to live in these habitats, most fish are readily recognizable as fish. The reason for this is that the physical and chemical characteristics of water impose a number of constraints on the functional design of fish. Most of the characteristics we

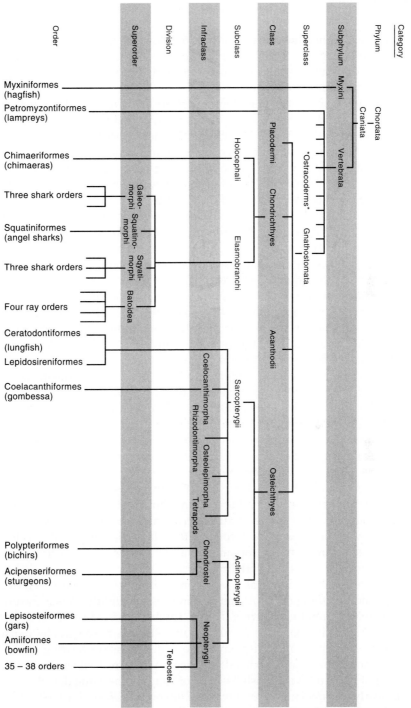

FIGURE 1.1 *A hierarchical classification of the major groups of fishes, showing presumed evolutionary relationships. Modified from Nelson 1984; copyright © 1984 by John Wiley and Sons and used with their permission.*

recognize as fishlike are adaptations to allow the most efficient use of the aquatic medium by mobile vertebrate predators. The characteristics of water exerting the greatest influence on fish design are its density, low compressibility, properties as a solvent, and transparency.

Water is about 800 times denser than air. This greatly reduces the effects of gravity on fish and enables them to remain suspended in the water column with little effort compared to the effort required by most birds to stay airborne. In fact, most fish are neutrally buoyant, so virtually all muscular effort can be devoted to movement and little is wasted on counteracting the pull of gravity. In addition, more thrust can be obtained by pushing against water than against air, as the futile flapping of a fish on land demonstrates. On the other hand, the high density of water means that it resists movement through it. Fish typically solve this problem by being streamlined to lower the resistance of the water to their swimming; by having a high proportion of their bodies devoted to the muscles needed for forward motion; and by having efficient means of shoving the body and tail fin against the water column to thrust themselves forward.

The resistance of water to motion is the result not only of its density but also of its virtual incompressibility. Movement through air is made considerably easier by the fact that air compresses slightly along bodies moving through it, flows by smoothly, and so does not have to be completely displaced. Water, in contrast, literally has to be pushed out of the way by organisms moving through it. This creates turbulence along the sides and in the wake of the organism and increases further the drag of the water. While the incompressibility of water creates problems for fish, they are also able to take advantage of it. Each fish has an extremely sensitive sensory system, the lateral-line system, that can detect small amounts of turbulence and water displacement created either by its own motion or by the motion of other organisms or objects. Using this system, fish can detect nearby stationary objects, other fish, and food organisms. The lateral-line system is particularly useful when visual cues are lacking. Fish (mainly teleosts) also use the incompressibility of water to help them in eating and breathing. Quick expansion of the mouth and gill chambers allows water to rush in, carrying food and oxygen into the chambers along with the water. This "pipette effect" is particularly well developed in fishes that feed on small, mobile organisms, and it results in jaw structures very different from those of terrestrial vertebrates.

While water behaves as if incompressible for the purposes of movement, feeding, and breathing of fish, it can be compressed slightly. This is fortunate, because it enables sound to be carried. In fact, sound is carried farther and faster in water than it is in air (1433 m/s versus 335 m/s) thanks to the greater density of water. As a consequence, most fish have an excellent sense of hearing, even though they lack the external ears associated with hearing in terrestrial vertebrates. External ears are not needed because fish tissue is of roughly the same density as water and so is nearly transparent to sound waves. However, the sound waves can be intercepted internally by structures that are either much denser than water (otoliths) or much less dense than water (swim bladders). Because most fish can hear well, it is not surprising to find that many also make sounds for communication. A single toadfish, for example, when engaging in its courtship rites, can produce sound that may reach 100 db in loudness. The "silent world" of the oceans is largely a myth, at least as far as fish are concerned!

Perhaps the most important characteristic of water that enables it to support life, including fish, is its property as the nearly universal solvent. The waters of the world contain complex mixtures of dissolved gases, salts, and organic compounds, many of which are needed by fish to sustain life and are taken up either directly through the gills or indirectly through food organisms. The most important of the gases is oxygen, which is present in extremely small amounts compared with that found in air (1 to 8 ml of oxygen per liter of water; 210 ml of oxygen per liter of air). Although the gills of fish are incredibly efficient at extracting oxygen from water, the low availability of oxygen in water can limit the metabolic activities of fish. In fresh water, where oxygen supplies may become depleted, many fishes are able to breathe air at least for short periods of time. In order to extract what oxygen is available in the water, fish must expose a large, highly vascularized gill surface area to the water. As a consequence, other substances also may pass between the environment and the fish. Fish eliminate waste products (especially carbon dioxide, ammonia, and heat) through the gills; but they may also take in harmful substances, including pollutants such as heavy metals and pesticides. The large area of exposed gill also makes fish very sensitive to changes in the concentration of salts in the water, accounting in part for the difficulty most fish have in moving between fresh and salt water.

A final important characteristic of water to fish is its low penetrability to light as compared with air. Even in the clearest water, light seldom penetrates deeper than 1000 m, and in most water the depth of penetration is considerably less. Since the lighted (photic) zone is the zone in which algae and aquatic plants grow and where grazing invertebrates are concentrated, it is not surprising that most fish are found there. Indeed, a majority of fish rely primarily on sight for prey capture. However, many fishes have sensory structures, such as barbels and electric organs, that allow them to find their way about at night or in muddy water, or in other low-light situations. Below the lighted zone of the oceans are complex communities of fish that produce their own light in order to signal each other and to attract prey.

As the following chapters will reveal, there are many exceptions to the preceding generalities about fish. Each fish species has its own unique combination of adaptive traits that enables it to survive in its own particular environment. These traits reflect the rich evolutionary history of fishes. They provide the notes for the complex sonata of systematics whose playing has traditionally been the showpiece of ichthyology. Today, the concert has been joined by other equally complex pieces featuring the physiology, ecology, and behavior of fish. Increasingly, the pieces are merging into a grand symphony of modern ichthyology. This book is only a program guide to that dynamic, but always unfinished, symphony.

HISTORY OF ICHTHYOLOGY

Ichthyology has its origins in the writings of Aristotle (384–322 B.C.). Aristotle made observations that allowed him to distinguish fish from whales and to recognize about 115 species of fish. He was the first to set down a myriad of basic facts about fish, such as that the sex of sharks can be determined from the structure of the pelvic fins and that certain sea basses change sex as they grow older. Unfortunately, for nearly 2000 years after Aristotle few original observations about fish were recorded because Aristotle was considered to have completely covered all areas of natural history. Aristotle's grip on ichthyology (and science) was finally broken in the sixteenth century by natural historians such as Pierre Belon (1517–1564), H. Salviani (1514–1572), and G. Rondelet (1507–1557). Belon published a natural history of fishes in 1551, in which he classified about 110 species according to anatomical characteristics. From 1554 through 1557, Salviani published sections of a treatise on Italian fishes in which 92 species were described and illustrated. Rondelet in 1554 and 1555 published books that summarized much of what was known about fishes at the time. Essentially, Belon published the first modern systematic treatise on fish, Salviani the first regional faunal work, and Rondelet the first ichthyology text.

Knowledge of fishes subsequently expanded rapidly, stimulated in good part by the discoveries and reports of naturalist explorers. Preeminent among them was George Marcgrave of Saxony (1610–1644), whose *Natural History of the Fishes of Brazil* was published posthumously in 1648. The knowledge of European fishes also continued to grow, so when the English naturalists John Ray (1628–1705) and Francis Willoughby (1635–1672) published their *Historia Piscium* in 1686, they could describe 420 species, arranged in a reasonable classification system. Works such as these are perhaps most important because they were the foundation upon which Peter Artedi (1705–1734) built the classification system of fishes that has earned him the title of Father of Ichthyology. Artedi also critically reviewed the previous literature on fishes and recommended standard measurements and counts that are still the basis of fish taxonomy. Artedi drowned before any of his studies were published, but his notes and manuscripts were purchased by his good friend Carolus Linneaus (1707–1778). Linneaus edited this material and issued it in 1738. He later adopted Artedi's classification of fishes for his own *Systema Naturae,* which became the basis for all future classification systems.

The first attempt after Artedi's to organize the expanding knowledge of fishes was that of Marc Elieser Bloch (1723–1799) of Berlin. His massive volumes were the standard reference works on fishes until the publication of the volumes written by Georges Cuvier (1769–1832) and his pupil A. Valenciennes between 1828 and 1849. The influence of all three of these individuals on ichthyology would probably have been less if the French Revolution had not cut short the studies of B. G. E. Lacepède (1756–1826), who was consequently obliged to compose his five-volume work on fishes largely from memory or rough notes. Much of his immediate successors' time seems to have been spent correcting the errors he made. While such general works on fishes were being composed, the detailed studies of fish anatomy and physiology were also proceeding, resulting in Alexander Monro's *The Structure and Physiology of Fishes Explained and Compared to that of Man and Other Animals* (1785).

In the early nineteenth century, the most important ichthyological works were descriptions of regional fish faunas. The first major work for North America was *The Fishes of New York, Described and Arranged* (1815), by Samuel L. Mitchill (1764–1831); however, the most detailed of the early accounts was *Ichthyologia Ohien-*

sis (1820) by the eccentric Sicilian naturalist Constantine Rafinesque (1783–1840). Many of the fishes of the Pacific coast of North America were first described by a British navy surgeon, Sir John Richardson (1787–1865), in his *Fauna Boreali-Americana* (1836). In 1829 another treatise on the fishes of Brazil appeared, which was the first major work of Louis Agassiz (1807–1873). Only 21 at the time, Agassiz classified the fishes collected by Johann Baptiste von Spix (1781–1826), who had died after spending three years pursuing them in the Brazilian jungles. Agassiz's next works were a series of volumes on fossil fishes (1833–1844), which laid the foundation for evolutionary studies of fishes. This is ironic, because Agassiz himself was a fervent opponent of evolution. In 1846 Agassiz moved from Switzerland to Harvard University, where, besides convincing the American public of the importance of science in general, he continued to make many contributions to ichthyology.

Meanwhile, in Germany Johannes Müller (1801–1858) revised Agassiz's ideas on fish classification to produce a system that recognized most of the major groups we still recognize today. His system was improved by such leading scientists of the era as Ernst Haeckel (1834–1919), Thomas H. Huxley (1825–1895), Edward D. Cope (1840–1897), and Theodore Gill (1837–1914), who were all greatly influenced by the ideas of Charles Darwin. Curiously, one of the most prominent ichthyologists of the late nineteenth century did not accept evolutionary ideas. This was Albert Günther (1830–1914), who labored in the British Museum with its magnificent collections of fishes from all over the British Empire, to produce the eight-volume *Catalogue of the Fishes in the British Museum*. This was the last time anyone tried single-handedly to describe the fish fauna of the world, species by species. Günther's successor at the museum, George A. Boulenger (1858–1937), recognized the impossibility even of revising Günther's volumes after reworking the volumes on perciform fishes. Instead, he devoted much of his time to the fishes of Africa, producing the four-volume *Catalogue of the Freshwater Fishes of Africa* (1909). Working with Boulenger in the British Museum was A. S. Woodward, who reviewed what was known about fossil fishes and set the knowledge in an evolutionary framework.

Perhaps the one person who could have revised the British Museum *Catalogue* was David Starr Jordan (1851–1931). He, however, turned down the curatorship at the museum to continue his career in the United States, where he eventually became the founding president of Stanford University. For much of his career, Jordan occupied an Agassiz-like role as a great popularizer of science, but at the same time he was extraordinarily productive as an ichthyologist. Although Jordan worked with fishes from all over the world, he is best known as the author of *Fishes of North and Middle America* (four volumes, 1896–1900), coauthored with B. W. Evermann (1853–1932). Jordan was also the author of the standard ichthyology text of the early twentieth century, *Guide to the Study of Fishes* (1905).

As the twentieth century progressed, ichthyology became more and more diverse. Ecology, physiology, and behavior shared the field with the more traditional areas of anatomy and systematics. Yet if there is still a common thread that holds the diverse areas together, it is systematics, which perhaps accounts for the fact that the best-known ichthyologists of our century—such as Charles T. Regan (1878–1943), Leo S. Berg (1876–1950), and Carl L. Hubbs (1894–1979)—have made

their major contributions in this area. Regan's work on teleost anatomy and classification is the foundation upon which much of our more contemporary systems rest.
Berg described and organized the information on much of the fish fauna of Russia
and nearby areas. In addition, his *Classification of Fishes* (1940) was the standard reference work on the subject until recently. Hubbs, like Jordan, worked mainly on the
fishes of North and Central America, smoothing off the rough edges of Jordan's
work. His *Fishes of the Great Lakes Region,* coauthored with Karl F. Lagler, besides
being a classic regional work, is still the standard reference on taxonomic techniques
for fishes.

FISH CLASSIFICATION

Although describing new taxa of fishes, and organizing the taxa into systems that
demonstrate interrelationships is no longer the primary occupation of most biologists who work with fish, it is nevertheless of fundamental importance. In order to
understand the significance of the ecological, physiological, behavioral, and other
types of adaptations of fish, their evolutionary relationships must be understood as
well. Modern classification schemes are generally presumed to reflect the evolutionary relationships among fishes, because common structural features (upon
which most schemes are based) presumably reflect common ancestry. Because our
knowledge of most fishes is far from complete and because taxa higher than the
species level tend to be somewhat arbitrary, refinements and changes to accepted
classification systems are continually being proposed. Eventually these changes lead
to new systems that may bear little resemblance to the old systems on which they
are based. Indeed, the most prominent figures in much of the history of ichthyology
were individuals who organized the recent advances in the knowledge of fishes into
"new" classification schemes. Most classification schemes today are based in large
part on those of Regan (1929) and Berg (1940).

More recently, the provisional classification of the teleosts by Greenwood et al.
(1966) has had a major impact on the thinking of systematic ichthyologists and has
stimulated many further attempts at revising taxa within the bony fishes. Considerable attention is being paid by modern systematists to other groups of fishes as
well, so controversies over arcane, but important, details of classification are still
slowly raging in the literature. Nelson (1994) put much of this recent work together
in a classification system that will be largely followed in this book, except where
we choose not to accept some of the more controversial changes from Nelson (1984)
or where we prefer other schemes, especially for higher levels of classification. Some
of the more significant differences include:

1. We follow the analysis of Forey and Janvier (1993) for the classification of
   the earliest fishes, because they separate the hagfishes from the rest of the
   vertebrates.
2. We retain Osteichthyes as the all-encompassing word for bony fishes,
   rather than the word Teleostomi. This makes the tetrapods a subdivision

of the bony fishes, but as Nelson (1994) states: Tetrapods are "a divergent sideline within the fishes that ascend onto land and into the air and secondarily return to the water" (p. 68).

3. For the Chondrichthyes, the system of Compagno (1973) is followed, reflecting Compagno's convincing arguments that there are four distinct evolutionary lines of sharks and rays rather than just two.

Supplemental Readings

Berg 1940; Boulenger 1910; Cohen 1970; Compagno 1973; Greenwood, Miles, and Patterson 1973; Greenwood, Rosen, Weitzman, and Myers 1966; Horn 1972; Hubbs 1964; Jordan 1922; Lagler, Bardach, Miller, and Passino 1977; Lauder and Liem 1983; Lurie 1960; Myers 1964; Nelson 1994; Norman and Greenwood 1975; Patterson 1977; Wooton 1990.

PART II
STRUCTURE AND FORM

CHAPTER **2**

Form and Movement

The great ecological diversity of fishes is reflected in the astonishing variety of body shapes and means of locomotion they possess. Indeed, much can be learned about the ecology of a fish simply by examining its anatomical features or by watching it move through the water. Equally important to students of ichthyology (if not to the fish) is that these features also form the basis of most schemes of classification and identification. The purpose of this chapter, therefore, is to provide an overview of (1) external anatomy, (2) internal support systems (the skeleton and muscles), and (3) means of locomotion.

EXTERNAL ANATOMY

Although life in water puts many severe constraints on the "design" of fish, the presence of thousands of species living in a wide variety of habitats means that these constraints are pushed to their limits. This results in many very unlikely forms such as seahorses and lumpfishes. Understanding the significance of the peculiar external anatomy of such forms practically requires study on a case-by-case basis. On the other hand, species that are more recognizably fishlike (Fig. 2.1) can usually be placed in some sort of functional category through the examination of

body shape, scales, fins, mouth, gill openings, sense organs, and miscellaneous
structures (Fig. 2.2).

BODY SHAPE

Most fishes fall into one of six broad categories: rover-predator, lie-in-wait predator, surface-oriented fish, bottom fish, deep-bodied fish, and eel-like fish (Fig. 2.2).

Rover-predators have the body shape that comes to mind when most people
think of fish: streamlined (fusiform), with a pointed head ending in a terminal mouth,
and a narrow caudal peduncle tipped with a forked tail. The fins are more or less
evenly distributed about the body, providing stability and maneuverability. Such fish
typically are constantly on the move, searching out prey, which they capture through

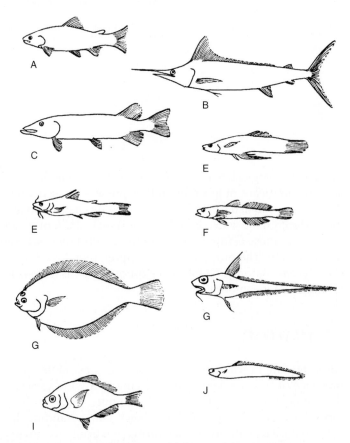

FIGURE 2.1 *Typical fish body shapes: (A) and (B) rover-
predator; (C) lie-in-wait predator; (D) surface-oriented fish;
(E) bottom rover; (F) bottom clinger; (G) flatfish; (H) rattail;
(I) deep-bodied fish; (J) eel-like fish.*

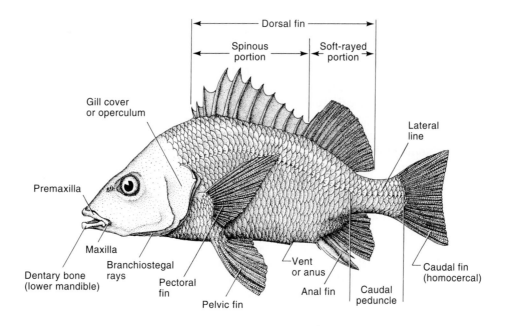

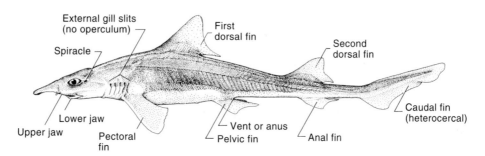

FIGURE 2.2 *External features of a bony fish (snapper, top) and cartilaginous fish (smoothhound shark, bottom). From Moyle 1993; © 1993 by Chris Mari Van Dyck.*

pursuit. Examples include many species of minnows (Cyprinidae), bass, tuna, mackerel, and swordfish. The rover-predator body shape is also characteristic of stream fish such as trout that spend much of their time foraging in fast water.

Lie-in-wait predators are mainly piscivores (fish eaters) that have a morphology well suited for the ambushing of fast-swimming prey. The body is fusiform, but it is also elongate, often torpedolike. The head is flattened and equipped with a large mouth filled with pointed teeth. In many species the mouth is largely contained in a long, pointed snout. The caudal fin tends to be large, and the dorsal and anal fins are placed far back on the body, often in line with each other. This arrangement of the fins gives a barely moving fish the large amount of thrust it needs to launch itself at high speed at passing fish. The narrow frontal profile that these fish present, coupled with their cryptic coloration and secretive behavior, also makes them less visible to their prey. Members of this group include the freshwater pikes (Esocidae), barracuda (Sphyraenidae), gars (Lepisosteidae), needlefish (Belonidae), and snook (Centropomidae).

Surface-oriented fish are typically small in size, with an upward-pointing mouth, a dorsoventrally flattened head with large eyes, fusiform body, and a posteriorly placed dorsal fin. The morphology is well suited for capturing plankton and small fishes that live near the water's surface, or insects that land on the surface. In stagnant water, the surface-oriented morphology is particularly suitable for taking advantage of the thin layer of oxygen-rich water that exists at the air-water interface. The mouth of the fish can be placed in the layer and the water then pumped across the gills. Most surface-oriented fish are stocky-bodied fresh or brackish water forms, such as mosquitofish *(Gambusia)*, many killifish (Fundulidae), and the four-eyed fish *(Anableps anableps)*, but a number of elongate marine forms, such as the halfbeaks and flying fishes (Exocoetidae), have similar adaptations.

Bottom fish possess a wide variety of body shapes, all of them adapted for a life in nearly continuous contact with the bottom. In most such fish the swimbladder is reduced or absent, and most are flattened in one direction or another. Bottom fish can be divided into five overlapping types: bottom rovers, bottom clingers, bottom hiders, flatfish, and rattails. *Bottom rovers* have a rover-predator-like body, except that the head tends to be flattened, the back humped, and the pectoral fins enlarged. Examples include forms as varied as (1) North American catfishes (Ictaluridae) with large mouths at the end of the snout (terminal mouths); (2) small armored catfishes (Loricariidae) with small mouths beneath the snout (subterminal mouths); and (3) sturgeons (Acipenseridae) with fleshy, protrusible lips located well below the snout (inferior mouth) that are used to suck plant and animal matter off the bottom. Many bottom rovers among the bony fishes have small eyes and well-developed barbels ("whiskers" equipped with tastebuds) around the mouth, indicating their ability to find prey at night or in murky water. Many sharks, with their inferior mouths, flattened heads, and large pectoral fins, can also be classified as bottom rovers.

Bottom clingers are mainly small fish with flattened heads, large pectoral fins, and structures (usually modified pelvic fins) that allow them to adhere to the bottom. Such structures are handy in swift streams or intertidal areas that have strong currents. The simplest arrangement is possessed by sculpins (Cottidae), which use their small, closely spaced pelvic fins as antiskid devices. However, other families of fishes, such as gobies (Gobiidae) and clingfishes (Gobiesocidae), have evolved suction cups. *Bottom hiders* are similar in many respects to the bottom clingers, but they lack the clinging devices and tend to have more elongate bodies and smaller heads. These forms usually live under rocks or in crevices, or lie quietly on the bottom in still water. The darters (Percidae) of North American streams are in this category, as are many blennies (Blennidae). However, the latter family contains species that range in form from "good" bottom hiders to more eel-like forms.

Flatfish have the most extreme morphologies of bottom fish. Flounders (Pleuronectiformes) are essentially deep-bodied fish that live with one side on the bottom.

In these fish the eye on the downward side migrates during development to the upward side, and the mouth often assumes a peculiar twist to enable bottom feeding. In contrast, skates and rays (Batoidea) are flattened dorsoventrally (depressiform), and mostly move about by flapping or undulating their extremely large pectoral fins. Not only is the mouth completely ventral on these fish, but the main water intakes for respiration (the spiracles) are located on the top of the head.

The *rattail shape* is another type of body shape that has independently evolved in both the Osteichthyes and Chondrichthyes. Groups such as the grenadiers (Macrouridae), brotulas (Ophidiidae), and chimaeras (Holocephali) have bodies that begin with large, pointy-snouted heads and large pectoral fins and end in long, pointed, ratlike tails. These fish are almost all inhabitants of the deep sea, and exactly why this peculiar morphology is so popular among benthic fish is poorly understood. The fishes live by scavenging and preying on the benthic invertebrates.

Deep-bodied fish are laterally flattened (compressiform) fish, with a body depth usually at least one-third that of the standard length (distance from snout to structural base of caudal fin). The dorsal and anal fins are typically long, and the pectoral fins are located high on the body, with the pelvic fins immediately below. The mouth is usually small and protrusible, the eyes large, and the snout short. Deep-bodied fish are well adapted for maneuvering in tight quarters, such as the catacombs of a coral reef, dense beds of aquatic plants, or tight schools of their own species. They are also well adapted for picking small invertebrates off the bottom or out of the water column. A majority of deep-bodied fish possess stout spines in the fins, presumably because in the course of their evolution they have sacrificed speed for maneuverability and developed spines for protection from predators. Although most deep-bodied fish are closely associated with the bottom, many open-water plankton feeders (e.g, herring) are also moderately deep bodied. This is largely the result of a sharp ventral keel, which functions to camouflage these silvery fish by eliminating ventral shadows, thus making them less visible to predators approaching from below.

Eel-like fish have elongate bodies, blunt or wedge-shaped heads, and tapering or rounded tails. If paired fins are present, they are small, while the dorsal and anal fins are typically quite long. Scales are small and embedded, or absent. In cross-section, their bodies can range from compressed to round. Eel-like fishes are particularly well adapted for entering small crevices and holes in reefs and rocky areas, for making their way through beds of aquatic plants, and for burrowing into soft bottoms. However, there are a surprising number that are also found swimming about in the open ocean, so the body shape is useful for other purposes as well. Examples of this group include the many eels (Anguilliformes), loaches (Cobitidae), and gunnels (Pholidae).

SCALES

The type, size, and number of scales can tell much about how a fish makes its living. The scales of bony fish range from a heavy coating of mail-like armor, to a few large bony plates on the back, to a dense covering of thin, flexible scales, to no scales at all (Fig. 2.3). Bony plates are large modified scales that serve as armor on a number of bottom-oriented fishes, such as sturgeons (Acipenseridae), many South American catfishes, poachers (Agonidae), and pipefishes and seahorses (Syngnathidae). Most such fish are rather slow in their movements. In contrast, typical scales usually cover the bodies of most free-swimming fish, apparently providing some degree of protection from predators while not excessively weighing the fish down. Fish that are fast swimmers or regularly move through the fast water of streams typically have many fine scales (e.g., trout), whereas those that live in quiet water and do not swim continuously at high speeds tend to have rather coarse scales (e.g., perch, sunfish).

Scales evolved independently in cartilaginous and bony fish (Chapter 13), as indicated by their fundamentally different structure. The *placoid scales* of sharks are tiny, tooth-like structures, while the scales of bony fish are layered plates, with bone as one of the layers. The ancestral condition for bony fish is represented by the heavy *ganoid scales* of gars (Lepisosteidae, Fig. 2.3) and the more derived condition by the *bony ridge (elasmoid) scales* of teleosts. The latter are of two basic types, cycloid and ctenoid. *Cycloid scales* are the round, flat, thin scales found on such fishes as trout, minnows, and herrings. *Ctenoid scales* are found on spiny finned teleosts *(Acanthopterygii)* and are similar to cycloid scales except for the tiny, comblike projections *(ctenii)* on the exposed (posterior) edge of the scales. The exact function of the ctenii is poorly understood, but they may improve the hydrodynamic efficiency of swimming. Curiously, the tiny placoid scales of sharks may be an independently evolved solution to the same "problem," because these scales, like ctenoid scales, make the exterior of the fish rough to the touch.

Although scales are usually considered an integral part of any fish, a surprising number of species lack them altogether or have just a few that are modified for other purposes. Such fish are by and large bottom dwellers in moving water (e.g., sculpins); fish that frequently hide in caves, crevices, and other tight places (many catfish and eels); or fast-swimming pelagic fish (swordfish and some mackerels). However, many fish that appear to be scaleless in fact have a complete coating of deeply embedded scales (most tunas and anguillid eels). It is also worth noting that many of the bottom-dwelling skates and rays do not have placoid scales, except as patches of bony armor or as spines (in sting rays).

FINS

Like scales, fins reflect the independent evolutionary history of bony and cartilaginous fishes (Fig. 2.2). In both groups, the fins are supported internally by sturdy fin rays. In sharks and rays, the fin rays are called *ceratotrichia* and are fairly stiff, unbranched, and unsegmented. In contrast, the *lepidotrichia* of bony fish are flexible, segmented, and branched. *Lepidotrichia* seem to start as embryonic spines *(actinotrichia)* which become covered with embryonic scales, which then replace the *actinotrichia* completely before emerging as fin rays. When this developmental process does not occur, true spines emerge, which are stiff, round in cross section, and unsegmented.

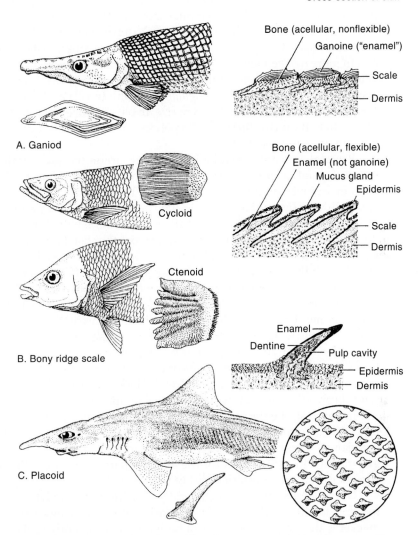

Cross-section of skin

FIGURE 2.3 *Examples of ganoid scales on gar, cycloid scales on sardine, ctenoid scales on snapper, and placoid scales on a shark. Ganoid scales after Dareff (1971), copyright © Fratelli, Fabbri Editori, Milan; cross sections after Hildebrand (1974), copyright © John Wiley. (From Moyle 1993; © 1993 by Chris Mari Van Dyck.)*

In all fish, the various combinations of location, size, and shape of the fins are closely associated with the different body shapes. Although the paired fins (pectorals, pelvics) and the unpaired fins (dorsal, anal, caudal, adipose) evolved together as a system that simultaneously propels, stabilizes, and maneuvers each fish, they will be discussed separately here, for convenience.

Pelvic fins are the most variable of the fins in terms of position. In more ancestral bony fishes, such as salmon, shad, and carp, and in sharks, the fins are located ventrally, toward the rear of the fish (termed *abdominal* in position). Most of these fish have rover-predator body shapes and the fins assist in steering and braking. In more derived teleosts, many of which are deep bodied, the pelvics are more anterior, below the pectoral fins (*thoracic* position, Fig. 2.1); occasionally they are even in front of the pectorals (*jugular* position). In eels and eel-like fish the pelvic fins are absent or greatly reduced in size, in part for ease of squeezing through tight places. In bottom-dwelling fish the pelvics are frequently modified into organs for holding on to the substrate.

Pectoral fins are generally located high up on the sides of deep-bodied fish, which depend on precise movements for picking prey from the bottom or water column. In rover-predators they tend to be more toward the midline of the fish, or below. In very fast swimming fish, such as tuna, and in very deep bodied fish that pick prey from the substrate (bluegill, many cichlids), the fins tend to be long and pointed. In slower moving rover-predators or other fish that need more surface area for stability while swimming, the fins tend to be more rounded. The pectoral fins of bony fish that rest on the bottom, such as suckers (Catostomidae) and sculpins (Cottidae), are usually broad, rounded, ventral in position, and spread out laterally. Other fish use enlarged pectoral fins for gliding (flying fish, Exocoetidae); for true flapping flight out of the water (freshwater hatchetfish, Gasteropelecidae); or "flying" in the water, in the case of many rays (eagle rays, Myliobatidae). In some fish, such as the "flying" gurnards (Dactylopteridae) and the tropical lion and turkey fishes (Scorpaenidae), enlarged pectoral fins are apparently used mainly for display, either to startle predators when suddenly opened (gurnards) or to signal predators (and conspecifics) to stay away from poisonous spines.

In contrast, the pectoral fins of sharks are rather like rigid wings that can be moved but not collapsed. These fins operate not only as stabilizers but also as "diving planes." Because of the latter function, they are normally set at an elevated angle of attack to generate lift for the anterior part of the body; the heterocercal tail provides lift for the posterior part of the body.

Dorsal and anal fins are generally long on rover-predators and deep-bodied fish, for stability while swimming. In fast-swimming pelagic fish, such as tuna and mackerel, the rearmost portions of both fins are frequently broken up into numerous finlets. When such fish are swimming at high speed, the forward portion of the dorsal fin may fold into a dorsal slot in order to reduce the resistance the additional surface area creates; likewise, the pectoral fins of such fish lie down into shallow pockets. However, even bony fish that lack these specializations will collapse the dorsal and anal fins and fold back the pectoral and pelvic fins when putting on a burst of speed. Interestingly, this method of reducing drag is not available to sharks, although a number of the mackerel sharks are capable of swimming at quite high speeds.

Another group of fish with long dorsal and anal fins are the eel-like fish. Their fins frequently run most of the length of the body and may unite with the caudal fin; such a configuration is necessary for the anguilliform locomotion discussed later in this chapter. In eel-like electric fish only one of the two long fins is developed. In such cases the fin is the principal means of propulsion, operated by sending waves of movement down the fin. The reason for this is that electric fish must keep their bodies rigid while swimming, to maintain a uniform electrical field about them.

The **caudal fin** has a shape that is strongly related to the normal swimming speed of a fish. The fastest-swimming fish, such as tuna and marlin, have a stiff, quarter-moon-shaped (lunate) fin attached to a narrow caudal peduncle. Fish whose survival depends upon frequent sustained swimming to live, have forked tails, the deepest forks occurring on the most active fish. Deep-bodied fish and most surface and bottom fish have tails that are square, rounded, or only slightly forked. The tails of most bony fish are *homocercal*, with upper and lower lobes being about the same size; while in the Chondrichthyes the tail is usually *heterocercal*, with the upper lobe being longer than the lower lobe. These two basic tail types do not so much reflect differences in ways of making a living as they do the evolutionary history of the fishes that have them (Chapter 13). In the homocercal tail, the vertebral column ends in modified vertebrae that support the fan-like tail structure; while in the heterocercal tail, the vertebral column actually extends into the upper lobe of the tail.

The **adipose fin** is a fleshy, dorsal appendage that is found in the trouts (Salmonidae), smelts (Osmeridae), lanternfishes (Myctophidae), and various catfish and characins. Although located between the dorsal and caudal fins toward the caudal peduncle, the small size and lack of stiffening rays make the function of this fin a bit of a mystery. It is possible that it has an important function in the swimming of fish in the postlarval stage of development, when other fins are poorly developed.

Spines. One of the most important attributes of the fins of fish is the presence or absence of spines on the dorsal, anal, and pectoral fins. The importance of spines is indicated by the fact they have developed independently in a number of different groups of fish. "True" spines are characteristic of most derived teleosts (Acanthopterygii); such spines are solid bony structures without any segmentation and are round in cross section. In contrast, the spines of catfish, carp, goldfish, and similar fishes are just stiffened, thickened rays, which are segmented, dumbbell-shaped in cross section, and often branched. The spines that precede the dorsal fin in some sharks are modified placoid scales, as are the stings of sting rays. Regardless of their structure and origin, spines are an effective and lightweight means of protection against predators. Dorsal, pectoral, and opercular spines are often located at the fish's center of mass, the usual target point of piscivorous (fish-eating) fish (Webb 1978a). Besides being uncomfortable for a predator to bite down on, spines greatly increase the effective size of a small fish. This is because once the dorsal, anal, and pectoral spines are locked into place, the fish can be grabbed only by a predator that can get its mouth around the spines. By increasing its effective size through the use of spines, a small fish reduces the number of predators available to prey on it, because large predators are almost always fewer than small predators. As a consequence of this factor, well-developed spines are found mainly in small to medium-sized fishes that actively forage for their food. As an additional disincentive to predators, many spines have poison glands associated with them, such as those found on scorpianfish (Scorpaenidae), some catfish, and sting rays.

OTHER STRUCTURES

The *mouth* tells much about the habits of a fish by its position, shape, and size. Not surprisingly, bottom-feeding fish have downward-pointing (inferior) mouths, while surface-oriented fish have upward-pointing (superior) mouths. For most fish, however, the mouth is at the end of the snout (terminal). The size and shape of the mouth is usually directly related to the size of the preferred food organisms. Thus fish that feed on small invertebrates by suction have a small mouth surrounded by protractile "lips" that, when protruded, form an O-shaped opening (the shape with the maximum ratio of area to perimeter length). However, fish that feed on large prey typically have an inflexible rim to the mouth, which is oval in cross section and frequently lined with sharp teeth. Beyond these general mouth types, the mouths of fish can show extraordinary shapes that reflect specialized modes of feeding, as discussed in the chapters on the fish of tropical reefs (Chapter 33) and tropical lakes (Chapter 29).

The *gill openings* of most bony fish are covered by a thin and flexible bony operculum that is an important component of the "two-pump" respiratory system possessed by most fish (Chapter 4). As a consequence, the gill openings and cover do not show a large amount of variability, except to be smaller on fish with low activity levels than on fish that are more active. In eels, the openings are typically reduced to a small hole, presumably because of the problems associated with raising and lowering the opercular bones under confined conditions. In the sharks and rays, the *spiracles*, small openings used for the intake of water for respiration (Fig. 2.2), are dorsally located in the bottom-dwelling rays, and laterally located in most sharks. In the most active species of sharks, however, the spiracular opening is greatly reduced in size because most of the respiratory water is forced through the mouth and across the gills while swimming.

Of the externally visible *sense organs* of fish, the eyes perhaps tell the most about habits. The size of the eyes, relative to the size of the fish, vary both according to the methods used to capture food and according to the light levels under which the food is taken. Well-developed eyes are found in most fish that are diurnal predators, although the largest eyes are present on fish that feed mainly at dusk and dawn, such as the walleye *(Stizostedion vitreum)*, or fish that live near the limits of light penetration in the oceans (see Chapter 35). Moderately small eyes are characteristic of fish that do not rely on vision for feeding, but especially of fish that feed on the bottom or feed at night. Such fish often have well-developed barbels around the mouth for taste and touch (catfish), or sensitive, fleshy lips (suckers, Catostomidae). Many cave-dwelling fish and deepsea fish have either tiny eyes or none at all, but typically do have extremely well-developed lateral-line systems. The lateral-line system is visible on most fish as a faint line of pores along the midline and as a series of lines on the head. This system detects movement of the water along the fish (Chapter 10).

SKELETAL SYSTEM

For convenience, the skeletal system is considered here to have three main components: the vertebral column, the skull, and the appendicular skeleton (Fig. 2.3).

The **vertebral column** in fish ranges in structure from a cartilage sheath around a notochord (hagfish), to a cartilaginous vertebral column (vertebrae without centra in lampreys but with centra in elasmobranchs), to one of partially ossified cartilage (ratfish), to one of solid bone (teleosts). Although the centra (round centers of the vertebrae) are aligned in a series in fish, the vertebrae lack elaborate interlocking processes, which are necessary in terrestrial vertebrates to counteract gravitational forces. The gars (Lepisosteidae) are an exception to this rule; they have interlocking vertebrae that resemble those of reptiles. The vertebral column of fish, of course, provides the structural base for swimming movements, and there is generally one vertebra per body segment. This system is admirably suited for withstanding the heavy compression load put on it by contractions of the large muscle masses during swimming.

Despite their apparent simplicity in structure compared with the vertebrae of terrestrial vertebrates, the vertebrae of fish are structurally specialized. The anteriormost vertebrae (the atlas and the axis) are structured for articulation with the skull. In minnows and catfish (Cypriniformes) the upper portions of the first three to four vertebrae are actually separated from the vertebrae themselves and form a chain of tiny bones that connect the swimbladder to the inner ear, for acute hearing (Chapter 10). At the other end of the spinal column, the posteriormost vertebrae are modified into a series of flattened elements (penultimate vertebrae, hypurals, epurals, and urostyle), which articulate with the rays of the caudal fin. Between these two sets of highly modified vertebrae are the trunk vertebrae, most of which bear ventral (pleural) ribs. These ribs extend ventrally from centra and extend between adjacent muscle masses. In addition to the ventral ribs, most bony fish also have dorsal ribs that extend between dorsal muscle masses but are usually just loosely associated with the vertebral column. When such ribs or intermuscular bones are well developed, as in minnows, suckers, and pikes, they can be a real nuisance and an occasional hazard to individuals who eat fish.

Both teleost and elasmobranch trunk vertebrae also feature dorsal (neural) processes that form an arch to accommodate the spinal cord. The neural arches of all vertebrae together compose the neural canal. In bony fishes a neural spine prominently extends from each neural arch to provide points of attachment for dorsal (epaxial) musculature. In like manner, fusion of the transverse processes of the vertebrae creates a hemal canal on the ventral side of the vertebrae located posterior to the body cavity. The hemal canal carries the primary blood vessels supplying and draining all the caudal musculature (Chapter 4). In many cases, a hemal spine extends ventrally from each hemal arch and provides a site of ventral (hypaxial) body musculature attachment. In laterally flattened teleosts both the neural and hemal spines are very long so as to give adequate support to the body musculature. They resemble a delicate "double comb."

The **skull** of fish (Fig. 2.4) is an extremely complex structure that represents a design compromise among frequently conflicting uses of the head region. It is (1) the entry point for food and for water for respiration; (2) the site of major sensory organs; (3) a protective container for brain, gills, and other organs; (4) the attachment site for many major muscle masses; and (5) a streamlined entry point necessary for efficient swimming. In lampreys and hagfish the skull is little more than a cartilaginous trough for the brain from which other cartilages are suspended to support the mouth parts and the gills. Superficially, the skull of the sharks and rays is also relatively simple; it consists of (1) a solid-appearing chondrocranium that is molded around the brain and sense organs of the head; (2) the jaws, which largely consist of the palatoquadrate cartilage (upper jaw) and Meckel's cartilage (lower jaw) supported by elements of the hyoid arch; and (3) the branchial cartilages supporting the gills. Despite its simple appearance, the chondrichthyan skull is quite complex in many subtle ways (e.g., position and size of foraminal and fenestral openings, development of rostrum), and is important in the study of taxonomy and evolution.

The skull of bony fish is an elaborate puzzle of articulating bones that differs from the elasmobranch skull in many fundamental ways, among them that (1) in general, the optic rather than the olfactory areas are well developed; (2) the relative positions of many of the elements are quite different; and (3) the important parasphenoid and opercular bones have no equivalents in the elasmobranchs. The skull of bony fish is highly variable. Bones important in the skull of one group may be totally absent from another, and equivalent bones are often difficult to define among major taxonomic groups. However, for convenience, the skull can be divided into five elements: the neurocranium, the suspensorium, the jaws, the opercular bones, and the branchiohyoid apparatus.

The *neurocranium* is the braincase and the most solid portion of the skull, yet it typically consists of 40 to 50 bones (counting the small bones around the eyes and optic region). In ancestral bony fishes, including the modern gars, the neurocranium is a solidly fused unit with strong connections (often fused) to the other portions of the skull. In more derived bony fish, while there remains a solid "core" of bone around the brain (the various frontal, parietal, occipital, optic, and sphenoid bones), the rest of the neurocranium and the skull are rather loosely articulated to provide the expansion capabilities needed for suction feeding and the two-pump respiratory system. Another development in derived bony fishes is the presence of parietal and pterotic crests and the fossae ("trenches") between them on which trunk muscles insert. This reflects changes in methods of swimming.

Connecting the neurocranium and the jaws is a series of bones (hyomandibular, symplectic, quadrate, pterygoids, etc.) collectively called the *suspensorium*. This series of bones has undergone rather dramatic changes in shape, size, and position during the course of evolution from ancestral fishes to modern teleosts and to the tetrapods. The *jaws* have also undergone rather dramatic changes in bony fishes, related to the change from a firm biting mouth to a flexible sucking mouth. In the course of this change the principal bone of the upper jaw has changed from

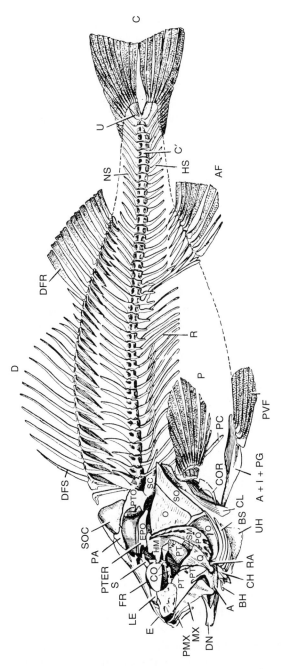

FIGURE 2.4 *The teleost (Perca) skeleton:* A *angulo-articular;* A + I + PG *actinosts + interneural + pelvic girdle;* AF *anal fin;* BH, *basihyal;* BS *branchiostegal rays;* C *caudal fin;* C' *caudal vertebral centrum;* CL *cleithrum;* CH *cerato-hyal;* CO *circumorbitals;* COR *coracoid;* D *dorsal fin;* DN *dentary;* DFR *dorsal ray fin;* DFS *dorsal fin spine;* E *ethmoid;* FPO *epiotic;* FR *frontal;* HM *hyomandibular;* HS *hemal spine;* IO *interoperculum;* LE *lateral ethmoid;* MX *maxillary;* NS *neural spine;* O *operculum;* P *pectoral fin;* PA *parietal;* PC *post-cleithrum;* PMX *premaxillary;* PO *preoperculum;* PT, PT', PT" *ecto-, metapterygoid;* PTER *pterotic;* PTO *posttemporal;* PVF *pelvic fin;* Q *quadrate;* R *rib;* RA *retroarticular;* S *sphenotic;* SC *supraclei-thrum;* SM *symplectic;* SO *subop-erculum;* SOC *supraoccipital crest;* U *urostyle;* UH *urohyal. (Modified from Dean 1895.)*

the maxilla to the premaxilla (see Chapter 13), and the principal bones bearing teeth have changed. In contrast, the principal bones of the lower jaw (dentaries) have remained fairly constant. The *opercular bones* have also remained fairly constant in bony fish, although the teleosts have added an interopercular bone on each side to increase the efficiency of the operculum as a respiratory pump. In more ancestral bony fish the interopercular bone is just another branchiostegal bone (ray), part of the *branchiohyoid apparatus* that makes up the floor of the mouth and the support for the gills. The branchiostegal rays are a fanlike series of bones that make up the floor of the branchial chamber and provide much of its expansion capabilities, which are so important for suction feeding and respiration.

The **appendicular skeleton,** compared with the skull, is relatively simple, consisting of the internal supports for the various fins. In the Chondrichthyes the support for the pectoral fins consists of a series of coracoid and scapular cartilages that form a U-shaped bar attached to the fins on either end. The pelvic girdle is even simpler, consisting solely of a connecting bar, the *ischiopubic cartilage*. In bony fish the girdles are more complex. In the pectoral fins the rays articulate with a series (usually five) of radial bones, which in turn articulate with the scapula and coracoid. These bones are attached to those of the cleithral series, but particularly the cleithrum itself, a large bone that is firmly united with the body musculature and is joined, via the supracleithrum, with the skull. The girdle of the pelvic fins of bony fish is relatively simple, usually consisting of just one basipterygial bone on each side. These bones are usually united with each other or, in more derived teleosts, with the cleithrum of the pectoral girdle (when the fins are in the thoracic or jugular position). For the dorsal and anal fins, the internal supports consist of basal cartilages in the Chondrichthyes and a series of small bones called pterygiophores in the bony fishes (one pterygiophore for each ray or spine in most teleosts). Because they interidigitate with the neural spines of the vertebrae, the dorsal pterygiophores are frequently called interspinous bones.

MUSCULAR SYSTEM

In almost all fish, the large muscles of body and tail used for swimming comprise the majority of the body mass, although there are many other smaller muscles associated with the head and fins, often as parts of complex interacting systems. The body muscles are divided vertically along the body length into sections, the *myomeres* (myotomes), which are separated by sheets of connective tissue. The myomeres are basically shaped like a W on its side, so that they fit into one another like a series of cones. The myomeres on the right and left halves of the body are separated by a vertical *septum*. A horizontal septum separates the muscle masses on the upper and lower halves of the body. The upper muscles are called the *epaxial muscles* and the lower muscles the *hypaxial muscles*. In addition, there is usually a lateral band of muscles that run along or slightly below the midline of the fish.

On inspection, fish muscles can often be divided into red (slow), white (fast), and pink (intermediate) muscle. Red muscle has many capillaries per cubic millimeter. The tissue appears red from the high concentrations of red oxygen-binding pigments in the blood (hemoglobin) as well as in the muscle tissue itself (myoglobin). The high capillary density and presence of the pigments ensure that the red muscle receives an adequate oxygen supply for its abundant mitochondria to sustain the fish's high levels of continuous swimming. Therefore, continuously active fish (e.g., bonito, marlin) have a large proportion of red muscle. In general, red muscle fibers metabolize fat aerobically, so their power output is dependent on their oxygen supply. Fish of "intermediate" activity levels often have the lateral band of muscles, which is always red, well developed and/or have various red fibers scattered in the white muscle that makes up most of the body mass. For example, examinations of body muscle cross sections show that the greatest proportion of red muscle occurs in the lateral bands at the caudal peduncle in both bluefish (Pomatomus saltatrix) and striped bass (Morone saxatilis). The red bands average 18.6% and 10.9%, respectively, of the total musculature in this region (Freadman 1979). Evolutionarily derived tunas (e.g., Thunnus) carry their red muscle bands deeper toward the body core than more ancestral tunas (e.g., Sarda), which leaves room for heat-exchanging vasculature in Thunnus (Sharp and Dizon 1978). Presumably this arrangement fits the stiff-body (thunniform, see below) swimming mode and aids Thunnus in conservation of metabolic heat, permitting faster muscular contractions and higher swimming velocities (Chapter 5).

The white muscle fibers are thicker than the red, have a poorer blood supply, and have no high-oxygen-affinity pigment such as myoglobin. As one might expect from the characteristics of this comparatively poor oxygen-delivery system, white muscle contraction is not as dependent on oxygen supply. White muscle usually converts glycogen to lactic acid via anaerobic pathways. Thus white muscle is most useful for short bursts of swimming and dominates the muscle mass of moderately active to "sluggish" swimmers. For example, dogfish sharks have almost all white muscle and can use up 50% of available muscle glycogen in about two minutes (Bone 1966). The fast (white) fibers exert tensions that are 2.7-fold greater than the slow (red) ones, albeit at a fourfold increase in energy cost to the dogfish (Altringham and Johnston 1986). After this burst of activity, the fish "repays its oxygen debt" by aerobic conversion of lactate to glycogen and glucose, in the red muscle, cardiac muscle, and liver (Hochachka and Somero 1984). In plaice (Pleuronectes platessa), however, the gluconeogenic conversion of lactate to glycogen occurs slowly in the white muscle (Batty and Wardle 1979).

"Staging" in red and white muscular activity has been shown in several fishes (Roberts and Graham 1979). That is, white muscle fibers in chub mackerel, mosaic red and white mixed fibers in salmonids, and pink and white fibers in common carp are recruited for only moderate increases in swimming speed. Roberts and Graham (1979) detected white muscle contractions from implanted electromyographic electrodes at swimming velocities as low as two body lengths per second in chub mackerel. Guppy and Hochachka (1978) have shown how shifts in muscle pH, oxygen tension, temperature, and biochemical substrates can reversibly alter aerobic and anaerobic enzyme activities in skipjack tuna white muscle. Thus some species conform to the classical differentiation of red and white muscle function (e.g., bluefish, striped bass, and herring [Clupea harengus]) while others (e.g., chub mackerel, rainbow trout, coalfish [Pollachius virens], and common carp) show a broader range of "white" muscle activity (Freadman 1979). Adaptations to low temperatures in red muscle include increased capillary densities (enhancing blood flow through muscle tissues) and increased cellular mitochondrial densities (increasing aerobic potential) in common carp (Johnston 1982). Egginton and Sidell (1989) found increased cellular mitochondrial and lipid droplet densities (which may accelerate O_2 flux via increased O_2 solubility) in cold-acclimated (5°C) striped bass, compared with warm acclimated (25°C) ones. These adaptations presumably maintain swimming performance in the face of slowed metabolic and diffusional processes at cold temperatures.

Pink muscle is a fast muscle used at swimming velocities too high for red muscle to sustain, but too low for recruitment of white muscle in common carp (Johnston et al. 1977). In goldfish (*Carassius auratus*) pink muscle is used similarly to red at slow velocities, whereas brown trout (*Salmo trutta*) use pink muscle at much higher velocities (Davison and Goldspink 1984).

LOCOMOTION

Fish move by a variety of means. The simplest means is the passive drift of many larval forms, but such drifters quickly metamorphose into forms more capable of active, directed movement. Although various fish species have evolved the ability to burrow, walk or crawl on the bottom, glide, and even fly, swimming is by far the most important means of locomotion.

To swim forward (or backward!), most fish utilize rhythmic undulations of part or all of their bodies or fins. The sides of the body and the fins exert force on the relatively incompressible surrounding water through the sequential contraction of the myomeres. The relatively stiff vertebral column provides compression resistance, so the body bends from side to side rather than shortening. In sharks, there is a helical collagen network in the skin, to which the myomeres attach distally, which acts as an external tendon for more efficient transmission of muscular force to the tail (Wainright et al. 1978). Changes in collagen fiber angle during swimming prevent loss of tension or skin wrinkling on the concave side of sharks.

Figure 2.5a shows how the lateral flexures at the appropriate angle of attack propel fish forward. The flexures typically move backward along the body with increasing amplitude and at a speed somewhat greater than the forward progress of the fish. As this propulsive wave moves posteriorly, the water adjacent to the fish is accelerated backward until shed at the posterior margin of the caudal fin, producing thrust (Lighthill 1969) much like the propeller on a boat. The more undulatory waves a fish can exert against the surrounding water, and the faster and more exaggerated the waves are, the more power the fish can generate. If other factors such as drag from body features and shape are held constant, fish that generate more power can accelerate more quickly and swim at faster velocities.

Webb (1971) measured the mean wavelength of rainbow trout to be 0.76 times the fish's length, which is a constant at all swimming velocities greater than 0.3 body lengths per second. To increase swimming velocity, trout increase both tail beat frequency (lateral movements per minute) and amplitude (lateral deflection

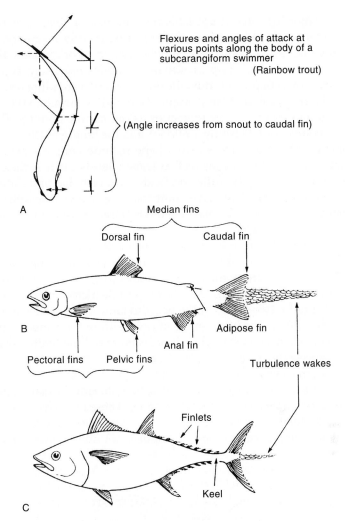

FIGURE 2.5 *Generalized swimming features of fishes.*

per movement). The thrust (forward-directed force) generated by this propulsive wave is a function of forces produced by the body flexures and the rearward velocity of the propulsive wave and is limited by decreased hydrodynamic efficiency at high tail beat frequencies and amplitudes. An inevitable consequence of this forward movement is a trail of vortices (turbulence) in the water behind the fish (Fig. 2.5b,c).

It should be obvious from the wide variety of body shapes of fish that, despite the basic approach to swimming just discussed, there is considerable variation in just how fish swim. It is possible to divide these swimming methods into four basic types: anguilliform, carangiform, ostraciform, and swimming with the fins alone (Fig. 2.6).

Anguilliform swimming is characteristic of flexible, elongate fish, such as eels (Anguilliformes). The whole body of such fish is flexed into lateral waves for propulsion. Just as an oar surpasses a pole in rowboat propulsion, the flattened posterior surface of most eels improves their swimming efficiency. Typical eel median "fins" consist of a continuous dorsal-caudal-anal fin extending around the posterior half of the fish. A similar fin configuration and swimming style is also found in such evolutionarily widespread groups as the marine gunnels (Pholidae), the anadromous lampreys (Petromyzontidae), and the lungfish (Dipnoi). Anguilliform swimmers without a strict eel-like shape include certain elasmobranchs (e.g., nurse sharks, Orectolobidae) as well as some teleosts, such as the cods (Gadidae), when swimming slowly (Wardle and Reid 1977). Fish that undulate their bodies into less than one full wavelength, yet more than one-half wavelength (at speeds greater than one body length per second), are often placed in a separate movement category: *subcarangiform swimming*.

Carangiform swimming is intermediate between the anguilliform and ostraciform extremes and is named after the jacks (Carangidae). Carangiform swimming, involves throwing the body into a shallow wave (up to one-half wavelength within the body length) with the amplitude increasing from very small at the head and anterior two-thirds of the body, to large at the posterior edge of the caudal fin (Webb 1975a). The body shape of carangiform swimmers is typically fusiform, tapering to a narrow caudal peduncle and then broadening to a large, forked caudal fin. Species normally thought of as carangiform types (e.g., jacks, drums, snappers, tunas, mackerels) are swift swimmers.

The fastest-cruising fish (tunas, billfish, lamnid sharks) are often placed in the separate *thunniform swimming* category. These fish have a low-drag fusiform shape and undulate a narrow caudal peduncle stiffened by a keel and a large, slim, lunate (moon-shaped) caudal fin for propulsion. With its "swept-back," tapered tips and

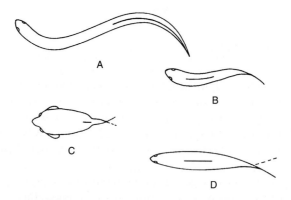

FIGURE 2.6 *Swimming modes of fishes: (A) anguilliform; (B) subcarangiform; (C) ostraciform; and (D) carangiform.*

"scooped-out" center, the lunate tail provides efficient power for fast underwater movement. Frictional drag is minimized by the high-aspect-ratio design of the tail. By having a small surface area per span length or distance between lobe tips (high-aspect ratio), propulsive force is maximized while energy wasted on lateral displacement of water (and consequent creation of excessive vortex wakes) is minimized. The vertically large tail allows a greater mass of water to be accelerated to the rear, increasing forward thrust.

Ostraciform swimming, named after the boxfish family (Ostraciidae), also involves flexing the caudal peduncle, but not to generate high velocities. By contracting the entire muscle mass on one side of their bodies and then the other, these swimmers oscillate the caudal fin to produce a sculling type of locomotion. Fish with this type of locomotion, mainly the trunkfishes, cowfishes, and boxfishes (Tetraodontiformes), rely on armor (plus spines and toxins) rather than speed to protect them from predators. The small isocercal (not differentiated into lobes) caudal fin also is in keeping with their low swimming velocities.

Swimming with fins alone is characteristic of a surprising number of teleosts, including forms that use their body musculature for swimming when high speed or sustained swimming is necessary. The ray-and-membrane fin design allows these fishes to undulate individual fins or fin pairs rather than their bodies to achieve precise movements. Examples of this type of swimming are found among, but not limited to, fish inhabiting areas of dense vegetation or coral or rock reefs. Wrasses (Labridae) of tropical coral reefs can utilize a rowing action of the pectoral fins for forward propulsion. In contrast, triggerfish (Balistidae) use alternate dorsal and anal undulations with some pectoral adjustments. The beautiful (and poisonous) lionfish *(Pterois volitans)* of shallow tropical waters moves by deliberate fanning of the caudal, anal, and second dorsal fins when the feathery pectorals and dorsal spines, capable of injecting painful venom, are held erect. Blake (1983) and Webb and Weihs (1983) give complete accounts of swimming hydrodynamics.

ENERGETICS OF SWIMMING

The energy costs of swimming have long fascinated investigators. Many attempts have been made to measure the relationship between thrust and drag in swimming fish. These have ranged from the pioneering efforts of Houssay (1912), who harnessed fish to a balance device that measured swimming power by measuring the weight lifted, to the more sophisticated efforts of Webb (1971), who attached wire grids or plastic plates of various resistances to the dorsal surface of fish swimming in a tunnel respirometer. Bainbridge (1958) showed that for goldfish, trout, and dace the swimming speed at any tail beat frequency increased for longer specimens. As a general rule, a doubling of body length corresponds to a 150% increase in velocity per body flexure. The relationship worked out for small fish is $V = kL^b$, where V is the mean swimming velocity (in meters per second), L is fish length (in meters), k is a constant, and the exponent $ß$ has been determined experimentally, usually between 0.5 and 0.6 (Wu and Yates 1978). When sudden bursts of swimming are required, the value of the exponent β is typically about 0.8, a value determined for fish as varied as dace, goldfish, and barracuda. One factor which complicates this relationship is that smaller fish are typically capable of faster tail beat frequencies, which also can increase swimming velocities (Wardle 1975). However, when speed is normalized as body lengths per second, the relationship between speed and tail beat frequency becomes predictable for a range of fish lengths (Fig. 2.7a). When this information is coupled with that of Brett (1965) (Fig. 2.7b), Wohlschlag et al. (1968), and others who described the relationship between energetic costs and swimming velocities, estimates regarding a fish's metabolic demands can be made on free-swimming animals by counting tail beat frequencies (Feldmeth and Jenkins 1973).

Temperature is an important factor in the swimming dynamics and energetics of fish. A 10°C rise in temperature (from 13°C to 23°C) is accompanied by a 22% decrease in water viscosity, which presumably reduces hydrodynamic drag. Moreover, warm muscles tend to operate more efficiently by exerting more force per contraction. Stevens (1979) found that temperature acclimation affected the swimming muscles of rainbow trout and largemouth bass (Micropterus salmoides). At a constant swimming velocity, tail beat frequencies were lower (i.e., longer stride lengths) for both species acclimated to a higher temperature. Similarly, Webb (1978b) found that trout benefit from warmed environments by increased acceleration rates, which should enhance their attack success on prey. Chapter 5 discusses a vascular heat exchanger system found in several continuously cruising fishes that keeps red muscle mass up to 20°C warmer than the surrounding water. In contrast, striped bass acclimated to cold (5°C) water increase their aerobic capacity by increasing mitochondrial and lipid droplet densities in red muscle (Egginton and Sidell 1989). These lipid droplets facilitate the muscles' aerobic metabolism by their high O_2 solubility and use as aerobic fuel.

Exercise conditioning (training) increases aerobic capacity and improves swimming performance in several fishes. One measure of fish swimming performance is the critical swimming velocity (U_{crit}), the fish fatigue velocity after "stepped" velocity increases in a variable-speed swimming tunnel (Brett 1964). Largemouth bass increased its U_{crit} and its aerobic capacity, as measured by blood hemoglobin concentration, with exercise conditioning (Farlinger and Beamish 1978). The aerobic capacity of rainbow trout red and white muscle, as measured by capillary density, increased with exercise conditioning (Davie et al. 1986). Young-of-the-year striped bass increased their red:white muscle ratio, another measure of aerobic capacity, after 60 days conditioning at "slow" (0.5–1.2 body lengths/sec), "medium" (1.5–2.4 bl/sec), or "fast" (2.4–3.6 bl/sec) velocities, compared with non-conditioned controls (Young and Cech 1994). The striped bass also significantly increased their U_{crit} when conditioned at the higher velocities for 50–60 days (Fig. 2.8). Swimming performance benefits for the "fast" fish persisted for 56 days after conditioning had stopped. Exercise conditioning may equip hatchery-reared fish with increased survival abilities. Thus, exercise-conditioned Atlantic salmon (Salmo salar) apparently return to spawn in greater numbers than non-conditioned fish (Wendt and Saunders (1973).

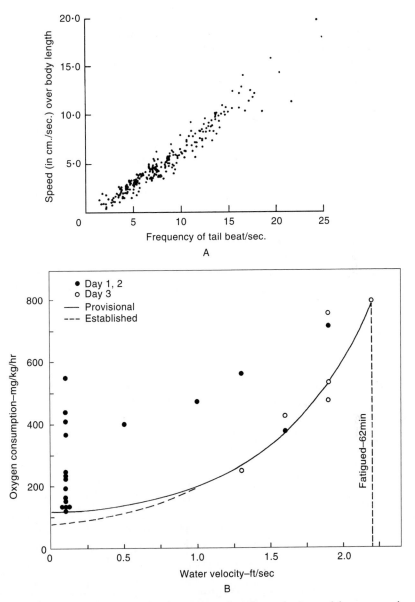

FIGURE 2.7 *(A) Relationship between swimming velocity and frequency of caudal undulations (tail beats) for dace,* Leuciscus leuciscus. *(From Bainbridge 1958.) (B) Relationship between swimming (water) velocity and oxidative metabolic (oxygen consumption) rate for juvenile sockeye salmon. (From Brett 1964.)*

Webb (1971) determined that the power required to propel a trout is exponentially proportional to their swimming speed and is approximately 2.8 times greater than that required to propel a rigid fish model of equal dimensions. In steady swimming, the average thrust equals the average total drag on the fish. For the fish to keep moving, the inertial forces of motion must be larger than the viscous forces of the surrounding water. Thus Reynold's number (Re), Re = VL/v is always greater than 1, where V is the mean swimming velocity, L is the length of the fish, and v is the coefficient of kinematic viscosity of the fluid. Values of Reynold's number typically range from 10^4 to 10^8 for fish swimming normally (Wu and Yates 1978). Viscosity effects at such high Reynold's numbers are mostly confined to a thin boundary layer adjacent to the body surface, especially in more streamlined fish. In species (tunas, marlin, etc.) with small turbulence wakes (Fig. 2.5), the maximum thickness of the boundary layer (at the tail end) is generally not more than a few percent of

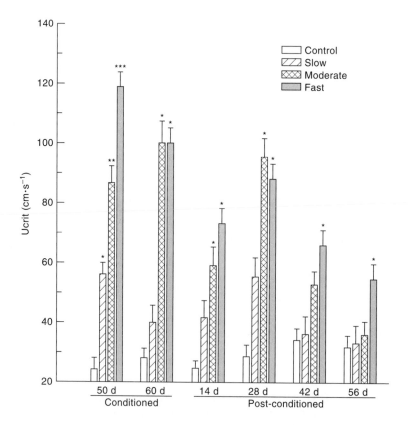

FIGURE 2.8 *Mean (± SE, n=12) critical swimming velocities (U_{crit}) of juvenile striped bass exercise conditioned at different flow velocities for 50 and 60 days and at 14, 28, 42, and 56 days post-conditioning; * significantly greater than control, ** significantly greater than * and control, *** significantly greater than **, *, and control; p<0.05. (From Young and Cech, 1994,* Can J. Fish. Aquat. Sci. *51:1519–1527.)*

the body thickness (Wu and Yates 1978). There is evidence that the mucous coating on a fish reduces the frictional drag (Rosen and Cornford 1971). It is also hypothesized that the swim and glide intermittent swimming pattern may be more efficient than continuous swimming in fish that are migrating at fairly high velocities (Weihs 1974; Blake 1983).

In studies of trout fast-start acceleration, Webb (1975) found that rainbow trout expend 18% of the total work of acceleration to overcome frictional drag. This study also demonstrated that both trout and green sunfish *(Lepomis cyanellus)* display uneven rates of acceleration during a fast start initiated by a mild electric shock. These species initially tended to accelerate maximally. Even though velocity and distance covered increased with time, acceleration rate actually decreased in the milliseconds after a fast start. To capture prey or avoid predation from larger predators, this behavior would seem to have high survival value. Greater velocities would be attained and increased distances covered in a shorter time than with a constant acceleration rate, at an increased energy cost of only 2% to 3% of the total expended.

Supplemental Readings

Alexander 1967; Blake, 1983; Egginton and Sidell 1989; Moyle 1976a; Webb 1975a; Webb and Weihs 1983; Wu and Yates 1978.

CHAPTER 3

Respiration

Respiration in an aquatic environment presents different problems when compared with respiration in air. Most terrestrial vertebrates have internal lungs that must be ventilated by bidirectional (tidal) movement of air to replenish the oxygen supply at the gas exchange surfaces. In contrast, most fish have external gills that are ventilated by a unidirectional flow of water, created either by branchial pumping or passively, by simply opening the mouth and operculi while swimming forward. Not having to accelerate and decelerate the water in a bidirectional pattern obviously saves the fish valuable energy. The fine sieve structure of the gills (Fig. 3.1) enables them to extract oxygen very efficiently from the water. This efficient oxygen uptake is vital to fish, since the dissolved oxygen content of water is very low. Water contains about 1/30 as much oxygen per volume as does the atmosphere above it. This low oxygen availability has undoubtedly contributed to the evolutionary development of the gills, which are characterized by large surface areas and extremely efficient gas exchange, and to the many, often bizarre, mechanisms some fishes use to extract oxygen directly from the air. The low availability of oxygen has also placed limits on rates of oxygen uptake and consequently on fish metabolism.

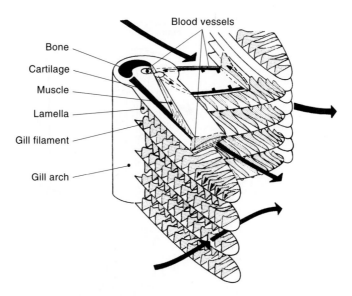

FIGURE 3.1 *Diagram of teleost gill structure. Large arrows indicate direction of water flow; small arrows show direction of blood flow. (Modified from Hughes and Grimstone 1965.)*

GILLS

Gills are the main site of gas exchange in almost all fishes. The gills consist of bony (Fig. 3.1) or cartilaginously stiffened arches that anchor pairs of gill filaments. In sharks the pairs of gill filaments are separated by a fleshy septum. The numerous, minute lamellae that protrude from both sides of each filament are the primary sites of gas exchange. However, not all the blood flow in the gills is directed to the lamellae. "Nonrespiratory" basal blood channels or venolymphatic sinuses (Fig. 3.2) may carry a significant fraction of the gill blood. Booth (1979) found that resting rainbow trout perfused about 58% of their lamellae with blood. Trout in hypoxic (low dissolved oxygen) water or injected with epinephrine (e.g., simulating stress or excitement) perfused more than 70% of their lamellae. Conversely, injections of acetylcholine decreased perfused lamellae to about 43%. These results indicate that rainbow trout can "recruit" lamellae in response to environmental hypoxia, presumably to increase functional gill surface area, and that they regulate blood flow distribution in the gills by cholinergic (acetylcholine-sensitive) and adrenergic (epinephrine-sensitive) receptors (Booth 1979).

The lamellae are made up of thin epithelial cells on the outside and thin basement membranes and supportive pillar cells on the inside (Fig. 3.3), allowing blood cells to flow through the interior without significant changes in shape (Hughes and Grimstone 1965). Oxygen is taken up by diffusion across the thin lamellar membranes. Because the blood and the water move in opposite directions, gas exchange

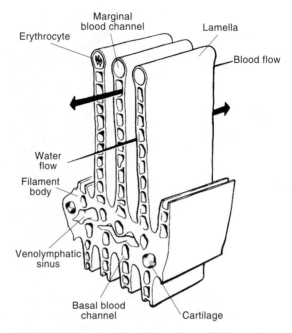

FIGURE 3.2 *A section through a gill filament and several lamellae of a teleost, drawn approximately to scale. (From Randall 1982.)*

efficiency is maximized by countercurrent exchange. Countercurrent flow ensures a steady oxygen tension gradient along the entire diffusion surface. Thus the blood can be oxygen saturated to a greater degree than with a parallel flow arrangement. Van Dam (1938) reported oxygen utilizations (extraction efficiencies) as high as 80% by a rainbow trout. When a parallel flow was experimentally induced by reversing the ventilatory water in the tench *(Tinca tinca)*, utilization dropped to less than 10% (Hughes 1963). The actual rate of oxygen uptake depends on the surface area of the lamellae, the thickness of the gill epithelia across which the oxygen moves, and the

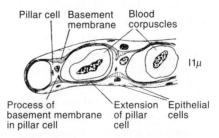

FIGURE 3.3 *Section through gill lamella. (Modified from Hughes 1963.)*

TABLE 3–1 COMPARISON OF GILL DIMENSIONS IN SEVERAL TELEOST FISHES

Species	Thickness of lamellae (μ)	Lamellae (per mm)	Distance between lamellae (μ)	Distance between blood and water (μ)	
Ice fish (*C. aceratus*)	35	8	75	6	⎫ Sluggish
Bullhead	25	14	45	10	⎬ species
Eel	26	17	30	6	⎭
N. tessellata	20	17.5	35	2	⎫
Sea scorpion	15	14	55	3	
Trout (5 kg)	15	20	40	3	
Flounder	10	14	70	2	Active
Icefish (*C. esox*)	10	18	40	1	⎬ species
Trout (400 g)	12	23	35	3	
Roach	12	27	25	2	
Coalfish	7	21	40	<1	
Perch	10	31	25	<1	⎭
Herring	7	32	20	<1	⎫ Very active
Mackerel	5	32	25	<1	⎭ species

Source: Modified from Steen and Berg 1966.

oxygen (tension) gradient across the membranes. Consequently, in order to increase rates of oxygen uptake from water, highly active fishes typically have larger gill surface areas and extra thin gill epithelial layers (Table 3-1). In order to increase gill surface area, fishes have two main evolutionary "options": increasing the number of lamellae by spacing them more closely together, or increasing the length of the lamellae. The latter option is seldom found because of the fragility of the delicate lamellae. Some tunas have evolved lamellae that are fused at the tips between adjacent filaments to add rigidity and hence protect the lamellae from damage from the high ventilatory flows (Muir and Kendall 1968). Both the close lamellar spacing and the thin epithelia usually associated with the lamellae of active fish decrease the distance across which oxygen in the water must diffuse to enter the blood and thereby increase the rate of diffusion. Gas diffusion rates also depend on the gas tension gradient across the respiratory surface. As oxygen diffuses from the water through the lamellar surfaces and into the relatively oxygen-depleted blood, diffusion slows or stops if fresh, oxygen-rich water is not continuously provided. Renewing this water is called *ventilation* of the gills.

Gill ventilation. In most bony fishes ventilation is accomplished by synchronous expansion and contraction of the buccal and opercular cavities to provide a nearly continuous unidirectional flow of water over the gill surfaces. In the first phase of the pumping cycle, water enters the mouth by expansion of the buccal cavity. The water is then accelerated over the gills by a simultaneous contraction of the buccal

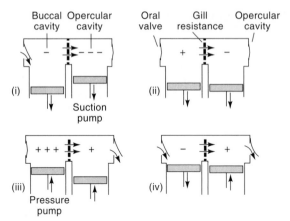

FIGURE 3.4 *Diagrammatic representation of the two-stage (buccal and opercular) pump for ventilating the gills of bony and cartilaginous fishes. The first three phases actively pump water through the gill sieve. The last phase shown (iv) does not pump a significant flow but accounts for only a very brief part of the cycle. (From Hughes 1963.)*

cavity and expansion of the operculi. After the branchial cavity contracts, expelling the water out the opercular openings, the cycle begins again (Fig. 3.4). Interruptions of this cycle produce brief reversals of flow or "coughs" which fish use to clear foreign matter or excess mucus from the gills. The frequency of these coughs in brook trout *(Salvelinus fontinalis)* has been used as a sublethal indicator of excessive copper concentrations in fresh water (Drummond et al. 1973). The greater the volume of water passed over the gills, the faster the "boundary" water is replaced at the lamellar surfaces, maximizing the oxygen tension gradient and, therefore, the diffusion rate. Sharks and rays use fleshy flaps of skin to create a ventilatory current through the branchial cavity.

Varying the ventilation volume is one adjustment that fish can make to influence the rate of gas exchange at the gills. Roberts (1975) has shown that at least one species from each of eight teleostean families ceases branchial movements and passively ("ram") ventilates at a high, "critical" swimming velocity. Presumably these critical velocities are evolutionarily determined to maximize energetic efficiency by using the swimming musculature both to propel the fish and to ventilate the gills adequately.

Another example of ventilation volume adjustments to influence gas exchange rates is exhibited by most fish that encounter water with low amounts of oxygen. In this case the oxygen tension of the inspired water is reduced and diffusion of oxygen across the gills slows as a result of the decreased oxygen gradient. The typical response to hypoxia is a higher ventilatory water flow. To increase the volume of water pumped over the gills, there must be an increase in either the number of buccal and opercular strokes per minute (ventilatory frequency) or the volume pumped with each stroke (ventilatory stroke volume). Commonly a fish will increase both in response to hypoxic conditions (Table 3-2). Increases in ventilation volume maximize the oxygen tension difference by rapid displacement of water next to the lamellar surfaces. Even though the oxygen extraction efficiency per volume of water (or percent utilization) is often reduced at high ventilatory flows, a sufficient amount of oxygen can normally be taken up to maintain respiratory homeostasis (Table 3-2).

Aquatic cutaneous respiration. In some fish some aquatic gas exchange takes place across the skin. Diffusion through the skin is known to play an important role in the respiration of larval fish. For example, the larvae of the swamp eel *(Monopterus albus)* of Southeast Asia display an extensive respiratory capillary network just below the epithelial surfaces of the median fins, the pectoral fins, and the yolk sac before the gills have developed. Interestingly, this species also increases the movement of water posteriorly over the body surfaces, countercurrent to the anteriorly flowing blood, to optimize oxygen uptake when exposed to hypoxic water (Liem 1981). Cutaneous surfaces account for 96% of the respiratory surface area in larval (0.045 g wet weight, 3.7 days posthatch) chinook salmon *(Oncorhynchus tshawytscha).* The branchial area of developing gills exceeds the cutaneous area only when these young salmon reach 2.5–4.0 g (Rombough and Moroz 1990). Significant cutaneous respiration has also been measured in several adult forms. Measurements of cutaneous respiration in six freshwater teleosts mostly matched the oxygen demand of the skin itself. Thus in crucian carp *(Carassius carassius),* yellow perch *(Perca fluviatilis),* brook trout, and brown trout the skin is not an oxygen exchanger for the benefit of other tissues. Only in the scaleless black bullhead *(Ameivrus melas)* does the skin function as a minor respiratory organ, supplying about 5% of the total oxygen demand (Nonnotte 1981). Cutaneous oxygen diffusion also matches cutaneous oxygen consumption in the marine plaice *(Pleuronectes platessa)* (Steffensen and Lomholt 1985).

TABLE 3–2   MEANS OF STRIPED MULLET (BODY WEIGHT = 100$_G$) VENTILATORY RESPONSES TO HYPOXIA

Variable	Units	Ambient conditions	Hypoxic conditions
Inspired dissolved O_2 concentration	mg O_2/l	8.81	3.48
O_2 consumption rate	mg O_2/h	12.05	11.94
Ventilation volume	ml water/min	36	171
Ventilatory frequency	strokes/min	60	95
Ventilatory stroke volume	ml water/stroke	0.60	1.80
Percentage utilization of oxygen	%	66	39

Source: Modified from Cech and Wohlschlag 1973, with permission, from *Journal of Fish Biology.* Copyright by Academic Press, Inc. (London) Ltd.

AIR-BREATHING FISHES

Behavioral means also have evolved in fish to cope with hypoxic water. Whereas some species swim to the surface and inspire the oxygen-rich water next to the atmosphere (Kramer and McClure 1982), others have evolved the ability actually to leave the water and breathe air. Air-breathing fish in aquatic habitats often breathe synchronously (Kramer and Graham 1976), presumably to minimize individual notice by terrestrial predators (Gee 1980).

Other fish that migrate short distances over land or are exposed to long-term dewatering or severe drought conditions have also evolved aerial respiratory adaptations. These adaptations range from modifications of the gills, to use of the skin, to special respiratory structures in the mouth and gut, to true lungs.

Modified gills. The walking catfish *(Clarias batrachus)* of Southeast Asia and more recently of Florida (Chapter 20), represents an example of a fish with modified gills. These catfish feature thickened, widely spaced lamellae on the dorsal side of the filaments and branched, bulbous dendritic structures dorsally emanating from the second and fourth gill arches. These dendritic structures resemble "respiratory trees" and reside in suprabranchial cavities (Jordan 1976). The thickened and bulbous shapes of these modified gills ensure adequate support in air. Ordinary gills, having numerous closely spaced filaments and lamellae, tend to stick together and functionally lose much of their surface area when removed from water. Another requirement for respiratory surfaces is that they remain properly moist. The walking catfish moves on land mainly when it is raining (Jordan 1976). Juvenile monkeyface prickleback *(Cebidichthys violaceus)* of the California intertidal zone can survive air exposure periods of several hours (e.g. during low tides). Using "standard" gills and, probably, cutaneous surfaces, they lower their overall O_2 demand by becoming very quiescent, as they hide beneath rocks (Edwards and Cech 1990). Several other intertidal fishes, such as sculpins (Cottidae), apparently have similar abilities to survive short-term air exposure under damp conditions (Yoshiyama and Cech 1994).

Skin. The extent to which fish use cutaneous respiration is poorly known. It is best documented in European eels *(Anguilla anguilla),* which can migrate short distances across land. By diffusion through a well-vascularized skin and to a lesser extent across the gills, they are able to use the atmosphere for respiration (Berg and Steen 1965). Desiccation of the body surface is avoided by limiting terrestrial sojourns to nocturnal movements through moist grass.

Mouth. Electric eels *(Electrophorus electricus),* in contrast to "true" eels, are among the obligate air-breathing fishes. This species has a well-vascularized area in the buccal cavity, where most of its required oxygen is taken up. Whereas this region has a large surface area from surface convolutions and papillae, the gills have degenerated over evolutionary time. The electric eel surfaces at intervals of about one minute to replenish the oxygen supply in its mouth and will drown if forcibly kept immersed (Johansen et al. 1968).

Two other genera that use modified areas of the mouth for aerial gas exchange are the Asian climbing perch *(Anabas testudineus)* and the North American mudsucker *(Gillichthys mirabilis).* Both of these examples have evolved bimodal breathing capabilities to feed or escape predators by moving out of the water.

Gut. *Hoplosternum, Ancistrus,* and *Plecostomus* are three genera of tropical catfishes that have parts of their gut specialized for oxygen uptake by actually swallowing air. In these and most other air-breathing fishes, elimination of respiratory carbon dioxide occurs primarily at a site different from that of oxygen uptake. Since the gut is not closely associated with the external environment, the highly water-soluble carbon dioxide is excreted primarily at the gills.

Lungs and swimbladders. Another example of a gas-specific exchange location comes from the famous lungfishes (Dipnoi). The South American *(Lepidosiren)* and African *(Protopterus)* lungfishes are obligate air breathers. The latter forms have adapted to extensive drought conditions which may completely dry up their environments. By breathing air through a small vent to the atmosphere, these fish survive extensive dry periods in the mud of dried-up lakes and rivers in an estivated state. When their habitats refill with water, they surface to inspire air into well-sacculated and heavily vascularized lungs. On the other hand, most of the carbon dioxide is eliminated directly into the water through vestigial gills. The Australian lungfish *(Neoceratodus)* is not subjected to such lengthy drought conditions in its natural environment and will perish if experimentally denied access to water for extensive periods. Other facultative air breathers that use a modified swimbladder for some gas exchange function include the bichir *(Polypterus* spp.), the bowfin *(Amia calva),* and gars *(Lepisosteus* spp.).

FISH OXYGEN REQUIREMENTS

Fish need energy to move, to find and digest food, to grow, and to reproduce, in addition to maintaining the body and internal environment. Energy stored in their food must be metabolically converted in order to power these various bodily functions. Oxygen, along with an organic substrate, is needed for all oxidative metabolic processes. When sufficient oxygen is unavailable—for example, during hypoxia or burst swimming—some anaerobic metabolism is likely. Many fish use glycolysis and accumulate lactic acid. Goldfish convert the lactate to ethanol in red and white muscle, presumably to minimize adverse effects of the metabolic acidosis (Shoubridge and Hochachka 1980). The ethanol also triggers behavioral seeking of cooler water, lowering total energy requirements (see below) via the thermoregulatory center in the brain (preopticus periventricularis) (Crawshaw et al. 1989).

Oxidative (or aerobic) metabolic pathways are dominant in organisms that have a fairly reliable oxygen source because they are biochemically more efficient than anaerobic pathways. The amount of oxygen a fish requires for these processes over a given length of time is called its *oxygen consumption rate.* Oxygen consumption rate can be affected by a variety of factors. Four of the most significant of these are body weight, level of activity, environmental temperature, and feeding. In general, larger fish use more total oxygen per hour than smaller fish do (Fig. 3.5), although per unit body weight, smaller fish use more oxygen than larger specimens. In similar manner, swimming fish use more oxygen than resting animals (Fig. 3.6). Moreover, fish in warmer water generally have higher oxygen consumption rates than those in cooler water (Fig. 3.7). Pacific cod *(Gadus macrocephalus)* increase O_2 consumption rates by 41–48% after feeding (Paul et al. 1988). This extra energy is needed for digestion and growth (Chapters 7, 8). The apparatus generally used to measure fish oxygen consumption (oxidative metabolic) rates is called a *respirometer. Sealed* and *open* (flow-through) respirometers may be used to measure *routine, active,* and—with special precautions—*standard* or *resting* metabolic rates of fishes. Measuring active rates of fish swimming at various velocities is commonly used to estimate standard metabolic rates by extrapolation back to a swimming speed of 0 lengths/s (Fig. 3.6). Subtraction of the standard metabolic rate from the active metabolic rate yields the *scope for activity,* which is a useful index in determining the relative amount of non-maintenance energy reserves. Fish with more reserves are better able to move, grow, reproduce, and resist diseases and parasitism.

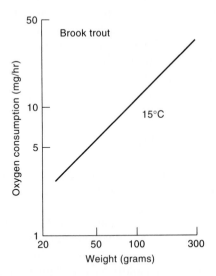

FIGURE 3.5 *The influence of body weight on total oxygen consumption rate for brook trout at 15°C. (Modified from Beamish 1964.)*

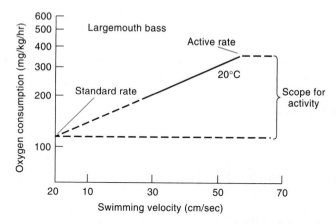

FIGURE 3.6 *The effect of swimming velocity on the oxygen consumption rate of largemouth bass. Extrapolation back from the data to 0 cm/s estimates the standard metabolic rate. Subtraction of the standard metabolic rate from the active rate gives the scope for activity. (Modified from Beamish 1970.)*

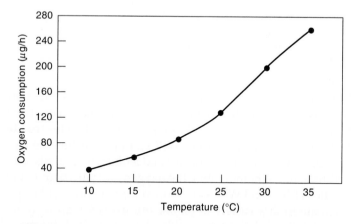

FIGURE 3.7 *The influence of temperature on the routine oxygen consumption rate of mosquitofish. (Data from Cech et al. 1985.)*

Supplemental Readings

Berg and Steen 1965; Cech 1990; Cech and Wohlschlag 1973; Hughes 1963; Johansen et al. 1968; Hoar and Randall 1984.

CHAPTER 4

Blood and Its Circulation

BLOOD

Fish blood, like that of other vertebrates and many invertebrates, is composed of blood corpuscles (cells) suspended in plasma that is circulated throughout the body tissues. The cells are of two basic types, erythrocytes (red blood cells, RBCs) and leukocytes (white blood cells, WBCs). In this section we will first describe the nature and function of erythrocytes and leukocytes and discuss in detail the structure and function of hemoglobin, the oxygen-carrying pigment of the blood.

Both RBCs and WBCs are formed from hemocytoblast precursor cells that may originate from a variety of organs but usually mature after they enter the bloodstream. In hagfish the primary blood-forming site is the mesodermal envelope surrounding the gut (Jordan and Speidel 1930). Percy and Potter (1976) have shown that adult lampreys *(Lampetra)* synthesize blood cells from the fatty tissue dorsal to the nerve cord. Elasmobranch fishes may produce blood cells from the Leydig organ (situated in the esophagus), the epigonal organ (around the gonads), and the spleen. The Leydig organ produces granulocytic and lymphocytic WBCs in the deepwater shark *Etmopterus spinax* (Mattisson and Fänge 1982), whereas the Atlantic nurse shark *(Ginglyostoma cirratum)* lacks this organ and produces these cells from the epigonal organ. The *white pulp* portion of the spleen produces more lymphocytes, and the *red pulp* portion produces erythrocytes and some granulocytes in the

Atlantic nurse shark (Fänge and Mattisson 1981). The spleen of elasmobranch and teleost fishes is supplied by splanchnic (autonomic) innervation which stimulates this organ to contract during stressful states, such as during hypoxia (Fänge and Nilsson 1985). Besides direct nervous stimulation, hormone (adrenergic or cholinergic) stimulation also causes contractions of the Atlantic cod *(Gadus morhua)* spleen (Nilsson and Grove 1974). Splenic production of RBCs may consist either of immature erythrocytes or of cells that differentiate into erythrocytes after entering the blood (Fänge and Johansson-Sjöbeck 1975). Teleostean hemopoietic (blood-forming) sites are primarily the kidney and spleen (Satchell 1971), whereas lymphomyeloid (lymphocyte- and granulocyte-producing) tissue is also found in the cranium of holocephalans *(Chimaera)* and sturgeons *(Acipenser)* as well as surrounding the heart of sturgeons (Fänge 1984). The thymus constitutes another lymphomyeloid tissue in the juvenile stages of many jawed fishes, but often regresses in sexually mature individuals (Fänge 1984). Fish bone has no marrow for hemopoiesis.

Erythrocytes

Red blood cells are usually the most abundant cells in fish blood (up to 4 million/ mm^3). They contain hemoglobin and largely function in carrying oxygen from the gills to the tissues. Like the erythrocytes of other nonmammalian vertebrates, fish RBCs are generally nucleated and show a wide range of sizes among different species. Elasmobranchs typically have larger RBCs, although fewer in number, than teleosts (Table 4-1). Even within the teleosts, fish having more erythrocytes per milliliter of blood generally have smaller RBCs. Within this group the more active species tend to have more erythrocytes than do sedentary ones (Table 4-1). Perhaps the smaller cell size in these active species presents a shorter mean diffusion path length for essential respiratory gases such as oxygen. Shorter path lengths and more erythrocytes would increase the efficiency of oxygen uptake at the gills and its delivery to the oxygen-requiring swimming muscles. Open-ocean pelagic species such as albacore and Atlantic shortfin mako sharks, which use physiological thermoregulation to warm red muscle masses (Chapter 5), characteristically have the highest hematocrit and hemoglobin levels (Table 4-1).

Because the oxygen demands of fish vary with stage of life history and environmental conditions, the number of red blood cells per milliliter varies as a way of balancing the energy costs of producing RBCs with those of pumping blood to the tissues. Blood that is low in RBCs obviously has to be pumped through the body at a greater rate than blood that is high in RBCs, if the oxygen demand is high. Since it has been demonstrated, for three species of freshwater fish, that the teleost heart requires up to 4.4% of the total energy of the fish (Cameron 1975), the number of RBCs can have a significant effect on its overall energy balance, including growth (Chapter 8). Indeed, rainbow trout experimentally made anemic show significant increases in the volume of blood pumped by the heart (cardiac output) (Cameron and Davis 1970). However, when oxygen demands of tissues are relatively low, such as when water temperatures are low and the fish are not very active, large numbers of RBCs are not required and the number tends to drop (RBCs live up to 150

TABLE 4–1 HEMATOLOGICAL CHARACTERISTICS OF VARIOUS FISHES

Species	Erythrocyte number (cells × 10^6/mm^3)	Hematrocrit (%)	Hemoglobin concentration (g %)	Mean erythrocytic volume (μ^3)	Blood oxygen capacity (volumes %)	Source
Spiny dogfish (*Squalus acanthias*)	0.09	18.2	—	650–1010	—	Thorson 1958 Wintrobe1934
Blue shark (*Prionace glauca*)	—	22.3	5.70	—	—	Johanson-Sjöbeck and Stevens 1976
Oyster toadfish (*Opsanus tau*)	0.69	—	6.84	—	—	Eisler 1965
Winter flounder (*Pseudopleuronectes americanus*)	2.21	23	5.36	107	8.30	Bridges et al. 1976
Common carp (*Cyprinus carpio*)	1.43	27.1	6.40	186	12.50	Houston and DeWilde 1968
Striped mullet (*Mugil cephalus*)	3.08	26.9	7.14	88	8.36	Cameron 1970a
Pinfish (*Lagodon rhomboides*)	2.66	32.9	7.59	124	7.78	Cameron 1970a
Spotted sea trout (*Cynoscion nebulosus*)	3.25	32.2	6.99	99	8.56	Cameron 1970a
Bluefish (*Pomatomus saltatrix*)	3.85	—	13.41	—	—	Eisler 1965
Atlantic shortfin mako shark[a] (*Isurus oxyrinchus*)	—	40.8	14.30	—	—	Emery 1986
Albacore[a] (*Thunnus alalunga*)	—	53.0	17.20	—	21.8	Barret and Williams 1965 Cech et al. 1984

[a]Species that use physiological thermoregulation (Chapter 5).

days, at least in tench *[Tinca tinca]*, at 18°C [Hevesy et al. 1964]). Thus in active fishes there are often seasonal changes in RBC production. For example, winter flounder *(Pseudopleuronectes americanus)* have a peak in RBC production during late spring and early summer in waters off Maine (Fig. 4.1). Cameron (1970) has shown that changes in RBC counts (and in total hemoglobin concentration, Hb) in pinfish *(Lagodon rhomboides)* are of some significance in meeting seasonal increases in respiratory demands. However, he points out that other adjustments, in erythrocyte size and in the rate of blood circulation, would also be required to meet the nearly tenfold change in respiratory metabolism associated with seasonal temperature extremes. In the striped mullet *(Mugil cephalus)*, changes in RBC numbers and Hb are associated not only with seasonal temperature changes (Cameron 1970b) but also with spawning activity, with its high energy demands (Fig. 4.2). Increases in RBC number during the spawning season have also been recorded for fish as diverse as common carp (Fourie and Hattingh 1976) and the redbelly tilapia *(Tilapia zilli)* (Ezzat et al. 1973), so the phenomenon may be widespread among teleosts. It is also worth noting that RBC counts may also be affected by other environmental factors, particularly pollutants. Destruction of erythrocytes through the inhibition of vital metabolic pathways in the cell appears to be one of the reasons chlorine in water is so harmful to fish (Grothe and Eaton 1975; Buckley 1976).

Leukocytes

White blood cells are less abundant ($20,000/mm^3$ to $150,000/mm^3$) than red ones in fish blood and function in a variety of ways in ridding the body of foreign material (including invading pathogens), along with providing a mechanism for blood

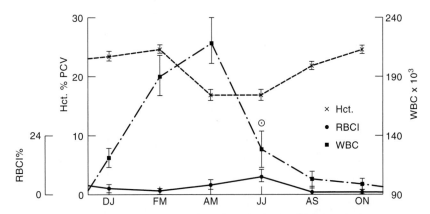

FIGURE 4.1 *Bimonthly mean values (±SE) of microhematocrit, immature red blood cells, and leukocytes (WBCs) for winter flounder* (Pseudopleuronectes americanus) *from Casco Bay, Maine. The notation signifies the highest mean RBCI, which occurred during the third week in June. (From Bridges et al. 1976.)*

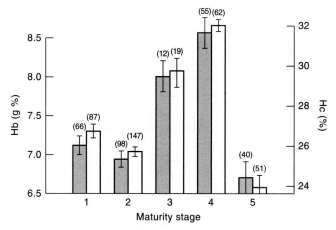

FIGURE 4.2 *Mean hemoglobin and hematocrit levels at different reproductive maturity stages. Histogram bar heights indicate mean values; vertical lines indicate ±1 SE; numbers in parentheses indicate sample size; stippled bars indicate total hemoglobin concentration; open bars indicate percent of packed cell volume (hematocrit). Maturity stages: 1 = immature (gonads very small or absent); 2 = mature (gonads mature but small); 3 = prespawning (gonads enlarged but not secreting reproductive products); 4 = ripe (reproductive products flow easily from fish); 5 = postspawning (gonads somewhat enlarged but empty). (From Cech and Wohlschlag 1981.)*

clotting. Measurements of change in total WBC number or in the percentages of the various types can often lead to a better understanding of the physiological or pathological state of the animal. Circulating WBC number can also vary through the year in some fish species. Bridges et al. (1976) describe a pattern of total and differential (separate) WBC counts in winter flounder, which generally shows an inverse rela-

TABLE 4–2   BOHR EFFECTS OF FISHES CHARACTERIZING VARIOUS ACTIVITY LEVELS

Activity level	Species	Temperature (°C)	Bohr effect $\dfrac{\Delta \log P_{50}}{\Delta \text{pH}}$	Source
Lower	Brown bullhead (*Ameivrus nebulosus*)	9, 24	−0.31	Grigg 1969
	Flounder (*Platichthys flesus*)	15	−0.55	Weber and De Wilde 1975
Higher	Rainbow trout (*Oncorhynchus mykiss*)	15	−0.57	Eddy 1971
Highest	Atlantic mackerel (*Scomber scombrus*)	25	−1.2	Hall and McCutcheon 1938

Mature erythrocytes

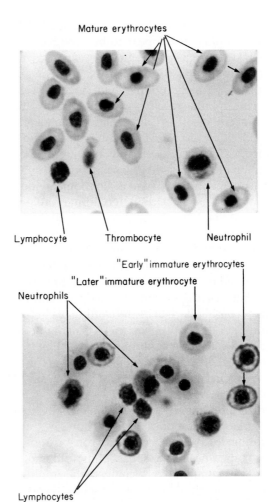

Lymphocyte   Thrombocyte   Neutrophil

"Early" immature erythrocytes

"Later" immature erythrocyte

Neutrophils

Lymphocytes

FIGURE 4.3 *Winter flounder blood cells.*

tionship with fish condition or health. Sick individuals would presumably make more WBCs to synthesize antibodies or phagocytize bacteria. Sample photomicrographs of winter flounder blood cells are shown in Fig. 4.3. There are often several types of leukocytes found in fish blood, and different roles have been attached to their presence. The principal types of WBCs are lymphocytes, thrombocytes, monocytes, and granulocytes.

Lymphocytes can vary in size (4.5 μm to 12 μm in diameter) among species. Their morphology, on the other hand, is more consistent. They are dominated by the nucleus, with only a narrow rim of basophilic cytoplasm, in which there are a few mitochondria and ribosomes. The number of lymphocytes varies among species (and with counting technique!). Ellis (1977) found that 12×10^3 lymphocytes/ mm^3 was the representative value for plaice. However, the number of lymphocytes can vary with the season, following general WBC seasonal trends (Fig. 4.1). Teleostean lymphocytes appear to be produced by thymus, spleen, and kidney (Fänge 1984), although specific antigen responses may differ among cells produced by each organ (Ellis 1977).

The primary function of fish lymphocytes seems to be to act as the executive cell of specific immune mechanisms by means of antibody production. Klontz (1972) reported a large increase in cells resembling small lymphocytes in the kidney of rainbow trout, which was correlated with high antibody production, two to three days after antigen injection. Hildemann (1970) and Hogarth (1973) have described the accumulation of cells resembling small lymphocytes at the graft points of rejected tissue transplants in fish. There is also some evidence that fish lymphocytes may demonstrate phagocytic activity (engulfing foreign cells) or give rise to cells (e.g., macrophages) that have this ability (Klontz 1972; Weinreb and Weinreb 1969).

Thrombocytes of fishes may appear as spiked, spindle, oval, and lone nucleus forms in stained blood smears prepared on microscope slides. The various thrombocyte shapes may well be different forms of the same cell because changes in shape can be observed in live preparations. From his work on plaice, Ellis (1977) believes that thrombocytes originate in splenic tissue. Wardle (1971) has shown the function of thrombocytes in plaice to be the clotting of circulating fluids. Clots are produced by spreading of the thrombocytic cytoplasm into long threads that cross-link the denuded nuclei, forming a fibrous network that traps circulating corpuscles.

Monocytes comprise a small proportion of the WBC population, unless foreign substances are present in the tissues or bloodstream. Thought to originate in the kidney, monocytes (termed "macrophages" by some workers) concentrate at and phagocytize foreign particles. Morphologically, therefore, the cell outline may be quite irregular from pseudopod formation.

Granulocytes are leukocytes with conspicuous cytoplasmic granules. There are three basic types: eosinophils, basophils, and neutrophils. The names of the three types reflect the comparative visibility of the granules when the cells are treated with acidic (e.g., eosin), basic, and neutral stains, respectively. Neutrophils are the most commonly encountered fish granulocyte, comprising up to 25% of the total leukocytes in brown trout (Blaxhall and Daisley 1973). In addition to the neutral-staining (e.g., gray) cytoplasm, fish neutrophils often have an eccentric nucleus which is divided into several lobes.

Granulocytes are formed in the kidney and the spleen to a lesser extent in teleosts (Ellis 1977). Fänge (1968) determined the Leydig organ to be the site of granulocyte formation in elasmobranchs. Granulocytic function is still open to question. Neutrophils apparently migrate to sites of bacterial infection, where they may be phagocytic (Finn and Nielson 1971) or otherwise bactericidal (Fänge 1984). In rainbow trout, neutrophilia (i.e., having increased numbers of circulating neutrophils) often corresponds to stress (Weinreb 1958).

Basophils have been reported in goldfish, Australian lungfish (*Neoceratodus forsteri*), common carp (except an Israeli strain), and Pacific salmon; but have been reported to be absent in the blood of anguillid eels, plaice, yellow perch (*Perca flavescens*), brown and rainbow trouts, and lampreys (Ellis 1977). Ellis also reported much confusion and contradiction in the fish hematological literature as to the presence or absence of eosinophils in fish. Although still unclear, basophil and eosinophil functions seem related to antigen sensitivity, stress phenomena, and phagocytosis (eosinophils) (Ellis 1977).

Hemoglobin

Hemoglobin (Hb) is a respiratory pigment that vastly increases the binding power of the blood for oxygen. For example, in the Port Jackson shark *(Heterodontus portjacksoni)* at 20°C, 93% of the oxygen carried by the blood is reversibly bound to the hemoglobin while 7% is physically dissolved in the plasma at saturation (Grigg 1974). In colder environments the plasma percentage may increase (12% in the Antarctic nototheniid *Trematomus bernacchii* at -1.5°C). Indeed, the Antarctic crocodile icefishes (family Channichthyidae) carry no hemoglobin in their blood at all. The icefishes survive because (1) their metabolic oxygen requirements are low and the environmental dissolved oxygen is high in the consistently cold Antarctic waters; (2) their sluggish activity levels are adequate to catch sufficient quantities of the plentiful krill and small fish; and (3) special cardiovascular adaptations (e.g., comparatively large heart and blood volume with relatively low resistance capillaries) promote efficient movement of their blood (Holeton 1970).

Despite this evidence that some fish can get along without hemoglobin, its importance to most fish is difficult to overstate. However, hemoglobin is not just a single type of molecule but really a class of structurally similar molecules that vary in their structure and in their affinity for oxygen under different conditions. This variability will become evident in the next sections on (1) hemoglobin structure, (2) the role of hemoglobin in blood oxygen affinity, and (3) factors affecting blood oxygen affinity.

Hemoglobin structure. Fish hemoglobin is of two basic types, monomeric and tetrameric. Monomeric hemoglobins consist of single-heme polypeptide molecules, each with a molecular weight of about 17,000 daltons. They are characteristic of lampreys and hagfish. Tetrameric hemoglobins are characteristic of all other fishes. They are composed of four chains of amino acids (two α chains and two ß chains), much like mammalian hemoglobins, and have molecular weights of approximately 65,000 daltons. There are many different kinds of tetrameric hemoglobins, and several kinds may be found in one fish! For example, four kinds of hemoglobin are found in rainbow trout blood (Binotti et al. 1971), two in American eel *(Anguilla rostrata)* blood (Poluhowich 1972), and three in goldfish blood (Houston and Cyr 1974). The significance of synthesizing more than one hemoglobin type appears to be related to the different functional properties of each, so different combinations of hemoglobin types reflect adaptations to different environments or ways of life.

Multiple hemoglobins are especially adaptive in migratory species which experience considerable environmental variation. For example, the catadromous American eel has one hemoglobin with a high oxygen affinity in saltwater conditions and one with a high affinity in freshwater conditions. Poluhowich (1972) suggests that the polymorphic hemoglobins assist in the acclimation of these eels to environments of different salinity by maintenance of an approximately constant blood oxygen affinity.

The goldfish hemoglobins are functionally differentiable by their responses to temperature (Houston and Cyr 1974). Goldfish acclimated to 2°C had two different hemoglobins, while others held at 20°C and 35°C featured three. Because the observed concentration of the third hemoglobin did not exceed 12.5% of the total concentration in any individual, its physiological importance may be minor, and a warm-temperature function for this component has yet to be demonstrated. However, Houston and Rupert (1976) have shown that the third Hb can be made to appear and disappear with temperature changes from 3°C to 23°C and vice versa, respectively, within *three hours.* Thus this rapid synthesis of the third hemoglobin in goldfish probably stems from rearrangement of the α and ß subunits in other hemoglobins rather than from synthesis of a new hemoglobin or production of a new type of erythrocyte (Houston and Gingras-Bedard 1994).

Hemoglobin polymorphism for activity levels has also been hypothesized for species of suckers (Catostomidae). Powers (1972) has presented evidence that the desert sucker *(Catostomus clarki)* possesses a pH-insensitive hemoglobin which maintains a high oxygen affinity even when the oxygen affinities of other hemoglobins are drastically reduced due to increases in circulating lactic acid from violent muscular activity. This species typically lives in fast water. In the same stream, however, lives the Sonora sucker *(Catostomus insignis),* which does not possess this hemoglobin. This species is therefore found mainly in the slower-water portion (e.g., quiet pools) of their streams. Although these hemoglobin types may enlarge the inhabitable environment for species that carry them, they may also function to increase intracellular buffer capacity (Chapter 6) in RBCs (Weber 1990).

Changes in hemoglobin types with age have also been demonstrated in fishes. Coho salmon, for example, show changes with the progression from alevin to fry or presmolt stages. Giles and Vanstone (1976) believe these changes are controlled genetically and may be related to known changes in the hemopoietic origin of the erythrocytes during development. Certainly the pattern of Hbs seems more fixed in developing cohos than in goldfish because exposure of the salmon fry and presmolts to extremes of temperature, salinity, and dissolved oxygen produces no detectable variation in hemoglobin types (Giles and Vanstone 1976).

Blood oxygen affinity. Figure 4.4a shows the blood oxygen dissociation curves of a Sacramento blackfish *(Orthodon microlepidotus),* and Fig. 4.4b shows those of a rainbow trout. Hyperbolic curves like those from blackfish blood result from the paucity of interaction among the four subunit hemes (O_2-binding sites) characteristic of tetrameric molecules. The subunit independence results in curves similar to those of the monomeric hemoglobin of agnathans. The steep, hyperbolic curve of the blackfish hemoglobin displays its ability to be 50% saturated with oxygen (half of the highest possible content, or half of capacity) at only 2 mm Hg P_{O2} at 20°C.[1]

---

[1] Note that 2 mm HgP_{O2} = partial pressure (P) of oxygen equal to 2 mm mercury (Hg) pressure.

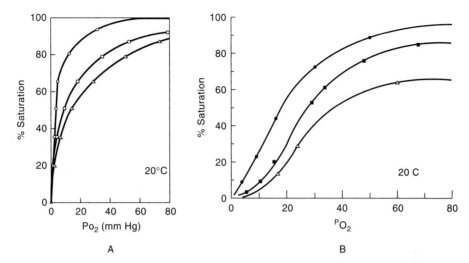

FIGURE 4.4 *(A) Blood oxygen dissociation curves for Sacramento blackfish equili-brated at 20°C and three* P_{CO_2} *levels: <1 mm Hg* P_{CO_2} *(○), 5 mm Hg* P_{CO_2} *(□), and 10 mm Hg* P_{CO_2} *(△). (From Cech, Mitchell, and Massingill, unpub. data.) (B) Blood oxygen dissociation curves for rainbow trout blood equilibrated at 20°C.* ● = 0 mm Hg P_{CO_2}, ■ = 3 mm Hg P_{CO_2}, and △ = 7 to 8 mm Hg P_{CO_2}. *(From Cameron 1971a.)*

This is termed the *half-saturation value* (or P_{50}) and reflects the affinity of the hemo-globin for oxygen. The low P_{50} of the Sacramento blackfish (2 mm Hg) indicates a high blood oxygen affinity. By comparison, the rainbow trout blood features a higher P_{50} (17 mm Hg) or *lower* blood oxygen affinity.

The importance of this difference is especially apparent in hypoxic environ-ments. For example, if the P_{O_2} of the water is only 32 mm Hg (about 20% of air sat-uration), fish can raise their arterial P_{O_2} to only about 25 mm Hg in the gills, despite the efficiency of this countercurrent gas exchanger. At 25 mm Hg, the Sacramento blackfish can saturate its arterial blood to about 90% (Fig. 4.4a), whereas the rain-bow trout can saturate its blood to only about 65% (Fig. 4.4b). This ability to satu-rate the blood to the 90% level under these conditions is obviously an advantage to a fish living in poorly oxygenated water, such as sloughs or stagnant pools, or in hypolimnetic parts of lakes. The higher-percent saturation achieved by the blackfish means that a greater content of oxygen is reversibly bound by the hemo-globin for transport to the tissues to meet the metabolic oxygen (content) require-ments of the fish.

The evolutionary advantages inherent in the sigmoid curve characteristic of the trout include the unloading of oxygen at the tissues at a fairly high P_{O_2}. Typifying quite active fish in well-oxygenated waters, the high P_{O_2} of the inspired water en-sures full oxygenation of the blood while traversing the gills. Fish with sigmoid curves with a fairly steep middle segment can unload and reload large quantities (contents) of oxygen over a quite narrow P_{O_2} range. This steep portion of the curve represents the physiologically most efficient P_{O_2} range for O_2 uptake and delivery for the species. As the steep portion of sigmoid curves is usually shifted to the right (compared with hyperbolic curves), the active fish with sigmoid curves operate most efficiently in well-oxygenated environments (streams, well-mixed oligotrophic lakes, shallow ocean areas).

Oxidized (rather than oxygenated) hemoglobin, which cannot function as a respiratory pigment, is termed *methemoglobin* (MetHb) and may occur in significant quantities in fish blood. Cameron (1971b) found 11% of the total hemoglobin in pink salmon *(Oncorhynchus gorbuscha)* was methemoglobin, as was 21.7% of the hemoglobin in hatchery steelhead (sea-run rainbow) trout (Meade and Perrone 1980). Although it is not clear why high percentages of MetHb occur in the few species examined, it is known that energy is required to reduce the MetHb back to the less stable, functional form (Cameron 1971b).

Factors affecting blood oxygen affinity. The dynamics of fish hemoglobin-oxygen binding and dissociation have evolved to optimize gas transport to oxidative tissue sites. Numerous factors can influence the blood oxygen affinity. Among the most important are pH, carbon dioxide concentrations, temperature, and organic phosphate concentrations.

Carbon dioxide concentration and pH effects are often interrelated and are physiologically the most important factors affecting blood oxygen affinity. Figure 4.5 shows the effect of pH and P_{CO2} on winter flounder blood oxygen affinity. The decrease in affinity with decreasing pH or increasing P_{CO2} (Bohr effect) normally works to "drive off" oxygen from the hemoglobin, thereby raising the plasma P_{O2} and facilitating its diffusion to surrounding tissues. The Bohr shift is calculated by dividing the shift or change in log P_{50} by the change in pH associated with the shift. Table 4-2 shows that more active fish species tend to have larger (absolute value) Bohr shifts. This tendency is presumably adaptive, as exercise provokes greater oxygen demands of the red swimming muscles. The larger Bohr effect increases the O_2 diffusion rate across the capillary walls to meet this demand. Moreover, violent or high levels of sustained exercise activates the primarily anaerobic white muscles, incurring an oxygen debt. Lactic acid, the glycolytic end product of this metabolism, decreases blood pH even further, possibly magnifying the Bohr shift. However, Nikinmaa et al. (1984) showed that striped bass *(Morone saxatilis)* maintain their *intracellular* pH in somewhat swollen RBCs despite marked *extracellular* (plasma) acidification from exercise-induced lactic acid increases. The intracellular pH and arterial oxygen content were apparently protected via endogenous epinephrine (adrenaline) secretions during the exercise, because both of these variables were lower in exercised striped bass injected with the beta-adrenergic antagonist propranolol. Figure 4.6 shows a model for this adrenergic response in rainbow trout RBCs (Nikinmaa 1986). This adrenergically mediated Na^+/H^+ exchange across the rainbow trout RBC is stimulated under stress conditions when cortisol secretions (see Chapter 6) increase the number of membrane adrenoreceptors (labeled as 1 in Fig. 4.6), enhancing adrenaline binding (Reid and Perry 1991). The exchange apparently also shows seasonal variations (Cossins and Kilby 1989).

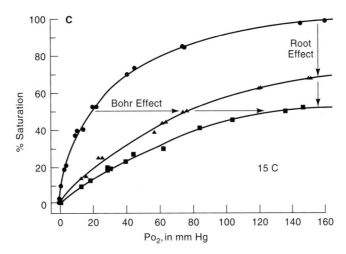

FIGURE 4.5 *Blood oxygen dissociation curves for winter flounder* (Pseudopleuronectes americanus) *blood equilibrated to three levels of P_{CO2} at 15°C:* ● = *<1 mm Hg P_{CO2} (mean pH = 8.02),* ▲ = *8 mm Hg P_{CO2} (mean pH = 7.48), and* ■ = *24 mm Hg P_{CO2} (mean pH = 7.17). (Modified from Hayden et al. 1975.)*

The Root effect (Root 1931) is another pH- or P_{CO2}-induced shift, except that blood oxygen capacity rather than affinity is affected (Fig. 4.5). The Root shift is now thought of primarily as an extreme Bohr shift, and the molecular basis of this phenomenon may be associated with a special hemoglobin within a complement of multiple hemoglobins. Increases in P_{CO2} or decreases in pH lower the oxygen capacity (oxygen content at 100% saturation). This effect is found only among fish hemoglobins and typifies species with swimbladders and retia mirabilia (red organs). Sharks have no swimbladders and no Root effect associated with their hemoglobins. As described in detail in Chapter 5, the unique features of these retial coun-

TABLE 4–2   BOHR EFFECTS OF FISHES CHARACTERIZING VARIOUS ACTIVITY LEVELS

Activity level	Species	Temperature (°C)	Bohr effect $\frac{\Delta \log P_{50}}{\Delta pH}$	Source
Lower	Brown bullhead (*Ameiurus nebulosus*)	9, 24	–0.31	Grigg 1969
	Flounder (*Platichthys flesus*)	15	–0.55	Weber and De Wilde 1975
Higher	Rainbow trout (*Oncorhynchus mykiss*)	15	–0.57	Eddy 1971
Highest	Atlantic mackerel (*Scomber scombrus*)	25	–1.2	Hall and McCutcheon 1938

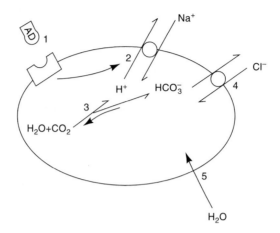

FIGURE 4.6 *A model for the adrenergic response of rainbow trout red cells. Binding of adrenaline to membrane receptor (1) activates the sodium/proton exchange (2), which extrudes protons and shifts (3) the reaction $H_2O + CO_2 = H^v + HCO_3^w$ to the right by removing one of the end products. Accumulation of bicarbonate (4) leads to increased efflux of HCO_3^w and influx of chloride. The accumulation of sodium and chloride draws (5) osmotically obliged water into the cell, and cell volume increases. (From Nikinmaa 1986.)*

tercurrent exchangers and the Root effect makes swimbladder inflation possible at great depths. Baines (1975) found a large Root effect characterizing the hemoglobin of relatively deepwater rockfishes (*Sebastes*, Scorpaenidae) he studied off the California coast. Scorpaenids from shallower water, which have less extensive vertical migrational patterns, had smaller Root effects. Finally, in the strictly shallow-water California scorpionfish (*Scorpaena guttata*), which has no swimbladder, no Root shift could be detected.

Winter flounder have no swimbladder yet display a significant Root effect (Fig. 4.5). Like many other teleosts that depend on vision to feed, winter flounder possess a choroid rete or countercurrent vascular organ behind the retina of the eye (Wittenberg and Haedrich 1974). The Root effect may play a significant role in delivering sufficient oxygen to the retina tissue, which has a high oxygen demand (Hayden et al. 1975).

Aspects of carbon dioxide transport in the blood are covered in more detail in Chapter 6, in the section concerning acid-base balance. Regardless, it is germane here to explain the carbon dioxide equilibrium curve which relates carbon dioxide loading (content) in the blood with the partial pressure of carbon dioxide (P_{CO_2}). There is typically significant carbon dioxide loading with little change in P_{CO_2} within the normal physiological range of P_{CO2} (less than 10 mm Hg), with some flattening out at higher tensions (Fig. 4.7). Carbon dioxide–combining power is greater in fishes (e.g., carp) adapted to living in stagnant, high P_{CO2} environments and is lower for fishes typifying low carbon dioxide habitats (e.g., trout and mackerel). Figure 4.7 also shows the increased carbon dioxide–combining power of deoxygenated Hb (Haldane effect) due to the pH rise accompanying blood deoxygenation (Grigg 1974). The magnitude of the Haldane effect also varies among species.

   Temperature effects on blood oxygen affinity and capacity of fish hemoglobins are most noticeable in stenothermal species. Figure 4.8 shows that increases in temperature depress both oxygen affinity and oxygen capacity of tench blood. The extra oxygen delivery to the respiratory tissues (e.g., from blood oxygen affinity loss) when oxygen demand is elevated by increased temperatures would seem to be an adaptive advantage. However, instead of exerting a selective effect like the Bohr shift (i.e., working primarily at the tissue sites where P_{CO2} is high and/or pH is low), the temperature effect in these ectotherms works equally well at the gills! Thus large temperature effects would not appear advantageous to species inhabiting environments that exhibit large temperature fluctuations or to species that move quickly from one temperature to a different one. The effect of temperature on the oxygen

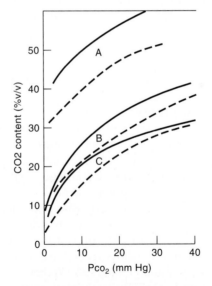

FIGURE 4.7 *Representative carbon dioxide equilibrium curves: (A) common carp; (B) Atlantic mackerel; and (C) rainbow trout. Solid lines and dotted lines represent deoxygenated and oxygenated blood, respectively. (Modified from Grigg 1974.)*

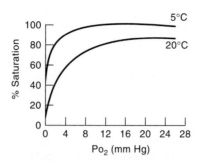

FIGURE 4.8 *Oxygen dissociation of tench* (Tinca tinca) *blood at 5°C and 20°C. (Modified from Eddy 1973.)*

affinity and capacity of hemoglobin can be quantified by the apparent heat of oxygenation (ΔH) from a form of the van't Hoff equation (Riggs 1970). The "living fossil" coelacanth *(Latimeria chalumnae)*, living in the quite thermally stable depth of 200 m to 400 m in the ocean, has hemoglobin displaying a ΔH of -10.42 kcal/mol (Wood et al. 1972). The more eurythermal winter flounder of coastal marine environments has a hemoglobin ΔH of -7.7 (Hayden et al. 1975). Species confronting wide temperature variations, such as the globally migratory bluefin tuna *(Thunnus thynnus)* (Rossi-Fanelli and Antonini 1960), display a Hb ΔH value of -1.8. Cech et al. (1984) showed a reverse temperature effect (ΔH = +1.72) for the warm-bodied albacore, in which oxygen is bound to the hemoglobin despite rapid warming of the blood in countercurrent retia (Chapter 5).

Organic phosphate effects are also important to the reversible binding of fish hemoglobins with oxygen. Gillen and Riggs (1971) have shown that concentrations of naturally occurring organic phosphates can profoundly influence $Hb-O_2$ affinity. They found adenosine triphosphate (ATP) to be the primary phosphorylated compound in Rio Grande perch *(Cichlasoma cyanoguttatum)*; and they found that ATP additions depress oxygen affinity, increase the Bohr effect, and modify heme–heme interactions. In carp RBCs, guanosine triphosphate (GTP) plays a greater role than ATP in blood oxygen affinity regulation (Weber and Lykkeboe 1978). Intraerythrocytic organic phosphate concentration decreases enhance oxygen uptake efficiency in fishes exposed to environments that are warm (Grigg 1969) or hypoxic (Greaney and Powers 1978; Weber and Lykkeboe 1978). In the spiny dogfish *(Squalus acanthias)* GTP also exerts a greater effect than ATP, but urea *increases* oxygen affinity (Weber et al. 1983).

CIRCULATION

The cardiovascular system of most fish is a closed system typically consisting of a heart as the pump in line with branchial (gill) and systemic capillary beds connected by arteries and veins (Fig. 4.9). In contrast, hagfish circulatory systems have acces-

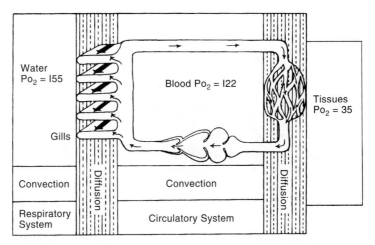

FIGURE 4.9 *The sites of convective and diffusional transport of oxygen in the circulation of a fish. The partial pressures of oxygen quoted are those of aerated water, arterial and venous blood in rainbow trout. (From Satchell 1971.)*

sory inline hearts. Lungfish also differ with the presence of a pulmonary circulation and partial mixing of oxygenated and deoxygenated blood in the heart (Randall 1970). A variety of circulatory adaptations can be found in fishes having accessory respiratory surfaces, for example, in cavities, at the skin, or in the gut (Satchell 1976). Given the diversity of circulatory adaptations in fishes, it is instructive to examine aspects of the cardiovascular anatomy to understand circulatory function better. Of paramount importance is the heart.

Heart Structure

Propulsion of blood through the circulatory system of the majority of teleosts and elasmobranchs is accomplished by a four-chambered heart, two chambers of which effect significant acceleration of the blood. All four chambers are in line and pump only venous blood. Except for a few air-breathing fish, all flow of blood is to the gills. The heart and gills are closely associated because fish hearts are located the farthest anterior of all the vertebrates. The heart is enclosed in a *pericardium*, which is more rigid in elasmobranchs than in teleosts (Satchell 1971).

The first chamber of the fish heart is the *sinus venosus*, which functions as a manifold. That is, venous blood from the hepatic circulation and the ducti cuvieri are collected in this relatively thin-walled chamber and directed to the *atrium* through the sino-atrial valve by a delicate lining of cardiac muscle (Fig. 4.10). While the sinus venosus provides the initial transition from smooth to pulsatile flow, the atrium provides the first significant circulatory acceleration of the blood. Compared with the sinus venosus, the atrium is a relatively large chamber which lies dorsal to the ventricle and funnels down to the atrio-ventricular ostium and two-flap valve.

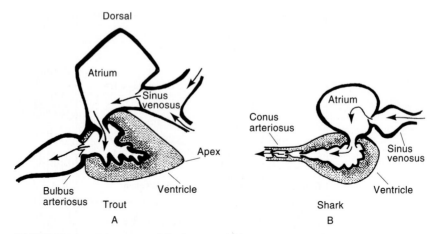

FIGURE 4.10 *Diagrams of the heart in (A) a trout (teleost) and (B) a shark (elasmobranch). (Modified from Randall 1968.)*

The *ventricle* is also a relatively large chamber featuring heavy walls of cardiac muscle (Fig. 4.10). It is pyramid-shaped in elasmobranchs and conical in teleosts, with the apex pointing posteriorly. The heavy muscle and efficient geometry of the ventricle provide the main propulsive force for circulatory flow. Ventricular walls may be composed of two layers of muscle. The cortex is relatively dense cardiac muscle (myocardium) which generally receives oxygen and nutrients from the coronary artery. The cortex is well developed in active species such as skipjack tuna (*Euthynnus pelamis*) and rainbow trout (Cameron 1975). Santer and Greer Walker (1980) found that 73 of 93 teleostean species examined had no ventricular cortex. These were generally more sluggish species compared with the 20 that had ventricular cortexes. All 14 elasmobranch species examined had a cortex (Santer and Greer Walker 1980). The inner layer of the ventricular myocardium consists of a spongy mesh supplied with oxygen and nutrients only by the venous blood it pumps.

In contrast to the atrium or ventricle, the fourth chamber (*conus arteriosus* in elasmobranchs, lampreys, hagfish, and holosteans; *bulbus arteriosus* in teleosts) does not increase the acceleration of the blood. It functions as an elastic chamber to dampen the extremes of pressure and intermittent flow from the ventricle into a less-pulsed, continuous flow to the ventral aorta and the gills. The bulbus wall consists only of elastic tissue and layers of smooth muscle and features no valves (Priede 1976). Conversely, the conus can have many valves (up to 72 in gars [*Lepisosteus*]!) as well as cardiac musculature in the walls. It is felt that the more rigid membrane (pericardium) that houses the heart in elasmobranchs produces a more active "rebound" between contractions of the heart, which assists in its filling from the veins. The conal valves ensure that significant reverse flow of the blood back into the heart does not occur during this rebound. The conus is more poorly developed in lampreys and hagfish, which have a single pair of valves. Despite the presence of in-line hearts (Fig. 4.11), hagfish have the lowest vertebrate blood pressures (e.g., 8 mm Hg in the ventral aorta, Forster et al. 1991).

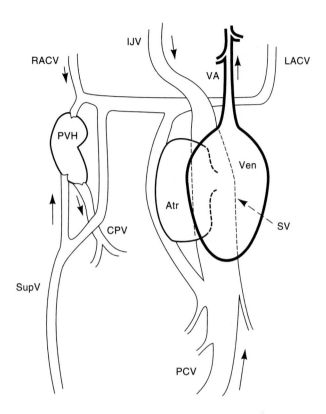

FIGURE 4.11 *Simplified diagram showing the arrangement of the heart, portal vein heart and venous system in the hagfish* Myxine glutinosa. *Atr, atrium; CPV, common portal vein; IJV, inferior jugular vein; LACV, left anterior cardinal vein; PCV, posterior cardinal vein; PVH portal vein heart; RACV, right anterior cardinal vein; SupV, supraintestinal vein; SV, sinus venosus; VA ventral aorta; Ven, ventricle. (From Forster et al. 1991.)*

Johansen and Hanson (1968) have summarized the differences in heart structure in lungfish and amphibians associated with the evolutionary transition from aquatic to atmospheric breathing. The most dramatic difference is the partial division in the lungfish heart associated with the separate return of blood (pulmonary vein) on the left side of the heart from the lungs. This separate return emanates from a special pulmonary vascular circuit which is coupled in parallel with the normal systemic (body) and branchial (gill) circulation. The *partially divided* ventricle moves the arterial (from the lungs) and venous (from the body) blood through a bulbus cordis which largely maintains separation of the two flows by spiral ridges that twist throughout its length. The arterial blood is conveyed to the body, while the venous blood passes through the functional gills, some of it subsequently entering the lung. The extent of separation of flows in the heart correlates with the dependence on air breathing. The Australian lungfish, which cannot withstand lengthy air exposure, displays the least separation. African and South American lungfish, which must withstand periodic droughts in their natural habitats, show more complete separation of flows.

Myocardial Electrical Activity

Typically for a vertebrate, most fish hearts are myogenic (i.e., no nervous signal from the brain is necessary for each heartbeat) and show a complex electromyogenic waveform. Although the actual sites of the primary pacemaker nodes are still obscure, evidence gathered for some teleosts suggest islets of pacemaker cells in the sinus venosus and atrium (Satchell 1971). Kisch (1948) demonstrated that many areas of the myocardium can show pacemaker activity.

Fish electrocardiograms (ECG) showing the progression of electrical phenomena through a cardiac cycle are obtained by implantation of bipolar electrodes under the skin, commonly spanning the pericardial area. The electrodes are wired to an appropriate amplification and display system consisting of an oscilloscope, physiological recorder, or computer. Figure 4.12 shows the ECG of an elasmobranch, the Port Jackson shark. The chronological sequence of chamber depolarizations (contractions) shows the synchronous movement of blood through the heart:

Wave	Chamber myocardium depolarized
V	Sinus venosus
P	Atrium
QRS	Ventricle
B	Conus arteriosus (elasmobranchs only)

The T wave is usually the only ECG wave visibly indicating chamber muscle repolarization (ventricle).

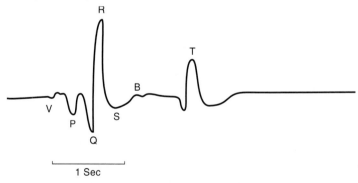

FIGURE 4.12 *The electrocardiogram of the Port Jackson shark* (Heterodontus portusjacksoni). *(From Satchell 1971.)*

Cardiac Flow

The ventricular pumping rhythm induces the systolic (contraction)/diastolic (relaxation) rhythmic flow in the ventral aorta. The bulbar pressure pulse-dampening effect as measured in lingcod *(Ophiodon elongatus)* is seen in Fig. 4.13. The systolic/diastolic wave form of pressure is also detectable in the dorsal aorta, even though the branchial vascular network of the gills drops the blood pressure by one-quarter to one-third. For example, in winter flounder, bulbus arteriosus mean pressure = 29 mm Hg and dorsal aorta mean pressure = 22 mm Hg. This difference (7 mm Hg) represents a 24% pressure drop through the gills (D'Amico Martel and Cech 1978).

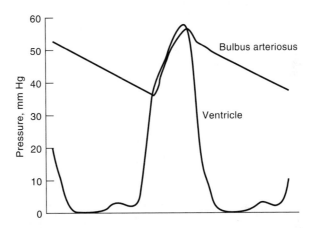

FIGURE 4.13 *Rectilinear records of blood pressure during one heartbeat of a lingcod (2.0 kg, 15°C). (Modified from Stevens et al. 1972.)*

Blood pressures in hagfish are very low despite the presence of the branchial and several accessory hearts. The various hearts work independently of each other to perfuse various parts of the body with blood (Randall 1970):

Hagfish heart	Blood source	Blood destination
Branchial	Body, liver	Ventral aorta
Portal	Gut, anterior cardinal vein	Liver
Caudal	Subcutaneous sinuses	Anterior body

Teleost hearts are generally 2 to 5 times more powerful pumps than those in elasmobranchs and 10 to 25 times more powerful than the hagfish's branchial heart (Sidell and Driedzic 1985). The hagfish heart is fueled by carbohydrates, the elasmobranch heart by carbohydrates and ketone bodies, and the teleost heart by carbohydrates and fatty acids (Sidell and Driedzic 1985). The hagfish caudal heart consists of a cartilaginous plate and attached skeletal musculature along with a pair of lateral sacs with valves to regulate the direction of blood flow. Movement of the muscles forces blood anteriorly.

Body undulations during swimming have also been implicated in blood flow in higher fishes. Satchell (1965) recorded increased blood flows in the caudal vein of a Port Jackson shark trunk preparation when electrical stimulation produced swimming-type movements. He also found valves in the caudal vein that allowed only anterior movement of the blood. Sutterlin (1969) described similar valves in the ventral segmental veins of brown trout. Isolated heart studies by Bennion (1968) revealed that increased filling volume (venous return) produces an increased force of contraction (inotropism) by the heart. Mediated by stretch receptors in the myocardial wall, this response (Starling's law of the heart) acts to increase the volume of blood pumped per contraction (cardiac stroke volume or Q_{sv}). The cardiac stroke volume and frequency (heart rate or HR) determine the circulatory flow rate (cardiac output or $\dot{Q}$).

Cardiovascular Control

Fish control their hearts and cardiovascular systems with several aneural and neural mechanisms. Venous return is one of the controls that can be produced by a variety of factors.

Aneural cardiovascular control. Aneural cardiovascular control is effected by changes in blood volume, by direct responses of heart muscle to temperature changes, and by secretions of various organs. Along with swimming movements in certain species, changes in blood volume also affect venous return. Mobilization of blood into the general circulation has been associated with the spleen, liver, or a blood sinus in various species. Temperature acts as another aneural regulator of circulation by direct action on the pacemakers in the myocardium (Randall 1970). Table 4-3 shows the positive chronotropic effect (increased heart rate) of temperature on winter flounder as the water temperature increased from 10°C to 15°C. These heart rate increases caused an elevated cardiac output at these temperatures, even though the amount of blood pumped per contraction did not change. This increase in blood flow provides an increased delivery of oxygen throughout the body, which is operating at a higher metabolic rate at the warmer temperatures (Cech et al. 1976).

Secretions of hormones that affect either the heart or the relative constriction or dilation of the blood vessels represent an important category of aneural cardiovascular regulators in fishes. Catecholamines such as epinephrine affect both the heart and the resistance to flow in various vascular beds. Nakano and Tomlinson (1967) have shown that levels of circulating catecholamines (epinephrine and norepinephrine) rise with exercise in rainbow trout. Epinephrine stimulates heart rate increases at relatively low temperatures (e.g., 6°C), and cardiac stroke volume increases in warmer water (e.g., 15°C) (Bennion 1968). Studies using blocking agents (e.g., inderal) have shown that the heart has receptor sites that are primarily epi-

TABLE 4–3   VALUES OF CARDIOVASCULAR VARIABLES OF WINTER FLOUNDER AT SPRING AND AUTUMN TEMPERATURES

Variable[a]	Units	Mean ± SE (with number of fish) at:		Level of significant difference[b]
		10ºC	15ºC	
HR	Beats/min	35 ± 1 (18)	62 ± 2 (18)	<0.01
V_{O_2}	ml/min	0.25 ± 0.01 (20)	0.45 ± 0.02 (20)	<0.01
Q	ml/min	14.7 ± 1.0 (16)	24.6 ± 3.1 (16)	<0.01
Q_{SV}	ml/beat	0.43 ± 0.05 (15)	0.41 ± 0.05 (15)	NS
Body weight	g	635 ± 40 (20)	681 ± 42 (20)	NS

Source: Modified from Cech et al. 1976.

[a] Variable abbreviations: HR = heart rate; V_{O_2} = oxygen consumption rate; Q = cardiac output; and Q_{sv} = cardiac stroke volume.

[b] As determined by the *t* test (Snedecor and Cochran 1967).

nephrine sensitive. The interplay of temperature, myocardial stretching, and epinephrine as controlling mechanisms determine the frequency/stroke volume characteristics under the various conditions. Other studies have shown that primarily norepinephrine-sensitive receptors predominate in constricting systemic vascular beds, whereas epinephrine-sensitive receptors dilate gill vasculature in rainbow trout (Wood and Shelton 1975). Removal and metabolism of circulating catecholamines apparently also occurs in the gills (Colletti and Olson 1988).

Neural cardiovascular control.   The hearts of all fish except hagfish are innervated by a branch of the tenth cranial nerve (vagus) (Randall 1970). Stimulation of the lamprey vagus produces an increased heart rate (positive chronotropism), whereas elasmobranch or teleostean vagal stimulation slows the heart rate. Because these stimuli mimic effects of acetylcholine, these fibers are termed *cholinergic.* Several factors may alter the level of vagal tone (level of fiber excitement), although stimuli threshold levels vary considerably between species. Light flashes, sudden movements of objects or shadows, touch, or mechanical vibrations usually promote a bradycardia (decreased heart rate) in teleosts and elasmobranchs by increasing the level of vagal tone. Atropine injections sufficient to block cholinergic innervation (the vagal nerve supply to the heart) attest to the neural origin of these responses. Stevens and Randall (1967) found no vagal tone in resting rainbow trout, but did find that atropine injections into a largescale sucker (*Catostomus macrocheilus*) increased the resting heart rate from 38 beats per minute to 55 beats per minute. Swimming in this sucker also reduced the inhibitory vagal tone, thereby elevating heart rate. Several teleosts also possess (adrenergic) *stimulatory* fibers from the vagus as an additional neural control mechanism (Gannon and Burnstock 1969; Holmgren 1977; Donald and Campbell 1982).

Armed with such a variety of aneural and neural control mechanisms, fish have much built-in flexibility for circulatory adjustments to environmental or other changes (see reviews by Laurent et al. 1983 and Farrell 1984). For example, environmental hypoxia invokes a bradycardia, an increased cardiac stroke volume, elevated peripheral resistance of both branchial and systemic blood vessels, and enhanced gas exchange efficiency in many teleosts and elasmobranchs (Satchell 1971). Changes in gas exchange efficiency may be linked to changes in blood distribution in the gills (e.g., lamellar recruitment; see Chapter 3). The reflex bradycardia has been described for the California grunion *(Leuresthes tenuis)* and the California flying fish *(Cypselurus californicus)* during exposure to air (Garey 1962). Both of these species have "standard" gills and are exposed to the atmosphere for short time periods (e.g., only 42 seconds for the flying fish and up to a few minutes for the spawning grunion; see Chapter 9). In contrast, the Indian climbing perch *(Anabas testudineus)*, which has labyrinthine organs specialized for air breathing and spends much of its time out of the water, shows an initial tachycardia (increased heart rate) just after taking an air breath. Hypoxic exposure increases catecholamine (including epinephrine) concentrations in spotted dogfish *(Scyliorhinus canicula)* (Butler et al. 1978), and epinephrine protects myocardial contractility in rainbow trout during anoxia (Gesser et al. 1982).

These circulatory patterns may be linked to maximization of oxygen uptake and delivery and, possibly, conservation of cardiac energy in the case of the bradycardic responses. Of course, to best understand the physiological response pattern of a fish to hypoxia (or any other change), the ventilatory, hematological, circulatory, and other affected systems must be considered as well. Apparently the receptors that detect low oxygen levels and provoke the bradycardia and increases in gill ventilation (see Chapter 4) are located on the dorsal part of the first gill arches in rainbow trout (Daxboeck and Holeton 1978; Smith and Jones 1978). Singh (1976) has pointed out the importance of carbon dioxide and pH (along with oxygen) receptors in the air-breathing *Anabas, Clarias,* and *Heteropneustes.*

The degree of cardiovascular control possible in fish is demonstrated by the spiny dogfish. Surgical closure of various gill slits was shown to prevent water ventilation of isolated gill arches. By selective vasodilation and constriction, blood was largely directed away from the nonventilated arches toward those receiving ventilatory irrigation (Cameron et al. 1971). As vascular resistance is a function of the fourth power of vessel diameter, minute constrictions or dilations of vessels will significantly affect peripheral resistance and flow. Thus the dogfish successfully maintained an efficient ratio of water flow (ventilation) to blood flow (cardiac output). Ventilation/perfusion ratios of approximately 10:1 to 20:1 have presumably evolved in gill breathers as fish blood oxygen capacities approximate 10 to 20 times the oxygen capacity of water. The matched flows ensure efficient oxygen diffusion. Absolute matching (stroke to stroke) of the ventilatory water pump and the cardiac pump is relatively rare in fish, with few exceptions (e.g., rainbow trout in hypoxic water).

Supplemental Readings

Blaxhall 1972; Cameron 1971a, b; Ellis 1977; Fänge 1984; Farrell 1984; Forster et al. 1991; Ferguson 1976; Holeton 1970; Houston and Rupert 1976; Laurent et al. 1983; Randall 1970; Riggs 1970; Satchell 1971, 1976; Weber 1990; Weber and Lykkeboe 1978; Wood and Shelton 1975.

CHAPTER 5

Buoyancy and Thermal Regulation

Morphologically, the gas-secreting structure of "closed-end" swimbladders found in derived teleosts and the heat-exchange organs in some large, active, oceanic fish are very similar. Both involve exchanges, of gas in one case and of heat in the other, across blood vessel walls in an ordered countercurrent (opposite direction) exchange network. Conceptually, this common factor brings these functionally somewhat disparate areas together in this chapter.

BUOYANCY

Neutral buoyancy (weightlessness) allows fish to minimize the energy cost of staying at a particular depth to feed, hide, reproduce, or migrate. Because an active fish can exert a *propulsive* force greater than 25% to 50% of its body weight for only brief periods, continuous effort to support its body by muscular power alone would be energetically costly (Marshall 1966). It is not surprising, therefore, that various ways of achieving neutral buoyancy have evolved among fishes. Essentially four strategies[1] are recognizable: (1) incorporation of large quantities of low-density com-

---

[1]The term "strategy" in this sense implies a direction dictated by the principles of natural selection. "Strategy" does *not* imply a conscious mode of action by the fish either at birth or during its life.

pounds in the body; (2) generation of lift by appropriately shaped and angled fins and body surfaces during forward movement; (3) reduction of heavy tissues such as bone and muscle; and (4) incorporation of a swimbladder as a low-density, gas-filled space.

The use of low-density compounds to reduce the overall density of the body is characteristic of most sharks and a few teleosts. In many sharks large quantities of lipids (specific gravity: 0.90–0.92) and the hydrocarbon squalene (sp. gr.: 0.86), found especially in the large livers, bring the total body mass toward neutral buoyancy in seawater (sp. gr.: 1.026). Furthermore, the characteristic heterocercal tail of sharks along with the positive angles of attack of the leading edges of the pectoral fins and the surface of the head provide additional lift while swimming. Hydrodynamic drag is minimized in the more pelagic sharks, which have relatively smaller fins and larger, fatty livers.

Among teleosts, only a few marine species such as sablefish (Anoplopomatidae), pelagic medusa fishes (Stromateidae), and shallow-water rockfish (Scorpaenidae) use low-density (triglyceride) oils to lessen negative buoyancy (Lee et al. 1975). The oils are found mainly in the bones. At least one deepsea fish, *Acanthonus armatus* (Ophidiidae), has an enlarged cranial cavity (approximately 10% of the head volume) which is mostly filled with watery fluid (Horn et al. 1978). This fluid has a total osmotic concentration almost one-half of those found in the plasma or perivisceral fluid and about one-quarter of that of the seawater environment. The cranial position of the "light-fluid" reservoir nicely balances most of the heavy body components (otoliths, gill rakers, pharyngeal teeth, and cranial spines) that are also located there.

Fish of deep (more than 1000 m) oceanic midwaters characteristically have reduced skeletal and muscular tissues. Food is scarce in these environments, and tissues that are energetically expensive to maintain—such as swimbladders—and compounds that are expensive to synthesize—such as body lipids—are usually reduced or absent. It is also likely that the cartilaginous skeleton (sp. gr. = 1.1) of elasmobranchs and some bony fish is partly an adaptation to decrease body density. Bone has a specific gravity of 2.0.

The major problem with the preceding methods of regulating density is that they either greatly restrict the activity of fish (reduced tissues), or make it difficult for a fish to regulate its density in response to changes in pressure, temperature, and salinity. The swimbladder is an "invention" of bony fish that overcomes these problems and has no doubt been largely responsible for their success.

Swimbladders allow precise control of buoyancy because the volume of gas they contain can be regulated with comparative ease. Because of the increased density of seawater, fish are more bouyant in it than in fresh water. Hence, with typical teleostean skeletal and body composition, swimbladders occupy about 5% of the marine teleost's body volume and about 7% of the freshwater forms.

Swimbladders are of two basic types, *physostomous* and *physoclistous*. Physostomous swimbladders have a connection (pneumatic duct) between the swimbladder and the gut. Physoclistous swimbladders lack this connection. Fish with physostomous swimbladders include many of the more ancestral, soft-rayed teleosts, including herrings, salmonids, osteoglossids, mormyrids, pikes, cyprinids, characins, catfishes, and eels. Physostomous fish inflate their swimbladders by gulping air at the water's surface and forcing it through the pneumatic duct into the swimbladder by a buccal force mechanism (Fänge 1976). It is, therefore, not surprising that physostomes are largely shallow-water forms. Additional swimbladder inflation is needed for neutral buoyancy at deeper depths. Swimbladder volume at the surface, 1 atmosphere gas pressure, is proportionately decreased with each 10 m (= 1 atmosphere hydrostatic pressure) descended. Thus, a fixed swimbladder volume at the surface would be reduced to ½ at 10 m (2 atmospheres total pressure), ⅓ at 20 m, ¼ at 30 m, and so on. Therefore, the amounts of gas needed at depth would be so great that it would be impossible for the fish to submerge!

Deflation of the physostomous swimbladder is accomplished by a reflex action, the *gass-puckreflex* (gas-spitting reflex), which is initiated when reduced external pressure makes the fish too light, releasing gas via the pneumatic duct into the esophagus. Pneumatic sphincter muscles (both smooth and striated muscle tissue), under nervous control, guard the entrance to the pneumatic duct. Fänge (1976) attributes the release of gas to a relaxation of the sphincter muscles, a contraction of smooth muscles in the swimbladder wall (under similar nervous control), the elasticity of the swimbladder wall, and contractions of body wall muscles. The importance of gas diffusion mechanisms (i.e., with the blood) for physostome swimbladder inflation or deflation is probably minimal. Although the number of species investigated is comparatively low, only a few species (e.g., eels [*Anguilla, Conger*], whitefish [*Coregonus*]) show the richly vascularized wall structures specially adapted for gas exchange (Fänge 1976).

In contrast to physostomous fish, fish with "closed" (physoclistous) swimbladders have special structures associated with the circulatory system for inflating or deflating the swimbladder. Presumably because these structures "free" fish from dependency on the surface, over two-thirds of all teleosts (especially the more derived, spiny-rayed species) are physoclistous. A *gas gland* and associated *rete mirabile* (meaning "wonderful net") are the source of inflation gas in these swimbladders. By biochemical additions of acid (hydrogen ions, or protons) and solutes to the blood entering the gas gland, dissolved gas partial pressures increase and inflate the swimbladder via gas diffusion. The gas gland tissue produces acid via the glycolytic transformation of glucose, and it produces CO_2 via dehydration of HCO_3^- and the transformation of glucose via the tricarboxylic acid cycle and the pentose phosphate shunt (Fig. 5.1). The protons apparently move across the cell membranes into the afferent blood, acidifying it. Some of the CO_2 also moves into the afferent blood and hydrates, forming more protons and HCO_3^-. Some of the protons and CO_2 bind to the hemoglobin in the RBCs, driving O_2 off of the hemoglobin via rapid (50 msec) Bohr and Root ("Root off") effects and increasing the plasma oxygen partial pressure (P_{O2}). The resulting P_{O2} gradient between the plasma and the swimbladder lumen moves O_2, via diffusion, through the gas gland into the lumen (Fig. 5.1). Some CO_2 also diffuses into the lumen down the PCO_2 gradient (Pelster and Scheid 1992). In addition, inert gases (e.g., N_2) diffuse into the lumen via a reduced gas solubility in the blood induced by the addition of solutes such as lactate ("salting out"

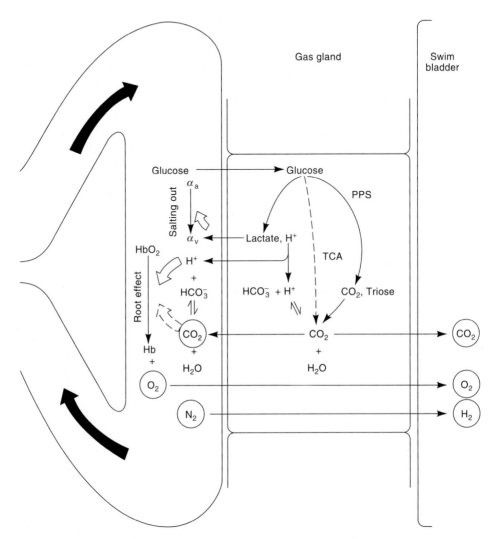

FIGURE 5.1 *Gas gland cell metabolism and its influence on the physical solubility of inert gases or the release of gas from chemical binding sites in the blood (open arrows). Solid arrows indicate movement of substances. TCA: tricarboxylic acid cycle; PPS: pentose phosphate shunt. (From Pelster and Scheid 1992.)*

effect, Kuhn et al. 1963). The rete consists of a tight bundle (rather than net) of thousands of afferent (running toward) and efferent (running from) capillaries surrounding each other, with only 1 μm separating afferent and efferent blood (Steen 1970). This structure provides for an efficient countercurrent exchange of blood gases and HCO_3^-, H^+, and lactate ions from efferent to afferent capillaries, as shown for one capillary pair (Fig. 5.2). These diffusive movements result from elevated gas partial pressures and solute concentrations in the efferent blood. High efferent P_{O2} is facilitated by the comparatively prolonged (10 sec) "Root-on" shift (return of full

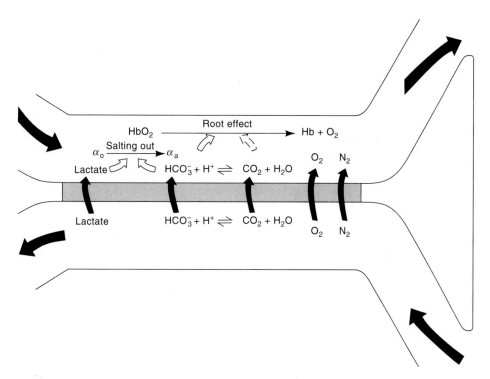

FIGURE 5.2 *Movements of gases and solutes in the rete mirabile and the resulting countercurrent concentration of gases and solutes. Open arrows indicate influences on inert gas solubility and hemoglobin-O_2 binding characteristics. (From Pelster and Scheid 1992.)*

hemoglobin capacity for O_2), minimizing hemoglobin-O_2 binding in the rete (Steen 1970). The resulting build-up of gas and solutes in afferent capillaries "multiplies" the gas secretory functions in the gas gland such that exceedingly high gas pressures (up to 300 atmospheres in some deepsea fish) can be generated in the swimbladder. Kobayashi (1990) measured P_{O_2} increases from 40 to 281 mm Hg and corresponding pH decreases from 7.82 to 7.33 along the length of European eel (*Anguilla anguilla*) afferent rete capillaries. The higher the partial pressures and the lower the pH, the greater effect of further acidification as afferent blood reaches the gas gland. Kobayashi et al. (1990) found that P_{O_2} decreases from 293 to 44 mm Hg and pH increases from 7.10 to 7.64 along the efferent capillaries in the same eels. These eel data demonstrate both the P_{O_2} and proton (efferent to afferent) gradients and the high efficiency of the countercurrent arrangement. The longer the retial capillaries, the more complete is the gas exchange and the more efficient is the filling of the swimbladder at depth. Investigations on deepsea fish show a good correlation between retial capillary length and habitat depth. Fish found between 1500 m and 3500 m may have retial capillaries 25 times longer than those of fishes found between 150 m and 500 m (Marshall 1971). Multiple layers of guanine crystals dramatically reduce the O_2 conductance of the swimbladder wall (Lapennas and Schmidt-Nielsen 1977).

Deflation of the physoclistous swimbladder is accomplished by diffusion of gas back into the bloodstream via a richly vascularized area adjacent to the enclosed gases. The more soluble gases, including CO_2 and O_2 in blood, are preferentially reabsorbed, leaving a higher percentage of less soluble gases (e.g., N_2) in the lumen. This area may be an "oval" patch of densely packed capillaries on the dorsal wall of the swimbladder or may consist of the posterior lining of the swimbladder wall, the functional area of which is regulated by anterior/posterior movements of a mucosal "diaphragm."

THERMAL REGULATION

Most fish, as cold-blooded vertebrates or ectotherms, have body temperatures close to that of their environments because of metabolic heat losses via the skin or gills. The low rate of metabolic heat production, compared with mammals, and the high heat capacity of water result in continuous heat losses and cool bodies for most fish. The sea raven (*Hemitripterus americanus*) remains at a temperature very close to its environment and probably loses most of its heat conductively through its skin (Stevens and Sutterlin 1976). The albacore tuna (*Thunnus alalunga*), in contrast, is one of several fish that can physiologically maintain warmer parts of its body by the use of heat-exchanging retia (see below), and primarily loses heat convectively through its gills (Graham 1983). Field and laboratory studies have shown that many fishes prefer water of particular temperatures over others (see review by Reynolds and Casterlin 1979). Thus examples of both behavioral and physiological temperature-regulating mechanisms are found in fishes.

Behavioral thermoregulation concerns the movements of fish from one water mass or area to another characterized by a warmer or cooler temperature. As temperature affects rates of metabolism and digestion so profoundly (Chapters 4 and 7), some fish may "select" a particular temperature to conserve energy or to run their metabolic machinery (i.e., enzymes) at its most efficient temperature. For example, Brett (1971) found that sockeye salmon (*Oncorhynchus nerka*) select a warm temperature (15°C) at a depth of approximately 11 m to digest the food eaten at their dusk feeding during the short Canadian summer nights. In contrast, the fish go deeper (37 m) to 5°C water between the dawn and dusk feeding periods. Thus during the longer daytime period, the fish conserve energy by lowering their body-maintenance energy requirements in the colder water (Chapter 4).

Human-induced thermal changes in aquatic environments have further stimulated investigations of fish thermoregulatory behavior. For example, Neill and Magnuson (1974) consistently captured bluegill, largemouth bass, longnose gar (*Lepisosteus osseus*), small rockbass (*Ambloplites rupestris*), pumpkinseed (*Lepomis gibbosus*), large yellow bass (*Morone mississippiensis*), and common carp in the heated outfall plume waters of an electrical power generating plant located on Lake

Monona, Wisconsin. Although localized food sources (e.g., zooplankton for the bluegill, small fish for the longnose gar) influenced the preference of some of these species for the 2°C to 4°C warmer thermal plume area in summer, concurrent laboratory studies using a shuttlebox apparatus showed that the consistent plume residents tested had higher preferred temperatures than the one species that consistently avoided the thermal plume, yellow perch.

Physiological thermoregulation in fish, to a significant degree, is exhibited only by several continuous-swimming species. Each of the "warm-bodied" species leads a pelagic marine existence and has heat-exchanging retia mirabilia to conserve heat produced by the fish's metabolism (Carey et al. 1971). These fish also have the major arteries and veins for blood transport between the heart and gills and the heat exchanger located close to the skin (Fig. 5.3). This enables them to transport the cool (i.e., near water temperature) blood to and from the heat exchanger without absorbing much of the heat produced by the swimming muscles. The structure of these retia is similar to that of the physoclistous swimbladder, the gas-secreting retia described in the buoyancy section of this chapter. Essentially, by means of a bundled arrangement of afferent and efferent blood vessels, heat (instead of gas) is exchanged by convection across the walls of these many vessels running parallel to each other. The absence of localized blood acidification, such as in the physoclistous swimbladder gas gland, minimizes gas exchange in the heat-exchange retia. Although hemoglobin usually loses its affinity for oxygen with temperature increases such as those experienced by arterial blood in the rete (Chapter 4), O_2 delivery to the red swimming muscles of albacore is maintained despite retial warming because of a reverse temperature effect of the albacore hemoglobin. This special hemoglobin increases its oxygen affinity with warming between 10 and 30°C and its carbon dioxide affinity with cooling, minimizing oxygen loss to the venous blood in the rete (Cech et al. 1984). Also, the larger vessel diameter (10 times as large: 0.1 mm rather than 0.01 mm) and thicker vessel walls (compared with the swimbladder rete capillaries) further slow the diffusion of oxygen molecules, which diffuse at a rate 10 times slower than heat. Because of the countercurrent flow, the metabolic heat is efficiently conserved in the rete, which surrounds the red swimming muscles (Fig. 5.3). The efficiency of this heat exchanger is 95% as a thermal barrier between the gills and red muscle in skipjack tuna (*Katsuwonus pelamis*) (Neill et al. 1976).

Although the number and position of heat-exchanging retia vary among the various tunas and mackerels (Scombridae) and lamnid sharks that possess retia, all of them are capable of fast, continuous swimming. Warm muscles confer swimming performance advantages to these species. Stevens and Carey (1981) showed that the facilitated diffusion of O_2 by myoglobin and, consequently, red muscle metabolism are greatly enhanced at warmer temperatures. Because warm muscles can contract faster than cool ones, presumably the heat exchanger allows these predatory fishes to exert more swimming thrust and thus outswim the squid and smaller fishes that compose their diet. For example, the grouper (*Epinephelus*), which does not have the special circulatory adaptations for metabolic heat conservation, has an internal temperature of 0.3°C above that of the water it lives in, whereas the swimming muscles of albacore tuna show a 12°C elevation (Carey et al. 1971).

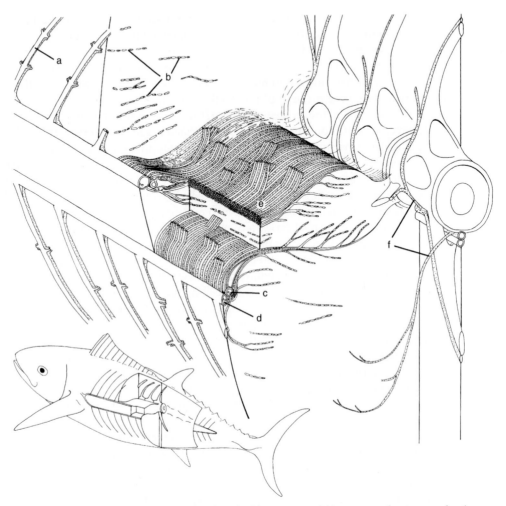

FIGURE 5.3 *Circulation in the muscles of a bigeye tuna: (A) segmental artery and vein; (B) vascular bands; (C) cutaneous artery; (D) cutaneous vein; (E) rete mirabile; (F) arterial branches from dorsal aorta. (From Carey and Teal 1966.)*

"Warm-bodied" fish, however, do not have constant body temperatures (such as in mammals or birds) but have temperatures that fluctuate with that of the environment. The core temperature of the largest of these "warm-bodied" species, the bluefin tuna, seems least affected by environmental temperature, apparently because of the great thermal inertia that is inherent in large bodies. In some situations this may work to their disadvantage by causing overheating of the muscle mass when exercising. Thus larger tuna adopt a cyclical pattern of depth distribution to "cool off" below the thermocline if surface waters are too warm for continuous occupancy. Although the largest of the warm-bodied tunas may have the most stable internal temperatures, black skipjack tuna *(Euthynnus lineatus)* as small as 207 mm (fork length) can elevate muscle temperatures significantly above that of the ambient water (Dickson 1994). The ability of "warm-bodied" fish to sense changes in their thermal environment may operate either by neural comparisons of water temperature (external surface of the fish) with temperature deep inside the body, or by the blood temperature gradient across the heat exchanger (Neill et al. 1976). Regardless, it is now apparent that bigeye tuna *(Thunnus obesus)* can sense thermal differences between body and water and respond with 100 to 1000-fold changes in whole body thermal conductivity (Holland and Sibert 1994). Carey (1982a), Graham (1983), and Brill et al. (1994) provide useful reviews of heat transfer processes in fishes.

Carey (1982b) described a "brain heater" in swordfish *(Xiphias gladius)* from highly modified eye muscles that locally warms brain and eye tissues and, presumably, contributes to foraging success in cold, deep (to 600 m) oceanic depths. Subsequent studies indicate that this type of regional endothermy has evolved twice, once in billfish *(Istiophoridae)* and once in scombrids (the butterfly mackerel, *Gasterochisma melampus*, Block 1991). The brain heater tissue has an exceedingly high mitochondrial volume (a measure of aerobic metabolic capacity and activity) and high activity of the aerobic enzyme, citrate synthase (Block 1991; Tullis et al. 1991). The high percentages of mitochondria (55–70%, depending on species), sarcoplasmic reticulum (SR, the highly organized intracellular membrane system that regulates calcium uptake, release, and storage, 25–30%), and transverse (T) tubules, as well as the lack of organized contractile elements, equip the brain heater cells for

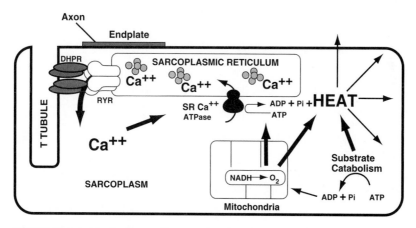

FIGURE 5.4 *Excitation—thermogenic coupling in the billfish heater cell. A nervous inpulse stimulates thermogenesis via the same molecular components found in the EC coupling pathway in "standard" skeletal muscle. Heat would be produced as a consequence of the Ca^{2+} release and reuptake at the SR and the resulting stimulation of substrate oxidation at the mitochondria. The high mitochondria and myoglobin content provides ample ATP and O_2 for the Ca^{2+}-mediated thermogenic cycle. Ca^{2+} may stimulate the heater cell's mitochondrial mechanism, contributing to heat generation. (Reproduced, with permission, from the* Annual Review of Physiology *Volume 56,* © *1994, by Annual Reviews Inc.)*

both rapid and sustained calcium cycling and heat production (Block 1994). In skeletal muscle, the signal for calcium release (and consequent muscle contraction) is initiated at the neuromuscular junction, and the action potential spreads down the T tubules, initiating a molecularly mediated release of Ca^{2+} from the SR along the excitation–contraction (EC) coupling pathway. It is thought that the similar depolarization of the T tubules in brain heater cells conformationally changes its voltage sensing molecule (dihydropyridine receptor, DHPR) and, via a molecular bridge, the SR Ca^{2+} release channel (ryanodine receptor, RYR), regulating SR Ca^{2+} release (Figure 5.4). Ca^{2+} is rapidly "pumped" back into the SR via a SR Ca^{2+} ATPase-mediated system that requires energy, increasing relative ADP and P_i concentrations in the cytosol. Increased mitochondrial uptake of ADP stimulates oxidative processes and substrate catabolism, producing more heat (Block 1994).

Supplemental Readings

Block 1994; Brill et al. 1994; Carey 1982a; Carey et al. 1971; Fänge 1976; Gee 1983; Graham 1983; Kuhn et al. 1963; Neill et al. 1976; Neill and Magnuson 1974; Neill et al. 1972; Steen 1971.

CHAPTER **6**

Hydromineral Balance

Living cells require an environment characterized by particular concentrations of certain substances (including ions) dissolved in water. Thus in fish, the internal environment must have the necessary combinations of ionized salts, alkalinity, and dissolved organic compounds despite an external environment that may have a very different combination of these factors. Special problems such as movement between freshwater and saltwater environments, stress induced by netting or transport, or survival in habitats subject to freezing add to the complexity of maintenance of the appropriate internal environment in some fishes. The following sections concerning osmoregulation, ion regulation, stress responses, freezing resistance, and acid-base balance address the "strategies," dynamics, and diversity of hydromineral balance in fish.

OSMOREGULATION

Fish can be divided into four groups or strategies of regulation of internal water and total solute concentrations. The first osmoregulatory strategy is used by the hagfish (Myxiniformes) and is characterized by no regulation at all. Hagfish are all strictly marine and are stenohaline (able to tolerate only a narrow range of salinities). Thus the total salt concentration in their body fluids is very similar to that of seawater;

77

hagfish are the only "vertebrates" (see Chapter 1) with this characteristic (Schmidt-Nielsen 1975). They can be described as osmoconformers rather than osmoregulators. However, hagfish do not have to withstand large changes in internal osmolality (total dissolved solute particles), because they live only in marine environments of quite constant salinity. As Table 6-1 shows, however, hagfish do show some individual (Na^+) ion-regulatory ability (see the ion regulation section in this chapter).

TABLE 6–1   PLASMA SOLUTE CONCENTRATIONS IN MMols/L

Habitat	Species	$[Na^+]$	$[Ca^{2+}]$	$[K^+]$	Urea	Total salts (mOsm/l)
M	Hagfish (Mysine glutinosa)[a]	549	5	11	—	1152
F	Lamprey (Lampetra fluviatilis)[b]	120	2	3	—	270
M	Dogfish (Squalus acanthias)[c]	263	7	4	357	1007
M	Anglerfish (Lophius americanus)[d]	198	2	3	—	—
M	Moray eel (Murena helena)[b]	212	4	2	—	—
F	Bass (Micropterus dolomieu)[e]	120	3	3	—	—
F	Whitefish (Coregonus clupoides)[b]	141	3	4	1	—
	Seawater [f, g]	~450	~20	10	—	1000
	Fresh water [h, i]	<1	<1	<1		1–10

Sources: [a]Bellamy and Chester-Jones 1961; [b]Robertson 1954; [c]Murdaugh and Robin 1967; [d]Forster and Berglund 1956; [e]Shell 1959; [f]Schmidt-Nielsen 1975; [g]von Arx 1962; [h]Hutchinson 1957; [i]Royce 1972.

The second strategy is that which encompasses all marine elasmobranchs. Like most vertebrates, the elasmobranchs maintain an internal inorganic salt concentration equal to about one-third that of seawater (Table 6-1). However, large quantities of organic salts (primarily urea, secondarily trimethylamine oxide or TMAO) in their blood bring the total osmotic concentration up to that of seawater (Table 6-1). Yancey and Somero (1980) found that the typical 2:1 concentration ratio of urea: methylamines (e.g., TMAO) protects the elasmobranchs' enzymes from the usual perturbing effects of urea. Despite a total salt concentration that approximates that of the sea, elasmobranchs possess considerable abilities to regulate the concentrations of individual ions. The coelacanth (Latimeria chalumnae), a bony fish, uses this osmoregulatory strategy as well.

The fish using either one of these two strategies of osmoregulation have solved a major problem regarding water balance. Water diffuses quite easily across thin membranes such as the skin, and especially those in the gills. Elasmobranch gills are quite water-permeable (Evans 1984). However, because the internal total salt concentration of elasmobranchs mimics that of their environment, passive water influx (inflow) or efflux (outflow) is minimized. Passive Na^+ and Cl^- effluxes are minimized due to low permeability of elasmobranchs to these ions (Evans 1979).

The third osmoregulatory strategy is that of the marine teleosts. The salt concentration of their internal environment is approximately one-third that of their environment (Table 6-1). Thus they operate *hyposmotically* and tend to lose water continually by diffusion to the more saline environment. These teleosts continually replace lost water by drinking (ingesting) seawater. Naturally, this also results in a large intake of salts, which must be excreted at a concentration higher than that ingested. Special (chloride) cells in the gill filament and opercular skin epithelia eliminate much of the excess salt via active transport. Teleost kidneys cannot produce a urine more salty than the blood (Schmidt-Nielsen 1975).

The fourth strategy has evolved in freshwater teleosts and elasmobranchs that operate *hyperosmotically*. Because their internal environment (one-third the salt concentration of seawater) is more concentrated than their environment (Table 6-1), they continually gain water by diffusion. The excess water is continually excreted by well-developed kidneys as a large volume of dilute urine (up to one-third of the body weight per day). Control of diuretic (urine-producing) processes is influenced by blood pressure changes induced by pituitary hormones (e.g., *arginine vasotocin*) (Sawyer et al. 1976). Some salts are unavoidably lost through the urine and by diffusion through the gill tissues. Diffusional losses are reduced due to *prolactin*, another pituitary hormone (see below). Although some of these solutes are replaced with those taken in with food, most are taken up at the gills, using active transport mechanisms. Thus an energy-requiring salt pump operates in chloride cells of the gills in these fishes as well, except that ions are pumped inward, rather than the reverse as exhibited by the marine teleosts. In especially ion-deficient (soft) mountain water, chloride cells have been found to be well developed on gill lamellae as well as filaments in rainbow trout (Laurent et al. 1985). There are few freshwater elasmobranchs, possibly because of their high permeability to water. The remarkable Amazon stingray *(Potamotrygon)*, a stenohaline freshwater species, displays an interior milieu strikingly similar to that of the freshwater teleosts with essentially *no* urea. The more euryhaline (meaning broad salt tolerance) sharks, such as the bull shark *(Carcharhinus leucas)*, which can ascend rivers, have a urea concentration about one-third that found in the marine elasmobranchs (Thorson et al. 1973).

Most fish are stenohaline and have the osmotic machinery needed to cope with the relatively constant salt concentration (whatever it may be) of their immediate surroundings. However, diadromous fishes (e.g., lampreys, salmon, eels), which move between freshwater and marine environments as part of their regular existence, must possess more versatility in dealing with environmental salinity. Keys (1933) moved a European eel from a freshwater environment to a marine one and measured an osmotic water loss from the body equal to 4% of the total body weight in 10 hours. The weight loss slackened as the eel began to drink seawater, and an equilibrium returned after one to two days. If Keys inflated a balloon in the esophagus of the eel, preventing the ingestion of seawater, the weight loss continued until the animal died of dehydration. Transfer of the eels from salt water into fresh water promoted a weight gain from passive water diffusion. The eels again reached an equilibrium in one to two days, when urine production increased to excrete the excess water.

Whether a fish is diadromous, freshwater, or marine, osmoregulation is usually one of the energy "costs" it has to pay just to stay alive. Indeed, growth rates and swimming performance of fishes may be affected by how much energy they must put into osmoregulation. For example, Brocksen and Cole (1972) measured the food consumption and assimilation, growth, and oxygen consumption in several stenohaline fishes from the Salton Sea, California. Using test salinities of 29, 33, 37, 41, and 45 parts per thousand (ppt), they showed that juvenile bairdiella (*Bairdiella icistia*) grew more efficiently at 37 ppt when held at 25°C. In contrast, substantially more food was required at both higher and lower salinities. On the other hand, sargo (*Anisotremus davidsoni*) showed optimal feeding efficiency at 33 ppt. Juvenile corvina (*Cynoscion xanthulus*) displayed optimal assimilation efficiency at 37 ppt. Wohlschlag and Wakeman (1978) demonstrated that another euryhaline sciaenid, the spotted sea trout (*Cynoscion nebulosus*), operates at maximum metabolic efficiency (maximum scope for activity) at approximately 20 ppt salinity, although the fish is found in a wide range of salinities in estuaries. Gibbs and Somero (1990) calculated that the energetic cost of osmoregulation is proportional to total metabolic rate across a variety of marine teleosts: higher for shallow-water forms with higher metabolic rates and lower for deep-living fish with lower metabolic rates. The exception was the presumed high metabolic rates in deep-living fish near hydrothermal vents where the seawater is geothermally warmed (from seafloor cracks along its spreading centers) and food is abundant.

IONIC REGULATION

Even if a fish has blood that has nearly the same osmotic concentration as seawater, energy still must be expended in regulation of solutes because the concentrations of individual ions will differ between the internal and external environments. To maintain an optimal ionic composition, active, energy-consuming processes are needed. These processes, and the organs involved, vary considerably among fish, although in terms of general "strategies" of ionic regulation fish fall into five main groups: lampreys and hagfish, elasmobranchs, saltwater teleosts, euryhaline teleosts, and freshwater teleosts.

Lampreys and Hagfish. The lampreys (Petromyzoniformes) and hagfish (Myxiniformes) have had long, separate evolutionary histories (Chapter 13), and this is reflected in the distinctness of their methods of ion regulation. Lampreys have ion concentrations and regulatory mechanisms similar to those of teleosts and so will not be discussed any further here. Hagfish, in contrast, are not only isosmotic with seawater but have a rather similar ionic composition as well, although some differences are detectable. For example, *Myxine glutinosa* demonstrates a sodium concentration [Na^+] somewhat greater than that of seawater (Table 6-1). The low Na^+ concentration in the secreted slime which coats its body probably helps maintain plasma [Na^+], as McFarland and Munz (1965) could find no evidence of Na^+ active transport across the gut, gills, or skin. The divalent ions Ca^{++}, SO_4^{--}, and Mg^{++} are all present in lower concentrations in hagfish than in seawater. However, Mg^{++}, K^+, SO_4^{--}, and PO_4^{--} are secreted into the glomerular filtrate by the mesonephric duct cells and appear in the urine at higher concentrations than in the plasma (Munz and McFarland 1964; McFarland and Munz 1965). Moreover, the slime has high concentrations of Ca^{++}, Mg^{++}, and K^+.

Elasmobranchs. While the retention of urea and other compounds has provided an efficient solution to the problem of water balance in sharks and their relatives, they still must eliminate the excess Na⁺ and Cl⁻ they ingest. Excretion of these ions is in fact the principal function of the rectal gland, which is found only in elasmo-branchs (Burger and Hess 1960) and the coelacanth. The rectal gland secretes a fluid that has Na⁺ and Cl⁻ concentrations approximating those of seawater (twice those in the plasma) (Silva et al. 1977a). In spiny dogfish, rectal glandular secretions can be produced by hypertonic injections of NaCl into the bloodstream (Burger 1962), and removal of the rectal gland provokes steady increase in plasma [Na⁺] (Forrest et al. 1973a). Silva et al. (1977a) have shown that the Cl⁻ secretion rate into the lu-men of dogfish rectal glands is dependent on the Na⁺ concentration. These authors hypothesize that the movement of Na⁺ and Cl⁻ from the blood (or perfusate) across the glandular wall into the lumen results both from active transport "sodium pumps" catalyzed by the special enzyme Na⁺-K⁺-dependent adenosine triphos-phatase (Na⁺-K⁺-ATPase) and from electrical forces inducing movement of these charged ions toward electrical homeostasis. This mechanism is essentially the same as that found in the chloride cells, which are so numerous in the gills of marine teleosts (see below). Rectal glands show evolutionary *regression* in elasmobranchs adapted to fresh water (Oguri 1964). Marine elasmobranchs also use their kidneys and gill chloride cells to excrete excess salts, but the density of gill chloride cells is probably only 10–20% that found in marine teleosts (Jampol and Epstein 1970, Shut-tleworth 1988).

Marine teleosts. Marine teleosts maintain a total ionic concentration in the plasma about one-third that of seawater. Since most of the ions needed by the fish are pre-sent in excess in the environment, the principal method used by marine teleosts for maintenance of ionic balance is selective excretion, particularly of Na⁺ and Cl⁻ (Fig. 6.1). Since the gills have a relatively high permeability to monovalent ions, Na⁺ and Cl⁻ move passively from seawater into the plasma. In addition, when seawater is ingested to replace water that has diffused into the environment, monovalent ions, as well as water, are absorbed in the intestine. Teleostean kidneys are of little help in the excretion of these ions because they do not have the ability to form a urine more concentrated than the blood. Indeed, many marine teleosts (e.g., oyster toad-fish *[Opsanus tau]* and plainfin midshipman *[Porichthys notatus]*) have an "evolu-tionary regressive" *aglomerular* kidney to minimize water losses! Instead, special large cells in the gills actively transport the excess monovalent anions against the concentration gradient back into the environment. Catlett and Millich (1976) de-scribe these "chloride cells" as being larger than the flat cells of the gills specialized for respiratory gas exchange. The chloride cells (termed alpha chloride cells by Pisam [1987] to distinguish them from beta chloride cells found in freshwater teleosts) are located on the filaments at the base of lamellae. They feature an abun-dance of energy-providing mitochondria, display extraordinary development of cy-toplasmic microtubules, and contain the Na⁺-K⁺-ATPase system also found in elas-mobranch rectal gland secretory tissue (Fig. 6.2). The Na⁺-K⁺-ATPase is located along the basolateral areas and in the extensive microtubular system of the chloride cell,

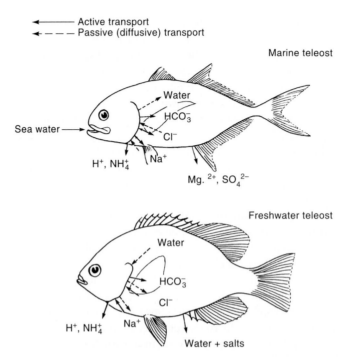

FIGURE 6.1 *Passive and active routes of salt and water exchange.*

and actively transports Na$^+$ out of the cell in exchange for K$^+$ (Karnaky 1986). This enzyme system has been elucidated with a specific pharmacological poison (ouabain, a glycosidic African arrow poison) and functions to maintain a high Na$^+$ gradient, with high [Na$^+$] in the tubules and the adjacent plasma and low [Na$^+$] in the chloride cell cytoplasm (Silva et al. 1977b). This high Na$^+$ gradient drives a linked Na$^+$-Cl$^-$ carrier system (inhibitable by furosemide, a diuretic), increasing the cytoplasmic [Cl$^-$]. The buildup of Cl$^-$ inside the chloride cell also increases the cell's electronegativity, and Cl$^-$ follows its electrochemical gradient (including a negative to positive *transmembrane* potential) by passively moving out of the apical pit area into seawater (Fig. 6.2). Na$^+$ probably exits passively to seawater via shallow tight junctions between chloride cells or between chloride cells and accessory cells, driven by the positive-to-negative *transepithelial* potential (Karnaky 1986). Utida and Hirano (1973) have shown that both Na$^+$-K$^+$-ATPase concentrations and numbers of chloride cells increase with increasing environmental salinity in gill preparations of Japanese eel *(Anguilla japonica)* (Fig. 6.3).

While the gills are the principal site of monovalent ion excretion, the kidneys eliminate excess divalent ions, such as Mg^{++} and SO$_4^{--}$. Such ions are present in only small amounts and so do not present the problems of the abundant monovalent ions.

Euryhaline and diadromous teleosts. The study of euryhaline and diadromous (meaning "to run across") teleosts can provide considerable insight into the mech-

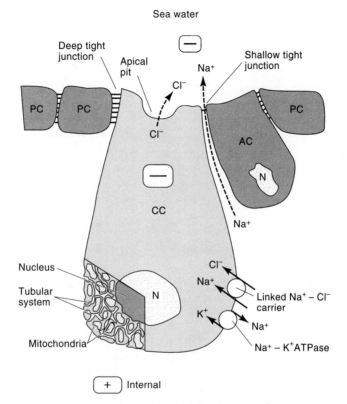

FIGURE 6.2 *A schematic model for the movement of Na+ and Cl- by chloride cells of seawater-adapted teleosts. Achloride cell (CC) is shown with a nucleus (N), connected by a shallow tight junction to an accessory cell (AC). Pavement cells (PC) are connected by deep tight junctions. Part of the chloride cell's ultrastructural detail of many mitochondria and extensive microtubule system is shown in inset. Cellular mechanisms are explained in the text. (Redrawn from Karnaky 1986.)*

anisms and energy costs of ionic regulation because such fish often endure dramatic changes in their external environments. Euryhaline forms are typically estuarine and intertidal inhabitants that experience continual shifts in external salinity dictated by tidal rhythms as well as wind, storm, or river-flow variations. Diadromous species spend part of their life cycle in fresh water and part in salt water, as rather stenohaline inhabitants except during the hormone-mediated transitions. Evans (1967a, b) studied an example of the former group, the intertidal black prickleback (*Xiphister atropurpureus*), whose plasma [Na+] and [Cl-] levels are stable when individuals are immersed in dilutions of seawater down to 31% seawater. Na+ and Cl-concentrations fall about 15% after transfer to environments with salinities between 10% and 31% of seawater. Salinities below 10% seawater are not in the tol-

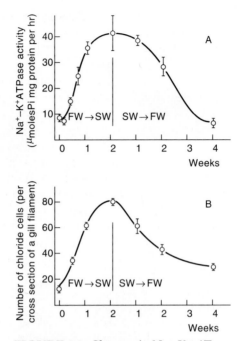

FIGURE 6.3 *Changes in Na+-K+-AT-Pase activity and number of chloride cells following transfer of Japanese eel* (Anguilla japonica) *from freshwater to seawater. (FW-SW) and vice versa (SW-FW). (From Utida and Hirano 1973; in* W. Chavin, Responses of Fish to Environmental Changes.*)*

erable range, apparently because of the prickleback's inability to retard Cl⁻ losses from passive diffusion.

Whereas prolactin can be thought of as the "freshwater" hormone, cortisol (a steroid hormone from the interrenal tissue associated with the kidney) can be thought of as the "seawater" hormone. Anguillid eels are catadromous fish that migrate down rivers as adults to spawn in the ocean. Forrest et al. (1973b) noted that plasma cortisol concentration showed a five- to seven-day increase in freshwater-adapted American eels *(Anguilla rostrata)* when they were transferred to seawater. Cortisol injection experiments support the notion that this transient peak morphologically prepares diadromous or euryhaline fishes for survival in hypertonic environments (Evans 1984). For example, injection of cortisol into freshwater tilapia *(Oreochromis mossambicus),* a euryhaline teleost, stimulated an increase in chloride cell density (Foskett et al. 1981). Conclusively, direct exposure of freshwater-acclimated tilapia opercular membranes to cortisol increased chloride cell density, size, and Na+-K+-ATPase activity (McCormick 1990). Adaptive mechanisms such as increased Na^+ excretion and Na^+-K^+-ATPase activity at the gills, increased water permeability of the urinary bladder (to retain water), and the increased uptake of ions and water in the gut (related to seawater drinking) have been associated with such cortisol-stimulated changes (Matty 1985).

Changes in diadromous fishes' ion-regulatory abilities are typically associated with ontogenic changes, mediated by hormones. Adult salmon and some trout are anadromous fish that migrate up rivers from the ocean (or a lake) to spawn. Young salmon and trout from the spawn migrate down the rivers to salt water after changing from a freshwater (parr) form to a saltwater-capable (smolt) form. Saltwater readiness in young trout and salmon ranges from a modest springtime rise in resistance shown by underyearling steelhead trout and other trouts and charrs to complete tolerance and survival in chum (*Oncorhynchus keta*) and pink (*O. gorbuscha*) salmon alevins! For most salmonids, tolerance of marine conditions develops in the spring, prior to the seaward migration of the silvery smolts (see Chapter 19). Hoar (1976) pointed out the importance of lengthening springtime photoperiods for timing these changes. On a finer scale, Grau et al. (1981) showed that plasma thyroxine surges, which occur in coho salmon (*O. kisutch*) during their smoltification period, correspond to new moon phases during spring. New moon–related swift ebbing currents and dark nights may decrease predation vulnerability of the young coho during their movements down rivers to the estuary. A few weeks after the thyroxine peaks, increased plasma cortisol concentrations (Specker and Schreck 1982) and the cortisol-related changes in chloride cells, urinary bladder, and intestine (see above) are observed (Loretz et al. 1982), and the coho smolts migrate to the sea. Besides cortisol, the pituitary hormone, growth hormone (GH), also plays an important role in the parr-smolt transformation among anadromous salmonid species (Barrett and McKeown 1988c). For example, freshwater-acclimated sea-run brown trout (*Salmo trutta*) yearlings regulate plasma ions better and survive in greater numbers after seawater exposure with injections of both GH and cortisol, compared with noninjected controls (Madsen 1990).

Studies of several species have demonstrated the role of prolactin in preventing Na^+ diffusive loss in freshwater-adapted fish and in minimizing increases in passive Na^+ loss as euryhaline forms pass from seawater to fresh water. For example, hypophysectomy (removal of the anterior lobe of the pituitary, where prolactin is synthesized) of freshwater-acclimated mummichogs promotes a marked drop in plasma electrolytes compared with sham-operated controls (Maetz et al. 1967). The many ion-regulatory roles of fish prolactin are essentially opposite those of cortisol (see above) regarding various physiological and morphological changes in the gills, gut, kidney, and urinary bladder of various species (see review by Hirano [1986]).

It is apparent that gill ionic permeabilities in many species are also affected by the concentration of calcium (Ca^{++}) in the water, although the actual site and mode of Ca^{++} action on the membrane has yet to be determined. It is known that addition of 10 mM Ca^{++} to fresh water will reduce prolactin synthesis rates by 50% in the cichlid *Oreochromis mossambicus* (Wendelaar Bonga et al. 1985). The sodium efflux from the plains killifish (*Fundulus kansae*) in fresh water is reduced 50% when 1 mM Ca^{++} is added to the water (Potts and Fleming 1971). Calcium can also reduce Na^+

permeability across the branchial epithelia of fish in seawater, such as European eels (Cuthbert and Maetz, 1972). Carrier and Evans (1976) demonstrated that the euryhaline marine pinfish *(Lagodon rhomboides)* tolerates essentially fresh water (5 *mM* Na⁺) if 10 *mM* Ca⁺⁺ is also present. Transfer of the pinfish to calcium-free fresh water stimulates substantial Na⁺ efflux. Pinfish left in calcium-free fresh water for 2.5 hours died with less than 50% of the body Na⁺ concentrations found in those acclimated to calcium-supplemented seawater. These results help explain why Breder (1934) observed several marine fish species living in a freshwater lake on Andros Island of the Bahamas. Analysis of this lake water showed it to have an unusually high (1.0 *mM* to 1.5 *mM*) Ca⁺⁺ concentration.

Freshwater teleosts. The hyperosmotic state of the freshwater teleosts dictates that small ions such as Na⁺ and Cl⁻ are continually being lost to the environment by diffusion across the thin epithelia of the gills (Fig. 6.1). Solutes are also continually lost in the large volumes of dilute urine which is produced to expel the excess water passively taken up by diffusion across the gills. Although some of the salts are regained via food sources, most of the Na⁺ and Cl⁻ needed to regain internal ionic homeostasis is taken up by active transport mechanisms in the gills.

From the pioneering work of Krogh (1939) and of Maetz and Garcia Romeu (1964), a model describing ion-exchange mechanisms across the gills in freshwater teleosts has been formulated. These ion-exchange mechanisms apparently reside in epithelial cells including chloride cells. These beta chloride cells (Pisam et al. 1987) occur on gill filaments between lamellae and, in very soft (low dissolved ion concentrations) water, on gill lamellae. They resemble chloride cells in marine fish in that they contain mitochondria, the tubular system, and Na⁺-K⁺-ATPase; but they are less numerous, usually occur singly, lack the apical crypt, and generally assist movement of Na⁺ and Cl⁻ into the fish rather than out (Eddy 1982). Fig. 6.4 diagramatically shows current ideas concerning these Na⁺ and Cl⁻ uptake mechanisms. It is not known whether all of these movements take place in beta chloride cells or in other (e.g., flat epithelial) types. These ion-exchange mechanisms serve several functions besides maintenance of [Na⁺] and [Cl⁻] in the fish. The Na⁺ exchange for NH₄⁺ conveniently rids the fish of part of its ammonia production, the principal waste product of protein digestive breakdown (see Chapter 7). Injections of NH₄⁺ into freshwater goldfish thereby stimulated Na⁺ influx (Maetz and Garcia Romeu 1964). Both the Na⁺ exchange for H⁺ and the Cl⁻ exchange for HCO₃⁺ tend to maintain internal acid-base homeostasis (see the acid-base balance section in this chapter). Thus just two ion-exchange mechanisms provide for maintenance of appropriate internal [Na⁺] and [Cl⁻]; elimination of some potentially toxic NH₃ (as NH₄⁺); elimination of some metabolic CO₂ (as HCO₃⁺); adjustment of internal [H⁺] and [OH⁻]; and maintenance of ionic electrical balance.

Evans (1977) reported results indicating the same exchange in four species of *marine* fish. Apparently, *active* (besides passive) uptake of Na⁺ and Cl⁻ via these active transport ion-exchange pumps may be *necessary* for adequate excretion of NH₄⁺, H⁺, and HCO₃⁺. If this mechanism to take up Na⁺ and Cl⁻ is functional in marine teleosts, one may ask why marine species are all not more euryhaline. After drink-

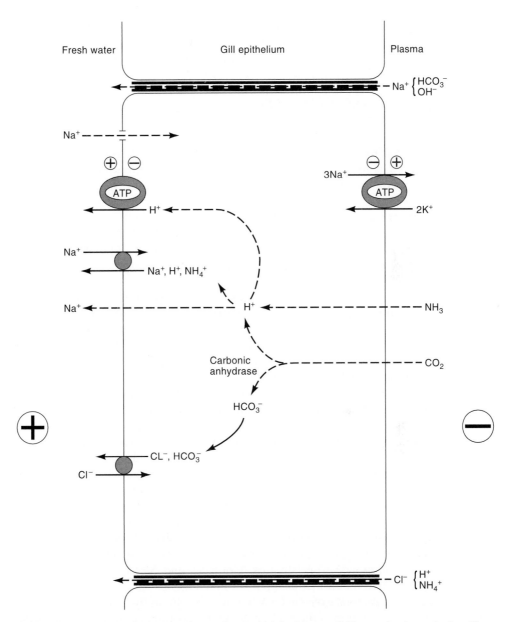

FIGURE 6.4 *Current ideas on the mechanism(s) for Na+ and Cl– uptake through the gills of a freshwater fish, based on experiments with intact fish and perfused gill preparations. The cell types involved have not been conclusively identified, hence they are not labeled. Carrier-mediated processes are indicated by solid arrows, diffusive processes by dashed lines. Paracellular movements of HCO₃–, OH–, H+, and NH₄ (acid-base equivalents) are shown in white to indicate that they may be dependent variables constrained by differential strong cation (Na+) and anion (Cl–) outfluxes. (From Wood and Marshall, 1994,* Estuaries *17:34–52.)*

ing rates, urine flows, and permeability differences have been considered, the relative inefficiency of NaCl *uptake* by the marine fish compared with diffusional NaCl losses in fresh water probably represents the limiting factor (Evans 1975).

STRESS RESPONSES AND EFFECTS

Stressors such as extremely vigorous exercise, netting and handling, and pronounced hypoxia (including air exposure) stimulate physiological changes (including increased gill permeability and possible hydromineral imbalances) in fish. These changes are either adaptive, allowing fish to respond to an emergency; or detrimental, leading to adverse effects and possible mortality. Less severe and short-term stressors usually lead to responses such as mobilization of glucose for metabolic needs (Barton and Iwama 1991, Reid et al. 1992). They also promote lamellar recruitment for enhanced gas exchange (Booth 1979), and mobilization of more epinephrine receptors on RBC membranes for maintenance of blood O_2 transport (Reid and Perry 1991) (Figs. 6.5, 4.6). Long-term or especially severe stressors lead to decreased growth, increased metabolic exhaustion and disease incidence, and possible mortality (Barton and Iwama 1991). Mediated by corticosteroids such as cortisol (in teleosts) and catecholamines such as epinephrine, stress responses and effects are typically accompanied by increased permeability to water and small ions (Pic et al. 1974). This permeability is especially acute in the gills, where most of the catecholamine uptake and removal from the circulation occurs (Nekvasil and Olson (1986a, b). Thus stress will invoke a loss of water (and some gain in ions) in marine fish and a water gain (and some ion loss) in freshwater fish. These increased diffusive movements are probably due to the epinephrine-stimulated increases in "exposure" of blood (at higher pressures due to increased cardiac output [Farrell and Jones 1992; Randall and Perry 1992]) to the environment across thin membranes (due to lamellar recruitment; see Chapter 3). Exercised Nile tilapia *(Tilapia nilotica)* adapted to seawater tended to increase plasma osmotic pressure (from water loss). The same fish tended to decrease osmotic pressure (from water uptake) with exercise after adaptation to fresh water (Farmer and Beamish 1969). This trade-off between enhanced O_2 uptake and gill permeability is probably more costly for less active species (e.g., sunfish) from lakes than for more active ones (e.g., trout and shiner minnows) from streams (Gonzales and McDonald 1992). These authors showed that the former group has a much higher Na^+ ion loss to O_2 gas gained ratio after vigorous exercise (chasing in a tank) than the latter group.

Minimization of the external to internal osmotic gradient and incorporation of exercise conditioning can minimize capture, handling, and transport stresses–induced osmotic problems under fish culture conditions. Transportation of excitable freshwater fish in salt solutions similar to their blood (isosomotic) reduces handling mortality due to permeability changes (Hattingh et al. 1975). Truck-transport stress of largemouth bass was reduced and related mortality eliminated when fish were treated for diseases, starved for 72 hours before loading, lightly anesthetized, hauled at a cool temperature in physiological concentrations of salts, and allowed

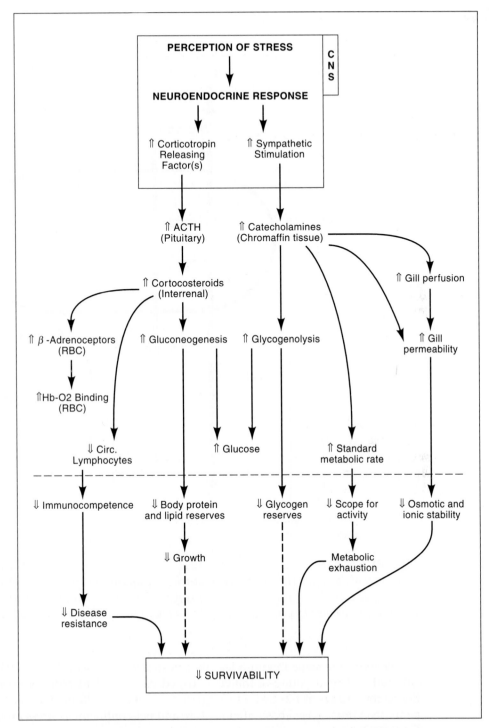

FIGURE 6.5 *Adaptive (above dashed line) and maladaptive (below dashed line) aspects of the major endocrine–metabolic stress response pathways in fish. (Modified from Barton 1988.)*

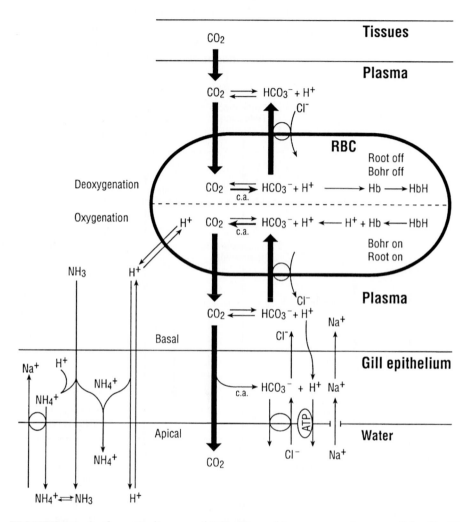

FIGURE 6.6 *A schematic diagram of CO_2, H^+, and ion movements across fish gills. The upper part of the figure (i.e., deoxygenation-related pathways in erythrocyte) takes place at tissue sites; the lower part of the figure (oxygenation) takes place at the gill. Carbonic anhydrase is denoted by c.a. (Modified from Randall 1982 and Lin and Randall 1991.)*

to recover in the same medium less the anesthetic (Carmichael et al. 1984). Both cultured and wild young-of-the-year striped bass that had been exercise-conditioned for 60 days at 1.2–2.4 body lengths/sec regulated plasma ions significantly better than unexercised bass, after capture and net-confinement stress (Young and Cech 1993b).

FREEZING RESISTANCE

Because their body fluids are either hyperosmotic or isosmotic with their environments, hagfish, marine elasmobranchs, and freshwater teleosts are not subject to freezing as long as their environment remains unfrozen. However, because the marine environment has a higher salt concentration than their body fluids and consequently a lower freezing point, marine teleosts can freeze to death even though the water around them is still liquid. To prevent this, many cold-water marine teleosts possess macromolecular antifreeze compounds in their blood. These antifreeze compounds are peptides or glycopeptides, having molecular masses of 2.5 to 20 kilodaltons and consisting of many repeating units rich in the amino acid alanine. Apparently the hydroxyl groups on the antifreeze molecules bond with oxygen molecules on the surface of the ice crystals forming in the blood. The antifreeze molecule is consequently adsorbed onto the ice crystal surface, interfering with the ice crystal growth and depressing blood freezing point (DeVries 1984). Consequently, demersal Antarctic fish such as the naked dragon fish *(Gymnodraco acuticeps)*, *Trematomus bernachii*, and *T. hansoni* can be found resting on anchor ice (DeVries and Wohlschlag 1969). This mechanism does not change the melting point, leading to a difference between melting and freezing points (typically of 1-1.6°C) termed *thermal hysteresis*. Smaller antifreeze peptides penetrate the skin increasing its effectiveness in preventing ice crystal propagation (Valerio et al. 1992). An aglomerular kidney is considered part of the freezing-resistance system in Antarctic fish, as the glycoproteins are conserved rather than filtered out of the blood. Moreover, energy is not needed for glycoprotein reabsorption, thereby lowering the energetic cost of low-temperature osmoregulation in these forms (Dobbs et al. 1974).

Duman and DeVries (1974a) showed that winter flounder *(Pseudopleuronectes americanus)* from Nova Scotian waters display seasonal changes in serum freezing point. Their serum freezing point is lowered from -0.69°C during the summer (water temperature 17°C) to -1.47°C in the winter (water temperature -1.2° C). Macromolecular antifreeze production (from the liver) allows this species to depress its serum's freezing point adequately during the colder months, when the release of an antifreeze synthesis inhibitor (made in the pituitary) is blocked by the central nervous system (Fletcher et al. 1984). Acclimation to cold temperatures alone promotes antifreeze production in several Nova Scotian fishes. However, a combination of both warm temperatures *and* long photoperiods was necessary as a "fail-safe" system to lose the antifreeze completely over a period of three to five weeks. From studies on the high cockscomb *(Anoplarchus purpurescens)* taken from cold Alaskan waters and from more mild California intertidal waters, genetically based population differences in antifreeze production are apparent. Upon acclimation to cold water, the Alaskan individuals were capable of producing the antifreeze compounds, whereas the Californian population could not (Duman and DeVries 1974b).

ACID-BASE BALANCE

The control of internal acid-base conditions within a certain range is essential for life in fish. For example, the catalytic properties of enzymes and the "regulatory responsiveness" of intracellular proteins to various enzyme regulatory functions are highly sensitive to solution conditions, including pH and ionic strength (Hochachka and Somero 1984; Somero 1986). Because the ionization constant of water (K_w) changes with temperature, the pH of water and weakly buffered aqueous solutions (including blood) also changes with temperature. For example, Cech et al. (1984) measured a 0.016 pH unit decrease for each °C increase in blood temperature for albacore *(Thunnus alalunga)* between 5°C and 35°C. Thus, rather than trying to keep a constant blood pH, fishes subjected to diurnal or seasonal temperature changes maintain a constant $OH^-{:}H^+$ ratio (relative alkalinity).

Hydrogen ions are continually produced by the fish's metabolic processes, e.g., from the hydration of metabolically produced CO_2. Dissolved carbon dioxide is hydrated and dehydrated in aqueous solutions according to the reaction:

$$CO_2 + H_2O \rightleftharpoons H_2CO_3 \rightleftharpoons H^+ + HCO_3^-.$$

These hydrogen ions (protons) must be buffered in the circulation until they can be excreted. Figure 6.6 shows the pathways for H^+ and CO_2 excretion in fish. The upper part of Fig. 6.6 shows what happens at the tissue (e.g., red muscle) capillaries, while the lower part shows what happens at the gill lamellae. As CO_2 is produced at the tissues it diffuses across the capillary walls into the plasma. A small portion of this plasma CO_2 forces the preceding equilibria to the right, slowly forming HCO_3^- and lowering blood pH (increased $[H^+]$). A much larger portion of the CO_2 diffuses across the membranes of the red blood cells (RBCs), and a fraction of this binds with the hemoglobin to form carbaminohemoglobin. As much of the hemoglobin may be in the reduced state (deoxygenated), the hemoglobin's CO_2 capacity is relatively high (see discussion of the Haldane effect in Chapter 4). Most of the CO_2 in the RBCs is very quickly converted to HCO_3^- and H^+ by the enzyme *carbonic anhydrase* (Fig. 6.6). The hemoglobin binds and, therefore, buffers the H^+. Because the HCO_3^- level in the plasma is much lower in the absence of the enzyme catalysis, "excess" HCO_3^- produced in the RBCs diffuses into the plasma, establishing a HCO_3^- equilibrium across the RBC membrane. Because of the HCO_3^- movement across the membrane, the RBC becomes more positively charged than the plasma, and Cl^- diffuses into the RBC to alleviate the electrical disequilibrium. Cameron (1978) demonstrated this "chloride shift" in RBCs of a marine snapper *(Lutjanus aya)* and the freshwater rainbow trout. The chloride shift brings more osmotically active particles (Cl^-) from the plasma in the RBCs. Thus water enters these RBCs along with the Cl^-, ensuring an osmotic equilibrium. This induces a slight swelling of the RBCs and causes the RBC volume (hematocrit) in venous blood to exceed that of the arterial blood by 2-3% in the same fish (Stevens 1968).

As the venous blood enters the gills, 95% of the carbon dioxide is in the form of plasma bicarbonate (Cameron 1978). Dissolved CO_2, which moves easily across gill epithelia, diffuses across the lamellar epithelium into the water, which usually has a high absorbing capacity for CO_2. This decrease in plasma CO_2 activates the dehydration of CO_2, relatively slowly in the plasma and very rapidly in the RBCs. Consequently, most of the plasma HCO_3^- diffuses back into the RBCs (in exchange for Cl^-), where the catalyzed dehydration produces dissolved CO_2, which rapidly moves across the RBC membranes and the gill epithelia. A small fraction of the *epithelial* CO_2 is catalytically hydrated to HCO_3^- and H^+, which are ultimately "exchanged" for Cl^- and Na^+, respectively (Fig. 6.6). Lin and Randall (1991) found evidence for an ATP-powered, H^+ excreting pump on the outside membrane of rainbow trout gills. H^+ (possibly as NH_4^+, from combination with NH_3) produced in the plasma or RBC is also excreted in exchange for either Na^+ or H^+ (Fig. 6.6).

Although hyperventilation acts to "wash out" blood CO_2 and raise arterial pH—for example, after exercise in striped bass (Nikinmaa et al. 1984)—acid-base balance is primarily controlled by adjustments of the bicarbonate equilibrium system (Randall and Cameron 1973). In another example, exposure of rainbow trout to hypercapnic (high PCO_2) water induced an initial "respiratory acidosis" with a high blood PCO_2 (matching that of the environment) and, consequently, lowered blood pH. Over the next few days, blood pH almost completely recovered (acidosis almost completely compensated) by plasma $[HCO_3^-]$ increases at the elevated PCO_2 (Janssen and Randall 1975).

The general "exchanges" of H^+ for Na^+ and of HCO_3^- for Cl^- generally balance the acid-base and ionic requirements in elegant fashion (Fig 6.4). However, this link can force unwanted adjustments in one system while compensating for a disturbance in another. The osmotic problems that fish confront in maintaining their acid-base balance are among the main reasons they have a hard time surviving in highly acid waters, such as in streams draining many mines or in lakes contaminated by acid rain or snow. Rainbow trout show significant increases in $[H^+]$ and decreases in total CO_2 after two days' exposure to water with a pH = 4. Compensatory rises in hemoglobin concentration apparently offset Root-shifted losses (Chapter 4) in blood O_2 capacity (Neville 1979). Another major problem in low-pH environments concerns excessive Na^+ losses from the body. Because high environmental $[H^+]$ can inhibit H^+ excretion associated with Na^+ uptake across gill epithelia (Fig. 6.6), acid-exposed teleosts often die from insufficient plasma NaCl. For example, Leivestad and Muniz (1976) attributed the death of brown trout exposed to low-pH conditions in the Tovdal River in southern Norway to extreme reductions in plasma NaCl. Lampreys have lower overall blood-buffering capacities compared with teleosts, leading to more dramatic blood pH decreases and mortality increases when they are immersed in water at pH = 4 (Mattsoff and Nikinmaa 1988). Most fish will avoid low pH environments if possible (Peterson et al. 1989).

Supplemental Readings

Barton and Iwama 1991; Evans 1979, 1984, 1993; Hazel 1993; Heisler 1988, 1993; Hoar 1976; Karnaky 1986; Shuttleworth 1988; Wood and Marshall 1994.

CHAPTER 7

Feeding, Nutrition, Digestion, and Excretion

Fish must have an energy source to run the body machinery (metabolism). They also require an adequate amount of essential amino and fatty acids plus vitamins and minerals to sustain life and promote growth. This chapter therefore examines feeding, food requirements, and the resulting dynamics in fish.

FEEDING

Fish can be classified broadly on the basis of their feeding habits as detritivores, herbivores, carnivores, and omnivores. Within these categories fish can be characterized further as (1) euryphagous, having a mixed diet; (2) stenophagous, eating a limited assortment of food types; and (3) monophagous, consuming only one sort of food. A majority of fish, however, are euryphagous carnivores. Often the feeding mode and food types are associated with the body form and digestive apparatus. For example, longer guts with greater surface areas typify species that feed on detritus and algae and take in a high percentage of indigestible material such as sand, mud, or cellulose. In contrast, carnivorous species tend to have shorter gut lengths. Among carnivorous fish, however, gut lengths are often greater in those fish that prey on small organisms (relative to their own size) than those that prey on large organisms. Thus the herbivorous, euryphagous Sacramento blackfish (*Or-*

thodon microlepidotus) has a vastly longer gut than the carnivorous Sacramento squawfish *(Ptychocheilus grandis)*, which feeds largely on other fish. The Sacramento hitch *(Lavinia exilicauda)* has an intermediate gut length (Fig. 7.1) corresponding to its diet of small zooplankters (Kline 1978). Digestive area can also be increased through the use of spiral valve intestines, found in the Chondrichthyes and in ancestral bony fishes, such as sturgeons and lungfishes. A spiral valve is a longitudinal fold that spirals down the length of the intestine, much like a spiral staircase down a lighthouse (Fig. 7.2).

Overall food demand is a direct function of a species' metabolic rate. Chapter 3 discusses effects of body size, temperature, and activity on aerobic metabolic rate. Feeding rates can also be directly measured in the laboratory. Measurements of gastric evacuation rates quantify feeding rates, incorporating the relative digestibility of prey (Bromley 1994). For example, Hopkins and Larson (1990) showed that marine rockfish *(Sebastes*, a euryophagous predator) digest fish faster than shrimp, and shrimp faster than crab. They determined that *friability,* the ease with which a food

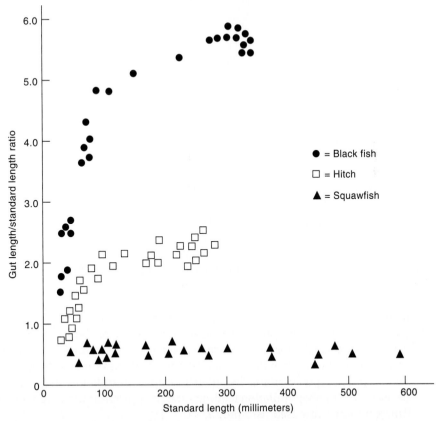

FIGURE 7.1 *Relationship between the relative length of gut and fish standard length for Sacramento blackfish, hitch, and Sacramento squawfish. (From Kline 1978.)*

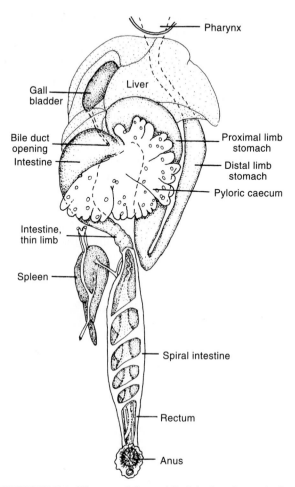

FIGURE 7.2 *Viscera of the paddlefish showing spiral valve intestine. The proximal limb of the stomach normally lies in the midline of the coelom. The diffuse pancreas is omitted from this illustration. (From Wiesel 1973.)*

item is fragmented in the stomach, may be an important factor in determining evacuation patterns. Chitinous exoskeletons are found on both shrimp (lighter exoskeleton) and crab (heavier); this may delay enzymatic attack or interfere with the emptying of chyme from the stomach. Laboratory measurements of gastric evacuation rates along with stomach contents samples from field-caught specimens can be used to estimate population feeding rates, if appropriate (regurgitation-free) capture techniques are used (Bromley 1994).

Structures in the buccal-pharyngeal cavity often correlate with food type and feeding habits. For example, the pharyngeal pad (or palatal organ) situated dorsally at the entrance to the esophagus has been implicated in removing excess water from

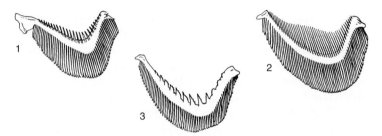

FIGURE 7.3 *Gill rakers of planktophagic and predatory fishes. (A) powan* (Coregonus lavaretus); *(B)* Coregonus muksun *(Pall.); (C) pike-perch* (Lucioperca lucioperca L). *The first two species feed on planktonic crustacea, and the pike-perch ingests larger prey. (From Nikolsky 1963, with permission, from* The Ecology of Fishes. *Copyright by Academic Press Inc. [London] Ltd.)*

the ingested food of common carp (Jara 1957). In contrast, the pharyngeal valve hanging from the roof of the pharynx of parrot fish (Scaridae) probably assists in the placement of pieces of coral for grinding by the pharyngeal teeth and lubrication from epithelial mucus cells (Kapoor et al. 1975). Likewise, the bony or cartilaginous gill rakers protruding from each gill arch can be specialized for modes of feeding (Fig. 7.3).

Many of these gill raker specializations can be found in the sunfish family (Centrarchidae). In piscivorous members of the family, such as the largemouth bass *(Micropterus salmoides)*, the gill rakers are short, stout, widely spaced, and pointed. They function mainly in preventing the prey from escaping through (and damaging) the gills but may also partially descale fish as they pass by the rakers. The shortest and stubbiest gill rakers in the family are possessed by members, such as the redear sunfish *(Lepomis microlophus)*, that are specialized for feeding on snails. Gill rakers of intermediate length, thickness, and spacing are found in euryphagous species, such as bluegill *(L. machrochirus)*. The longest and finest gill rakers in the family are those of the crappies *(Pomoxis* spp.), reflecting the importance of zooplankton in their diets, which they "pick" individually from the water column. Among fish in general, the finest, most closely spaced gill rakers are possessed by a type of *suspension-feeding* species that directly strain plankton out of the water, such as the Atlantic menhaden *(Brevoortia tyrannus)*. Large schools of this abundant clupeid decrease the phytoplankton as well as the dissolved oxygen concentrations of the waters they swim through (Oviatt et al. 1972). Dense concentrations of the food organisms in the water stimulate faster swimming by the menhaden (to 2.5 body lengths per second). Durbin and Durbin (1975) showed that the feeding response of menhaden is linked to the presence of comparatively large zooplankton or the larger phytoplankton rather than to much greater densities of the small phytoplankters, which are filtered less efficiently. Juvenile Sacramento blackfish switch from particle feeding to suspension feeding at a small metabolic cost (ca. 1% of total metabolic energy costs), presumably to maximize energy intake (Sanderson and Cech 1992). Suspension-feeding subadult and adult blackfish use gill rakers that resemble brushy tufts to guide, rather than strain, food particles to a sticky palatal organ on the roof of the mouth (Sanderson et al. 1991). Food and mucus are apparently rubbed or sloughed off the palatal organ into the esophagus. Feeding efficiency (>95%) via particle guiding in blackfish is not adversely affected by hypoxic water conditions when spreading gill rakers from hyperventilation (increased ventilatory stroke volume) would compromise direct particle straining (Cech and Massingill 1995).

Mouth structure is also related to the feeding modes and habits of fish. Mouth structure is highly variable, and this variability explains in part the evolutionary success of both teleosts and elasmobranchs (Chapter 12). The ancestral mouth consists of firm jaws lined with sharp teeth for grasping active prey. Such jaws are still possessed by many piscivorous fishes (such as barracuda and pike). More common among modern fish are jaws modified for suction feeding. In suction-feeding fish the jaw is shortened to limit the gape while the expansibility of the buccal (mouth) cavity is maintained, resulting in increased water velocity through the smaller mouth when the cavity is expanded or contracted. In elasmobranchs, such as skates (Rajidae), eagle rays (Myliobatidae), and nurse sharks (Orectolobidae), the strong oral suction created allows them to feed effectively on benthic invertebrates. In teleosts, three primary motions are involved in the expansive phase of suction feeding: the elevation of the neurocranium, the depression of the mandible, and the depression of the "floor" (hyoid) of the mouth (Lauder 1985). The major musculoskeletal couplings involved in these movements are shown in Fig. 7.4. Lauder (1983) showed that bluegill adduct their gill bars to firmly close the connection between the buccal and branchial (gill) cavities during suction feeding. This protects the delicate gill lamellae from hydraulic damage during suction feeding. Alexander (1970) trained fish to take rings of earthworm off the free end of a nylon tube connected to a pressure transducer and recorder. Negative pressures from -80-cm water (18°C) in the temperate black bullhead (*Ameivrus melas*) to -400-cm water (27°C) in the tropical butterfly fish (*Pterophyllum scalare*) were measured.

The feeding of many sharks represents an unusual type of predation, that of taking bites from prey larger than the predator. The sawtooth edges on the awl-shaped teeth of the lower jaw and the bladelike teeth of the upper jaw teeth, coupled with a head-shaking action, provide for efficient cutting through flesh of larger, slow-moving or disabled animals. The well-developed jaw musculature and the unique position of the hyomandibular cartilages provide support and positioning for the jaws when the mouth is open to effect a deep, gougelike bite (Moss 1977). In contrast, filter-feeding elasmobranchs such as the basking shark (*Cetorhinus maximus*), whale shark (*Rhincodon typus*), and manta rays (Mobulidae) have comparatively weak jaw musculature and reduced dentition. Instead, numerous, elaborate gill rakers function to strain small organisms from immense ventilatory water flows.

NUTRITION

Most of our knowledge concerning fish dietary requirements comes from experimental nutrition studies conducted on cultured species, primarily salmonids. These studies have demonstrated the relative importance of dietary proteins, lipids, and

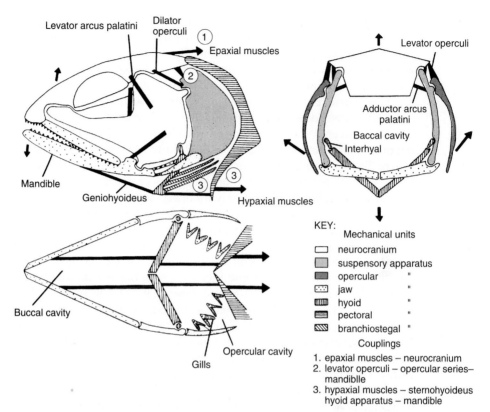

FIGURE 7.4 *The major muscles and mechanical units in the head of a teleost fish. Three major musculoskeletal couplings are involved in the expansive phase of prey capture: (1) the epaxial muscles coupling, which causes cranial elevation; (2) the levator operculi coupling, which mediates mandibular depression via the opercular apparatus and interoperculomandibular ligament (ligament l_1); and (3) the hyoid coupling, which also governs mandibular depression via the mandibulohyoid ligament (l_2). (From Lauder 1985. Reprinted by permission.)*

carbohydrates for growth (anabolism) and for energy to run the bodily machinery (catabolism). Proteins, which consist of chains of amino acids, seem to be essential mainly for growth, although they may also be used for catabolic functions. The importance of proteins for growth has been shown in numerous nutritional studies that omit proteins containing amino acids the fish are not capable of synthesizing themselves. For example, Halver (1957) fed experimental groups of chinook salmon (*Oncorhynchus tshawytscha*) diets devoid of single amino acids and compared their growth rates with control animals fed diets containing all the amino acids. He found that their growth rates were greatly reduced because new structural proteins (for muscle, bone, etc.) could not be synthesized when one or more amino acids composing the specific protein chain were missing. Missing amino acids can also provoke developmental vertebral abnormalities such as scoliosis and lordosis (Halver and Shanks 1960). These nonsynthesizable amino acids therefore become "essential" in the diet of the fish. Ten amino acids that have been shown to be essential for fish are arginine, histidine, isoleucine, leucine, lysine, methionine, phenylalanine, threonine, tryptophan, and valine. The *quantities* of the various required amino acids needed, however, vary among species, and excessive amounts of any one acid may also be detrimental to growth and survival.

In wild fish, proteins are often an important source of energy for meeting metabolic demands. For example, rainbow trout in the wild feed largely on aquatic and terrestrial invertebrates, making protein a high percentage of their natural diet, far beyond what is needed for growth. In cultured fishes, however, the protein fraction of the diet usually comes from fish meal and is a comparatively expensive part of the feed. To minimize their monetary costs of operation, fish culturists include protein in quantities sufficient only for anabolic processes and substitute lipids or, especially, relatively inexpensive carbohydrates for a source of energy.

A significant energy cost is incurred in breaking down (hydrolyzing) the large, complex protein molecules to amino acids and in synthesizing new proteins (growth) following a meal. This cost is termed the *specific dynamic effect* (SDE) or *specific dynamic action* (SDA), and increases with the amount of protein in the diet. Thus Schalles and Wissing (1976) calculated that 12.6% to 16.1% of the ingested energy was used by bluegills to digest, assimilate, and resynthesize protein from diets containing 23.9% to 45.3% protein, respectively. Brown and Cameron (1991) showed that growth was an important component of the SDA process by infusing a normal ration of essential amino acids directly into the bloodstream of channel catfish *(Ameiurus nebulosus)* and measuring a peak 56% increase in metabolism (measured as O_2 consumption rate) 4 hours after infusion. Significantly, the excreted ammonia accounted for only 21% of the total infused amino acids' nitrogen, indicating tissue incorporation of most of the nitrogen. Conclusively, infusion of either (nondigestible) D-stereoisomer essential amino acids or a protein synthesis inhibitor (cycloheximide) into the catfish failed to produce the metabolic elevation.

Carbohydrates and lipids constitute the other available energy sources in foods. In natural aquatic environments, lipids are found in both animal and plant sources, while carbohydrates are found almost exclusively in plants. The low digestibility of carbohydrates by carnivores such as trout and salmon contributes to the low energy value gained from their ingestion. A salmonid extracts only 1.6 kcal of energy from 1 g of carbohydrate fed, while gaining 3.9 kcal/g for ingested protein and 8.0 kcal/g for lipids. The salmonid culturist must thus balance the low feed costs of carbohydrate sources (e.g., grains and cereals) with their low nutritional value. Of the carbohydrates, monosaccharides are the most digestible, followed (in order) by disaccharides, simple polysaccharides, dextrins, cooked starches, and raw starches (Halver 1976). Some herbivorous and omnivorous fishes, such as anchovies (Enqraulidae), sea catfish *(Arius felis)*, and channel catfish may utilize gut microbes to break down cellulose, the plant structural carbohydrate (Stickney and Shumway 1974). The bacteria having this cellulase activity are either maintained in the gut or regularly brought in with ingested detritus (Prejs and Blaszczyk 1977).

The seaweed-eating sea chubs (Kyphosidae) have apparently taken this ability to full fermentative capacity. Volatile fatty acids (VFA) are the nutritive end products of microbial fermentation of plant materials such as celluloses, fiber, starches, and sugars (Bergman 1990). Two species of *Kyphosus* from Australian marine waters produce high VFA concentrations in caecal pouches containing a diverse microflora, near the posterior end of their intestines (Rimmer and Wiebe 1987). Two Hawaiian *Kyphosus* species, along with the warm-temperate halfmoon *(Medialuna californiensis)*, produce a full complement of 6 VFAs (Kandel et al. 1994), which are rapidly absorbed at the site of production and contribute substantially to these herbivores' energy requirements (Bergman 1990).

Lipids represent a rich source of energy for fish in general. Besides their high specific energy value (8.0 kcal/g), they are also almost completely digestible (Halver 1976). The high lipid content of a diet consisting of small fish maximizes growth by sparing the ingested protein for tissue synthesis. For example, rapid growth rates are typically achieved by predaceous fishes such as the mackerels, billfishes, salmon, pikes, and sharks. Besides being an energy source, lipids provide essential fatty acids, such as linolenic acid (Millikin 1982). Fatty acids are used in the construction of fats or oils (triglycerides) to be stored by a fish for use as an energy source at a later time. A classic example are Pacific salmon, which accumulate lipids at sea and expend them while fasting during migrations upstream to spawn. Experiments with catfish *(Ictalurus)* have shown that body lipids synthesized by fish for energy storage parallel those ingested in terms of saturation (completeness of hydrogen bonding of constituent fatty acid carbon chains) (Andrews and Stickney 1972).

The relative importance of lipids and proteins as energy sources is also shown by their mobilization by fishes during periods of starvation, which can be a regular occurrence in the life cycle of many fish. For example, winter flounder *(Pseudopleuronectes americanus)* inhabiting coastal Maine waters fast while in deeper water during the period from January to May (Bridges et al. 1976). Pacific salmon as well as Atlantic salmon and steelhead trout fast during their spawning migration. As no carbohydrates, protein, or fat are taken into the body during a fast, the fish must use compounds stored in body tissues. Savitz (1971) showed that bluegill utilize body protein and, especially, fat to meet body energy demands when fasting. The quantities of body fat and protein are significantly reduced in the starved fish, while inorganic content (ash) remains about constant. Protein depletion is presumably accomplished by the high concentration of proteolytic enzymes found in fish muscle (Siebert et al. 1964). Losses in body fat or protein as seen in bluegill are rarely reflected in significant body weight changes in the fish. Instead, the metabolized fat or protein is replaced by water to make up the body weight difference. For example, the whole body water content of sockeye salmon was shown to increase from about 60% to 77% during the spawning migration, while the sum percentage of lipid plus water was approximately constant at 80% (Idler and Bitners 1959). The familiar phenomenon of ascending salmon possessing an atrophied gut but still striking an angler's bait represents an interesting contradiction. Even if food were swallowed, the degeneration of the digestive tract and the significant decrease in gastric enzyme secretion indicate that very little of the food could be digested.

At the other end of the feeding spectrum, it is of interest to know what happens when fish have unlimited food available to them. In their investigation of unrestricted feeding in juvenile rainbow trout, Grayton and Beamish (1977) found that trout held at 10°C would consume only just under 4% of their wet body weight per day of dry, prepared trout pellets. The trout would consume this quantity whether they were offered pelletized food in unlimited quantities twice daily or up to six times a day. As one would expect, growth rate also did not vary with feeding frequencies from two to six feedings per day. In contrast, Balon (1977) describes deep-bodied, obese body shapes associated with an extreme abundance of food. Deep-bodied salmonids (including rainbow trout), pikes (Esocidae), carps, and others have been described in cultured or natural environments where food is very abundant. As described in Chapter 8, fish tend to grow throughout their lives but increase more in girth rather than length toward the ends of their lives.

DIGESTION

Digestion in fish concerns the breakdown of foods by enzymatic and, in many cases, acidic secretions in the gut. The diversity of foods found in the guts of fish attests to the variety of morphological and chemical adaptations that have evolved for digestion. The esophagus of fish often contains many mucus cells and functions as a lubricated transit tube between the buccal-pharyngeal cavity and the lower gut. The lower gut of many fish (especially carnivorous ones) contains a true stomach, characterized by a smooth muscle *(muscularis mucosa)* layer of tissue. On the other hand, development of a gizzard (for masticatory as well as secretory digestive processes) as found in mullets and shad is a stomach specialization for microphagous food habits.

The gastric mucosa of the stomachs of carnivorous fish produces a protease (protein breakdown) enzyme (e.g., pepsin) with an optimal activity at a pH of 2 to 4. Hydrochloric acid is also secreted by the gastric mucosa glands in these species, creating the low-pH environment. Gastric acid secretions are stimulated by stomach distension, which apparently activates cholinergic (mimicking acetylcholine response) neural fibers. The "secretory" signals of these fibers to the acid glands can be blocked with injections of the neural-blocking agent atropine. The rates of both gastric acid secretion and of pepsin secretion are influenced by temperature. As temperatures increase (up to a point), the rates of secretion also increase. These increased secretions largely account for the threefold to fourfold increases in digestion rate that follow 10°C increases in temperature (Kapoor et al. 1975).

Proteins are also broken down in the alkaline medium of the intestine by the action of the enzyme trypsin. Trypsin is secreted by pancreatic tissue, which may be concentrated in a compact organ as in mackerel or diffusely located in the mesenteric membranes surrounding the intestine and liver. Some fish possess one or more pyloric caeca (see Fig. 9.1), which are blind pouches of secretory tissue located near the pyloric valve at the stomach-intestine junction. Trypsin may be secreted from the caecal tissue or the pancreatic tissue, which commonly envelopes the caeca.

Fish also have enzymes that break down carbohydrates (carbohydrases) and fats (lipases). The pancreas appears to be the primary site of carbohydrase (e.g., amylase, which breaks down starch) production, although the intestinal mucosa and pyloric caeca represent additional production sites in various species. The pancreas is presumably also the primary site of lipase production. However, lipase activity has been found in extracts of the pyloric caeca and upper intestine as well as the pancreas in mackerel, menhaden, scup (*Stenotomus chrysops*), and searobins (Triglidae) (Chesley 1934).

Both the presence and the quantity of digestive enzymes seem to correlate with the diet of fish. Herbivorous and omnivorous fish which have no stomachs also lack pepsin as a low-pH, proteolytic enzyme (Kapoor et al. 1975). However, omnivorous species have amylase activities in the gut many times that found in carnivorous species (Volya 1966). Initiation of gastric secretions of pepsin and acid in white sturgeon (*Acipenser transmontanus*) larvae is concomitant with the switch from endogenous (yolk) to exogenous (feeding) nutrition (Buddington and Doroshov 1986).

Compounds broken down by actions of pharyngeal teeth, gizzards, and/or secretions of acid and enzymes are subsequently absorbed through the intestinal wall. Absorption (or assimilation) can be estimated by the difference between the quantity and quality (energy value in kilocalories or joules[1]) of the food ingested and of the feces excreted. These estimates are made even more precise when fecal nitrogen and calories from nonfood sources (e.g., sloughed gut wall) are taken into account.

As in other animals, the metabolic conversion of biochemical compounds, either to provide energy or to synthesize other compounds (e.g., enzymes, structural proteins, stored triglycerides), requires particular cofactors to proceed. The cofactors, which are largely unavailable in the body, constitute the vitamins. The vitamin requirements of fish probably vary somewhat with species, although only a few species (mostly of commercial value) have been investigated (Table 7-1). Dietary deficiencies of the vitamins that are essential for life and growth provoke a variety of physiological disturbances (Table 7-2). As with the research into essential amino acids, most of the vitamin deficiencies were determined by single vitamin deletions in an otherwise complete diet.

EXCRETION

Digestive breakdown of either lipids or carbohydrates yields water and carbon dioxide as end (waste) products. Water is either conserved, excreted, or diffused away depending on the salinity of its environment (Chapter 6). Carbon dioxide enters into the bicarbonate equilibrium system, and most is excreted at the gills (Chapter 6). Protein digestion yields nitrogenous compounds in addition to carbon dioxide and water. In teleosts, these nitrogenous wastes take the form of ammonia, a potentially toxic substance. Thus teleosts are primarily *ammoniotelic*. Despite its toxicity, ammonia has many advantages over urea or uric acid as the chief excretory product of nitrogen metabolism as long as the animal resides in an environment with abundant water. First, the small molecular size and high lipid solubility permits un-ionized ammonia (NH_3) to diffuse easily across the gills. Second, ionized ammonia (NH_4^+) is exchanged for Na^+ at the gills for maintenance of relative alkalinity and

---

[1]Note that 4183 joules = 1 kilocalorie (kcal).

TABLE 7-1 VITAMIN REQUIREMENTS FOR GROWTH[a]

Vitamin (mg/kg dry diet)	Rainbow trout	Brook trout	Brown trout	Chinook salmon	Coho salmon	Carp	Eel	Goldfish	Yellowtail	Channel Catfish
Thiamine	10–12	10–12	10–12	10–15	10–15	R[b]	R	R	R	R
Riboflavin	20–20	20–30	20–30	20–25	20–25	7–10				R
Pyridoxine	10–15	10–15	10–15	15–20	15–20	5–10		R	R	R
Panothenate	40–50	40–50	40–50	40–50	40–50	30–40			R	R
Niacin	120–150	120–150	120–150	150–200	150–200	30–50				R
Folacin	6–10	6–10	6–10	6–10	6–10	?				R
Cyanocobalamin	R	R	R	0.015–0.02	0.015–0.02	?				R
myo-Inositol	200–300	R	R	300–400	300–400	200–300				R
Choline	R	R	R	600–800	600–800	1500–2000				R
Biotin	1–1.2	1–1.2	1.5–2	1–1.5	1–1.5	1–1.2	R		R	R
Ascorbate	100–150	R	R	100–150	50–80	R		R	R	R
Vitamin A	2000–2500	R	R	R	R	1000–2000		R	R	
Vitamin E[c]	R	R	R	40–50	R	80–100		R	R	R
Vitamin K	R	R	R	R	R				R	R

Sources: From Halver 1972.

[a] Fish fed at reference temperature with diets at about protein requirement.

[b] R = required.

[c] Requirement directly affected by amount and type of unsaturated fat fed.

TABLE 7–2 VITAMIN DEFICIENCY SYNDROMES

Vitamin	Symptoms in salmon, trout, carp, catfish
Thiamine	Poor appetite, muscle atrophy, convulsions, instability and loss of equilibrium, edema, poor growth
Riboflavin	Corneal vascularization, cloudy lens, hemorrhagic eyes—photophobia, dim vision, incoordination, abnormal pigmentation or iris, striated constrictions of abdominal wall, dark coloration, poor appetite, anemia, poor growth
Pyridoxine	Nervous disorders, epileptiform fits, hyperirritability, ataxia, anemia, loss of appetite, edema of peritoneal cavity, colorless serous fluid, rapid postmortem rigor mortis, rapid and gasping breathing, flexing of opercles
Pantothenic acid	Clubbed gills, prostration, loss of appetite, necrosis and scarring, cellular atrophy, gill exudate, sluggishness, poor growth
Inositol	Poor growth, distended stomach, increased gastric emptying time, skin lesions
Biotin	Loss of appetite, lesions in colon, coloration, muscle atrophy, spastic convulsions, fragmentation of erythrocytes, skin lesions, poor growth
Folic acid	Poor growth, lethargy, fragility of caudal fin, dark coloration, macrocytic anemia
Choline	Poor growth, poor food conversion, hemorrhagic kidney and intestine
Nicotinic acid	Loss of appetite, lesions in colon, jerky or difficult motion, weakness, edema of stomach and colon, muscle spasms while resting, poor growth
Vitamin B_{12}	Poor appetite, low hemoglobin, fragmentation of erythrocytes, macrocytic anemia
Ascorbic acid	Scoliosis, lordosis, impaired collagen formation, altered cartilage, eye lesions; hemorrhagic skin, liver, kidney, intestine, and muscle
p-Aminobenzoic acid	No abnormal indication in growth, appetite, mortality

Source: From Halver 1972.

internal ion balance (Chapter 6). Third, conversion of ammonia to either urea or uric acid requires energy. Thus in contrast to terrestrial forms, less energy is required to complete nitrogenous compound catabolism and, in teleosts, the end products resulting from this catabolism are largely released at the gills rather than the kidney. For example, common carp and goldfish excrete six to ten times as much nitrogen at the gills as at the kidney. Of the total nitrogenous excretion, 90% is in the form of ammonia, and only 10% consists of urea (Smith 1929).

Elasmobranchs as well as coelacanths excrete urea as the primary nitrogenous end product (i.e., are *ureotelic*). As discussed in Chapter 6, much of the urea is retained in these marine fish, giving their body fluids a near isosomotic relationship with their environment. The elasmobranch kidney filters urea from the blood plasma at the glomerulus. Much of the urea is subsequently recovered from the filtrate by active tubular resorption, preventing major losses of urea in the urine (Schmidt-Nielsen 1975).

Lungfish and, to varying degrees, teleosts possess the biochemical machinery to be either ammoniotelic or ureotelic. For example, the African lungfish must sometimes endure extensive droughts. When the aquatic environment is drying up, the lungfish constructs a cocoon of mucus in the bottom mud and estivates there until the water returns. The African lungfish is mostly ammoniotelic while aquatic but shifts to complete ureotelism while estivating, and survives by metabolizing the proteins in its muscles. This shift is made possible by high concentrations of the necessary enzymes for urea production in its liver tissue (Janssens and Cohen 1966). Nontoxic urea may accumulate in the blood of estivating lungfish to concentrations of 500 mmol/L after a three-year estivation (Smith 1961). In contrast, the liver of Australian lungfish possesses only 1% of the concentration of urea-synthesizing enzymes found in African lungfish. This finding is in accord with the obligatory aquatic habits of the Australian lungfish (which does not estivate).

In contrast, some water-breathing teleosts, such as toadfish *(Opsanus beta)* and the Magadi tilapia *(Oreochromis alcalicus)*, also have the necessary liver enzymes for substantial ureogenesis (Mommsen and Walsh 1991; Randall et al. 1989). Toadfish are intermittently ureotelic, such as during confinement in a small volume of water (Walsh et al. 1994). The Magadi tilapia are exclusively ureotelic, apparently to survive in their extremely alkaline (pH=10) lake ecosystem (Randall et al. 1989). The relative dearth of H^+ (protons) in such a highly alkaline environment makes excretion of NH_3^- virtually impossible. Three reasons for this phenomenon are the potentially low blood to water NH_3^- gradient, the high buffer capacity of Lake Magadi water (inhibiting NH_3^- to NH_4^+ conversion in water passing over the gills), and the inhibition of Na^+/NH_4^+ exchange (Chapter 6) across the gill membranes (Wood et al. 1989).

Supplemental Readings

Andrews and Stickney 1972; Balon 1977; Budker 1971; Goldstein et al. 1967; Grayton and Beamish 1977; Halver 1972, 1976; Holmgren et al. 1983; Horn 1989; Kapoor et al. 1975; Lauder 1983, 1985; Love 1970; Millikin 1982; Nikolsky 1963; Savitz 1971; Stickney and Shumway 1974; Wood 1993.

CHAPTER 8

Growth

Most fish continue to grow throughout their lives. Consequently, growth has been one of the most intensively studied aspects of fish biology because it is a good indicator of the health of individuals and populations. Rapid growth indicates abundant food and other favorable conditions, whereas slow growth is likely to indicate just the opposite. Growth can be defined as the change in size (length, weight) over time or, energetically, as the change in calories stored as somatic and reproductive tissue. The energetic definition is particularly useful for understanding the factors that affect growth in fishes because ingested food energy *(I)*, measured in calories, must emerge either as energy expended for metabolism *(M)* or growth *(G)*, or as energy excreted *(E)* (Brett and Groves 1979). This can be simply expressed in the equation

$$I = M + G + E \qquad (1)$$

As explained in Chapter 3, metabolic energy expenditures can include calories expended for body maintenance and repair, for digesting food, and for movement. Excreted energy can take the form of feces, ammonia, and urea, and the small quantities of mucus and sloughed epidermal cells of the skin. The remaining factor in the energy equation is growth.

FACTORS AFFECTING GROWTH

Because growth is usually positive (e.g., increase in weight over time), a positive energy balance in metabolism is indicated. Metabolism is the sum of anabolism (the tissue synthesis or "building up" aspect of metabolism) plus catabolism (the energy-producing breaking of chemical bonds or "tearing down" aspect). Thus the rate of anabolism exceeds that of catabolism in a growing fish. The principal factors controlling anabolic processes are growth hormones secreted by the pituitary and steroid hormones from the gonads (see next section). However, the growth rate of fish is highly variable because it is greatly dependent on a variety of interacting environmental factors such as water temperature, levels of dissolved oxygen and ammonia, salinity, and photoperiod. Such factors interact with each other to influence growth rates, and with other factors such as the degree of competition, the amount and quality of food ingested, and the age and state of maturity of the fish.

Temperature is among the most important environmental variables. For example, growth in desert pupfish (*Cyprinodon macularius*) increases with temperature up to 30°C before falling off some at 35°C. Brett et al. (1969) measured the weight gain in fingerling sockeye salmon (*Oncorhynchus nerka*) at several ration (meal size) levels. As for pupfish, maximal growth rates in the young salmon are achieved at intermediate temperatures (15°C). It is also noteworthy in Brett's study that the maintenance ration (ration at zero growth) increased with temperature, reflecting the increased standard or maintenance metabolism (M in equation [1]) at warmer temperatures (Chapter 3). At any particular temperature, there often is an optimal ration for maximum growth. For example, juvenile mosquitofish (*Gambusia affinis*) show increased food consumption and growth with increasing temperature to a 30–35°C peak, with ad libitum (excess) rations (Fig. 8.1). Growth rate decreases dramatically with reduced (20% of ad libitum) rations, and the growth peak shifts to 25°C, presumably due to increased metabolic (M) demands. Gross efficiency (G/I) is maximal at 25-30°C (Fig. 8.1). Fish that vertically migrate on a diel basis between strata of different temperatures can optimize their feeding and digestive efficiencies to maximize growth. Juvenile Bear Lake sculpin (*Cottus extensus*) shorten gut evacuation time in warmer (13–16°C) surface waters of Bear Lake at night, allowing them to feed at the bottom (30-40 m deeper, 5°C) the following day. This alternation of temperatures increases their growth by 300%, compared with fish held at a constant 5°C (Neverman and Wurtsbaugh 1994). Overall, fish tend to prefer temperatures at which their growth is maximal (Jobling 1981).

Dissolved oxygen levels, although temperature dependent, are often by themselves an important factor affecting the growth rates of fishes. Stewart et al. (1967) measured a significant reduction in growth rate and food conversion efficiency in juvenile largemouth bass when dissolved oxygen concentrations fell below approximately 5 mg/l at 26°C. Presumably, the reduced oxygen below this threshold precludes "extra," aerobic, energy-requiring activities such as growth and reproduction above maintenance energy costs. These fishes (called *oxygen regulators* and including largemouth bass, channel catfish, striped mullet, Sacramento blackfish, and others) maintain a homeostatic level of metabolism as oxygen levels are reduced. In some cases, attempts to swim to more favorable environments will be made by these species.

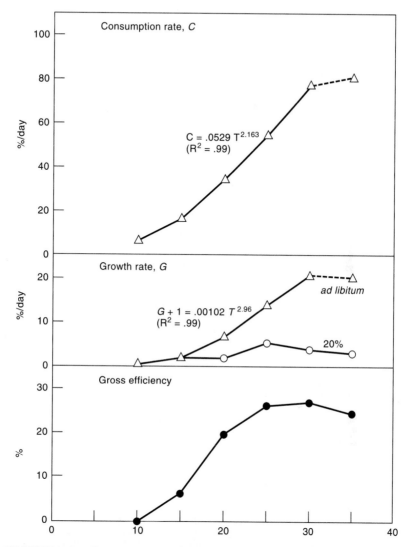

FIGURE 8.1 *Effects of temperature on instantaneous food consumption rate, instantaneous growth rate, and gross efficiency, of juvenile mosquitofish fed ad libitum. Growth rates of fish fed at 20% of ad libitum also are shown. All data are based on dry weights of fish and food. Regression lines for consumption and growth rates were fitted for temperatures from 10 to 30°C. (From Wurtsbaugh and Cech 1983.)*

Ammonia is the primary excretory product of fish, but if it is present in high concentrations, it will slow growth rates. For example, juvenile channel catfish display a linear drop in weight gain with increasing ammonia in their water (Fig. 8.2). Although the mechanism of growth inhibition by ammonia is still unknown, there

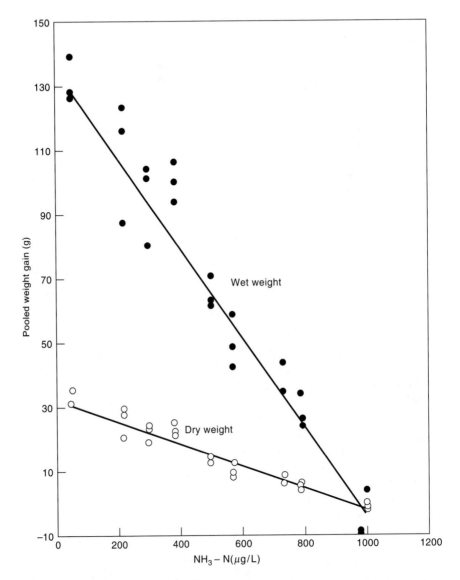

FIGURE 8.2 *Effects of nonionized ammonia on growth, measured in terms of pooled weights of the fish in each aquarium. (From Colt and Tchobanoglous 1978.)*

may be a relationship with food consumption rates. Juvenile lake trout *(Salvelinus namaycush)* have been found to decrease their food consumption rate along with their growth rate at un-ionized ammonia concentrations >198 µg/l (Beamish and Tandler 1990). Obviously, this information has important applications in fish culture systems. Culture systems designed to maximize growth rate must have either high flows of fresh water to carry away excreted ammonia, or ammonia-removal systems such as green plants or "biological filters" utilizing appropriate bacteria. It is generally acknowledged that un-ionized ammonia (NH_3) in the water produces more toxic effects on fish than an equal concentration of the ionized form (NH_4^+). As the relative proportion of the two forms depends on water pH, regular pH monitoring is an essential part of the operation of intensive freshwater-fish culture systems. Although ammonia is a "natural" compound, its effects on fishes are typical of many pollutants, which also reduce growth rates when present at sublethal levels.

Salinity also affects growth rate. The euryhaline (broad salt tolerance) desert pupfish shows maximum growth rate at 35 parts per thousand (ppt) salinity compared with both higher and lower salinities (Kinne 1960). Growth is altered as other energy-demanding components (such as ion and osmoregulatory active transport systems) respond to environmental characteristics. These responses increase maintenance energy requirements *(M)*, which will decrease growth rate *(G)* if *I* and *E* remain constant (Brett 1979). This topic is discussed more completely in Chapter 6.

Competition, either within or among species, for limited food supplies may slow growth. Swingle and Smith (1940) showed that bluegill, a species in which the adults and young both eat virtually the same aquatic invertebrates and are not cannibalistic, become stunted when the population size reaches a particular level. Fertilization of the pond will increase the invertebrate food base and consequently bluegill total biomass. However, the average size of the bluegills remains small as growth slows and some reproduction continues.

Food availability also interacts with other factors, particularly temperature, to affect the growth of fishes on a seasonal basis. For example, Gerking (1966) found marked seasonal differences in growth (length increases) in northern Indiana bluegill populations (Fig. 8.3). Bluegill growth was accelerated during the warmer months of plentiful food. Figure 8.3 also shows the reduced rate of growth (especially gains in length) consistent with advancing age in bluegill, also typical of most other fishes. Striped mullet from south Texas coastal waters show cycles of seasonal growth similar to those of bluegill, except that growth virtually ceases during the warmest months of midsummer through midautumn. This leveling off of growth when food is abundant can probably be attributed to excessive water temperatures reducing assimilation efficiency (Cech and Wohlschlag 1975, 1981). Photoperiod (day length) may also affect seasonal growth phenomena. For example, Hogman (1968) found a close association between growth of lake whitefish (*Coregonus clupeaformis*) and seasonal photoperiod but no relationship between the spring water temperatures and growth.

Age and maturity are usually the best predictors of relative growth rates in fishes, although the absolute growth rates are strongly influenced by environmental factors. Thus fish typically grow very rapidly in length in the first few months or years of life, until maturation. Then increasing amounts of energy are diverted from growth of somatic tissues to growth of gonadal tissues. As a consequence, growth rates of mature fish are much slower than those of immature fish. Partly because of the amount of gonadal tissue, however, mature fish are typically heavier per unit of length than immature fish. This is reflected in their higher condition factor *(K)*, an index of "plumpness":

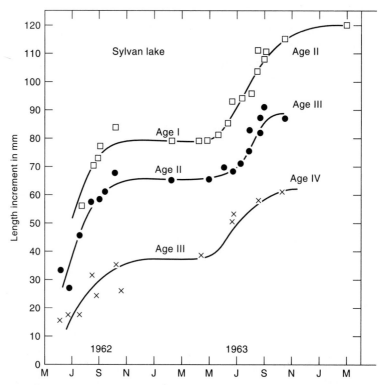

FIGURE 8.3 *Seasonal gain in length of a population of bluegill (Lepomis macrochirus) by age groups. The growth increment varies with season and decreases with age and size. (From Gerking 1966.)*

$$K = \frac{W(100)}{L^3} \qquad (2)$$

where *W* is the weight of the fish in grams and *L* is the length in centimeters. The condition factor is frequently used by fisheries biologists as an indicator of the health of a fish population. If the fish in a population have high *K* values, then there is probably plenty of food available to support both somatic and gonadal growth.

Exercise Conditioning (training) has been shown to increase growth in several fishes. For example, Young and Cech (1993) found that young-of-the-year striped bass, continuously swimming for 60 d at 1.2–2.4 body lengths/sec, grew 7–10% faster than unexercised (<0.2 bl/s) control fish. Houlihan and Laurent (1987) report that rainbow trout continuously swimming at 1 bl/s for 42 d grew 118% faster than unexercised controls! Increased growth rates associated with exercise conditioning have been attributed to various factors in different species. These include: (1) better food conversion efficiency (Davison and Goldspink 1977); (2) increased growth hormone levels (Barrett and McKeown 1988a, 1988b); (3) increased protein synthesis rates (Houlihan and Laurent 1987; Christiansen et al. 1989); (4) decreased antagonistic behavior (East and Mangan 1987); and (5) decreased stress levels (Woodward and Smith 1985). Young and Cech (1994) found that significant conditioning-related growth increases were still detectable in striped bass 56 d after conditioning (60 d swimming at 1.5-2.4 bl/s) had stopped!

GROWTH REGULATION

Photoperiodic and other factors affecting growth rates may well act through variations in hormone secretions. Fish growth hormone is synthesized in the alpha cells of the pars distalis (anterior lobe) of the pituitary gland (Donaldson et al. 1979). Removal of this tissue (hypophysectomy) results in a cessation of growth in species investigated (including poeciliids, salmonids, and sharks). On the other hand, mammalian growth hormone injections increase growth rates of juvenile coho salmon *(Oncorhynchus kisutch)*, apparently because food conversion rates are improved. Possible mechanisms involved with this improved food conversion rate include stimulation of stored fat mobilization (for an energy source), positive effects on protein synthesis, or stimulation of insulin production or release (Markert et al. 1977). Thyroid and gonadal steroid hormones have also been used to increase growth in various species. The thyroid hormone triiodothyronine (T3) increased growth of underyearling coho salmon when added to their diet, whereas thyroxine (T4) additions increased food consumption but not growth (Higgs et al. 1979). T3 additions increased both growth and food consumption of rainbow trout (Matty 1986). Two synthetic androgens, dimethazine and norethandrolone, increased the growth rate of juvenile rainbow trout when either compound was added to a pelleted diet. These weight gain increases were due to both the increased protein synthesis rate and the improved food conversion efficiency (Matty and Cheema 1978). Two natural androgens, testosterone and 11-ketotestosterone, improved the food conversion efficiency of common carp when added to their diet (Lone and Matty 1982).

GROWTH RATE MEASUREMENTS

Growth rate in fish can be determined by measuring changes in size over time. In practice, it is usually measured by changes in body weight (mass) or length per unit of elapsed time. Growth rates of fish are generally measured by one of six methods.

1. **Raise in a controlled environment.** A fish (or egg or larva) of known age is placed in a tank, small pond, or cage in a larger water body. Its length or body weight is measured at time intervals for growth rate calculations. For example, instantaneous (or specific) growth rates (GR) in % body weight/day can be calculated from: $GR = 100 \cdot (\log_e W_f - \log_e W_i)/(t_f - t_i)$, where W and t are body weights and times (usually, days), respectively, at the initial (i) and final (f) experimental times (Ricker 1979, Wurtsbaugh, and Cech 1983). This method is especially valuable for assessing growth of cultured fishes, where feeding rates, temperatures, and other factors may be controllable.

2. **Mark and recapture.** A fish is marked (or tagged) and released when an initial measurement of size is made. The fish is recaptured at a future date and measured again. The growth rate is calculated from the change in size over the time period the marked animal spent in its habitat. It should be established that the marking method does not significantly alter the behavior, feeding rate, etc. Marks may consist of clipped fin rays, liquid nitrogen "cold brands," pigmented epidermis from high-pressure spray painting, or fluorescent rings on bones or scales (visible under ultraviolet light) from incorporation of tetracycline or 2,4-bis(N,N'-dicarboxymethylaminomethyl)fluorescein (DCAF) in the diet (Weber and Ridgway 1962; Hankin 1978). Tags may also vary considerably, from externally attached discs, plates, and streamers to small implantable metal rods detectable in a magnetic field, and passive individual transponders (PIT tags) that emit a unique code to a nearby receiver. Although these fish provide more realistic data concerning growth rates in their natural setting, they are more difficult to recapture compared with those in which the first method is used.

3. **Length-frequency distribution.** Length-frequency distributions are produced by measuring the lengths of individuals sampled from a population and plotting the number of fish (frequency) of each length caught. This is especially useful as a technique with young fish, and the individual peaks often separate by age classes (Fig. 8.4). By comparing the mean lengths between age classes, one can determine approximate growth rates at various ages. For example, in Figure 8.4 the

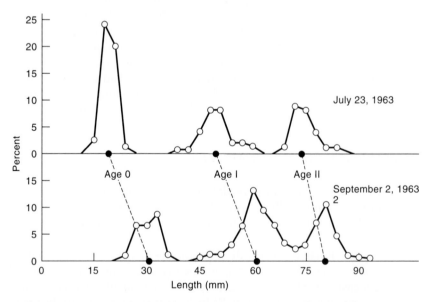

FIGURE 8.4 *Percentage length frequencies of pond smelt* (Hypomesus olidus) *from Black Lake, Alaska, in middle and late summer. (Unpublished data from Fisheries Research Institute, University of Washington, Seattle, Washington.) (From Royce 1972.)*

difference between age class 0 (young of the year) fish and age class I (between second and first "birthdays") fish is 49 mm - 20 mm = 29 mm. Thus these grow at a mean rate of 29 mm (length) per year in their first year of life (when sampled in late July). In this example, the growth increment declines with increasing age from 29 mm to 24 mm per year (between year classes I and II).

4. **Back-calculation from rings on hard structures.** Juvenile fish have the same number of bones and scales as very old, much larger individuals of the same genetic stock when rearing takes place under similar conditions. And, for many species, the rate of growth in diameter of the bones, spines, and scales is proportional to the growth rate (length) of the fish. For many reasons scales are the hard structure most commonly examined. The relative transparency of scales, the ease of sampling them, and the minimal damage to the fish make them desirable to work with. Scales grow by fibroblast cells in the fibrillar plate region supplying collagen (a protein) and by calcification ($CaCO_3$) of the outer surface. Figure 8.5 shows the proliferation of cells at the scale margin which enlarge the diameter of the scale. These additions to the scale diameter are formed repeatedly at a relatively constant rate over time and are distinguishable as growth rings (*circuli*) when the scale is magnified (Fig. 8.6). Periods of slow growth are discernible in magnified scales as areas of closely spaced circuli. Closely spaced circuli may occur on an annual basis from:

a. decreased metabolism and appetite in cold seasons, especially in temperate water;
b. fasting periods associated with spawning and unavailability of food; or
c. partial scale decalcification (resorption) in females with developing eggs and young.

These annual variations in the circuli pattern are termed *annuli*. Thus age can be determined by counting the annuli, and fish lengths at each year can be back-

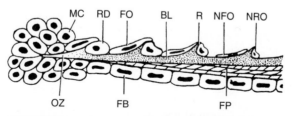

FIGURE 8.5 *Schematic diagram showing the structure of the anterior margin of a teleostean fish scale and the scale-forming cells. BL bony layer, FB fibroblast, FO flattened osteoblast, FP fibrillary plate, MC marginal cell, NFO necrotic flattened osteoblast, NRO necrotic round osteoblast, OZ osteoid zone, R ridge, RO round osteoblast. (From Kobayashi et al. 1972.)*

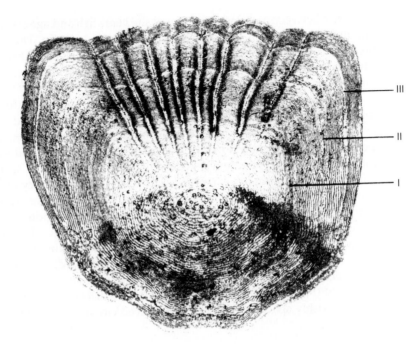

FIGURE 8.6 *A scale of a kelp perch* (Brachyistius frenatus) *from Bodega Bay, California. Shown are three annuli (magnification = 14X). (Photo by Samuel Woo, Illustration Services, University of California, Davis.)*

calculated by measuring the linear distance (radius) from the "focus" of the scale to each annulus (Fig. 8.6). For example, the length at *n* years can be calculated by using the following formula (Lee 1920):

$$L_n = a + \frac{(L - a)(V_n)}{V_r} \tag{3}$$

where

L_n = fish length at *n* years
a = a constant that often approximates fish length at time of scale formation
L = fish length at time of capture
V_n = scale radius distance from focus to nth annulus
V_r = scale radius from focus to scale edge

From these back-calculations of length at different years, growth rates can be estimated. Table 8-1 shows back-calculated standard lengths for striped mullet from South Texas coastal waters.

TABLE 8–1 MEAN BACK-CALCULATED STANDARD LENGTHS IN MILLIMETERS OF STRIPED MULLET

Age class	(n)*	Standard lengths (mm)				
		I	II	III	IV	V
1+	(39)	132				
2+	(71)	127	194			
3+	(54)	122	188	234		
4+	(12)	125	178	227	266	
5+	(3)	127	183	213	249	286
Means		127	186	225	258	286
Growth increments			59	39	33	28

Source: From Cech and Wohlschlag 1975.

n* = Sample size in each age class.

Daily increments of growth have been detected on fish otoliths ("ear stones") (Pannella 1971). The widths of these increments average 1 μm to 2 μm in larval anchovies *(Engraulis)* and 3 μm to 4 μm in larger hake *(Merluccius)* but are difficult to count where annual rings are formed. Thus using daily growth increments for age estimates is particularly effective in young fish (less than one year) and in tropical species having poorly differentiated annuli (Brothers et al. 1976). Advances in otolith microchemistry (e.g., microspectrometric analysis) have shown potential to record prior events in the life of the fish. For example, strontium is present in higher concentrations in sea water than in fresh water. Increased strontium content in otolithic layers indicates marine, rather than freshwater, habitation of Japanese eels *(Anguilla japonica)* during the period the layers were deposited (Tzeng and Tsai 1994). Either daily or annular rings on hard structures need to be *validated*. Using methods such as oxytetracycline baths (for larvae) or injections to make a fluorescent marker ring, or by sampling a population over an extended period, the time period between annular, daily, or other rings can be determined (Summerfelt and Hall 1987).

5. **Radiocarbon uptake method.** Ottoway and Simkiss (1977) describe a method in which living fish scales, plucked from the epidermis, are incubated in a medium containing the simple amino acid glycine which has been radiotagged with ^{14}C. The rate at which the [^{14}C]glycine is incorporated into the collagenous structure of the scale (protein synthesis rate) after an incubation of less than four hours is measured by the level of beta radiation emitted by the scale. Faster growth rates of fish should accompany increased ^{14}C incorporation by the scale, as measured in a scintillation counter.

6. **RNA/DNA Ratio Method.** The RNA/DNA ratio method is another measure of protein synthesis (tissue elaboration) rate as an index of instantaneous growth rate. Whereas deoxyribonucleic acid (DNA) content is constant per cell, and ribonucleic acid (RNA) content is a function of the cell's protein synthesis rate, the RNA/DNA ratio reflects this rate per number of cells in a tissue sample (Haines 1980). This ratio correlates well with measured weight gains in golden shiners

(Notemigonus crysoleucas) (Bulow 1970). However, growth rate comparisons based on RNA/DNA ratios should be limited to the same species and to restricted size and life history stages (Bulow 1987).

Supplemental Readings

Brett 1979; Brett and Groves 1979; Donaldson et al. 1979; Kinne 1960; Matty 1986; Ottaway and Simkiss 1977; Ricker 1979; Royce 1972; Summerfelt and Hall 1987; Weatherley 1972; Webb and Brett 1972.

Reproduction

The success of any fish species is ultimately determined by the ability of its members to reproduce successfully in a fluctuating environment and thereby to maintain viable populations. Since each fish species lives in a unique set of ecological conditions, it has a unique reproductive strategy, with special anatomical, behavioral, physiological, and energetic adaptations.

REPRODUCTIVE ANATOMY

The reproductive strategies of fishes are often clearly reflected in the anatomical differences between the sexes. Internally, of course, the sexes of most fishes can be easily distinguished by examination of the gonads, at least during the spawning season. Both the testes of males and the ovaries of females are typically paired structures that are suspended by mesenteries across the roof of the body cavity, in close association with the kidneys (Fig. 9.1). During the spawning season, the testes are smooth, white structures that rarely account for more than 12% of the weight of a fish, while the ovaries are large yellowish structures, granular in appearance, that may be 30% to 70% of a fish's weight.

The testes are rather similar among the various groups of fishes, although the path of the sperm may show considerable variation. Thus in lampreys, hagfish, and

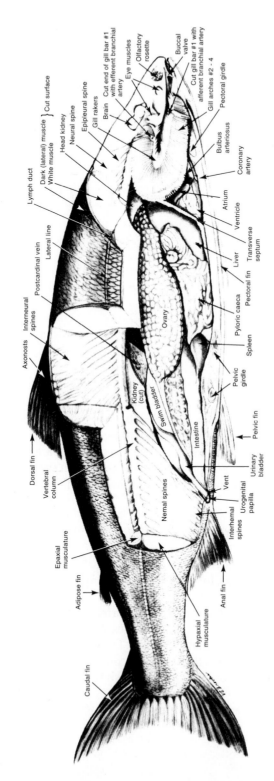

FIGURE 9.1 *Semidiagrammatic drawing of an adult female salmon, with portions cut away, showing the location and identity of various external and internal features.* (From L. S. Smith and G. R. Bell 1975. A Practical Guide to the Anatomy and Physiology of Pacific Salmon. *Fish. Mar. Serv. Misc. Spec. Publ. 27:14.*)

salmon, sperm are shed directly into the body cavity and exit through an abdominal pore or pores. In contrast, in the Chondrichthyes sperm pass through a duct that is shared with the kidney and may be stored in a seminal vesicle for a short period of time before being expelled. A similar situation exists in most non-teleost bony fishes, although a seminal vesicle is usually lacking. In teleosts there are usually special separate sperm ducts. The means of passing eggs from the ovary to the outside are similar to those for sperm, although special modifications of the oviducts (and/or ovaries) are common in fishes that retain the fertilized eggs and/or young; this is particularly true if nutrients are supplied to the developing young by the mother (see the next section of this chapter).

While the internal differences between the sexes are generally obvious in mature fish, it is frequently difficult to distinguish the sexes externally. Indeed, many fishes that are mass spawners show virtually no sexual dimorphism or dichromatism (color differences), even when spawning. At the opposite end of the spectrum are fishes that are permanently and obviously dimorphic or dichromatic. Many of these species have internal fertilization, so the males have penislike intromittent organs. In most such cases, such as sharks or poeciliid fishes (e.g., guppies), the intromittent organ is a modified fin. Because intromittent organs evolved independently in many groups, they show considerable anatomical variation, ranging from the barely noticeable thickening of the anal spine region of the surfperches (Embiotocidae), to the elongated movable anal rays of the Poeciliidae, to the complex claspers of the anal fin of the sharks and rays.

The most widespread type of sexual dimorphism is size. In egg-laying fish in which the males are territorial during the breeding season, the males are often larger than the females, as in salmon. However, in such species there are also nonterritorial males that are typically smaller than the females; these species utilize an alternative reproductive strategy discussed later in this chapter.

In most fishes with sexual differences in size, it is the female that is larger or at least achieves a larger size. Thus the record-sized individuals of many game fishes such as striped bass and sturgeon (Acipenseridae) are females. Among live-bearing fishes, females as a rule are larger than males. What males may lack in size they often make up for in bright coloration. Sexual dichromatism is mostly a seasonal phenomenon among fish, because bright colors that are likely to increase reproductive success by attracting mates are also likely to attract predators. Exceptions to this "rule" are found primarily among tropical fish in which the breeding season lasts through much of the year, so the males are more or less continuously on display. Males of dichromatic fishes often have temporary structural modifications as well. Best known are the bizarre hooked mouths (kypes) and humps characteristic of many spawning salmon. More widespread, however, are breeding tubercles and contact organs, which Wiley and Collette (1970) noted were found in at least 25 families of fishes. Breeding tubercles are tiny, keratinized bumps that grow on the fins, head, and body scales during the breeding season. Contact organs are similar but have an internal core of bone as well. Both types of structure are found primarily in males on the body parts that are likely to come in contact with females or other males during the spawning season. These tubercles seem to function in assisting the males to maintain contact with females during spawning, in stimulating the females during spawning, and in assisting the defense of territories and nests. For ichthyologists the breeding tubercles and contact organs have proved to be very useful taxonomic tools, because the number and pattern differ among species.

BREEDING BEHAVIOR

Fish have a fascinating array of reproductive behavior patterns. Not surprisingly, such behavior is highly adaptive and is strongly correlated with the overall ecology of each species and with its morphological adaptations. It is thus possible to construct a classification of fishes based on their methods of reproduction and the means by which fish protect their developing embryos and young (Balon 1975a, 1984; Table 9-1). In this system, fish can be (1) nonguarders, (2) guarders, or (3) bearers.

Nonguarders are fish that do not protect their eggs and young once spawning has been completed. They fall into two basic groups: those that simply scatter their eggs in the environment (open substrate spawners) and those that hide the eggs as part of their spawning behavior (brood hiders). The open substrate spawners by and large spawn in groups, without elaborate courtship behavior or specialized reproductive structures. Often the spawning groups are quite large, with males outnumbering the females. The spawning behavior is very difficult to describe precisely because typically all that can be observed is a swirling mass of fish.

Pelagic spawners are very common among marine fishes. They spawn in open water, often near the surface. Many such spawners are schooling fishes, such as tuna (Scombridae) and sardines (Clupeidae). Some river-dwelling anadromous fishes, such as shad *(Alosa)*, are also pelagic spawners, often seeking out areas where the flows are most favorable for successful spawning. Although pelagic spawning is most often associated with pelagic fishes, many benthic fishes temporarily rise off the bottom to spawn. This is particularly true of fishes associated with coral reefs, such as wrasses (Labridae) and parrotfishes (Scaridae). One of the main functions of pelagic spawning seems to be to assure that the young become widely dispersed by water currents.

In order to become widely dispersed, the eggs, embryos, and larvae of pelagic spawners have to be buoyant; and buoyancy is achieved either through the presence of oil globules or through high water content. One of the problems with this, however, is that the mortality of eggs and young is extremely high, either because they are carried to unfavorable areas or because they are eaten by pelagic predators. To compensate, females have extremely high fecundities, and spawning periods are often protracted since all the eggs can rarely be released by a single spawning act. The shortest spawning periods are found in temperate-zone pelagic fishes, since optimal conditions for embryo and larval survival are likely to be highly seasonal. In pelagic spawners associated with tropical reefs, spawning may be a nearly daily activity for months, with each female producing a small number of eggs each day. In these fishes, the breeding behavior may be extremely complex and variable. Indeed, some of the most complex mating systems known are found in such fishes, involving territoriality, harems, leks, and sex changing.

TABLE 9–1   A CLASSIFICATION OF REPRODUCTIVE STRATEGIES OF FISHES BASED ON SPAWNING HABITATS

I. Nonguarders

   A. Open substrate spawners

      1. Pelagic spawner

      2. Benthic spawners

         a. Spawners on coarse bottoms (rocks, gravel, etc.)

            (1) Pelagic free embryo and larvae

            (2) Benthic free embryo and larvae

         b. Spawners on plants

            (1) Nonobligatory

            (2) Obligatory

         c. Spawners on fine substrates

      3. Terrestrial spawners

   B. Brood hiders

      1. Benthic spawners

      2. Crevice spawners

      3. Spawners on invertebrates

      4. Beach spawners

II. Guarders

   A. Substratum choosers

      1. Rock tenders

      2. Plant tenders

      3. Terrestrial tenders

      4. Pelagic tenders

   B. Nest spawners

      1. Rock and gravel nesters

      2. Sand nesters

      3. Plant-material nesters

         a. Gluemakers

         b. Nongluemakers

      4. Froth nesters

      5. Hole nesters

      6. Miscellaneous-materials nesters

      7. Anemone nesters

III. Bearers

   A. External bearers

      1. Transfer brooders

      2. Auxiliary brooders

      3. Mouth brooders

      4. Gill-chamber brooders

      5. Pouch brooders

   B. Internal bearers

      1. Faculative internal bearers

      2. Obligate internal bearers

      3. Livebearers

Source: After Balon 1975a, 1984.

Benthic spawners are typically freshwater species without elaborate courtship rituals. Very often when spawning is observed, there is one female closely followed by several males who fertilize the eggs as the female releases them. The eggs and embryos are either adhesive and stick to whatever surface on which they are laid, or are laid in long strings that are wrapped around objects, or drop into interstices and cracks where they take on water, swelling enough to wedge themselves in place. The free embryos and larvae of these fishes may be either pelagic or benthic. Those that are pelagic (such as those of sturgeons [Acipenseridae] or smelt [Osmeridae]) become active or buoyant immediately after "hatching," whereas those that are benthic stay close to the spawning area until they can swim freely. In lakes or shallow ocean waters, plants are often important substrates for the adhesive embryos of benthic spawners. Some fishes always spawn on such plants. For example, common carp and pikes (Esocidae) generally spawn only on vegetation that is flooded by high water in the spring. If such material is not available, spawning usually does not take place or is much less successful. Once the embryos hatch, the young remain among the plants; some of them have adhesive organs on their heads with which they can stick to the stems of the plants.

Brood hiders are fish that hide their eggs in one way or another but do not show any parental care beyond spawning. A majority of these species are benthic spawners that build nests in which the eggs are buried. The females of salmon and trout, for example, excavate nests (redds) by digging with their tails. The redds are defended by both sexes from other members of the same species. The most vigorous defenders, however, are the brightly colored males. Once the eggs are laid, fertilized, and buried (by the female), the nest site is abandoned. Many North American minnows (Cyprinidae) build nests as well, although a number of species build piles of stones rather than depressions. The males of these species also defend the nest sites and have well-developed tubercles on the head and body to assist them in doing this.

Guarders go a step further than the brood hiders in their reproductive behavior, because they guard the embryos until they hatch and frequently tend the larval stages as well. Because tending the embryos usually means being tied to a specific location, territoriality (often implying competition for egg-laying sites) and elaborate courtship behavior are the usual state of affairs among the fishes of this group. Except among the cichlids, the embryos are almost always guarded by males, who not only protect them against predators (including other members of the same species) but typically keep oxygen levels high around the embryos by fanning currents of water across them, and keep the embryo mass free of dead embryos and debris. The amount of time spent guarding can range from a few days to over four months (Antarctic plunderfish [*Harpagifer bispinis*]). Guarding species can be broken into two groups, those that do not build nests (substratum choosers) and those that do. The differences between substratum choosers that merely clean off a suitable area of bottom, and fish that build slightly more elaborate structures, however, are often slight.

Nest spawners construct some sort of structure, cavity, or pit in which the eggs are laid and fertilized and the embryos defended. The young are often defended in the nest as well, and in some species the parents even herd schools of young around for a period of time. Pit nests can be made of a wide variety of material, but most common are nests of gravel and rock. Such nests are typically shallow depressions that are carefully constructed and tended by territorial males. Most sunfishes and black basses (Centrarchidae) construct nests of this sort, often in colonies. The males defend the embryos and young until the young become too active to be kept in the nest. In some cichlids, eggs are laid and incubated in one nest depression but the young are tended (by both parents) in one or more additional depressions constructed nearby. A few species construct nests in sandy bottoms. Either the eggs and embryos in such nests have special adaptations, such as semibuoyancy, to reduce the possibility of being smothered, or the parent fish must spend considerable time handling them. In areas where bottoms are muddy, nest-building fish commonly build nests of plant material. Usually plant-nesting fishes construct loose aggregations of material in which the eggs are laid. One special type of plant-nest builder uses a kidney secretion to glue the pieces of plant together to form a tight nest. The main examples of this type of nesting are the sticklebacks (Gasterosteidae), in which the male builds a tube, usually attached to rooted plants or placed in a small pit. By means of a complicated courtship ritual a female is enticed into a nest, where she deposits some eggs after being nudged by the male. After the eggs are laid, he chases the female out and fertilizes them. This process is repeated several times until there are enough embryos in the nest, at which time the male begins to incubate them by fanning currents of water across them. After the embryos hatch, the male guards the young for several days, first in the nest and then in a school outside the nest.

Perhaps the most common type of nest among fish are those in caves, cavities, or burrows. Such nests are characteristic of fish that live in active habitats such as the rocky intertidal zone or streams. For stream-dwelling fishes, the typical cave nest is the underside of a flat rock in midstream, where there is plenty of current to keep the water well oxygenated. Sculpins (Cottidae) and many darters (Percidae) deposit their eggs in clusters on the roofs of such shelters and guard the embryos until they hatch. In quieter water, minnows such as the fathead minnow *(Pimephales promelas)* lay their eggs on the underside of a log or board, in an area that has been cleaned off by the male. Spawning males develop a thick, horny pad on their heads which is used for rubbing algae and other material off the spawning surface. Many large catfishes (Ictaluridae) lay their eggs in cavities ranging from hollow logs, to old muskrat burrows, to oil drums, where the embryos are guarded by the males. These catfish also guard schools of the young for one or more weeks after they emerge from the nest.

Bearers are fish that carry their embryos (and sometimes their young as well) around with them, either externally or internally. Fishes that carry their embryos externally have developed a wide variety of ways of doing so, ranging from short-term attachment of embryos to the fish until a suitable place to put them is found (transfer brooders) to the carrying of embryos and young in special pouches. Good examples of various kinds of bearers can be found among pipefishes and seahorses (Syngnathidae). In this family, only the males do the brooding. After the eggs are fertilized, the female places the embryos on the male. Herald (1959) points out that there is a continuum of forms in the Syngnathidae starting with skin-brooding pipefishes, progressing through pipefishes with open brood pouches on their bellies, and ending with seahorses, which have closed pouches with only one opening. In seahorses, after an extended courtship period, the female deposits eggs in the pouch (marsupium) of the male, by means of a penislike oviduct. The eggs are fertilized as they enter the marsupium, and 25 to 150 embryos may be incubated. After hatching, the free embryos are carried in the pouch until they are capable of fairly active swimming, at which time they are expelled by the brooding male.

Another way of carrying externally spawned young internally is found in mouth brooders. This method is found in families as diverse as the sea catfishes (Ariidae), cichlids (Cichlidae), cardinal fishes (Apogonidae), and bonytongues (Osteoglossidae). Mouth brooders carry the large, yolky embryos about until they hatch, and typically carry the free embryos about as well. Even after the young become active, they usually are closely associated with the parent fish for a period of time and may flee back into the mouth cavity when threatened. In cichlids—although both sexes may participate in some species—it is usually the female that carries the embryos, which she picks up quickly after spawning.

Internal bearers have many similarities to pouch brooders, although fertilization is internal and females always carry the embryos and/or young. Internal bearers typically produce only a small number of large, active young, a strategy characteristic of all sharks and rays (See Chapter 15) and a few bony fish families. There seems to be no strong correlation between internal bearing and the elaborateness of courtship behavior. In guppies and other live-bearing poeciliids, courtship behavior is barely noticeable, and the most important trait of males that successfully copulate with females seems to be persistence (although in fact there are subtle interactions among competing males and other courtship-related behaviors). In contrast, some surfperches (Embiotocidae) have fairly elaborate courtship behavior, with males establishing breeding territories to attract passing females.

The first step in the evolution of live-bearing fishes can be seen in *facultative internal bearers.* These consist of a few species of *oviparous* (egg-laying) killifishes in which eggs retained by the female are accidentally fertilized during the normal process of spawning on the substrate. They usually have only a short period of embryonic development before being laid. The next step in the evolutionary process is found in *obligate internal bearers,* in which all the embryos are retained by the female although the only source of nutrition for the embryos is the egg yolk, as in externally spawned eggs. This situation is also referred to as *ovoviviparity* and is characteristic of marine rockfishes (Scorpaenidae) and the Lake Baikal sculpins (Comephoridae). This strategy allows these fish to have fecundities approaching those of pelagic fish with external fertilization, but also enables them to protect their young during their most vulnerable stage of development. In contrast, sharks and rays with this strategy produce a relatively small number of embryos, and they are retained for a few weeks to 16 or more months. The shorter time spans are characteristic of species that eventually deposit their embryos in the environment, surrounded by a horny capsule; while the longer periods are characteristic of sharks that retain the embryos until they are ready to emerge as actively swimming young (Wourms 1981).

Given the advantages of retaining the embryos internally, it is not surprising to find that a number of fishes have developed means to provide additional nutrition for their young while the female is carrying them and then give birth to large, active young *(viviparity).* Viviparous fishes provide nutrition for their young by a variety of means. The biggest variety is found in the sharks (see Chapter 15), but the teleosts also show a considerable variety of methods. In the surfperches the young develop in the ovary of the mother and obtain nutrients through the close contact of the extra-large fins with the ovarian wall. Most poeciliid embryos have highly vascular pericardial tissue that loops around the neck and is in close contact with the ovarian wall of the mother. The number of young produced by each female is small, although in poeciliids several broods in different stages of development may be carried at once, so production of young may be nearly continuous when conditions are favorable.

DEVELOPMENTAL ADAPTATIONS

It should be obvious from the previous section that the adaptations of the eggs, embryos, larvae, and juveniles of a fish species reflect the reproductive behavior and ecology of the parent (Blaxter 1974; Russell 1976; Braum 1978; Balon 1981). In describing these adaptations, it is useful to divide the life history of a fish into five major developmental periods: embryonic, larval, juvenile, adult, and senescent periods (Balon 1975b). For convenience these periods can be further divided into more or less arbitrary developmental phases. This classification scheme was developed both to provide some consistent terminology for the enormously confusing literature on fish development and to support the saltational theory of development (Balon 1979, 1980). According to this theory, development proceeds gradually through each period until a point is reached when a rather abrupt change in habits is possible, such as the change from an embryo which cannot capture food to a larva which can. The change is accompanied by further, rather rapid changes in morphology and physiology. Once a new developmental threshold is reached through this process, development proceeds gradually again. The contrasting theory of development is that the process is continuous and gradual, so that all designated periods or phases are arbitrary.

Embryonic period. The embryonic period is the period in which the developing individual is entirely dependent on nutrition provided by the mother, either by means of yolk from the egg, by a direct placentalike connection (in viviparous fishes), or by some compromise between the two methods. The period begins at fertilization. The period can be usefully divided into three phases: cleavage egg, embryo, and free embryo. The *cleavage phase* is the interval between the first cell division and the appearance of recognizable predecessors of the organ systems, but especially the neural plate. The *embryonic phase* is the interval in which the embryo becomes recognizable as a vertebrate because the major organ systems begin to appear. It ends at hatching. Although hatching is a major, recognizable event in the life of a fish (at least from our perspective), the exact state of development an embryo may be in at hatching not only varies among species but may vary within a species, depending on environmental conditions. In any case, once the embryo is free of the egg membranes, the *free embryo phase* begins. During this phase, the embryo ceases to be curled up, becomes increasingly fishlike, continues to rely on its yolk or mother for nutrition, and usually remains in the same environment it was in for the previous two stages. This phase may range from very lengthy (e.g., in salmon embryos in the spawning beds) to nonexistent (in cyprinodont fishes with rapid life cycles).

Larval period. The beginning of the larval period is signified by the appearance of the ability to capture food organisms. During this period special larval structures may develop, often related to respiration. The period ends when the axial skeleton is formed and the embryonic median fin-fold is gone (Fig. 9.2). In marine fishes the period is often lengthy, lasting from one to two weeks (sardines, rockfishes) to many months (anguillid eels). For those fishes with pelagic larvae (and

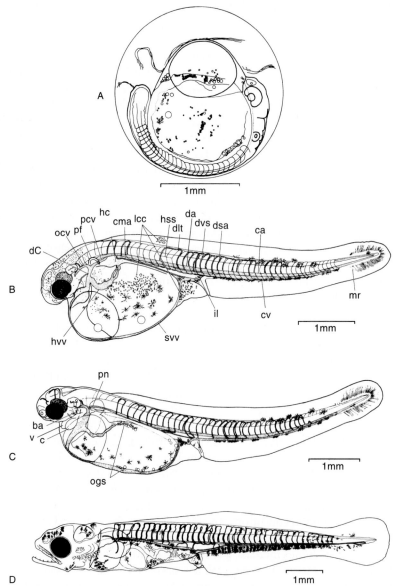

FIGURE 9.2 *Some stages in the development of the walleye* (Stizostedion vitreum). *(A) Embryo at age 3 days, 50 minutes. (B) Embryo at 6 days, 18 hours, which has been removed from the egg membrane to show structures* (acv *anterior cardinal vein,* ca *caudal artery,* cv *caudal vein,* da *dorsal aorta,* dC *duct of Cuvier,* dlt *dorsal longitudinal trunk of the segmental muscles,* dsv *dorsal segmental vein,* dsa *dorsal segmental artery,* hc *hepatic capillaries,* hss *horizontal skeletogenous septum,* hvv *hepatic vitelline vein,* il *intestinal loop of caudal vein,* lcc *large clear cells,* mr *mesenchyme rays,* pcv *posterior cardinal vein,* pf *pectoral fin bud,* svv *subintestinal vitelline vein). (C) Embryo at 8 days, 1 hour, immediately after hatching. (D) Larva at 17J days. (From McElman and Balon 1979.)*

free embryos), it is often the major period of dispersal as well as the period of highest mortality, because of the vulnerability of the larvae to predation and starvation (see Chapter 34). In freshwater fishes pelagic larvae are present mainly in lake- or river-dwelling forms, such as sunfishes (Centrarchidae), pike-perches (Percidae), and whitefishes (Salmonidae), but are absent from most stream-dwelling forms. Such forms typically have benthic larvae (Cottidae, many Cyprinidae) that exist only for short periods and often live in heavy cover, such as flooded beds of vegetation. In live-bearing fishes, the larval period may be absent or very short (and internal). In salmon and trout, the alevins that emerge from the gravel and begin feeding seem to be vestigial larvae because while they possess many larval characteristics, they are more like true juvenile fishes in their overall appearance and behavior (Balon 1980).

Juvenile period. Although the change from larva to juvenile may involve a dramatic metamorphosis, as in the transformation of the leptocephalus larva of an eel to an elver, usually the change is more subtle. The period begins when the organ systems are fully formed or nearly so. Juveniles are recognizable by the presence of fully formed fins as well; in appearance they are miniature adults, although they often possess distinctive color patterns that reflect the distinct habitats they typically occupy. The juvenile period lasts until the gonads become mature and is usually the period of most rapid growth in the life of a fish.

Adult period. Once the gonads are mature, a fish is an adult. The onset of the period is reflected in spawning behavior and often in the development of reproductive structures and color patterns.

Senescent period. Few fish reach this period of "old age," when growth has virtually stopped and the gonads are degenerate and usually not producing gametes. While the period may last for years in sturgeon, it lasts for only a few days in Pacific salmon. In male Siamese fighting fish *(Betta splendens)*, the period may last over a year, over one-third of the lifespan (von Saal and Finch 1988).

PHYSIOLOGICAL ADAPTATIONS

The complex behavioral adaptations that fishes have evolved to ensure reproductive success are obviously of little use if reproduction takes place at a time when environmental conditions are unfavorable for the survival of the young. Thus the reproductive cycles of fishes are closely tied to environmental changes, particularly seasonal changes in light and temperature. These two factors are often most important because they can act, directly or through sense organs, on glands that produce hormones, which in turn produce the appropriate physiological or behavioral responses. This can be demonstrated by examining the reproductive cycle of the longjaw mudsucker *(Gillichthys mirabilis)* in San Francisco Bay, California (De-Vlaming, 1972a,b,c).

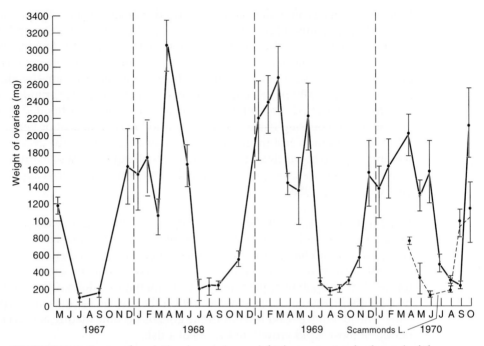

FIGURE 9.3 *Seasonal variation in ovarian weight (mean ± standard error) of the Alviso population (solid line) and Scammons Lagoon population (broken line) of long-jaw mudsucker. (From DeVlaming 1972a.)*

In the mudsucker the testes and ovaries develop between late September and mid-November, although ovarian development typically continues through early December (Fig. 9.3). Spawning occurs from December to June, with each individual spawning more than once. Gonads of both sexes regress abruptly in July and remain regressed through August and September. Laboratory studies show temperature to be the primary environmental factor regulating the reproductive cycle in the mudsucker, although photoperiods also play a role. For example, temperatures of less than 20°C are required for gonadal development under any experimental light regime. However, at low temperatures, short photoperiods (equivalent to those of late autumn) accelerate gonadal development. Temperatures higher than 22°C to 24°C inhibit spawning in mudsuckers regardless of photoperiod because they inhibit the transformation of spermatogonia to spermatocytes in males (spermatogenesis) and inhibit the formation of the vitelline membrane in females. The latter is the final stage in vitellogenesis, the process of providing high-energy stores of yolk for the developing oocytes. Following vitellogenesis, the oocytes are stored in the ovary for maturation and eventual release from the follicle (ovulation). After ovulation, the oocytes must be spawned within a short period of time, if they are to be viable. Thus both ovulation and the final stages of sperm maturation must be precisely timed for successful spawning. Both processes are stimulated not only by temperature and photoperiod but also by the presence of suitable substrates for spawning (muddy bottoms for burrows in the case of mudsuckers) and the presence of mates in a state of reproductive readiness. Indeed, one of the functions of courtship behavior is to stimulate ovulation and spermatogenesis (Stacey 1984). Males of some species actually produce pheromones to stimulate ovulation in females (Chen and Martinich 1975). There is evidence that the terminal nerve, which is situated alongside the olfactory nerve, mediates these responses to pheromones (Demski and Northcutt 1983).

The relative importance of the various external factors in stimulating reproduction varies considerably among species. In threespine sticklebacks (*Gasterosteus aculeatus*), increasing daylight is the single most important factor in gonad maturation, although appropriate temperatures and substrates are necessary for spawning. In contrast, for common carp, photoperiod is of minor importance compared to temperature regime (Davies et al. 1986). Water chemistry can also affect maturation; low pH created by acid rain, for example, can create severe problems in the gonadal maturation of rainbow trout (Weiner et al. 1986).

Internally, the gonadal maturation processes are regulated by the production of gonadotropic releasing hormone by the hypothalamus and gonadotropic hormones by the anterior portion of the pituitary gland (neurohypophysis) (Fig. 9.4). Thus removal of the neurohypophysis in mudsuckers inhibits the production of sperm cells in males and blocks vitellogenesis in females. These same processes can be stimulated, regardless of temperature, by the injection of gonadotropic hormones into the fish. This latter fact is now taken advantage of by fish culturists, who routinely inject various carps and catfishes with pituitary extracts to induce spawning on a prescribed schedule. Some species can be induced to spawn with pituitary extracts from other animals, even species of mammals.

When the gonadotropic hormones stimulate the gonads to develop, they also stimulate the gonads to produce gonadal steroid hormones, which stimulate reproductive behavior and the development of secondary (nongonadal) sexual characteristics. In males the production of nuptial colors, breeding tubercles, and other secondary sexual characteristics is stimulated by androgens produced in the testes (or cells adjacent to them). The steroid hormones regulate their own production through inhibition (negative feedback) of the hypothalamus and pituitary (Fig. 9.4).

ENERGETIC ADAPTATIONS

It should be obvious from the previous sections that fish invest a great deal of energy in reproduction, both in behavior and in the production of gonadal tissue. Indeed, life history strategies of fish can be viewed as finding ways to balance the amount of energy put into reproduction with that put into growth and metabolism (Williams 1966). Among fish species (and even within species) there is enormous variation in the amount of energy invested in the various aspects of reproduction, such as spawning migration, courtship behavior, parental care, and egg and sperm production. There are many factors contributing to this variation, and in this

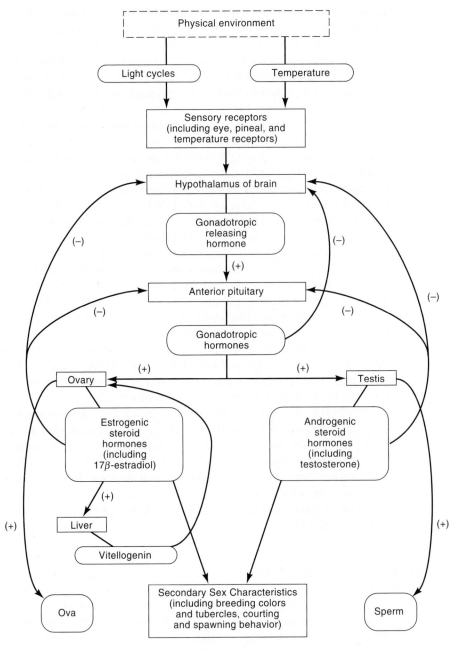

FIGURE 9.4 *Pathways for reproductive stimulation (+) and inhibition (-), consisting of substances or factors (circled) that regulate structures or behaviors (boxed) among various adult fishes. Inhibitory pathways shown here are often stimulatory in juveniles.*

section we will examine some of the more general factors: (1) reproductive effort, (2) age of onset of reproduction, (3) fecundity, (4) survivorship rates, and (5) frequency of reproduction. A key concept to understanding the importance of these five factors is *fitness,* which is a measure of how likely an individual is to have offspring that will also reproduce successfully.

Reproductive effort is a measure of the amount of energy (or time) invested in the production of offspring. The most easily measured index of this is the size of the gonads, compared with body size. Because ovaries are much larger than testes, it is generally assumed that females invest more energy in reproduction than males. Even in pelagic fishes, where males have to produce enormous amounts of sperm to assure fertilization of the eggs, the ovaries are several times larger than the testes. A consequence of this disproportionate investment is, in theory, that females are much more careful about mate choice than are males, to avoid waste of their reproductive effort on less fit males. This idea goes back at least to Charles Darwin. The differences in energetic investment may be less than is usually thought, however. In the lemon tetra *(Hyphessobrycon pulchripinnis),* for example, the amount of sperm extruded by males decreases with each successive spawning act, and females therefore discriminate against recently spawned males in their selection of mates. This greatly limits the number of matings possible for males and indicates that they too have to be fairly discriminating in their choice of mates (Nakatsuru and Kramer 1982).

Differences in gonadal investment between sexes is also partially evened out by the greater investment on the part of males in reproductive structures (breeding tubercles, etc.), and in reproductive behavior such as courtship and territoriality. The investment of energy in reproductive behavior, coloration, and structures can be interpreted as a way in which both males and females are assured that their reproductive effort is not wasted by matings with less fit individuals of the same species or with members of closely related species. In addition, in many species many males are excluded from mating. Mortality of males is also often higher than that of females because of their conspicuousness, as the result of color patterns or behavior, during the spawning season.

The territorial behavior of many fishes, such as the sunfishes (Centrarchidae) and the sticklebacks (Gasterosteidae), combined with external fertilization of the eggs, predisposes the males for parental care as a way of further protecting their investment in the zygotes. The fact that parental care in fishes is generally performed by the males (including those of nonterritorial species such as pipefishes and seahorses) indicates that this is another way of equalizing the energetic investments of the sexes in reproduction. Parental care in such fishes is apparently more "cost effective" than merely increasing the output of the gonads (Blumer 1979; Gross and Sargeant 1985)!

The age of onset of reproduction is another factor that varies with sex, because males typically mature at smaller sizes and younger ages than females. For both sexes, however, the age at first reproduction depends in good part on the nature of the environment in which the population of concern lives as well as the nature of the population itself. Where the environment is favorable for growth and favors high adult survival, fishes will tend to delay reproduction; but if conditions are unfavorable, so that growth and adult survival are low, reproduction tends to take place at a younger age. For example, in Europe there are two distinct forms of the brown trout *(Salmo trutta)* whose life history tactics reflect the environments in which they live (Alm 1949). The lake-dwelling form inhabits a fairly predictable and productive environment and so grows to a large size and spawns first when five to seven years old. The stream-dwelling form, in contrast, lives in a much less predictable and productive environment and so grows more slowly and matures in three to five years. On an energetic basis, it appears that in a more predictable environment natural selection favors females that delay reproduction in order to invest their energy in producing large numbers of large eggs, because egg size and number tend to increase with size of the female; while in a less predictable environment natural selection favors females that reproduce as quickly as possible, since the probability of survival from one year to the next is low. A similar pattern has been found for the number of young produced in different environments by live-bearing fish (Baltz and Moyle 1982).

The nature of the population to which a female belongs also influences the age of reproduction. Females that belong to an expanding population tend to reproduce at an earlier age than those in more stable populations. Part of the reason for this is that expanding populations tend to be in favorable environments, so that a larger size can be achieved at a younger age. Natural selection may also favor, in this situation, females that can fill the "empty" space most quickly with the most young, especially if juvenile mortality is exceptionally low. A well-managed commercial fishery can take advantage of this by keeping a fish population in a perpetually expanding state, since a typical fishery removes both a large number of fish and the larger individuals. Thus the fishery can, in theory, reduce intraspecific competition, increase growth rates, and favor females that reproduce at a young age and small size.

Fecundity is the most common measure of reproductive potential in fishes because it is a relatively easy measurement to make; it is the number of eggs in the ovaries of a female fish. In general, fecundity increases with the size of the female, with the relationship

$$F = aL^b$$

where F = fecundity, L = fish length, and a and b are constants derived from the data (Bagenal 1978). With this relationship, larger fishes produce considerably more eggs than do smaller fishes, both absolutely and relative to body size (number of eggs per gram of body weight). This means that the energetic investment in reproduction tends to be higher in the larger members of a species (i.e., they have larger ovaries in relation to body wieght). Smaller females tend to invest more in growth (particularly in the first year or so of life). In contrast, in males the size of testes tends to increase in a linear fashion throughout life. Sargent and Gross (1986) argue that this is a major reason that males are usually the sex that provides parental care in fishes; males have more energy to invest in parental care in comparison to females who are putting most of their energy into production of eggs.

While the exponential relationship between fecundity and size in females seems to hold true for many species (but especially for species that produce large numbers of eggs and spawn just once each year), there are many factors that complicate the interpretation of fecundity data, especially in relation to the investment of energy. Some of these complications are the relationship between fecundity and (1) fertility, (2) the frequency of spawning, (3) parental care, (4) egg size, (5) population density, and (6) environmental factors (Bagenal 1978).

Fertility contrasts with fecundity in that it is the actual number of young produced rather than the number of eggs. Since in terms of measuring reproductive success, the number of young produced is what really counts, fertility should be a better measure than fecundity. Unfortunately it is extremely hard to measure, because young fish typically disperse immediately after hatching. For many species, however, fecundity is probably a fairly close approximation of fertility. This is especially true in viviparous fish. In many other species the relationship between fecundity and fertility is not clear, because many eggs may be laid but not fertilized, or eggs may be developed in the ovary but then resorbed. In fishes that spawn repeatedly over long periods of time (called *fractional spawners*), there may be eggs in the ovary in several stages of development, and it is very difficult to determine the contribution of the immature eggs to the season's spawning. In fishes with *parental care*, the relationship between fecundity and fertility is obscured by the limitations placed on the parents by the number of young for which they can effectively care. Thus in mouthbrooding cichlids, the fecundity is often considerably higher than the number of embryos capable of being brooded (Welcomme 1967).

Parental care is just one of a number of factors that seems to be related to *egg size*. Most important of these factors is size of the female, because egg size often (but not always) increases with the size of the parent. The advantage of larger eggs seems to lie in the greater ability of larger young to survive. As Svardson (1949) pointed out, each population of fish seems to achieve a balance between egg size and number that produces the greatest number of young. Rounsefell (1957) found that within the Salmonidae, river spawners produce larger eggs than lake spawners and that, in anadromous forms, species with the longest freshwater stages produce the largest eggs, demonstrating fine evolutionary "tuning" to environmental factors.

Although the evolutionary adjustment of fecundity to *environmental conditions* (such as food supply) is important, equally important is the ability of fishes to adjust egg production on an annual basis in relation to environmental variation. Usually, this adjustment seems to be related to food supply. When food is plentiful, there is plenty of energy available for investment in reproduction, beyond what is required for maintenance and growth. As a result, well-fed fishes produce more and frequently larger eggs. Wooten (1973) found that threespine sticklebacks (*Gasterosteus aculeatus*) were exceptionally fecund in food-rich environments. A female in such situations could produce two to three times her weight in eggs over a season, despite the limitations placed on egg production by the abilities of the males to care for the eggs and young. High availability of food leading to high fecundities is often related to the lack of intense intraspecific competition. Thus when population levels are low, reproductive success is likely to increase; whereas when they are high it is likely to decrease, providing an effective feedback mechanism for density-dependent population regulation (see Chapter 34 for an example of this). This mechanism also allows fishes to adjust their populations to other unfavorable conditions that reduce the availability of food, such as unfavorable water temperatures and oxygen levels.

Survivorship rates are inversely related to fecundity; fishes with high fecundities have very high death rates, especially through the free embryo and larval stages. Indeed, much research on commercially important fishes with pelagic larvae has focused on factors affecting larval survival, because it has been recognized that a very small increase or decrease in the survival rate of the larvae can have enormous impact on the adult fish population. In these fishes any individual larva has a very low probability of survival. At the opposite extreme, viviparous fishes, such as the poeciliids, surfperches, and many sharks, produce a small number of young that have a fairly high probability of surviving to adulthood. Curiously, if all appropriate measurements could be made, it is likely that the amount of parental investment per successful offspring is about equal in the two groups or at least shows equal variability.

What are the advantages of these two divergent reproductive strategies if the energetic investment is about the same? Williams (1975) argues that highly fecund fishes are capable of making rapid genetic adjustments to environmental change because even with such high mortality rates, larval deaths are not entirely random, so the survivors are likely to have high fitness in the particular set of local or short-term environmental conditions that exist. In addition, highly fecund fishes are capable of rapidly adjusting their populations to environmental changes. For example, under favorable conditions that increase larval survival rates, even a small number of adults can produce a large number of successful offspring. Alternatively, under unfavorable conditions, only a small number of fish will survive the larval stages regardless of the number of spawning adults. Essentially in such fishes, the number of young surviving to adulthood is independent of the number of parents. This strategy is likely to be characteristic of fishes that live in environments where food availability fluctuates in an unpredictable fashion from year to year, and in which competition is usually not a major problem.

In contrast, the populations of large, low fecundity fishes are not as capable of responding genetically to short-term environmental fluctuations as high fecundity fishes, but their young have much greater capabilities as individuals of adjusting to the fluctuations or of avoiding unfavorable conditions. Because of their large size, the young of these fishes are also much more capable of avoiding predators and potential competitors. However, the high frequency of small pelagic eggs among teleost fishes argues that this has been a major factor contributing to their success.

The **frequency of reproduction** is another characteristic of fish life history strategies that appears to reflect the predictability of the environment in which the fishes live. The two basic strategies here are semelparity and iteroparity. *Semelparity* is "big bang" reproduction, where the adults spawn and die (as among Pacific salmon), while *iteroparity* is repeated reproduction (characteristic of most fishes). The reason for the commonness of iteroparity lies in the fact that most environments are unpredictable enough so that there is no guarantee that young in any particular spawn will survive to adulthood. If conditions are favorable, a semelparous fish may have very high reproductive success; but if they are unfavorable, it may lose out completely. Thus most fishes increase their fitness by adopting a "bet-hedging" strategy of not putting all their energy into one spawn (Murphy 1968).

A study that demonstrates very nicely the advantages of iteroparity and semelparity is that of Leggett and Carscadden (1978) on American shad *(Alosa sapidissima)*. They examined the reproductive strategies of this anadromous species in rivers of the Atlantic coast of North America, from Florida to New Brunswick, and found that the degree of iteroparity increased with the latitude of the river. Florida populations are entirely semelparous, while those in New Brunswick are 55% to 77% iteroparous, with intermediate populations having intermediate values for the frequency of repeat spawners. The fecundity of the northern populations is lower than that of the southern populations, indicating that they devote less of their energy to reproduction than the southern shad and so will have more in reserve for postspawning survival. The northern shad even swim at slower speeds during migration as an energy-conserving measure (Glebe and Leggett 1981). The differences in strategy seem to be the result of differences in environment; the northern rivers are a harsher and more variable environment for the eggs and larvae, while the southern rivers are more benign.

ALTERNATIVE REPRODUCTIVE STRATEGIES

This chapter so far has largely discussed fish reproduction as if all species had two well-defined sexes and 1:1 sex ratios. In fact, this is not the case. Some alternatives include: (1) alternate male strategies, (2) hermaphroditism, (3) parthenogenesis, and (4) hybridogenesis.

Alternative male strategies are likely to develop in species in which large aggressive males can dominate spawning, creating opportunities for small males to engage in cuckoldry. In salmon and trout, for example, *jack* males are common. These are small silvery males that migrate upstream along with the standard large hook-nosed males and spawn by sneaking into redds to release sperm simultaneously with a mated pair. This behavior is an *evolutionary stable strategy* for reproduction because it is favored by natural selection just like the "standard" strategy of large males (Gross 1984). Such alternative methods have also been recognized in many other species including parrotfishes (Scaridae) and wrasses (Labridae) on tropical reefs, and bluegill sunfish *(Lepomis macrochirus)* in fresh water. In bluegill there are two alternatives to being a large male who defends a nest in a colony of similar males and lures passing females into the nest (Gross 1982). One alternative method is *sneaking*, as described for salmon, where a small male hides near an active nest and dashes in to release sperm when the resident male is spawning with a female. Another method is for a small male (called a *satellite male*) to hover above a nest containing a pair of courting sunfish and to slowly descend into it, reaching the pair in time for spawning. The satellite males manage to do this because they mimic females in coloration and behavior. Both sneaker and satellite males are usually badly chewed up by irate parental males by the end of the spawning season, but their strategy is nevertheless a successful one (giving them high fitness) because they do not have to spend any energy on parental care and they can spawn at a much younger age than the parental males. Parental males may be six or seven years old before they are large enough to compete successfully for the best nest sites, while the sneakers and satellites may be only two or three years old.

Hermaphroditism, where one individual can be either male or female, is known from at least 14 families of teleost fishes (Shapiro 1984). Hermaphrodites can be either *synchronous,* where individuals possess both ovarian and testicular tissue, or *sequential,* where individuals change sex. Synchronous hermaphrodites are uncommon. In black hamlets (*Hypoplecturus nigricans,* Serranidae) individuals take turns releasing sperm and eggs during spawning. Because such egg trading is advantageous to both individuals, hamlets are typically monogamous for short periods of time, a situation unusual in fishes (Fischer and Peterson 1987). In sequential hermaphrodites, the most common pattern is for a female to change into a male (protogyny). This often happens when a large dominant male controlling a harem of females is removed by a predator (or experimenter). Within a few days, the largest female in the harem becomes a dominant male and takes over the missing male's function (Shapiro 1984). This pattern is common in coral reef fishes, such as the parrotfishes (Scaridae), wrasses (Labridae), and groupers (Serranidae).

Parthenogenesis, a form of asexual reproduction, occurs in species where all individuals are female. The curious phenomenon of unisexuality is characteristic of a number of fishes but is best studied in a complex of Mexican mollies (Poeciliidae). The first of these all-female species to be discovered was the Amazon molly *(Poecilia "formosa")* (Hubbs and Hubbs 1932). Studies revealed that the Amazon molly and similar unisexual species were sexual parasites on other species of the same genera from which they originally were derived as hybrids (Schultz 1989). The sperm from males of the host species is required to activate the development of the eggs of the Amazon molly, but union of the male and female chromosomes does not occur, so only genetically uniform females are produced.

Hybridogenesis is another variation on the unisexuality theme and is best known from a group of Mexican mollies *(Poeciliopsis)* (Schultz 1989). In this case, the mating between the female and the host male results in fertilization of the egg, and a true hybrid is formed. However, during oogenesis in the hybrid females, the chromosomes contributed by the host male are lost in meiosis, so that only the female genes are passed on to the next generation. The result is a self-perpetuating strain of all female fish. To make matters even more complicated, some unisexual populations of *Poeciliopsis* exist that are actually trihybrids. The trihybrids apparently result when hybridogenetic females mate with males from a third species, resulting initially in fish that are hybrids between the original maternal species and the new species. However, in this new hybrid some chromosomal reassortment takes place, resulting in eggs containing at least some genetic material from the third species. The new hybrid females then mate with the males that produced the original hybridogenetic fish, resulting in female progeny with characteristics of all three of the original species.

One of the interesting questions posed by the unisexual "species" (= clones) is: Why are they so successful? There is little question that they are indeed successful; they are widespread and often more abundant than the parent species. This is attributed to a combination of factors such as (1) the heterosis (hybrid vigor) exhibited by the hybrids (e.g., larger size, higher survival rates); (2) the increased reproductive potential of an all-female population; and (3) the specialization of clones for taking advantage of particular aspects of the environment. However, these factors offer only a partial explanation, since the unisexual species have two other problems to overcome: the low genetic variability expected in the absence of genetic recombination and the continued dependence of the unisexual fishes on bisexual males for reproduction. The first problem is minimized by the fact that the unisexual populations have apparently arisen repeatedly, so that each "species" in fact represents many different clones, each with a different origin and different ecological requirements. When individuals from two clones coexist, they may segregate ecologically from one another (reflected in dentition and feeding behavior) as well as from the parent bisexual species (Balsano et al. 1989). The continued dependence of the unisexual fish on the bisexual males is a problem because unisexual fish cannot afford to be so successful in their competitive interactions with bisexual fish that they eliminate them. In addition, there could be strong selection pressures on the host species to develop mechanisms for not wasting reproductive effort on the parasitic unisexual fishes. However, although males of bisexual species do have a preference for the appropriate females, they do mate freely with receptive unisexual females. Sperm does not seem to be a limited resource for which females compete (Balsano et al. 1989).

SEX CHANGE IN FISH

As the discussion on hermaphroditic fish indicates, the sex of many species of fish is not necessarily fixed but is determined by the social and physical environment in which the fish lives. For example, anemone fishes (Pomacentridae) live in monogamous pairs in single anemones, protected from predators by the stings of the anemone. Female anemone fish are typically larger than the males because a male does not have to vigorously compete for mates once he has paired with a female. However, if the female dies, a juvenile anemone fish quickly moves in; such fish are always male. The resident male then turns into a female and reproductive advantages of the large female–small male combination continues (Fricke and Fricke 1977). An example of environmentally determined sex occurs in the Atlantic silverside *(Menidia menidia)*. Silverside larvae that develop at low temperatures are more likely to become females than larvae that develop at high temperatures (Conover and Kynard 1981). More disturbingly, there is growing evidence that pollutants may cause sex changes in fish by disrupting endocrine cycles. In this situation, sex changes in fish may serve as early warnings of potential effects of pollutants on humans (Bortone and Davis 1994).

Supplemental Readings

Bagenal 1978; Balon 1975a, b, 1979, 1980, 1984; Barlow 1984; Breder and Rosen 1966; Chan and Yeung 1983; Gross 1984; Gross and Sargeant 1985; Pitcher 1986; Potts and Wootton 1984; Stearns 1976; Wooton 1990.

CHAPTER **10**

Sensory Perception

Fish sense the world around them in a diversity of ways. While most fish have the "terrestrial" senses of sight, hearing, smell, and taste that we can comprehend from our own experience, they also possess sensory means for detecting stimuli such as water particle displacement and electrical currents, for which we have little empathy. Such modes take advantage of the physical and chemical properties of water and work in conjunction with the more "conventional" sensory modes. In this chapter, therefore, aspects of chemoreception (smell and taste), mechanoreception (hearing, orientation, and lateral-line detection of water disturbances), electroreception, and vision are covered.

CHEMORECEPTION

Odors and tastes are quite distinguishable to the great majority of terrestrial animals; olfactory organs, stimulated by airborne molecules, are more sensitive and chemical-specific than gustatory organs, which are generally stimulated by contact with dilute solutions. In fish, both types of organs have similar sensitivities to "contact" stimuli of chemicals dissolved in water, but are distinguished by the location of the sensory receptors as well as processing centers in the brain.

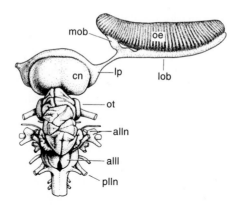

FIGURE 10.1 *Dorsal view of the brain of the bonnethead shark (*Sphyrna tiburo*):* alll *anterior lateral-line lobe,* alln *anterior lateral-line nerve,* cn *central nucleus,* lob *lateral division of the olfactory bulb,* lp *lateral pallium,* mob *medial division of the olfactory bulb,* oe *olfactory epithelium (organ),* ot *optic tectum,* plln *posterior lateral-line nerve,* II *optic nerve,* III *oculomotor nerve,* V *trigeminal nerve,* VII *facial nerve,* VIII *statoacoustic nerve,* IX *glossopharyngeal nerve,* X *vagal nerve. (From Northcutt 1978.)*

Olfaction

The olfactory receptors are usually located in olfactory pits, which have incurrent and excurrent channels (nares) divided by a flap of skin. Water is induced to flow through olfactory pits by movements of cilia within the pit, by the muscular movement of the branchial pump, by swimming, or by a combination of these. Odors are perceived when the dissolved chemical makes contact with the olfactory rosette, a multifolded epithelium rich in receptor cells, located in the olfactory pit (Fig. 10.1). Fish relying heavily on olfactory cues have elongated rosettes with many receptor cells located in elongate olfactory pits. In anguillid eels such elongate olfactory rosettes can detect certain chemicals such as ß-phenylethanol in concentrations of 1×10^{-13} *M* (Teichmann 1962)! Seasonal variations in sensitivity suggest that cyclical hormone action may influence the threshold level of detection.

At least two types of olfactory exceptor cells detect and encode chemical signals (Hara 1986). Olfactory stimuli are communicated via lateral or medial divisions of the olfactory bulb (Fig. 10.1) to the olfactory lobe of the brain via the first cranial nerve. Species that rely heavily on olfactory information, such as anguillid eels, moray eels, and sharks, display oversized olfactory bulbs and lobes. A few fish, such as some of the puffers (Tetraodontidae), have greatly reduced bulbs and lobes consistent with the evolutionary loss of the olfactory organs and pits. These puffers probably rely entirely on sight for feeding.

Olfactory cues have been shown to be important to some adult fish in locating spawning streams. For example, salmon apparently use olfaction in locating their natal stream, once they are in the vicinity of the river mouth (Hasler and Scholz 1983). Thus salmon are thought to be imprinted with odors as presmolts and smolts as they migrate down rivers and streams to a larger body of water where they spend the majority of their adult life (Chapter 19). The chemical nature of the attracting odors is not well known. Bodznik (1978) recorded sensory responses from the olfactory lobes of sockeye salmon (*Oncorhynchus nerka*) and found that the inorganic ion calcium could be used as an upstream odorant cue substance. Hara et al. (1984) demonstrated that salmon skin mucus (e.g., from juvenile fish of a previous spawn) contains species-specific amino acid combinations that stimulate olfactory neurons. Li et al. (1995) showed that adult sea lampreys (*Petromyzon marinus*) are olfactorily stimulated by two bile acids, allocholic acid and petromyzonol sulfate, released from conspecific larvae in the streambed.

Studies on nurse sharks (Orectolobidae) show a distinct gradient-searching activity (klinotaxis) for food detection. By detection of a stronger chemical concentration in the olfactory rosette on one side of its head, the shark turns in that direction. Thus tacking motions through the odorant field lead the shark to the odor source. Experimentally plugging the water channels on one side of its head will produce a continuous circling in the opposite direction. The extremely wide head of hammerhead sharks (Sphyrnidae) should be particularly useful in locating odor sources when only dilute concentrations are detectable because of the increased separation of the nares. Particular amines and amino acids attract teleosts as well as elasmobranchs. Sutterlin (1975) found glycine and alanine to be especially attractive to winter flounder (*Pseudopleuronectes americanus*), while alanine and methionine attracted Atlantic silversides (*Menidia menidia*) most effectively.

Taste

Taste or gustatory chemoreception is especially useful in the identification of both food and noxious substances. Whereas the olfactory receptors are localized in the nares, taste buds are commonly located on several exterior surfaces of the fish besides in the mouth. Bottom fishes, such as catfish, have considerable numbers of taste receptors on their skin, fins, and barbels. The high gustatory sensitivity of the barbels extends the usefulness of these chemoreceptors a reasonable distance from the fish, presumably to aid in finding food in murky water. A similar "distant touch" sense might be inferred from the presence of taste buds on the free pelvic fin rays of some codfish and threespot gourami (*Trichogaster trichopterus*). Other structures bearing recognizable taste buds include the well-developed lips of some minnows (Cyprinidae) and the suckers (Catostomidae). Suckers may have 41 to 57 taste buds in a 1.3-mm² field (Miller and Evans 1965). Taste buds have also been described on the palatal organs in the buccal cavities of various cyprinids, catostomids, cobitids, and salmonids as well as on the gill rakers and arches, primarily in freshwater fish (Kapoor et al. 1975).

Whereas the cutaneous taste buds are innervated by branches of the facial (cranial nerve VII) nerve (Fig. 10.1), the sensory signals from the internal taste buds (e.g., those in the pharyngeal cavity and palate) are transmitted to the glossopharyngeal (IX) and vagus (X) nerves. In species having a palatal organ, the total number of taste buds is considerably augmented, and the terminal centers in the visceral sensory column of the medulla are correspondingly enlarged as *vagal lobes* (Kapoor et al. 1975). Just as the olfactory lobes of the brain are grossly enlarged in fishes relying heavily on olfactory sensory information (e.g., Atlantic eels, sharks), the facial and/or vagal lobes of the medulla display a marked enlargement in species that find food by taste. For example, the vagal lobes are larger than the remainder of the brain in suckers, reflecting the large number of taste buds found on the palatal organs and their "mouth-tasting" behavior (Miller and Evans 1965). These correlations between brain morphology and feeding habits have prompted researchers to categorize teleostean taxa into one of (usually) three overlapping groups: (1) fish that feed by sight and taste and show prominent optic lobes, facial lobes, and relatively large vagal lobes; (2) those that detect food using barbels and have enlarged facial lobes with less prominent vagal lobes; and (3) sight-feeding species possessing well-developed optic lobes and poorly developed facial and vagal lobes (Khanna and Singh 1966).

The functional importance of taste receptors to catfish has been demonstrated by the fact that surgical removal or sectioning of optic and olfactory senses does not prevent catfish from swimming to a food source in still water. When taste reception is surgically blocked on one side of the catfish, it continually circles toward the side of intact reception until, eventually, the food is found. Thus the bilateral taste receptors in catfish function much as the sensitive olfactory system does in some other fish to indicate the directionality of a food source. Further, surgical removal of the facial lobes of the medulla prevents catfish from locating and ingesting food. In contrast, removal of the vagal lobes does not inhibit the fish's finding of food or taking it into its mouth but prevents swallowing, which is controlled via the glossopharyngeal and vagus nerves (Atema 1971). Interestingly, sharks and rays show no sensory elaboration (including enlarged medullary lobes) for taste functions (Kapoor et al. 1975). Elasmobranchs rely primarily on olfaction, vision, and electroreception to locate their food.

ACOUSTICO-LATERALIS SYSTEM

The acoustico-lateralis system of fish senses sounds, vibrations, and other displacements of water in their environment. It has two main components, the inner ear and the neuromast/lateral-line system. Besides sound detection, the fish inner ear functions to orient or "balance" the animal in three-dimensional space, giving it a feeling of the direction in which gravity is acting even when suspended in lightless, pelagic habitats. In this section, hearing will be considered first, followed by aspects of spatial equilibrium and balance and a discussion of the lateral-line system.

Hearing

The nature of sound transmission in water has had an important influence on the evolution of hearing in fish. Because of its greater density, water is a much more efficient conductor of sound pressure waves than is air. Therefore, sounds will carry much farther and travel 4.8 times as fast underwater. Sound consists of extremely small fluid motions (vibrations) which have a discernible *particle displacement* component close to the sound source ("near field") as well as a *sound pressure* component that persists through the more extensive "far field." The extent of the near field increases at lower sound frequencies. For example, at 100 Hz, the near field extends to approximately 2.3 m from the source of the sound (Popper and Fay 1977). Within the near field, vibrations are detected in comparatively direct fashion by both teleosts and elasmobranchs, via the inner ear and/or the lateral line.

Structure of the inner ear. Figure 10.2a and b shows diagrammatic representations of teleostean inner ears. The dorsal part (pars superior) includes three semicircular canals (through the horizontal, lateral, and longitudinal planes) with their respective ampullae (fluid inertia-sensing chambers). The utriculus with its utricular otolith (ear stone) completes the pars superior, which mainly functions as an equilibrium system and gravity detector. The ventral part (pars inferior) consists of the sacculus and lagena, which also contain otoliths, and functions primarily in sound detection. As sound vibrations (e.g., in the near field) impinge on a fish, the whole fish moves to and fro with the particle displacement of the water. The inertia of the comparatively dense otoliths (approximately three times the total fish density) in their chambers causes the otoliths to lag somewhat behind the movements of the fish. The otoliths are suspended in fluid and surrounded by ciliary bundles emanating from sensory hair cells. This layer of hair cells constitutes a sensory epithelium (macula) in each chamber. Thus the differential amplitude and phase motions of the otolith with respect to its chamber cause the otolith to bend some of these cilia mechanically. Bending the cilia causes the sensitive hair cellular membranes to deform, thereby stimulating neural transmissions to the auditory center of the brain, where they are processed and comprise the sense of "hearing."

At higher frequencies the amplitude of fish displacement decreases, and more sound energy is needed for otolithic stimulation. The sensitivity of hearing in the far field is increased by anatomical devices that can transform sound pressure into displacement movements so as to provide a movement differential between the sacculus/lagena and their respective otoliths. The gas bubble in the swimbladder provides this acoustical transformation in many bony fish. Because the gas is far more compressible than water, it pulsates when exposed to sound. The pulsating surface of the swimbladder acts to vibrate the tissues of the fish surrounding it. This provides the necessary particle movement for otolithic/auditory nervous stimulation, especially in species having a close association of the swimbladder and the auditory apparatus (pars

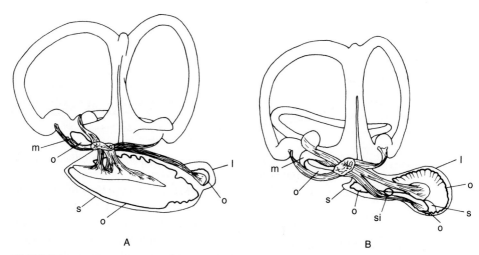

A   B

FIGURE 10.2 *Drawing of a medial view of the inner ear of (A) zander,* Stizostedion lucioperca, *and (B) ide,* Levcisus idus, *modified from drawings by Retzius. Only the auditory portions of the ear are labeled. The nerves shown in both figures are the auditory portions of the eighth nerve.* l Lagena, m *utriculus,* o *otolith of each otolithic organ,* s *sacculus,* si *transverse canal. (From Popper and Fay 1973.)*

inferior). Among three species of squirrelfish (Holocentridae), the species having the shortest distance between swimbladder and inner ear also has the most sensitive (lowest-intensity threshold) hearing. Certain squirrelfishes, along with the tarpon (Elopidae), featherbacks (Notopteridae), deepsea cods (Moridae), and sea breams (Sparidae), all have a forked, forward extension of the swimbladder ending close to the ear. Herrings (Clupeidae) and mormyrids feature a similar swimbladder extension which actually enters the cranial auditory capsule and lies close to the inner ear.

Minnows, catfish, and other otophysan teleosts connect the auditory system to the swimbladder with a chain of small bones called *Weberian ossicles*. The ossicles connect the pulsating swimbladder wall (tunica interna) with a Y-shaped lymph sinus (sinus impar), which abuts the lymph-filled transverse canal joining the sacculi of the right and left ears (Fig. 10.3). In studies on the goldfish, deflation of the swimbladder significantly decreased the hearing sensitivity at frequencies above 150 Hz. Swimbladder deflation of another otophysid *(Ictalurus)* revealed an even greater loss of high-frequency sensitivity, whereas the same procedure on the perciform *Tilapia*, which lacks Weberian ossicles and a close swimbladder-ear connection, had no significant effect on its already poor sense of hearing.

Sharks, skates, and rays also show evidence of hearing sounds or vibrations, especially at lower frequencies. Sharks seem especially attracted to *irregularly* pulsed sounds, perhaps signaling a crippled prey. However, they seem to have little sensitivity to high-frequency sounds. This low-frequency range correlates well with near-field displacement hearing and the fact that elasmobranchs have no swimbladders which may act as a sound pressure transducer. For example, the auditory sensitivity of the horn shark *(Heterodontus francisci)* is maximal at 40 Hz. Cartilagi-

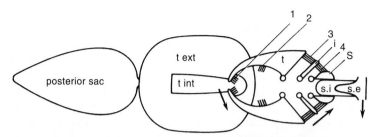

FIGURE 10.3 *Diagrammatic dorsal view of the swimbladder and Weberian apparatus of a typical member of the Cyprinidae. The anterior parts (right) are drawn to a larger scale than the posterior ones. Arrows indicate movements resulting from enlargement of the swimbladder. The axes about which the ossicles pivot are indicated by circles. t.ext. tunica externa, t.int. tunica interna seen through the slit in the tunica externa, 1,2,3,4 ligaments, t tripus, i intercalarium, s scaphium, s.i. sinus impar, s.e. sinus endolymphaticus. (From Alexander 1966.)*

nous fishes generally have endolymphatic ducts which connect the inner ear with the environment. Some of these species, which cannot produce calcareous otoliths, apparently use exogenous material for otoliths. Fänge (1982) found sand grains held together by a gelatinous material in the endolymph of two electric rays (Torpedinidae).

Many shark species also show an ability to directionally locate pulsed, low-frequency sounds from as far as 100 m, which is well into the far field (Popper and Fay 1977). It is possible that the taut skin over the parietal fossae of the shark's ears serves in "drumlike" fashion to induce fluid movements on the canal-based sensory organ, the macula neglecta. The functional similarities between this auditory system and the tympanic membrane and associated structures of higher vertebrates are striking (Myrberg 1978). Presumably, the differences in amplitude or time of the sounds received at the right and left ears give the shark a general direction to the source of the sound. Because of the vertically oriented axis of the macula neglecta in sharks, sound bounced off the surface of water bodies may also be useful in determining direction. In this case, the air-water interface would mimic the far-field sound transduction of the swimbladder wall in some teleosts. Thus it is possible that sharks (and other fish) may increase their auditory sensitivity and directionality by swimming just below the water surface (Popper and Fay 1977).

Equilibrium and Balance

The dorsal part (pars superior) of the inner ear is concerned with spatial equilibrium and balance in fish. The utriculus connects to three semicircular canals in teleosts and elasmobranchs (Fig. 10.2a,b). Lampreys have only two such canals, and hagfish make do with one. The three canals (also termed the *labyrinth*) in jawed fish are filled with lymph (endolymph), and function to inform the fish as to angular accelerations through space. Because the three canals are more or less aligned in the horizontal, vertical, and lateral planes, changes in pitch (head up or down), yaw (head from side to side), roll (rotation about the head-to-tail axis), straight-line acceleration or deceleration, or any combination of these are detectable. Each canal has an ampulla (bulbous area) containing a sensory hair cell area and a gelatinous cupula attached to the hair cell cilia. The cupula extends into the canal path, partially blocking the flow of endolymph. Angular accelerations, either from swimming/turning movements of the fish or from water currents moving the fish, are detected as the endolymph lags behind the movements of the labyrinth. The appropriate cupula(e) are bent by the pressure of the endolymph, thereby stimulating the hair cells. Thus the sensory hair cell system as a mechanoreceptor parallels that of the hearing and lateral-line systems. Changes in the pattern of the continuous trains of nervous impulses from the hair cells to the balance/equilibrium center in the medulla provoke the appropriate motor responses by the fish, such as eye movements to maintain a stable visual field and fin movements to restore body equilibrium. Even at rest in quiet water, some fishes, such as northern pike *(Esox lucius)*, constantly make pectoral fin movements to maintain balance. This species, among others, has denser tissues in the dorsal part of its body (bone, muscle) than in the ventral part (swimbladder, viscera). Thus its center of gravity (balance point) is dorsal to its roll axis (midline through body profile), and the fish always tends to roll to one side or the other to reach stability—ventral side up!

Lateral Line

The lateral line of fish provides a *ferntastsinn* or "distant touch" sense (Dijkgraaf 1962). By means of mechanoreceptors, similar to those in the auditory and equilibrium systems, water movements around the fish can be detected. The receptors are called *neuromasts,* and each consists of individual hair cells with an attached cupula (Fig. 10.4). Water movements bend the protruding cupula, which stimulates the hair cell by bending the attached cilia (sense hairs). All fish, including hagfish and lampreys, have at least some free (individual) neuromasts on the body surface or at the bottom of shallow pits or grooves (Dijkgraaf 1962). Most teleosts and elasmobranchs have also developed lateral-line canals, in which the neuromasts lie between canal pores that open to the environment (Fig. 10.5). The cupulae of the canal neuromasts are sensitive to movements of the watery endolymph fluid through the canal. Like the auditory and equilibrium hair cells, the neuromasts continually send neural impulses to the brain, even when undisturbed. As in the sensory cells of the auditory and equilibrium systems, the neural impulse frequency is increased as the cupulae are flexed in one direction and decreased when flexed in the other direction. Thus the pattern of impulses from the free or canal neuromasts imparts a direction to the disturbance. Most of the lateral-line organs of the head region are innervated by sensory fibers of the lateralis anterior root of cranial nerve VII (facialis). The remaining organs of the system are innervated by the lateralis posterior root of the vagus (X). The fibers of both roots unite with those of the labyrinth nerve (VIII) in the acoustic tubercle of the medulla oblongata.

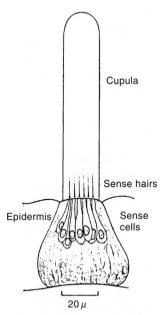

FIGURE 10.4 *Superficial neuromast of a bony fish* (Phoxinus). *Characteristic features are the bottle-shaped sense cells, each bearing a hair, and the jellylike cupula ensheathing the hairs. (From Dijkgraaf 1962.)*

The lateral-line system is developed and used in various ways by fish exhibiting different modes of life. For example, the roach *(Rutilus rutilus)* and the stone loach *(Noemacheilus barbartulus),* which inhabit streams, both have extensive canal neuromast systems. In contrast, another loach that lives in still water has no canals (Alexander 1967). In general, more active fish have a greater percentage of canal neuromasts compared with free neuromasts. Presumably, the canals offer some "protection" from the continuous stimulation of water rushing past the laterally lo-

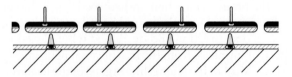

FIGURE 10.5 *Longitudinal lateral-line canal section. Black denotes epidermis; spacious striation denotes subepidermal tissues; dots denote cupulae. (From Dijkgraaf 1962.)*

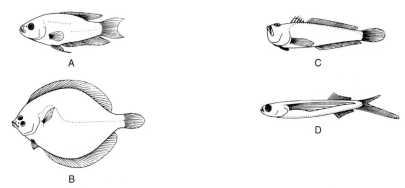

FIGURE 10.6 *Secondary displacement of lateral line on trunk in connection with dorsal shift of pectoral fin [(A) paradisefich,* Macropodus viridi-auratus; *(B) flounder,* Pseudorhombus *sp.]; or as an adaptation to special modes of living [(C) stargazer,* Uranoscopus scaber; *(D) flyingfish,* Exocoetus volitans]. *(From Dijkgraaf 1962.)*

cated neuromasts. Thus the canal-based receptors can still function to detect weak local water displacements during rapid swimming (Dijkgraaf 1962). Figure 10.6 shows a dorsal displacement of the lateral line in the region of the pectoral fins in two species where this fin may drive water against the canal during locomotion. In these cases a straighter lateral line would generate more "noise" from locomotion alone and provide less sensitivity to external water disturbances. Similarly, lateral-line placements on the dorsal side of the demersal stargazer (Fig. 10.6c) and the ventral side of the flying fish (Fig. 10.6d) show selection toward the direction where water movements would be critical for survival.

Parts of the lateral-line system are often specialized for detecting prey. The lateral line of the antarctic fish *Pagothenia borchgrevinki* seems tuned to the frequencies produced by the swimming motions of its planktonic prey (Montgomery and Macdonald 1987). Surface-oriented fish such as killifish *(Fundulus)* sense surface ripples from struggling insects by using the short canal neuromast system on the flattened dorsal surface of their head. Blind cavefish, such as *Typhlichthys osborni,* have rows of free neuromasts on the head which stand out in ridges, presumably to aid the cavefish in locating food so precisely that it can be ingested without sight (see Chapter 30). The deepsea gulper eel *(Eurypharynx)* features groups of neuromasts on the ends of stalks projecting from its body, which aid lightless detection of prey (Marshall 1966).

Neuromast function can also be useful to fish for stimuli other than localized water disturbances from distant objects. As fish swim they push some water in front of their heads, like a boat creates a bow wave. The amount of water pushed or displaced depends on the size of the fish and the shape of the head. The water displaced forward rebounds from objects in front of the swimming fish. The rebounds or increases in resistance in front of the fish are apparently sensed by the neuromasts on the head, allowing avoidance of the obstacle. Fish with very sensitive cephalic neuromast systems seem to be especially skilled in object avoidance. Hahn (1960) found that blind cavefish could navigate better through a barrier of thick, fixed rods than thin ones when placed equal distances apart. Presumably this system also accounts for the avoidance of transparent aquarium walls when naive fish are first introduced into an aquarium, even in total darkness. Experiments with adult saith *(Pollachius virens)* fitted with opaque eye covers showed that schooling behavior continued when these fish were placed among nonblinded individuals as long as their lateral line remained intact. Five blinded saith with their lateral lines cut at the operculum failed to school at all (Pitcher et al. 1976). In addition, near-field sounds are detected by lateral-line neuromasts at frequencies up to 200 Hz because of the accompanying water displacements. On the other hand, sensitivity to temperature change or physical touch stems from general cutaneous endings of spinal nerves, not from lateral-line receptors. Trained minnows *(Phoxinus)* could not distinguish between warm and cold jets of water from a pipette located posterior to the point where the spinal cord was sectioned, even though the water movements (of either temperature) were detected by the lateral-line neuromasts.

ELECTRORECEPTION

The primary function of the external pit organs of teleosts is the reception of minute electrical currents in the water. These pit organs open to the surrounding water via canals filled with an electrically conductive gel. Specializations for electroreception are widespread among fishes, *except* among teleosts, which are represented by relatively few groups (Bullock et al. 1983). The freshwater examples, including the gymnotids (Gymnotidae), the electric catfishes (Malapteruridae), and the African electricfishes (Mormyriformes), have very short canals (300 μm). In contrast, marine catfish *(Plotosus)* have longer canals resembling similar structures found in marine elasmobranchs, called *ampullae of Lorenzini*, which range from 5 mm to 160 mm in length. The longer ducts in the marine species compared with those living in fresh water are related to the electrical conductivity differences between the environments compared with those of the skin and body tissues. Specifically, the relatively low resistivity of the skin and the somewhat greater resistivity of the internal tissues compared with the seawater environment make the marine animal quite transparent to external voltage gradients. In contrast, freshwater fish have relatively good conducting tissues compared with their environment. However, their skin has high electrical resistance, causing large voltage drops compared with the other tissues. Thus freshwater fish electroreceptors need be only skin deep to sample a maximum change in potential. In both cases the gel-filled canals terminate at sensory cells in the more bulbous pit portion of the organ.

An array of electroreceptors (Fig. 10.7) capable of detecting weak electrical currents can be very helpful to a fish in perceiving aspects of its environment. For example, sensitivity to the electrical phenomena generated by the movement through the earth's magnetic force field, that resulting from the depolarization and repolarizations of a contracting muscle, or even the electrical transmissions from a conspecific individual may have adaptive value. Lissman (1963) described both electrical reception and transmission used by the mormyrid and gymnotid fishes to

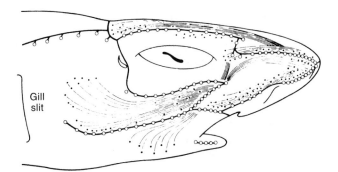

FIGURE 10.7 *Location of sense organs on the head of the spotted dogfish* (Scyliorhinus). *Openings of the ampullae of Lorenzini are shown by black dots. The open circles show the pores of the lateral-line system and the black lines show its location. (From Dijkgraaf and Kalmijn 1963.)*

probe their turbid African and South American stream environments (see Chapter 11). The rigid body posture of these electric fishes, with locomotion generated by undulation of the long anal (gymnotid) or dorsal (mormyrid) fins, may make the electrolocation process easier (Alexander 1967). Body undulations would continually change the distances and orientations among the electric organs and receptors, complicating the processing of the electroreception information.

Kalmijn (1971) demonstrated that predaceous marine elasmobranchs can locate prey by electroreception alone. For example, the spotted dogfish shark *(Scyliorhinus canicula)* can locate a flounder buried in sediment, even when concealed by an electrically conductive agar plate. The dogfish was not attracted to buried chopped fish or to live flounder covered by an electrically insulating sheet of polyethylene. Conclusively, the shark tenaciously dug out two electrodes emitting a biological-strength electrical current, which were buried in sediment. Nighttime field studies showed that smooth dogfish *(Mustelus canis)* also responded more strongly to short-term electrical rather than olfactory stimulation. As an applied use of this information, the U.S. Navy's antishark screen (a large polyvinyl bag suspended from an inflatable collar) provides good electrical as well as visual and olfactory insulation for a mariner with skin cuts in shark-infested waters (Kalmijn 1978a).

Any electrical conductor moving through a magnetic field induces an electrical field through the conductor. Thus a fish having dorsally and ventrally located electroreceptors and swimming across the earth's north-south magnetic field should be able to detect the induced electrical currents (Fig. 10.8). These induced currents are of sufficient strength for detection by sharks swimming as slowly as 2 cm/s, proving the feasibility of an electromagnetic compass sense (Kalmijn 1978b). When the eastbound shark depicted in Fig. 10.8 turns to the north or south, the potentials vanish. Turns toward the west induce potentials of the opposite polarity. The discovery of magnetite crystals in the ethmoid region of skulls suggests another avenue of research concerning geomagnetic orienteering in fishes. Walker

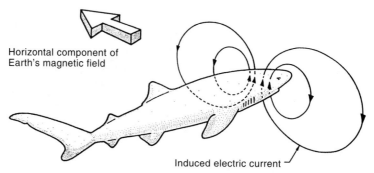

Horizontal component of
Earth's magnetic field

Induced electric current

FIGURE 10.8 *A shark swimming through the earth's magnetic field induces electric fields that provide the animal with the physical basis of an electromagnetic compass sense. (From Kalmijn 1974.)*

et al. (1984) found magnetite crystals in a dermethmoid bone sinus of the yellowfin tuna *(Thunnus albacares)*, a species known to behaviorally respond to earth-strength magnetic fields.

VISION/PHOTORECEPTION

The eye of a fish is the primary receptor site of light from its surroundings. It is worth noting as well that the pineal organ is also sensitive to light in some fish and appears to have importance in the control of circadian rhythmicity (Kavaliers 1979). The eyes of all vertebrates have many similarities. A notable feature of the typical teleost eye is the cornea of constant thickness (Fig. 10.9). This cornea imposes no optical alterations (convergence or divergence) on incoming light. Thus all the focusing of light occurs at the spherical lens, which has the highest effective refractive index (1.65) among the vertebrates (Marshall 1966). As in other vertebrate eyes, the lens consists of water and structural proteins. High concentrations of soluble protein in the lens confer the high refractive index.

The teleost eye lens protrudes through the pupilar opening in the iris, and the eye bulges from the body surface. Therefore, the field of view includes a considerable arc forward, continuing laterally to almost directly behind the fish. The alternating head movements of anguilliform or subcarangiform swimmers with coordinated eye movements (Harris 1965) tend to eliminate the blind spot to the rear. Light focused by the lens is projected in the appropriate pattern of light, shade, and (often) color on the retina, the light-sensitive cell layer in the eye. Because the spherical lens is eccentrically located in the elliptical eye of teleosts, the lens-retinal distance varies, determining relatively near-field (close-up) vision in front of the fish and comparatively far-field vision to the side. Presumably this "nearsightedness" to the front coupled with the binocular depth-perception capabilities allow fish to seize their prey accurately and avoid obstacles.

The elasmobranch lens, on the other hand, is slightly flattened on the optical axis. Most elasmobranchs have a unique ability to dilate and constrict the pupil of

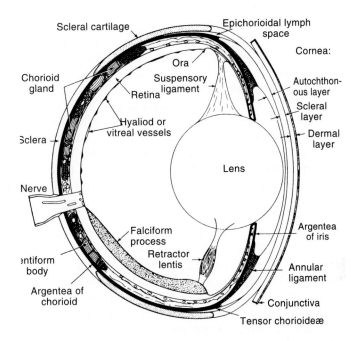

Scleral cartilage
Epichorioidal lymph space
Cornea:
Ora
Chorioid gland
Suspensory ligament
Retina
Autochthonous layer
Scleral layer
Hyaliod or vitreal vessels
Sclera
Dermal layer
Lens
Nerve
Falciform process
Argentea of iris
Retractor lentis
 entiform body
Annular ligament
Argentea of chorioid
Conjunctiva
Tensor chorioideæ

FIGURE 10.9 *Diagrammatic vertical section of a typical teleost eye. Not all structures shown are present in every teleost eye; for example, hyaloid vessels are not present in conjunction with a falciform process. (From Walls 1942.)*

the eye, comprising another mechanism to regulate incoming light levels, although some deepsea sharks have fixed pupils (Kuchnow 1971). The constricted, light-adapted pupil takes the shape of a pinhole in the blacktip shark *(Carcharhinus limatus)*, a vertical slit in the lemon shark *(Negaprion brevirostris)*, a horizontal slit in the bonnethead shark *(Sphyrna tiburo)*, and an oblique slit in the nurse shark *(Ginglystoma cirratum)*. Sawfish *(Pristis)* and skates *(Raja)*, among others, have an *operculum pupillare* or opaque projection that descends ventrally to shield part of the pupillary opening. In contrast, the nictitating membrane (semiopaque eyelid) present in some sharks probably functions more to protect the eye than to reduce incoming light levels (Gruber 1977).

Adjustments in focus for near or far vision (optical accommodation) are accomplished by movement of the lens without changing its shape by muscles within the eye. The specific muscles within the eye that are responsible for these movements differ in lampreys, elasmobranchs, and teleosts. For example, in teleosts the lens is pulled inward by a retractor muscle (Fig. 10.9), while in elasmobranchs it is pulled outward by a protractor muscle. The four-eye fish *(Anableps anableps)* displays an aspherical lens and two-part retina as structural adaptations associated with its life at the air-water interface. The lens thickness differences allow for the density differences of the two media.

The retina is made up of a dense packing of (often) both rod and cone cells for discrimination of light images. Incoming light must penetrate a clear layer of nerve cells and fibers to reach the photochemically active tips of the rods and cones (Fig. 10.9). The closer spacing of the rods and the connection of many rods to one neural fiber allows for reasonably fine image definition of "lightness and darkness," especially in dim light. The more widely spaced cone cells are each connected to an individual nerve fiber and provide vision of higher resolution as well as in color, but only in reasonably brightly lit surroundings (Marshall 1966). Gruber et al. (1975a) measured a rod:cone cell ratio of approximately 10:1 in the retinas of four species of requiem sharks (Carcharhinidae) and about 6:1 in three species of the more active mackerel sharks (Lamnidae). As light strikes the rods or cones, it is absorbed by the light-sensitive pigment (e.g., rhodopsin, porphyropsin) in the cell. Visual pigments are organic dyes consisting of an opsin protein complexed onto a short-chain prosthetic or chromophore molecule (e.g., retinal) related to vitamin A (Gruber and Cohen 1978). These pigments are located in the photoreception area of the retina, giving it its characteristic purple or pink coloration. For example, rhodopsin constitutes up to 35% of the dry weight of the rod outer segments. The pigments reversibly bleach out when exposed to light, and each has a characteristic absorption spectrum. The maximum absorption of the visual pigments of "typical" shallow-water dogfish sharks *(Squalus)*, skates, and rays (Myliobatidae) occurs at wavelengths around 500 nm, which is typical for rhodopsin (Gruber and Cohen 1978). Denton and Warren (1956) reported high densities of a golden-colored pigment ("chrysopsin") in the retinas of three teleosts living below 500 m depth. As one would predict from the spectral shift in light penetrating to deeper strata, the absorbance maximum of chrysopsin is shifted toward the blue (shorter-wavelength) end of the spectrum by about 20 nm. Parallel evolution of "deepwater" visual pigments is found among three elasmobranch species (caught at 1150 m) containing pigments that absorb maximally from 472 nm to 484 nm (Denton and Shaw 1963). Most temperate-freshwater teleosts have three cone pigments that absorb light maximally at about 455, 530, and 625 nm (Loew and Lythgoe 1978). Rainbow trout show similar spectral sensitivity peaks and most likely can distinguish different colors (Douglas 1983). In all cases, pigmental absorption of light stimulates the retinal cells to send impulses via the optic nerve (Fig. 10.9) to the optic lobe on the same side of the brain. The reception and integration of the visual image in the brain then provokes the appropriate motor response (e.g., to the muscles and/or fins).

The choroid coat underlies the retinal layer and primarily functions to supply nutrients and oxygen to the retina with its high metabolic demand. Most teleosts possess a pigmented choroid projection into the posterior portion of the interior of the eye; this is called the *falciform process* (Fig. 10.9). The falciform process is highly vascularized and probably serves a nutritive function (Munz 1971). In addition, a choroid gland (or rete) is present in most teleosts (and the bowfin *[Amia calva]*) behind the retina. The countercurrent arrangement of blood vessels of the choroid rete makes it eminently suited for oxygen delivery to the retina, in similar fashion to the rete mirabile of physoclistous swimbladders (Chapter 3). Wittenberg and Haedrich (1974) described the presence and relative size of choroid retia in several species of North Atlantic fishes. Invariably, the fishes that rely heavily on sight, such as bluefish *(Pomatomus saltatrix),* have the best-developed choroid retia. Presumably, localized modification (e.g., acidification) of the blood next to the rete drives oxygen off the hemoglobin via the Root shift, much as in the swimbladder rete (Chapter 5). Hayden et al. (1975) attributed the significant Root shift in the swimbladderless winter flounder to choroid rete function in this demersal sight feeder. Wittenberg and Wittenberg (1962) measured the partial pressure of oxygen (PO_2) in the vitreous humor of living marine fish. Those species having the best-developed choroid rete also had the highest vitreous PO_2 (250 mm Hg to 820 mm Hg). Teleosts with smaller retia had lower PO_2 values (20 mm Hg to 210 mm Hg), while elasmobranchs and those teleosts that lacked the choroid rete had the lowest PO_2 values (10 mm Hg to 20 mm Hg).

The choroid layer of elasmobranchs also contains the *tapetum lucidum* or reflecting layer. It is the reflecting layer that produces eyeshine when a direct beam of light is trained on the eye, especially under darkened conditions. Many teleosts also have tapeta lucida, but most are located in the retinal pigment epithelium (Nicol and Zyznar 1973). The reflecting material of the tapetum varies among fish. Guanine crystals comprise the primary reflecting substance in the bigeye *(Priacanthus arenatus),* the bream *(Abramis brama),* the bay anchovy *(Anchoa mitchilli),* and all the elasmobranchs investigated. A lipid reflecting substance is found in at least six teleost families, yellow "melanoid" substances occur in gars (Lepisosteidae) and catfish, and a pteridine is found in the gizzard shad *(Dorosoma cepedianum)* (Zyznar and Nicol 1973).

In all cases, the tapetal layer functions to increase the visual sensitivity of retinal pigments by shining most of the transmitted light back through the retina. The arrangement of choroidal tapetal plates reflects light back in the same direction from which it first stimulates the retina, preserving image clarity. Whereas most benthic and deepsea elasmobranchs have tapeta lucida that function continuously, pelagic species from well-lit waters can cover the reflecting layers by moving dark pigment between the tapetal plates. Occlusion of the reflecting layer prevents "overloading" of the retinal pigments under brightly lit conditions. With the onset of darkness, the occluded tapetum becomes completely shiny after one hour. Gruber and Cohen (1978) point out that the light reflection from elasmobranch tapeta approaches 90% at certain wavelengths. This layer gives elasmobranchs a light sensitivity approximately equal to that of sympatric teleosts (without tapeta), which typically have twice the concentration of visual pigment per unit area of retinal surface.

Fish tissues other than the eyes may also show receptivity to light. The pineal gland, dorsally located on the brain, is one of these tissues. Gruber et al. (1975b) showed that the chondrocranium of three shark species is modified for light transmission in that seven times more light impinged on the pineal receptors than on surrounding areas of the brain. Hamasaki and Streck (1971) found evidence that the pineal of *Scyliorhinus* responds to changes in illumination approximating 4×10^{-6} lumens/m^2, which is far below the intensity of moonlight at the water surface. Thus the pineal may function as an ultrasensitive light sensor closely connected to the brain, and may be used to cue the fish's behavior to changes in light intensity on a daily and seasonal basis. Larval sea lampreys show a photosensitivity (escape response) when the lateral skin of the tail is illuminated. Apparently the photoreceptor signals are carried by a trunk lateral-line nerve, because bilateral sectioning of this nerve significantly diminishes this sensitivity (Ronan and Bodznick 1991).

Supplemental Readings

Alexander 1966, 1967; Bullock et al. 1983; Dijkgraaf 1962; Gruber and Cohen 1978; Hara 1986; Hasler and Scholz 1983; Kalmijn 1978; Loew and Lythgoe 1978; Marshall 1966; Munz 1971; Myrberg 1978; Nicol and Zyznar 1973; Northcutt 1978; Popper and Fay 1977; Sorensen and Scott 1994.

CHAPTER **11**

Behavior and Communication

The anatomical and physiological characteristics of a fish are best understood when explained in relation to their effects on its behavior. Thus much of the space in the chapters on the major fish groups (Chapters 14 through 24) is spent describing behavior patterns. Similarly, descriptions of fish behavior are important to the chapters on ecology (27 through 36) because ecology is the study of organism-environment interactions, and the most conspicuous manifestation of these interactions is behavior, particularly behavioral change in response to environmental change. For this chapter it is convenient to divide the subject of behavior into seven categories (which are not necessarily mutually exclusive): (1) migratory behavior, (2) schooling behavior, (3) feeding behavior, (4) aggressive behavior, (5) resting behavior, (6) reproductive behavior, and (7) interspecific interactions. Reproductive behavior is covered in Chapter 9; interspecific interactions, which include predator-prey, mimicry, and symbiotic relationships, are covered in the ecology chapters; thus, only the first five areas will be discussed in this chapter.

Because so much behavior involves interactions with other fish of the same or different species, it is important to understand how fishes communicate. Therefore, the latter half of this chapter will be devoted to communication using visual, auditory, chemical, tactile, and electrical signals.

MIGRATORY BEHAVIOR

Mass movements of fish from one place to another, on a regular basis, are common. Such migratory behavior can range in occurrence from seasonal to daily. The daily migrations are typically for feeding and/or predator avoidance (see Chapters 33 and 35), so only long-term patterns will be discussed here. The general patterns are usually broken up into three basic patterns: oceanodromy, potamodromy, and diadromy. *Oceanodromy* refers to fish that migrate entirely within saltwater, while *potamodromy* refers entirely to species that migrate within fresh water. *Diadromy*, the phenomenon of migrating between the two environments as a regular part of the life cycle, is broken into:

1. **catadromy**, moving from fresh to salt water to spawn;
2. **anadromy**, moving from salt to fresh water to spawn; and
3. **amphidromy**, moving between the two environments for purposes other than spawning (McDowall 1988).

Whatever they are labeled, fish migrations are often quite spectacular. Tuna, salmon, and eels, for example, may migrate thousands of kilometers in relatively short periods of time, often arriving within a relatively narrow time span at a fairly specific locality. Two questions will be addressed here: "Why do they do it?" and "How do they do it?"

Why fish migrate is a fascinating question because in many cases the energetic investment in migration is quite high, and often migrating fishes do not feed. The catadromous eels that migrate to the Sargasso Sea near Bermuda cease feeding once they enter salt water, as do anadromous salmon once they enter fresh water, some to swim hundreds of kilometers upstream. Most such migrations are for spawning, allowing the eggs to be laid in places favorable for their development and for the survival of the newly hatched larval stages. As Harden-Jones (1968) points out, many such migrations have a triangular pattern. The adults swim against a current (ocean or stream) to the spawning grounds; the currents then carry the helpless young to favorable feeding areas; once the young reach a certain size and are active swimmers, they migrate to the adult feeding grounds. This pattern has several advantages: (1) it greatly increases the probability of the larval stages finding their way to the proper habitats; (2) it reduces the likelihood of intraspecific competition for food among different age classes, a problem most likely to affect plankton-feeding fishes such as herring; and (3) it reduces the probability of cannibalism.

The use of migration to separate the different life history stages seems to be one of its main characteristics, regardless of the environment in which it occurs. River- and lake-dwelling fishes often migrate into small tributary streams to spawn in riffle areas. The young may then use the small streams as nursery areas, before moving down to the adult habitat. Many lake-dwelling species migrate only as far as suitable spawning grounds in shallow waters of the lake itself. In fishes such as the sunfishes (*Lepomis*) and crappies (*Pomoxis*), the young become pelagic after hatching and drift about in the surface waters for several weeks before settling down to the bottom and then moving inshore, where they school in large numbers in shallow weedy areas or other protected habitats. A similar pattern is typical of many marine benthic species, such as various flounders (Pleuronectidae) and rockfishes (Scorpaenidae). Some of the most prolonged larval stages, however, are found in amphidromous gobies that live in the streams of Hawai'i and other islands. The larvae wash downstream as soon as they hatch and then spend a month or more at sea before returning to the streams as 20 mm long post-larvae (McDowall 1988). Not only do these tiny fish manage to find their way to a stream but once there they proceed to move upstream long distances, ascending major waterfalls. They climb over the falls through the use of their specialized pelvic fins, which are modified into a sucking disk.

While perhaps a majority of fish migrations are related to reproduction and the separation of the life history stages, many are also in response to changing environmental conditions, particularly temperature, and the movements and abundance of food organisms. The seasonal movements of albacore *(Thunnus alalunga),* for example, appear to follow the development of the 14°C isotherm in the North Pacific. In herring *(Clupea harengus)* the northward movement in spring in the North Sea is related to the warmth of the inflowing Atlantic waters; the warmer the water, the greater the blooms of plankton upon which the herring feed. Increasingly, knowledge of the responses of migratory fish to temperature, salinity, and other oceanographic conditions is being used to predict how good fishing is likely to be in a given area, sometimes several months in advance.

One factor that greatly increases the predictability of the migrations of many fishes is their ability to find their way back to a "home" area, particularly a spawning area. Homing has been well documented in nonmigratory as well as migratory fishes. Many tide pool fishes, for example, can find their way back to their home pool, using olfactory and visual clues, after being displaced several hundred meters (Gibson 1986). The most studied of homing fishes, however, have been the Pacific salmon *(Oncorhynchus)* because they have been shown to return with an amazing degree of accuracy to the stream and area in which they were spawned, after wandering for several years and thousands of kilometers through the Pacific Ocean. A. D. Hasler and his students have shown rather conclusively that the precision of homing is due to the ability of the salmon to recognize the distinctive odor of their home stream, and that they become imprinted on this odor as they transform into smolts, just prior to their outward migration (Hasler and Scholz 1978). Not only are migrating salmon capable of recognizing the odor of their home stream, but they also recognize, and use as navigational cues, the odors of other streams they pass on their way up the main rivers. Furthermore, there is evidence that salmon may also respond to chemicals (pheromones) given off by conspecifics, such as juveniles inhabiting a stream, and are able to discriminate between water that contains fish from the same population and that from other populations (Groot et al. 1986). Such abilities can permit a great deal of precision in homing. Mechanisms other fishes use for the precise location of home areas have not been as well studied, but besides odor, it is likely that topographic cues, currents, and salinity and temperature gradients are important.

The recognition that migratory fishes can home precisely has led to the widespread acceptance of the idea that they can also navigate precisely over long distances. This has resulted in an extensive search for mechanisms of orientation. The most likely mechanisms proposed have been (1) orientation to gradients of temperature, salinity, and chemicals; (2) sun orientation; and (3) orientation to geomagnetic and geoelectric fields (Leggett 1977).

As the previous discussion has indicated, fish can detect gradients in the water and do orient to them, often timing migrations on the basis of seasonal changes in such factors as temperature and salinity. However, such phenomena fluctuate from year to year and frequently cover wide areas, and thus they seem to be poor candidates as cues for the precise nature of the homing observed. It is possible that migrating salmon may be able to detect sequential changes in the chemical content of the oceanic water masses they move through, much as they detect changes in the streams they pass through, but direct evidence for this is limited. The evidence that fish can navigate by orienting to the position of the sun is somewhat better. For example, Hasler et al. (1958) tied small floats onto white bass *(Morone chrysops)* and noted that on sunny days bass displaced from their spawning grounds had a strong directional bias when released, while on cloudy days such bias was lacking. Unfortunately, evidence that fish widely use the sun compass for navigation is limited. Indeed, for both salmon and American shad *(Alosa sapidissima)*, correctly oriented migrants have been observed both at night and on cloudy days.

Evidence is stronger that migratory fishes can detect and orient to the earth's magnetic fields. These fields are weak but can be detected by many migratory fishes, particularly when additional electric fields are generated by the movement of oceanic currents through them. The strongest evidence for the use of geomagnetic fields for navigation is for anguillid eels, which migrate long distances in deep water, have an extreme sensitivity to the fields, and have different directional responses to them, depending on their developmental stage (Leggett 1977).

In the search for precise mechanisms of fish orientation, many bits of evidence suggesting that migrations are not always very accurate have been overlooked. Tagged salmon frequently show up in the wrong streams many miles distant from their home streams. Tagging studies of various migratory fishes frequently note that dispersal from the tagging site is essentially random in direction, even though a majority of the marked fish do end up in the home area. Furthermore, in orientation experiments, outright "mistakes" by fish are common and the overall orientation of fish to the factor being tested (e.g., sun azimuth) tends to be rather general and not exact. In fact, Saila (1961) was able to demonstrate that the homing of winter flounder to inshore spawning areas could be explained largely on the basis of random search movements of fish that will not go deeper than 40 m. A majority of these fish will find the coastline during the spawning period and then subsequently find their way to the spawning area partially through random searching and partly through the use of environmental cues, such as topography and water chemistry. Similarly, salmon may not need highly precise navigational abilities to reach a general area of coastline that contains their spawning stream. All they may need is some cue, or multiple cues, to get them swimming in the general direction. Cues can include food availability, currents, and temperature and chemical gradients, as well as sun direction and geomagnetic fields (Patten 1964). By using a combination of cues, most of the fish can reach their home region and, once there, use more precise mechanisms, particularly olfaction, to find the home stream. However, the jury is still not in on the subject because it does not seem to make a great deal of sense for fish to waste time and energy on generalized movement if more precise navigational methods are possible.

Migrations of fish generally seem to have evolved as a mechanism to place adult fish in a favorable place for feeding and to place larval and juvenile fish in a favorable place for survival. Most salmon, for example, feed on fish in the ocean and grow much larger than would be possible on the limited resources of the streams and rivers in which they spawn. This results in a great increase in fecundity, giving anadromous forms a tremendous advantage over resident forms. Gross et al. (1988) provide evidence for this pattern by showing that anadromous fish are most common in northern latitudes, where ocean productivity exceeds freshwater productivity, while catadromous fish are most common in tropical latitudes where ocean productivity is typically low. It is not always advantageous to migrate, however, as is indicated by the commonness of resident populations of fish in the headwaters of coastal streams that are derived from anadromous forms. For example, Snyder (1989) found that the inland populations of threespine stickleback (*Gasterosteus aculeatus*) in coastal streams had lost the inherited ability to migrate that characterized populations only a few km downstream. The reason for this loss was apparently that the energy requirements of migration were just too costly for upstream populations of this tiny fish. However, while the upstream populations were less robust and fecund than the anadromous sticklebacks, they *were* persisting in places where the anadromous forms clearly could not.

SHOALING

Shoaling is perhaps the most fascinating social behavior pattern possessed by fish, although most attention has been focused on the most spectacular aspect of shoaling, schooling. A school of fish often seems to have a mind of its own, moving in a coordinated fashion through complicated maneuvers with its members precisely spaced within it. A *shoal* is any group of fishes that remains together for social reasons, while a *school* is a polarized, synchronized shoal (Pitcher and Parrish 1993). This distinction is necessary because experimental studies indicate that schooling is just one extreme in the entire phenomenon of shoaling, and that fish shift in and out of schools on a regular basis. A shoal can go from the classic polarized organization to an amorphous mass in a matter of seconds, depending on whether or not its members are traveling, feeding, resting, or avoiding predators (Fig. 11.1). The shape of a shoal can also vary widely. Traveling shoals, for example, range in shape from long, thin lines, to ovals and squares, to more amoeboid shapes. However, fast-moving traveling schools most typically assume a wedge shape, while feeding shoals are usually more or less circular.

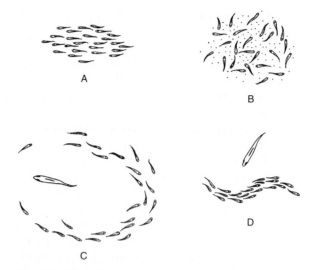

FIGURE 11.1 *Common patterns of shoaling:*
(A) traveling school; (B) planktivores feeding;
(C) encirclement of a predator; and (D) streaming
school avoiding predator. (After Radakov 1972.)

Shoaling is of considerable interest because of its prevalence; Shaw (1978) estimated that 25% of all fishes shoal throughout their lives and that about half of all fishes spend at least part of their lives shoaling. Most of the important commercial fish species also shoal, and their behavior greatly increases their vulnerability to capture in large numbers. In many commercial species, the largest shoals form during migrations, when smaller shoals join together. Radakov (1972) mentions "chains" of shoals of migrating mullet *(Mugil)* in the Caspian Sea that were 100 km long! In the North Atlantic, herring shoals are sometimes encountered in the winter that occupy 279 million m³ to 4580 million m³, with densities of 0.5 fish/m³ to 1.0 fish/m³ (Radakov 1972).

How do fish school? Obviously, the precise structure and movements of polarized schools require precise sensory contacts among the individuals within the schools. The fact that most schools (but not necessarily shoals) break up at night indicates that vision is the main sensory link. Many laboratory experiments with temporarily blinded fish also demonstrate the importance of vision. Shaw (1978) has proposed that one way in which vision can be used to maintain the regular spacing noted in schools is through the *optomotor reaction*. This is the response fish have when placed in a container around which alternating vertical black and white stripes are rotating. The fish "stops" the motion of the stripes by fixing on one stripe and swimming at the same speed at which it is rotating. This response is quite useful to schooling fish, because position in a school can be maintained by visually fixing on the sides of neighboring fish, especially on the conspicuous dark lateral stripe possessed by so many schooling fishes.

The importance of vision in schooling does not mean that other senses are not important as well. Because the lateral-line system is so sensitive to water movement, it is quite likely that fish use the regular turbulence created by neighboring fish as another cue to help maintain spacing. It is also possible that pheromones or sounds may play a role in schooling, although there is no direct evidence for either one.

Why do fish shoal? Various hypotheses have been put forward, including: (1) increased hydrodynamic efficiency, (2) reduced risk of predation, (3) increased efficiency of food finding, and (4) increased reproductive success.

Hydrodynamic efficiency. The idea that shoaling increases the efficiency of swimming applies mainly to schooling. It is very appealing because of the regular spacing that seems to characterize fish in schools, and because fish in shoals tend to be uniform in size. However, to gain hydrodynamic advantages each fish must maintain rather precise positioning within a school in order to take advantage of the hydrodynamic lift created by its neighbors. By and large, measurements of fish positions within schools have not found this to be true (Pitcher and Parrish 1993).

Reduced predation risk. Shoaling reduces predation risk in two main, interacting ways: dilution and confusion (Pitcher and Parrish 1993). The *dilution effect* relies on simple safety in numbers (Parrish 1993). When predators do attack, large shoals are particularly advantageous because of the reduced probability that any one individual will be eaten. In any one attack, a smaller percentage of a large shoal will be eaten than of a small one (Major 1978). The *confusion effect* is based on the common observation that shoaling fish tend to get eaten mostly when they have been separated from the shoal; many of the attack strategies of predators can thus be best interpreted as efforts to break up shoals so individuals can be picked off. Most small shoaling fish are silvery, and it is difficult for a visually oriented predator to pick an individual out of a mass of twisting, flashing fish and then to have enough time to "fix" on that prey and grab it before it disappears into the shoal.

Shoaling fish that are captured are individuals that have become separated from the main shoal somehow (Major 1978). Thus when a predator approaches, typically a shoal will initially bunch up into a tight, weaving school. One of the reasons that attacks on shoaling fish are often more successful at dawn or dusk than during the day is presumably the reduced effectiveness of flashing scales in confusing the predators at those times. Shoals of fish also confound their predators by complicated maneuvering. One maneuver is called "flash expansion" in which a shoal of fish explodes in all directions and then reassembles quickly, never giving the predator a chance to focus on an individual (Pitcher and Parrish 1993). A more common maneuver is for a school to divide in two, turning away from the predator in two directions and finally joining again behind it. The effect of this is to constantly leave the predator isolated in a large, empty pocket in the school, from which the predator finds it very difficult to attack effectively because its every movement can be closely monitored by individuals in the school. Indeed, one of the general advantages of swimming in a shoal is being accompanied by a large number of eyes that make it virtually impossible for a predator to approach during the day without being detected.

Despite the many antipredator advantages of shoals, shoaling fishes are still the favorite prey of most pelagic predators, and many effective hunting strategies have been evolved to overcome the defenses of the shoal. One strategy for the predator is simply to attack at low light levels when shoals are more dispersed and the predator is more difficult to spot. Another strategy is to swim along with a school and grab fish that make defensive errors and become separated from it, or that are sick or injured. This strategy, used by stalking predators such as cornetfish (Fistulariidae), has a relatively low success rate (Parrish 1993). A more effective strategy is to attack in schools. When a school of jacks (Carangidae) attacks a school of herring (Clupeidae), the school of herring cannot respond as effectively as to a single predator, especially when the jacks hunt cooperatively and separate out clusters of fish from the main shoal or literally ram into the shoal. Shoals of small fish can be devastated when a school of predators drives them to the surface of the water and then flocks of seabirds dive down on them from above.

Increased efficiency of food finding. Schooling by predators may increase the probability of their detecting a school of prey, just as shoaling in plankton-feeding fish may increase the probability of detection of suitable patches of plankton. Fish in shoals monitor each other's behavior closely, and feeding behavior in one fish quickly stimulates food-searching behavior in others (Pitcher and Parrish 1993). However, for planktivores, this advantage may be partially compensated for by having to share the patch with many other fish; fish in the rear of a school moving through a patch of plankton are likely to encounter much lower densities of plankton than those in the front. Another disadvantage is that fish are less vigilant when feeding in shoals and may allow predators to approach more closely than when not feeding.

Reproduction. For fish that shoal throughout their lifetimes, little energy has to be expended in finding a mate when spawning time comes around. For fish that migrate long distances, schooling may increase the accuracy of homing because the average direction sought by fish in a school is more likely to be a better choice than that chosen by an individual migrating singly.

FEEDING BEHAVIOR

The feeding behavior of fish is as diverse as their morphology, which more often than not reflects their general method of feeding (Chapter 2). However, while most fish are specialized in their feeding to a greater or lesser degree, their actual diet at any given time depends on the availability of both typical and atypical food items as well as on the presence of potentially competing fish species. When a major hatch of mayflies occurs in a lake, for example, almost every fish large enough to capture them will do so, although normally adult mayflies would be taken mainly by fish with adaptations for surface feeding. Similarly, fish that normally filter-feed on plankton will on occasion selectively feed by "picking" large individual zooplankters, including larval fish. Rainbow trout usually feed on drifting organisms in streams but may become benthic feeders when drift is hard to see, even though this mode of feeding is generally less efficient (Tippets and Moyle 1978). Other fishes may regularly switch between two or more modes of feeding, depending on the abundances of different kinds of prey. Bay gobies *(Lepidogobius lepidus)*, for example, will hop up from the bottom to seize swimming prey or bite the substrate to obtain benthic prey, especially polychaete worms (Grossman et al. 1980). Obviously, the feeding behavior of fishes is influenced by many factors, including characteristics of the environment, the predators, and the prey.

In an effort to understand just how and why predators select their prey, a general theory of *optimal foraging* has been developed (Hart 1986). The basic idea behind this theory is that natural selection will favor predators that maximize the efficiency of their capture of prey. Thus the feeding "strategy" adopted by a fish at any time should be one that allows it to take in the most or highest quality food with the least amount of effort (energy expenditure). Because the principal ways a predator expends energy in feeding are in searching for and pursuing prey, handling the prey, and then digesting it, an optimal foraging strategy should balance these factors in such a way that the total energy expenditure is minimized, even if the cost of one of the factors is higher than it could be. For example, it does not "pay" a carnivorous largemouth bass to browse on algae, even though the algae may be very easy to find and handle, because the fish will presumably expend more energy passing it through the gut than it can extract from it. On the other hand, it may pay the bass quite well to select slender, soft-rayed minnows over deep-bodied, spiny sunfish because the handling time is likely to be considerably less. Similarly, the bass is most likely to select for larger minnows over smaller ones, because the search time per gram of fish ingested will be less.

Although, as the preceding example indicates, the morphological characteristics of the prey can greatly influence prey selection, the most important factors are usually size and availability. For example, bluegill sunfish in aquaria will select all size classes of zooplankton prey equally, if all are present at low densities; they simply grab the prey as they encounter them. However, if the densities of all sizes of the prey are greatly increased, the fish will select only the largest sizes (Werner and Hall 1974). An interpretation of such an experiment is that when food is scarce, a fish will capture any prey item for which there is likely to be a net gain of energy for the fish, no matter how small; whereas when food is abundant, the fish will select the prey that produce the most energy for the least amount of effort (resulting in more energy available for growth and reproduction). Likewise, Fausch (1984) showed that juvenile trout and salmon will select places to forage in a stream where energy gain can be maximized. Dominant fish therefore choose the very best spots to hang out, the slow-moving places near the fast water that delivers lots of food. However, Ringler (1979) noted that brown trout in aquaria would abandon, for short periods of time, areas where prey were most abundant to check out other areas. They also continued to take small amounts of small "suboptimal" prey long after preferred, larger prey became abundant. While such behavior kept the trout from completely optimizing their diets in the aquaria, in the wild it would be highly adaptive because prey size, availability, and location are likely to fluctuate considerably.

As these experiments indicate, a number of factors influence the choice of prey. Sculpins in streams, for example, apparently choose prey not only on the basis of size and abundance but on the basis of activity pattern (both time of day and amount of activity), how hard-shelled they are, and where they live in the streams.

Obviously, an optimal foraging strategy for a fish must include other factors besides maximizing the energy obtained per prey item; perhaps most important is reducing the risk of predation. Thus an optimal strategy for a small, crevice-dwelling bottom fish might be to minimize the time spent foraging, in order to minimize exposure to predation. Such a fish could presumably obtain more food by foraging more continuously but would increase its own probability of being eaten as it spent more time away from cover. An optimal foraging strategy here would balance energy gains against survival probabilities. In fact, balancing these two factors is a continuous problem for fish because diets and predators change with life history stage. In streams, the earliest life stages of many species are on the stream edges where food is abundant and the water is too shallow for larger fishes that might prey on them. However, as they grow larger, they become increasingly desirable as prey for herons and other wading birds, forcing them into deeper water. Their increased size has made them less vulnerable to medium-sized piscivorous fish but more desirable to large ones that hang out in deeper water. As a result, intermediate-sized prey fish tend to be most abundant at intermediate depths, near suitable cover (Power 1987). In another variation on this theme, Harvey (1990) found that, in an Oklahoma stream, larval cyprinids were most abundant in pools that contained large predatory bass, because the bass kept the pools free of fish small enough to prey on the larvae and were too large to prey on the larvae themselves.

AGGRESSIVE BEHAVIOR

Aggressive interactions among fish are frequently observed, particularly in aquaria. In form, such interactions range from direct charges of one individual at another, which may result in bites or fights, to elaborate ritualistic displays involving modified swimming, flaring of gill covers and fins, and changes in color, to barely detectable movements. The best known aggressive interactions among fishes are those related to reproduction and the defense of breeding territories because they are part of elaborate sets of conspicuous, ritualized behavior (Chapter 9). Just as important to many fishes, but much less conspicuous, is aggressive behavior associated with the defense of food and space (cover). Trout and juvenile salmon, for example, frequently defend feeding territories in streams. Such territories generally center around a rock or some other object that shelters the fish from the currents but provides a good view of food organisms drifting downstream. Proximity of the territory to cover, for protection from predators, may also be important. The most frequently observed form of territory defense is the "nip," where a defending fish charges an intruder and attempts to nip its caudal peduncle or side. When the intruder is the same size or smaller than the defender, it usually flees quickly. Occasionally an intruder will not flee at once, and more elaborate displays result, most conspicuously lateral displays in which the two fish swim side by side in a rigid fashion, with opercula and fins flared. Three factors seem to be of greatest importance in deciding which fish wins a bout: prior residency, size, and results of previous encounters. A fish that already lives in a territory is likely to defeat an intruder unless that intruder is considerably larger than the defender. The displacement of small fish by larger fish can result in frequent shifts in the patterns of territories in trout and salmon streams, because larger fish also require larger territories. In trout, several fish of different sizes may coexist in the same area, with the larger fish being dominant over the smaller fish but not driving them away (T. Jenkins 1969). Such dominance hierarchies presumably exist in part because the smaller trout feed on smaller prey, and so are not competing too much with the larger trout for food, and because the smaller trout may actually help the larger trout defend the area against intruders.

It has been implied in the preceding discussion that aggressive behavior has an adaptive significance. The gain in food availability is assumed to offset the costs of patrolling a territory and chasing away intruders. Thus among tide-flat-dwelling bay gobies, winners of aggressive encounters are able to consume more food than losers under conditions of artificial food shortage (Grossman 1979). Likewise, in the case of reef-dwelling damselfishes, the density of filamentous algae, upon which they feed, is much higher in the territories than outside of them. Further discussions of the ecological significance of aggressive behavior can be found in the ecology chapters.

RESTING BEHAVIOR

Although it is not often acknowledged in studies of fish behavior, most fishes spend a good part of each 24-hour period in an inactive state. On coral reefs there are marked differences between the day and night fish faunas, in large part because day-active fishes hide in crevices and caves in the reef at night, where they rest quietly, while night-active fishes are inactive in the crevices during the day. Many species even change color patterns when at rest. In lakes, many fish become pale at night and rest quietly on the bottom, under logs or on beds of aquatic weeds. Often such fish are so torpid that a diver can swim up to one and touch it, something that would be impossible to do during the day (Emery 1973). Some pelagic fishes, such as tuna, that must swim to keep water moving across the gills are presumably active all night long; but other pelagic fishes, such as herring, tend to remain in a quiescent state in the water column. The polarized school of the day becomes an unpolarized shoal at night, but the members remain close enough to each other so that schooling can resume as soon as there is enough light. The inactivity of many fish at night is presumably an energy-conserving measure.

COMMUNICATION

Communication is, according to E. O. Wilson (1975, 176), "the action on the part of one organism that alters the probability pattern of behavior in another organism in a fashion that is adaptive to one or both of the participants." This definition implies that the signals given off by a fish, as well as the mechanisms to receive those signals, are highly adaptive. Therefore, fish employ a rich variety of signals in their efforts to communicate with one another: visual, auditory, chemical, and electric.

Visual Signals

For most fish, vision is the most important sense for finding food and for communicating with other fish. Thus it is not surprising to find that there is an enormous variety of visual signals among fish, from subtle movements of the body and fins to bright colors arranged in elaborate patterns. Because colors and color patterns are so important for visual communication, this section will discuss (1) how they are produced by fish, (2) their general significance, and (3) the specific significance of some of the most common types of color patterns.

Colors in fish are of two basic types, pigments (biochromes) and structural colors. **Pigments** are colored compounds that are located primarily in chromatophores, cells located mainly in the dermis of the skin (but also in the epidermis, in the peritoneum, in the eyes, and in the various organs). Chromatophores are highly irregular in shape but usually appear as a central core giving out many branched processes. This shape permits the rapid color changes frequently observed in fish; when the pigment granules are concentrated in the center portion, the overall appearance of the fish will be paler than when the granules are dispersed through the branches. The hues change through the combined action of chromatophores containing pigments of different colors overlying one another, or by the internal changes of chromatophores containing more than one pigment.

The internal control of the chromatophores, and consequently color patterns, is complex, involving both hormones and nerves. As might be expected, the initiation of a color change usually comes from visual cues. A flounder placed with its head on one background and its body on another will have a body color matching that of the background around the head. Likewise, body coloration can be experimentally altered by fitting the fish with colored transparent eye lenses or by changing the intensity of illumination. Visual stimuli are carried to the chromatophores by sympathetic nerves, by special hormones secreted by the pituitary, or by both. The method used depends on the type of chromatophore and on the species of fish. Nonvisual cues may also cause color changes, as indicated by the sensitivity of the nerves associated with chromatophores to such substances as adrenalin (epinephrine) and acetylcholine. Adrenalin and its relatives cause pigment granules in the chromatophore to aggregate, rapidly making the fish lighter in color, while acetylcholine will make them disperse slowly. Thus fish that are frightened may undergo rapid color changes and then slowly revert back to their original colors when the danger is past.

There are many different kinds of pigments found in fish (Fox 1978), but the most frequently encountered types are carotenoids, melanins, and purines. Carotenoid pigments are those responsible for the bright reds and yellows frequently seen in fish, and greens as well, when yellow carotenoids overlie a blue structural color. Melanins are mainly dark red, brown, and black and form the background coloration of most fishes. Purines (mostly guanine in fish) are crystalline substances that perhaps should not be classified as pigments because they are colorless and are often nonmotile in the chromatophores. However, they have the peculiar reflective qualities that produce the silvery sheen of pelagic fish and the iridescent colors of many reef and freshwater tropical fish. In fact, most of the **structural colors** of fish (colors produced by light reflecting from structures rather than by pigments) are caused by light reflecting from purine crystals located in special chromatophores. The silvery color of pelagic fish, for example, is created by the stratum argenteum, a sheet made up of layers of guanine-containing cells (iridophores) that is capable of reflecting most of the light that hits it, much like a mirror. Because the light is scattered as it is reflected, it appears silvery; if the crystals or iridophores are aligned in such a way that the light waves are reflected back in parallel, iridescent colors are created.

What is the adaptive significance of the complex color patterns of fish? Color patterns in general seem to have three main purposes: thermoregulation, intraspecific communication, and evasion of predators (Endler 1978). The role of color patterns in fish in thermoregulation is not known, but it is not likely to be great, given the closeness of fish body temperatures to environmental temperatures. Most color patterns of fishes can be viewed as compromises between the "need" to communicate with other members of the species and the "need" to avoid being eaten. The former need will favor bright, distinctive, and conspicuous coloration, while the latter will favor cryptic coloration. The fact that a particular color or color pattern may be either quite conspicuous or quite cryptic depending on such factors as background colors, water clarity, and visual capabilities of the predators means that the significance of color patterns must be interpreted carefully. Interpretation of the significance of color patterns is also complicated by the ability of many fishes to change colors, often quite rapidly in response to changing conditions, but particularly in relation to reproduction (Fig. 11.2). The compromising, multipurpose nature of color patterns in fishes can be best demonstrated by examining some of the more common patterns in fishes: (1) red coloration, (2) poster colors, (3) disruptive coloration, (4) countershading, (5) eye ornamentation, (6) eye spots, (7) lateral stripes, and (8) polychromatism.

Red coloration. The wavelengths in the red region of the spectrum are the first to be filtered out as light passes through water, yet bright red fishes are common. Fishes that are solid red in color are generally either nocturnal (such as the cardinal fishes [Apogonidae] or the squirrel fishes [Holocentridae]) or live at moderate depths (such as many rockfishes). In both situations red light is virtually absent from the water, so the fish are in fact cryptically colored. Red is also a cryptic color in tidepool fishes because many of them are found in close association with red algae. Many shallow-water fishes, however, do have red bands and other markings that seem to make them quite conspicuous. Such coloration is particularly common in the spawning males of freshwater fishes, such as minnows, salmon, trout, and sticklebacks. It can be argued that red is a good compromise color for spawning fish because it is highly visible at short distances—important for males trying to attract females for spawning—yet is likely to be difficult to see laterally for any distance,

FIGURE 11.2 *Color patterns of tilapia* (Tilapia mossambica): *(1) neutral pattern; (2) male territorial pattern; (3) aggression pattern; (4) arousal pattern; (5) female spawning pattern; (6) female brooding pattern; (7) frightened juvenile; (8) and (9) frightened adult. The arrows show probable direction of change of color pattern. (From Lanzing and Bower 1974.)*

especially if the water is turbid or shaded. The importance of hiding even small patches of red color that do not function in communication is demonstrated by white sturgeon *(Acipenser transmontanus)*, which have a small dorsal portion of their gill exposed. While the covered part of the gill is red, the exposed portion is darkly pigmented, like the skin of the sturgeon (Burggren 1978).

Poster colors. This is the name given by Konrad Lorenz to the bright complex color patterns so characteristic of coral reef fishes because he thought their primary function was advertisement of territory ownership. The most conspicuous, and most studied, of the poster-colored fishes are the butterfly fishes (Chaetodontidae), which are typically yellow or white with dark, contrasting stripes and other markings. For many reef fishes the bright colors may indeed be important for advertising territories, but it is now apparent that this is only one of a number of possible functions (Ehrlich et al. 1977). Many highly colored reef fishes are not territorial, while many territorial fishes, such as some damselfishes (Pomacentridae), are rather plain in color. For more gregarious species, the bright colors may serve to keep foraging individuals in contact with each other. Ehrlich et al. (1977) noted that when a pair of butterfly fish become separated, one of them may rise off the bottom in a brief display that helps to bring the two together again. Coloration may also be closely tied to sex and courtship; the complex polymorphic patterns of wrasses (Labridae) and parrotfishes (Scaridae), for example, reflect sex, status, and maturity.

Still other possible functions of poster colors lie in the realm of predator avoidance. Often fishes with bright colors can hide very effectively in the reef, partly because the reef itself is quite colorful and partly because the patterns may be disruptive in nature (see next section). In fact, it may be the patterns and not the colors that are most important for concealment because being invisible to reef predators is most important when light levels are low and colors hard to see. Thus the patterns could serve different purposes at different light levels. Brightly colored fishes may also be able to escape predators through the "flash effect," whereby a predator is confused when a fish approached from the side suddenly turns and "disappears" because only the narrowest profile is visible. On the other hand, bright colors may actually function as a warning in announcing a fish's presence to a predator because the fish is too poisonous or spiny to be worth pursuing (*aposematic coloring*). Indeed, the spiny nature of butterfly fishes is thought to account at least partially for their rarity in the stomachs of predatory reef fishes.

Disruptive coloration. Colors and patterns that disrupt the outline of fish make them less visible. Thus fishes that associate with beds of aquatic plants, such as sunfish (*Lepomis* spp.) and many cichlids, often have on their sides vertical bars that help them to blend in with the vertical pattern of the plants. Part of the effect of such patterns may be "flicker fusion" in the predator (Endler 1978), whereby the rapid movement of the vertical bars on the side of the fish across a field of vertical bars (plant stems) may cause them all to blend together in the eyes of the predator, much like motion picture film. The intriguing aspect of flicker fusion as camouflage is that it may permit a fish to have a color pattern that is conspicuous at rest but confusing when the fish is swimming rapidly. Many of the bright but irregular patterns of coral reef fishes or freshwater fishes of the tropics may function in this way, because they are often associated with irregular, dappled backgrounds.

The real masters at matching their backgrounds, however, are slow-moving bottom fishes, such as sculpins (Cottidae), darters (Percidae), flounders, and blennies. Flounders are famous for their ability to match their background, even to the point of coloring themselves in a fair imitation of a checkerboard when placed on one in the laboratory. Other fishes may break up their outlines by having cirri and other irregular growths that resemble seaweed, especially on the head.

Countershading. Countershading is the commonest way fish disguise themselves. Being dark on top helps to hide them from predators attacking from above, while being light on the bottom helps them to blend in better with the light streaming down from above. Its effectiveness in concealing a fish can be demonstrated simply by turning a countershaded fish upside down in the water and noting how conspicuous it becomes.

Eye ornamentation. The eye in fish, being naturally conspicuous, seems to be a focus for both the attacks of predators and for intraspecific communication. Thus there are two trends in eye ornamentation: to disguise the eye and to emphasize it. Disguising the eye is accomplished in a variety of ways, such as minimizing the contrast between the iris and pupil and then surrounding the eye with a matching background, having a line run through the eye that matches the pupil, and having a field of spots surround the eye of a size similar to the pupil. Eye lines are the most common form of eye disguise, and Barlow (1972) notes that such lines tend to be vertical on deep-bodied species but horizontal on slender-bodied species, so that they are consistent with body patterns.

Although disguising the eye is a common practice, particularly in reef fishes, much more common is emphasizing the eye with a striking pattern around it or with bright colors in the eye itself. In Caribbean reef fishes, a majority of the species have eyes with conspicuous coloration, mostly black, blue, and yellow (Thresher 1977). Usually, the dark pupil is emphasized by a light-colored iris and often with some supplementary markings, such as eye rings, as well. Presumably such conspicuous eyes have developed in reef fishes because of the ease with which they can find cover during the day, when such eyes would be most conspicuous, and because of their general importance for intraspecific signaling.

Eye spots. Among the commonest markings on the bodies of fish are single spots about the size of the pupil of the eye and often surrounded by light-colored pigmentation for emphasis. Such eye spots are most commonly located at the base of the caudal peduncle. They are found most often in the juveniles of tropical characins, cyprinids, and cichlids. Although it is possible that such spots may function as orientation marks for fishes in a school, their principal function seems to be to confuse predators into aiming attacks at the caudal area rather than the head, giving the fish greater opportunities to escape (McPhail 1977a). In some species, eye spots serve as recognition signals that inhibit cannibalism of juveniles by adults. In the poeciliid fish *Neoheterandria formosa* the midlateral spot that apparently serves such a function is retained in the adults as well, and is used as an appeasement signal during courtship (McPhail 1977b).

Lateral stripes. These are typically a single midlateral band, and are best developed in schooling fishes. They seem to serve the dual function of keeping school members properly oriented to each other and of confusing predators. Presumably the latter aim is achieved by the effect of visual fusion of the stripes of members of the school, increasing the difficulty of picking out individuals.

Polychromatism. Nowhere is the conflict between the need to be cryptically colored to avoid predators and the need to be bright to attract mates more apparent than in fishes that are polychromatic, with different patterns predominating in different populations depending on the degree of predation. In the midas cichlid (*Ci-chlasoma citrinellum*), gold morphs are dominant over plainer morphs, particularly in contests over food (Barlow 1973), yet the failure of the gold morphs to "take over" their habitats in the wild presumably reflects their greater vulnerability to predation. In the annual killifish (*Nothobranchius guntheri*), brightly colored morphs are dominant over dull morphs and so have greater reproductive opportunities early in the season. However, they are gradually picked off by predators, giving the dull morphs greater reproductive opportunities later in the season (Haas 1976a,b).

Special patterns. Besides general patterns, such as those just discussed, many species have special color patterns that fit their own particular lifestyles. The males of some cichlids have circles on their anal fins that resemble eggs; these are displayed just after a female has laid some eggs and taken them into her mouth. When she tries to pick up the dummy eggs as well, the male releases sperm, and the eggs in the mouth are fertilized. On coral reefs there are many fishes with special color patterns, such as the bright colors of cleaner fishes that advertise their presence to fish wanting to be "cleaned" and the patterns of fishes that mimic other fishes or invertebrates (see Chapter 33). In the deep sea, photophore patterns play much the same roles as color patterns in lighted environments.

Auditory Signals

The use of sound for communication among fish is common but far from universal, although the hearing of fish is usually keen (Hawkins 1993). In some species, however, the sounds produced can be very loud and continuous and be fundamental to their way of life, especially during reproduction, when courtship "singing" may occur. Fish produce sounds in three main ways: by rubbing of hard structures together (stridulation), by vibration of the swimbladder, and as incidental to other activities. Stridulation produces mainly low-frequency sounds, but this method is the most common means of deliberate sound production, presumably because it often requires little modification of existing structures. Thus some fishes can communicate just by grinding the pharyngeal or jaw teeth together in a regular fashion. Some filefishes (Balistidae) even have special ridges on the backs of their front teeth that are used for sound production. Another common stridulatory mechanism is to rub the specially roughened base of a fin spine (usually pectoral spines) against its socket. Sea catfishes (Ariidae) are particularly well known for their use of this mechanism. Many, perhaps most, stridulatory sounds are amplified by the fish's swimbladder, and often there are muscular connections between the sound-producing structure and the swimbladder.

In fishes with the most complex auditory signals, it is usually the swimbladder itself that serves as the sound-producing organ. There are many ways this is done, often involving major modification of the swimbladder, but the basic means is to vibrate the swimbladder either by moving special muscles attached to it or by rubbing it with adjacent structures. The special musculature may either be muscles that insert on the swimbladder and originate on the skull or vertebral column or musculature intrinsic to the swimbladder itself. In the former case, the sound produced by the muscles depends on their tension and rate of vibration. This mechanism is found in the noisier members of many families of spiny-rayed fishes and in some catfishes. The loudest and most elaborate sounds, however, seem to be made by fishes with intrinsic swimbladder musculature for sound production, such as the toadfishes (Batrachoididae), searobins (Triglidae), and gunnards (Dactylopteridae); although the drums (Sciaenidae) get their name and sound-producing reputation by vibrating muscles in the body walls next to the swimbladder.

Compared to the sounds of many terrestrial animals, the sounds produced by fish are not particularly elaborate. In general, fish have only limited abilities to make and detect sounds of different frequencies, perhaps the most important means of varying sound patterns in mammals and birds. Nevertheless, sounds produced by fish can be varied by changes in loudness (amplitude), duration, repetition rate, and number of pulses within a signal (Fine et al. 1977). The loudest calls produced by fishes seem to be those associated with agonistic behavior, especially territorial defense. During the courtship season of the plainfin midshipman *(Porichthys notatus)*, people living on houseboats in Sausalito, California, find their peace and quiet disrupted when the loud and persistent humming of many fish is transmitted through the hulls of their boats! Anemone fishes *(Amphiprion)* have an extremely loud call that is used in defense of an anemone against conspecifics, but a much quieter call is associated with close encounters and fighting between two fish. The calls of anemone fish can also be distinguished on the basis of their duration: the more intense a threat, the longer a call will last. The repetition rate of a signal and the number of pulses within it (i.e., its complexity) may also increase with the intensity of the interaction. In drums (Sciaenidae), the drumming sounds are produced when the fish are in schools and increase in intensity during certain times of the day. As the intensity of the drumming increases, the length of each call increases as well, as does its frequency of repetition. Such variation in calls may also serve to keep closely related species reproductively isolated from each other. For example, Gerald (1971) found that the courtship grunts of six species of sunfish could be distinguished from each other on the basis of duration and number of pulses per second.

Chemical Signals

As the discussion of the use of odors as migrational cues indicates, most fish have a well-developed sense of smell. Thus it is not surprising to find that chemicals produced by fish even in very small amounts are often important in intraspecific communication, especially in fish that do not have keen eyesight (such as catfish). The chemical nature of most of the substances used in communication by fishes is not known, but it is likely that many of them are produced specifically for that purpose. This is particularly true of compounds that when released into the water produce an immediate and fairly specific reaction in other fish of the same species (pheromones). The general areas in which pheromones have their most important uses are in reproductive behavior, individual recognition, and predator avoidance.

For reproductive behavior, pheromones are often important for recognition of both sex and sexual condition and may be necessary for the release of certain behavior patterns. In frillfin gobies *(Bathygobius soporator)*, for example, an ovarian pheromone will elicit courtship behavior in males, even in the absence of any females (Tavolga 1956). Similarly, blind gobies *(Typhlogobius californiensis)* react very differently to the invasion of their burrows by conspecifics depending on their sex; gobies of the same sex produce aggressive behavior, whereas those of the opposite sex produce more passive behavior. It has been demonstrated that this sexual recognition is accomplished largely through the detection of pheromones (MacGintie 1939).

In some species of fish, odors may be used not only to determine sex but also to identify individuals. In yellow bullheads *(Ictalurus natalis),* individuals recognize each other by odors and also associate the odors with rank in social hierarchies. Thus a subordinate fish will avoid an area of an aquarium into which the water from the tank of a dominant fish has been introduced, even though the dominant fish is not present (Bardach and Todd 1970). Some cichlids can identify their own young on the basis of odor as well, at least during the three weeks or so when parental care is necessary (McKaye and Barlow 1976).

Predator avoidance by means of chemical signals is accomplished through the use of fear scents or *Schreckstoff* (Smith 1982). These compounds are present in epidermal cells and are released into the water when the skin is broken. When the compound is detected, other fish of the same (or closely related) species immediately adopt some sort of predator avoidance behavior, such as diving into the vegetation, bunching up as a school, or becoming motionless. This ability is known mainly from fishes of the superorder Otophysi, although a few other fishes may possess it as well. Presumably, fear scents not only enhance the ability of the fishes to avoid predators (especially in turbid environments) but also inhibit cannibalism.

Electrical Signals

Every time a muscle contracts, it gives off a small electrical discharge. Water containing dissolved minerals is a good conductor of electricity. These two facts together mean that electricity is a means of communication readily available to aquatic organisms. Many fishes have specialized organs for detecting electrical impulses *(electroreceptors),* and the capacity to generate electricity for communication has evolved independently in six groups of fishes (Rajidae, Torpedinidae, Notopteridae, Mormyriformes, Gymnotiformes, and Siluriformes). Of these fishes, the mormyrids and the gymnotids, both inhabitants of turbid tropical fresh waters, are most dependent on electricity for intraspecific signaling. The signals produced by the electric organs of these fishes can be modified in complex ways, by varying such factors as discharge frequency, waveform, and the times between discharges. The signals are received in specialized lateral-line organs known as *electroreceptors.* As a consequence, electrical discharges can have all the functions visual and auditory signals have in other fishes, including courtship, agonistic behavior, and individual recognition.

Supplemental Readings

Endler 1978; Harden-Jones 1968; Leggett 1977; McKeown 1984; Pitcher 1993; Radakov 1972; Shaw 1978.

PART III
THE FISHES

CHAPTER **12**

Systematics

Systematics is the study of the evolutionary relationships among organisms. In modern usage it has become nearly synonymous with taxonomy, the science of describing and classifying organisms, because most classification systems of organisms are considered to reflect evolutionary relationships. Modern taxonomy had its beginnings, however, in the work of Carolus Linnaeus, who believed each species to be an unchanging entity, created by God. The binomial system of nomenclature he developed for species, and the hierarchical classification system he used for higher categories, proved to be exceedingly useful in organizing the rapidly expanding knowledge of animals and plants. Although Linnaeus's distinctions among species and, especially, higher categories were often rather arbitrary (by our standards), later workers (including many prominent ichthyologists; see Chapter 1) modified his system to reflect presumed evolutionary relationships among the various taxa. By the late nineteenth century, evolutionary trees were being drawn; ancestral, presumably primitive, forms were placed near the base of such trees, while successively higher branches led to more advanced, or at least more modern, forms. There were two main problems with such trees: (1) They implied that evolution is more or less linear, with each lineage somehow striving toward some perfect organism (e.g., humans); and (2) the location of the branches depended in good part on how a particular investigator felt about the relationships of the organisms or groups making up the tree.

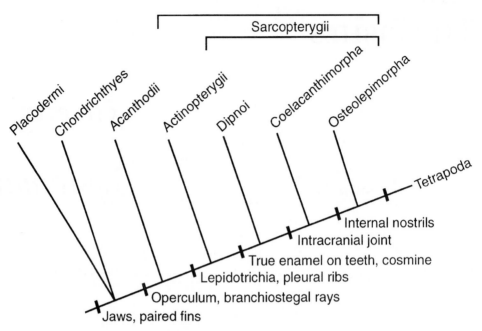

FIGURE 12.1 *Cladogram showing probable evolutionary relationships (phylogeny) among major groups of fishes, plus the tetrapods. The dark crossbars indicate ancestral characters that are shared by most members of the group ahead of each bar but not in the group behind the bar. The characters listed for each bar are only a few of the more obvious ones. The tetrapods are the uppermost group in the diagram because they were the last to evolve. The various groups are discussed in detail in Chapter 13. (Based on cladograms in Lauder and Liem [1983] and Bemis et al. [1986], which also show some alternative arrangements.)*

The modern descendants of such trees are hierarchical diagrams such as presented in Figure 1.1. Such diagrams are very handy for showing how major groups relate to one another, and they are designed to show evolutionary relationships. Nevertheless, they are still somewhat arbitrary, as there are no firm rules as to how the divisions are made or what makes, for example, the Chondrichthyes and Osteichthyes both a class. In an effort to make the decision-making process for the branches less arbitrary, the methods of *phylogenetic systematics* were developed by Willi Hennig and adopted by systematic ichthyologists (Nelson 1972a; Mayden 1992). This method works with branching diagrams, called *cladograms,* in which each branch represents a monophyletic group of organisms (populations, species, families, orders etc.). A *monophyletic group* is one that is assumed to have a common ancestor; therefore, all members share one or more distinctive derived characters. These characters can be defined precisely, and their presence or absence in groups allows the systematist to construct a cladogram of the groups following specific rules, rather than whims. Each cladogram essentially represents a series of evolutionary hypotheses. An example of a cladogram showing the phylogeny of the major groups of fishes is presented in Figure 12.1 along with some of the characters used to define each group. Detailed explanations of the method can be found in Lundberg and McDade (1990) and Mayden and Wiley (1992).

TAXONOMIC METHODS

The information used in developing an understanding of evolutionary relationships among fishes comes largely from detailed taxonomic studies, particularly careful descriptions of species. Such studies are the foundation of ichthyology (see Chapter 1) and are more necessary than ever, not only as a basis for evolutionary, ecological, and physiological studies but for conservation as well. Today, major decisions on land and water use are being made on the basis of arcane aspects of taxonomy that indicate whether an endangered population of fish is an entire species (and therefore unique), or whether it is part of a widely distributed species (and therefore less worthy of protection). The basic methods used in taxonomic studies fall into six categories: (1) morphometric measurements, (2) meristic traits, (3) anatomical characteristics, (4) color patterns, (5) karyotypes, and (6) biochemical characteristics.

Morphometric measurements are any standard measurements that can be made on a fish, such as standard length, snout length, length of longest ray on the dorsal fin, or depth of caudal peduncle. General instructions for making these measurements are found in Hubbs and Lagler (1964) and Strauss and Bond (1990). Since these measurements change as a fish grows, they are usually expressed as ratios to standard length (or some other measurement that is easily made). Even such ratios, however, are most useful if comparisons are made between samples of fish of approximately the same size and sex, because the growth of a fish is not always proportional in all directions, and sexual dimorphism is common among fishes (but often not obvious). In an effort to standardize morphometric measurements and make them more comparable among species, a *truss protocol* has been developed, in which a systematic set of measurements is made between anatomical "landmarks" on a fish such as a measurement of the distance between the base of dorsal fin to base of anal fin (Strauss and Bond 1990).

Meristic traits are often considered to be the most reliable taxonomic characteristics because most are easy to determine. Meristic traits include anything on a fish that can be counted, such as vertebrae, fin rays and spines, scale rows, pyloric ceca, and lateral-line pores. Because there is often considerable variation in these characteristics within a species, it is important to make the counts on enough individuals so that means, ranges, and standard errors can be determined. One of the biggest sources of variation in meristic counts is human error, especially on small fish. Such error is reduced if standard methods are used. Another source of variation is the conditions under which larval fish develop. Any factor that affects larval growth, such as temperature, dissolved oxygen concentration, salinity, or food availability, is likely to affect meristic characters (Barlow 1961; Johnson and Barnett 1975).

Anatomical characteristics are hard to quantify but are nevertheless important for species descriptions. They include shape, completeness, and position of the lateral line; position and size of internal organs; special anatomical features (such as air-breathing and electrical organs); secondary sexual characteristics (such as breeding tubercles on males); and the shapes, sizes, positions, and interrelationships of bones, nerves, and muscles. Most of these are yes-no characteristics: either a fish has them or it does not. As a consequence they can be definitive characteristics, useful for separating not only species but also higher taxa. However, even these characteristics are not always absolute, since occasionally individuals of a species are found that possess characteristics supposedly definitive for another, closely related species. Thus basibranchial teeth, usually a reliable feature for separating cutthroat trout from rainbow trout, are rarely found in "good" rainbow trout and are occasionally absent from "good" cutthroat trout.

Color patterns are perhaps the most variable characteristics of species, because they may change with age, time of day, or the environment in which a fish is found. Nevertheless they should be an important part of every species description, as color patterns are species specific, reflecting habitat, reproductive condition, sex, and methods of communicating with conspecifics (Chapter 11). The main problem with using color as a taxonomic tool is that it fades in preservatives, and descriptions of living fish tend to be highly subjective. However, some pigmentation patterns, such as dark spots and stripes, tend to be fairly permanent and can be used judiciously.

Karyotypes are descriptions of the number and morphology of chromosomes. The number of chromosomes per cell seems to be a rather conservative characteristic and so may be used as an indicator of the closeness of species interrelationships within families. The number and position of arms of chromosomes is even more conservative than chromosome number and is often equally useful in taxonomic studies. Thus in the course of an evolutionary change, two one-armed (acrocentric) chromosomes may fuse into a single two-armed (metacentric) chromosome, decreasing the chromosome number but not the number of arms. Another way chromosome number may increase is through polyploidy, which is the result of the failure of an entire set of chromosome pairs in a diploid cell to separate. The production of diploid gametes by this method is infrequent but common enough so that triploid and tetraploid individuals may result (Ohno 1974). Triploidy has been shown to be of significance in the origin of unisexual "species" of poeciliid fishes in Mexico. Tetraploidy appears to have been important in the evolution of some species (Ohno 1974) and hence an important taxonomic indicator. For example, carp, goldfish, and barbel all have approximately double the number of chromosome arms of other cyprinids, as do all members of the derivative family Catostomidae (Uyeno and Smith 1972), indicating that tetraploidy may have played an important role in the early evolution of these successful species. Similarly, salmon, trout, whitefish, and graylings (Salmonidae) all have double the number of chromosome arms of more ancestral members of the order Salmoniformes.

Biochemical characteristics are patterns in proteins and genetic material that are typically used to quantify genetic differences among populations. These techniques have come into vogue as a result of the rapid development of molecular biology in past decades. The principal biochemical techniques used are electrophoresis and various methods of analyzing DNA composition and structure. *Electrophoresis* evaluates the protein (allozyme) similarities of species. Proteins are encoded by loci on DNA, so analysis of variants in proteins encoded at different loci (= alleles) becomes a genetic measure. In this technique a tissue sample is treated mechanically to disrupt the membrane structure of the cells, thereby releasing water-soluble proteins. The resulting solution is placed in a gel, usually made of starch or agar, which is then subjected to an electric current. Each protein migrates in response to the current at a rate that depends on its molecular size and electric charge. The proteins (alleles) can then be identified, and the genetic similarity of individuals and species can be compared by noting the presence and absence of proteins as well as differences in their position in the gels. A slight difference in the molecular structure of a protein can result in its having a different net charge and hence a different position in the gel. The number of such differences encountered between two samples is considered to be an index of genetic similarity and, if the samples involve different species, of the closeness of their evolutionary relationship. Usually species have unique alleles or combinations of them which can be useful for identification of species, especially when there are doubts about the identity of morphologically similar species (Leary and Booke 1990).

Although electrophoresis has proven to be a powerful tool in systematics, more direct measures of genetic structure, techniques that make some measure of DNA sequencing, are displacing it for many studies. These techniques have the advantages of being able to use small samples of tissue (so the fish does not have to be killed to be characterized); of being able to use tissue from preserved or even fossil material; and of having the potential to measure variation of over 3 billion DNA sequences (Wirgin and Waldman 1994). Two basic kinds of DNA are present in cells, mitochondrial DNA and nuclear DNA. Mitochondrial DNA is particularly useful for analysis of populations within a species because it lacks recombination, it has a simple inheritance pattern (through the mother), and it evolves faster than nuclear DNA. On the other hand, nuclear DNA is much more abundant and contains about 3 billion nucleotide subunits, as opposed to 20,000 for mitochondrial DNA (but virtually all of them encode proteins). One technique for analyzing DNA is to compare the exact sequence of base pairs on a standard section of DNA, which can now be done (after some preparation!) by automated DNA sequencers. Another technique is to break up the DNA strands using standardized enzymes (restriction endonucleases) and then compare the number and size of the fragments using electrophoresis; this technique is known as DNA "fingerprinting." Wirgin and Waldman (1994) point out the many uses that are being found for DNA techniques in taxonomy and fisheries management, such as identification of distinct stocks of striped bass, salmon, and other fishes even when they are mixed in the ocean.

SPECIATION

One of the main purposes of taxonomy is to demonstrate how species or other categories differ from one another, while systematics deals with their evolutionary relationships. Because the evolutionary events on which systematics is based took place in the distant past and cannot be studied directly, it is important to study the processes that are leading to species formation at the present time. These processes can be surprisingly rapid.

In most cases it is assumed that the factor most important for species formation is geographic isolation of a population from related populations. In isolation, different selection pressures, combined with intrinsic factors such as size and makeup of the gene pool of the isolated population, result in divergence. A population that has its origin in a small number of individuals that became isolated from the main population may show differences that result from the unique genetic makeup of the "founding" organisms (the *founder effect*). Given sufficient time, this divergence will continue until the population is able to retain its genetic identity after it comes into contact again with other, similarly derived populations, even if some hybridization occurs. For example, Nelson (1968) found that two species of suckers (Catostomidae) evolved from a common ancestral population during the Pleistocene, after advancing glaciers isolated one portion of the population in the Columbia River drainage and the other portion in the eastern United States. In recent years, one species has, by natural means, entered the range of the other. The two species hybridize, but there appears to be little gene flow between them even though they are ecologically and reproductively still quite similar. In situations such as these, given time and continued lack of backcrossing, the two species can be expected to continue to diverge ecologically in the region of overlap, exaggerating whatever adaptive differences in morphology and behavior now exist *(character displacement)*.

In some situations, character displacement can occur very rapidly. In Lake Michigan, the native bloater *(Coregonus hoyi)* switched from plankton feeding to benthic feeding in the face of apparent competition from the introduced alewife *(Alosa pseudoharengus)*. In less than 20 years, the selection pressures for more efficient foraging on the bottom resulted in bloaters with both fewer and shorter gill rakers (Crowder 1984). This rapid shift seems to have been a key to the continued success of the bloater in Lake Michigan when other plankton-feeding fishes have suffered drastic declines.

While the rapid change in bloaters indicates that evolution can take place at a rapid pace under certain conditions, there is considerable debate as to how long it takes for species to become distinct from one another. Many, perhaps most, of the subspecies of fish we recognize evolved in response to Pleistocene or post-Pleistocene conditions, in less than 20,000 years. For example, the Cottonball Marsh pupfish *(Cyprinodon salinus milleri)* of Death Valley has been isolated from the form from which it is derived *(C.s. salinus)* for less than 4000 years. Similarly, Moodie and Reimchen (1976) indicate that populations of threespine sticklebacks on islands off the British Columbia coast have diverged to the species level in 8000 to 10,000 years. More usual estimates for the amount of time required for adaptive differentiation of fish to have reached the species level are between 100,000 and several million years (e.g., Avise et al. 1975).

While all allopatric (geographic) speciation offers the best explanation for most speciation events that have been studied, there are some examples that do not fit the model well and so are candidates for sympatric speciation. Sympatric speciation occurs when two forms diverge without geographic isolation. Perhaps the best (but unusual) examples of sympatric speciation in fishes occur in the formation of unisexual species of poeciliids through hybridization of two or three bisexual species (see Chapter 9). This type of speciation can even be repeated using laboratory populations of the bisexual species (Schultz 1973; Vrijenhoek 1994). Whether or not sympatric speciation can occur in more normal situations is not really known but the presence of "flocks" of similar species in lakes is suspicious. Most spectacular of these flocks are the hundreds of species of haplochromine cichlids that occur in the Great Rift Lakes of eastern Africa, where the nature of cichlid reproductive systems makes sympatric speciation particularly plausible (see Chapter 33).

NOMENCLATURE

One of the most frustrating aspects of ichthyology for anyone who is not a taxonomist is the constant changing of the scientific names applied to fishes, at all levels from subspecies to kingdom. The changes in names throughout the three editions of this text alone (starting in 1982) have been substantial, and names the authors learned as students often seem quaintly archaic. The changes are nevertheless necessary, reflecting that fish systematics is a dynamic field; the rate at which names change reflects the rate at which we are obtaining new information about fish and their interrelationships. To ease the problem for journeyman biologists of fish and fisheries in the United States and Canada, every ten years the American Fisheries Society issues a standardized list of the names of common and scientific names of fishes (Robins et al. 1991). This has allowed the development of nearly universal, constant common names for fishes, while keeping interested individuals informed of changes in scientific nomenclature. The rainbow trout, for example, has been called rainbow trout for about 50 years, while its scientific name has changed completely (see below). In this section, we will discuss scientific names for (1) higher levels than species, and (2) species.

Higher-level names. Textbooks like this one and most discussions of systematics use a hierarchical system of names to designate how species and higher groups are related to one another. This is largely the result of a tradition going back to Linneaus which fits a very human need to put things into categories for purposes of learning. Thus we have the basic Kingdom—Phylum—Class—Order—Family—Species structure to taxonomic systems, with various subdivisions to make finer distinctions (e.g. superclass, subclass, infraclass).

The basic assumption behind all this is that all classes, orders, and families are equivalent levels for all fishes, even though there is no really standardized way of doing this. A class in one taxonomic system may be a superclass in another one or an order in yet another. The fact remains that each name usually does enclose a group of fishes with a recognizable set of characters. The elegant analyses now possible through cladistics demonstrate that these groups do exist in reality; but where one draws a line on a cladogram to separate a class from an order, for example, is still arbitrary. Cleverly, names on cladograms are generally not preceded by the level labels. Despite this problem, the hierarchical system of names does help organize knowledge of fishes in human brains (at least in those of ichthyologists, reputed to be human) and will so be continued to be used.

Species names. Each species is assigned a unique two-part scientific name: the genus name and the species name, which is often followed by the name of the person who first described it and the year in which it was described. For example, the longnose dace is designated *Rhinichthys cataractae* (Valenciennes, 1842). Valenciennes' name is in parentheses because he assigned the fish the species name but the genus name was subsequently changed; if his name had no parentheses around it, that would mean the genus name had remained unchanged since the time he described the species (a rare occurrence). As long as the longnose dace is recognized as a distinct species, its species name will be *cataractae;* however, the generic name can change depending on how ichthyologists perceive it is related to other species. The genus *Rhinichthys* now contains seven or eight (depending on who is counting) rather similar-looking species.

The changes in scientific names in a species frequently reflect changes in our understanding of the nature and relationships of the species. A classic example of this is the rainbow trout, *Oncorhynchus mykiss* (Walbaum 1792), which for over 150 years was listed as *Salmo gairdneri Richardson, 1836*[1] (Smith and Stearley 1989). John Richardson described the trout from specimens he had collected from the Columbia River in 1836. However, Johann Walbaum had described a similar species, *Salmo mykiss,* from the Kamchatka Peninsula of Asia in 1792. The similarity of the two "species" was recognized for a long time but unambiguous evidence that they belonged to the same species was not collected until the 1970s and 1980s by Russian and Japanese workers. Resistance of American workers to recognizing Russian science, however, delayed adoption of the name *Salmo mykiss* for North American populations. By the strict rules of scientific nomenclature, the earliest name had precedence. However, by the late 1980s new work on the family Salmonidae, to which rainbow trout belong, indicated that rainbow trout were much more closely related to Pacific salmon of the genus *Oncorhynchus* than they were to Atlantic salmon and trout of the genus *Salmo.* Thus rainbow trout were placed in *Oncorhynchus* and because the Russian species name was finally accepted at the same time, rainbow trout became *Oncorhynchus mykiss* (Smith and Stearly 1989).

The use of scientific names for fish are created from a mixture of Latin and Greek root words, a tradition that dates back to the time when entire species descriptions were in Latin. It has been retained as a useful tradition, not tied to any modern language. The names of the fishes are generally descriptive of the fish in some way or tell something of its history or habits. Figuring out what the names mean is a bit like working a crossword puzzle—a very satisfying, if esoteric, exercise. For example, for the longnose dace, *Rhin-ichthys* translates as "nose-fish" (referring to the long snout) and *cataractae* refers to the fast water in which it lives. For rainbow trout, *Onco-rhynchus* means "hook-snout" (referring to the hooked snout that develops in spawning salmon), while *mykiss* is supposedly the common name given to the fish by the natives of the Kamchatka.

HYBRIDIZATION

Hybridization is common among fish species, especially in fresh water (Hubbs 1955; Schwartz 1972), and its significance in the evolution of fishes is much debated. In some situations it can lead to the formation of new species, such as the unisexual mollies or the tetraploid fishes mentioned previously. Alternatively, it can lead to the elimination of species, especially if human interference allows fishes to move

---

[1]This is not precisely true because there were a number of other names used for rainbow trout simultaneously, but none of them stuck. For example, for many years resident rainbow trout were known as *Salmo irideus,* while steelhead (searun rainbow trout) were known as *S. gairdneri.*

over natural barriers. Thus cutthroat trout have been eliminated from much of their native range in the Great Basin of the United States by hybridizing with introduced rainbow trout. For a variety of reasons, the rainbow trout phenotype usually becomes dominant when hybridization takes place, after a number of generations.

Although hybrids between many species are known, the mere fact that members of two species can mate with each other and produce offspring does not mean they belong to the same population or even that they are not reproductively isolated from each other. The important test of the significance of hybridization between two populations is whether or not, under *natural conditions,* significant gene flow between them occurs, resulting in introgression of characters and eventually a continuum of forms from one population to the next. Many species of fishes will freely interbreed in captivity, producing fertile hybrids that will backcross with either parent species; many varieties of aquarium fishes are the result of such hybridization between species. Some of the best examples of this are in swordtails (Poeciliidae), which rarely, if ever, hybridize in the wild. Even when hybridization between fish species does occur in the wild, reproductive isolation is usually maintained because the hybrids either die before reaching sexual maturity, are sterile, or have low survival and/or fertility.

Hybrid sterility, in which the hybrids develop to adulthood but prove to be sterile, seems to be fairly common in fishes. Among the best-known examples are crosses among species of the genus *Lepomis* (Centrarchidae), especially the bluegill–green sunfish cross *(L. macrochirus x cyanellus).* This hybrid is common where the two species occur together; it presumably results mostly from male green sunfish sneaking into bluegill nests and releasing sperm when a pair of bluegill is spawning. The hybrids that result are all male and exhibit hybrid vigor (heterosis) in that they typically grow faster than either parent species. During the spawning season they build nests and defend them with great vigor, dominating the nonhybrid fish. However, such fish are sterile, so no introgression occurs between the two species.

Hybrids that are fertile typically have low survival rates and poor success at reproduction. The reasons for this are complex but are presumably related in part to their intermediate nature. In most cases the two parent species have a competitive advantage over the hybrids in occupying their respective niches. Hybrids are likely to be successful only when environmental conditions are intermediate. Thus hybrids between two species of darters (Percidae) are abundant only in stretches of stream that have been altered by humans, creating an intermediate type of habitat (Loos and Woolcott 1969). This hybridization seems to be the result of deliberate matings between members of two species. However, it is much more common among fishes for the matings to be accidental, the result of the mixing of sex products when two species spawn in the same area at the same time. For example, Tsai and Zeisel (1969) found that hybrids among three species of cyprinids were common in a small stream in the eastern United States because all three species spawned simultaneously on the gravel nest mound of yet another species.

Supplemental Readings

Bell 1976; Cailliet et al. 1986; Lundberg and McDade 1990; Mayden 1992.

CHAPTER 13

Evolution

The evolutionary history of fish is a complex and fascinating topic. However, the frequent lack of a good fossil record for critical periods of fish evolution, coupled with the diversity and specialized nature of both modern and fossil fish groups, makes controversies over relationships among major groups common. Even as the fossil record becomes better known, the controversies continue and increase, for as the paleontologist Alfred S. Romer has noted, the increasing knowledge of fossil forms often leads to a "triumphant loss of clarity." Partly for this reason, recent studies of the evolutionary relationships among fishes rely heavily on comparisons among living forms and on the use of cladistics (Patterson 1977). However, the results of the new inquiries into the evolutionary relationships of fishes still produce many contradictions. Thus the relationships described here should be regarded as tentative and are necessarily oversimplified.

The chordate ancestors of fish and, of course, vertebrates in general are assumed to be sessile forms that had free-swimming larvae for dispersal. The basic vertebrate organization presumably evolved as the larval stage became more active, perhaps as a means of increasing the probability that the larvae would land on a suitable site for the adult stage. Eventually, however, larvae capable of reproduction evolved (neoteny), and finally the sessile adult stage was lost altogether. It is usually hypothesized that the typical vertebrate organization evolved as these neotenous forms assumed an increasingly planktonic existence in the oceans. Alternatively, the organization may have developed among forms adapted for bottom feeding on organic particles, much like modern lamprey larvae do (Mallett 1984).

An interesting question is *where* did this early evolution take place? It is generally assumed to have happened in the ocean because this is the habitat of other chordates (Phylum Chordata, to which the vertebrates belong), and marine deposits contain most early vertebrate fossils. However, Griffith (1994) suggests that the earliest vertebrates may have been anadromous, much like modern lampreys, with the early life history stages adapted for living in fresh water.

One of the difficulties with the anadromous origins hypothesis is explaining how the conodonts (Conodonta) fit in. The conodonts are an ancient group of organisms that are known almost entirely from tiny (< 2 mm) tooth-like structures that are abundant in ancient marine sediments. They first appear in the sediments in late Cambrian times (ca. 510 million years ago) and disappear 300 million years later. Recent discoveries of fossils of the conodont organism indicate they were most likely chordates; they had large eyes and eel-like bodies supported by a notochord, and were probably free-swimming (Briggs 1992). Analysis of the composition of the teeth indicates they have an outer coating of enamel over a layer of bone-like material, much like vertebrate teeth (Sansom et al. 1992) although there is some doubt that the enamel and bone are identical to that of vertebrates (Forey and Janvier 1993). If conodonts are indeed vertebrates, then they are the earliest known vertebrates by 40 million years (Fig. 13.1). This also opens up some intriguing questions about their phylogenetic relationships to the rest of the vertebrates and to the modern hagfishes (Myxini), which arguably can be excluded from the vertebrates because they lack bone and vertebrae (see Chapter 14).

OSTRACODERMS[1]

The earliest history of the vertebrates is necessarily speculative, because the first undoubted fossils are broken pieces of bony armor from jawless fish known as ostracoderms. The first fossils are found in marine deposits from the Ordovician period, about 460 million years ago, and they were abundant and diverse for about 100 million years (Forey and Janvier 1994). About 600 species have been described, representing about nine evolutionary lines that seem be as different from one another as the Chondrichthyes and Osteichthyes are from one another today.

Although the ostracoderms were quite diverse, they all had a basic body plan that seems to have limited their ability to become as ecologically diverse as later fish groups, which may explain in part why they eventually became extinct. The

---

[1]The ostracoderms (meaning shell-skinned) were once regarded as being a unified taxon of fossil jawless fishes as distinct from the modern lampreys and hagfishes, placed together in the Cyclostomata. All the jawless fishes were then placed within the Agnatha, with the idea that there were a number of distinct evolutionary lines within the ostracoderms, one which gave rise to the lampreys and another to the hagfishes. More recent research indicates the Agnatha represents several evolutionary lines rather than one, so the term is not used here.

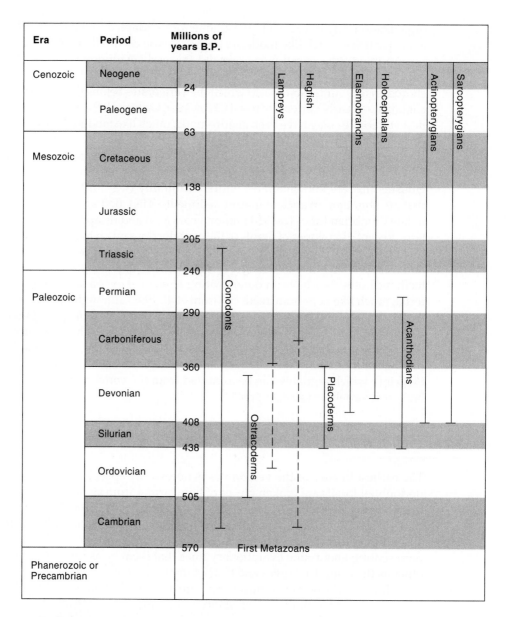

FIGURE 13.1 *Geologic periods and time lines of major groups of fish.*

ostracoderms were characterized by the lack of jaws, the lack of paired fins (with some possible exceptions), the presence of bony armor, an internal cartilaginous skeleton, and a heterocercal tail. The armor tended to be fairly massive around the head and more scale-like on the body. Most ostracoderms were quite small, less than 15 cm long and dorsoventrally flattened. Their overall body structure indicates that they were mostly bottom dwellers that lived by sucking up organic ooze and small

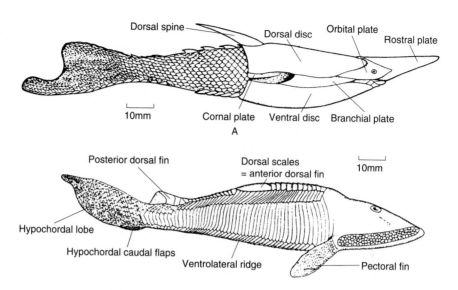

FIGURE 13.2 *Ostracoderms: (A)* Pteropsis rostrata *(Pteraspidiformes); and (B)* Hemicyclaspis murchisoni *(Cephalaspidiformes). (From Moy-Thomas and Miles 1971.)*

invertebrates. However, one curious group (the "fork-tailed thelodonts") was deep-bodied and large-eyed, suggesting other modes of existence were possible (Wilson and Caldwell 1993). The gills of ostracoderms, which were quite large, presumably served as food filters as well as respiratory organs much like those of the fishlike chordate, amphioxus. Ostracoderms presumably moved about much like tadpoles do, because most lacked the control of movement granted by paired fins. Later ostracoderms did develop bony, finlike structures behind the gill openings that undoubtedly increased their stability and maneuverability. In one group (Osteostraci), the fins appear to be true pectoral fins, indicating a close relationship of this group to jawed fishes (Forey and Janvier 1994). However, the habits of these advanced forms are a bit of a mystery because most of them also had reverse heterocercal tails (Fig. 13.2). Such a tail would tend to push the animals off the bottom.

The armor is one of the most interesting features of the ostracoderms because it represents the first undoubted bone. It is generally assumed that the bony armor evolved for protection against predators, although its use as an osmotic barrier in freshwater forms and as a phosphate storage mechanism have also been suggested (Halstead 1968). Thanks to the work of Swedish paleontologist E. A. Stensio and his students, who carefully sectioned and analyzed numerous ostracoderm fossils, many other details of ostracoderm structure are also known, including a surprising amount about the structure of the nervous system. Despite the growing amounts of information, there is still a great deal of uncertainty as to how the ostracoderms relate to the jawed vertebrates or to the lampreys and hagfishes. Forey and Janvier (1993, 1994) support the general idea that the ostracoderms are more closely related to the jawed vertebrates than are the lampreys, which in turn are more closely related to ostracoderms and jawed vertebrates than are the hagfishes. Their analysis indicates that the unarmored, boneless condition of lampreys and hagfishes represents the ancestral condition, rather than representing the result of secondary loss of ostracoderm armor (as has generally been thought).

PLACODERMI

The first major group of fishes to appear after the ostracoderms was the placoderms (Class Placodermi, meaning plate-skinned). Another group, the Acanthodii, actually appeared earlier in the fossil record and are important as the earliest known jawed fishes. However, they remained a minor element of the fish fauna for millions of years. The placoderms, which also possessed jaws, dominated the waters of the late Devonian period and died out completely in the lower Carboniferous period (about 350 million years ago). They were a highly diverse group of fishes, often very bizarre in appearance, but appear to share a common ancestry based on the structure of their armor, especially a ring of interlocking plates around the shoulder region (Young 1986). The large bony plate on the head region of most placoderms has a joint-like attachment to the bony plates covering the trunk. Besides their distinctive covering of dermal bony plates, placoderms have an internal body skeleton, paired fins, jaws, and a dorsoventrally compressed body (Fig. 13.3).

The development of this combination of characteristics permitted the placoderms to achieve a much greater ecological diversity than the ostracoderms. Indeed, the jaws, paired fins, and internal skeleton are characteristics fundamental to the fishes that eventually replaced them. At the same time, their bony armor, flattened bodies, and other specializations seem to have pretty much limited them to the role of bottom dwellers (with a few exceptions). Their success as bottom dwellers was considerable; this is perhaps best attributed to the development of jaws (from the first gill arch), which enabled them to become predators. During their Devonian heyday, large-jawed predators such as the arthrodires achieved lengths of 6m or more. The failure of the placoderms to evolve more advanced types of jaw suspension and true teeth, both characteristics of the Osteichthyes and Chondrichthyes, may have been partially responsible for their replacement by these two groups.

What is the significance of the placoderms in the evolution of modern fishes? No satisfactory answer to this question yet exists. They appear in the fossil record at a time when we would expect to find ancestors of the modern groups, yet they are so bizarre and specialized that it hardly seems possible they could have served as such ancestors. Seven distinct evolutionary lines within the placoderms are recognized (Young 1986), but none show any special affinities to modern fishes. As A.S. Romer (1966) indicated, it would make things much easier for students of fish evolution if the placoderms had never existed! There is some weak evidence that the placoderms are related to the Chondrichthyes (Moy-Thomas and Miles 1971; Young 1986); however, they are best regarded as a lineage independent of the other two main lines until more evidence is accumulated.

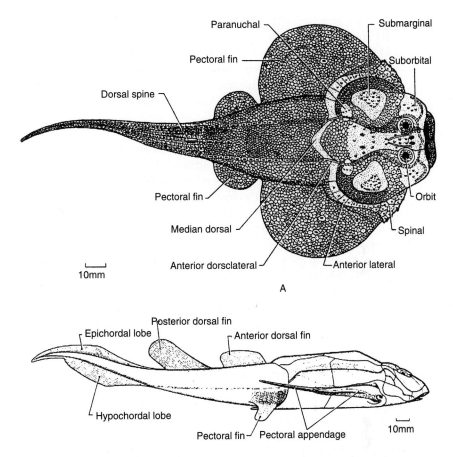

FIGURE 13.3 *Placoderms: (A)* Gemuendina, *dorsal view (Rhenaniformes); and (B)* Bothriolepis *(Antiarchiformes). (From Moy-Thomas and Miles 1971.)*

CHONDRICHTHYES

The cartilaginous fishes (class Chondrichthyes) are an easier group to define than the bony fishes (class Osteichthyes) partly because there are only about 850 species and partly because the fossil groups (with a few exceptions) are so poorly known that the characteristics of the living forms suffice for the entire class. Distinctive anatomical characteristics include: (1) cartilaginous skeleton, (2) teeth that are not fused to the jaw and are replaced in rows, (3) presence of unsegmented, epidermal fin rays (ceratotrichia), (4) single, ventral nostrils on each side of head, (5) spiral valve intestine, and (6) claspers on pelvic fins of males, indicating internal fertilization. They also lack features of bony fish described later in this chapter. Some fossil forms may lack some of the above features; for example, well-preserved sharks from upper Devonian deposits lack claspers.

The Chondrichthyes first appeared in the fossil record of the late Silurian period and they were common by the Devonian. Most deposits from which they are known are marine. This is in marked contrast to the bony fishes, which accomplished much of their early evolution in fresh water. Within the Chondrichthyes there are two distinct evolutionary lines, going back independently as far as the Devonian: the subclass Elasmobranchii (sharks and rays) and the subclass Holocephali (chimaeras).

Elasmobranchii. The elasmobranchs have been important predators in the oceans ever since the first sharklike forms appeared in the middle Devonian. Unfortunately, their lack of a bony skeleton means that good fossils are rare, although teeth and spines are often abundant as fossils. They seem to have achieved a successful combination of characteristics early in their evolution, and the greatest deviation from the basic body plan occurred when the rays (superorder Batoidea) appeared in the Jurassic period. The characteristics that distinguish the elasmobranchs are five to seven gill openings, plus a spiracle (secondarily lost in some forms); placoid scales; upper jaw (palatoquadrate cartilage) not fused to cranium, lower jaw attached with either amphistylic or hyostylic suspension (usually the latter in modern forms, which permits a large gape); and teeth numerous and rapidly replaced. With a few exceptions, elasmobranchs are top-level carnivores that are not particularly dependent on sight for prey capture (in contrast to most bony fishes).

The evolution of elasmobranchs is difficult to discuss, because it requires that leaps of imagination be made between the few well-preserved fossil forms and modern forms. The overall trend, however, is toward modest improvements of the basic Devonian shark design, with numerous side excursions into bottom-dwelling, invertebrate-feeding forms. The Devonian cladoselachian sharks (superorder Cladoselachimorpha, order Cladoselachiformes) had ancestral characteristics such as the lack of claspers, an elongate skull, amphistylic jaw suspension, and no anal fin; they also had broad-based, triangular, paired fins (Fig. 13.4). These early sharks had sharp, multicusped teeth (termed cladodont) and were undoubtedly predators on other fishes. However, when cephalopods and other molluscs radiated in the seas of the Carboniferous period, forms with flat, pavementlike teeth for crushing hard-shelled invertebrates became common. Curiously, while the cladoselachians were diversifying in salt water, another group—the xenacanth sharks (superorder Xenacanthimorpha, Xenacanthiformes)—were common in fresh water (Figure 13.4). They resembled the lobe-finned bony fishes in some respects but disappeared during the Triassic period.

During the Permian period, the cladoselachians were replaced by the hybodont sharks (superorder Selachimorpha, order Hybodontiformes), which are considered to be ancestral to the modern sharks, skates, and rays. The hybodont sharks seem to have been adapted for feeding primarily on large, active invertebrates (e.g., squid), because they had sharp teeth for biting in the front of their jaws but blunt teeth for crushing in the rear. During the Jurassic period, the hybodonts apparently gave rise to the modern lines of elasmobranchs: the three lines of sharks largely adapted for preying on bony fishes, albeit with many exceptions to this rule;

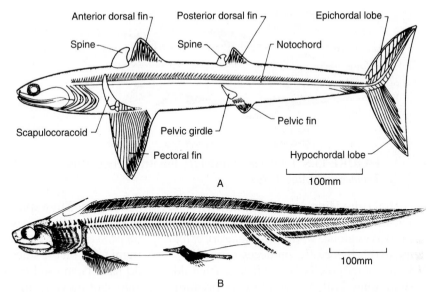

FIGURE 13.4 *Devonian Chondrichthyes: (A)* Cladoselache; *and (B)* Xenacanthus, *a freshwater form. (From Moy-Thomas and Miles 1971.)*

and the skates and rays (Batoidea), which are largely adapted for feeding on benthic invertebrates (also with many exceptions!). It should be emphasized, however, that ideas concerning the relationships of modern elasmobranchs are in a state of flux (Nelson 1994).

Holocephali. The Chimaeras (subclass Holocephali, order Chimaeriformes) are a strange group of bottom-dwelling, invertebrate-feeding fishes that have been present in small numbers apparently since the upper Devonian period. Among their more distinctive characteristics are a single gill cover over four gill openings, no spiracle, an upper jaw fused to the cranium, teeth consisting of only a few large flat plates (with very slow replacement when lost), and no scales. The males have a clasper on the head, in addition to ones on the pelvic fins. Modern-type chimaeras first appeared in the Jurassic period.

ACANTHODII

The so-called spiny sharks (Acanthodii) are the oldest known jawed vertebrates (having lived about 440 million years ago), so they have long excited the interests of students of vertebrate evolution. Despite their early appearance in the fossil record, they were somewhat specialized forms. Most were small (less than 20 cm long) with large eyes and flexible, streamlined bodies covered with bony, dentine-tipped scales. However, their most distinctive feature was the stout, ornamented spines in front of all fins. In the earliest acanthodians there were also two rows of

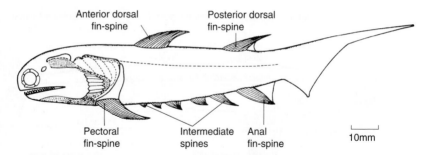

Anterior dorsal fin-spine

Posterior dorsal fin-spine

Pectoral fin-spine

Intermediate spines

Anal fin-spine

10mm

FIGURE 13.5 *Typical acanthodian,* Climatius reticulatus. *(From Moy-Thomas and Miles 1971.)*

ventral paired fins, one row on each side and each fin preceded by a spine (Fig. 13.5). The number of fins in a row was variable, and the presence of the row is frequently cited as evidence of the *fin-fold theory of the origin of paired fins* (and limbs). According to this theory, the predecessors of fins were lateral folds on the sides of the presumably tadpolelike early fishes. The folds would have been used for stabilizing swimming. With an evolutionary premium on control of movement, the fin-fold, by this theory, became subdivided into controllable segments, and eventually the intermediate segments were lost, leaving the standard two sets of paired fins. The multiple paired fins of early acanthodians represent the intermediate stage of the progression. Most acanthodians lacked the multiple paired fins and persisted as specialized plankton feeders in freshwater and marine environments well into the Permian period, long after the much more abundant and diverse placoderms had become extinct.

The relationship of the acanthodians to other fishes is controversial. Early workers usually placed them in with the placoderms, as just one more peculiar group. In the past 30 years or so, various workers have considered them to be an early offshoot of the Osteichthyes, while others have found them to be more closely related to the Chondrichthyes. Jarvik (1977) thought they had a surprising number of features (structure of the jaws, gill arches, and pectoral fins, etc.) in common with modern sharks; but the presence of such features as bony opercula, branchiostegal rays, and three otoliths argue in favor of bony fish affinities (Nelson 1994).

OSTEICHTHYES

The bony fishes (class Osteichthyes) are a large, diverse group, with a fairly rich fossil record. For this reason they are a hard group to define precisely. There is no one feature that distinguishes modern forms, but rather a common structural pattern, combined with the absence of the features characterizing the Chondrichthyes and Agnatha. The most distinctive elements of the osteichthyan structural pattern are the presence of lungs, bone, bony scales, and lepidotrichia.

Lungs (represented as swimbladders in derived forms) presumably indicate that the early steps of bony fish evolution took place in fresh water in a tropical region, where the ability to breathe air would be advantageous as protection against periods of stagnation. The history of the development of the lungs into a swimbladder that acts primarily as a hydrostatic (buoyancy) organ is an interesting one, because it reflects the overall structural changes that have taken place in the course of bony fish evolution. The first lungs were probably ventral outpouchings of the gut that evolved in fishes that survived in stagnant waters by swallowing bubbles of air and exchanging oxygen and carbon dioxide through the gut. Ventral lungs still characterize the South American and African lungfishes (Lepidosireniformes) and tetrapods. However, such lungs present problems to fish that swim about actively, because a pocket of air under the gut tends to make a fish top-heavy and subject to rolling over. The earliest solution to this problem seems to have been the development of a dorsal lung with a ventral opening. This situation is still found in the Australian lungfish (Ceratodontidae). The next step, found in most modern bony fishes, is to have a dorsal "lung" with a dorsal connection. Such swimbladders function primarily to keep the fish buoyant in the water. In many forms, the connection to the gut is lost altogether and gases enter and leave the swimbladder entirely through the circulatory system. In addition, a number of teleosts have secondarily lost the swimbladder entirely, largely as an adaptation to a bottom-dwelling existence.

    Bone, or at least some ossification, is present in most Osteichthyes, but it may be secondarily lost in a few forms such as the sturgeons and paddlefishes (Acipenseriformes) and the lungfishes. The skeletal structure of the head, although quite variable, also seems to have a general osteichthyan pattern, particularly in relation to the importance of dermal bone in making up the skull and jaws.

    Scales in ancestral bony fishes contain a layer of dermal bone overlaid by enamel, forming very solid but flexible armor. In more derived fishes, the bony layer has been lost and the scales consist of a thinly structured material called isopedine (Sire 1990). Scales, like bone and swimbladder, may be secondarily lost in some groups of fishes.

    Lepidotrichia, like scales, are of dermal origin, and are probably derived from scales. They form the soft rays of the fins, which are segmented and dumbbell-shaped in cross section.

    True bony fishes first appear in the fossil record of the lower Devonian period. Most of these early bony fish are from freshwater deposits, a good indication that bony fishes in general originally evolved in fresh water. The two major evolutionary lines of the modern Osteichthyes appear in the fossil record nearly simultaneously: Sarcopterygii (lobe-finned fishes) and Actinopterygii (ray-finned fishes).

SARCOPTERYGII

The relationships among the lobe-finned fishes and their relationships to other groups is a subject of heated (well, warm) debate and no doubt will continue to be. The reasons for this are that (1) modern forms are highly specialized; (2) smashed fossils that characterize the ancestral forms of a group are always subject to reinterpretation; (3) tetrapods (including humans) are a subgroup of the Sarcopterygii;

and (4) the modern fishes within the group are few and highly specialized. One of the distinctive features of this group are fins with bony leg-like supports. As a variation on the theme of Nelson (1994), we present the lobe-finned fishes as five subclasses: Coelacanthimorpha, Porolepimorpha, Dipnoi, Rhizodontimorhpha, Osteolepimorpha, and Tetrapoda. The porolepimorphs and rhizondontimorphs are obscure fossil groups that will not be discussed further, while the tetrapods are outside the study of ichthyology.

Coelacanthimorpha. The coelacanths are a distinctive group of predatory fishes with a long fossil record and one living form. They are easily recognized by their three-lobed (diphycercal) tail (with the vertebral column entering the middle lobe), forward-placed dorsal fin, and large cosmoid scales (see Chapter 16). They also have external nostrils (as opposed to having choana), no branchiostegal rays, a large swimbladder, and unbranched lepidotrichia (fin rays). One of the more fascinating aspects of their biology is that they evolved initially in fresh water, became inhabitants of shallow water marine environments, and then disappeared from the fossil record in the Cretaceous period. It was thus a major ichthyological event when in 1938 coelacanths (*Latimeria chalumnae*) were discovered to be still living in the deep waters off the African coast, in the Indian Ocean. At the time, it was thought they were the closest living relatives to the tetrapods, a sort of living "missing link," but more recent work has cast doubt on this theory. However, the arguments about its position in the grand scheme of tetrapod evolution are continuing.

Dipnoi. The lungfishes have been a very conservative group in their evolution and have never achieved much diversity of form. However, their evolutionary history is well known because they have lived throughout their history in fresh waters prone to stagnation and drying up and hence conducive to the making of fossils. On the basis of these fossils, the amount of change from the earliest known forms to the present-day forms has been plotted (Fig. 13.6). Lungfish evolution seems to have been most rapid early in their history, but the rate of change has been extremely slow for the past 200 million years or so. This change in lungfish over their history has largely been one of reduction; this includes reduction in the amount of bone and in the number of skull bones, loss of various hard layers from the scales, and loss of the separation between the dorsal, caudal, and anal fins. Besides lungs and a largely cartilaginous skeleton, modern lungfishes are characterized by internal nostrils, platelike teeth, a spiral valve intestine, and many other features (Rosen et al. 1981). Because they do seem to be intermediate in so many of their characteristics, in the nineteenth century lungfishes were considered to be the fishes most closely allied to terrestrial vertebrates. Subsequently the similarities were regarded as largely the result of convergent evolution, making the lungfishes only an interesting evolutionary sideshow. Rosen et al. (1981), however, examined some fossil lungfishes closely and revived the idea that the lungfishes are in fact the closest piscine relatives of the tetrapods. This conclusion is controversial; other analyses (see Bemis et al. 1986) seem to point to a more distant relationship between tetrapods and lungfishes.

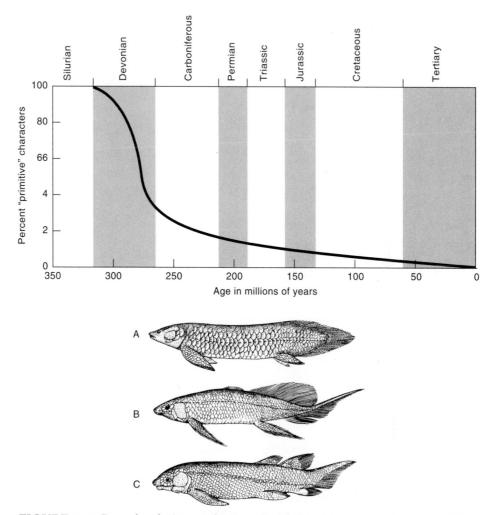

FIGURE 13.6 *Rate of evolutionary change in lungfishes, from ancestral characteristics (defined as those possessed by the Devonian genus* Dipnorhynchus*) to derived characteristics (those of the modern genus* Protopterus*). (After Westoll 1949.) The lungfishes illustrated are (A)* Neoceratodus *(recent); (B)* Scanmenacia *(late Devonian); and (C)* Dipterus *(middle Devonian).*

Osteolepimorpha. The osteolepids are of special interest to students of vertebrate evolution because they are intermediate in many ways between the first amphibians (Labyrinthodontia) and fish. Indeed, some authorities prefer to place the osteolepids and the labyrinthodont amphibians together in one group. The most dramatic characteristics that link the osteolepids and the early amphibians are the lobed fins, the means of jaw suspension, and the structure of the teeth (Fig. 13.7). The fins are lobed because they contain a series of bony elements that link them to the pelvic and pectoral girdles, much like tetrapod legs. The jaw suspension, like

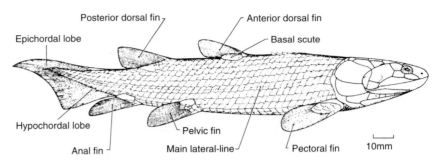

FIGURE 13.7 *An osteolepid sarcopterygian*, Osteolepis macrolepidotus. *(From Moy-Thomas and Miles 1971.)*

that of tetrapods, is autostylic, and the jaw connects directly to the brain case. The teeth have the complex foldings of the enamel—visible as grooves on the outside of each tooth—that are also found in labyrinthodont ("labyrinth tooth") amphibians. The osteolepids were mostly armored, air-breathing predators of tropical freshwater environments. They became extinct by the lower Permian period, replaced by the amphibians to which they gave rise.

For a long time, osteolepids and coelacanths were placed together as one evolutionary line. However, they differ in a number of fundamental ways: for example, osteolepids have internal nostrils (choana), branchiostegal rays, and branched lepidotrichia.

ACTINOPTERYGII

The subclass Actinopterygii (ray-finned fishes) contains most of the bony fish species that exist today. However, when they first appeared in the fossil record, in Devonian freshwater deposits, they were uncommon. By the beginning of the Carboniferous period some 360 million years ago, they had become the dominant freshwater fishes and had begun their invasion of the seas. The history of this group is one of constant change, with continuous "improvements" being made on the basic fish design, culminating in the modern teleosts. The ancestral features of the Actinopterygii include lepidotrichia, heavy ganoid scales, structurally distinctive pelvic and pectoral girdles, fins that are attached to the body by the fin rays (rather than with a fleshy lobe), branchiostegal rays, and no internal nostrils. The Actinopterygii can be divided into two major evolutionary groups, the infraclasses Chondrostei and Neopterygii. The odd African bichirs (with virtually no fossil record) are sometimes placed as a separate subclass (Brachiopterygii) because they are so distinctive structurally (Bjerring 1986). However, it is more likely that they are an early, specialized derivative of some early chondrostean line (Nelson 1994).

Chondrostei. The Chondrostei are the original ray-finned fishes, which achieved their greatest abundance and diversity in the Carboniferous period. The most important order within this group is the Palaeonisciformes, because the most ances-

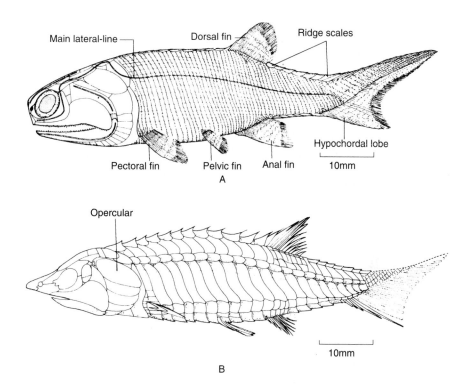

FIGURE 13.8 *Fossil Chondrostei: (A)* Moythomasia *(Devonian); and (B)* Phanerorhynchus *(Pennsylvanian). (From Moy-Thomas and Miles 1971.)*

tral and most numerous forms are placed within it and because its members probably gave rise to most of the Neopterygii. All modern chondrosteans (25 species) belong to the order Acipenseriformes, with its two highly specialized families, Acipenseridae (sturgeons) and Polyodontidae (paddlefishes) (see Chapter 16).

The ancient chondrosteans developed many of the body shapes, and presumably ways of living, that also characterize the more derived groups (Fig. 13.8). However, they also have many structural features considered to be ancestral because the fishes that replaced the chondrosteans had either lost or modified them. Among these features are (1) heavy ganoid scales (so called because the outer enamel layer is made up of a distinct substance, ganoine); (2) presence of a spiracle; (3) a heterocercal tail; (4) a cranium consisting of three strongly fused units of bone; (5) bones of upper jaw (maxilla and premaxilla) fused to cranium; and (6) no interopercular bone. In more derived fishes the structure of the skull is more complex and flexible, especially in relation to the jaws.

Neopterygii. This group contains most of the modern bony fishes and seems to be derived from one line of chondrosteans. Until recently, the neopterygians ("new fins") were generally divided into two infraclasses, Holostei and Teleostei. The holosteans were considered to be an intermediate evolutionary stage containing

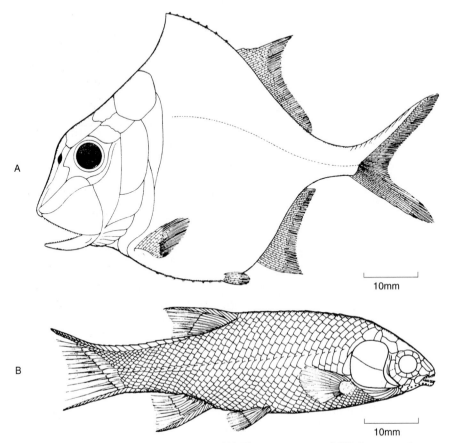

FIGURE 13.9 *Jurassic neopterygians: (A)* Platysomus; *and (B)* Acentropho-rus. *(From Moy-Thomas and Miles 1971.)*

many fossil forms as well as modern gars (Lepisosteiformes) and bowfin (Ami-iformes), two groups whose exact relationships to the teleosts are still uncertain (Olsen and McCune 1991). Although this classification system was convenient, it did not reflect the more complex reality of evolutionary trends among the fishes (see Fig. 1.1 for relationships). Early neopterygian fishes (Fig. 13.9) shared the seas and fresh waters with the chondrosteans through most of the Triassic, Jurassic, and Cretaceous periods but gradually became the dominant group. They presumably became dominant because of gradual but significant changes in structure that gave them a competitive edge over the chondrosteans. These changes culminated in the subdivision Teleostei, the dominant bony fishes today. The teleosts are a highly diverse group of fish that have a number of distinctive (but not necessarily exclusive) characters in common:

1. The operculum consists of four bones, including the interopercular bone (absent from chondrosteans), which is derived from a branchiostegal ray.
2. The tail is usually homocercal and partly supported by uroneural bones (modified from neural arches of vertebrae).

3. The scales, referred to as elasmoid scales, are made up of two thin layers, an external fibrous layer and an internal layer of isopedine.
4. The vertebrae are completely ossified and reduced in number from chondrosteans. Because of their structure, they are lighter and stronger as well.
5. The swimbladder is reduced in size and functions primarily as a hydrostatic organ.
6. Both the premaxillary and maxillary bones of the upper jaw are moveable. The premaxilla is usually the principal bone of the upper jaw.
7. The fins are highly maneuverable, giving teleosts good control over their movements.
8. The body shape is amazing in its variety, and a large number of the species are quite small (less than 30 cm long), enabling the teleosts to occupy niches and habitats not previously available to fishes.

STRUCTURAL CHANGES IN ACTINOPTERYGIANS

The characteristics of teleosts are the culmination of general trends in the evolution of actinopterygian fishes toward fishes that are capable of rapid and complex movements, have efficient respiratory systems, and are capable of using a wide variety of foods. This can be seen by examining the evolutionary changes within the Actinopterygii in some of the more obvious structures.

Scales. The general trend in scales has been a reduction in heaviness and complexity, along with an increase in flexibility. The heavy scales of chondrosteans must have served as a moderately flexible suit of armor. Such armor was a definite improvement over the solid sheets of bone used by the placoderms but still a heavy burden to carry around. It is probably significant that the surviving chondrosteans (sturgeons and paddlefishes) have no scales at all over most of their bodies. The early neopterygian scale, as found on modern gars, still had three layers, but the general trend in the group was to reduce the heaviness of these layers. This culminated in the thin, two-layered, elasmoid scale of teleosts, which is light and flexible. Many teleosts have gone a step further and eliminated scales altogether.

Branchiostegal rays. In fossil chondrosteans the floor of the branchial cavity is rather rigid, so water had to move across the gills by movements of the operculum, through the spiracle, or by simply being rammed across during swimming. The branchiostegal rays developed from bones in the floor of the branchial cavity. This increased the efficiency of active pumping of water across the gills. The efficiency of the "two-pump" respiratory system was further increased by the modification of one branchiostegal ray on each side to become part of the gill cover, as the interopercular bone. This bone, a definitive feature of teleosts, increased the size of the opercular cavity and hence the amount of water that could flow across the gills, as part of the two-pump respiratory system. A secondary, but equally important, function of the branchiostegal rays has been to permit feeding methods based on suction rather than grabbing. Thus the evolution of branchiostegal rays has been an important factor in the development of teleost diversity. Within the neopterygian fishes there is a general trend toward decreasing the number of branchiostegal rays, although a reverse trend is present in some groups.

Swimbladder. Presumably the swimbladder in the earliest actinopterygians functioned primarily as a lung, as it did for other bony fish groups. The general trend in actinopterygian evolution has been to increase the importance of the swimbladder's hydrostatic (buoyancy) function and to decrease its importance in respiration. In many teleosts the swimbladder is still connected to the gut by a tube, but the tube functions primarily as a means of regulating the volume of gas in the bladder to adjust buoyancy. In derived teleosts and in deepsea forms, even this connection is lost. In teleosts the swimbladder is also reduced in size. A final trend in swimbladder evolution has been for it to assume other functions in addition to being a hydrostatic organ. In many teleosts it serves as an amplifier of sound waves for hearing, and in some it is used for sound production as well. So specialized has the swimbladder become for nonrespiratory functions that most teleosts adapted for surviving in stagnant waters have developed other means for breathing air.

Jaws. In the course of actinopterygian evolution the jaws changed from being rigid, toothed structures adapted for biting and grabbing to much more flexible structures, often without teeth, adapted for feeding by a wide variety of methods. This is best illustrated by following the changes in the two principal bones of the upper jaw, the maxilla and premaxilla. In chondrosteans these bones are firmly united to the skull. The maxilla is the main bone of the upper jaw and possesses many sharp teeth. In ancestral neopterygian fishes the maxilla is reduced in size and is firmly attached to the skull only by its anterior portions. The premaxilla is greatly increased in size, and both bones still carry teeth. This arrangement developed in conjunction with branchiostegal rays and seems to be an intermediate step in the development of suction feeding. In most derived teleosts, the premaxilla is the dominant bone of the upper jaw and is largely free of strong attachments to other bones, so it can be easily extended. The maxilla in these fishes has become a sort of lever to increase the protrusibility of the premaxilla. The maxilla is usually without teeth, and they are frequently absent from the premaxilla as well. One of the results of having this type of mouth structure is that biting and chewing have to take place at some location other than the rim of the mouth. Thus predatory fish with protrusible premaxillae more often than not have pharyngeal teeth for this purpose. The flexible mouth also permits other types of feeding specializations to develop, such as plankton straining. In this case the O-shaped mouth opening is very efficient because it provides the maximum opening with the minimum perimeter. Suction feeding is most characteristic of the smaller invertebrate-feeding teleosts; large piscivorous forms tend to have a firm biting mouth with teeth, elliptical in cross section.

Tail. The original actinopterygian tail was heterocercal, but there seems to have been an inexorable trend in actinopterygian evolution toward the symmetrical, homocercal tail. The development of the homocercal tail is related in large part to the development of the swimbladder and neutral buoyancy, which eliminated the need for a heterocercal tail to provide lift. The homocercal tail is also advantageous for fast-swimming, pelagic forms (because it delivers uniform thrust); and for small, maneuverable forms that require a tail in which each ray can be controlled, for precise movements.

Fins. Two of the most important trends in fin structure have been the addition of spines and the changes in the positions of the pelvic and pectoral fins. True spines are characteristic of the most derived teleosts. Spines are antipredator devices that are usually best developed in fishes that cannot rely on speed to escape from their predators. Their development followed the loss of heavy bony scales and coincided with changes in the relative positions of the pelvic and pectoral fins. Basically, in more derived teleosts the pelvic fins are located immediately below, or even slightly anterior to, the pectoral fins, whereas in most other actinopterygians the pelvic fins are well behind the pectorals. The anterior positioning of the pelvic fins is associated with an increase in the maneuverability of the fish, because they are used for assisting the pectoral fins in controlling movement, rather than functioning primarily as stabilizers. The anterior positioning of the pelvic fins is also associated with the development of deep-bodied forms; even in deep-bodied chondrosteans the pelvic fins occupied a more anterior position than they did in elongate forms.

EVOLUTIONARY TRENDS WITHIN THE TELEOSTS

Modern teleosts seem to represent four distinct lineages (Figs. 1.1 and 13.10), although the relationships within and between the lineages are a matter of considerable debate. The present lineages were first recognized by Greenwood et al. (1966), who developed a provisional classification system that stirred up the modern debate on how teleosts are related to one another, a debate which was fueled by Lauder and Liem (1983). The first line (subdivision Osteoglossomorpha) is a very distinctive group of fishes, the bonytongues (Osteoglossiformes), represented by a few peculiar species scattered through the world fauna and by the 190 species of African electric fishes. The second line (subdivision Elopomorpha) includes three rather disparate orders—Elopiformes (tarpons), Anguilliformes (true eels), and Notacanthiformes (spiny eels)—that are united by the presence of a distinctive larval form. The third line (subdivision Clupeomorpha) is a highly specialized group of plankton feeders, the Clupeiformes (herrings, anchovies, etc.). The fourth line (subdivision Euteleostei) is the main line of teleost evolution, including over 22,000 species.

   The Euteleostei ("true teleosts") can be divided into a number of separate evolutionary lineages as well. One of the most distinctive (and largest) is the superorder Ostariophysi, the freshwater minnows, catfishes, and characins, which should perhaps be treated as yet a fifth line of teleostean evolution, rather than an early offshoot of the euteleostean line. A lineage with many generalized or ancestral euteleost characteristics is the Protacanthopterygii, containing the smelts, salmonids, and pikes. In contrast, the lineage with the most derived features is the

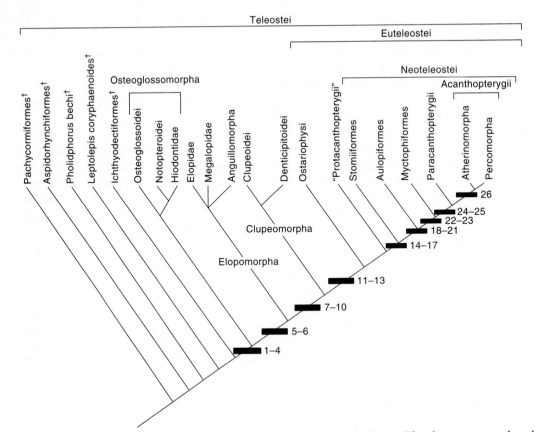

FIGURE 13.10 *Cladogram showing one version of a phylogeny of teleosts. The characters numbered at each dark bar are ancestral characters that can be found in all groups above the bar (although they may be lost secondarily) but not in the groups below the bar. Groups known from fossils only are indicated by a dagger. The characters indicated by each number are as follows:*

(1) presence of an endoskeletal basihyal bone; (2) four pharyngobranchials; (3) three hypobranchials present; (4) basibranchial and basihyal cartilages overlain by medium tooth plate; (5) two uroneurals extend anteriorly over the second ural centrum in support structure for caudal fin; (6) intermuscular bones present in abdominal and caudal regions of epipleural muscles; (7) retroarticular bone excluded from quadratomandibular joint surface; (8) toothplates fused with bones of gill arch; (9) neural arch on centrum of first ural vertebra reduced or absent; (10) articular bone of lower jaw fused with angular bone; (11) adipose fin present; (12) nuptial (breeding) tubercles present; (13) a membranous outgrowth of first uroneural bone in tail present; (14) retractor dorsalis muscle present; (15) rostral cartilage present; (16) tooth attachment to bone is distinctive; (17) portion of adductor mandibulae muscle of jaw has a tendon inserting on the quadrate, preopercular, or opercular bone; (18) neural spine on second preural vertebrae reduced; (19) tendon or retractor dorsalis muscle inserts on third pharyngealbranchial bone; (20) interoperculo-hyoid ligament present; (21) third epibranchial bone has toothplate fused to it; (22) pharyngohyoideus muscle inserts on urohyal bone; (23) fourth pharyngealbranchial reduced or absent; (24) ctenoid scales present; (25) premaxillary bone of upper jaw with expanded ascending and articular processes; (26) retractor dorsalis muscle inserts on third pharyngobranchial only. [Figure and information from Lauder and Liem (1983), which should be consulted for details.]

superorder Acanthopterygii ("spiny fins"), which contains numerous orders of the diverse spiny-rayed fishes, ranging from perch to seahorses to flounders. Between these two groups are other lineages whose relationships to the euteleosts and to each other is fairly fluid, although the cladogram developed by Lauder and Liem (1983, Fig. 13.10) is still largely valid, whether the groups are divided into four superorders as in Lauder and Liem (1983), or seven as in Nelson (1994, followed in this text). The relationships of the fishes within and between the lineages currently recognized are complex, so the classification system presented here will no doubt change as more is learned about them.

Supplemental Readings

Forey and Janvier 1993, 1994; Greenwood et al. 1966; Griffith 1994; Lauder and Liem 1983; Long 1995; Moy-Thomas and Miles 1971; Nelson 1984, 1994; Romer 1966; Rosen et al. 1981; Thomson, 1972; Westoll 1949.

CHAPTER 14

Hagfishes and Lampreys

PHYLUM CHORDATA
  Subphylum Myxini
    Class Myxini
      Order Myxiniformes
        Family Myxinidae (hagfishes)
  Subphylum Vertebrata
    Class Pteraspidomorphi[1]
    Class Cephalaspidomorphi
      Order Petromyzontiformes
        Family Petromyzontidae (lampreys)
      Order Anaspidiformes
      Order Galeaspidiformes
      Order Cephalaspidiformes

---

[1]The Pteraspidomorphi are an extinct group of ostracoderms, as are Anaspidiformes, Galeaspidiformes, and Cephalaspidiformes. Relationships among the various jawless (agnathan) fishes are highly uncertain.

The lampreys and hagfishes are slimy, eel-like, jawless, and without paired fins. They have long fascinated biologists as the only living representatives of the ancient creatures that gave rise to fish and humans. While they clearly possess many ancestral features, they also have many specializations that make them fascinating in their own right. As more has been learned about the two groups, it is clear that the lampreys and hagfish are as different from each other as either is from the jawed fishes (Table 14-1). Although superficially similar, lampreys and hagfishes are in fact extremely different (Table 14-1). The differences are so pronounced that arguments can be made to exclude the hagfishes from the vertebrates altogether, as is done here (see Chapter 13).

TABLE 14–1 DIFFERENCES BETWEEN ADULT LAMPREYS AND HAGFISHES, BASED ON INFORMATION IN HUBBS AND POTTER (1971), JANVIER (1981), AND PAPERS IN FOREMAN ET AL. (1985).

Characteristics	Lampreys	Hagfishes
Dorsal fin	One or two	None
Pre-anal fin	Absent	Present
Eyes	Well developed	Rudimentary
Extrinsic eye muscles	Present	Absent
Oral disc	Present	Absent
Lateral line system	Well developed	Absent
Barbels	Absent	Three pairs
Intestine	Ciliated	Unciliated
Spiral valve intestine	Present	Absent
Buccal glands	Present	Absent
Nostril location	On top of head	In front of head
Nasohypophysial sac	Does not open into pharynx	Opens into pharynx
External gill openings	Seven	One to 14
Internal gill openings	United	Separate
Cranium	Clearly cartilaginous	Poorly developed
Branchial skeleton	Well developed	Rudimentary
Vertebrae	Present	Absent
Spinal nerve pairs per body segment	Two	One
Ducts of Cuvier to heart	Right only	Left
Pronephric kidney	Absent	Present
Osmoregulation	Hyper- or hypoosmotic	Isosmotic
Eggs	Small without hooks	Very large with hooks
Cleavage of embryos	Holoblastic	Meroblastic

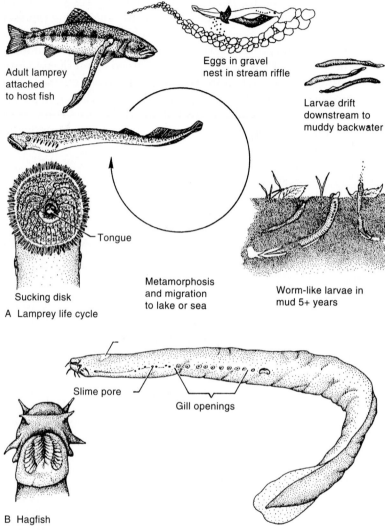

Adult lamprey attached to host fish

Eggs in gravel nest in stream riffle

Larvae drift downstream to muddy backwater

Tongue

Sucking disk

A Lamprey life cycle

Metamorphosis and migration to lake or sea

Worm-like larvae in mud 5+ years

Slime pore

Gill openings

B Hagfish

FIGURE 14.1 *Top: life cycle of the sea lamprey* (Petromyzon marinus). *Bottom: a typical hagfish* (Myxine). *(From Moyle 1993, copyright © 1993 by Chris Mari van Dyck.)*

HAGFISHES

Hagfishes are remarkable for their lack of striking external features (Fig. 14.1b). Linnaeus even classified them as worms! Wormlike, they live in part by scavenging on dead and dying fishes, so it is not uncommon for marine commercial fishermen who use set-lines or gill nets to find fish in their nets that have been burrowed into by hagfish. Once on deck the hagfish secrete incredible amounts of slime that sticks to both deck and fishermen (the stem *myxin* means slime). Despite these disadvantages, hagfish are now subject to fisheries themselves, for their tough skins. Leather items made out of "eel skin" are usually made of hagfish skin.

Structure. The most conspicuous structures on hagfish are the three pairs of barbels around the nostril and mouth, which are used as tactile organs. The single nostril connects to the pharynx and functions as the water intake for both respiration and the sense of smell. The eyes are rudimentary, visible mainly as shallow depressions on the top of the head. The ventral mouth is somewhat inconspicuous but contains a tongue with four rows of keratinized "teeth." These teeth work against each other and a cartilaginous dental plate to form a jawlike structure that is capable of tearing out pieces of flesh from dead fish. Along the sides of the body are from one to fourteen gill openings and a long series of pores that are the openings for the slime glands.

Hagfish also have such unusual features as a circulatory system with four "hearts" and a simple (pronephric) kidney, reflecting the fact that their internal salt concentrations are the same as that of sea water.

Life history. All of hagfish are marine. Most are found in water deeper than 25 m and at temperatures of less than 13°C, which means they are largely confined to temperate seas. Most hagfish are found in association with soft bottoms, into which they burrow and search for soft-bodied invertebrates as food. Although they prey extensively on invertebrates, hagfish apparently are also important scavengers on the ocean floor.

Hagfish are unknown from the stomachs of predatory fish. It appears that their main defense mechanism is their slime, with which they can coat themselves in large quantities quite quickly. The slime may also be used to coat dead fish and other "carrion" they encounter on the bottom, thereby making it unpalatable to other scavengers. In order to clear their gill openings and body surface of a heavy load of slime, hagfish have developed the remarkable ability to tie themselves in a knot, which passes down the body, pushing the slime away. The knotting behavior is also useful in giving hagfish extra leverage when taking a bite out of large fish. Little is known about reproduction in hagfish, except that each female lays only a small number (20 to 30) of large (2 cm to 3 cm), leathery eggs. The eggs have small hooklike structures on their ends for attaching to the bottom and to each other. When the young hatch from eggs, they are essentially miniature adults, so they do not undergo the dramatic metamorphosis of lampreys.

LAMPREYS

Lampreys have acquired an evil reputation in modern times because some species feed on fish also favored by humans, especially salmon and trout. Their habit of latching onto the sides of fish and sucking their blood and other body juices has caused them to be placed in the "nasty creature" category, along with vampires and leeches. This is despite the fact that their prey often survives the attack, which is not true of the prey of more conventional predators. Lampreys also have some value as a gourmet food item themselves. Indeed, Henry I of England died after overindulging himself in a dish of cooked lampreys. Lampreys are also useful as experimental animals; they are particularly useful for neurobiological studies because of their large nerves (Rovainen 1979).

Structure. The most distinctive feature of adult lampreys is their oral disc, with its numerous toothlike plates of keratin that cover the disc and tongue in species-specific patterns (Fig. 14.1a). These plates are used for grasping the prey and rasping the hole through which its fluids and tissues are sucked. Other features of lampreys (Table 14.1) also reflect the efficient means by which they have been able to take advantage of the abundant fishes that have replaced their ostracoderm ancestors. The sexes of spawning lampreys may be distinguished by the presence of an anal fin (ventral fin fold) on the female and of a penislike structure (genital papilla) on the male.

The larval lamprey *(ammocoete)*, in contrast to the adult, is adapted for living a secretive life buried in the mud of river backwaters, where it filter-feeds on algae and detritus. Structurally, the ammocoete has the most ancestral features of living vertebrates and is so different from the adult that the two were not connected until 1856. The eyes of ammocoetes are located beneath the skin of the head and are barely functional. In fact, the most important light-sensing organs are photosensitive cells in the tail. The fins are also barely visible and consist mostly of a low dorsal fold with a notch in the end to form the caudal fin. The most conspicuous feature of the ammocoete is the expanded pharynx, which is used for both respiration and feeding. Water is drawn into the pharynx by the movements of a special muscular structure (velum) in the anterior portion and by expansion and contraction of the posterior portion (branchial cavity). The water departs through seven gill slits on each side. In gill filaments and in the walls of the pharynx are goblet cells that secrete mucus. The mucus traps the particulate matter drawn into the pharynx and is swallowed in a continuous stream. This mechanism is very efficient but slow, so it requires dense concentrations of food to be effective (Mallatt 1982). Some mucus is also secreted to help stabilize the walls of the burrows in which ammocoetes live.

Distribution. Of the approximately 40 species of lamprey, four are known from temperate areas of the Southern Hemisphere, in South America, New Zealand, and Australia. The rest of the lampreys are widespread throughout the northern hemisphere.

Life history. One of the most fascinating aspects of lamprey biology is the presence of two distinct life history patterns. The most notorious lamprey species are those that migrate as adults to the ocean or large bodies of fresh water, where they prey on fish. Many of these predatory forms have given rise to nonmigratory "satellite species" that do not feed as adults (Vladykov and Kott 1977). The nonpredatory adults have poorly developed teeth, are small in size (usually less than 20 cm total length), and often inhabit small streams or streams located a great distance from the ocean or other sources of large fish. The adult stage generally lasts less than six months. Predatory species are most abundant as spawners in short coastal streams, but they may migrate as much as 250 km to 300 km up large streams. The adult stage of these species may last up to two years, although six to eight months of this time may be taken up with migrations, during which they do not feed. When feeding, they prey on a wide variety of fishes, concentrating on larger species. Vision seems to be the sense most involved in prey location, although there is some evidence that smell may be used as well. The lampreys grow rapidly on their diet of fish. Species that spend the predatory stage in the ocean reach a total length of 30 cm to 80 cm; those that spend this stage in fresh water seldom exceed 30 cm. The differences in sizes achieved by adults with different life history strategies is well illustrated by the lampreys of the Klamath River in Oregon and California. The anadromous Pacific lamprey *(Lampetra tridentata)* may reach lengths of 60 cm to 70 cm in this river. However, landlocked versions, which prey on fish in the lakes and reservoirs of the upper river, typically reach only 20 cm to 30 cm. The nonpredaceous species from this area seldom exceed 20 cm as adults.

Regardless of the size and feeding habits of the adults, the life cycle of lampreys from the time of spawning, through the ammocoetes stage, and through the period of metamorphosis shows the same basic pattern from species to species. The spawning adults generally choose a shallow, gravel-bottomed riffle as a spawning site, and spawning takes place in the late winter or early spring. The males tend to arrive first at the spawning site, and each begins to construct a nest depression by latching onto the larger stones in the site and pulling them downstream. Apparently attracted by olfactory cues released by the male, one or more females move into the nest site and help with nest construction. Spawning of each pair takes place repeatedly over a week or more. The eggs fall into the interstices of the gravel and then adhere to the gravel. The number of eggs per female varies with the species. The females of the anadromous sea lamprey *(Petromyzon marinus)* contain 124,000 to 260,000 eggs, whereas most females of nonpredatory lampreys contain only 1000 to 2000 eggs.

Newly hatched ammocoetes swim out of the nest and drift with the currents until they are swept into an area with a muddy bottom. They burrow into the mud and feed with only their oral hoods sticking out above the surface. The currents created by their feeding apparatus bring a steady stream of diatoms, desmids, detritus, and small invertebrates to the animal, although local depletions of digestible material apparently cause ammocoetes to change positions frequently. This stage usually lasts from three to seven years, and ammocoetes may grow to a total length in excess of 10 cm. Ammocoetes of the nonpredatory forms seem to spend one to two years longer as larvae than do those of the predatory forms.

Lampreys as predators. Under normal conditions, lampreys are "prudent" predators that do not seriously deplete the populations of their prey species. In some instances, prey species may have a very high incidence of scars from lamprey attacks. Such scars indicate that many of the fish that lampreys attack survive the experience. The attacks may seriously reduce the growth of the prey, but at least it is capable of reproducing itself. The outstanding exception to this general set of circumstances was the near-extinction of many fish populations following the invasion of the Great Lakes by sea lamprey. The lamprey moved into Lake Ontario about 1890 and into Lake Erie, via the Welland Canal, about 1921. By 1936 they were established in Lake Huron and Lake Michigan, and 10 years later they were established in Lake Superior. Following the invasion of each lake, the populations of the large fish species—such as lake trout, burbot, and lake whitefish—collapsed, as did the fisheries for them. The only exception to this was Lake Erie, which is too warm for the lampreys and has few streams suitable for spawning. An intensive research program following the disaster made the life cycle of the sea lamprey one of the best known of any aquatic vertebrate (Applegate 1950) and eventually resulted in the development of a poison that is rather specific for ammocoetes. Through the use of this lampricide and other control measures, the lamprey populations have been reduced, and most of the prey species have recovered their populations. However, the lamprey will never be eradicated from the Great Lakes, so continued control measures will be required to maintain the fish populations in them. It is interesting to note that in Cayuga Lake, New York, the sea lamprey manages to coexist with many of the same species that were depleted by lamprey predation in the Great Lakes. This seems to be a situation where predator and prey occurred together naturally and have coadapted so that both survive. Given enough time, presumably the same thing would happen to the Great Lakes. It is also worth noting that the control programs in the Great Lakes streams may be having a severely detrimental effect on the native nonpredaceous lampreys, which are being killed by the lampricide.

LESSONS FROM HAGFISHES AND LAMPREYS

Hagfishes and lampreys are continually teaching us new things about the evolution and biology of early vertebrates, as more is learned about their anatomy and physiology. There is also growing recognition that they are high successful creatures in their own way, preying or scavenging on the jawed fish that replaced the ostracoderms. They are not just "degenerate" ostracoderms as was once thought! In the Great Lakes, in fact, lampreys have exhibited an extraordinary capacity to colonize new habitats and to generate large populations, putting them in direct competition with human fishermen/predators. In less disturbed systems, lampreys are prudent predators that often do not kill their prey, indicating the importance of co-evolution in predator–prey systems.

Supplemental Readings

Applegate 1950; Brodal and Fange 1963; Foreman et al. 1985; Forey and Janvier 1994; Hardisty and Potter 1971; Vladykov and Kott 1979.

CHAPTER **15**

Sharks, Rays, and Chimaeras

CLASS CHONDRICHTHYES
  Subclass Elasmobranchi
    Superorder Galeomorphi
      Order Heterodontiformes
        Family Heterodontidae (horn sharks)
      Order Lamniformes
        Families Ondontaspididae (sand tigers), Mitsukurinidae (goblin shark), Pseudocarchariidae (crocodile shark), Lamnidae (mackerel sharks), Megachasmidae (megamouth shark), Alopidae (thresher sharks), Cetorhinidae (basking shark)
      Order Orectolobiformes
        Families Parascyllidae (collared carpet sharks), Brachaeluridae (blind sharks); Orectolobidae (wobbegons), Hemiscyllidae (bamboo sharks); Ginglystomatidae (nurse sharks), Stegostomatidae (zebra shark), Rhincodontidae (whale sharks)
      Order Carcharhiniformes
        Families Scyliorhinidae (cat sharks), Proscyllidae (finback cat sharks), Pseudotriakidae (false cat shark), Leptotchariidae (barbeled houndshark), Triakidae (houndsharks), Hemigaleidae (weasel sharks), Carcharhinidae (requiem sharks)

Superorder Squatinomorphi
   Order Squatiniformes
      Family Squatinidae (angel sharks)
Superorder Squalomorphi
   Order Hexanchiformes
      Families Chlamydoselachidae (frill sharks), Hexanchidae (cow sharks)
   Order Squaliformes
      Families Echinorhinidae (bramble sharks), Dalatiiae (sleeper sharks), Centrophoridae, Squalidae (dogfish sharks)
   Order Pristiophoriformes
      Family Pristiophoridae (saw sharks)
Superorder Batoidea
   Order Rajiformes
      Families Rhinidae, Rhinobatidae (guitarfishes), Rajidae (skates)
   Order Pristiformes
      Family Pristidae (sawfishes)
   Order Torpediniformes
      Families Torpedinidae (electric rays), Narcinidae (electric rays)
   Order Myliobatiformes
      Families Plesiobatidae (deepwater sting ray), Hexatrygonidae (longsnout sting ray), Dasayatidae (sting rays), Urolophidae (round sting rays), Gymnuridae (butterfly rays), Myliobatidae (eagle rays)
Subclass Holocephali
   Order Chimaeriformes
      Families Callorhynchidae (plownose chimaeras), Chimaeridae (shortnose chimaeras), Rhinochimaeridae (longnose chimaeras)

The sharks, rays, and chimaeras have long been held in low esteem by humans. As a group, they are generally considered to be vicious, inedible, and primitive. With a few notable exceptions, however, most members of this surprisingly diverse class possess none of these attributes. The common application of the word "primitive" to the group is particularly inappropriate because they are as specialized in their own way as are the teleosts among the bony fishes. The Chondrichthyes *are* less diverse than the teleosts, in the sense of having fewer species; and most of the species are predators on large invertebrates and fish, so extreme diversity in ways of making a living is also lacking. As predators, their success is undisputed. This success seems to be due to the particular combination of adaptive characteristics including those related to (1) buoyancy, (2) respiration, (3) external covering, (4) feeding, (5) movement, (6) sensory systems, (7) osmoregulation, and (8) reproduction. Because of their long separate evolution from the Osteichthyes, the Chondrichthyes have developed different solutions to the problems of being a fish. This aspect of their biology makes them particularly fascinating to ichthyologists.

Buoyancy. One of the major adaptive problems that the ancestors of modern fish groups had to "solve" in order to achieve a higher degree of ecological diversity was getting off the bottom and staying there without burning excessive amounts of energy. The ideal is to achieve neutral buoyancy, which many bony fishes have accomplished with a swimbladder. This particular solution does not seem to have been available to the Chondrichthyes, and this may be one of the main reasons why they never managed to occupy the niches typically occupied by small teleosts. One of the chondrichthyan solutions to the buoyancy problem was simply never to leave the bottom; a substantial number of modern forms are bottom dwelling (e.g., rays) or bottom oriented. Even these forms possess a feature that significantly reduces their average density: the cartilaginous skeleton. Other elasmobranchs benefit from the presence of huge oil-filled livers (oil is lighter than water) and/or the hydrodynamic lift created by the heterocercal tail while swimming, which also helps to keep them off the bottom (Chapter 3).

Respiration. The Chondrichthyes have three basic (but not mutually exclusive) means of respiration. First, slow-moving, bottom-oriented sharks have developed a "two-pump" respiratory system that works on the same principles as that of teleosts (Chapter 4) and provides for a steady flow of oxygenated water across the gills. Second, fast-moving sharks use "ram" ventilation, pushing the water across the gills in the process of swimming. Such sharks will die if they stop swimming. Third, the spiracles can be used to bring water to the gills, a technique especially favored by rays. The spiracles are small, round openings that immediately precede the principal gill openings on each side. In rays, they are located on the top of the head and thus can be used to draw water into the gill chambers while the fish is lying motionless on the bottom waiting to ambush prey or avoiding predators. Not surprisingly, the spiracles are greatly reduced or absent in pelagic sharks that ram water across the gills. In some pelagic sharks, however, the spiracles may operate as an independent respiratory system for supplying oxygen to the large muscles of the eyes.

External covering. All members of the Chondrichthyes have placoid scales in one form or another on the outside of their bodies. In skates and rays they are typically found only as a few rows of large denticles on the back, sometimes modified into spines (as in stingrays). In sharks the skin is filled with tiny, overlapping placoid scales, giving it a sandpaperlike feel. These scales form a lightweight, protective coat over the sides that seem to be particularly important in increasing hydrodynamic (swimming) efficiency. In fast-swimming sharks, there are channels between the scales that absorb turbulent flow, reducing the drag of the passing water (Moss 1984). Such placoid scales are characteristic of the oldest known sharks, yet it took the bony fishes several hundred million years to develop a scale covering (ctenoid scales) that apparently works as well as placoid scales for increasing the efficiency of swimming.

In more sluggish sharks, the placoid scales can be stouter and more projecting, often with sharp points, that work well as lightweight defensive armor. Placoid scales have been modified into a number of other structures as well, most conspicuously the "sting" of stingrays, the dorsal spines of dogfish sharks, and the defensive spines and denticles found on many skates. The teeth of sharks and rays are also modified placoid scales.

Feeding. Most members of the Chondrichthyes are specialized predators, and their dentition reflects this. Sharks that prey on large fish and marine mammals have triangular, bladelike teeth with which they can grab their prey and saw or snap off large chunks. The jaws of some such sharks can exert biting pressures in excess of 2800 kg/cm³. Because sharks cannot move their jaws back and forth in order to chew, when a large shark takes a bite out of a large prey, the shark must shake its head back and forth to get the "chewing" motion necessary. Each species of shark or ray has distinctive teeth that reflect the way it makes a living. Sharks that swallow their prey whole, usually fish, have teeth that come to long, thin points for holding onto the prey so it can be swallowed. Many small inshore sharks have rows of small sharp teeth that they use for feeding on small invertebrates. Some species will "graze" on the protruding siphons of clams, resulting in stomachs full of mysterious O-shaped rings of muscle. Many skates and rays have flattened, pavementlike teeth for crushing hard-shelled invertebrates. Some sharks, such as the horn sharks (Heterodontidae), have pointed teeth in front for grasping the prey but crushing teeth in the back of the jaw.

One of the more remarkable aspects of Chondrichthyan teeth is that they are continually being shed and replaced. Some sharks may consequently lose 30,000 teeth over their lifespan, dropping them either in rows or singly. Examination of the jaws of a shark reveals row upon row of teeth behind the front biting row, the next row ready to pop up as the outer one is lost. This results in a mouth full of ever-sharp teeth.

Aside from the teeth, the main reason sharks can ingest large prey is that their jaw suspension is hyostylic in most forms, which allows the gape to be maximized. The jaws are also rather loosely attached to the cranium, which increases their gape and flexibility. In rays, the loose connection has allowed the development of an ability to protrude the jaws a short distance for picking or pulling organisms off the bottom. This results in a structure very much like the suction mouth of teleost fishes.

Once the prey is ingested, it quickly reaches the large stomach, where the initial stages of digestion take place. From the stomach the food passes to the spiral valve intestine, a distinctive feature often considered to be primitive (presumably because only the most ancestral bony fishes possess one). In fact, the spiral value is a remarkably efficient way to increase the digestive surface area without increasing the length of the intestine.

Movement. How sharks and rays swim has already been discussed (Chapter 2), but it is worth emphasizing that the characteristic heterocercal tail of modern sharks is a complex organ that serves the fish well for propulsion, steering, and hydrodynamic stability. Some pelagic sharks (Lamnidae) have countercurrent exchangers in their circulatory system that permit them to be "warm-blooded" and increase the efficiency of their swimming (Chapter 3).

Rays use their pectoral fins for propulsion and literally fly through the water with their "wings."

Sensory systems. Sharks and rays have a number of remarkably well-developed sensory systems which act in concert to help them locate prey and find their way about the environment. This is unlike the teleosts, which tend to rely very heavily on vision. Probably the first sensory cues sharks and rays pick up when in search of prey are either odor, particularly from injured prey, or low-frequency sounds. Their well-developed olfactory organs attest to the keenness of their sense of smell. The peculiar head of the hammerhead shark, for example, permits a wide separation of the nostrils and may give the sharks an unusual ability to follow odor trails in the water, by turning toward the side where the odor is strongest. Low-frequency vibrations and turbulence created by struggling fish or even fish swimming in schools may also be detected at distances of a kilometer or more, either with the inner ear (vibrations) or with the lateralis system (turbulence).

At closer range, vision comes into play. Contrary to much of the literature on sharks and rays, their visual systems are well developed and used both during the day and during times when light levels are low (Gruber 1977). Many sharks possess both rods and cones, so it is possible that color vision may be present. When sharks are almost ready to seize their prey, nictitating membranes may cover the eyes, and other sensory systems take over. One of these is the electroreception system, which can detect the tiny electrical fields created by muscular movement. The ampullae of Lorenzini, located on the snout, may function in the latter capacity, as do sensory receptors on the lower jaw. The ampullae may also play a role in intraspecific communication, because many elasmobranchs, particularly among the skates and rays, possess weak electrical organs. After the prey is seized, it may be rejected because of taste. The Moses sole is a bony fish that is distasteful to sharks and will be rejected once bitten into. It is therefore a possible source of chemical shark repellents.

Osmoregulation. The osmoregulatory system of the Chondrichthyes is extremely efficient. The concentration of solutes in the body is actually close to or higher than that of seawater largely due to the retention of nitrogenous wastes, mostly urea and trimethylamine oxide, to which the gills are nearly impermeable. A large rectal gland is used primarily for the excretion of sodium and chloride ions, while the kidney excretes divalent ions (Chapter 6). This osmoregulatory system allows sharks and rays to readily adapt to fresh water by reducing urea concentrations in their tissues. There are a number of freshwater stingrays and some sharks frequently move long distances up large rivers, indicating that the scarcity of sharks and rays in freshwater systems is presumably due to ecological rather than physiological reasons.

Reproduction It is likely that the osmoregulatory and reproductive systems of Chondrichthyes evolved simultaneously, because the long gestation periods of the embryos, either in egg cases or in the body cavities of the females, would hardly be possible without the ability of the embryos to withstand high concentrations of their own waste products. In some sharks the embryos may be carried for nearly two years, although the concentration of urea around the embryos is periodically reduced by the ability of the female to flush the "uterus" with seawater.

The cartilaginous fishes, unlike most bony fishes, expend most of the energy used for reproduction in producing a relatively small number of large, active young. They have a wide variety of ways of doing this, from egg laying (oviparity) to live bearing (viviparity) and all stages in between (Wourms 1977; Compagno 1990; Wourms and Demski 1993).

Oviparity, or egg laying, is considered to be the ancestral means of reproduction in the Chondrichthyes and it is still characteristic of 43% of them, including many sharks, all skates (Rajidae), and probably all chimaeras. Most of these fish produce large eggs covered with tough, leathery cases that are deposited in the environment, where they may take as much as 15 months to hatch *(extended oviparity).* Many of the cases have tendrils at the corners, apparently for attachment to rocks and corals (Fig. 15.1). Those of skates are frequently washed up on beaches as "mermaids' purses." The eggs of the horn shark (Heterodontidae) are surrounded by a spiral shelf, which makes the eggs very difficult to remove from the rocky crevices in which they are wedged. The closest thing to parental care observed in sharks and rays has been female horn sharks carrying their eggs and nudging them into crevices. The young that emerge from the eggs are essentially miniature adults and they quickly disperse into nearby cover or shallow nursery areas. For a few sharks (e.g., some catsharks, Scyliorhinidae), the eggs spend little time in the environment because they are retained by the female until they are nearly ready to hatch. This *retained oviparity* clearly represents an intermediate step in the process that led to viviparity.

Viviparity, or live bearing, in the Chondrichthyes takes a number of forms: yolksac viviparity, uterine viviparity, cannibal viviparity and placental viviparity (Compagno 1990). Fish with *yolksac viviparity* (ovoviviparity) produce eggs, but the shells are thin and the eggs are retained in the uterus of the female. The shell soon disappears, and the young are retained in the uterus until fully developed. Like the young of oviparous forms, these young obtain their nutrition from a yolk sac. A modification of this method is found in sting rays and eagle rays (Myliobatiformes, 19% of all Chondrichthyes), which rely on *uterine viviparity.* In these rays, the mother secretes a nutrient-rich uterine fluid which is taken up by the developing young through the skin or epithelia in the gut. Another modification of yolk sac viviparity is *cannibal viviparity,* in which the young in each of the two oviducts consume unfertilized eggs produced by the mother. It is characteristic mainly of many of the large sharks in the Lamniformes (Gilmore 1993). The most extreme case of cannibal viviparity is that of the sand tiger *(Carcharias taurus)* and perhaps the thresher sharks *(Alops),* in which the first two young in the oviducts proceed to eat the other embryos in the oviduct with them. They have well-developed teeth to do this. The mother shark continues to produce unfertilized eggs for the nutrition of the two young, which are born at large sizes (90 cm or so) and as experienced predators.

The most derived form of viviparity is *placental viviparity,* found mainly in carcharhiniform sharks, in which most of the nutrients for the developing embryos are provided through a placentalike arrangement, including an umbilical cord. The placenta in these sharks is derived from a wall of the embryonic yolksac, which fuses with the uterine wall. Because the yolksac placenta evolved independently many times within the carcharhiniform sharks (in five families), there are a number of different arrangements. For example, in the Atlantic sharpnose shark *(Rhizopriondon terranovae),* the early nutrition of the young is through egg yolk and the placental connection does not develop until the yolk is largely consumed (Hamlett 1993); while in the spadenose shark *(Scoliodon laticaudus)* the embryo has virtually no yolk and the yolksac placenta develops while the embryo is still tiny (3 mm). Overall, the placental arrangement in the

FIGURE 15.1 *Egg capsule of a swell shark* (Cephaloscyllium ventriosum) *showing embryo inside. (After Springer 1979.)*

spadenose shark, with the complete dependence of the embryo on direct nutrition from the mother, is remarkably like that of mammals (Wourms 1993).

Viviparity is characteristic of 57% of all Chondrichthyes and is especially characteristic of large, active forms such as the requiem sharks and the eagle rays. Its presumed evolutionary advantage is that it allows young to be delivered into the environment at a large size, so there are lots of prey available to them, and few predators to prey on them. Females usually move into shallow protected areas to give birth and do not feed during the birthing period, perhaps as a mechanism to reduce cannibalism.

While the reproductive output of livebearing sharks and rays is generally low (few young, long gestation period), the spadenose shark, with the most highly developed form of placental viviparity, has a gestation period of only six months and produces 10–15 young that are about 15 cm long. This reproductive rate is about twice that of other placental sharks (Wourms 1993).

Life history. The reproductive strategy of sharks and rays is to produce a relatively small number of young over a lifetime, young that necessarily have high survival rates. To produce these young, livebearing forms have gestation periods of 6–22 months. Compared to teleosts, most sharks and rays are large in size. Recently developed methods of aging sharks and rays indicate that most are slow growing, long-lived, and have late ages of maturity. The best-studied shark is the spiny dogfish *(Squalus acanthias)*, which rarely grows larger than 1.2 m but regularly lives 70–80 years; females usually become mature at around 35 years of age and can theoretically produce 70–80 young in a lifetime (Saunders and McFarlane 1993). The similar-sized leopard shark *(Triakis semifasciatus)* lives 25–30 years and females become mature at around age 17 (Cailliet 1992), while the bat ray *(Myliobatus californica)* lives about 23 years (Martin and Cailliet 1988). On the other hand, the Atlantic sharpnose shark *(Rhizoprionodon terraenovae)* reaches a maximum length of 1.1 m at 9–10 years of age, and females become mature at age five (Cortes 1995). How long the really large sharks and rays live is not known but maximum ages of 70–100 years or more are likely, with ages at maturity of 20–30 years. Given that fecundities are low, gestation periods long, and reproductive intervals long, such sharks and rays can produce only a small number of young over a life time. While this "slow" life history pattern has clearly served sharks and rays well through the millennia, it is rapidly becoming their undoing. Fisheries for many species, but especially the larger ones, have expanded greatly in recent years. It is already abundantly clear that these species can be easily overfished and that recovery of a depleted population is likely to be slow at best. Species like the white shark *(Carcharodon carcharias)* are rare enough so that intensive fisheries could easily drive them to extinction.

DIVERSITY

While the preceding discussion indicates that the Chondrichthyes are a cohesive group taxonomically in that they share a common structural pattern, examination of the adaptations of the various groups within the Chondrichthyes demonstrates their diversity and has resulted in a rather split taxonomy. The number of orders and families, considering the number of species, is high compared to teleosts, for example. Of the two main lines of evolution within the Chondrichthyes, the Holocephali (chimaeras) are a small, fairly uniform group, while the Elasmobranchi (sharks and rays) are highly diverse. The major taxonomic groups of the elasmobranchs used in this book are those of Compagno (1973, 1977). His detailed anatomical studies (especially of jaw suspension, head musculature, and chondrocranial structure) indicate there are four main groups of elasmobranchs (galeomorph sharks, angel sharks, squalomorph sharks, and rays).

Elasmobranchi

Galeomorph sharks. The shark superorder Galeomorphi contains not only the sharks with the classic body shape that usually comes to mind at the word "shark" but also many of the sharks that diverge markedly from this shape (Fig. 15.2). The "typical" sharks are mostly in the families Lamnidae (mackerel sharks) and Carcharhinidae (requiem sharks). These sharks are mostly large, pelagic forms, with bladelike teeth. They are efficient predators on large fish, cephalopods, and marine mammals and are also responsible for most attacks on humans. The sharks that perhaps most deserve the reputation of man-eater are the white shark *(Carcharodon carcharias)*, the oceanic whitetip shark *(Carcharinus longimanus)*, the bull shark *(C. leucas)* and the tiger shark *(Galeocerdo cuvieri)*, although almost any shark will attack a human if provoked. Studies of shark behavior (e.g., Johnson and Nelson 1973) indicate that many attacks on humans may not be feeding attacks but defensive attacks on swimmers behaving in a way the shark interprets as threatening. Likewise, attacks on small submersible vehicles appear to be defensive responses to what the sharks perceive as a predator (Nelson et al. 1986). Klimley (1994) has documented that white sharks are very selective in the prey they eat and seem to prefer prey with high fat content, such as seals and sea lions; this may explain why they tend to spit out prey that are mostly muscle, such as sea otters, birds, and lean humans.

Three sharks in this superorder definitely not capable of biting attacks on humans are the whale shark *(Rhincodon typus)*, the basking shark *(Cetorhinus maximus)*, and the megamouth shark *(Megachasma pelagios)*, although male whale sharks apparently mistake boats on occasion for competitors and ram them. The whale shark, which has been measured at 12 m and may reach 18 m long, is the world's largest fish, while the basking shark runs a close second, with lengths approaching 15 m. Whale sharks and basking sharks are only distantly related to each other and have independently evolved mechanisms for straining plankton. Both have fine, elongate gill rakers for the straining, but those of the basking shark have developed from placoid scales, while those of the whale shark are cartilaginous rods with spongy material between that acts as a filter. The gill rakers of the basking shark are shed in the fall and regrown in the spring, and the sharks, at least in the North Sea, become inactive during the winter. The megamouth shark is a large (4-5 m) deepwater shark discovered in 1976. It has an extraordinarily large mouth through which it filters small shrimp and which may be lined with light producing organs (Taylor et al. 1983).

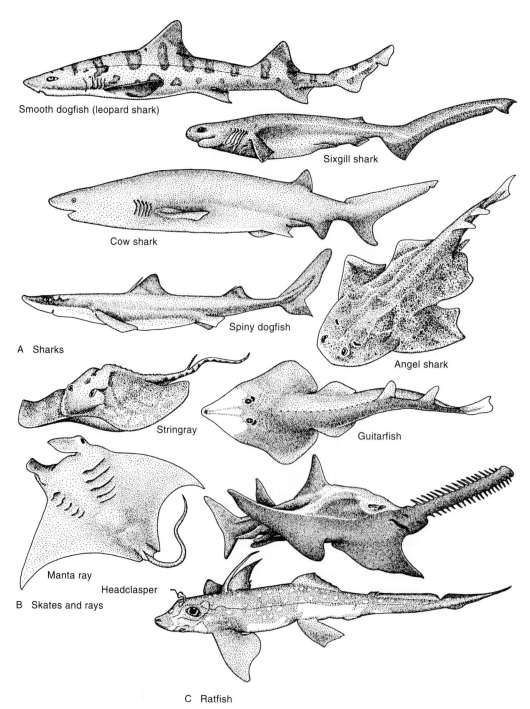

Smooth dogfish (leopard shark)

Sixgill shark

Cow shark

Spiny dogfish

A Sharks

Angel shark

Stringray

Guitarfish

Manta ray

Headclasper

B Skates and rays

C Ratfish

FIGURE 15.2 *Representative Chondrichthyes. Top to bottom: Carchariniformes: leopard shark* (Tri-akis semifasciata); *Hexanchiformes: sixgill shark* (Hexanchus griseus); *juvenile sixgill shark adult; Squatiniformes: angel shark* (Squatina californica); *Squaliformes: spiny dogfish* (Squalus acan-thias); *Myliobatiformes: stingray* (Dasyatis *sp.*) *Rajiformes: guitarfish* (Rhinobatos *sp.*); *Myliobati-formes: manta* (Manta birostris); *Pristiformes: sawfish* (Pristis perottei); *Chimaeriformes: chimaera* (Hydrolagus collei). *(From Moyle 1993, copyright c 1993 by Chris Mari van Dyck.)*

Among the more peculiar sharks in this superorder are the thresher sharks, with their extraordinarily long upper lobe of the caudal fin. The long lobe seems to be used for herding fish schools into tight balls, making them easier to attack. However, Budker (1971) questions the completeness of this explanation, noting that other sharks can accomplish such herding without an elongate tail and that the peculiar shape of the tail must decrease the swimming ability of the sharks. Another odd galeomorph group are the horn sharks (Heterodontidae), which are often considered to be one of the most ancestral groups of living elasmobranchs because they *look* primitive. However, as Compagno (1973) points out, they seem to have as many derived as ancestral characteristics and so are best treated as part of the galeomorph sharks. Because they are rather sluggish, shallow-water bottom dwellers, horn sharks are comparatively well studied (McLaughlin and O'Gower 1971).

Another peculiar group of sharks are the hammerhead sharks (*Sphyrna* spp.), with their broad head. One explanation for the head shape is that it provides a 'stereoscopic' sense of small, useful for tracking prey. However, a preferred prey of hammerheads is sting rays and the sharks have been observed holding down rays with their heads while taking bites out of them with their subterminal mouths (Strong et al. 1990). The heads of hammerheads frequently contain sting ray spines but the spines do not seem to deter the predation. Hammerhead sharks feed mainly at night and are known for their propensity to occur in large (100+ individuals) schools during the day. Given the large size of the fish (2+ m) defense from predators is an unlikely explanation of the schooling; Klimley (1985) speculates it allows for social interactions, presumably leading to breeding, to occur.

Much more typical of the galeomorph sharks are the many species of cat sharks (Scyliorhinidae), hound sharks (Triakidae), and bamboo sharks (Hermiscyllidae). These are elongate, medium-sized (50-200 cm) sharks, with flattened heads, small teeth, small livers, and a highly asymmetrical heterocercal tail, the lower lobe being small. These bottom-oriented sharks are abundant in shallow areas throughout the world. They cruise about feeding on small bony fish, squid, and various benthic invertebrates.

Angel sharks. The 13 species of angel sharks (Squatinidae) appear to be intermediates between sharks and rays. They are flattened like rays, yet the large pectoral fins are not attached to the head. They have large spiracles on top of the head, yet the five gill openings are as much lateral as ventral and the mouth is terminal rather than ventral. Like rays, they lack anal fins and have two small dorsal fins on the caudal region of the body. In most other details, however, they bear little resemblance to the rays, have many characteristics in common with both the squalomorph and galeomorph sharks, as well as many characteristics of their own. Because of their distinctiveness, Compagno (1973) places the angel sharks in their own superorder (Squatinomorpha), although other authorities have usually placed them in with the squalomorph sharks, the group with which they have the most in common. The flattened profile and blunt heads of angel sharks qualify them as bottom lurkers that ambush large prey (Compagno 1990). Their mouths are armed with spike-like teeth and are highly protrusible and expandable, so they can suddenly inhale unsuspecting passing fish.

Squalomorph sharks. The three orders in the superorder Squalomorphi superficially differ considerably from each other, but they are treated together because of considerable similarities in the structure of the chondrocranium (skull). The order Hexanchiformes contains only five species of peculiar sharks with six or seven gill openings that are largely inhabitants of deep water. The frill shark (Chlamydoselachidae, *Chlamydoselachus anguineus*) has an eel-like body and a terminal mouth. The first gill extends across the throat, from one side to the other. This shark has been considered to be related to the ancient cladodont sharks, because of its three-cusped teeth, but Compagno (1973) argues that the similarities to the ancient sharks are only superficial and that in most respects the frill shark is a modern form. The cow sharks (Hexanchidae) are a group of rather flabby, bottom-oriented sharks with weak jaws and small teeth. They apparently live mostly by scavenging. The teeth in the upper jaw are sharply pointed, while the teeth in the lower jaw are saw-like, suggesting that they feed by anchoring their head onto large dead animals (like whales) with their upper teeth and then sawing off chunks with their lower teeth.

The 74 sharks of the order Squaliformes are abundant and widely distributed. All have two dorsal fins, and many have spines preceding one or both fins. Although one of the sleeper sharks (Dalatiidae) may exceed 6 m in length, most of the squaliform sharks seldom exceed 2 m in length. In fact, the smallest sharks known are from this order. The tsuranagakobitozame[1] (Squalidae, *Squaloides laticaudus*) is mature at 11 cm to 15 cm. Another contender for smallest shark is the dwarf dogshark *(Etmopterus perryi)* from deep water (300 m) of the Caribbean Sea, which matures at 16-20 cm (Springer and Gold 1989). All these small sharks are apparently deep water dwellers and some are luminescent with photophores. There is some evidence that at least one of them *(Isistius brasiliensis)* may mimic the squid which they prey upon. This mimicry may also allow them to cut out small, round pieces of flesh from larger fishes, porpoises, and whales which mistake the sharks for prey. The evidence for this is the peculiar mouth and dentition of these sharks, a body shape that would seem to preclude the capture of fast-swimming prey (Fig. 15.3), and the commonness of the peculiar crater wounds on large fish and cetaceans (Jones 1971). As more has become known about these remarkable fish, they have acquired the name of "cookie-cutter sharks."

Perhaps the best known and most abundant squaliform shark is the spiny dogfish (Squalidae, *Squalus acanthias*), which commonly inhabits anatomy and ichthyology teaching laboratories. They are also found worldwide in temperate to subpolar waters, mostly along coastlines. They form huge schools which contain both sexes when the dogfish are immature but only one sex or the other when they are mature (Jensen 1966). They may migrate considerable distances. A dogfish tagged off Washington has been caught off Japan, while one tagged off Newfoundland was subse-

---

[1]A Japanese name meaning "dwarf shark with a long face" (Lineaweaver and Backus 1969).

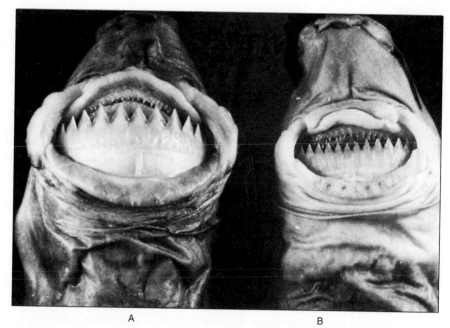

FIGURE 15.3 *Cookie-cutter sharks. (A)* Isistius plutodus; *and (B)* I. brasiliensis. *These small sharks grab onto the side of a larger fish, hold on with their strong suctional lips, and then cut along a cookie-shaped plug of flesh with their lower teeth. (Photo by L. J. V. Compagno.)*

quently caught in the North Sea (Templeman 1976). In many parts of the world they are an important commercial fish, but off North America they are still considered to be mostly a nuisance that preys on more valuable fish. In contrast to the abundant dogfish, bramble sharks (Echinorhinidae) are considered to be uncommon, although this is probably mostly a reflection of their deep water habitat. Despite their rather weak jaws and teeth, they are bottom-oriented predators that apparently feed by suction. Their rather flabby bodies are covered with a scattering of spinelike denticles, presumably for protection. Another squalomorph family with modified external denticles is the Pristiophoridae, the saw sharks. These fish have teeth attached to their snout, which is extended as a long, flat blade. In this respect they are like the true sawfishes (superorder Batoidea, family Pristidae), but the peculiar snout seems to have evolved independently in the two groups. In the saw sharks the teeth on the blade are unequal in size and are rather weakly attached, while in the sawfishes the teeth are all about the same size and are firmly held by sockets. Both forms, however, have flattened heads, although the gill openings are lateral on the saw sharks and ventral on the sawfishes. In both saw sharks and sawfishes the "saw" is used for slashing through schools of fish, after which they return to devour the pieces and incapacitated fishes. Some researchers think that similarities between the two forms is more than just coincidental and that saw sharks are in fact more closely related to rays than to other sharks (Nelson 1994).

Skates and rays. The 450-500 members of the superorder Batoidea are primarily adapted for bottom living, although a number of forms have developed the ability to "fly" through the water with their enlarged pectoral fins and have become nektonic. Even the bottom-dwelling forms are surprisingly diverse, although all members of the superorder are characterized by ventral gill openings, enlarged pectoral fins that attach to the side of the head, no anal fin, eyes and spiracles located on the top of the head, and pavementlike teeth. The most speciose of the Batoidea are the skates (family Rajidae), which are often extremely abundant, especially in water less than 1000 m deep. The tail of skates is very slender, usually without a caudal fin, and contains weak electric organs. It is common to find several morphologically similar species of skates, especially of the genus *Raja*, occurring together. These species segregate by subtle ecological factors such as temperature and depth preferences, and by feeding habits, reflected in specialized dentition. Closely related to the skates are the guitarfishes (family Rhinobatidae), which have a shark-like body. Most of the guitarfishes are small, shallow-water feeders on small crustaceans, although one species may exceed 3 m in length.

Perhaps the most remarkable of the batoids are the electric rays (families Torpedinidae and Narcidae), which can deliver as much as 200 V from the electric organs in their heads. Although electric rays are rather flabby, they use electric discharges to stun the active fish which make up most of their prey (Bray and Hixon 1978). The eyes of all electric rays are quite small, however, and a number of narcid rays are blind, so it is quite possible that they also use electricity for navigation. Another group of rays with formidable weapons are the sting rays (Dasyatidae and Urolophidae). The sting is a spine modified from a placoid scale with a venom gland at its base. The spine is whipped about most effectively by the tail, and, because sting rays feed mostly on crustaceans and other invertebrates, it must be used solely for defense against large predators. A number of sting ray species have independently evolved the physiological abilities to live in fresh water, in the tropical rivers of Asia and South America. These species have a small rectal gland and low urea concentration in the blood.

The eagle rays (Myliobatidae) are closely related to the sting rays and a number of species have venomous spines. The eagle rays fly through the water in schools, flapping their powerful pectoral fins. They have powerful jaws and teeth for crushing molluscs and appear to move around in search of concentrations of invertebrates. A group of eagle rays that are adapted for plankton feeding are the manta and devil rays. These rays are distinguished by large, scooplike appendages on the head that direct the plankton into the mouth. Like whale and basking sharks, manta and devil rays have fine gill rakers for straining out the plankton. The mantas are also the largest of the batoids, some achieving a pectoral fin span in excess of 6 m and weights over 1360 kg.

Holocephali

The chimaeras (subclass Holocephali) have had a long evolutionary history independent of the elasmobranchs, and their anatomy reflects it (see Chapter 13). The chimaeras are commonly known as ratfish because of their long, slender tail and large pointed head. This body shape is convergent to that of teleosts (e.g., Macrouridae) that also live on the bottom in deep water. There are only about 30 species of chimaeras, most of them in the family Chimaeridae. All apparently feed on bottom-dwelling crustaceans and molluscs and consequently have well-developed, pavementlike teeth for crushing. For defense, they all have a spine in front of the dorsal fin with an associated venom gland. All lay eggs with leathery coverings.

The chimaeras have many anatomical peculiarities. For example, the gill slits are covered with a gill flap like the operculum of bony fishes and most water for respiration is taken in through the nostrils. Males have complex, spiny claspers on the pelvic fins and an additional clasper on the head. How these are used in reproduction is not known.

LESSONS FROM THE CHONDRICHTHYES

There are two big lessons from this chapter. First, the Chondrichthyes when contrasted with the Osteichthyes, represent a clear alternative in fish design. They have hit upon many independent solutions to individual problems such as swimming, buoyancy, sensory perception, capturing prey, or being a flatfish. The modern Chondrichthyes are highly derived species with few "primitive" characteristics.

Second, the Chondrichthyes have a highly successful life style based long life, low reproductive rates, and high survival rates. This life style makes them highly vulnerable to human predation and other activities and so their abundance and diversity are rapidly being diminished.

Supplemental Readings

Bigelow and Schroeder 1948; Castro 1983; Compagno 1973, 1990; Lineaweaver and Backus 1969; Moss, 1984, Springer and Gold 1989; Wourms and Demski 1993.

CHAPTER 16

Relict Bony Fishes

CLASS OSTEICHTHYES
  Subclass Sarcopterygii
    Infraclass Dipnoi
      Order Ceratodontiformes
        Family Ceratodontidae (Australian lungfishes)
      Order Lepidosireniformes
        Families Lepidosirenidae (South American lungfishes), Protopteridae
        (African lungfishes)
    Infraclass Coelacanthimorpha
      Order Coelacanthiformes
        Family Latimeriidae (gombessa or coelacanth)
  Subclass Actinopterygii
    Infraclass Chondrostei
      Order Polypteriformes
        Family Polypteridae (bichirs)
      Order Acipenseriformes
        Families Acipenseridae (sturgeons), Class Polyodontidae (paddle-
        fishes)
    Infraclass Neopterygii

Division Ginglymodi
  Order Lepisosteiformes
    Family Lepisosteidae (gars)
Division Halecomorphi
  Order Amiiformes
    Family Amiidae (bowfin)

The bony fishes have a long and complex evolutionary history, yet the world's fish faunas are dominated by one group, the teleosts (Division Teleostei). Other groups of bony fishes have had similar heydays in the past but only a few scattered descendants (ca. 50 species) of these past groups persist in the modern fauna. Fortunately for students of evolution, the relict fishes represent many of the major lines of bony fish evolution. The relationships among the groups are highly controversial, as are their relationships to fossil forms and to tetrapods (Chapter 14). However, one of the most interesting questions to ask is how did these relict fishes manage to survive, when most of their relatives perished?

SARCOPTERYGII

The lobe-finned (Sarco-pterygii) fishes are the fishes most closely related to the tetrapods. Nevertheless, modern forms are so derived and so evolutionarily distant from the tetrapods that arguments about which are closer will probably go on indefinitely. The characteristics that unite members of this group with tetrapod ancestors are the presence of lobed paired fins and lungs. The lobed fins resemble the limbs of tetrapods; they are supported by internal skeletal elements that attach to pelvic and/or pectoral girdles. Modern lobe-finned fishes belong to two very different groups: the freshwater lungfishes (Dipnoi) and the marine coelacanths (Coelacanthimorpha).

DIPNOI

Modern lungfishes are in three distinct families, the Ceratodontidae of Australia, the Lepidosirenidae of South America, and the Protopteridae of Africa. Lungfishes are readily recognized by their elongate bodies and continuous rear fins that encompass dorsal, caudal, and anal fins. The Australian lungfish (*Neoceratodus forsteri*) most resembles the fossil forms, with its flipperlike fins, large scales, unpaired lung, and compressed body. In contrast, the South American (*Lepidosiren paradoxa*) and African (*Protopterus*, four species) lungfishes have fins that are reduced to filaments, small scales, paired lungs, and eel-like bodies. The Australian lungfish is relatively uncommon, confined to four rivers in Queensland. These rivers have low flows in the summer and the lungfish live in the deep pools that remain. Although their lung is functional in a limited way, even during the dry season the Australian lungfish seems to rely primarily on gill respiration. The lung supplements the gills during times of stress. The South American and African lungfishes live in swamps that are likely to dry up and they breathe air to survive. As the waters recede in their swamps, they dig burrows in the mud in which they can survive until the rains come. The African lungfishes undergo true estivation, which includes drastic metabolic changes. They line their burrows with a heavy coating of mucus, which dries to form a hard, impermeable cocoon. Each burrow is connected to the surface by a narrow tube plugged with mud except for a small hole. When the rains come, the plug dissolves, water enters the lung of the fish, and it awakens by coughing.

During estivation the oxygen consumption of the lungfish is reduced to extraordinarily low levels, and what metabolic energy is needed is derived entirely from the utilization of protein. The estivating lungfish live by metabolizing their own muscles. During this process, carbohydrate (glycogen) reserves actually build up and are consequently available for immediate use when the lungfish emerges from the cocoon. Another substance that builds up during estivation is urea (Chapter 7). Urea may build up in tissues to seven times its normal level, far beyond the levels toxic to most other bony fishes. Once the lungfish leave the cocoon, the urea is rapidly excreted and ammonia becomes the main nitrogenous waste product.

The African and South American lungfishes all hollow out nests in mud banks or bottoms. The female then lays the eggs in the nest and the male guards them. The newly hatched lungfish resemble salamander tadpoles in that they have external gills. Such gills, as well as the nesting behavior, are not characteristic of Australian lungfish, which lay their eggs on aquatic plants.

All lungfishes have dermal tooth plates. These tend to be flattened in fossil forms, apparently for crushing and grinding, but are more bladelike in living lungfishes. The South American and Australian lungfishes are omnivorous, and plant material is an important part of the diet; the African lungfishes are more carnivorous, preying on molluscs, crustaceans, and fish. On this diet some species may exceed 2 m in length, although fish longer than 1 m are seldom encountered.

COELACANTH

Probably no single event in the history of ichthyology has received more public attention than the discovery of the coelacanth *(Latimeria chalumnae)* in 1938. This discovery excited the public imagination because the coelacanth is large (up to 2 m long), is from deep water, was previously known only from fossils (the most recent being about 70 million years old), and would supposedly reveal much about the evolutionary transition between fish and tetrapods. The coelacanth brought instant fame to the South African ichthyologist J. L. B. Smith, who described it, and a certain celebrity, in scientific circles anyway, to Ms. M. Courtenay-Latimer (hence *La-*

timeria). Latimer was the curator of a small local museum who recognized the significance of the fish brought to her by a local fisherman, and so notified Smith. Unfortunately, a second specimen was not obtained until 1952. It had been caught nearly 3000 km north of the first collection locality, in the deep trenches around the Comoro Islands. All subsequent specimens have come from this area, where it is common enough so that the local fishermen have a name for it (gombessa). Since 1952 considerable research has been conducted on the coelacanth, although new discoveries about its biology are still being made (Musick et al 1991). For example, the fact that the coelacanth is ovoviviparous (i.e., retains the eggs in the body cavity where the young hatch and develop) was not discovered until 1975 (C. L. Smith et al. 1975). In 1987, the first observations on living coelacanths in their natural habitat were made using a small submarine. These observations revealed they did not "walk" on the bottom with their lobed fins as had been commonly supposed (Fricke et al. 1991). Instead, when feeding (at night), they drift in currents close to the bottom, with the head pointing downward at an angle and the paired fins used for stabilizers. During the day they aggregate in caves, resting quietly. Most coelacanths live at depths of 150–253 m and the limited number of resting caves at such depths may be a factor limiting their populations (Fricke et al. 1991). They feed on large bottom fishes, including small sharks, which they apparently detect with a special electric organ in the snout.

Coelacanths have a number of interesting anatomical adaptations. The bones of the paired fins articulate with the pelvic and pectoral girdles, much like those of tetrapods. While the skeleton is made up of both bone and cartilage, the vertebral column is essentially notochord constricted by cartilaginous neural and haemal arches (this is true of lungfishes as well). The fin "spines" are also cartilaginous and are hollow, hence the name coelacanth (*coel,* "hollow," *acanth,* "spine"). However, there is bone present in the large, highly modified cosmoid scales that cover the body. The skull and jaws are also partially bony and are well suited for a fish that swallows its prey whole. Unlike other living fishes, the coelacanth has an intracranial joint that allows the cranium to flex dorsally when the jaws are opened, in which the notocord functions as a hinge. In addition, the gape of the mouth is very wide and the head is capable of being moved somewhat independently from the trunk (Thomson 1973). Other unusual aspects of coelacanth biology include its osmoregulatory strategy and its fat-filled swimbladder. Coelacanths are nearly isosmotic with seawater, maintaining high concentrations of urea in the blood much like sharks and rays. The fat-filled swimbladder, combined with the reduced skeleton, presumably allows the coelacanth to be neutrally buoyant without the limitations of movement imposed by a gas-filled swimbladder.

ACTINOPTERYGII

The ray-finned (Actino-pterygii) fishes are the dominant fishes on the planet, with 42 orders, 431 families, and nearly 24,000 species (Nelson 1994). They have evolved into so many specialized forms that it is difficult to find common structural characters; thus the group is easiest to define by the absence of key characters of other major groups. The vast majority of the actinopterygians are teleosts, but the structure and ecology of the few remaining nonteleosts do give us some clues as to what the ancestral fish were like. The forms with the most ancestral characteristics are all placed in the Chondrostei, the name reflecting the largely cartilaginous skeletons of modern forms: the bichirs (Polypteriformes) and the sturgeons and paddlefishes (Acipenseriformes). Somewhat more derived in character but of uncertain relationship to the teleosts are the gars (Lepisosteiformes) and the bowfin (Amiiformes).

POLYPTERIFORMES

The bichirs seem to share a common ancestry with the early chondrosteans; however, they superficially resemble lobe-finned fishes. For example, in common with lungfishes and coelacanths, they possess lobed pectoral fins, although the supporting structures are so distinctive they probably evolved independently. In common with chondrosteans, bichirs possess spiracles, maxillary (upper jaw) bones firmly united to the skull, and ganoid scales. In common with both groups, bichirs possess such ancestral features as a spiral valve intestine, paired lungs that attach ventrally to the gut, and a heterocercal tail. In most features, however, the bichirs are quite distinct. The body is elongate and flexible, even though covered with a heavy armor of scales. The dorsal fin consists of 5 to 18 separate finlets, each supported by a single spine. They normally respire through gills but can breathe air when the oxygen content of the water becomes low. The larvae are also adapted for low oxygen levels by possessing external gills.

Most of the features of bichirs are adaptations for being predators on fishes and invertebrates in the swamps and rivers of tropical Africa. Although they may be locally abundant enough to be collected for the aquarium trade, there are only 10 species (Fig. 16.1).

ACIPENSERIFORMES

The sturgeons and paddlefishes are large fish with cartilaginous skeletons, a heterocercal tail, a spiral valve intestine, an upper jaw that does not articulate with the cranium, only one branchiostegal ray, fin rays that are more numerous than the supporting basal elements, and a notochord that persists in the adults. Otherwise, the sturgeons (Acipenseridae) and paddlefishes (Polyodontidae) are quite different from each other and probably are products of long separate evolutionary lines.

The sturgeons (26 species) are distinguished by five rows of bony scutes on the body that represent the remnants of ganoid scales and by a highly protrusible, bot-

FIGURE 16.1 *A bichir* (Polypterus). *(After Boulenger 1907.)*

tom-oriented mouth that is preceded by four barbels. Teeth are absent in adults. As their morphology indicates (Fig. 16.2), sturgeons feed on the bottom by sucking up organisms detected by their highly sensitive barbels. Although various types of garbage found in their stomachs indicate that they feed in part by scavenging, most of their diet is benthic invertebrates, with fish becoming increasingly important prey as the sturgeon grow larger. Most of the fish they eat are probably captured at night, when it is difficult for the prey to avoid a large sturgeon, even though the sturgeon are somewhat sluggish. The shovelnosed sturgeons *(Scaphirhynchus)* use their flat snouts for stirring up the bottom to expose the invertebrates upon which they feed.

Sturgeons are the largest fish found in fresh water, although the largest species are anadromous. The beluga sturgeon *(Huso huso)*, the main source of true Russian caviar, has been found to achieve lengths up to 8.5 m and weights of nearly 1300 kg. In North America there are apparently authentic records of white sturgeon *(Acipenser transmontanus)* growing to about 4 m and weights of 590 kg. Sturgeons have presumably been able to persist by adopting a life history strategy combining the large size, slow growth, and long life of sharks with the high fecundity and small egg size of teleosts. Because of their extreme value, large size, and vulnerability to both pollution and overfishing, most large sturgeon species are endangered today. Their value and reproductive habits, however, do make it possible to culture them successfully and sturgeon farms are now present in a number of places around the world.

The paddlefishes possess a long, paddlelike snout, whose function is apparently for detecting patches of prey by sensing electrical fields. Their skin is smooth and scaleless, except for a small patch on the caudal peduncle. Like most sturgeons, they possess a small spiracle, which is covered with a greatly elongated operculum. There are two species of paddlefish. One lives in the Mississippi River system and achieves lengths of about 2 m, while the other lives in the Yangtze River of China and may reach in excess of 5 m. North American paddlefish feed on zooplankton, which they capture by swimming through the water with mouth agape and filtering out the plankton with their many fine, elon-

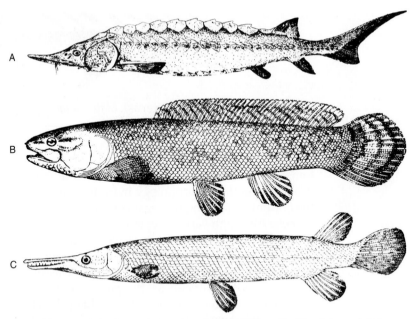

FIGURE 16.2 *(A) Sturgeon* (Acipenser); *(B) bowfin* (Amia); *and (C) gar* (Lepisosteus). *(From Jordan and Evermann 1900.)*

gate gill rakers. However, Chinese paddlefish apparently feed on fish. Both species are declining in numbers due to habitat changes and overexploitation.

LEPISOSTEIFORMES

The seven species of gars are among the most distinctive freshwater fishes. Their cylindrical bodies are covered with hard, nonoverlapping, diamond-shaped ganoid scales, and their hard bony heads have long snouts with sharp, conspicuous teeth. The long body and snout, coupled with the placement of the dorsal and anal fins near the tail, make gars superb lie-in-wait predators. Passing fish are seized sideways during a sudden dash from ambush by the gar, held firmly with the teeth, and eventually turned around and swallowed whole. The heavy armor that gars carry with them as protection against predators is made possible by large swimbladders, which make gars neutrally buoyant. The swimbladders are also used for air breathing. Gars are not obligate air breathers but become increasingly dependent on the lung for oxygen as water temperatures increase and the dissolved oxygen in the water decreases (Renfro and Hill 1970). Aside from the large, well-vascularized swimbladders, the most distinctive internal features of gars are the spiral valve intestine and the vertebral column with unique opisthocoelous vertebra; each vertebral centrum has a convex anterior surface and a concave posterior surface.

Although gars do not build nests, the eggs and probably the sac-fry are protected from predators by being toxic. The eggs are laid on aquatic vegetation, to which they adhere. The young cling to the stems with an adhesive disc on the head until the yolk sac is absorbed and they can swim actively. Most of the seven species reach a maximum length of 1 m to 2 m, but the alligator gar (*Atractosteus spatula*) can exceed 3 m. Gars are largely confined to the Mississippi River drainage, although one species is found in coastal drainages down to Costa Rica and another is found in Cuba.

AMIIFORMES

The bowfin (*Amia calva*) is another fish of the Mississippi River drainage, the last survivor of a once abundant group that coexisted with the dinosaurs. With its cycloid scales and functionally homocercal tail, it is similar in appearance to teleosts. However, its many sharp teeth, 10 to 13 branchiostegal rays, vestigial spiral valve intestine, stout body, solid jaws and head, and large lung also make it seem distinctly archaic. One of its distinguishing features is the bony gular plate under the lower jaws. Like teleosts, the bowfin has vertebrae that are concave at both ends (amphicoelous). The large lung is definitely advantageous to the bowfin in the warm summer waters in which it normally occurs. It is not an obligate air breather, but once the water temperatures exceed about 10°C, it supplements oxygen obtained through the gills with that absorbed through the lung. The rate of air breathing increases with increasing temperature (Horn and Riggs 1973). On occasion, bowfin can apparently survive entirely by air breathing while lying torpid in muddy burrows during periods of drought. There is some evidence that during such periods they, like lungfish, may actually metabolize muscle rather than fat. Although they cannot accumulate urea in their body tissues, they can reduce water demand by excreting urea and uric acid.

LESSONS FROM RELICT FISHES

These holdovers from fishes of earlier eras have persisted because of specializations that allow them to coexist with and frequently prey on more derived actinopterygians. Most relict fishes are large in size, many have heavy armor, and many are air-breathers. That they have been able to more than hold their own is indicated by the abundance of gars, bowfin, paddlefish, and sturgeons in the Mississippi River drainage, a river system where more "modern" fishes are abundant and diverse. However, although some of these forms have persisted for millions of years, their survival for the next hundred years is probematical.

Supplemental Readings

Herald 1961; Jessen 1973; McCosker and Lagios 1979; Musick et al. 1991; Pflieger 1975; Schaeffer 1973; Scott and Crossman 1973; J. L. B. Smith 1956; Thomson 1973.

CHAPTER 17

Teleost Offshoots

BONYTONGUES, HERRINGS, AND EELS

SUBDIVISION TELEOSTEI
  Infradivision Osteoglossomorpha
    Order Osteoglossiformes
      Families Osteoglossidae (bonytongues), Pantodontidae (butterflyfishes), Hiodontidae (mooneyes), Notopteridae (knifefishes), Mormyridae (elephantfishes), Gymnarchidae
  Infradivision Elopomorpha
    Order Elopiformes
      Families Elopidae (tenpounders), Megalopidae (tarpons)
    Order Albuliformes
      Families Albulidae (bonefishes), Halosauridae (halosaurs), Notacanthidae (spiny eels)
    Order Anguilliformes
      Families Anguillidae (freshwater eels), Heterenchelyidae, Moringuidae (spaghetti eels), Chlopsidae (false morays), Myrocongridae, Muraenidae (moray eels), Synaphobranchidae (cutthroat eels), Ophichthidae (snake eels), Colocongridae, Derichthyidae (longneck eels), Muraenesocidae (pike congers), Nemichthyidae (snipe eels), Congridae (conger eels), Nettastomidae (duckbill eels), Serrivomeridae (sawtooth eels)

Order Saccopharyngiformes
Families Cyematidae (bobtail snipe eels), Saccopharyngidae (swallowers),
Eurypharyngidae (gulpers), Monognathidae
Infradivision Clupeomorpha
Order Clupeiformes
Families Engraulidae (anchovies), Pristigasteridae, Chirocentridae (wolf
herring), Clupeidae (herrings)

TELEOSTEI

The Teleostei, based on sheer numbers of species and individuals, is the main line
of fish evolution. According to Nelson (1994), the group contains 42 orders, 431 families, and 23,681 species. It is a successful group because of a package of adaptations
that improved respiration, feeding, buoyancy, swimming, and reproduction (Chapter 13). The group is defined by the homocercal tail; Tele-ostei means "end-bone" referring to the specialized bones (uroneurals) at the end of the vertebral column that
support the symmetrical caudal fin. While the success of the teleosts overall has depended on the integrated design package, the success of evolutionary lines within
the teleosts has depended on specializations of various sorts; this includes specializations that have resulted in the abandonment of what seem to be basic teleost traits,
such as the two-pump respiratory system or the homocercal tail. The importance of
specialization is reflected in the three major lines of teleost evolution covered in this
chapter: the bonytongues (Osteoglossomorpha); the eels and tarpons (Elopomorpha); and the herrings (Clupeomorpha). While these three groups together contain
about 1400 species (roughly 6% of all teleosts) and include some of the most abundant fish in the world (herrings and anchovies), they are considered to be relict or
specialized offshoots of the main line of teleost evolution (the Euteleostei).

OSTEOGLOSSOMORPHA

The osteoglossomorphs are an unusual group of about 220 species of freshwater
fish, most of which (ca. 200 species) are in one African family, the Mormyridae. The
rest of the species are scattered about the continents and are generally considered
to be relics of a once much more abundant group. Although the fossil record is
scanty, osteoglossomorphs may have been a dominant element in the freshwater
fauna of the world before the emergence of the ostariophysan fishes. The relationships of the osteoglossomorphs to other fish groups are poorly understood,
presumably because they are such an ancient group. Their osteology is quite distinctive and ties the members of the Osteoglossomorpha together, if somewhat ten-
uously. Most osteoglossomorphs have most of their teeth located on the tongue
(osteo-glossid = bony-tongue) and on the roof of the mouth (or the parasphenoid).
They also have a caudal fin with 16 or fewer branched rays (most bony fishes have
more), no intermuscular bones on the back (epipleurals), cycloid scales with ornate

microsculpturing, and an intestine that curls around to the left side of the esophagous rather than to the right as in most other bony fishes (Nelson 1994). There are six living families in this group, all in the order Osteoglossiformes.

Osteoglossidae. There are only seven species in this family, yet they are found in the tropical areas of Africa, South America, Asia, and Australia. This distribution pattern is frequently cited as evidence for continental drift, because fossils for this family are found as far back as the Paleocene epoch. Bonytongues are conspicuous members of their local faunas, with heavy, elongate bodies covered with large scales (Figure 17.1). The dorsal and anal fins are long and placed on the rear half of the body. All apparently can breathe air with their lunglike swimbladders. Most of the species make their living as predators in tropical rivers. The arapaima *(Arapaima gigas)* of the Amazon River is one of the largest freshwater fish species, regularly reaching lengths of 2 to 3 m. The silvery arawana *(Osteoglossum bicirrosum)* occurs with the arapaima but reaches lengths of only about 1 m. It is characterized by two chin barbels and a remarkably large, angled mouth with which it can capture other fishes and small animals that fall into the water from the overhanging vegetation. It incubates its young in a special pouch in its mouth, as do the bony tongues *(Scleropages* spp.) of Australia and Asia.

The only member of the Osteoglossidae that is not predatory is *Heterotis niloticus* of western Africa (Fig. 17.1). This large fish (to 1 m) has its fourth gill arch modified into a spiral-shaped filtering apparatus. This organ secretes mucus in which phytoplankton and small bits of organic matter are trapped and then swallowed.

Hiodontidae. The two species in this family, the mooneye *(Hiodon tergisus)* and the goldeye *(H. alosoides),* are the most "normal"-looking fish in their entire superorder, because they superficially resemble clupeid fishes (Fig. 17.1). Their most distinctive external features are their large eyes, which have bright gold irises in the goldeye and gold-silver irises in the mooneye. The gold color in both species is from a tapetum lucidum that increases their ability to see at low light levels (see Chapter 10). Goldeye are known to feed mostly at night and to have only rods in their retinas (no cones). The goldeye and mooneye are found in the backwaters of the large rivers and lakes throughout the Mississippi River drainage system. They are also found in the Hudson Bay drainages and Arctic drainages (goldeye only) of Canada, where the goldeye is abundant enough to be an important commercial species. Both species take a wide variety of prey, but they are largely piscivorous as adults (Scott and Crossman 1973).

Notopteridae. The eight species of knifefish have long, strongly compressed bodies that taper to a point (Roberts 1992). They swim mainly through the rhythmic movements of the long anal fin, which extends from just behind the head to the tiny caudal fin, which it joins. They appear to be able to swim equally well forward or backward. The dorsal fin (absent from one species) is small and featherlike, so these fishes are commonly called featherbacks. The swimbladder is connected to the gut and is used for air breathing. Thus the knifefishes are extremely well adapted for living among submerged and emergent vegetation in stagnant backwaters and

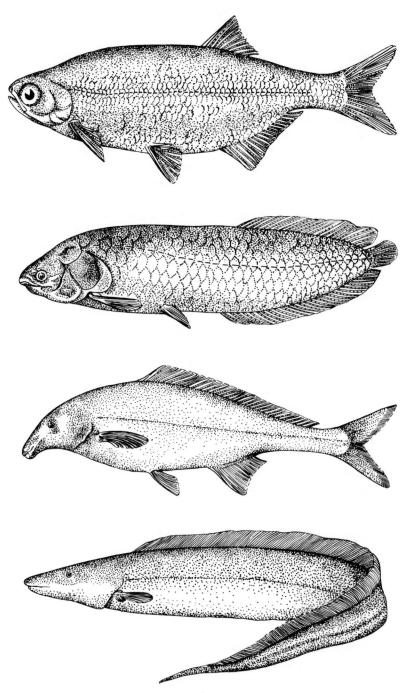

FIGURE 17.1 *Representative osteoglossomorph fishes: (A) goldeye (Hiodonti-dae); (B) African bonytongue (Osteoglossidae); (C) elephant fish (Mormyridae); and (D) electric fish (Gymnarchidae). ([A] from Jordan and Evermann 1900; [B], [C], and [D] after Boulenger 1907.)*

ponds of tropical Asia and Africa. They generally remain quietly in cover during the day but come out to prey on invertebrates and small fish in the evening. The large species, which may approach 1 m in length, are favored food fishes in Southeast Asia. A fish with habits and morphology similar to the knifefishes is *Gymnarchus niloticus*, a close relative of the mormyrids (Fig. 17.1). This species, however, uses its dorsal fin for propulsion rather than the anal fin. Also, like the mormyrids, it uses electricity for finding its way about.

Mormyridae. The elephantfishes are about 200 species of odd-looking fishes including species with a trunk-like appendage on the chin or snout (Fig. 17.1). This family is adapted for nocturnal living in muddy rivers and lakes in tropical Africa and is quite abundant in many areas. It has also successfully adapted to the reservoirs that now exist on many African rivers, and contributes significantly to the reservoir fisheries. One of the principal reasons for the success of this group seems to be their use of electric organs to find their way about, to detect prey, and to communicate with each other. Weak electric signals are produced by modified muscles in the caudal peduncle and an electrical field is set up around each fish. Anything that disrupts the field can be detected and identified with a surprising (to us) degree of precision. The electric signals can be modified by the fish to communicate with other fish by changing the shape of the field, the form of the waves, the discharge frequencies, the timing of the discharges, and the pattern of stopping and starting the discharges (Hopkins 1974). Thus the electric signals can be used in courtship, aggressive behavior, and other intraspecific encounters. Because each species has its own set of electrical patterns, recognition and avoidance of other species is also possible. This capability for acute discrimination between different types of electrical signals requires an extremely well-developed nervous system. The mormyrid cerebellum, in particular, is so large that, relative to body size, it is roughly the same size as that of humans. The complexity of the mormyrid brain is also reflected in their complex behavior patterns. Aquarists have long admired mormyrids for their learning abilities and the fact that many species engage in apparent "play" behavior, usually considered to be a sign of intelligence. The play usually consists of batting around a small object with the head.

The morphology of mormyrid fishes reflects the importance of electricity as a sensory modality. The eyes are small and the skin thick. All species usually swim slowly, with their bodies rigid, presumably to avoid distorting the electrical field they are generating. They rely primarily on the tail and/or dorsal fin for propulsion. As a consequence the tail is often deeply forked and the caudal peduncle very narrow, somewhat reminiscent of the arrangement in tunas. Despite the importance of the electrical system in mormyrids, they also possess a well-developed sense of hearing, which depends on the swimbladder for amplifying sound (Werns and Howland 1976). The swimbladder is quite small and located mostly in the head region, where it is in contact with the inner ear. Another peculiar feature of the Mormyridae is that many of the species have proboscis-like snouts or long extensions of the lower jaw. These species presumably feed by probing in the bottom mud for small invertebrates. Species without the protruding snout usually feed on plankton or small fish.

ELOPOMORPHA

The fishes of the Elopomorpha are morphologically extremely diverse. It includes the tarpons (which look like giant herrings), the streamlined bonefishes, the true eels, and the spiny eels (which look like a cross between a bonefish and a true eel). What links these diverse groups is the presence of leptocephalus larvae (Greenwood et al. 1966). These planktonic larvae are thin, transparent, and leaflike, drifting passively with currents. The leaflike body shape apparently allows the larvae to get a significant portion of their nutrition through the direct absorption of dissolved organic matter (Pfeiler 1986). Despite this seemingly basic link between the groups, the classification system used here for the Elopomorpha is far from being universally accepted by experts.

Elopiformes

This order contains eight species (two families) of streamlined, predatory fish with large cycloid scales and deeply forked tails (Fig. 17.2). While the presence of leptocephalus larvae seems to link them with the eels, the larvae are quite distinctive. Elopiform larvae have a forked tail and a distinct dorsal fin, while eel larvae have a rounded "tail" that merges with an elongate dorsal fin. The members of this order are all shallow-water tropical or subtropical marine forms that occasionally enter fresh or brackish water. Although not esteemed for eating, species such as the Atlantic tarpon *(Megalops atlanticus)* and the tenpounder *(Elops saurus)* are favorite sport fishes because of the spectacular, leaping fights they put on once hooked.

Albuliformes

There are only 29 species recognized for this order, but they represent two very different groups: (1) the bonefishes (Albulidae) and (2) the halosaurs (Halosauridae) and spiny eels (Notacanthidae). The union of these two groups is based on obscure details in structure because they look extremely different. The bonefishes are tarpon-like predators of shallow, tropical marine waters, while the 25 species of

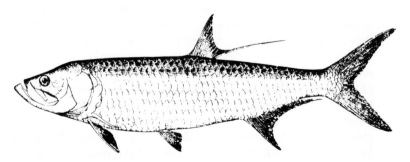

FIGURE 17.2 *An elopiform fish, the tarpon (Megalopidae). (From Jordan and Evermann 1895–1900.)*

halosaurs and spiny eels are eel-like forms from the deep sea (Fig 17.3). The sub-terminal mouths and body structure of halosaurs and spiny eels indicate that they probably make a living by pulling small invertebrates out of muddy bottoms. Al-though superficially similar to true eels, they differ from them in many important characteristics; these include the presence of both pelvic and pectoral fins, the flex-ible jaw structure, and the elongate anal fin, which merges with the caudal fin (if one is present). One of the most striking aspects of spiny eels is that the lepto-cephalus larvae may be quite large (up to 180 cm) but then metamorphoses into much smaller juveniles (D. G. Smith 1970).

Anguilliformes

The diversity of eels is not widely appreciated. Their public "image" has been formed largely by the culinary and sporting qualities of freshwater eels and by lurid descriptions of fierce moray eels attacking divers on coral reefs. Their image is not helped by the fact that most species are quite secretive in their habits, many are quite rare, and superficially there is not much variation in eel morphology. Eels are elon-gate fishes that (1) lack pelvic fins (and often pectorals as well); (2) have dorsal and anal fins that are continuous with the caudal fin (and hence a pointed tail); (3) have cycloid scales that are deeply imbedded in the skin or absent; (4) lack gill rakers; and (5) have a reduced skeleton; they also share many other characteristics.

Despite this seeming uniformity, there are over 730 species of eels, belonging to 15 families. These species are found in a wide variety of habitats, from freshwater lakes and streams, to coral reefs, to the deep sea, although most eels live in shallow tropical or subtropical marine habitats. All, however, have planktonic leptocephalus larvae; and in temperate regions eels of many species make extensive migrations to lay their eggs in places where oceanic currents will favor the growth, survival, and return "home" of their larvae. McCleave (1993), for example, documents the remarkable ability of different species of eels to spawn in different areas of the Sar-gasso Sea in order to take advantage of the various currents generated in the Sub-tropical Convergence Zone.

An idea of the diversity of eels can be obtained by briefly examining four of the families: Anguillidae, Muraenidae, Congridae, and Ophichthidae (Fig. 17.4).

Anguillidae. Although there are only 15 species in this family, it is the best known of the various eel families because most of the species live in fresh water and spawn in the ocean. They are "typical" elongate eels, however, in that each has a wedge-shaped head with a "hard" mouth that lacks the maxilla and premaxilla. The head also has gill openings that are far back and are covered with a small, flexible oper-culum. The branchial cavity is quite large, because the eels breathe mostly by "swal-lowing" water and moving it past the gills in pulses. The shape of the head greatly restricts the gape of an eel's mouth and hence the size of prey it can swallow whole. In order to eat a larger prey item, an eel will grab onto it and then spin around rapidly, until a chunk breaks off that can be swallowed (Helfman and Clark 1986). All these features make eels admirably suited for living secretive lives in crevices

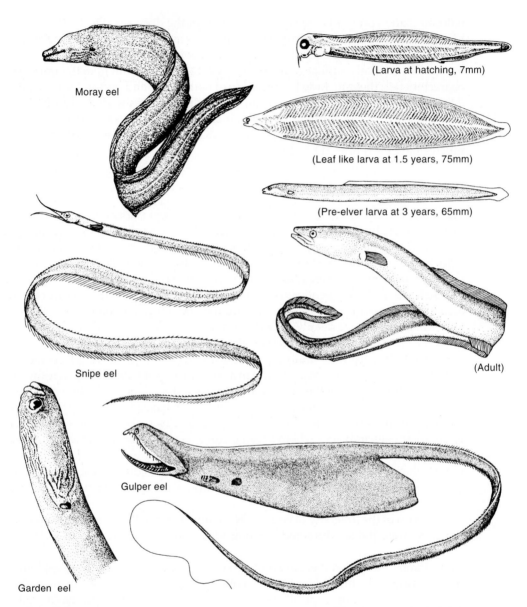

Moray eel

(Larva at hatching, 7mm)

(Leaf like larva at 1.5 years, 75mm)

(Pre-elver larva at 3 years, 65mm)

Snipe eel

(Adult)

Gulper eel

Garden eel

FIGURE 17.3 *Top right: stages in the development of anguillid eels (Anguillidae); left, top to bottom: moray eel (Muraenidae); snipe eel (Nemichthyidae); garden eel (Congridae); gulper eel (Eurypharyngidae). (From Moyle 1993, copyright 1993, C. van Dyck.)*

or burrows or among stalks of aquatic plants in which they can seek out equally secretive prey or ambush fishes that pass by.

   In the eastern United States the American eel *(Anguilla rostrata)* is an important (if declining) predator in many lakes and streams, and the closely related *A. anguilla*

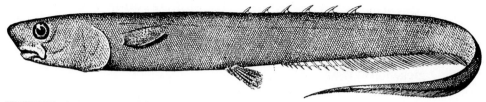

FIGURE 17.4 *Spiny eel (Notacanthidae). (From Goode and Bean 1895.)*

plays a similar role in European waters. After spending six to twelve years in these habitats and growing to 35–150 cm, both species transform from being cryptically colored green and yellow to being silvery. The silver eels then migrate out to sea and apparently seek deep water currents, with which they swim to their spawning grounds in the Sargasso Sea, a distance as much as 5600 km. Once there, they apparently spawn at great depths and die after spawning. The spawning grounds of the eels were located by Johannes Schmidt (1922) by plotting the distribution of leptocephalus larvae by size on a map of the Atlantic. The smallest larvae were found in the vicinity of the Sargasso Sea. To reach Europe, the larvae must drift with the currents for about three years; to reach North America, about one year. Once the leptocephali reach coastal waters, they metamorphose into elvers, which proceed to migrate into streams and estuaries.

Muraenidae. Moray eels are efficient predators of fish and invertebrates of reefs and rocky shores in tropical and temperate regions. They lack both paired fins and scales; they have hard, pointed heads with many teeth, small round gill openings, and a posterior set of nostrils set high on the head, usually between the small eyes. With such adaptations, they penetrate easily into the deep crevices of reefs to consume night-active fishes that are in hiding during the day and day-active fishes that are in hiding during the night. Most species have daggerlike teeth for grabbing their prey, but some have flattened teeth for breaking up hard-shelled invertebrates. Some morays grow as long as 3 m, but most do not exceed 1 m. Their colors range from drab yellow-green to bright yellow or red with spots or rings of white. While many morays are considered to be dangerous because they can give severe bites to an unwary diver, they are probably most dangerous as a cause of ciguatera fish poisoning. The flesh of tropical species of morays can become poisonous when they consume other fishes that have fed on the algae that produce the toxins (Halstead 1967). The fish have adapted to the toxins, but humans have not!

Congridae. Most of the 150+ species of conger eels resemble moray eels, except that they usually possess pectoral fins and that their teeth, rather than being sharp fangs, are stout and cone-shaped. They feed on a wide variety of prey, but mostly invertebrates. In temperate regions most conger eels are associated with shallow, rocky areas, but in tropical regions many of them instead construct burrows in soft bottoms. Most remarkable of the latter group are the garden eels (*Gorgasia, Heteroconger*). Garden eels are small, extremely elongated eels with moderately large eyes, rounded heads, and small mouths; they form colonies on sandy bottoms in areas of moderate currents. Each eel constructs a burrow from which it can extend its long (to 1 m) body and feed during the day on zooplankton carried by the current (Fricke 1970). When all the eels in a colony are feeding and waving about in the current, the colony has more the appearance of a field of seagrass than an aggregation of fish.

Ophichthidae. The family of snake and worm eels is the largest in the Anguilliformes, with about 250 species. Most are found in shallow water in tropical and subtropical areas, are small in size (less than 1 m), and are brightly colored. Despite their abundance, bright colors, and shallow-water habitat, they are rarely seen and are difficult to collect because they burrow into soft bottoms and are active mostly at night. Unlike the garden eels, they do not have permanent burrows but use them for a day and then abandon them. The "true" snake eels (subfamily Ophichthinae) have a finless, spikelike tail with which they can quickly penetrate sand and mud bottoms. The worm eels (Myrophinae) possess a caudal fin but are mostly found in soft mud bottoms. When in their burrows, snake and worm eels leave just their heads exposed. Consequently, they have exceptionally well-developed branchial pumping apparatus for moving water across the gills, and both sets of nostrils are located on the tip of the snout.

Saccopharyngiformes

This group of deepsea eels has pushed teleost morphology to its extreme, in good part by abandoning structures essential to most other fishes, such as opercular bones, branchiostegal rays, scales, pelvic fins, ribs, and swimbladders. The loss of so many structures is presumably an energy-saving measure for fish that live under extreme conditions with infrequent meals. The least modified members of the three families in this order are the bobtail snipe eels (Cyematidae); they still possess a caudal fin and traces of a maxillary bone in the mouth. They also have the most abbreviated bodies of any eels and elongate snipe-like snouts, which are apparently advantageous for the life of a midwater planktivore in the deep ocean. The other three families in this order have abandoned even more features (e.g., caudal fin, upper jaw bones) to focus on their role as predators capable of swallowing prey larger than themselves. The mouth and pharynx are extremely large and distensible, with small teeth for holding onto the prey. The gill openings are small and placed far back on the body, closer to the anus than to the tip of the snout in the gulper eels, while the tiny eyes are set near the tip of the snout. These fishes are among the largest (or at least the longest, up to 180 cm) bathypelagic fishes. Their watery flesh and poorly developed fins indicate that they do not actively pursue prey but hang suspended in the water column waiting for their prey to come to them. It seems likely that they attract their prey by using a light-producing organ at the tip of the tail. At present nine species of swallower eels (Saccopharynidae) and one species of gulper eel (Eurypharyngidae) are recognized. In addition, there are six species of small, gulper-type eels that are placed in a separate family (Monognathidae) because they lack an upper jaw and pectoral fins.

CLUPEOMORPHA

The herrings and their kin form one of the most well-defined teleost orders (Clupeiformes, the only living order in the Clupeomorpha). All are adapted for living in well-lighted surface water, where most species school and feed on plankton. Their most conspicuous adaptations for this way of life are silvery scales, a compressed, often keeled, body, a flexible mouth, and fine gill rakers. The silvery scales and compressed body function in reducing the visibility of the fish, since the scales scatter the light coming from above, while the compressed body reduces the profile visible from below. The mouth and gill raker structure are used for plankton feeding. More definitive are their skeletal characteristics, the structure of their lateral-line system, and the connection of the swimbladder with the inner ear by means of a narrow diverticulum of the bladder. The latter structure gives clupeids a sense of hearing that is among the most acute in fishes. Most clupeiform fishes belong to the families Clupeidae and Engraulidae.

Clupeidae. The herrings, shads, sardines, menhaden, and other clupeid fishes (about 180 species) can be readily recognized by their keeled (sawtooth) bellies and silvery, deciduous scales (Fig. 17.5). They play key roles in many food webs because of their abundance and their ability to feed on both zooplankton and phytoplankton. They tend to concentrate in coastal waters, in areas of upwelling, so they have long been important to humans, either as the object of commercial fisheries or as food for predacious fishes harvested by humans. Because they often have boom-or-bust population cycles, especially when under pressure from commercial fisheries (see Chapter 34), they may have considerable impact on human affairs. In the fourteenth century, for example, the power of the Hanseatic League declined when herring populations in the Baltic Sea, upon which the League depended for a steady source of fish for trade, collapsed.

While clupeids are usually thought of as marine fishes, many species are abundant in inland lakes and seas, and still others are anadromous. In North America the freshwater species (especially the gizzard shads, *Dorosoma* spp.) are valued mostly as forage for game fish; for this purpose they have been planted in lakes and reservoirs far outside their native ranges, with mixed results. In such situations they frequently have population explosions, taking advantage of the lightly exploited zooplankton populations. They also typically become important prey of the game fish, and growth rates of the game species may increase dramatically. Unfortunately, the introduced shad are often too successful and, through competition for zooplankton, may decrease the growth and survival rates of juvenile game fish (which typically feed on zooplankton) and of native planktivorous fish.

Like the freshwater clupeids, anadromous clupeids are found in many parts of the world: shad (*Alosa* spp.) are characteristic of coastal streams of eastern North America and Europe, and hilsa (*Hilsa kelee*) spawn in streams that flow into the Indian Ocean, from China to Africa. These fishes typically move upstream during periods of high water to spawn. Following spawning, the embryos and/or larvae are quickly washed downstream, and the young live initially in estuaries or nutrient-

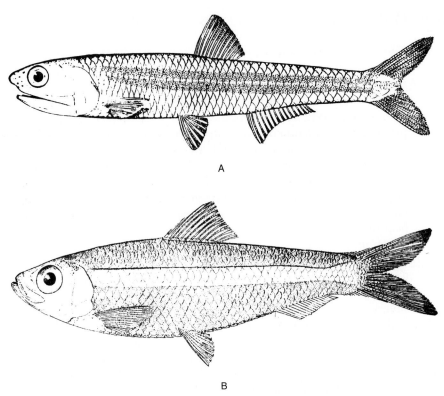

FIGURE 17.5 *Clupeiform fishes: (A) anchovy (Engraulidae); and (B) sardine (Clupeidae). ([A] from Jordan and Evermann 1895-1900; [B] from Jordan 1895.)*

rich coastal waters. It is worth noting that spawning migrations are characteristic of clupeids in general. Most of the marine species congregate for spawning in areas away from the adult feeding grounds. Herrings *(Clupea)* seek inshore areas with submerged plants or rocks to which they can attach their eggs; gizzard shads move to the upper ends of reservoirs, where the inflowing currents will keep their embryos suspended.

Engraulidae. The 139 species of anchovies can be distinguished from clupeids by their overhanging snout and long upper jaw, which extends behind the eye (Fig. 17.5). As a consequence of this mouth structure, anchovies can open their mouths to an incredible extent, producing a round opening that is efficient for filter feeding on plankton. The actual filtering apparatus is the numerous gill rakers on the first gill arch. Anchovies are usually small (less than 15 cm), translucent fish that inhabit inshore areas of the oceans where plankton densities are high, although a few tropical species inhabit fresh water. Many anchovies are important commercial species; their populations, like those of the clupeids, may fluctuate considerably in response to changing oceanographic conditions, and may collapse dramatically when overfished.

LESSONS FROM THREE DIFFERENT TELEOST LINES

There are clearly many ways to be a successful teleost. The bonytongues can be regarded as early successes that faded as other teleost groups evolved. However, they managed to leave specialized remnant species on all continents, and the African electric fishes found a way to maintain high numbers and diversity through specialized adaptations to murky waters. The eels have taken one particular morphological pattern and diversified in astonishing ways, occupying a wide array of habitats from streams and lakes to the open ocean to coral reefs to the deep sea. Likewise, the clupeiforms developed into specialized plankton feeders with relatively few species but extraordinarily high numbers, especially in coastal areas. One key to the success of both eels and clupeiforms is their ability to make long migrations, including migrations into fresh water, that separate life history stages.

Supplemental Readings

Blaxter 1985; Bullock 1973; Gosline 1971; Herald 1961; Hopkins 1974; McCleave 1993; Sinha and Jones 1975; Tesch 1977.

CHAPTER 18

Minnows, Characins, and Catfishes

SUBDIVISION TELEOSTEI
  Infradivision Euteleostei
    Superorder Ostariophysi
      Series Anotophysi
        Order Gonorynchiformes
          Families Chanidae (milkfish), Gonorynchidae (beaked sandfishes), Kneriidae, Phractolaemidae (snake mudhead)
      Series Otophysi
        Order Cypriniformes
          Families Cyprinidae (minnows and carps), Gyrinocheilidae (algae eaters), Catostomidae (suckers), Cobitidae (loaches), Balitoridae (river loaches)
        Order Characiformes
          Families Citharinidae, Hemiodontidae, Curimatidae, Anostomidae (headstanders), Erythrinidae (trahiras), Lebiasinidae, Ctenoluciidae (pike-characins), Hepsetidae (Kafue pike), Gasteropelecidae (freshwater hatchetfishes), Characidae (characins)
        Order Siluriformes
          Families Diplomystidae, Ictaluridae (North American catfishes), Bagridae (bagrid catfishes), Olyridae, Cranoglanididae (armor-

head catfishes), Siluridae (Eurasian catfishes), Schilbeidae (schilbeid catfishes), Pangasiidae, Amphiliidae (loach catfishes), Sisoridae (sisorid catfishes), Amblycipitidae (torrent catfishes), Akysidae (stream catfishes), Parakysidae, Chacidae (squarehead catfishes), Clariidae (airbreathing catfishes), Heteropneustidae (airsac catfishes), Malapteruridae (electric catfishes), Ariidae (sea catfishes), Plotosidae (eeltail catfishes), Mochokidae (upside-down catfishes), Doradidae (thorny catfishes), Ageneiosidae (barbelless catfishes), Auchenipteridae (driftwood catfishes), Pimelodidae (longwhisker catfishes), Cetopsidae (whale catfishes), Helogenidae, Hypophthalmidae (loweye catfishes), Aspredinidae (banjo catfishes), Trichomycteridae (parasitic catfishes), Callichthyidae (armored catfishes), Scoloplacidae (dwarf catfishes), Loricariidae (suckermouth armored catfishes), Astroblepidae (climbing catfishes)

Order Gymnotiformes

Families Sternopygidae (glass knifefishes), Rhamphichthyidae (sand knifefishes), Hypopomidae, Apteronotidae (ghost knifefishes), Gymnotidae (knife eels), Electrophoridae (electric eel)

The superorder Ostariophysi contains over 6500 species, over one-quarter of the known fish species. More importantly, nearly three-fourths of all freshwater fish species belong in this superorder. They are the dominant freshwater fish on all continents except Australia and Antarctica. Thus, to appreciate the adaptations of fish in this group is to appreciate what it takes to live in freshwater environments, which are frequently turbulent, turbid, and subject to extreme fluctuations in temperature and water chemistry. Such environments are also often small, isolated, and fragmented, making them subject to extreme and rapid changes from both human and natural causes. The fact that this superorder contains some of the most abundant species of freshwater fish and some of the most important species for aquaculture is a tribute to their adaptability. As this chapter will demonstrate, the ancestors of the minnows, characins, and catfish developed a suite of adaptations that has allowed them to dominate fresh water and to diverge early from the evolutionary stream of other euteleostean fishes.

Some of the characters that fishes in this group share include:

1. Fright substances (*Schreckstoff*) are present. Schreckstoff is released into the water when a fish is injured and causes a fright reaction in members of the same or closely related species.
2. A swimbladder is present and usually has two chambers.
3. Unculi are present (Roberts 1982). Unculi are small, unicellular projections on various parts of the body that may provide a rough surface for clinging or scraping.
4. Breeding tubercles are well developed, including a keratinous cap.
5. The upper jaw (premaxilla) is easily extended, for suction feeding.
6. The pelvic fins are abdominal in position.

GONORYNCHIFORMES

Prior to Greenwood et al. (1966), the Ostariophysi did not include the Gono-rynchiformes but only the fishes placed here under the Otophysi. This is because the series Otophysi is the most cohesive of all the major teleost taxa; its members are easily recognized by a number of distinctive features. The Gonorynchiformes lack most of these distinctive features, but the members of this order have enough in common with the otophysan fishes to be considered derivatives of the forerun-ners of the Otophysi (Rosen and Greenwood 1970).

There are only four families and about 35 species in this order, most of them small freshwater fishes. Aside from the various family specializations, they are not a particularly distinctive group. They have small, usually toothless mouths and epi-branchial organs (modified gill rakers) for breaking up the particles of food they ingest. Their first three vertebrae are modified in such a way as to suggest the con-dition that permitted the development of the distinctive Weberian ossicles of the Otophysi. The best-known member of the Gonorynchiformes is the milkfish (*Chanos chanos*), the sole member of the family Chanidae (Fig. 18.1). This is a marine and brackish-water species that is one of the most important food fishes of Southeast Asia. The adults are large (to 1.8 m), active fish, with silvery sides and deeply forked tails. They feed mostly on planktonic algae. They are extremely tolerant of a wide range of temperature and salinity, and so are successfully raised in brackish and freshwater ponds. The fish used for pond culture are collected as fry in estuaries and other inshore areas.

The gonorynchiform family with the most species (27) is the Kneriidae, a group of small, loachlike freshwater fish of Africa. These fish are well adapted for living in swift streams. They have fine (or no) scales, subterminal and protractile mouths, elongate bodies, and large pectoral fins that when placed together can form a sucker to enable the fish to cling to rocks in strong currents. Some species are also air breathers, which enables them to survive in stagnant pools. The kneriids are of special interest because they provide some idea of what the early ancestors of the otophysan fishes may have been like.

OTOPHYSI

This group is the main line of ostariophysan evolution, with 6500 species. The tax-onomic arrangement of the Otophysi presented here is that of Fink and Fink (1981), who regard the Cypriniformes (minnows, etc.) as the probable ancestral group for the rest of the orders, with the Characiformes (Characins) being derived early in the evolutionary history of the Otophysi. The catfishes (Siluriformes) were derived somewhat later and themselves gave rise to the South American electric fishes (Gymnotiformes).

The Otophysi have a tremendous range of body forms and sizes, yet they are united by a number of distinctive skeletal features. Most obvious of these features is the Weberian apparatus. This is a chain of bones that connects the swimbladder

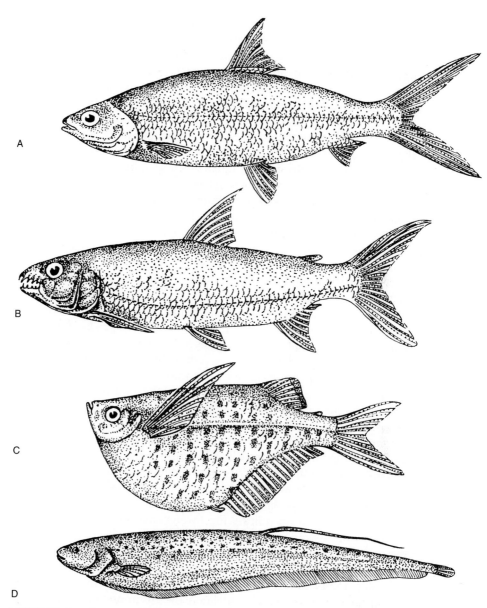

FIGURE 18.1 *Representative ostariophysan fishes: (A) milkfish* (Chanos, Chanidae, *Gonorynchiformes); (B) characin* (Astyanax, Characidae, Characiformes); (C) *freshwater hatchetfish* (Gasteropelecus, Gasteropelecidae, Characiformes); *and (D) electric knifefish* (Sternarchus, Apteronotidae, Gymnotiformes).

to the inner ear, giving the fishes a sensitive sound-reception system similar in function to that of the inner ear in mammals. The connecting bones are modified portions of the first four or five vertebrae. It is presumed that the acute sense of hearing from the Weberian apparatus is particularly useful in turbid water or at night, when most catfish are active. Another feature of major importance is the protractile upper jaw (absent in most characins), which in combination with pharyngeal teeth allows for a diversity of feeding techniques. The pharyngeal teeth permit the separation of the grabbing and chewing functions of the mouth, important for fish that feed mostly on active prey. The many specializations in pharyngeal dentition present in the Otophysi, from molariform grinding teeth, to comblike teeth for breaking up fine materials, to sharp teeth for piercing prey, have undoubtedly contributed to the success of these fish in much the same way that the specialized jaw teeth of mammals have contributed to their success on land.

Other otophysan features that seem to be particularly important contributors to their success are their fear scent, their generally small size, and their reproductive strategies. Like the keen sense of hearing, the fear scent is likely to be particularly useful under conditions, common in fresh water, where a predator is hard to see. Once the scent has been released, the fish may flee the area, hide, or school more closely even though the predator is not visible, so any additional attacks by the predator are likely to be less successful. The use of fear scents by these fishes is a reflection of the fact that most of the species are highly social and school during at least one stage of their life history. It also reflects the fact that most otophysan fishes are quite small, even as adults. There are a number of species that reach 1 m to 2 m in length, but they are decidedly a small part of the total. Most of these large forms are either piscivores or detritivore/herbivores. Small size seems to be advantageous for feeding on the myriad of small aquatic invertebrates, as well as on the terrestrial invertebrates that fall into the water. Small size is also advantageous for the occupation of the numerous microhabitats in fresh water, such as between rocks in fast streams or among the aquatic vegetation in lakes; or for the occupation of small or intermittent waterways where low oxygen levels and shallow water are likely to discriminate against large fish. Yet another advantage of small size lies in the ability of the fish to reach maturity quickly. Freshwater environments, but particularly streams, fluctuate from season to season and from year to year; wet years and droughts may alternate with one another on an irregular basis. Thus the availability of conditions necessary for successful reproduction may vary considerably from year to year and from place to place. Mobile, small fish with early maturity can quickly take advantage of favorable conditions and flood the environment with young, thus maintaining large populations as long as the favorable conditions exist.

CYPRINIFORMES

This order contains the Cyprinidae and specialized cyprinid relatives: the Catostomidae and the four families of loaches. Together, these fish dominate the fresh waters (but especially streams) of North America and Eurasia and, to a lesser extent, Africa. The nearly 2700 species in the order are diverse in their external appearances, but most possess protractile mouths without teeth and specialized pharyngeal teeth. Their heads are scaleless, and with the exception of a few loaches, all lack an adipose fin.

Cyprinidae. The minnow or carp family is the largest family of fishes, with over 2000 species. They are distinguished from other members of the suborder by their pharyngeal teeth (one to three rows, but never more than eight teeth per row) and thin lips (upper jaw usually bordered only by the premaxilla). Although most have only soft rays in the fins, rays that have been modified into spines are present in some forms, most notably common carp *(Cyprinus carpio)* and goldfish *(Carassius auratus)*. Remarkably, considering the number of species involved, cyprinids all have body plans that are mainly variations on the "classic" fish theme, with fusiform to moderately deep bodies, large eyes, conspicuous scales, abdominal pelvic fins, and small terminal or subterminal mouths (Fig. 18.2). Nevertheless, the cyprinids show considerable morphological, physiological, and behavioral diversity (Winfield and Nelson 1991). Most are diurnal predators on small invertebrates, but some are piscivorous and others feed on algae, higher plants, and organic ooze. Cyprinids include the smallest freshwater fish known, *Danionella translucida*, which is mature at 10–11 mm in length (Roberts 1986), as well as a number of large species that reach 2–3 m in length. Many species exhibit various forms of parental care of the eggs and young but many also simply scatter their eggs in selected places in the environment, sometimes making long migrations to do so.

In North America there are about 286 species of cyprinids, over 40% of them small, silvery "shiners" of the genera *Notropis* and *Cyprinella* (Mayden 1991). The shiners are often the most abundant, or at least the most conspicuous, fishes in small streams and lakes of eastern North America, where they form large schools in shallow water. It is not unusual to find five to ten species of small cyprinids living together in these habitats, and studies to determine how groups of such similar species can coexist have contributed much to our understanding of stream ecology. One of the most interesting and abundant of the eastern stream minnows is the central stoneroller, *Campostoma anomalum* (Jenkins and Burkhead 1993). The stoneroller is an herbivore with a hard plate on the lower jaw for scraping algae from rocks and a long intestine (eight times body length) for digesting it. Schools of stonerollers are so abundant in places that they can keep the rocks clean of algae; thus algae grow well only in pools where predatory fish keep the stoneroller populations low (Power and Matthews 1983). Stonerollers are also well known for the many large tubercles that cover the stout heads of large (10–28 cm) multicolored breeding males. The males build nests on the bottom of riffles, which are defended from other males by way of the breeding tubercles. During the spawning season, it is not unusual to find males missing eyes or dying from the results of encounters with other males. Like antlers, the breeding tubercles are shed by surviving males at the end of the breeding season.

Bright breeding colors, nuptial tubercles, and some type of nest building are actually characteristic of many North American cyprinids, so for a few weeks each year they can rival their tropical relatives in brilliance. A number of these cyprinids have developed the curious habit of using nests of other fishes, mostly those of larger cyprinid species or centrarchid basses, for spawning. Nests of the large

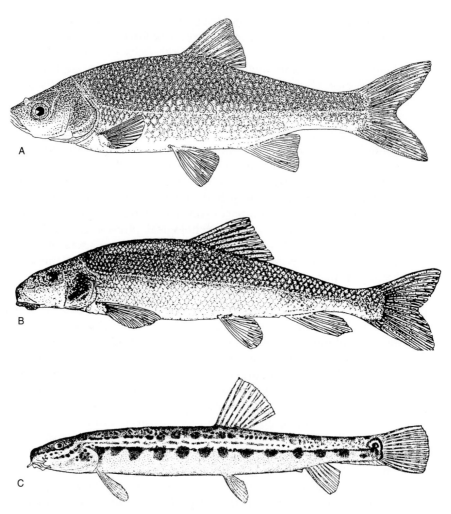

FIGURE 18.2 *Representative cypriniform fishes: (A) Loach* (Cobitus *spp., Cobitidae) (From Nichols 1943); (B) sucker* (Catostomus occidentalis, *Catostomidae) (From Moyle 1976a); (C) tui chub* (Gila bicolor, *Cyprinidae) (From Moyle 1976a).*

cyprinids, fallfish *(Semotilus corporalis)* and hornyhead chub *(Nocomis biguttatus)*, may be used for spawning simultaneously by as many as three species of small cyprinids, resulting in occasional hybrids among the species.

In eastern North America a large majority of the cyprinids have a maximum length of less than 10 cm, although some species may reach 25 to 30 cm. In the major drainages of western North America, however, a majority of the species are large, commonly exceeding 25 cm as adults (Moyle and Herbold 1987). Largest of these western species are the four piscivorous squawfishes *(Ptychocheilus)*. The Colorado squawfish *(P. lucius)*, now an endangered species, is reported to have reached nearly 2 m in length and a weight of 45 kg. Presumably these pikelike cyprinids evolved in western rivers because the true pikes (Esocidae) and centrarchid basses, the main large piscivores of the Mississippi and associated drainages, were absent. In altered habitats into which the basses and pike have been introduced, squawfish often gradually disappear.

Southeast Asia is generally considered to have become the center of cyprinid evolution because the cyprinids are extraordinarily numerous and diverse there as well as on the Indian subcontinent. Most African cyprinids belong to genera also found in Asia and are apparently derived from them. Many of these species are the small, bright, colorful, and highly active forms favored by aquarists, usually known as barbs, rasboras, and "sharks." Many Eurasian cyprinids also grow to respectable sizes and are important sport and commercial fish. In Great Britain large cyprinids, including the common carp, are much sought after by anglers, often in catch-and-release fishing contests. Because of their ability to grow rapidly to harvestable sizes in ponds on diets of organic ooze, plants, and small invertebrates, a number of the Asiatic carps—such as common carp, grass carp *(Ctenopharyngodon idella)*, and silver carp *(Hypophthalmichthys molitrix)*—are among the most important aquaculture animals in the world.

Catostomidae. The suckers are a small (68 species) but very successful family of fishes (Fig. 18.2). Throughout North America they are among the most abundant fishes, particularly in streams and rivers. Their success can be attributed to the tolerance most species have of a wide variety of environmental conditions and to their feeding habits. Most species are bottom browsers, sucking up organic ooze, algae, and small invertebrates through their subterminal mouths with fleshy lips. The food ingested is then broken up by comblike pharyngeal teeth (one row of 16 or more teeth) and digested in a long, winding intestine. A majority of the suckers are moderate-sized (40 to 80 cm), streamlined forms belonging to the genera *Catostomus* and *Moxostoma*. Species of these genera are most characteristic of streams, where they are often abundant. Other species of suckers have become adapted for life in large, fast-moving rivers. Most extreme in this regard are the razorback sucker *(Xyrauchen texanus)* of the Colorado River. The back of the razorback sucker rises steeply behind the head to form an inverted keel. Water flowing past this keel apparently pushes the fish against the bottom, allowing it to feed and move in swift water. An evolutionary trend in suckers in the opposite direction is toward lake living. Suckers adapted for living in quiet water, such as carpsuckers *(Carpoides)* and buffalo suckers *(Ictiobus)*, are large, deep-bodied forms. While many of these forms are still bottom feeders, a number have developed terminal mouths and fine gill rakers that enable them to feed on plankton.

Cobitidae. This family (110 species) of small fish favored by aquarists is largely adapted for living in the streams of Eurasia. The loaches are most diverse in Southeast Asia, but one species has managed to invade North Africa, and the Japanese weatherfish *(Misgurnus anguillicaudatus)* has become established through introductions in both California and Michigan. Most loaches are small (to 30 cm) fishes that range in body shape from wormlike to chunky (with a flattened belly). All have subterminal mouths with three or more pairs of barbels (Fig. 18.2). As might be expected, most are secretive bottom dwellers that feed on small invertebrates and plant matter. A closely related family is the Balatoridae (= Homalopteridae), the river loaches. Many of these loaches are adapted for life in fast-flowing streams in southern Asia. Some of the species are small dacelike fish that have subterminal mouths and large pectoral fins, and actively forage among the rocks. Others are highly specialized for browsing on algae growing on rocks in torrential streams and have a ventral sucking disc. It is created by the pelvic and pectoral fins joining on a flattened belly. This arrangement allows them to live in faster-flowing water than probably any other fishes.

CHARACIFORMES

The characins are confined to Mexico, South and Central America (ca. 1350 species), and Africa (ca. 200 species), with the exception of the Mexican tetra *(Astyanax mexicanus)*, which has managed to invade North America. In South America, characins, together with catfish, totally dominate the freshwater fish fauna. Although the many species possess a wide array of specialized features, as a group they are readily recognizable. In the past this has resulted in the placing of all species in just one family, the Characidae. However, recent workers have split up this group in recognition of its diversity; but the 10 families listed here are bound to change in number and composition as our understanding of the characiform fishes increases.

Most characins are diurnal predators, with large eyes (absent in some cave-dwelling forms), no barbels, and numerous teeth set in the jaws. Their jaws are not very protractile and most possess rather unspecialized pharyngeal teeth. They tend to be small, bright (often silvery) in color, and have fusiform or laterally compressed bodies that are completely covered with cycloid scales. Most possess an adipose fin, a short dorsal fin located midway on the body, abdominal pelvic fins, and a caudal fin with usually 19 principal rays.

Characidae. This is the largest and most varied of the characin families (ca. 885 species). Its members are found in Africa, South and Central America, and North America (the Mexican tetra). The family Characidae essentially contains the various characins that lack the features used to characterize the other nine families (Fig. 18.1). All have good sets of jaw teeth; most are predatory, including the fearsome-looking piranhas *(Serrasalmus* spp.) and African tigerfish *(Hydrocynus* spp.—which can reach 1.4 m). While there is no doubt that piranhas are well-developed predators, their predation on humans and large mammals seems to have been exaggerated. Most human "victims" of piranhas may have drowned first and then been scavenged by the fish. A number of close relatives of the piranhas are vegetarians and some have piranha-like jaws, with strong teeth, that enable them to invade flooded Amazon jungles to feed on fruit and seeds falling from trees. Such species support important indigenous fisheries. Other smaller species, such as the tetras, support fisheries and aquaculture operations to provide brilliantly colored fish for the aquarium trade.

Other families. The nine other characin families are small groups of rather specialized species (Roberts 1969; Nelson 1994). Three of the families (Ctenoluciidae, Hepsetidae, Citharinidae) contain fishes with pikelike morphologies; most are lie-in-wait predators on other fishes, although some have peculiar beaklike snouts that enable them to pluck scales and pieces of fin from other fishes. The Erythrinidae are also largely piscivorous as adults. In contrast, many members of the South American family Curimatidae are deep-bodied, bottom-feeding fishes of moderate size with subterminal, suckerlike mouths. Members of the African family Citharinidae are somewhat similar, although they are more adapted for picking invertebrates from the bottom than for sucking up algae, ooze, and small invertebrates. Perhaps the most remarkable fishes are the freshwater hatchetfishes (Gasteropelecidae), which have a compressed head and body and large breast muscles, giving them a deep-bodied appearance (Fig 18.1). These fish are arguably the only "true" flying fish because they fly short distances, out of the water, with rapid beats of their pectoral fins, rather than relying on gliding.

SILURIFORMES

The catfishes are one of the most distinctive groups of fish. While their Weberian apparatus and fear scents link them to other otophysan fishes, their distinctive morphology is also indicative of a long independent evolutionary history. In general, it appears that the catfishes have diversified for being active after dark or in turbid water, thereby reducing interactions with the vision-oriented cypriniforms and characiforms. This diversification has produced over 2400 species of catfishes, about 1440 of which reside in the New World. Although any group of fish with so many species is bound to have its share of bizarre forms, most catfish are readily recognizable by their whiskery snout, containing one to four pairs of barbels (invariably one of the pairs is supported by the maxilla), as well as by their small eyes, a head that is usually flattened, an adipose fin, and a streamlined body that is either without scales or covered with heavy, bony plates. Most also have a stout spine leading each pectoral and dorsal fin, which can lock into place. Some species have venom glands associated with the spines. Although catfish are readily recognizable on the basis of their external anatomy, their most definitive features, which separate them from other otophysans, are osteological:

1. They lack the symplectic, basihyal, and subopercular bones in the skull and intermuscular bones in the body. The latter feature makes them especially desirable as food fish, in contrast to the carps.
2. The premaxilla is usually covered with small teeth, but they are absent from the maxilla, which is reduced to a rod to support the barbels. The only exception to this is found in *Diplomystes*, a South American genus considered to have the most ancestral characters of all catfish.

3. Small teeth are usually present on the vomer, on the roof of the mouth.
4. The Weberian apparatus is generally more complex than that of other otophysans.

Most catfish are small in size, reaching 10 cm to 30 cm, although a number of species can exceed 1 m in length. Probably the largest is the wels *(Silurus glanis)* of Europe, which may reach 5 m and 300+kg. In contrast, many members of the South American family Trichomycteridae attain lengths of only 2 to 3 cm. The larger catfish are much favored as food fishes, while many of the smaller forms are popular as aquarium fish.

The systematics of the catfishes is just beginning to be understood. For example, there is no widespread agreement as to how the 34 families listed here relate to each other. The problem of determining interrelationships among the families is somewhat simplified by the fact that each continent has been an independent center of catfish radiation, so in most cases each family is confined to just one continent. Thus South America has 14 families of its own, Eurasia 10, Africa 3, and North America 1. Three other families are found in both Eurasia and Africa, while the remaining two (Ariidae and Plotosidae) are mostly marine. The 14 species of catfish found in the fresh waters of Australia are members of the two marine families.

Ictaluridae. The North American catfish family contains about 45 species of rather unspecialized catfish (Fig. 18.3). All are scaleless and dark in color (except for cave forms), with large, flattened heads that support eight barbels (two on the snout, two on the maxillae, and four on the chin). These catfishes can be divided into three distinct groups: the large species sought by anglers *(Ameiurus, Ictalurus, Pylodictis);* the small, secretive madtoms *(Noturus);* and the blind cave catfishes *(Satan, Trogloglanis, Prietella).*

The species in the first group of catfishes were originally native to warm waters east of the Rocky Mountains, with the exception of one species in Mexico. Thanks to their popularity as food fish, they have been spread by humans to suitable waters throughout North America, as well as to Europe. The second group, the madtoms, are a widely distributed but poorly known group of 25 to 30 species of small (less than 10 cm) catfishes. Most live in small to moderate-sized streams, where they hide under rocks, logs, and trash (such as old automobile parts and beer cans) during the day, coming out to forage on invertebrates at night. Besides their secretive habits, their main protection against predators seems to be stout spines, whose effectiveness is increased by the mild venom associated with them. Like all members of the Ictaluridae, madtoms exhibit a high degree of parental care, building nests and then guarding the eggs and young. The species in the third group, the cave catfishes, are small, white, blind, and known from only a few specimens, some collected from wells.

Clariidae. The 100+ air-breathing catfishes are members of the most widely distributed catfish family, occurring in a wide range of habitats from South Africa

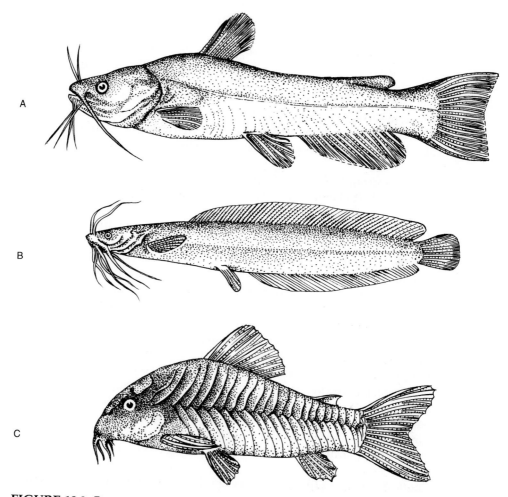

FIGURE 18.3 *Representative siluriform fishes: (A) bullhead* (Ameiurus, Ictaluridae); *(B) air-breathing catfish* (Clarias, Clariidae); *and (C) armored catfish* (Callichthys, Callichthyidae).

through most of Africa and the southern half of Asia over to Java and the Phillippine Islands. Their bodies are rather elongate (some species are remarkably eel-like), their heads flattened with four pairs of long barbels, and their dorsal and anal fins long (Fig. 18.3). The adipose fin is frequently absent. Their most distinctive feature, however, is the air-breathing organ made up of modified gill filaments on particular gill arches. These gill filaments are supported by a treelike structure with a cartilaginous "trunk" so they do not collapse (as do normal gill filaments) when exposed to air (Chapter 4). The posterior portion of the gills is normal and can be used for aquatic respiration, although most species of clariids seem to depend at least partially on aerial respiration. Surprisingly, many clariids are found in large lakes and rivers, where oxygen levels are normally high. A number of such species support important fisheries. However, many other species are found in low-oxygen waters, and some are capable of moving for short distances across land to colonize new areas. The latter forms "walk" on the tips of their stout pectoral spines by using them as pivots as they shove themselves along by flexing their bodies. The species best known for this activity is the so-called walking catfish *(Clarias batrachus)*, which has become established, presumably by escapees from aquaria and tropical fish farms, in such places as Guam, Hawaii, and Florida. In Florida it is considered to be a pest because it has spread rapidly, to the detriment of populations of more desirable fishes, despite periodic die-offs caused by cold weather (Courtenay et al. 1974).

Other Eurasian and African families. Throughout much of Africa and southern and eastern Asia (to Japan), the "typical" catfishes belong to the family Bagridae. Ecologically, morphologically, and economically they are similar to the ictalurid catfishes of North America. In Europe and northern Asia, the typical catfish role is played by 100+ members of the family Siluridae. However, members of this family diverge markedly from the classic catfish shape of the bagrids by having a long anal fin, short (or no) dorsal fin, no adipose fin, strongly compressed trunk, and (for catfish), large eyes. Alexander (1966a) interprets these features and others as being adaptations for a more pelagic mode of existence than is true of most catfish. The small glass catfishes *(Kryptopterus)* are in fact completely pelagic, as evidenced by their diurnal activity and semitransparency, which should offer them camouflage in open waters. The 45 species of the African and Indian family Schilbeidae have a morphology similar to the silurids, including "glass catfish" species *(Physalia)*. The remaining families in this group have various specializations. For example, five families (Amblycipitidae, Amphiliidae, Akysidae, Olyridae, Sisoridae) contain mostly small species adapted for life in fast-moving streams; the Heteropneustidae have lunglike extensions of the gill cavity they use for air breathing; and the electric catfishes (Malapteruridae) have powerful electric organs they use for stunning prey.

South American catfishes. The 14 families and 1300+ species of catfish in South America rival the characins in their diversity (Fig. 18.3). Over a third of the species belong in the family Loricariidae, a group of heavily armored, attenuated catfish. Most are adapted for scraping or sucking algae from the bottom in streams and can use their suckerlike mouths for holding onto rocks in fast water. Two other families of armored catfish are the Callichthydae and the Doradidae. Members of both families tend to be moderately deep bodied (but flattened ventrally) and protected with large, bony plates and spines. The callichthyids are characteristic of waters that frequently become stagnant and so they swallow bubbles of air, which are absorbed in a highly vascularized portion of the hind gut. Like the clariid catfishes of Africa and Asia, many of these catfish are capable of moving overland on their stout pectoral spines.

The remaining families of South American catfishes all have smooth bodies. The Pimelodidae fill the "typical" catfish role, being widely distributed (including Central America and Cuba), abundant (300 species), and large enough to support fisheries for them. However, the bodies of pimelodids tend to be much more flattened than those of the ictalurid and bagrid catfishes, and they possess extremely long barbels (three pairs). Eight other families of smooth catfish are mostly distinguished by their minor morphological variations on the typical catfish theme. The most deviant of the smooth catfish families is the Trichomycteridae, which make up 155+ species of small, elongate catfishes that lack the adipose fin. Some of them seem to be parasitic on other fishes, entering their gill cavities and feeding on gill filaments and blood. Still other species apparently hide themselves in sand, mud, or leaf litter and snatch scales from passing fishes.

Marine catfishes. The only families in the Otophysi whose member species are primarily found in salt water are the Ariidae (sea catfishes) and the Plotosidae (eeltail catfishes). The sea catfishes are unspecialized-looking catfishes found in tropical and subtropical waters over much of the world but particularly in estuarine waters. On the east coast of the United States, the gafftopsail catfish *(Bagre marinus),* so named because of its large dorsal fin, and the sea catfish *(Arius felis)* are common fish that move in and out of the estuaries on a seasonal basis. They swim about, feeding on benthic invertebrates, in noisy schools, the noise being created by the clicking of pectoral spines and the vibration of the swimbladder. The males of these two species, as well as of other species in the family, incubate the eggs in their mouths.

The eeltail catfishes look as if they have the head of a catfish welded onto the body of a stout eel. They are widely distributed in the Indian and Pacific oceans, where a number of the species have colonized the fresh waters of Australia and other islands. Their spines are particularly toxic.

GYMNOTIFORMES

The 60+ species of electric knifefishes are found entirely in the fresh waters of South America, where they presumably share a common ancestor with modern catfishes (Fink and Fink 1981). All have electric organs and, as a result, they are remarkably similar to the mormyrids of Africa, although they evolved independently (Fig. 18.1). The electric organs are used for navigation and for detection and capture of prey organisms, at night or in murky water. The distinctive morphology of the gymnotiformes can be largely explained as an accommodation to the efficient use of their electric organs. Their bodies are eel-like, and because much of their muscle mass has been converted to electric organs, they can create large electric fields around them. Because of the large electric organs and the need to keep the body fairly rigid to create a uniform electric field, the fish propel themselves, slowly and gracefully, through wavelike movements of their long (140+ rays) anal fin. Using this fin, they can move either forward or backward. Each individual fin ray actually moves in a circular pattern, made possible by the way they connect to the internal supporting bony element (pterygiophore). Other fins on the gymnotoids are minimal; the pelvic fins are absent, the caudal absent or very small, the pectorals small, and the dorsal absent or reduced to a few filaments. The viscera of the gymnotoids are confined to a relatively small anterior part of the body. The gills are small with small openings, reflecting both the leisurely activity patterns of the Gymnotiformes and the ability of many of them to breathe air. The dependence on electric organs for sensory input is indicated by the small eyes of gymnotiformes, although some sand knifefishes (Rhamphichthyidae) have an attenuated, fingerlike caudal region that apparently enables them to feel their way into protective cover, which they frequently enter backward.

Perhaps the best known of the gymnotiform fishes is the electric eel (*Electrophorus electricus*), the only member of the family Electrophoridae. It inhabits the backwaters and shallow streams of the Amazon region of South America. About half the body musculature of this fish has been converted into electric organs; together they can produce 350 V to 650 V, depending on the length of the fish, although the amperage is low (less than 1 A). These extraordinary electrical powers are used both for defense and for stunning the fish upon which it feeds. The eels also have two other, much smaller sets of electrical organs, one of which is used for navigation. Apparently, the main prey of electric eels are other electric fish, which they detect using their electrical sense organs (Westby 1988). The eels make themselves "invisible" to their prey by turning off their own electrical systems and waiting in ambush. Prey fish that detect a waiting eel attempt to confuse them by shutting down their own electrical activity for a few seconds, at irregular intervals.

LESSONS FROM THE OTOPHYSI

The otophysans demonstrate how the "right" combination of behavioral, physiological, morphological, and life history traits has allowed one major evolutionary line of fish to dominate freshwater environments. Presumably interactions within the group led to the evolution of catfish, which are active primarily at night and can therefore use resources less available to day-active cyprinids and characins. Likewise, the knifefishes evolved electrical sensory systems to handle the highly turbid conditions of tropical rivers, paralleling the evolution of mormyrid fishes in Africa. In shallow-water marine environments, and to a lesser extent in lakes, spiny percomorph fish predominate, fish that largely rely on vision for feeding. The ostariophysans are also frequently vision-oriented, but it is clear from the development of their superb sense of hearing and well-developed sense of taste that visual cues are often of secondary importance to them. This in turn reflects the frequent lack of water clarity and the turbulence of stream environments.

Supplemental Readings

Alexander 1966a,b; Fink and Fink 1981; Jenkins and Burkhead 1994; Moyle 1976a; Nelson 1994; Pflieger 1975; Sawada 1982; Sterba 1959; Winfield and Nelson 1991.

CHAPTER 19

Pike, Smelt, and Salmon

SUBDIVISION TELEOSTEI
   Infradivision Euteleostei
      Superorder Protacanthopterygii
         Order Esociformes
           Families Esocidae (pikes), Umbridae (mudminnows)
         Order Osmeriformes
           Families Argentinidae (herring smelts), Microstomatidae;
           Bathylagidae (deepsea smelts), Opisthoproctidae (barreleyes),
           Leptochilichthyidae, Alepocephalidae (slickheads), Platytroctidae
           (tubeshoulders), Osmeridae (smelts), Salangidae (oriental icefishes),
           Sundasalangidae (sundaland noodlefishes), Retropinnidae (New
           Zealand smelts), Lepidogalaxiidae (salamanderfish), Galaxiidae
           (galaxiids)
         Order Salmoniformes
           Families Salmonidae (salmon, trout, whitefish),

Anyone who wishes to gain an understanding of how modern fish systematics progresses through the use of cladistics and other techniques should explore the history of Protanthopterygii. A good place to start is with J. S. Nelson (1994), who notes that the large number of recent analyses "might suggest that we now have a strong

basis for classifying this taxon; however, much disagreement exists in the conclusions of these authors" (p. 175). The high level of interest in this group is reflected
in its name: Prot (original)- acanth (spine)-pterygii (fin). This name indicates that
the group is supposed to contain fishes most similar to the presumed ancestors of
the spiny rayed fishes (Acanthopterygii) which dominate the oceans of world. Although the systematists generally seem to agree that somewhere in this group of
rather specialized fishes there are some ancestor-like fishes, just which ones they
are and how they relate to each other and to other groups is debatable.

The superorder as constituted here contains 310+ species divided up into three
distinct orders. The fish in these orders lack spines, but most possess an adipose fin.
Their pelvic fins are abdominal in position and widely separated from the pectoral
fins (the pelvic and pectoral girdles are not connected), which are placed low on the
body. The scales are cycloid, and the upper jaw contains both the maxilla and the premaxilla, the latter not protractile. The swimbladder is connected to the gut with a duct.

From an ecological perspective, the superorder contains three rather different
kinds of fish: freshwater predators, diadromous species, and deepsea species. This
variety alone should raise suspicions as to their relatedness. The diadromous fishes
are among the most studied of fishes because they include the valuable and much-
favored salmonids and smelts, plus the curious galaxiids of the southern hemisphere.

ESOCIFORMES

This order contains just 10 species, all confined to fresh water: five species of pike
(Esocidae) and five species of mudminnow (Umbridae). The pikes and mudminnows are widespread in North America and northern Eurasia. The body morphology of all the species is that of the lie-in-wait predator, with dorsal and anal fins
placed far back on the body, about equal in size, and aligned with each other. The
adipose fin is lacking, as are pyloric cecae, teeth on the maxillary bone, and the
mesocoracoid bone in the shoulder girdle.

The pikes, with their elongate snouts and forked tails, are classic lie-in-wait
predators and are important piscivores in weedy lakes and other slow-moving bodies of water. In North America and Europe they are favorite sport fishes, especially
the circumpolar northern pike (Esox lucius), which may reach 24 kg to 26 kg (1.3 m),
and the muskellunge (E. masquinongy) of eastern North America, which may reach
32 kg (1.6 m). Pike generally capture their prey with a sudden rush from cover. They
grab the prey sideways, impaling it on sharp teeth before retreating to cover to turn
the prey around and swallow it head first. Pike require flooded vegetation for
spawning and nursery areas for the young, so stabilization of lake levels and stream
flows by humans is frequently detrimental to their populations.

In contrast to the pikes, the mudminnows are all small, rarely reaching 20 cm,
and have blunt snouts and rounded tails. However, all are voracious lie-in-wait
predators on invertebrates. They are most characteristic of weedy ponds, lakes, and
backwaters, where temperatures may be very warm and oxygen levels low. At least
one species (Umbra limi) has a limited ability to breathe air. The mudminnows are

of particular interest to zoogeographers because they are obligatory freshwater fishes with a distinct family distribution pattern. The three species of *Umbra* are found in Atlantic coast drainages of North America, the Mississippi River system, and Europe, respectively; *Novumbra hubbsi* (Olympic mudminnow) is confined to the Olympic peninsula of Washington; and *Dallia pectoralis* (Alaska blackfish) is widely distributed in arctic North America and Siberia (see Chapter 25). Blackfish are extraordinarily abundant in some arctic lakes and ponds and have been used by the native people as food for themselves and their dogs.

OSMERIFORMES

This order is a curious mixture of somewhat elongate predators on small invertebrates, most with an adipose fin, a maxillary bone included in the upper jaw, no radii on their cycloid scales, and common skeletal characteristics. They can be conveniently broken up into three suborders that may or may not actually be closely related to one another: Argentinoidei (deepsea smelts), Osmeroidei (true smelts), and Galaxoidea (southern hemisphere smelts).

Deepsea smelts. The 160+ species, from seven families, in this suborder are all small, deepsea, smeltlike fishes with large or tubular eyes. They are either silvery in color (Argentinidae, Microstomatidae, Bathylagidae, Opisthoproctidae) or black (Leptochilichthyidae, Alepocephalidae, Platytroctidae). Many lack the adipose fin, and only a few have photophores. However, they all possess an epibranchial (crumenal) organ for grinding up small prey. This organ consists of a small diverticulum located just behind the fourth gill arch. The gill rakers from both sides can fit into this pouch, where they interdigitate with one another to break up the food particles.

One of the more peculiar adaptations present in some members of this suborder, including the 10 known species of barreleyes or spookfishes (Opisthoproctidae), is tubular eyes. Such eyes are pointed upward and contain exceptionally large numbers of rods. The fishes that possess such eyes are apparently capable of binocular vision under extremely low light conditions. Fishes with tubular eyes typically prey on small active invertebrates toward the lower limits of light penetration; the upward-pointing eyes enable them to locate prey silhouetted against the light above.

True smelts. Within this grouping are "true" smelts of the northern hemisphere (Osmeridae) and the curious noodlefishes (Salangidae, Sundasalangidae) of Asia. Within the Osmeridae (Figure 19.1) there are only about 13 species but these species are often enormously abundant in the coastal areas of the northern hemisphere. Some species are entirely marine (although confined to inshore areas), some are entirely freshwater or brackish-water dwellers, and some are anadromous. All make excellent eating, but only about half the species are regularly sought as food by humans. Smelts are generally small in size (usually less than 20 cm, although some species may reach 40 cm), but they are still voracious pelagic carnivores, consuming both zooplankton and small fish. The mouth is well equipped with small teeth,

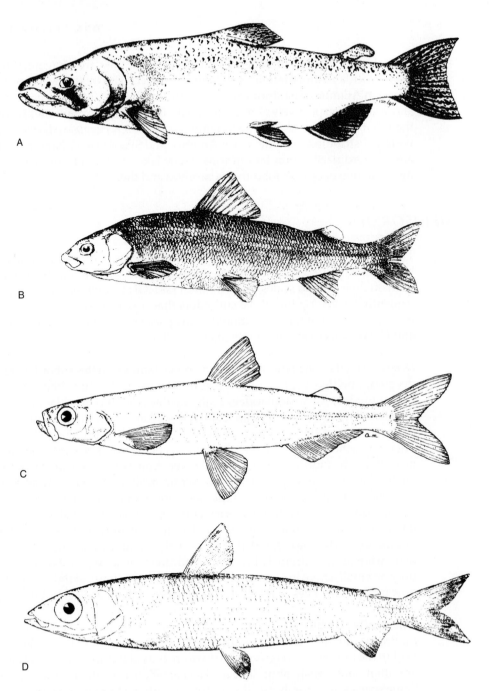

FIGURE 19.1 *Representative protacanthopterygian fishes: (A) chinook salmon* (Oncorhynchus tshawytscha, *64 cm, Salmonidae); (B) mountain whitefish* (Prosopium williamsoni, *28 cm, Salmonidae); (C) delta smelt* (Hypomesus transpacificus, *8 cm, Osmeridae); and (D) Atlantic argentine* (Argentina silus, *36 cm, Argentinidae). [(A), (B), and (C) from Moyle 1976a; (D) from Goode and Bean 1895.]*

including those on the maxilla and premaxilla. As in salmonids, the adipose fin is present; but in contrast to this, the axillary process on the pelvic fin is absent and the number of pyloric ceca ranges from zero to eleven. Smelts are silvery in color and, as McAllister (1963) notes, have "a curious cucumber odor" that is caused by a specific chemical but has unknown function. Smelts generally seek out gravelly areas for spawning, either beaches or riverine riffles, and lay adhesive demersal eggs. When they aggregate for spawning they are very vulnerable to capture by humans. Spawning periods are also when whales, predatory fish, and sea birds move into inshore areas to feast on the concentrated fish.

The noodlefishes (or icefishes) are also the subject of important fisheries, in Japan, China, and Southeast Asia. Like the true smelts, the 11 species are small (to 15 cm) and often very abundant, especially in brackish-water lakes and bays (Saruwatari and Okiyama 1992). These fish are elongate, scaleless, and nearly transparent due to a poorly ossified skeleton. These and other characteristics can be regarded as typical of larvae, and so noodlefish have long been regarded as neotenic (adult fish possessing larval traits) (Roberts 1984).

Southern hemisphere smelts. Throughout the coastal and fresh waters of Australia and New Zealand are found a group of small, often trout-like fishes that fall into three (or more) families: Galaxiidae, Retropinnidae, and Lepidogalaxiidae. The galaxiids are an especially fascinating group to zoogeographers because of their occurrence in fresh water on all the southern continents except Antarctica. They are found in Australia, Tasmania, New Zealand, southern South America (including Tierra del Fuego and other islands), South Africa, and New Caledonia. Most of these areas have endemic genera and species, but one species, *Galaxias maculatus,* is apparently present in all regions where galaxiids are found except South Africa. The distribution pattern of the galaxiids can be explained by the former connection of the continents and their subsequent separation through the processes of continental drift (see Chapter 25). On the other hand, McDowall and Robertson (1975) argue that the distribution of *G. maculatus* can be at least partially explained by the fact that larvae of this species are planktonic and marine and are capable of being carried to distant shores by oceanic currents.

Despite their far-flung distribution pattern, galaxiids are a readily recognizable group. They are small (usually less than 15 cm), elongate fishes that lack an adipose fin but have a dorsal fin placed far back on the body, above the anal fin. The caudal fin is usually rounded, the pectoral fins large, and the pelvic fins small or absent in some species. Scales and maxillary teeth are lacking. Most of the 50 or so species spend their entire life cycle in fresh water, but a few spawn in estuaries and have marine larvae. *G. maculatus* seems to move downstream to spawn in response to lunar cycles, since it lays its eggs among grasses flooded by high spring tides. When the tides ebb, the eggs are stranded among the grasses but hatch when the next high tide covers the grasses, about two weeks later (McDowall and Whitaker 1975). In streams, galaxiids are the approximate ecological equivalents of salmonids in the Northern Hemisphere but they have suffered badly in competition with introduced trout.

One of the more curious galaxiid relatives is the salamander fish *(Lepidogalax-ias salamandroides)*, a tiny (<60 mm) fish discovered in southeastern Australia in 1961, where it inhabits acidic, ephemeral streams and ponds (Berra and Allen 1989). It is eel-like and has a wedge-shaped head, which allows it to burrow into damp sand

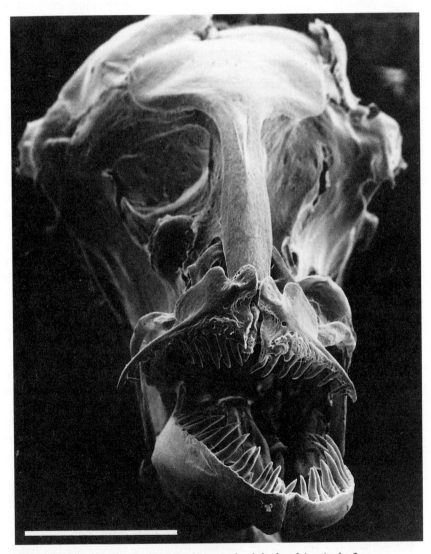

FIGURE 19.2 *Scanning electromicrograph of the head (top) of a 3 cm Australian salamanderfish,* Lepidogalaxias salamandroides *(bottom). The salamanderfish is a small, osmeriform species that lives in acidic, ephemeral streams in south Australia and uses its teeth for the capture of large prey. From Berra and Allen (1989). (Photos by Clay Bryce [left] and Tim Berra [right].)*

or litter when the water disappears (Figure 19.2). Following rains, it emerges quickly and preys on insects with its surprisingly formidable teeth.

SALMONIFORMES

This order contains just one family, the Salmonidae, with about 70 species. The Salmonidae can be divided up into three readily recognizable groups, usually treated as subfamilies (but often as families): Salmoninae (salmon and trout), Coregoninae (whitefishes), and Thymallinae (graylings). Salmon and trout have fine scales (more than 110 in the lateral line), a short dorsal fin, and teeth on the maxillary bone of the upper jaw. Whitefishes have coarse scales (fewer than 110 along the lateral line), a short dorsal fin, and no teeth on the maxillary bone. Graylings have moderately large scales (70 to 110 in the lateral line), a long, sail-like dorsal fin, and teeth on the maxillary bone.

Salmonids are the dominant fishes in the cold-water streams and lakes of North America and Eurasia, where they support major sport and commercial fisheries. Because of the favor they find with anglers and their ease of propagation, salmonids now dominate the cold fresh waters of the Southern Hemisphere as well. A member of the family is readily recognized by its streamlined body, forked tail, adipose fin, axillary process by the pelvic fins, and large number of pyloric ceca (11 to 210) and branchiostegal rays (7 to 20) (Fig. 19.1). Most species grow to at least over 20 cm, and the largest species is the chinook salmon (*Oncorhynchus tshawytscha*), which may grow nearly 1.5 m long (57 kg).

Perhaps no group of fishes has been more studied than the Salmonidae, as their presence in numerous examples in this book attests. The reason for this high interest in them is their mystique as sport fish combined with their value in commerical fisheries and aquaculture. Because of their abundance and their occurrence in

streams and hatcheries near research centers, they also are convenient to study. As a group, the salmon and trout are highly adapted for survival in the cold and fluctuating waters of the northern hemisphere. Most species are anadromous or are derived from anadromous forms. Nonanadromous forms have apparently evolved repeatedly, as populations of anadromous fish become trapped above new barriers or otherwise find it evolutionarily advantageous not to go to sea.

The advantages of anadromy to salmon and trout are considerable. First, it provides a superb dispersal mechanism that has allowed rapid recolonization of regions suddenly made available by retreating glaciers or other events. Second, the abundance of small fish in the ocean permits rapid growth. In the ocean, salmon and trout grow extremely rapidly and can consequently produce more (and larger) eggs than fish that spend their entire life cycle in fresh water. A 500-g rainbow trout that has lived in a stream for four years will typically produce fewer than 1000 eggs, whereas a 4-kg anadromous trout (steelhead) of the same age will produce 4000 or more eggs. The advantage of continuing to use streams for spawning is presumably the protection they afford the embryos and young from marine predators, including other salmon and trout. The embryos are particularly well protected, because they are buried in riffles, in gravel beds that permit penetration of oxygen-rich water but few predators. By the time the young fish have emerged from the gravel, they are large in size (for newly hatched fish) and quite active, so they are capable of avoiding most invertebrate predators and of feeding on a wide range of prey items themselves. Despite the advantages of anadromy, it is variable trait among the salmonids. It is obligatory in some species of Pacific salmon and in the Atlantic salmon *(Salmo salar)*, optional for most species of trout, and not present at all in some species of char, most notably the lake char *(Salvelinus namaycush)*. Most species of whitefish and grayling are also not anadromous.

While anadromy is not a universal feature of the salmonids, most species do undertake spawning migrations and possess a series of distinctive life history stages. A special set of terminology has arisen in association with these stages, thanks to the interest of them by salmon and trout anglers. The eggs are laid in a depression dug in the gravel, called a **redd**. The embryos develop into **alevins** or sac fry, small fish that still possess a yolk sac. As the yolk sac is absorbed and the alevins emerge from the gravel, they become **fry**. The small, active fry develop a series of bars on their sides (parr marks) and are then called **parr**, a stage that may last a few months or years. Stream-dwelling trout frequently retain the parr marks throughout their life. In anadromous populations parr transform into silvery **smolts** and migrate to the sea. Since the parr-smolt transformation is in preparation for a dramatic change in habitat, it includes profound changes in morphology, physiology, and behavior (Hoar 1976). In the ocean (or large lakes) the smolts gradually become mature adults and return to their home streams for spawning. Some males, called **jacks** or **grilse**, return to spawn at an early age and small size. Spawned-out fish are termed **kelts**.

In both inland and coastal drainages, the migratory tendencies of salmonid fishes tend to promote the creation of isolated populations that become quite distinct in their morphology and color patterns. Behnke (1992) documents the fascinating diversity of native trout populations around the American West that we are just beginning to appreciate. High mountain populations of cutthroat and rainbow trout in particular often develop into distinctive, spectacularly colored forms that can be described as subspecies. Good examples include the brilliant green and red Colorado cutthroat trout and the three subspecies of golden trout in California. Less appreciated perhaps is the tendency of whitefish to develop distinctive morphological types when isolated in lakes. Before the invasion of non-native fishes caused extinctions of several species of *Coregonus*, the Laurentian Great Lakes had a "flock" of species/forms that was segregating by temperature and depth (Smith 1968).

Despite the enormous interest in salmonids, including whitefish and grayling, many species, runs, and populations are extinct or in danger of extinction. There are lots of factors working together to produce this situation; foremost among these are the destruction of habitats in which the fish spawn and rear their young, and the construction of dams that deny them access to spawning areas or change the nature of the streams. Salmon and trout require cold water of high quality, preferably flowing through relatively undisturbed watersheds. Increasingly, such habitats are not available. Salmonids are relatively easy to culture, but hatchery programs have generally hurt wild populations even as they allow fisheries to continue.

LESSONS FROM PIKE, SMELT, AND SALMON

1. The pikes, smelts, and salmonids may have many characteristics that make them reasonable representatives of the ancestors of more derived groups of fishes, but they also are highly specialized and successful fishes in their own right.

2. Life cycles that entail movements between fresh and salt water can be very successful in terms of numbers of individuals produced by a species, but the total number of species that can adopt such strategies seems to be limited.

3. Systematics is a dynamic field, and major changes within and between taxonomic groupings can be expected. This is a healthy trend because it indicates we are gaining increased understanding of evolutionary relationships.

Supplemental Readings

Gosline 1971; Hart 1973; Herald 1961; McAllister 1963; Moyle 1976a; Nelson 1994; Rosen 1973; Scott and Crossman 1973.

CHAPTER 20

Anglerfish, Barracudinas, Cods, and Dragonfish

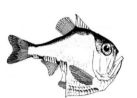

---

[1]Nelson (1994) divides this superorder in two, placing the Aulopiformes in the Cyclosquamata and the Myctophiformes in the Scopelomorpha. While there is considerable doubt that the two orders have common ancestry (Johnson 1992), their exact relationships are not well understoood so we have retained them in one superorder.

Omosudidae, Alepisauridae (lancetfishes)
Order Myctophiformes
Families Neoscopelidae, Myctophidae (lanternfishes)
Superorder Paracanthopterygii[2]
Order Percopsiformes
Families Percopsidae (troutperches), Aphredoderidae (pirate perch), Amblyopsidae (cavefishes)
Order Ophidiiformes
Families Carapidae (carapids), Ophidiidae (cuskeels), Bythitidae (viviparous brotulas), Aphyonidae, Parabrotulidae (false brotulas)
Order Gadiformes
Families Ranicipitidae (tadpole cod), Euclichthyidae (eucla cod), Macrouridae (grenadiers), Steindachneriidae (luminous hake), Moridae (flatnose cods), Melanonidae (pelagic cods), Macruronidae (southern hakes), Bregmacerotidae (codlets), Muraenolepidae (eel cods), Phycidae (phycid hakes), Merlucciidae (merluccid hakes), Gadidae (cods)
Order Batrachoidiformes
Family Batrachoididae (toadfishes)
Order Lophiiformes
Families Lophiidae (goosefishes), Antennariidae (frogfishes), Brachionichthyidae (handfishes), Chaunacidae (sea toads), Ogcocephalidae (batfishes), Caulophrynidae (fanfins), Neoceratiidae, Melanocetidae (black devils), Diceratiidae, Himantolophidae (football fishes), Diceratiidae, Oneirodidae (dreamers), Thaumatichthyidae, Gigantactinidae (whipnoses), Centrophrynidae (deepsea anglerfish), Ceratiidae (seadevils), Gigantactinidae, Linophrynidae (netdevils)

In this chapter, we have entered the freeway leading into the most complex metropolis of teleost evolution, sometimes called Neoteleostei (new teleosts). The exits eventually lead to between 15,000 and 16,000 species. A major problem (from a human point of view) is that the freeway is still under construction and in many cases the locations of exits, major and minor, have not been decided. This is not surprising considering the complexity of the task of the systematists, who must find ways to fit an incredibly diverse array of fishes into a common plan. Most of the fishes (ca. 13,500) are located in the Acanthopterygii, the dense aggregation of spiny-rayed fishes that dominate the shallow inshore waters of the oceans, treated in the next chapters. However, that still leaves about 2,000 species that exited early from the main line and have successfully exploited a wide variety of environments, but

---

[2]Nelson (1994) inserts two other superorders in front of the Paracanthopterygii: Lampridiomorpha, containing the Lampridiformes, and Polymixiomorpha, containing the family Polymixiidae. Here we stick with Nelson (1984) which places these fishes within the Percomorpha (Chapter 22). There seems to be little doubt that they do have an ancestral relationship with the percomorph fishes (Johnson and Patterson 1993); the unresolved question is just how close that relationship is.

especially the deep sea, the soft-bottomed environments on continental shelves, and caves in fresh water. Their specializations obscure their relationships with the Acanthopterygii and with each other but make them some of the most curious fishes known. Three major groups are discussed together in this chapter, as much for convenience as for any other reason.

STENOPTERYGII

The Stenopterygii ("narrow-fins") have a mixture of ancestral and derived teleost characteristics and seem to have had a long independent evolutionary history. They are tropical to temperate deepsea fishes, with photophores and large mouths with teeth on both the maxilla and premaxilla (Fig. 20.1). Many species have an adipose fin. The scales, if present, are cycloid. Most species are black in color, although a few are silvery. This group includes the most abundant fishes in the world (bristlemouths), as well as some of the most fearsome-looking small predators (dragonfishes).

Gonostomatidae. The bristlemouths are extraordinarily abundant in many parts of the world's oceans; members of the genus *Cyclothone* are probably more numerous than any other fishes. However, all of the 75 known species are quite small (most under 5 cm long) and live at great depths, so they cannot be exploited. Bristlemouths have large, horizontal mouths with numerous small teeth, typical of fish that feed on large prey, yet they also have fine gill rakers, typical of fish that feed on small prey (Fig. 20.1). This arrangement may partially explain their success, since it enables them to feed on whatever prey comes along, regardless of size. The bodies of bristlemouths are elongate and somewhat rounded and are lined with light organs (photophores).

Sternoptychidae. In many deep areas of the oceans, the marine hatchetfishes (ca. 50 species) are second in abundance only to the bristlemouths. These small (to 10 cm) fish are indeed hatchet-shaped, with deep, extremely compressed bodies (Fig. 20.1). Not only does the belly taper to a thin edge, but the top of each fish has a "blade" made of fused pterygiophores (the internal bony supports for fin rays). The sides of the body are silvery and contain numerous large photophores. The eyes and mouth are all turned upward and the eyes of some species are tubular. These features are all indicative of the fact that most species of hatchetfish move up and down the water column, preying on copepods and other migrating zooplankton. The slender profile of these fish when seen from above or below, coupled with the light-scattering abilities of their silvery sides and their photophores, serves to conceal them from both predators and prey.

Stomiidae. The barbelled dragonfishes are a diverse group of dark-colored deepsea predators, each equipped with a chin barbel and a large, fang-rich mouth that allows some species to capture prey larger than themselves. The viperfishes (*Chauliodus* spp.) have extraordinary fangs and an ability to swing open their mouths to swallow very large prey (Fig. 20.1). The scaleless dragonfishes (subfamily Melanostomiinae, 160+ species) and loosejaws (subfamily Malacosteinae, 15 species) are

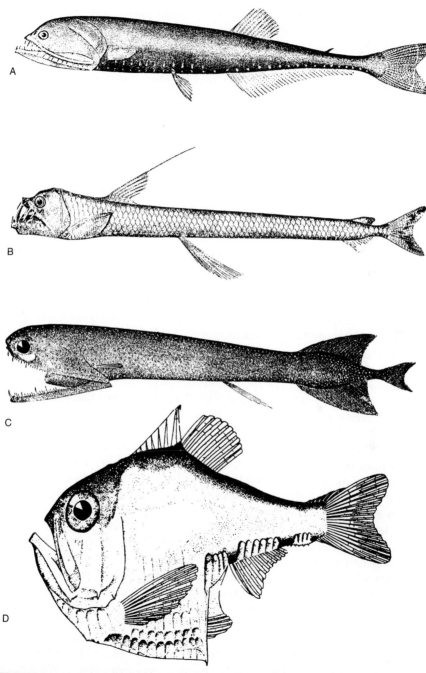

FIGURE 20.1 *Representative stomiiform fishes: (A) bristlemouth* (Cyclothone elongata, *8 cm); (B) viperfish* (Chauliodus sloani, *35 cm); (C) loosejaw* (Malacosteus niger, *12 cm); and (D) hatchetfish* (Argyropelecus olfersi, *3 cm). [(A), (B), and (C) from Goode and Bean 1895; (D) from Jordan and Evermann (1900).]*

elongate, lie-in-wait deepsea predators with rows of tiny photophores (Fig. 20.1). Their jaws are large with many sharp teeth, and the long chin barbel of most species has a luminescent "lure" at the end, presumably for attracting prey. The maximum size of these fishes is 10 to 25 cm. The black dragonfishes (*Idiacanthus* spp.) are similar in many respects to the preceding families, except that their bodies are nearly eel-like, with elongate dorsal fins. The black dragonfishes also possess extremely peculiar larvae that are colorless and have eyes on the tips of long stalks. Although these fishes can achieve lengths between 35 and 40 cm (but only 25 to 30 g in weight), only the females reach such sizes. The males are much smaller and apparently serve only for reproduction, because they lack teeth, the chin barbel, and a functional digestive tract.

SCOPELOMORPHA

These fishes are, in many respects, similar to the salmoniform fishes, and the two groups have previously been lumped together in the Salmoniformes (Greenwood et al. 1966). Both groups have many ancestral features, such as soft-rayed fins, the presence (usually) of an adipose fin, abdominal pelvic fins, and various skeletal features; but the Scopelomorpha also differ from the Salmoniformes in many important respects, such as the exclusion of the maxillary bone from the gape of the mouth (although the upper jaw is not protrusible) and the presence of a physoclistic (closed) swimbladder. This superorder contains 14 families with about 560 species, most of which inhabit deepsea environments where they prey on fish and invertebrates. The diversity of the group is reflected in the fact that eight of the fifteen families contain fewer than ten species each.

Aulopiformes. This order is a mixed bag of odd deepsea fishes, plus one family of inshore fishes—the lizardfishes, Synodontidae—that are united by the unique structure of the gill arches. Most of the deepsea forms are small (<50 cm) predators capable of devouring a wide range of prey species, including other fishes nearly their same size. The 55+ species of barracudinas (Paralepididae) look like miniature barracudas, complete with sharp teeth (Fig. 20.2). They have large eyes but no swimbladder. Barracudinas, although typically less than 15 cm long, seem to be important in marine food chains, because they prey on smaller deepsea fishes and are themselves extensively preyed upon by such predators as salmon, tuna, and swordfish. The daggertooth (*Anotopterus pharao*) is similar to the barracudinas, except that the jaws are enlarged, with numerous bladelike teeth. Extremely large jaws and teeth are also characteristic of other families in the order, and the sabertooth fishes (Evermannellidae) are capable of swallowing fish larger than themselves. Both the sabertooth fishes and the pearleyes (Scopelarchidae) have telescopic eyes that point upward, enabling them to see their prey from below. While these fishes are spectacular predators, they are less than 50 cm long and rarely receive much public attention. This is not true, however, of the lancetfishes (Alepisauridae), which may exceed 2 m in length and occasionally wash up on beaches. Besides having long

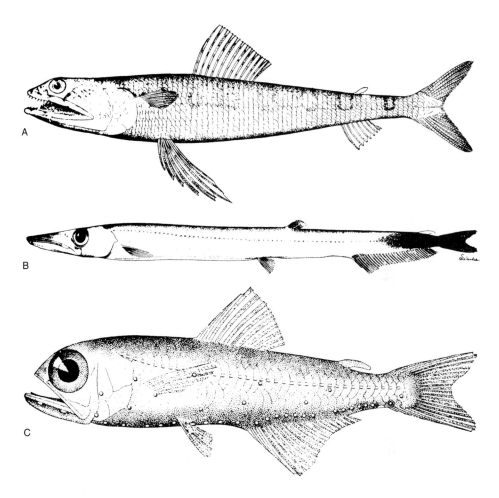

FIGURE 20.2 *Scopelomorph fishes: (A) lizardfish* (Synodus); *(B) barracudina* (Lestidium); *and (C) lanternfish* (Myctophum, Myctophidae). *(From Jordan and Evermann 1895, 1900.)*

fangs and elongate bodies, these fish have an enormous, sail-like dorsal fin. They seem to be among the largest fish that spend full time in the mesopelagic region of the world's oceans, feeding on all other fish present. A number of rare deep sea fishes are known mainly from specimens obtained from lancetfish stomachs.

All the previously mentioned aulopiform fishes inhabit the water column of the deep sea, but some of the most curious members are deepsea bottom-dwellers. These small, slender fishes belong to two basic groups, the greeneyes (Chloropthalmidae) and the spiderfishes and grideye fishes (Ipnopidae). The greeneyes have exceptionally large eyes of a pale green color, which permit them to see in the dim light that exists just above the bottom at the edge of the continental shelf. There they feed on small, pelagic invertebrates. In deeper water, the spiderfishes (18 species) play a similar role, except that they "stand" on the bottom with the extraordinarily long rays on their pelvic and caudal fins (see Fig. 35.2). These fishes have tiny eyes, and it seems likely that they detect the small invertebrates they prey on with the long, independent rays of their pectoral fins (Sulak 1977).

The exception to the rule that aulopiform fishes inhabit the deep sea is the family Synodontidae, although even two of its species are deepwater dwellers. The lizardfishes are moderate-sized (25 to 50 cm) benthic fish that live mainly in the shallow waters of tropical and subtropical areas. Some species, such as the Atlantic lizardfish *(Synodus foetans)*, inhabit temperate waters as far north as Cape Cod. Lizardfish have a vaguely lizardlike appearance, with their flattened bony heads, large scales on the body and head, and large mouths in pointed snouts (Fig. 20.2). The mouth contains numerous long, pointed teeth useful for holding onto the prey they ambush. Lizardfish conceal themselves by resting quietly on their large pelvic fins on rocky bottoms or coral reefs, or by partially covering themselves with sand in soft-bottomed areas.

Myctophiformes. Most (235) of the species of myctophiform fishes are lanternfish (Myctophidae) (Nafpaktitis 1978). They are a remarkably abundant group that can be found in all the oceans of the world. They generally live between 200 m and 1000 m in the open ocean, but some have been observed at depths greater than 2000 m, and others have been found at the surface at night. They are often an important part of the deep scattering layer, so called because sound produced by sonar units of ships bounces off the thousands of swimbladders in a school, at times giving the impression of a false bottom. The lanternfishes are small, with blunt heads, large eyes, and rows of photophores on the body and head (Fig. 20.1). The photophore patterns are different for each species, and they are also different for the sexes within each species (which led some early investigators to describe the males and females as separate species). It is not unusual for several species of lanternfish to be caught together in sampling devices. How they manage to coexist is an interesting question, because most are generalists in their feeding, apparently taking whatever prey of suitable size are available (Tyler and Pearcy 1975). It is possible that there is some segregation by depth preferences and by patterns of vertical migration.

PARACANTHOPTERYGII

The Paracanthopterygii (para = like) are a major evolutionary line of predominantly marine fishes (1200+ species) that possess many ancestral osteological and myological features but also possess many of the derived features of the Acanthopterygii. Among the derived features that characterize most (but not necessarily all) species are (1) an elaborate and protractile premaxilla; (2) spines on the dorsal, anal, and pelvic fins; (3) reduced numbers of pelvic and caudal fin rays; (4) ctenoid scales; and (5) pelvic fins in the thoracic or jugular position (Fig. 20.3). There is good reason to doubt, however, that the Paracanthopterygii represent a single unified evolutionary line (Nelson 1994).

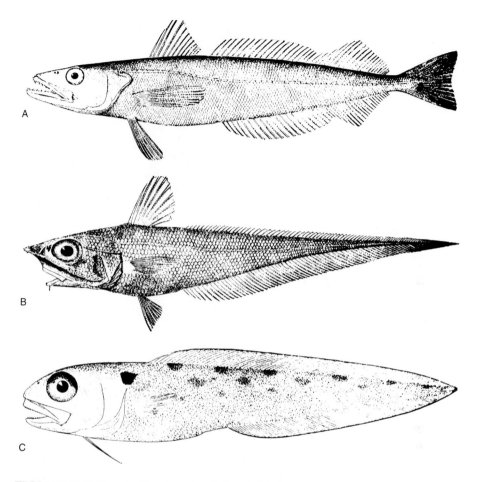

FIGURE 20.3 *Paracanthopterygian fishes: (A) hake* (Merluccius); *(B) grenadier* (Coelorhynchus); *(C) cusk-eel* (Otophidium, Ophidiidae). *(From Goode and Bean 1895.)*

Percopsiformes

This order contains just three families and nine species of peculiar North American freshwater fishes, all small (less than 20 cm) in size. The species have an interesting mixture of ancestral and derived characteristics. The premaxilla forms the entire margin of the upper jaw but is not protractile. The pelvic fins (if present) are "subthoracic" in position in that they are located close to the pectorals but slightly behind them. Spines are weakly developed. Scales are either ctenoid or cycloid.

The two species of troutperch (Percopsidae, Fig. 20.4), with their adipose fins, ctenoid scales, and weak dorsal, pelvic, and anal fin spines, look like a cross between trout and perch. The pirateperch *(Aphredoderus sayanus)*, the sole member of the Aphredoderidae, is more perchlike with its ctenoid scales, spines in the dorsal and

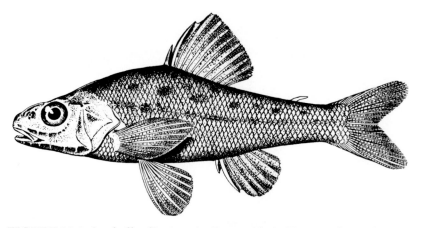

FIGURE 20.4 *Sandroller (Percopsis, Percopsidae). (From Jordan and Evermann 1900.)*

anal fins, subthoracic pelvic fins, and, most distinctively, its anus in its throat. In contrast to the pirate perch, the eight species of Amblyopsidae have cycloid scales, spines on the anal and dorsal fins (optional), and no pelvic fins (except in one species). They are adapted for living mainly in caves and springs of the limestone regions of the southeastern United States (Fig. 20.5).

Ophidiiformes

Most members of this order are distinctly eel-like with long tapering tails. Their pelvic fins, when present, are located on the chin, where they are reduced to just one or two fin rays. Many cusk-eels and brotulas (families Ophidiidae, Bythitidae, and Aphyonidae) are also inhabitants of the deepsea bottom and may show extreme adaptations for living there, such as poorly developed eyes. Some of the deepest-living fishes known are brotulas (see Fig. 35.1). Curiously, some brotulas have managed to adapt to the water of caves, including brackish and fresh water. These forms are typically blind or have reduced eyes. The cave forms occur in a wide range of localities, from the Bahamas, to Cuba, to the Yucatan Peninsula of Mexico, to the Galapagos Islands. The largest family in the order, the cusk-eels (Ophidiidae, 160+ species) also occurs in a wide range of habitats, from tide pools to the deepest parts of the ocean. However, most species are small and not particularly common.

In many respects, the most remarkable fishes in this order are the 27 species of pearlfish (Carapidae), because some live in close association with marine invertebrates, such as sea cucumbers, clams, sea urchins, and starfish (Trott 1981; Smith et al. 1981). Their relationships with the invertebrates range from commensalism to parasitism. In the latter case, certain species live inside the body cavity of sea cucumbers, where they feed on the internal organs (Fig. 20.6). Pearlfish are small (to 30 cm) with elongate, slender bodies that taper to a fine point. The pelvic, caudal, and sometimes the pectoral fins are absent, and scales are small or absent. This morphology allows a pearlfish to back into the body cavity of its host species through

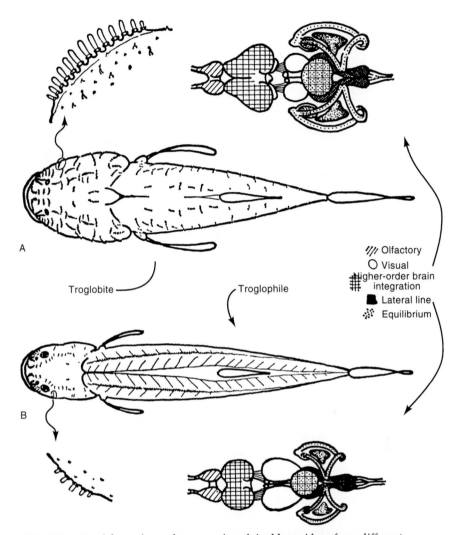

Olfactory
Visual
Higher-order brain integration
Lateral line
Equilibrium

Troglobite

Troglophile

A

B

FIGURE 20.5 *Adaptations of two species of Amblyopsidsae from different cave habitats. A. The northern cavefish lives in total darkness and has a well-developed lateral-line system. The sections of the brain dealing with the lateral line are also well developed. The head is larger and has more sensory canals for detection of obstacles than that of the spring cavefish (B), which lives in caves that have some light. The longer fins of the northern cavefish allow it to "row" slowly and efficiently search for prey. (From Poulson and White [1969]; copyright 1969, American Association for the Advancement of Science.)*

the mouth or anus. The anus of a pearlfish is located close to the head, allowing the fish to void wastes without emerging far from the host. Besides the peculiar way of life of the adults, pearlfish are also noted for their complex life cycle. They pass through two larval stages: a vexillifer stage, which is planktonic, and a tenuis stage,

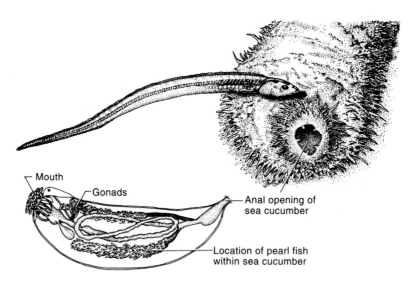

Mouth

Gonads

Anal opening of
sea cucumber

Location of pearl fish
within sea cucumber

FIGURE 20.6 *A pearlfish (Carapidae) and its host, a sea cucumber. (From Moyle 1993, copyright © 1993 by Chris Mari van Dyck.)*

which is benthic. The larval forms are different enough from the parents so that the first ones known were described as distinct species.

Gadiformes

This order contains over 480 bottom-oriented marine fishes, some of which play major ecological roles in their respective communities (but particularly in the benthic communities of deep water). They are a fairly uniform group from a taxonomic perspective, with many distinctive anatomical features (Markle 1989). Gadiform fishes typically have elongate bodies (often tapering to a point at the tail) with long dorsal and anal fins. It is not unusual for these fins to be broken up into two or three sections (especially the dorsal fins). The pelvic fins are either thoracic or jugular in position, or absent. There are no spines. All of them have small, cycloid scales. Because they are predators on fish and invertebrates, most have large terminal or subterminal mouths, often with barbels.

Macrouridae. The grenadiers or rattails are an important group (285 species) of benthic fish found in deep water throughout the world, although they are most abundant in tropical and subtropical areas. All have large heads and long, tapering bodies. The dorsal and anal fins are continuous with the sharply pointed caudal fin (Fig. 20.4). The grenadiers are major predators and scavengers of the deepsea bottom. They can be photographed in large numbers by suspending a camera over a bucket of dead fish lowered to the bottom. Although their preference for deep water makes them difficult to catch, there is considerable interest in developing commercial fisheries for grenadiers.

Moridae. The flatnose cods are moderate-sized (50 to 70 cm) deepsea fish that are apparently very abundant on the upper continental slope throughout the Atlantic, Pacific, and Indian oceans. The ca. 100 species resemble hake in many respects but can be distinguished from them by their pointed snout, which is quite flat over the mouth, and by their swimbladder, which connects to the inner ear. Two closely related species of *Antimora* are abundant off the Atlantic and Pacific coasts of North America.

Merlucciidae. The merluccid hakes are often placed in the Gadidae but differ from them by having one or two dorsal fins, no chin barbel, and the first ray of the first dorsal fin hardened into a "spine" (Fig. 20.4). A few species have a long, pointed tail in which the anal, caudal, and dorsal fins are united. All have terminal mouths with sharp teeth, indicative of their tendency to be piscivorous. The true hakes (*Merluccius*, seven species) are found at moderate depths over much of the world, near coastlines. Although their flesh is not as prized as that of the cods, the hakes now rank among the most important commercial fishes of the world because of their abundance and ease of capture with trawls.

Gadidae. The "true" cods are distinguished from other cod-like fish by their separate caudal fin and by the dorsal fin, which is divided into two or three sections. None of the fins have spines, the swimbladder is physoclistous, and a chin barbel is usually present. As might be expected from their morphology, the cods are bottom-oriented species, feeding on such animals as crabs, fish, and molluscs. Some species make extensive seasonal migrations for spawning and feeding. Besides the classic cods *(Gadus)*, the commercially important members of this family are haddock *(Melanogrammus aegelfinus)*, and pollock *(Pollachius, Theragra)*. In the Arctic, some cold-adapted species of cod are the dominant predators (see Chapter 36) and have some importance as commercial fish. One species of cod, the burbot *(Lota lota)*, is confined to cold freshwater lakes and rivers of North America and Eurasia.

The cod family contains only about 55 species, but most of them are highly desired food fish and so have long played an important economic and nutritional role for Western peoples. The Atlantic cod *(Gadus morhua)* has been particularly important because of its size, abundance, and ease of capture. At least 100 years before the formal colonization of North America, European fishermen (particularly the Portuguese) were capturing cod by hook and line off the coast of North America and landing in Newfoundland to dry and salt their catches. The importance of the cod fisheries to the early development of America is indicated by the fact that since 1784 the effigy of a cod has been prominently displayed in the Massachusetts statehouse. This, of course, has not kept the cod populations from collapsing due to overfishing. At one time it was thought that the Grand Banks and other fishing areas had an inexhaustible supply of cod, haddock, and similar fishes. Cod in particular have such high reproductive potential (e.g., a six-year-old female can produce 5 million eggs) that it was often assumed they could replace themselves under almost any fishing pressure. Today (1995), the cod fisheries of North America are almost nonexistent and the ecosystems on which they depend are in disarray. Recovery of the ecosystems and the fisheries will be a long and painful process.

Batrachoidiformes

This order contains just the toadfish family (Batrachoididae), which contains only about 69 species. What the order lacks in species it makes up for in conspicuousness, because toadfishes are commonly encountered in shallow marine waters, especially off North America. As the common name suggests, toadfish have a flat, toadlike head with protruding, dorsally located eyes and a large mouth. The body is squat, and usually without scales. The pelvic fins are jugular in position, and spines are present in the dorsal fin. In some South American forms the spines are hollow and associated with venom glands. Perhaps the best-known toadfish is the oyster toadfish *(Opsanus tau),* which can make incredibly loud sounds by vibrating its swimbladder and has the habit of laying its eggs (which it defends vigorously) in old cans and other trash. Midshipmen *(Porichthys)* are also well-known members of this family, since they are one of the few inshore fishes that have numerous photophores. They also make loud noises when courting, to the annoyance of people who live in boats anchored near a spawning area; the hulls of the boats can pick up and even amplify the loud buzzing sound.

Lophiiformes

All the 280–300 members of this order are called anglerfishes, because most possess a fishing pole (illicium) on the head, complete with an artificial lure (esca). The illicium and esca develop from the first ray of the spinous dorsal fin. Anglerfish are inactive forms with large heads and mouths (Fig. 20.7), cryptic coloration, scales small or absent, small gills, jugular pelvic fins (if present), no ribs, and swimbladders that are physoclistic when present (Pietsch and Grobecker 1987). Anglerfish fall into two ecological groups: (1) those that live on the bottom or attached to drifting seaweed, usually in shallow water (families Lophiidae, Brachionichthyidae, Antennariidae, Chaunacidae, Ogcocephalidae); and (2) those that live in the Bathypelagic Zone (the remaining 11 families). The fishes in the first group lie hidden on the bottom and wave the illicium and esca around to attract potential prey. The esca mimics particular types of organisms; at least one species of anglerfish (*Antennarius* sp.) has an esca that looks remarkably like a small fish (Pietsch and Grobecker 1978). Most species in the latter four families of the first group have muscular pectoral fins that look like arms and are used either for "walking" across the bottom or for clinging onto floating seaweed. Most of the shallow-water anglerfishes are small in size, but some goosefishes (Lophiidae) may reach 1.3 m in length and a weight of nearly 32 kg. Despite their ugly appearance, such fish are quite edible and are sometimes referred to as the "poor man's lobster."

While the shallow-water anglerfishes are extremely peculiar in appearance, many of the deepsea anglers can be described only as bizarre. They are, by and large, small, soft-bodied forms without scales or pelvic fins but with large mouths and teeth, dark-colored bodies, and a variety of illicia and esca. However, the angling organs are present only on females; the males exist primarily for reproduction and in many species live attached to the females (see Chapter 35 for a discussion of reproductive strategies). As in the shallow-water forms, the esca seems to mimic other

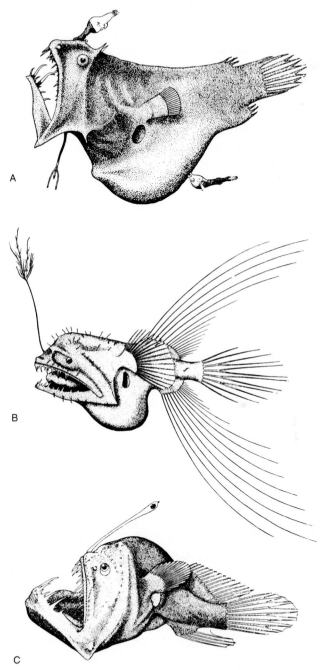

FIGURE 20.7 *Deepsea anglerfishes (Lophiiformes): (A) netdevil* (Linophryne); *(B) fanfin anglerfish* (Caulophryne); *and (C) black devil* (Melanocetus). *Life size of these fish is 5 cm to 10 cm. Note the small male attached to the large female in (A). (From Regan and Trewavas 1932.)*

organisms to attract them to the anglerfish. Because most potential prey organisms in the deep sea are luminous, the esca contains a light organ, in which light is produced by symbiotic bacteria (O'Day 1974). This light attracts not only prey but also (because the esca is different for each species of anglerfish) males. As might be expected of an organ that is important for both prey capture and reproduction and that is likely to become damaged by animals attracted to it, the illicium is apparently capable of regeneration (Pietsch 1974). In addition to the esca, some deepsea anglerfish have barbels that also produce light. Curiously, these barbels do not contain light-producing bacteria but have an intrinsic light-producing system (Hansen and Herring 1977).

LESSONS FROM ODDS AND CODS

The many bizarre, to us, shapes of the deepsea fishes make perfect sense in the extraordinary environment in which they live (Chapter 35), and demonstrate the extreme flexibility of the basic teleost body plan. Although teleosts are primarily a vision-oriented group, abandoning vision as a major sensory mode has been done repeatedly, whether to live in the caves or the deep sea. The opposite response to lightless conditions has been to evolve means of producing light, adaptations that have presumably developed independently in the three major evolutionary lines discussed here. In short, the process of natural selection has produced teleosts that have found ways to use energy extremely efficiently in resource-poor environments.

In contrast, the cods and their relatives have found ways to become extremely abundant in resource-rich benthic environments of northern seas, maximizing the possibilities of the small-egg/high-fecundity life history strategy. When conditions are good, these fish can flood the pelagic environment with larvae; and the adults live long enough to persist through times when conditions are bad. Humans, of course, have found ways to overcome the astonishing ability of these fish to maintain high populations.

Supplemental Readings

Fitch and Lavenberg 1968; Hart 1973; Herald 1961; Nelson 1994; Pietsch and Grobecker 1987.

CHAPTER 21

Silversides, Flying Fish, and Killifish

Infradivision Euteleostei
   Superorder Acanthopterygii
   Series Atherinomorpha
     Order Atheriniformes
       Families Bedotiidae, Melanotaeniidae (rainbow fishes),
       Pseudomugilidae (blueeyes), Atherinidae (silversides),
       Notocheiridae (surf sardines), Telmatherinidae (sailfin
       silversides), Dentatherinidae, Phallostethidae
     Order Beloniformes
       Families Adrianichthyidae, Belonidae (needlefishes),
       Scomberesocidae (sauries), Exocoetidae (flying fishes),
       Hemiramphidae (halfbeaks)
     Order Cyprinodontiformes
       Families Aplocheilidae (rivulines) Profundulidae (Middle
       American killifishes), Fundulidae (killifishes), Valenciidae,
       Anablepidae, Poeciliidae (livebearers), Goodeidae (splitfins),
       Cyprinodontidae (pupfishes)

This is the first chapter devoted to the Acantho-pterygii (spiny-fins), the most diverse group of fishes, with over 250 families and 13,500 species.

As might be expected from such a diverse group, the taxonomic relationships of these fishes are complex, and our concepts about them are changing as more is learned about various species and groups. This is particularly true of the higher categories of classification, which are groups with presumed common ancestry. In this text, we divide the acanthoptergyians into two main presumptive evolutionary groups, the Atherinomorpha (this chapter) and the Percomorpha (next three chapters), following Nelson (1984)—even though good arguments can be made for adding additional groups or for creating different groupings of orders within the groups (Nelson 1994). What all acanthopterygian fishes have in common are structural anatomical details of the mouth, pharyngeal jaws, and paired fins that permit increased efficiency of feeding and movement.

The features used to link the three orders placed in the Atheriniomorpha are also anatomical details, such as the absence of spines or serrations on the opercular bones, the rarity of ctenoid scales, the lack of an orbitosphenoid bone, and the connection of the pectoral girdle to the skull with Baudelot's ligament. This diverse group (ca. 1300 species) is also linked by their generally surface-oriented body shapes; most species have large eyes, flattened heads, upturned mouths, and dorsal fins placed far back on the body. The members are either livebearers or else lay eggs, each of which has a long filament that attaches it to the spawning substrate. While some atherinomorphs, such as flying fish and needlefish, are abundant marine fish, most live in estuarine or inland environments, including some of the harshest environments that support fish of any type.

ATHERINIFORMES

The 285+ atheriniform fishes are mostly elongate species, with terminal mouths, large eyes, and two dorsal fins. The first dorsal fin is made up of weak spines, and a similar spine usually precedes the anal fin as well. The lateral line is weak or absent, while deciduous cycloid scales are present. About 160 of the species are silversides (Atherinidae), slender, silvery fishes with abdominal pelvic fins and large scales (Fig. 21.1). Silversides are often extremely abundant in inshore regions of lakes, estuaries, and various shallow marine environments. They are schooling, diurnal planktivores. Perhaps the most famous of the atherinids is the grunion *(Leuresthes tenuis),* which deposits its eggs in the sands of the beaches of Southern California during high spring tides (see Chapter 32). In lakes, silversides are frequently important forage fishes for predatory game fishes. This and their supposed potential for control of nuisance insects have resulted in the introduction of the inland silverside *(Menidia beryllina)* into lakes and reservoirs in California, Oklahoma, and elsewhere. Such introductions often seem to create more problems than they solve.

The atherinids have apparently given rise to two families of moderately deep-bodied freshwater fishes, the rainbow fishes (Melanotaeniidae) and the blueeyes (Pseudomugilidae). The rainbow fishes (53+ species) and the blueeyes (15 species) are small, brightly colored fish with compressed bodies and subthoracic pelvic

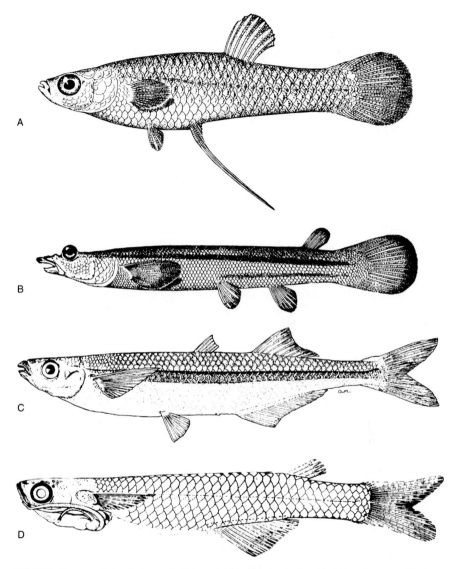

FIGURE 21.1 *Atherinimorph fishes: (A) male mosquitofish* (Gambusia affinis, *Poeciliidae); (B) four-eyed fish* (Anableps anableps, *Anablepidae); (C) topsmelt* (Atherinops affinis, *Atherinidae); and (D)* Ceratostethus *male (Phallostethidae). ([A] and [B] from Jordan and Evermann 1900; [C] from Moyle 1976a; [D] from Roberts 1971.)*

fins. They are confined to the fresh waters of Australia, New Guinea, and adjacent islands. A number of species are confined to isolated desert springs or similar habitats.

Perhaps the most curious family in this group is the Phallostethidae (19 species), which reside in brackish and fresh waters of Southeast Asia (Fig. 21.1). They are small, elongate translucent fishes distinguished by an extremely complex copulatory organ (priapium) located on the throat of the males, part of which is used to hold the female during copulation; the priapium is derived from bones of the pelvic girdle (Parenti 1989). Despite internal fertilization, the females are egg-layers.

BELONIFORMES

This order unites the killifish-like medakas (Adrianichthyidae, 18 species), with the flying fishes (Exocoetidae, 50+ species), halfbeaks (Hemiramphidae, 85+ species), needlefishes (Belonidae, 30+ species), and sauries (Scomberesocidae, four species). The medakas are abundant inhabitants of fresh and brackish waters of tropical Asia. The ricefishes (*Oryzias* sp.) are important for laboratory studies because of their ease of rearing in captivity and their high reproductive rates. The other four families are made up of small to moderate-sized epipelagic fish (Fig. 21.2). Most are marine, but about one-third of halfbeaks and needlefishes live in fresh water. The four families are all characterized by having the single dorsal and anal fins about equal in size and located close to the tail. The pelvics are abdominal in position, and none of the fins have spines. The lateral line is well developed and low on the body, which is typically long and narrow.

The members of the three families can readily be distinguished by their unique specializations. The flying fishes have long pectoral fins which they use for gliding after they jump out of the water. The length of the glide is increased by sculling motions of the lower lobe of the tail, which is larger and longer than the upper lobe and possesses extra, stiffened rays (Davenport 1994). Some species have enlarged pelvic fins as well, which assist in the gliding. The "flying" of these fish appears to have developed as a means of escaping predators; larger individuals can gain nearly a meter of altitude and glide as far as 100 m, although most flights are lower and shorter. Adult flying fish have blunt snouts and small, unspecialized mouths. However, the juveniles of some species have elongated lower jaws such as those possessed by halfbeaks (as do juveniles of needlefishes). The fact that some halfbeaks also have enlarged pectoral fins for making longer leaps from the water further indicates the close relationship between the two groups. The elongate lower jaw of halfbeaks apparently functions in directing small, surface-oriented zooplankters into the mouth of the fish, since halfbeaks capture such prey while swimming in schools close to the surface of water. In contrast to halfbeaks, needlefish and sauries prey on small fishes, as their long jaws with pointed teeth attest. The needlefishes are elongate fishes that look like unarmored gars, while the sauries are even more terete. Both groups are speedy, pelagic fishes. The speed of the sauries is enhanced by the five to seven finlets behind both the dorsal and the anal fins, much like those possessed by tuna. Despite their speed, these fish (but particularly the sauries) are important prey for larger predators, such as tuna and swordfish. One reason for this, perhaps, is that the stocks of sauries in many parts of the oceans are relatively unexploited by humans because of their difficulty of capture. This situation is changing rapidly.

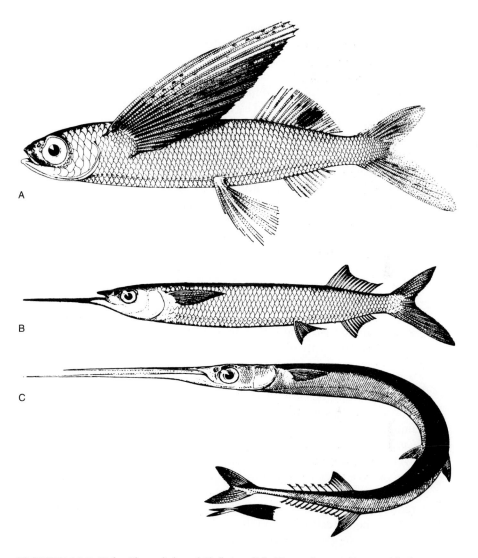

FIGURE 21.2 *Beloniform fishes: (A) flying fish* (Cypselurus, *Exocoetidae);
(B) halfbeak* (Hemiramphus, *Hemiramphidae); and (C) needlefish* (Belone,
Belonidae). (From Jordan and Evermann 1900.)

CYPRINODONTIFORMES

Throughout the tropical and temperate world, wherever there is water too saline,
too warm, too small, too isolated, or too extreme in its fluctuations in quality for
most fish, chances are reasonably good that it will be inhabited by one or more
cyprinodontiform species. By and large they are small (less than 15 cm) omnivores,
although many species are such efficient predators on insects that they are used for

mosquito control, while other species are capable of digesting blue-green cyano-bacteria. Their omnivory is one feature that allows them to live in harsh environments. Another is their surface-oriented morphology, which enables them to pump the thin oxygen-rich layer of water at the air-water interface across the gills, an ability especially useful for life in warm stagnant waters. Their ability to colonize unusual places is also enhanced by their diverse reproductive strategies. Despite their hardiness and versatility, however, cyprinodontiform fishes have more than their share of threatened species. This is because many of their habitats, ranging from desert springs to coastal salt marshes, have been destroyed, modified, or polluted by humans. This is particularly true for the many endemic species that have adapted to peculiar local conditions.

As a result of their surface orientation, these fishes are frequently called top-minnows. They are distinguished from similar true minnows (Cyprinidae) by the presence of small teeth in the jaws, and the group is sometimes referred to as the "tooth-carps" (Cyprino-don = carp-tooth). The pelvic fins are reduced or absent in many species, and fin spines are absent. Scales are generally cycloid, although the males of a few species develop ctenoid scales. The lateral line is usually well developed on the head but absent from the body, the nostrils have double openings, the upper jaw is bordered by a protractile premaxilla, and the caudal fin is symmetrical and often rounded. The evolutionary diversity of this order has been hidden by the superficial similarity of the many species around the world (Parenti 1981, 1984).

Aplocheilidae. The 220+ rivuline species include some with some remarkable reproductive strategies. Individuals of *Rivulus marmoratus,* for example, contain both ovaries and testes and engage in internal self-fertilization (Harrington 1961). Equally remarkable are the life cycles of the annual fishes, mostly of the genera *Cynolebias* (pearlfishes) and *Nothobranchius* (nothos). These fish complete their life cycles in a year. Eggs are deposited in the mud of the pond bottoms, where they can survive after the pond dries up. When the rains come again, the eggs hatch quickly and the pond is soon populated with fish again. At least one species, the redtail notho *(Nothobranchius guentheri),* grows from egg to spawning adult in four weeks, the fastest such growth known in fish (Haas 1976a,b). The annual life style evolved independently in Africa (nothos) and South America (pearlfishes).

Fundulidae. The approximately 50 species of killifish are scattered throughout North America (into southeastern Canada and the Yucatan of Mexico). Morphologically, the killifishes are the least specialized of the cyprinodontiform fishes, and most other families in the group are defined according to how they diverge from the standard killifish pattern. Many of them are brightly colored and are favored as aquarium fishes. All lay eggs, and many exhibit territorial behavior at breeding time. Killifish are successful in a wide range of habitats, including lakes, streams, salt marshes, and estuaries.

Cyprinodontidae. There are over 100 species of pupfish, which are renowned for their ability to live in conditions of extreme isolation, temperature, and salinity in

North and South America and the Mediterranean region of Europe and Africa. Pupfish got their name from the mistaken notion that the brightly colored males busily engaged in the serious business of reproduction were "playing" like puppies. The name has contributed to their popularity in the United States, however, and made it easier to protect obscure species and their unusual habitats, especially desert springs. One of the most remarkable fish in this remarkable group is the Devil's Hole pupfish (*Cyprinodon diabolis*) which occupies the smallest known range of any animal species. Devil's Hole is a pocket of water on a desert hillside in Nevada that is fed by a deep aquifer; the pupfish, however, live mainly on a shallow shelf about 20 m^2 in area. The fish subsist on the sparse growth of algae on the shelf and on the small invertebrates associated with it. Their population fluctuates between 200 and 700 individuals, reflecting their small body size (15–20 mm). They have evolved a number of energy-saving features to survive, including lack of pelvic fins, reduced pigmentation, and elimination of the vigorous courtship behavior of other pupfishes. Another extreme environment for pupfish occurs on the floor of Death Valley, California; there the Cottonball Marsh pupfish (*C. salinus milleri*) regularly experiences salinities up to 4.6 times that of sea water, and water temperatures from nearly freezing in winter to 40°C in summer, with daily fluctuations of 14-15°C. Despite their remarkable survival abilities, pupfish in many areas are endangered because of diversion of the meager water sources that feed the habitats in which they live (Minckley and Deacon 1991).

A major contrast to the desert pupfishes are the Andean pupfishes (*Orestias* spp.), which consist of 43 species that inhabit high-elevation lakes and streams of the Andes Mountains of South America. Twenty-three of these species inhabit Lake Titicaca, which is large (8100 km^2), cool (11°C to 16°C), and located at 3803 m elevation. The Andean pupfish species have, in the absence of competing species from other groups (except one catfish species), taken the basic cyprinodont morphology to its limits. In Lake Titicaca, species have evolved into a rather peculiar-looking array of piscivores, planktivores, insectivores, and grazers. All are clearly recognizable as cyprinodonts, yet some are deep-bodied (inshore forms), others are slender-bodied (offshore forms), and others are large with big mouths (piscivores) (Parenti 1984).

Poeciliidae. The family name Poeciliidae was formerly used only to encompass about 190 species of small livebearing fishes, now relegated to the subfamily Poeciliinae. However, mode of reproduction has proven not to be entirely reliable as a family-level character, so the family now includes 110 additional species that were formerly lumped with the killifishes and pupfishes. In this account, however, we will discuss only the livebearers in which the anal fin of the male is highly modified into a copulatory organ, the gonopodium (Meffe and Snelson 1989). The livebearers are small; most rarely exceed 10 cm in length, and some species have a maximum length of only 2 to 3 cm. They are found in warm, fresh, or brackish water at low elevations from northeastern Argentina to the southeastern United States, and in the West Indies as well. They are most numerous in Central America, perhaps because this region is so unstable geologically. Poeciliids in general are well suited for maintaining populations in such areas because:

1. They have a broad tolerance of extremes in temperature, salinity, and dissolved oxygen.
2. They are small in size, so a large population can exist in a small area.
3. They will eat whatever food is available.
4. Livebearing frees them from the need to have special substrates for spawning and assures high survival of the young, even under adverse conditions.
5. Many species are unisexual, giving them unusual adaptive abilities (see Chapter 9).
6. Their quick attainment of maturity results in high reproductive rates that can produce rapid population expansion under favorable conditions.

These same factors help to explain the success of livebearers such as guppies (*Poecilia reticulata*), mollies (*Poecilia* spp.), and swordtails (*Xiphophorus* spp.) as aquarium fish, as well as the ability of guppies to establish populations in sewage treatment plants (into which they are frequently flushed by aquarists tired of their prolific charges).

The factors are also important reasons why mosquitofish (*Gambusia affinis* and *G. holbrooki*) have proved to be such successful mosquito-control agents, resulting in their being introduced into warm waters throughout the world (Fig. 21.1). In the process of becoming established around the world, mosquitofish have probably displaced similar native fishes in many areas, although this has been documented mainly in the American Southwest. Their success as mosquito-control agents has also led to reduced consideration, in many parts of the world, of native fishes that might be equally useful in mosquito control (such as annual rivulines).

Other families. Other families of cyprinodontiform fishes contain few species but a number of interesting adaptations. The Goodeidae (40 species) includes 36 livebearing species largely confined to the Rio Lerma basin in the highlands of Central Mexico, where the various species are specialized for a wide variety of niches (Fitzsimmons 1972). The male copulatory organ is a muscular "pseudophallus," since the anal fin is only slightly modified. The embryos obtain nutrients from a placenta-like affair called a trophotaenia. The four-eyed fishes (Anablepidae, three species) are also viviparous, but they are distinguished by their remarkable eyes, each of which is divided into two parts with separate pupils (Fig. 21.1). With this system they can see simultaneously both above the water and beneath it. These fish forage in shallow water in both fresh and brackish water environments.

LESSONS FROM THE ATHERINOMORPHA

The atherinomorphs demonstrate how a basic body pattern (large eyes, upturned mouth, flattened head, abdominal pelvic, rearward dorsal fin) can be modified for life under extreme conditions or for specialized life styles. The Atheriniformes have classically fishlike bodies, advantageous for living in the large shoals in which they are often found. In the Beloniformes, the fish retain the terete body (or stretch it out) and develop elongate jaws or pectoral fins or both. In the Cyprinodontiformes, the body is small and often chunky, ideal for living in shallow, isolated habitats. This body form is also present in some atheriniforms (rainbow fish, blueeyes) that live in similar environments. The atherinomorphs' success seems to depend on an ability to live under conditions that most fish find difficult: silversides are abundant in estuaries and salt marshes; killifish and their kin thrive in water that is near their physiological limits in terms of temperature and salinity; flying fishes and halfbeaks live in the well-lighted surface waters where they would seem to be exceptionally vulnerable to predation. Finally, the atherinomorphs show a complete array of reproductive strategies, from the small pelagic eggs of the sauries, to the livebearing poeciliids, to the all-female "species" found among silversides and livebearers. The adaptability of many species within this group is demonstrated by the explosive success of introductions of mosquitofish, mollies, guppies, and various silversides into human-altered environments. On the other hand, this group has more than its share of endangered species, usually species that cannot escape when humans dry up or pollute their isolated habitats, or introduce predators into them.

Supplemental Readings

Herald 1961; Meffe and Snelson 1989; Miller 1948; Minckley and Deacon 1991; Naiman and Soltz 1981; Nelson 1984; Parenti 1981, 1984, 1989, 1993; Rosen 1964.

CHAPTER 22

Opahs, Squirrelfish, Dories, Pipefish, and Sculpins

Families Parazenidae (parazen), Macrurocyttidae, Zeidae (dories), Oreosomatidae (oreos), Grammicolepididae, Caproidae (boarfishes)

Order Gasterosteiformes

Families Hypoptychidae (sand eel), Aulorhynchidae (tubesnouts), Gasterosteidae (sticklebacks), Pegasidae (seamoths), Solenostomidae (ghost pipefishes), Syngnathidae (pipefishes and seahorses), Indostomidae, Aulostomidae (trumpetfishes), Fistulariidae (cornetfishes), Macrorhamphosidae (snipefishes), Centriscidae (shrimpfishes)

Order Synbranchiformes

Families Synbranchidae (swamp eels), Chaudridae, Mastacembelidae (spiny eels)

Order Dactylopteriformes

Family Dactylopteridae (flying gurnards)

Order Scorpaeniformes

Families Scorpaenidae (rockfishes), Caracanthidae (orbicular velvetfishes), Aploactinidae (velvetfishes), Pataecidae (prowfishes), Gnathanacanthidae (red velvetfish), Congiopodidae (racehorses), Triglidae (searobins), Bembridae (deepwater flatheads), Platycephalidae (flatheads), Hoplichthyidae (ghost flatheads), Anoplopomatidae (sablefishes), Hexagrammidae (greenlings), Normanichthyidae, Rhamphocottidae (grunt sculpin), Ereuniidae, Cottidae (sculpins), Cottocomephoridae (Baikal sculpins), Comephoridae (Baikal oilfishes), Abyssocottidae (deepwater Baikal sculpins), Hemitripteridae, Agonidae (poachers), Psychrolutidae (fathead sculpins), Bathylutichthyidae, Cyclopteridae (lumpfishes), Liparidae (snailfishes)

PERCOMORPHA

The percomorph fishes are an immensely variable and successful group, making up about half of all known fish species. Representatives can be found in most major habitats and their food and feeding mechanisms are as varied as the group itself. Despite this variability, most members are easy to place in this series because of their common structural plan. One reason for the structural similarities is that, while there are species that live in habitats as diverse as the deep sea and swift streams, most live either in shallow-water marine habitats or in lakes, especially in tropical regions. Most also live in, on, or in close association with the bottom. The general percomorph plan includes (1) pelvic fins that, if present, are thoracic or jugular in position, and pectoral fins that are placed high on the body; (2) fin spines present; (3) protractile premaxilla; (4) upper and lower sets of pharyngeal teeth; (5) swimbladder either physoclistous or absent; (6) pelvic fins usually with one spine and five rays each, caudal fin usually with 15 branched rays, and spinal column usually with 24 vertebrate; (7) small spines usually on bones of head and/or operculum; (8) pleural ribs, (9) absence (usually) of specializations common in other major groups, such as photophores, otophysic connections (e.g., Weberian apparatus of Ostariophysi) and viviparity; (10) ctenoid scales (usually); and (11) well-developed eyes. Many of the groups listed under the Percomorpha lack one or more of these characteristics, but whether the condition is ancestral (and therefore reason to exclude the group from the Percomorpha) or secondarily lost is often not certain.

This mosaic of characteristics (and others) have made the percomorph fishes successful because they have been modified, in concert with one another, into an extraordinary array of specializations. A majority of these specializations are those that allow the fishes to take advantage of the complexity of benthic inshore habitats in both salt and fresh water. These specializations fall into three general categories: predator avoidance, feeding, and social (especially reproductive) behavior.

Predation avoidance. Perhaps the single most important percomorph characteristic that has reduced predation pressure is the presence of spines. Spines increase the effective diameter of small fish and thereby increase the minimum size of their predators. Big predators are fewer than small predators, and even they are likely to prefer prey in which the edible body size is close to the effective diameter for easy swallowing. Spines thus give fish the type of protection otherwise available mainly through the use of heavy armor, which greatly reduces mobility. With spines a fish can afford to be small, slow-moving, and day-active, and to have a body shape advantageous for something other than a speedy escape from predators. The maneuverability of percomorph fishes, which results from the placement of the paired fins and from the fine control they possess over buoyancy provides further protection from predators. The fish can turn quickly, dive into cover, and, in some species, swim backwards. Of course, many percomorph fishes have abandoned both stout spines and swimbladders (and, in many cases, pelvic fins) in favor of a completely benthic existence in which small size, cryptic coloration, secretive habits, and unusual body shapes offer protection from predation; examples of these are blennies, flounders, and sculpins.

Feeding specializations. Both the cryptic benthic forms and the more conventional percomorph fishes have a wide array of feeding specializations. Most of these are designed for capturing small invertebrates, but specializations exist for feeding on everything from organic ooze to plant material to large fish. These specializations are made possible by a flexible mouth for sucking in or grabbing prey, combined with pharyngeal dentition for breaking up, grinding, or holding it. The acute vision of most percomorph fishes (the result of the tight pattern of cones in the retina) allows, in addition, precise location of prey.

Behavior. As might be expected of fish that exhibit such varied and complex feeding habits, their behavior in general is quite complex. Many are highly social, exhibiting either schooling or territorial behavior. In addition, many interact symbiotically with other organisms. To accomplish these various inter- and intraspecific interactions, the percomorph fishes have developed a variety of means of communication, including rapid color changes, sound production, and stereo-typed movements (fin and body language). The ability of the percomorph fishes to develop complex behavior patterns has presumably contributed to their success by increasing the number of "niches" open to them and by helping the species to maintain their genetic integrity.

Because the series Percomorpha contains 10 orders, over 230 families, and roughly 12,000 species, only the largest or most representative families in each order will be discussed. Most of the families not discussed are small and poorly known (although they do invariably have fascinating specialized features of their own). This chapter will cover six relatively small percomorph orders, plus the large Scorpaeni-formes. Chapter 23 will cover only the immense order Perciformes, while Chapter 24 will cover the highly derived Pleuronectiformes and Tetraodontiformes.

LAMPRIDIFORMES

This order contains a bizarre mixture of large, often brightly colored pelagic fishes. Most species apparently live at depths between 100 and 1000 m and so are rarely seen, despite broad, often worldwide, distribution patterns. Their diversity of form is indicated by the fact that 7 families are recognized, but only 19 species. Most of these species lack many of the "typical" percomorph characteristics, such as spines and ctenoid scales, which is why they can arguably be placed in the Paracanth-opterygii (Chapter 20). The mouth is highly protrusible, because not only the pre-maxilla but also the maxilla can be pushed outward. Protrusibility is especially characteristic of the tube-eye *(Stylephorus chordatus)*, which has a membranous pouch connecting the mouth to the cranium. The pouch can be expanded to a volume nearly 38 times that of the closed buccal cavity, creating the tremendous suction pressure for drawing in planktonic organisms (Pietsch 1978b). Most have an elongate dorsal fin. In body shape they range from extremely deep-bodied (Lam-pridae, Veliferidae) to extremely elongate (Lophotidae, Regalecidae). Most spec-tacular of the deep-bodied forms are the two species of opahs (Lampridae). Not only are they large (up to 1.5 m), disc-shaped, and laterally compressed, but they are bril-liantly colored: The body is dark blue on top, shading to a silver-flecked green and iridescent purple on the sides, and then to pink on the belly; the fins and jaws are vermillion. How these colors function is not known because opahs are found mostly below 100 m, where they feed on other fish, squid, octopus, and crustaceans. In marked contrast to opahs are the two species of oarfish (Regalecidae). These fish are extremely attenuated, reaching lengths of 8 m; the anterior rays of the dorsal fin are modified into a peculiar red "cockscomb" over the head, and the pelvic rays are modified into long filaments. Their mouth and eyes are quite small, and they seem to feed mainly on pelagic crustaceans. Apparently, they normally maintain themselves in the water column in a vertical position, which enables them to see their prey silhouetted against the downstreaming light (Pietsch 1978b). Because oarfish are only rarely seen on the surface, the appearance of a "monster" oarfish in a coastal area is likely to arouse a considerable amount of attention.

STEPHANOBERYCIFORMES AND BERYCIFORMES

The fish in these two orders are a mixed bag of mostly deepsea or nocturnal species that possess a number of ancestral osteological features. Many of the 16 families and over 200 species are poorly known, so the composition and status of both orders is fluid. Some of the families are well represented in fossil deposits of the Cretaceous period, and during the later portions of that period they may have played the dominant role in inshore waters now played by perciform fishes.

The Stephanoberyciformes are soft, rounded, toothless deepsea predators that include the gibberfishes, pricklefishes, and whalefishes. The three families of whalefishes have a vaguely whale-like appearance but are only from 10 to 30 cm long. The deepsea forms in the Beryciformes are mostly small and chunky, with large (or no) scales and, usually, conspicuous spines on the body and/or fins. A few species have photophores. The deepsea species make up all the beryciform families except the Holocentridae, Moncentridae, and a few species in the Trachichthyidae, Anomalopidae, and Berycidae. The shallow-water fishes are characterized by large eyes, bright red coloration, and rather conventional perchlike bodies. One of the Trachichthyidae, the orange roughy (*Hoplostethus atlanticus*), has become an important commercial fish species off New Zealand and Australia in recent decades. Because the roughy is slow-growing and late-maturing, the fisheries are mining the populations of large individuals and have been sustained mainly by the discovery of new, unexploited populations.

The bright red squirrelfishes (Holocentridae, 60+ species) are the largest and most widely distributed family in the Beryciformes and are found throughout the tropical and subtropical marine regions (Fig. 22.1). Most species inhabit coral reefs or shallow rocky areas in which they hide during the day; they come out at night, often in amazing numbers, to feed on zooplankton in the water column. As a group they are rather noisy fish, communicating with each other through a variety of clicks, croaks, and grunts. Some species of lanterneye fishes (Anomalopidae) are also active at night over reefs. These fish have a large light-emitting organ beneath each eye, which apparently functions in enabling the fish to see prey, in confusing predators (it can be quickly covered with a lid), and in intraspecific communication (Morin et al. 1975).

ZEIFORMES

The zeiform fishes are a curious mixture of six families and 39 species (Fig. 22.1). Most live in the deep sea, but a number of the better-known forms occur at only moderate depths, in midwater, and may actually support small fisheries. Most zeiform fishes have deep, compressed bodies with ctenoid scales and a few well-developed fin spines. Their heads are large, with extremely distensible jaws that enable them to capture the fishes and large crustaceans on which they feed. Anatomically, these fishes have a mixture of ancestral, derived, and specialized percomorph features, so they are usually linked with the Beryciformes. Perhaps the best-known fishes in this

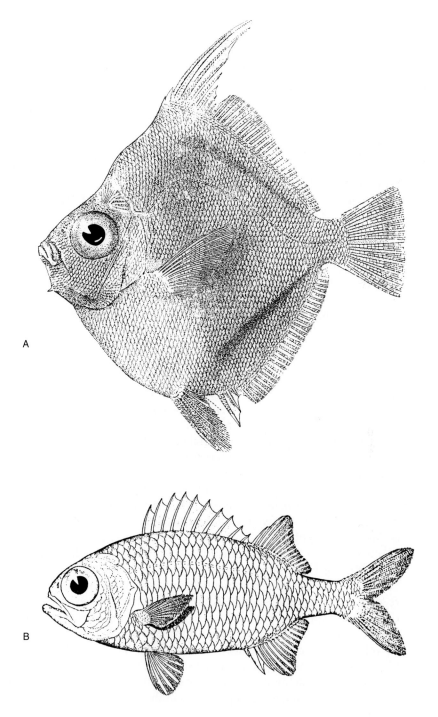

Figure 22.1 Percomorph fishes with ancestral characteristics: (A) boarfish (Antigonia, *Zeiformes); (B) squirrelfish* (Myripristis, Beryciformes). *(From Jordan and Evermann 1900.)*

order are the dories (Zeidae), which are readily recognized by the large, upward-angled mouth, silvery color, and long filaments on the dorsal fin.

GASTEROSTEIFORMES

This order is small (ca. 260 species) but contains some of the most unusual and best-known teleost fishes, such as the seahorses, pipefishes, and sticklebacks. It is divided into two suborders, which are so different from each other that they are often treated as separate orders: the Gasterosteoidei (Hypoptychidae, Aulorhynchidae, Gasterosteidae) and the Syngnathoidei (the remaining eight families). The two groups are treated together here, following the suggestion of Pietsch (1978), who has demonstrated that the seamoths (Pegasidae) are intermediate in structure between the two groups. Previously, the seamoths had been placed in an order by themselves. The problem with defining this order, even with the seamoths included, is that there are few anatomical features possessed by all members, since each group has its own bizarre specializations. However, most have armor plates of one sort or another and small mouths. Also, there is enough overlap between groups to link all the families listed, although the development of these characteristics shows considerable variation, as the following accounts should demonstrate.

Gasterosteidae. The sticklebacks are the one family in this order with body shapes approaching that of "normal" fish (Fig. 22.2). They are small fishes that live in either fresh or salt water (or both) and are found throughout the Northern Hemisphere, usually in close association with coastlines. They are readily recognized by the presence of 3 to 16 isolated spines on the back that precede the dorsal fin, large eyes, small upturned mouths, and narrow caudal peduncles. Most possess a row of bony plates on each side. Sticklebacks are territorial nest-builders, and their elaborate reproductive behavior is perhaps the best documented of any animal species (see Wooton 1976, 1984), thanks to their abundance in the wild and the ease with which they reproduce under artificial conditions. Their physiology (mostly as related to reproduction) has also been well documented. Only seven or eight species of stickleback are usually recognized, but two of these—the threespine stickleback (*Gasterosteus aculeatus*) and the ninespine stickleback (*Pungitius pungitius*)—are widespread in northern Asia, North America, and Europe. Haglund et al. (1992) note that ninespine sticklebacks on the three continents form distinct evolutionary lineages that can be recognized as separate species. A similar situation may exist for threespine stickleback. These "species," however, are in fact complexes of hundreds of divergent populations. Many of these populations may have the characteristics of "good" species, reflecting the ability of sticklebacks to adapt to local conditions, such as food supply, substrates, and abundance of predators. This nightmare for traditional taxonomists has been a dream for students of evolution and genetics, providing many fascinating insights into general problems in these fields (Bell 1976a,b).

Pegasidae. The five species of seamoths have excited the interest of biologists ever since the first dried specimens were imported to Europe from China by early explorers. They

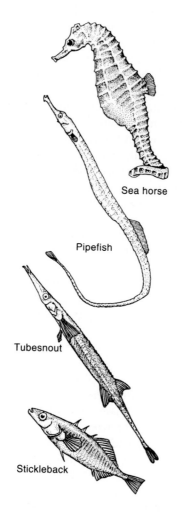

FIGURE 22.2 *Representative Gasterosteiformes. Top to bottom: seahorse (Syngnathidae); pipefish (Syngnathidae); tubesnout (Aulorhynchidae); and stickleback (Gasterosteidae). The fish are arranged to represent steps in the hypothetical evolution of the seahorse from a stickleback-like ancestor. The modern fishes shown, of course, are not directly ancestral to the seahorse. (From Moyle 1993, copyright © 1993 by Chris Mari van Dyck.)*

are small (to 15 cm) marine fishes that are completely encased in bony plates and have winglike pectoral fins and long, bony snouts. The mouth, rather than being at the end of the snout, is underneath it and is a uniquely complicated structure that can be folded when not in use into a cavity beneath the snout. When the fish is feeding, the mouth unfolds and the buccal cavity expands, creating a powerful suction device (Pietsch 1978a).

Syngnathidae. The pipefishes (200 species) and seahorses (25 species) are a family that has sacrificed streamlining and speed for armor, cryptic coloration, and secretive behavior. They are nevertheless very successful and are found in shallow marine waters the world over and occasionally in fresh water as well. All are long and thin, are encased in bony rings, have tubelike snouts with the mouth at the end, and lack pelvic fins (Fig. 22.2). Pipefishes propel themselves with their tails. Seahorses employ the dorsal and pectoral fins, having converted the caudal peduncle into a prehensile organ for holding onto plant stems; consequently, seahorses swim upright in a very slow and unfishlike manner. To compensate in part for their slow swimming, the tubelike mouth of syngnathids allows them to suck in small crustaceans from some distance, after locating the prey precisely with their apparently binocular vision.

One of the most fascinating aspects of syngnathid biology is the means by which they care for the eggs and young. Each male seahorse has a sealed brood pouch on the underside of the tail with a tiny opening on the top. The female lays her eggs in this brood pouch, where they are incubated and hatched. The young are expelled once they are capable of swimming on their own. In the pipefishes there are brood pouches as well, but they are open down the middle or sealed with overlapping flaps. In the most primitive species the brood pouch is completely lacking, and the female merely attaches the eggs to a bare spot on the belly of the male.

Aulostomidae and Fistularidae. The trumpetfishes (three species) and cornetfishes (four species) are long (0.8 m to 1.8 m), extremely slender fishes generally associated with tropical reefs. The snout is especially long but tipped with a surprisingly large mouth, which enables them to capture other fishes. As their body shape and fin placement indicate, they are lie-in-wait predators that conceal themselves either by hanging in the water column above the reef, by hanging close to the reef itself (often at an angle to it), or by associating closely with large browsing fish (e.g., parrotfishes).

SYNBRANCHIFORMES

Fish in this order are convergent on true eels (Anguilliformes) with elongate bodies, no pelvic fins, small gill openings, and hard mouths. The two main groups, swamp eels and spiny eels, are otherwise quite different from each other.

Synbranchidae. Swamp eels (15 species) enjoy a wide distribution in the fresh and brackish waters of tropical Africa, Asia, Australia, and South America. Pectoral fins are present only in the larval stages; dorsal and anal fins are reduced to small folds, without rays, in the caudal region; and the caudal fin is reduced or absent. Scales are absent or confined to the caudal region. The eyes are small or absent in cave-dwelling species. The gill membranes are united and continuous, so there is only one, continuous ventral gill opening. The gills themselves are often quite small, because swamp eels are capable of breathing air, either through the vascularized lining of the gill pouch or through a pair of lunglike sacs off the gill pouch. Some species are capable of moving across land for short distances, while others may burrow into the mud and survive even if the covering water evaporates. Swamp eels are nocturnal predators on small fishes. They also have the distinction of being the only freshwater fishes known to be protogynous hermaphrodites (capable of changing sex with increasing size and age). They are often large enough (up to 1.5 m) and abundant enough to support fisheries for them.

Mastacembelidae. Spiny eels (60 species) live in the fresh waters of tropical Africa and Asia. They have soft dorsal and anal fins placed far back on the body, often joining with the tail (Fig. 22.3). Each soft dorsal is preceded by a row of stout, isolated spines which can inflict painful wounds on any fisher person unfortunate enough to grab one around the middle. Their most peculiar feature is their pointed snout, which has a fleshy appendage at the end. The appendage has three lobes, the two side lobes containing the anterior nostrils. The appendage is apparently used for finding invertebrates on and in the soft bottoms of the backwaters commonly inhabited by these eels. The only other family in this order (Chaudhuriidae) contains just three species, which lack the appendage on the snout, as well as the dorsal spines and the scales.

DACTYLOPTERIFORMES

Superficially, the seven species of flying gurnards (Dactylopteridae) that make up this order resemble searobins (Triglidae). Like the searobins, they have an armored head with large, dorsal eyes, bony plates on the body, large pectoral fins with free inner rays that can be used to "walk" over the bottom, and the ability to make loud sounds (Fig. 22.3). The flying gurnards differ from the searobins by the arrangement of the pectoral fins; by their use of hyomandibular stridulations to produce sound rather than "twanging" the swimbladder; and by the presence of two long, free spines just before the dorsal fin. Although the large pectorals have given rise to the supposition that these small fish (30 to 50 cm) can fly, it appears that the pectorals are used mainly to frighten potential predators. When a gurnard is startled, the brightly patterned pectorals are flashed open, startling the predator.

SCORPAENIFORMES

With nearly 1300 species in 24 families, the Scorpaeniformes are one of the largest teleost orders. Most members of the order are bottom oriented and so possess large, rounded pectoral fins, large heads, rounded caudal fins, and bodies and heads with many spines and/or bony plates. All possess a *suborbital stay* on each cheek, a ridge of bone that runs across the operculum below the eye. As a result, the Scorpaeniformes are frequently referred to as the mail-cheeked fishes. Most members of this group are found in marine environments at depths of less than 100 m, but a number of species are freshwater forms.

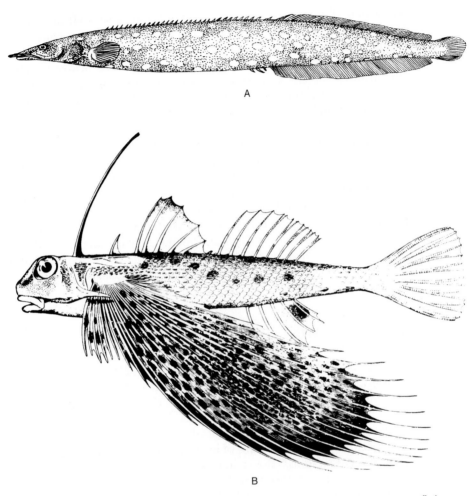

FIGURE 22.3 *Top: spiny eel* (Mastacembelus, *Synbranchiformes*). *Bottom: flying gurnard* (Dactyloptena, *Dactylopteriformes*).

Scorpaenidae. The rockfishes and scorpionfishes, with over 380 species, are the largest family in the order. They are mostly found in the Indian and Pacific oceans; only about 60 species are known from the Atlantic. Off the Pacific coast of North America alone there are over 65 species of rockfish *(Sebastes),* many of them morphologically similar to each other and found together, apparently in mixed aggregations. This complex of species presents some interesting problems in evolution and ecology. One way in which the species segregate is by depth; those found in the deepest water are typically bright red or orange in color, because at that depth such coloration serves as camouflage. However, the color patterns of many inshore forms are also quite bright, and this may serve to advertise that they possess toxic spines in the dorsal, anal, and pelvic fins. The spines are not only toxic but also stout and numerous; when combined with the head and operculum spines, they give the fishes a very prickly appearance.

Scorpionfish have large heads, large mouths and eyes, and stout, laterally compressed bodies with large pectoral fins (Fig. 22.4). Scales are either absent or very fine and ctenoid. Most scorpaenids are bottom-oriented predators, although many species enter the water column to feed on shoals of fish and squid. Many species also enter the water column to mate and to give birth to their young. The livebearers have not sacrificed much in the way of total egg production; their eggs are tiny and retained in the body cavity after fertilization, but the larvae are released immediately after hatching. Thus a 45-cm Pacific ocean perch *(Sebastes alutus)* may give birth to over 300,000 young. This same fish is likely to be 15 to 20 years old. Large (50–70 cm) rockfish of most species are typically 25—50 years old and some may live as long as 140 years, making them among the oldest fish known (Beamish and McFarlane 1987). Such slow growth is fairly typical of scorpaenids and is one reason that the commercially important species, such as Pacific ocean perch and Atlantic redfish *(S. marinus)*, have been so easy to overexploit. Both species were once enormously abundant in their respective northern oceans but now support only modest fisheries.

While scorpaenids are generally known as rockfishes in northern waters, where they support valuable sport and commercial fisheries, in tropical waters they are usually known as scorpionfishes because of the extreme toxicity of the spines. Most spectacular are the turkeyfishes and tigerfishes of coral reefs *(Pterois* spp.), which have bright bodies crossed with white and black stripes that extend onto the extremely long rays of the pectoral and dorsal fins. These species are toxic and act as if they are well aware of the fact; they cruise the reefs during the day and have been known to swim aggressively toward human swimmers, toxic spines angled forward. In contrast to the turkeyfishes, the stonefishes *(Synanceia)* are rather dull in color. They sit quietly on reefs and are extremely well camouflaged. However, they possess the most deadly fish venom known. It is a neurotoxin that can actually be injected by a stonefish into the foot of a hapless wader by means of venom glands at the base of hypodermic-like hollow dorsal spines.

Triglidae. The searobins or gurnards (100 species) are a widely distributed group of marine fish adapted for living on soft ocean bottoms at moderate depths. Typically they are red in color, with large eyes set toward the top of a head covered with heavy, bony plates (Fig. 22.4). The body may be covered with such plates as well. The mouth is subterminal and quite protrusible. The benthic invertebrates on which searobins feed are apparently located in part through the use of two or three fingerlike, independent rays that are part of each pectoral fin. These rays are used to probe the bottom and also to rest on. The swimbladder of searobins is large and muscular and is used for sound production. They are perhaps the noisiest fish on the Atlantic coast of North America.

Cottidae. The sculpins are a large (300+ species) family of bottom-dwelling fishes. With the exception of about five species, all are confined to the marine coastal

A

B

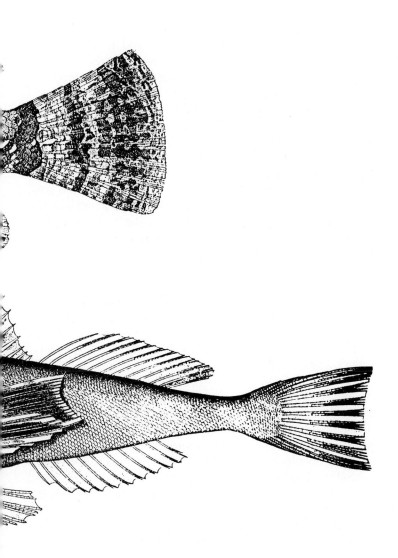

FIGURE 22.4 *Scorpaeniformes: (A) scorpionfish (Scorpaena, Scorpaenidae); and (B) searobin (Trigla, Triglidae). [(A) from Jordan and Evermann 1900; (B) from Goode and Bean 1895.)] (C) Sculpin (Oligocottus, Cottidae); and (D) snailfish, with ventral view to show sucker (Liparis, Cyclopteridae). (From Jordan and Starks 1895.)*

waters and fresh waters of the Northern Hemisphere. They are characterized by a broad, flattened head that usually has conspicuous spines and large, dorsal eyes, a smooth body (scales embedded, absent, or modified into tiny prickles), lack of a swimbladder, and large pectoral fins (Fig. 22.4). Many species of sculpin live in turbulent water, such as that found in the intertidal zone of oceans, in swift streams, or in the wave zone of lakes. They maintain themselves in these habitats by hiding beneath objects or by taking advantage of their negative buoyancy and hydrodynamic body shape. Presumably, when their pectoral fins are spread out and the fish face into a current, the current flows over them, actually pressing them to the bottom.

Perhaps the best-known members of this family are the freshwater sculpins of the genus *Cottus*, called bullheads in Europe. They inhabit coldwater streams and lakes and consequently are frequently accused of competing with or preying on trout and salmon, charges that are usually not justified (Moyle 1977). Like other members of the family, however, they are efficient predators on active benthic invertebrates.

Two other scorpaeniform families that are confined to fresh water, the Abyssocottidae (37 species) and the Comephoridae (2 species), are derived from cottid ancestors. Most of the species are found only in ancient Lake Baikal in the Soviet Union. They, and some cottid species, have radiated into a number of unsculpinlike niches, including that of pelagic planktivores. Some species are important as commercial fishes and as food for various endemic predators, such as the Baikal seal.

Agonidae. The poachers and alligator fishes make up a curious family of about 44 species with a bipolar distribution pattern. However, most of the species occur in the northern Pacific. They are small (25 to 30 cm), elongate fishes that are covered with bony plates, so that many species look somewhat like a cross between a sculpin and a pipefish. They are bottom dwellers (no swimbladders) and are frequently common in shallow marine waters, but their biology is poorly known.

Cyclopteridae. The lumpsuckers (Cyclopterinae, 26+ species) are found in the temperate and arctic portions of the Northern Hemisphere, while the snailfishes have a bipolar distribution pattern. The members of this family tend to have rather flabby bodies, globular in shape. The pelvic fins are modified into a large sucking disc (or absent altogether), and the gill openings are small; both features are indicative of the inactive life these fishes live. The lumpsuckers are found attached to the bottom and to drifting objects but are often caught in midwater as well. Despite their repulsive appearance, created by their lumpy build, complete with wartlike tubercles, lumpsuckers are favored foodfishes (they reach 60+ cm) not only of humans but of sperm whales, seals, and sleeper sharks. The eggs are frequently sold as lumpfish caviar.

Liparidae. The snailfishes (195+ species) are somewhat more fishlike in appearance than the related lumpsuckers, but their skin is without scales and jellylike in texture. They also possess a sucking disc. They favor cold waters and are common in both the Arctic and the Antarctic, as well as in deep water (down to 7 km). Some species lay their eggs in the gill cavities of crabs and other crustaceans.

LESSONS FROM PERCOMORPHS: I

The first four orders discussed in this chapter are (or have been) regarded as most resembling the ancestral condition of percomorph fishes. It is interesting and probably significant that most of the members of this order are deepsea or open-sea fishes, adapted for life away from the shallow-water habitats dominated by the Perciformes. The deepsea environment in particular is shared with a wide variety of other fishes of ancient lineages. In contrast, the sticklebacks and seahorses and their kin are usually found with perciform fishes and seem to defend themselves with heavy armor and good disguises. The synbranchiform eels are also very cryptic species. Within both groups, species may be few but numbers are often high.

The scorpionfishes are most abundant in shallow-water marine environments. They have evolved a very successful strategy as bottom-dwelling ambush predators, protecting themselves from predators by both concealment and poisonous spines. Smaller species, especially the cottids, can live in turbulent environments where food is abundant. Perhaps because of the abundance of active perciform predators, most scorpianfishes engage in some sort of parental care, from nest-brooding to livebearing. Rockfish have successfully combined livebearing with the teleost small-egg/high-fecundity strategy, with each female giving birth to thousands of larvae. Rockfish, and many other of the larger species in the percomorph orders discussed in this chapter, have opted for life in the slow lane. Under natural conditions, the cryptic, toxic-spined adults have high survival rates, so it pays for them to delay reproduction, even though growth rates are slow. Individuals can live long and thereby produce lots of young when conditions are good, even if those conditions are infrequent. This life history strategy, of course, makes them extremely vulnerable to fisheries, which select for the largest individuals and can quickly push populations to collapse.

Supplemental Readings

Hart 1973; Johnson 1993; Mayden 1992; Nelson 1994; Wooton 1990.

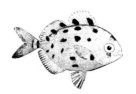

CHAPTER *23*

Perciformes

SNOOKS TO SNAKEHEADS

SUBDIVISION TELEOSTEI
    Infradivision Eutelostei
        Superorder Acanthopterygii
           Series Percomorpha
               Order Perciformes
                   Suborder Percoidei
                       Families Centropomidae (snooks), Chandidae (Asiatic glassfishes), Moronidae (temperate basses), Percichthyidae (temperate perches), Acropomatidae (ocean basses), Serranidae (sea basses), Ostracoberycidae, Callanthiiidae, Pseudochromidae (dottybacks), Grammatidae (basslets), Plesiopidae (roundheads), Notograptidae, Opistognathidae (jawfishes), Dinopercidae, Banjosidae, Centrarchidae (sunfishes), Percidae (perches), Priacanthidae (bigeyes), Apogonidae (cardinalfishes), Epigonidae (deepwater cardinalfishes), Sillaginidae (smelt-whitings), Malacanthidae (tilefishes), Lactariidae (false trevallies), Dinolestidae (longfinned pike), Pomatomidae (bluefishes), Nematistiidae (roosterfish), Echeneididae (remoras), Rachycentridae (cobia), Coryphaenidae (dolphins), Carangidae (jacks), Menidae

(moonfish), Leiognathidae (ponyfishes), Bramidae (pomfrets), Caristiidae (manefishes), Emmelichthyidae (rovers), Lutjanidae (snappers), Lobotidae (triple tails), Gerreidae (mojarras), Haemulidae (grunts), Inermiidae (bonnetmouths), Sparidae (porgies), Centracanthidae, Lethrinidae (emperors), Nemipteridae (threadfin breams), Polynemidae (threadfins), Sciaenidae (croakers), Mullidae (goatfishes), Pempheridae (sweepers), Glaucosomatidae (pearl perches), Leptobramidae (beach-salmon), Bathyclupeidae, Monodactylidae (moonfishes), Toxotidae (archerfishes), Coracinidae (galjoens), Drepanidae, Chaetodontidae (butterflyfishes), Pomacanthidae (angelfishes), Enoplosidae (oldwife), Pentacerotidae (boarfishes), Nandidae (leaffishes), Kyphosidae (seachubs), Arripidae (Australasian salmon), Teraponidae (grunters), Kuhliidae (flagfishes), Oplegnathidae (knifejaws), Cirrhitidae (hawkfishes), Chironemidae (kelpfishes), Aplodactylidae, Cheilodactylidae (morwongs), Latrididae (trumpeters), Cepolidae (bandfishes)

Suborder Elassomatoidei

Family Elassomatidae (pygmy sunfishes)

Suborder Labroidei

Families Cichlidae (cichlids), Embiotocidae (surfperches), Pomacentridae (damselfishes), Labridae (wrasses), Odacidae, Scaridae (parrotfishes)

Suborder Zoarcoidei

Families Bathymasteridae (ronquils), Zoarcidae (eelpouts), Stichaeidae (pricklebacks), Cryptacanthodidae (wrymouths), Pholidae (gunnels), Anarhichadidae (wolffishes), Ptilichthyidae (quillfish), Zaproridae (prowfish), Scytalinidae (graveldiver)

Suborder Notothenioidei

Families Bovichthyidae, Nototheniidae (cod icefishes), Harpagiferidae (plunder fishes), Bathydraconidae (Antarctic dragonfishes), Channichthyidae (crocodile icefishes)

Suborder Trachinoidei

Families Chiasmodontidae, Champsodontidae, Pholidichthyidae (convict blenny), Trichodontidae (sandfishes), Pinguipedidae (sandperches), Cheimarrhichthyidae, Trichonotidae (sanddivers), Creediidae (sandburrowers), Percophidae (duckbills), Leptoscopidae (southern sandfishes), Ammodytidae (sand lances), Trachinidae (weeverfishes), Uranoscopidae (stargazers).

Suborder Blennioidei

Families Tripterygiidae (threefin blennies), Dactyloscopidae (sand stargazers), Labrisomidae, Clinidae (clinids), Chaenopsidae (pikeblennies), Blenniidae (combtooth blennies)

Suborder Icosteoidei

Family Icosteidae (ragfish)
Suborder Gobiesocoidei
  Family Gobiesocidae (clingfishes)
Suborder Callionymoidei
  Families Callionymidae (dragonets), Draconettidae
Suborder Gobioidei
  Families Rhyacichthyidae (loach gobies), Odontobutidae,
  Eleotridae (sleepers), Gobiidae (gobies), Kraemeriidae (sand
  gobies), Xenisthmidae, Microdesmidae (wormfishes), Schind-
  leriidae
Suborder Kurtoidei
  Family Kurtidae (nurseryfishes)
Suborder Acanthuroidei
  Families Ephippidae (spadefishes), Scatophagidae (scats),
  Siganidae (rabbitfishes), Luvaridae (louvar), Acanthuridae (sur-
  geonfishes)
Suborder Mugiloidei
  Family Mugilidae (mullets)
Suborder Scombrolabraciodei
  Family Scombrolabracidae
Suborder Scombroidei
  Families Sphyraenidae (barracudas), Gempylidae (snake mack-
  erels), Trichiuridae (cutlass fishes), Scombridae (mackerels and
  tunas), Xiphiidae (billfishes)
Suborder Stromateoidei
  Families Amarsipidae, Centrolophidae (medusafishes), Nomei-
  dae (driftfishes), Ariommatidae, Tetragonuridae (squaretails),
  Stromateidae (butterfishes)
Suborder Anabantoidei
  Families Luciocephalidae (pikehead), Anabantidae (climbing
  gouramies), Helostomatidae (kissing gourami), Belontiidae
  (gouramis), Osphronemidae (giant gourami)
Suborder Channoidei
  Family Channidae (snakeheads)

The Perciformes, with over 9200 species, is the largest order of vertebrates. They are extremely diverse, but most species are adapted for life as predators in the shallow or surface waters of the oceans or for life in lakes. Perciform fishes usually have the following characteristics: (1) fin spines present; (2) dorsal fins either double or made up of two distinct parts, the lead part spiny; (3) adipose fin never present; (4) pelvic fins thoracic or jugular in position, or absent; (5) pelvic fins with one spine and five or fewer rays; (6) pectoral fins on side of the body, with a vertical insertion; (7) 17 or fewer principal caudal fin rays; (8) scales ctenoid or absent (but cycloid in a few forms); (9) premaxilla the only bone bordering the upper jaw; (10) orbitosphenoid, mesocoracoid, and intermuscular bones absent; and (11) swimbladder physoclistous or absent.

Within the Perciformes, general lines of evolution are indicated by the 19 suborders, although nearly 57% of the species are found in just eight families (Gobiidae, Cichlidae, Labridae, Serranidae, Blenniidae, Pomacentridae, Sciaenidae, and Apogonidae). In contrast, many of the 149 families recognized here contain fewer than 20 species. The relationships of the various groups within the Perciformes and its families are constantly shifting. J. S. Nelson (1994), for example, places the mullets (Mugilidae) in a separate superorder (Mugilomorpha) of their own, reflecting frustration with trying to figure out where they belong in the great scheme of teleost classification. In this chapter, we will discuss every suborder but can usually only sample the diversity within each one.

PERCOIDEI

This suborder contains over 2850 species. By and large they have the classical perciform appearance: deep to moderately elongate body, two dorsal fins, large mouth and eyes, ctenoid scales, and thoracic pelvic fins. Most are inshore, diurnal (or crepuscular) predators, and those of any size are usually harvested by humans for food. Some of the most popular saltwater and freshwater game fishes, such as striped bass, snook, bluefish, jacks, snappers, croakers, perches, and sunfishes, belong to this suborder.

Serranidae. The 450 species of sea basses are large, piscivorous fishes associated with tropical and temperate reefs and inshore environments. They can be distinguished from most similar species by (1) presence of three spines on the operculum; (2) complete lateral line; (3) caudal fin often rounded; (4) no scaly process in the axillae of the pelvic fins; and (5) A long, continuous dorsal fin, with from seven to thirteen spines. Most species are hermaphroditic, a trait first noticed by Aristotle around 300 B.C. The hermaphrodites typically are female when small and convert to males when large, although in some species male and female gonads develop simultaneously.

In recent years, three "new" families have been split off from this family: Moronidae (6 species), Percichthyidae (22 species), and Acropomatidae (40 species). These basses can be best distinguished from the sea basses by the presence of only two spines on the operculum, a tail that is usually forked, and the absence of hermaphroditism (Fig. 23.1). In North America the four species of **Moronidae** are found in fresh water and estuaries and are much sought after as sport and commercial fishes. The best known of these species is the striped bass (*Morone saxatilis*), the "rockfish" of the East Coast; this was introduced into California in the 1870s, where it quickly became extraordinarily abundant. In the 1970s and 1980s, both populations showed large-scale declines in abundance due to the deterioration of environmental conditions in estuaries on both coasts.

Centrarchidae. The sunfish are a family of 29 freshwater species that are native only to North America. They are most characteristic of warm-water lakes and sluggish streams. Since the black basses (*Micropterus*), sunfishes (*Lepomis*), and crappies (*Po-*

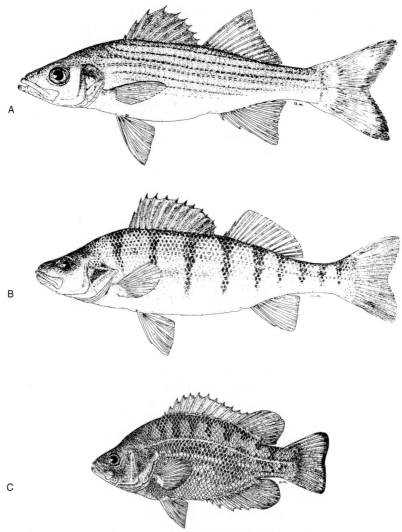

FIGURE 23.1 *Perciformes, Percoidei. Top: striped bass* (Morone, *Moronidae); Middle: yellow perch* (Perca flavescens, *Percidae). Bottom: Sacramento perch* (Archoplites interruptus, *Centrarchidae). (From Moyle 1976a.)*

moxis) are very popular sport fishes, many populations have been established far outside their native ranges. The largemouth bass *(M. salmoides)* in particular, has become established in ponds and lakes throughout the world. In a number of localities, such as Lake Atitlan, Guatemala, the establishment of largemouth bass has been responsible for the disastrous decline of native fishes and fisheries. In the Central Valley of California introduction of various centrarchids from the eastern United States was accompanied by the near disappearance of the one native centrarchid, the Sacramento perch *(Archoplites interruptus)* from its native habitats. The centrarchids are recognizable as fishes that are deep bodied (or moderately deep bodied), with the spinous and soft dorsal fins joined together and with moderately forked tails (Fig. 23.1). They are nest-builders with well-developed parental behavior.

The pygmy sunfishes (Elassomatidae) were formerly placed in the Centrarchidae but are now regarded as quite distinct (e.g., the lack a lateral line, have cycloid scales, and have only five branchiostegal rays). Following Nelson (1994), they are placed here in a separate suborder **(Elassomatoidei)** until systematists have figured out what to do with them. The pygmy sunfishes are six species of small (25 cm), attractive fish from the southeastern United States.

Percidae. This family is widely distributed in fresh waters of the Northern Hemisphere, but about 90% of the over 160 species are found in North America east of the Rocky Mountains. The reason for this is the presence of 155 species of darters *(Etheostoma, Percina, Ammocrypta)* in the streams and lakes. These are small, elongate bottom-dwelling fishes with small mouths and conspicuous eyes, and with the swimbladder reduced or absent. Although they are secretive fish that pick small invertebrates from the bottom, many are brightly colored, especially when spawning. In small, warm streams darters are usually second in abundance only to cyprinids. Aside from the darters, the North American percids contain two other groups of fishes: the perches *(Perca)* and the pike-perches *(Stizostedion)* (Figure 23.1). They are largely inhabitants of lakes and large rivers and are highly prized foodfish. The most favored of these fish is the walleye *(S. vitreum),* a species that prefers deep, cool water and has large, reflective eyes that help it detect and capture other fishes in dim light.

Apogonidae. The cardinalfishes are superficially similar to the beryciform squirrelfishes, but they are usually smaller (5 to 15 cm as adults) and possess two short and well-separated dorsal fins. Like the squirrelfishes, most are red in color, have large eyes, and are active mainly at night. A majority of the over 195 species are associated with tropical reefs, where they hide in crevices and caves (often with squirrelfishes) during the day and emerge in large schools to feed on plankton at night. A few species have managed to invade the freshwater streams and mangrove swamps of Pacific islands, while a few others inhabit deep (to 1200 m) water. They are unusual among coral reef fishes in that many, perhaps most, of them are mouth brooders.

Pomatomidae. A text on fish would be remiss if it did not mention the nearly cosmopolitan bluefish *(Pomatomus saltatrix),* famous for its voracious appetite and sharp teeth and celebrated by John Hershey in his 1987 book *Blues:*

> It has such an elegant hull. It is so wicked and wild when it's hooked. It has such a cruel eye and such passionate jaws. . . . It's so full of life! And it's true to life; there is nothing fake or soft about it; life is harsh. I've said it before and I'll say it again: I'm deeply in awe of the bluefish. (p. 186)

Echeneididae. The remoras or sharksuckers are among the most specialized of perciform fishes. The specializations of the eight species of remora center around the remarkable sucking disc on top of their head. This disc is formed from the spiny dorsal fin and contains 10 to 28 slatlike transverse ridges, which are modified spines. When a remora presses this disc against a large fish, turtle, or whale, the ridges are erected to create a powerful suction and the remora becomes very difficult to dislodge. The disc is fused to the upper jaw and consequently forms part of the snout, beyond which projects the lower jaw. The body of remoras is smooth (small, cycloid scales) and fusiform, and the fish are good swimmers, but their dependence on rides from other fish is indicated by the absence of a swimbladder. Some remoras will pick parasites and diseased tissues from their hosts, but it is unlikely that such activity compensates for the energy expended by the host to carry one or more remoras. On the other hand, the remoras get a free ride, enjoy the protection of a large fish, and probably make short forays away from their host to capture small fish.

Carangidae. Although the body shapes of the over 140 species of jacks and pompanos range from torpedolike to nearly platelike, all are fast-swimming predators. This is reflected in their deeply forked tails and narrow caudal peduncles; the fine, cycloid scales (often absent or modified into scutes along the lateral line); the deeply sloping heads (with large eyes and mouth); and, usually, the laterally compressed bodies. Carangids range in color from silvery to metallic blue or green to bright yellow or gold. Adult size ranges from about 25 cm to 2 m. Most jacks are schooling fish that feed by making rapid, slashing attacks at shoals of smaller fish, especially herrings and anchovies.

Lutjanidae. The snappers are among the most important foodfishes in tropical and subtropical waters. There is nothing remarkable about their morphology, which may in part explain their success (125 species); they are generalized, bottom-oriented predators. The typical snapper is heavy bodied, with a continuous dorsal fin, slightly forked tail, fully scaled body, and triangular head with a large mouth located at the apex of the triangle. The mouth is protractile and equipped with many teeth, usually including some large canine teeth. Most are brightly colored, ranging from bright red to yellow to iridescent blue, often with contrasting stripes and bars. Most species are associated with tropical reefs, submerged banks, or inshore areas. They have also shown themselves to be quite adaptable; the red snapper (*Lutjanus campechanus*), an important commercial species in the South Atlantic and Gulf of Mexico, is one of the more abundant fish around oil platforms, shipwrecks, and artificial reefs.

Haemulidae. The grunts (over 150 species) are a much more attractive family than their name suggests; schools of them with iridescent yellow, blue, and orange stripes are commonly seen over tropical reefs. At night these color patterns are altered, and the grunts of many species leave the reefs to forage on hard-shelled invertebrates that live in the surrounding flats. The invertebrates are crushed with the grunt's formidable pharyngeal teeth. They are called grunts because they also use their pharyngeal teeth for making rude sounds, sounds that are amplified by the swimbladder.

Sciaenidae. The croakers or drums are another group of noisy, bottom-oriented, invertebrate crunchers. Despite many similarities, they can be distinguished from the previous four families by their deeply notched dorsal fins, rounded or emarginate caudal fin (rather than forked or straight), and one or two anal spines (rather than three). In addition, many possess one or more chin barbels. Internally, croakers are notable for their multibranched swimbladder and huge otoliths. Both features are presumably related to the fact that croakers produce loud sounds, especially during spawning season, by vibrating muscles associated with the swimbladder. Since the 270 species are often inhabitants of turbid estuaries, bays, and rivers, it is quite possible that their elaborate sound-producing and sound-receiving systems may assist them in finding their way about and in communicating with one another. The well-developed lateral line (extending into the rays of the tail) is also indicative of their murky habitats. In North America there are about 34 species of croakers, many of them important as sport and commercial fishes, including the famous "blackened redfish" of gourmet Cajun restaurants (red drum, *Sciaenops ocellatus*). The freshwater drum *(Aplodinotus grunniens)*, is an important commercial species throughout much of the Mississippi River drainage.

Chaetodontidae. It is unusual to see a photographic view of a reef that does not include at least one individual of the over 110 species of butterflyfish or the closely related angelfishes (**Pomacanthidae,** 74 species). They are all extremely colorful, with striking patterns of stripes and spots on multihued backgrounds of colors that include most of the visible spectrum. However, yellow does seem to be the most common color. The colors are well displayed because butterflyfishes are thin in cross section but nearly circular in side view, with large dorsal and anal fins. The spectacular patterns are made even more noticeable by the constant activity of these fishes during the day.

   Butterflyfishes and angelfishes are remarkable not only for their coloration but for their feeding specializations. Most have small, protractile mouths with many tiny teeth. Different species are specialized for feeding on invertebrates at different depths in crevices, as indicated by the length of the snout. Others specialize on prey types such as zooplankton, coral polyps, sponges, and polychaete worms, since each food type requires particular morphological and behavioral specializations to be fed upon efficiently (Motta 1985).

LABROIDEI

The suborder Labroidei contains six fascinating families and over 2200 species, which all possess highly specialized pharyngeal jaws that have allowed them to diversify and prey on a wide variety of food items. Three of the families (Pomacentridae, Labridae, Scaridae) contain large numbers of species that are especially important on tropical reefs. It also contains the cichlids, which are extraordinarily diverse in tropical lakes, and the surfperches (Embioticidae), famous for their spiny viviparity.

Cichlidae. The cichlids are over 1300 species of freshwater and brackish-water fishes inhabiting Africa, South America, Central America, and parts of Asia and North America. Their most amazing characteristic is their tendency to form flocks of extremely specialized species in large lakes, especially in Africa; lakes Malawi, Victoria, and Tanganyika contain among them about 900 endemic species of cichlids (Fryer and Iles 1972; Ribbink 1990). This number is actually conservative, because new species from these lakes are continually being described. Sadly, as many as 200 species have been lost from Lake Victoria in recent years as the result of introduction of the predatory Nile perch (*Lates* sp.), perhaps in combination with overfishing and other factors. This has been one of the greatest mass extinction events in recent times.

A major factor that promotes speciation in the cichlids is that most species have a strong feeding orientation toward the bottom, a heterogeneous environment with a wide variety of invertebrates and plants to feed on. The tendency in lake-dwelling cichlids is to specialize in feeding on just one type of food, such as filamentous algae growing on rocks or fly larvae living in sand (see Chapter 29). According to Liem (1974), the extraordinary ability of the cichlids to specialize is the result of the unique and complex structure of the pharyngeal "jaw" apparatus, which permits efficient grinding and chewing of ingested food, using highly specialized teeth. The pharyngeal jaws free the mouth to develop specializations just for food-gathering, such as long, forcepslike teeth for picking up small invertebrates from plants or pulling scales from other fish.

As might be expected of substrate-feeding fishes, most cichlids are deep bodied, with large, spiny fins, rounded tails, protractile mouths, and well-developed eyes. Many are brightly colored, although many also have color patterns to match the substrate. Many of the more colorful forms, such as discus fishes *(Symphysodon)*, angelfishes *(Pterophyllum)*, South American cichlids *(Cichlasoma)*, and jewelfishes *(Haplochromis)*, are favorite aquarium fishes; this preference is increased by the ease with which they breed in captivity. Reproductive behavior is often elaborate, and many species brood the developing embryos in the mouth of the female.

Embiotocidae. The surfperches form a small (23 species) but abundant family that is found only along the northern Pacific coasts of North America and Asia. One species, the tule perch *(Hysterocarpus traski)*, is confined to fresh water in California. Externally they are not particularly remarkable, being moderately deep-bodied percoid fishes, with cycloid scales and small mouths that are handy for picking up small invertebrates (DeMartini 1969). However, when discovered in the early 1800s, they greatly aroused the interests of biologists, including Louis Agassiz, because they are viviparous. The young develop in uteruslike sacs in the ovary and obtain most of their nutrition from the body fluids of the mother. This is possible because the dorsal, pelvic, and anal fins of the embryo are greatly enlarged, highly vascularized, and in close contact with the tissues of the mother, allowing transfer of nutrients to take place. When born, the young are 3 to 5 cm long, and they may become sexually mature a few weeks after birth. The number of young produced per female varies among the species; those living in the most variable environments produce the most young, while those living in more predictable environments produce fewer young (Baltz 1984).

Pomacentridae. The damselfishes are another group of deep-bodied, conspicuous fishes characteristic of tropical reefs. Their conspicuousness stems not just from bright color patterns, for many are in fact rather plain, but from their abundance and activity. Many of the over 315 species in the family actively defend territories on reefs not only against members of the same species but against many other species as well (see Chapter 33). The functions of the territories are multiple, but one of the most important appears to be in providing food for the fish, because defended areas typically have much heavier growths of algae than do undefended areas and the main food of many damselfishes is filamentous algae.

Damselfishes that do not defend garden territories fall mostly into two general categories: shoaling fish that feed on plankton above the reef, and fish that are commensal with anemones. The plankton-feeding forms are similar in body shape to the territorial forms; both types seem to represent a compromise between the convenience of being deep bodied for hovering and picking out small food items, and having the ability to flee quickly to cover when a predatory fish approaches. The latter "need" places a limit on just how deep bodied they become, and results in a forked tail. The plankton-feeding and territorial forms also have large eyes and small, protractile mouths. The teeth of territorial forms are incisorlike, for nipping off pieces of algae, whereas the teeth of the plankton-feeders are conical or villiform, for holding onto small prey. The group of 27 species of damselfish that live in close association with anemones are generally small, brightly colored forms, many with rounded tails. These fish actually live among the tentacles of the invertebrates and have a mucus layer that seems to inhibit the anemones from stinging them.

Labridae. With over 500 species, this is one of the largest perciform families. Although there is considerable variation in body shape and size among the wrasses, most can be quickly recognized by (1) the pointed snout; (2) the small to moderate-sized mouth containing conspicuous, outward-pointing teeth; and (3) the solid, semicylindrical body with cycloid scales, long dorsal fin, and square or slightly rounded tail. Most are less than 12 cm long, but members of the genus *Cheilinus* may reach 2.3 m. Whether they occur in tropical or temperate regions, wrasses are usually brightly colored, diurnal fishes that live by picking up small invertebrates. Perhaps the best-known trait of wrasses is that a number of them are cleaners that pick parasites from other fishes. Such fish are usually solitary or live in pairs and may behave very aggressively toward other wrasses. Most noncleaner wrasses behave in a similar manner, although a few species, especially wrasses that inhabit temperate regions, are shoaling fishes. On the Atlantic coast of North America two such species are the cunner *(Tautogolabrus adspersus)* and the tautog *(Tautoga onitis)*, both of which have some value as commercial and sport fish.

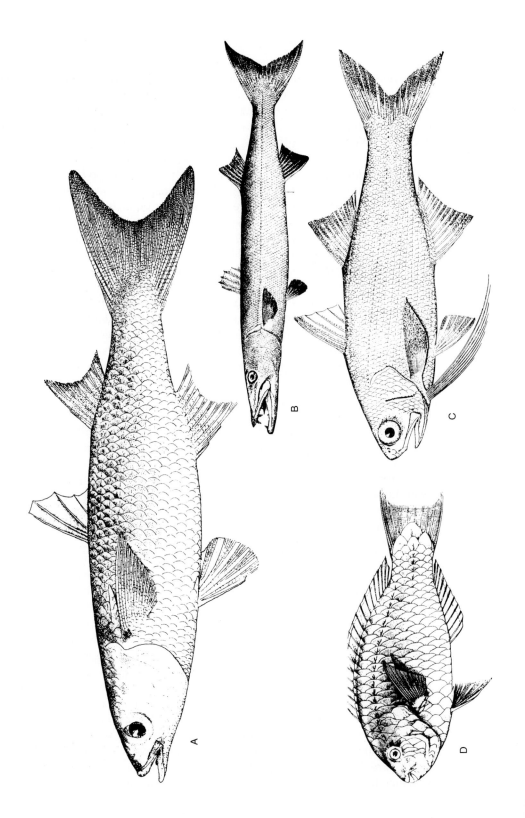

Scaridae. The over 80 species of parrotfish look like large, heavy-bodied wrasses that have their jaw teeth fused into a solid, parrotlike beak. They also have heavy pharyngeal teeth consisting of solid units of bone (Fig. 23.2). These structures permit parrotfish to scrape algae and invertebrates from hard surfaces of the reef and then to crush the ingested material. They move about the reefs in conspicuous small schools during the day and hide in caves and crevices at night. A few species secrete a mucus cocoon about themselves when at rest, presumably to foil night-feeding predators such as moray eels.

Perhaps the most remarkable feature of parrotfish, however, is their color patterns, which change dramatically with age and sex (which may also change), reflecting extremely complicated mating systems. Robertson and Warner (1978) recognize three basic color phases in parrotfishes: a **juvenile phase,** an **initial phase** (characteristic of young adults), and a **terminal phase** (characteristic of large, dominant males). Depending on the species, males and females may or may not have different color patterns, and color patterns may or may not be reversible. To complicate matters further, parrotfish populations may contain two types of patterns of sexual development: fishes that have their sex genetically fixed **(gonochorists)** and fishes that can change sex from female to male **(protogynous hermaphrodites).** In many species much of the mating is controlled by large, terminal-phase males (which are often protogynous hermaphrodites) who defend permanent territories, each containing a harem of females. In these situations the smaller, initial-phase males manage to spawn largely by **sneaking** and **streaking** (Robertson and Warner 1978). Sneaking occurs when a small male manages to get a member of a harem to spawn with it within the territory of the terminal male; streaking occurs when a male dashes into a territory and spawns with a female just as the terminal male is also spawning. Not all species have permanent territories; some resort instead to either group spawning or lek spawning. In the latter case, the terminal males defend territories only temporarily and mate with females, singly or in groups, that enter the territory. The preceding discussion only partially reflects the complexity and variety of mating systems in the Scaridae (and the Labridae as well).

ZOARCOIDEI

The 320 species in this group are all elongate fishes with long dorsal and anal fins and small (or absent) pelvic fins. Most live in temperate to arctic waters of the Northern Hemisphere although, curiously, there are a few species of eelpout (Zoarcidae) that live in Antarctic waters. Although many of the species are offshore or deep-

FIGURE 23.2 *Representative perciform fishes: (A) mullet (*Mugil, Mugiloidei*); (B) barracuda (*Sphyraena, Scombroidei*); (C) threadfin (*Polydactylus, Percoidei*); and (D) parrotfish (*Scarus, Labroidei*). ([A] from Jordan and Starks 1895; [B], [C], and [D] from Jordan and Evermann 1900.)*

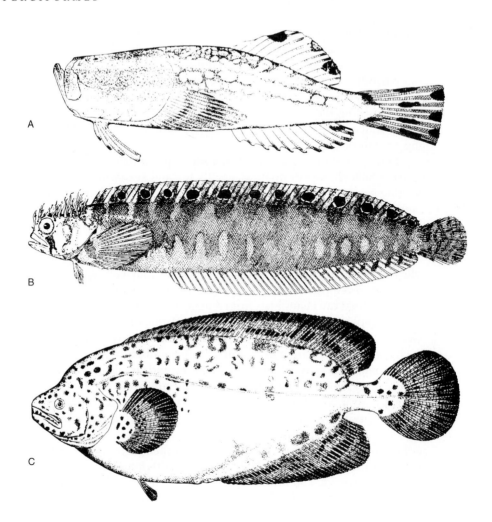

FIGURE 23.3 *Representative perciform fishes: (A) stargazer* (Astroscopus, *Uranoscopidae, Trachinoidei); (B) mosshead warbonnet* (Chirolophis nugator, *Stichaeidae, Zoarcoidei); and (C) ragfish* (Icosteus aenigmaticus, Icosteoidei). *([A] from Jordan and Evermann 1900; [B] from Jordan and Starks 1895; [C] from Goode and Bean 1895.)*

water bottom dwellers, many pricklebacks (Stichaeidae, Fig. 23.3) and gunnels (Pholidae) are common in tide pools. The penpoint gunnel (*Apodichthys flavidus*), like a number of other intertidal fishes, has red, green, and brown forms; the green forms are found among beds of green algae in the upper intertidal zone, the brown forms among brown algae in the lower intertidal zone, and the red forms in deep water, among red algae (Winkler 1988). The largest members of this suborder are the wolffishes (Anarhichadidae), which reach 2.5 m and are famous for their ferocious appearance and tendency to lunge at divers who get too close, especially when the fish are guarding a nest of embryos.

NOTOTHENIOIDEI

The over 120 species of notothenioid fishes are the dominant fish of the Antarctic, although a few species are also found along the coasts of southern South America, Australia, and New Zealand. The remarkable morphological and physiological adaptations of these fishes are discussed in Chapter 36.

TRACHINOIDEI

There are 13 families and about 210+ species in this suborder, most of them dwellers in the sandy bottoms of shallow waters. They bury themselves in sand to ambush prey, which they suddenly engulf in their large, upward-pointing mouths. The weeverfishes (Trachinidae) and the stargazers (Uranoscopidae) also have poisonous spines that can inflict painful injuries on waders and other predators (Fig. 23.3). The stargazers have, in addition, electric organs, formed from modified eye muscles, that they probably use for detection of prey. However, some species can deliver up to 50 V, so these organs may also function in stunning the prey. When buried, stargazers can inhale water through their nostrils, which open into the branchial cavity. Some species also have a wormlike lure growing from the floor of the mouth, which can be moved about to attract prey.

A recent addition to this suborder are the sand lances (Ammodytidae, 18 species), which are small, shoaling fishes. They are abundant enough in inshore waters of the Northern Hemisphere to be of major importance in marine food chains leading to larger, commercially exploited fishes. They are elongate, rarely exceeding 30 cm, with deeply forked tails, long dorsal fins (without spines), reduced or absent pelvic fins, cycloid scales, and no swimbladder (Fig. 23.4). Their heads are pointed, with projecting lower jaws. The latter characteristic is apparently an adaptation that allows them to burrow quickly, head first, into sand when attacked by predators. Despite this important defense mechanism, shimmering schools of sand lances are frequently found offshore, feeding on zooplankton.

BLENNIOIDEI

The blennioid fishes range from eel-like to sculpin-like in body shape and include nearly every conceivable combination of these two conditions. The pelvic fins are either absent or small and are located in front of the pectoral fins. Most have long dorsal and anal fins, which are fused with the caudal fin in eel-like forms. The suborder contains over 730 species in six families.

Clinidae. The clinids are an enormously variable group of about 75 species that mostly inhabit the intertidal zone. They are perhaps the most common group of intertidal fishes in Australia and South Africa, but they are not unusual elsewhere (particularly along the Pacific coast of North America). Many species have the elongate body and blunt head so typical of blennies, but they are distinguished from the Blenniidae by the predominance of spines in the dorsal fin (many more than rays) and the presence of patches of fixed, conical teeth in the mouth. Some species have pointed snouts and laterally compressed heads and bodies. Most species have small cycloid scales, although scales are absent from one species. Their reproductive habits vary considerably; a number of species are viviparous, so the males have intromittent organs. Some of the most distinctive of the clinids are the fringeheads (*Neoclinus*) of the California coast, 20-cm-long blennylike fishes with long, fleshy cirri over the eyes and extraordinarily large mouths. The common name of one species is the sarcastic fringehead.

Blenniidae. Combtooth blennies are an important part of the rocky inshore marine fauna over much of the world, but especially in tropical and subtropical regions. The common name stems from the numerous closely packed teeth present on their jaws, although a few species also possess daggerlike teeth on each side of the lower jaw. Most of the 345 species have blunt heads, usually topped by cirri, and moderately long, scaleless bodies with dorsal fins containing more rays than spines. Many species have pelagic larvae or postlarvae, so they can quickly colonize disturbed areas of coastline, such as new breakwaters. Wherever they are, blennies tend to be secretive in their behavior but eclectic in feeding, consuming both invertebrates and algae. One of the more famous exceptions to this characterization of the blennies is the sabertooth blenny (*Aspidontus taeniatus*), which mimics cleaner wrasses so that it can sneak up on unsuspecting fishes in order to take bites out of their fins and tails. As the name implies, these are among the blennies that have large jaw teeth; the large teeth are not used for feeding, however, but for aggressive displays to members of the same species.

ICOSTEOIDEI

There is but one family (Icosteidae) and one species in this suborder. The ragfish (*Icosteus aenigmaticus*) of the deep waters off the Pacific coast of North America is well described by its scientific name, which means "puzzling fish with soft bones." The adults can exceed 2 m in length and are extremely flabby, with a largely cartilaginous skeleton and no spines, scales, or pelvic fins. The body shape of the adult is somewhat troutlike, with a blunt head and chocolate brown color. The juvenile fish, in contrast, are deep bodied, with rounded tails, pelvic fins, and a blotched brown and yellow color pattern (Fig. 23.3). It is not surprising, therefore, to find that the juveniles were originally described as a different genus and species from the adults.

GOBIESOCOIDEI

The 120 species of clingfish have been moved back and forth between the Paracanthopterygii and the Acanthopterygii, their true nature well hidden by their specializations. Clingfish are designed for clinging to rocks in the pounding surf of the intertidal zone or to swaying fronds of kelp. They are mostly small, tadpole-like fish with pelvic fins united into a large sucking disc. They lack scales, spines, and a swimbladder.

CALLIONYMOIDEI

The dragonets (Callionymidae, 130 species; Draconettidae, 7 species) are small, colorful, goby-like inhabitants of tropical reef areas. The callionymids have the principal opening of each operculum as a nearly dorsal notch, which permits the fish to remain partially buried on the bottom but still capable of taking in water for respiration. A number of dragonets are covered with evil-smelling mucus, which apparently decreases their desirability to predators. They are best known, however, for the brightness of the males in contrast to the females and the readiness with which they court and spawn in aquaria.

GOBIOIDEI

The gobioid fishes form a quite distinctive group of bottom dwellers, on the basis of both osteology and external morphology, and so perhaps should be given the status of a separate order. They usually lack both lateral line and swimbladder; they have gill membranes that are joined to the isthmus (i.e., have opercula that are not free at the bottom); they have a short, spiny dorsal fin (one to eight spines), and pelvic fins that either are united to form a sucking disc or at least are close together. This suborder contains over 2100 species in eight families, 8–9% of all fishes.

Gobiidae. The total number of species in the Gobiidae—1875—is only slightly smaller than that of the Cyprinidae. Gobies are found worldwide in both fresh and salt water, with the bulk of the species associated with shallow tropical and subtropical environments. Despite their wide distribution and richness of species, the gobies are a readily recognizable group (Fig. 23.4). They are characterized by (1) a sucking disc created by the pelvic fins; (2) two dorsal fins, the first consisting of two to eight flexible spines; (3) a rounded caudal fin; (4) a blunt head dominated by relatively large eyes; (5) visible scales, either cycloid or ctenoid; and (6) small size (few reach 20 cm, and most are shorter than 10 cm). Their success seems to be best explained by their remarkable ability to adapt to habitats or microhabitats inaccessible to most other fishes, such as (1) cracks and crevices in coral reefs, (2) burrows of invertebrates, (3) mud flats, (4) mangrove swamps, (5) fresh water on oceanic islands, and (6) inland seas and estuaries.

The cracks and crevices of coral reefs, and other inshore habitats, provide homes for perhaps a majority of goby species. Many of these gobies are very small; in fact, the smallest known vertebrate is *Trimmatom nanus,* a goby from the Chagos Islands in the Indian Ocean, which is mature at 8 to 10 mm (Winterbottom and Emery 1981). Many of these reef gobies are brightly colored and live symbiotically with other reef

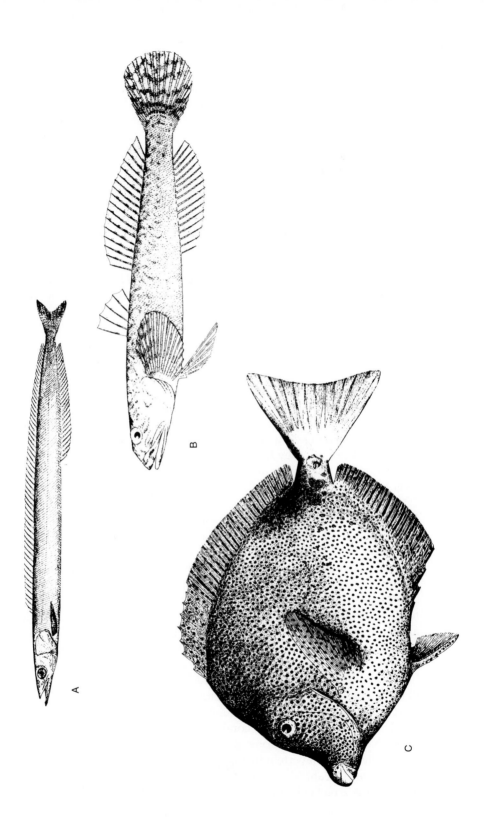

animals. Some species are found only in the "chimneys" of sponges, others in the arms of branched corals. While these are probably commensal relationships, some gobies associated with sea urchins appear to behave as parasites, because they browse on the tube feet of the urchins (Teylaud 1971). In Atlantic reefs, *Gobisoma* gobies leave their crevices to pick ectoparasites from other fishes.

When gobies are found on soft bottoms, they typically live in the burrows of invertebrates, ranging from polychaete worms to shrimp to clams. On tide flats some gobies manage to survive by breathing air and "walking" across the mud. The longjaw mudsucker *(Gillichthys mirabilis)* absorbs oxygen from the air in its large and highly vascularized mouth cavity. It is also capable of making "sojourns" from one muddy pool to another (Todd 1968). However, the most extreme examples of a goby adapted to the terrestrial environment are the mudskippers *(Periopthalamus),* which inhabit the mangrove swamps and mud flats of the tropical Indian Ocean. These fishes actually climb out of the water, along mangrove roots, seeking terrestrial insects (Nursall 1981). They "walk" on their pectoral fins, propelled in part by the tail, and breathe air trapped in highly vascular opercular cavities.

Another characteristic of the mudskippers is their tolerance of low salinities. Indeed, this seems to be a characteristic of the family, because gobies have invaded freshwater habitats throughout the world but particularly on oceanic islands and in Asia. On the islands they are frequently the principal native freshwater fishes, and many are amphidromous, spending part of their life cycle in the ocean (Chapter 11). The island gobies include the world's smallest freshwater fish, *Pandaka pygmaea* of Luzon (Phillipines), which mature at 10 to 12 mm. In Asia, gobies are common in inland waters from estuaries to rivers to brackish inland seas. In the Black and Caspian seas they are abundant enough to be exploited commercially, despite their small size. Some of these gobies have been spread to the Laurentian Great Lakes through the ballast water of ships, as have Asian gobies to western North America and Australia.

Schindleriidae. The two species of *Schindleria* are very peculiar indeed. They are tiny (2 to 3 cm) surface-dwelling fishes of the tropical Pacific. They would be classified as larvae with adults unknown except that they become sexually mature. Like larval fishes, they are elongate and transparent and have a poorly developed skeleton, except for the bones of the jaw, which bear fine teeth. They are extremely abundant in many areas, especially around Hawaii.

KURTOIDEI

Only two species (*Kurtus,* Kurtidae) are placed in this suborder, both of them rather peculiar but abundant fishes of the estuaries and streams of southeast Asia, New Guinea, and northern Australia. They are unmistakable fishes with their deep,

FIGURE 23.4 *Representative perciform fishes: (A) sand lance* (Ammodytes, *Ammodytidae, Trachinoidei); (B) arrow goby* (Clevelandia ios, *Gobioidei); and (C) surgeonfish* (Acanthurus, *Acanthuroidei). ([A] and [C] from Jordan and Evermann 1900; [B] from Jordan and Starks 1895.)*

compressed bodies, long anal fins, deeply forked tails, small cycloid scales, large upward-oriented mouths, and, most of all, depressed foreheads topped by a hook-like structure of modified dorsal fin spines. The latter feature is found only on males and is used to carry eggs. This has earned them the names of nurseryfish or humpheads.

ACANTHUROIDEI

Although this suborder is small, it contains some of the most conspicuous and colorful fishes on tropical reefs: the surgeonfishes and moorish idols (Acanthuridae, 72 species) and the rabbitfishes (Siganidae, 27 species). Surgeonfishes are deep-bodied fishes of moderate size (20 to 30 cm) that are extremely compressed laterally. They tend to have beaklike snouts with small mouths and incisorlike teeth that are used for scraping algae from rocks and coral (Fig. 23.4). Their name comes from the scalpel-like spines they possess on the caudal peduncle, which generally point forward when erected. A few species that engage in picking ectoparasites from other fishes are called doctorfishes. Moorish idols (*Zanclus canescens*) resemble surgeonfishes in body shape and mouth structure but lack the "scalpels" on the tail. They are readily recognized by their strong black-and-white striped pattern and symmetrical dorsal and anal fins. In fact, moorish idols are probably the most familiar of all reef fishes; stylized versions of them are standard decorations on shower curtains, tiles, towels, bathroom wallpaper, and other water-related items.

MUGILOIDEI

The mullets (Mugilidae) are the sole family in this suborder, but they have been lumped with many other groups, especially assorted families in the Atheriniformes. The 80 species of mullets are readily recognizable, with their thick yet streamlined bodies, forked tails, hard-angled mouths, large, cycloid or faintly ctenoid scales, subabdominal pelvic fins, and two widely separated dorsal fins, the first containing just four spines (Fig. 23.2). The streamlined body of the mullets is necessary both to avoid the numerous predators that attack their schools in the shallow inshore waters they inhabit, and to speed them along in their spawning migrations, many of which closely follow coastlines. The main reason the mullets favor the inshore environment is for feeding. They subsist largely on organic detritus and small algal cells which are scooped up when the fish swim at an angle to the bottom, running their mouths through the sediment. The larger particles are retained by their fine gill rakers and then ground up in their gizzardlike stomachs. Digestion takes place in an extraordinarily long intestine (five to eight times the body length), which is necessary because much of the material ingested is sand and other indigestible matter.

SCOMBROIDEI

The scombroid fishes are only about 135 species distributed among five families, but these species are usually characterized by superlatives for their value as food-fishes, their speed, their voraciousness as predators, their long migrations, the sport they provide anglers, and their peculiarities of anatomy and physiology. Curiously, they have lost the protractile upper jaw so characteristic of teleosts and have instead a solidly fused unit to support a biting mouth, much like more ancestral bony fishes.

Sphyraenidae. Barracudas are fearsome predators on other fishes, with elongate, pikelike bodies, protruding lower jaws, formidable pointed teeth in the jaws, two widely separated dorsal fins, forked tails, and tiny or nonexistent gill rakers. Their body plan is an interesting compromise between that of the lie-in-wait predator and that of an active predator (Fig. 23.2). Barracudas swim about actively in clear water, often in schools, searching for prey. Their narrow head-on profile and silvery color reduce their visibility to potential prey; their long caudal region, assisted by posteriorly placed dorsal and anal fins, allows them to put on a quick burst of speed to close the gap between them and their prey. This strategy is particularly effective when light levels are low. The great barracuda (*Sphyraena barracuda*) of the Atlantic may reach lengths of nearly 2 m and has been known to attack divers, but such attacks are rare and virtually unknown in the other 19 species. However, they are excellent food fish and favored sport fish.

Scombridae. There are only about 50 species of mackerels and tunas, and they make up less than 10% of the total catch by weight of marine fish. However, their monetary value is extremely high because of the favor they find as food fish, particularly with Americans and Europeans. Tuna and mackerel are the top carnivores of the epipelagic zone of the tropical and subtropical seas. Their prey consists of small schooling fish and squid, which they locate and capture through high-speed swimming, also in schools. Thus most of the features that characterize the scombrids are adaptations for fast and continuous swimming. Their bodies are beautifully stream-lined: spindle-shaped and oval to round in cross section (Fig. 23.5). The skin is smooth, with tiny cycloid scales; its coloration tends to be shades of iridescent blue or green on top of the fish, countershading to silver and white below. The first dorsal fin, while made up of stout spines, depresses into a groove on the back while the fish is swimming rapidly. The soft dorsal and anal fins are short, identical in shape and size, and located opposite one another just in front of rows of small finlets that run down the caudal peduncle to the tail. The tail fin is deeply forked to lunate in construction (high aspect ratio) and provides the tremendous thrust needed to maintain high speeds. The caudal peduncle is very narrow and contains mainly the bony keel on each side (created by the flattening of the caudal vertebrate) and the tendons running to the tail from both red and white muscle. Because the tendons run over the keel, the keel acts as a pulley, to increase the amount of pull exerted by the muscles. In many species the swimbladder is reduced or absent, en-

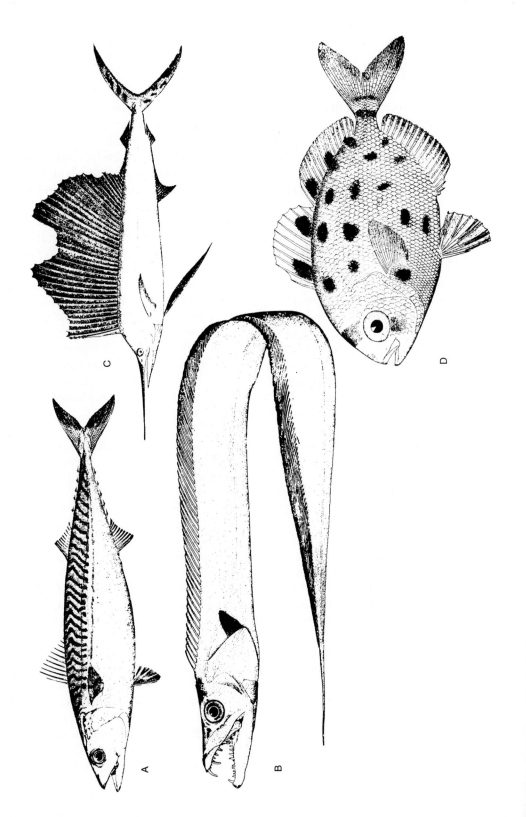

abling the fish to move throughout the water column in search of deep water as well as surface prey.

The respiratory pump system in scombrids is reduced because constant rapid swimming forces plenty of water across the gills. In the larger scombrids the circulatory system has been modified with countercurrent exchangers in order to reduce loss of the heat generated by the tremendous muscular activity. This in turn increases the efficiency of the muscle (see Chapter 5).

Xiphiidae. The 12 species of billfish roam the surface waters of tropical and subtropical seas, readily recognizable as swordfish *(Xiphias gladius)*, sailfish (*Istiophorus* spp.), spearfish *(Tetrapturus* spp.), and marlin (*Makaira* spp.). These fish all have a long bill derived from the premaxilla; they have two anal fins, no true spines in the dorsal fin, and reduced or absent pelvic fins (Fig. 23.5). The sword of the swordfish is flat and, at its maximum extent, about one-third the length of the fish (which may reach 4.5 m). The sword of other species is rounded in cross section and is generally less than one-quarter the total length (up to 4 m). Billfish capture other fish for food by swimming through schools and slashing the bill back and forth, stunning or injuring the prey in the process. Swordfish apparently can also spear large fishes with their snouts.

STROMATEOIDEI

In this curious group of six families and 65 species, the juveniles are, for the most part, better known than the adults. The reason for this is that, with the exception of members of the Ariommatidae (which are bottom-oriented deepsea fishes), juvenile stromateoid fishes are associated with jellyfish or drifting objects in the epipelagic region. The juveniles found with jellyfish swim among the tentacles, dodging the stinging nematocysts, to which they are *not* immune. With this association they obtain not only protection from large piscine predators but food as well, because they nibble on the tentacles. These juveniles, in contrast to the adults, have a well-developed swimbladder and a color pattern of vertical stripes. The rather drab and unremarkable-looking adults (Fig. 23.5) are mostly also pelagic and may compensate in part for the reduced or absent swimbladder by having a high lipid content of the body and a reduced firmness of muscle and bone. However, exceptions to this are the 13 species of deep-bodied, iridescent butterfishes (Stromateidae), which do have a high lipid content but are nevertheless negatively buoyant. The butterfishes are active inshore species that apparently move freely up and down the water column feeding on coelenterate medusae, ctenophores, and

FIGURE 23.5 *Pelagic perciform fishes: (A) tuna* (Thunnus, Scombridae); *(B) cutlass fish* (Trichiurus, Trichiuridae); *(C) sailfish* (Istiophorus, Xiphiidae)—*[(A) through (C) all Scombroidei]—and (D) driftfish* (Psenes, Nomeidae, Stromatoidei). *([A] and [C] from Jordan and Evermann 1900; [B] and [D] from Goode and Bean 1895.)*

other soft-bodied animals. Like other stromateoid fishes, which also feed on such organisms, they possess tooth-covered pharyngeal sacs just behind the last gill arch (Horn 1984).

ANABANTOIDEI

The gouramis are a group of five freshwater families well known to aquarists through such species as the climbing gourami (Anabantidae, *Anabas testudineus*), the Siamese fighting fish (Belontiidae, *Betta splendens*), the kissing gourami (Helostomatidae, *Helostoma temmincki*), and the giant gourami (Osphronemidae, *Osphronemus goramy*). The over 80 species in these families are mostly small (less than 10 cm), surface-oriented fishes with moderately deep bodies, rounded tails, and long anal fins (Fig. 23.6). Internally, they have two particularly distinctive features: a long body cavity, so that the swimbladder extends into the caudal region, and a labyrinthine (suprabranchial) organ (Liem 1963). The labyrinthine organs permit the gouramis to breathe air. They are made up of elaborately folded layers of highly vascularized skin that cover modified lamellae from the first functional gill arch. The organs occupy much of the gill chamber as well as an extra chamber on its roof. The gills have become reduced in size as a consequence, and gouramis suffocate if deprived of access to the surface. Gouramis breathe by swallowing bubbles of air, holding them in the labyrinthine organs for extended periods of time, and then forcing them out through the gill covers. The air bubbles taken in by the gouramis are also important for hearing and reproduction. When in the chambers of the labyrinthine organ, the air bubbles are right next to the sides of the cranium containing the inner ear. In gouramis, membranous "windows" are present at this point, so vibrations picked up by the air bubbles are easily transmitted to the inner ears (Alexander 1967). For reproduction, male gouramis expel air bubbles through their mouths and build a nest of froth on the surface of the water, into which eggs are laid by the female and subsequently tended by the male. The froth nests and labyrinthine organs of the gouramis are obviously adaptations for life in the stagnant waters of tropical Asia and Africa in which they live.

CHANNOIDEI

The 21 known species of snakeheads (Channidae) are famous for their voraciousness as predators. For this purpose they have a large mouth with an underslung, well-toothed jaw, large eyes, and a thick, elongate body with long dorsal and anal fins (Fig. 23.6). Like the gouramis with which they typically occur, snakeheads have a labyrinthine organ in the gill chamber, but it is quite different in structure from that of the gouramis. Other adaptations of snakeheads for life in stagnant waters are eggs that float (by means of oil droplets) at the surface, where they are guarded by the males; and the ability of some species to move overland by "swimming" in an eel-like fashion.

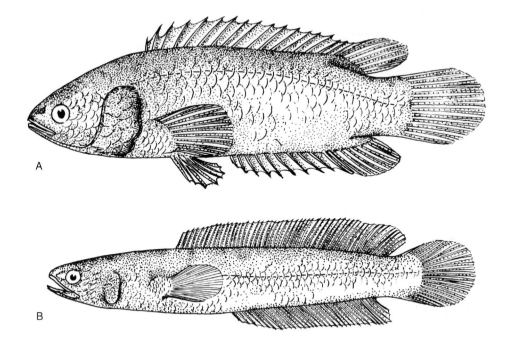

FIGURE 23.6 *Representatives of tropical freshwater perciform suborders: Top: climbing perch* (Anabas, *Anabantidae, Anabantoidei); Bottom: snakehead* (Channa, Channidae, Channoidei).

LESSONS FROM THE PERCOMORPHA II

The extraordinary success of the perciformes is clearly related to three factors: (1) a basic suite of adaptive characters that has allowed them to take advantage of complex shallow-water habitats; (2) an evolutionary "willingness" to abandon key general adaptations, such as spines, in favor of specializations; and (3) complex behavior patterns, including interactions with other species. Many of the species are small and cryptic, but many others are brightly colored day-active fishes that are protected by their spines and behavior. Others are large and predatory. If there are any two external features that unite the diverse members of this group, it is the large and maneuverable pectoral fins, placed near the center of gravity, and the large eyes. These two features characterize fish that rely on precise movement and vision to capture prey.

Another important (but less obvious) adaptation of perciform fishes, and of teleosts in general, is the dominance of small free embryos (eggs) in reproduction, usually with pelagic larvae for dispersal. Thus many perciform fish have high fecundities; the record is probably the louvar (*Luvarus imperialis*, Luvaridae), in which a 1.7-m-long individual can produce over 47 million eggs (Nelson 1994). The advantages of this strategy include wide dispersal of the young in ocean currents and the ability to put large numbers of young into the environment when conditions are good. This strategy is the complete opposite of the Chondrichthyes, where emphasis is placed on producing a few large young, usually by livebearing. It is interesting, however, that even a few perciform fishes (e.g. Embiotocidae) have adopted the chondrichthyan strategy.

Supplemental Readings

Bigelow and Schroeder 1953; Hart 1973; Nelson 1994; Pitcher 1993; Ribbink 1990; Wooton 1990.

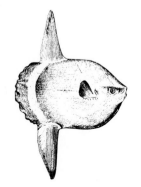

CHAPTER 24

Flounders, Puffers, and Molas

SUBDIVISON TELEOSTEI
  Infradivision Euteleostei
    Superorder Acanthopterygii
      Order Pleuronectiformes
        Families Psettodidae, Citharidae, Bothidae (lefteye flounders),
        Achiropsettidae (southern flounders), Scopthalmidae;
        Paralichthyidae (sand dabs), Pleuronectidae (right-eye flounders),
        Samaridae, Achiridae (American soles), Soleidae (soles),
        Cynoglossidae (tonguefishes)
      Order Tetraodontiformes
        Families Triacanthodidae (spikefishes), Triacanthidae (triplespines),
        Balistidae (triggerfishes), Monacanthidae (filefishes), Ostraciidae
        (boxfishes), Triodontidae (threetooth puffers), Tetraodontidae
        (puffers), Diodontidae (porcupinefishes), Molidae (ocean sunfishes)

The two orders considered here contain fishes that are so modified it is difficult to figure out with whom they share common ancestry among the Acanthopterygii. It is certainly not each other! The flatfishes and puffers are usually placed at the end of fish classification schemes on the assumption that they are the most derived groups of fishes and descended somehow from highly derived perciform-like ancestors.

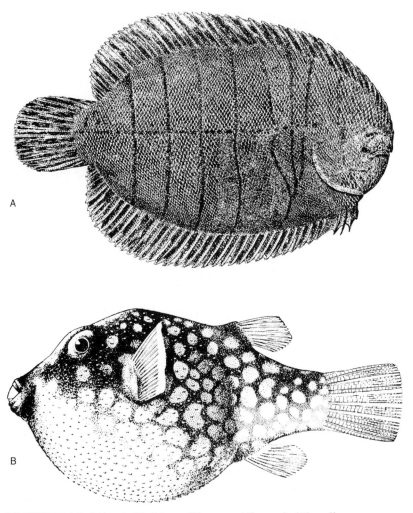

FIGURE 24.1 *(A) sole* (Achirus, *Pleuronectiformes); (B) puffer* (Canthigaster, *Tetraodontiformes);* Page 341: *(C) ocean sunfish* (Mola mola, *Tetraodontiformes). (From Jordan and Evermann 1900.)*

PLEURONECTIFORMES

There are few problems in recognizing a member of the flatfish order, because it is the only group of fishes in which the adults are not bilaterally symmetrical. One side of the body is white and eyeless, while the other side is dark-colored and has both eyes (Fig. 24.1). Flatfish lie on the bottom with the pale side down and the dark side up. Since they are very flat, secretive in their behavior, and able to change color to match the substrate, flatfish are masters at hiding from both predators and prey. Most flatfish remain close to the bottom even while swimming, which is accom-

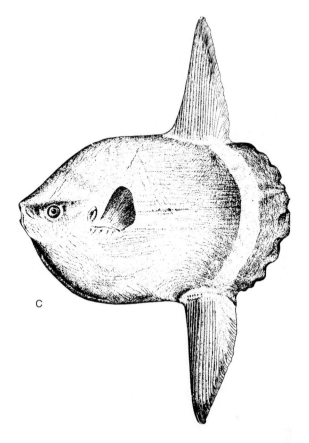

C

plished by undulating motions of the body; presumably the efficiency of this type of swimming is improved by the long dorsal and anal fins, which together with the caudal fins may almost completely encircle the body. These fins are usually without spines and very flexible. As might be expected in such fishes, the swimbladder is absent in adults and the body cavity is very small. Within the limits of their peculiar morphology, flatfish are very diverse, with over 570 species in 11 families.

One of the most fascinating aspects of flatfish biology is the change that takes place as the pelagic, bilaterally symmetrical larvae become benthic, asymmetrical juveniles (Fig. 24.2). The most visible parts of this process are the change in pigmentation patterns and the migration of one eye across the top of the head to its final resting place close to the other eye. This involves not only the movement of the eye but also changes in nerves, blood vessels, skull bones, and muscles. One of the features used to distinguish various flatfish groups is whether or not they have both eyes on the left or right side of the body. Left-eyed flatfishes rest on the right side of the body, and vice versa. Some species, however, such as the starry flounder *(Platichthys stellatus)*, have both right- and left-eyed forms. Flatfish are found mostly on soft bottoms of continental shelves, although a few species inhabit the continental slope and others may invade fresh water. On continental shelves they have a worldwide distribution and are abundant, often supporting important fisheries. The large number of flatfish species means that many species coexist with each other. Ecological segregation is reflected in differential depth distributions (see Chapter 32) and in different feeding habits, as reflected in the structure of the mouth and pharyngeal teeth. Piscivorous species, such as halibut *(Hippoglossus)*, have large symmetrical mouths, lined with tiny teeth for grasping, and sharply pointed pharyngeal teeth. Species that feed by taking chunks out of the siphons of clams and other buried invertebrates have asymmetrical mouths (favoring the down side) with chisel-like teeth for biting and molariform pharyngeal teeth for grinding.

Flatfish are favored food fish, so a great deal is known about some species, especially European plaice *(Pleuronectes platessa)* and halibut (*Hippoglossus* spp.). Fisheries often catch a mixture of flounders, soles, sanddabs, turbots, and tonguefish, with an occasional whiff or hogchoker. Because Pacific halibut *(H. stenolepis)* are so valuable and competition for them among fishermen in Alaska was so severe, the fishing season has been reduced to one frantic 24-hour period! In contrast, in the fishery in British Columbia, where the number of fishermen is restricted, the season lasts for months.

TETRADONTIFORMES

If degree of alteration of the basic Acanthopterygian body plan is the key to determining how "derived" a fish group is, then this order includes the most derived of all teleosts. While perhaps the best indications of this are found internally, in modifications of the skeleton (they lack, for example, parietals, nasals, infraorbitals, and lower ribs), the tetraodontiform fishes are also visibly different from other fishes. To begin with, they come in a variety of body shapes that are the antithesis of the fusiform bodies of "typical" fish, ranging from globular to triangular to extremely compressed. All are slow swimmers, propelled either by a rounded caudal fin, by sculling with the pectoral fins, or by movements of the dorsal and anal fins, which are typically symmetrical and placed far back on the body. Presumably because of the vulnerability of such fish to predators, most possess some form of protection such as inflatable, spine-covered bodies, body armor (often of scales), stout fin spines that can be locked erect, tough leathery skin, and/or poisonous flesh. Gill openings are small, usually just holes on the side of the fish, in front of the pectoral fins. The food of tetraodontiform fishes is mostly invertebrates that have heavy shells or other armor. As a result, the fish have stout teeth in the jaw, or toothlike bones fused into a beak. The maxillae and premaxillae are also fused to each other. This hard jaw is powered by large muscles. The pharyngeal teeth are also stout and provide additional crushing abilities. Most of the 340 or so species in this order are associated with coral reefs, which are dominated by hard-shelled invertebrates, although a few live in fresh water.

Balistidae. The triggerfishes are typified by the 20-cm-long humuhumunukunukuapuaa of Hawaiian reefs. Most members of this family (40 species)

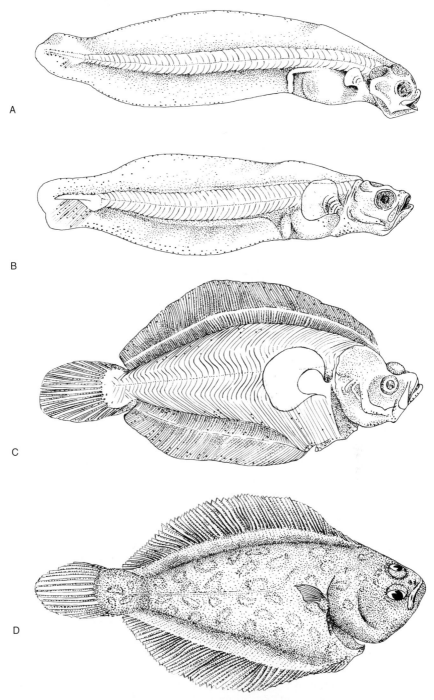

A

B

C

D

FIGURE 24.2 *Metamorphosis of halibut* (Hippoglossus stenolepis) *from a pelagic larva to a bottom fish. Note the migration of the eye from one side to the other. (After Thompson and Van Cleve 1936.)*

and the related **Monacanthidae** (filefishes, 95 species) are slow-moving, solitary, often brightly colored reef-dwellers; they have laterally compressed bodies, tiny mouths, and no pelvic fins. Triggerfish are so named because the stout first dorsal spine can be locked rigidly into place by the second spine (the "trigger").

Triodontidae, Tetraodontidae, and Diodontidae. The more than 140 species in these three families have the outer bones of the jaws modified into strong, beaklike structures for shearing off corals and other such invertebrates (Fig. 24.1). The beaks are divided by sutures, which give them the appearance of teeth. However, the number of "teeth" is distinctive and is handy for distinguishing the three families: Diodontidae means two-toothed; Triodontidae, three-toothed; and Tetraodontidae, four-toothed. For protection these slow-moving fishes rely on their ability to puff themselves up and on their toxicity. In order to inflate themselves the puffers and porcupine fishes suck water into a ventral diverticulum of the stomach. This greatly increases their diameter, especially in the species that possess spines or prickles on the sides. Fishes unfortunate enough to be caught by humans will inflate themselves with air. The toxin possessed by many of these fishes, called tetrodotoxin, is found mostly in the internal organs and can be fatal to humans. This has not kept the puffers from being a favored food (fugu) in Japan, although they must be cleaned by licensed cooks. Presumably the risk involved in eating fugu enhances the flavor.

Molidae. The three species of molas are unlike any other members of the order. They are adapted for life as sluggish pelagic predators on jellyfish or other large invertebrates that come close enough to be sucked in. While they possess the fused "teeth" in the jaws typical of the order, in most respects they are unique. They are large, flattened fishes that lack a caudal peduncle but do have a fin of sorts running along the posterior edge of the body, immediately behind the tall, short-based dorsal and anal fins (Fig. 24.1). Pelvic fins and swimbladder are absent, as are spines, although the body is covered with a tough leathery skin. Despite these disadvantages, molas are commonly observed jumping out of the water, although how they do it is a mystery. The mouth is small and has sharp-edged plates of fused teeth. These fish feed by grazing on various kinds of jellyfish, although fish (such as the leptocephalus larvae of eels) are occasionally found in their stomachs. Two of the species *(Mola mola, Masturus lanceolatus)* may reach 3 m in length and weigh 1500 kg. Because such large fish are typically observed on the surface (and are often called, as a result, ocean sunfish), they can be a hazard at times to boats. A collision of a large sharptail mola with a submersible vehicle at 670 m in depth led Harbison (1987) to suggest that this species may be more an inhabitant of the mesopelagic zone than the surface waters, especially since large jellyfish are most abundant at depths well below the surface.

The molas are considered to be the most fecund of all vertebrates, producing upward of 300 million eggs. They are not considered to be highly desirable as food because the flesh is flabby and often parasite-ridden. Nevertheless, they are being fished commercially to supply the sashimi market in Japan. Despite their large size, the yield of edible flesh in a mola is low, roughly 20% of the body weight, because of the large cartilaginous skeleton and thick skin.

LESSONS FROM FLATFISH AND PUFFERS

Flatfish. There are two major, independent evolutionary lines of fish that are flat bottom-huggers: flatfish and rays. A majority of both groups are cryptic in behavior, modest in size, and feed on bottom-dwelling invertebrates, which they catch with many tiny sharp teeth. A few larger species use their flatness to lie in ambush for other fishes. Both groups are very diverse (570 flatfish vs. 460 rays), abundant, and widespread, although rays have a slight advantage in being considered less desirable to eat by humans. In a way it is curious that flatfish are so successful, when you consider that rays were already common when flatfish were still figuring out how to distort their bodies into flatness. Arguably, rays hit upon a much more elegant solution to the problem by simply flattening out a basic morphology already headed in that direction. The original shark morphology in turn reflects less reliance on vision for prey-finding than seems to be true of bony fishes, resulting in sub-terminal mouths and elongate snouts. The ancestral condition in bony fishes seems to be large eyes and terminal mouths. Perhaps this is also the reason why some rays have reversed the trend and become pelagic, flying through the water with grace virtually unmatched by other fish. Flatfish will often enter the water column to feed or move, but their movements would rarely be called elegant or graceful! Still, the migration of the eye across the head in flatfish has got to be regarded as one of the developmental wonders of the animal world.

Puffers. A general trend in bony fish evolution has been a reduction in armor in favor of increased maneuverability. The puffers and their kin, however, have reinvented the concept of armor in order to survive as slow-moving crunchers of hard-shelled invertebrates, in the evolutionary arms race that is taking place on tropical reefs. Those without heavy bony plates typically are covered with spines, which can be erected when the body is inflated with water. In addition, many of the species are highly toxic, which also discourages predators. The fact that even the toxic species are eaten, however, is a tribute to human omnivory.

Supplemental Readings

Bigelow and Schroeder 1953; Fitch and Lavenberg 1968; Gordon 1977; Hart 1973; Herald 1961; Nelson 1994.

IV
ZOOGEOGRAPHY

CHAPTER 25

Zoogeography of Freshwater Fishes

The study of fish zoogeography is alternately one of the most fascinating and one of most frustrating areas of ichthyology. It is fascinating because the explanation of the world patterns of fish distribution requires putting together knowledge from many other areas of ichthyology, such as ecology, physiology, systematics, and paleontology, as well as from other disciplines such as geology and biogeography. It is frustrating, however, because so much of our knowledge of these areas is nonexistent, fragmented, or incomplete, so that any attempt to explain fish distribution patterns, particularly over large areas, is bound to contain gaps that have to be bridged with guesswork.

Nevertheless, the acceptance of continental drift as a concept that explains many perplexing geological problems has led to the solution of many zoogeographic puzzles, so that worldwide patterns of fish distribution have become much easier to understand. This has been particularly true for freshwater fishes (Berra 1981). Therefore, this chapter will summarize (1) the broad zoogeographic patterns of freshwater fishes; (2) the fish faunas and drainage patterns of the major continental areas; and (3) the zoogeographic history of freshwater fishes, especially the minnows, characins, and catfishes (Otophysi).

ZOOGEOGRAPHIC TYPES

There are two basic types of fish found in fresh water, euryhaline marine fish and obligatory freshwater fish. **Euryhaline marine fish** are those that are primarily marine but are capable of entering fresh water for extended periods of time, and so are frequently characteristic of the lower reaches of coastal streams. Most commonly it is juveniles that inhabit fresh water, perhaps to avoid predation. However, adult forms of such fish as the large bull sharks *(Carcharinus leucus)* and sawfishes (*Pristis* sp.) that move in and out of Lake Nicaragua are important in some areas. Euryhaline marine forms are generally most important in freshwater systems where the obligatory freshwater fish fauna is not well developed.

Obligatory freshwater fish are those that must spend at least part of their life cycle in fresh water. For zoogeographic studies, two basic types can be recognized: freshwater dispersants and saltwater dispersants. **Freshwater dispersants** belong to fish families whose members by and large are incapable of traveling for long distances through salt water. The distribution patterns of these families are best explained through the use of overland (freshwater) routes of dispersal and through plate tectonics (Rosen 1974). Freshwater dispersants include the primary and secondary freshwater fishes of Myers (1951). As D. E. Rosen (1974, 1975a) points out, the distribution patterns of most secondary freshwater fish (fish characteristic of fresh water but with distribution patterns seeming to indicate saltwater dispersal) can often be better explained on the basis of continental drift than on the basis of long-distance movements through salt water. In addition, many primary freshwater fish (those supposedly incapable of entering salt water) have been shown to be tolerant of a wide range of salinities. Typical examples of freshwater dispersants include most of the Otophysi and families such as the Esocidae (pikes), Percidae (freshwater perches), Mormyridae (African electric fishes), Poeciliidae (livebearers), Lepisosteidae (gars), and Cichlidae (cichlids). Freshwater dispersants dominate the fresh waters of most of the world (Fig. 25.1).

Saltwater dispersants are those fishes whose distribution patterns can be explained in large part by movements through salt water. Even in this group, however, there are many families whose broad distribution patterns in freshwater environments are related to continental movements. Saltwater dispersant fishes are of two basic types: diadromous fishes and freshwater representatives of marine families. Diadromous fishes are those that regularly move between fresh water and salt water, spending different parts of their life cycle in each environment (see Chapter 11 for further definitions). Diadromous fishes are frequently important members of the faunas of coastal streams, especially if the region is geologically young. In most areas where they occur, diadromous species have given rise to numerous nonmigratory forms, which if isolated from the parent stock may evolve into distinct species. This has happened repeatedly in families such as the Galaxiidae, Salmonidae (Fig. 24.1), and Petromyzontidae (lampreys).

If a region lacks a well-developed fish fauna of freshwater dispersants, it is quite likely that the fauna will be made up of a mixture of diadromous species and species

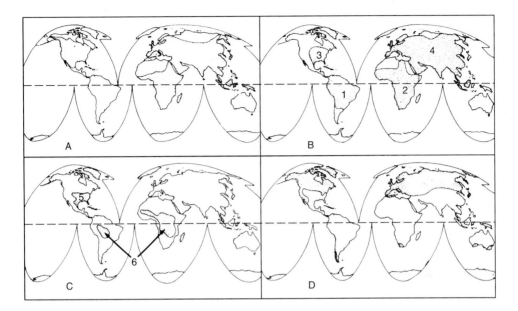

FIGURE 25.1 *Representative distribution patterns of freshwater fish families: (A) distribution of the Cyprinidae, a widely distributed family of freshwater dispersants that is absent from South America and Australia; (B) distribution of four families of freshwater dispersants largely confined to one continent (1 Gymnotidae, 2 Mormyridae, 3 Centrarchidae, and 4 Cobitidae); (C) distribution of two ancient groups of freshwater dispersant fishes (5 Lepisosteidae, 6 Lepidosireniformes); and (D) distribution of two saltwater dispersant families, Salmonidae (Northern Hemisphere) and Galaxiidae (Southern Hemisphere). (From Rosen 1975a.)*

that are otherwise representative of marine families. A good example of the latter group are the sculpins of the genus *Cottus* (Cottidae), which have a circumarctic distribution, mostly in streams dominated by salmonids. However, some of these marine-derived species are quite successful members of well-developed freshwater fish faunas, such as the many freshwater herrings (Clupeidae) and freshwater puffers (Tetraodontidae).

The classification system of zoogeographic types presented here is quite arbitrary and is set up mostly as a means of simplifying the explanation of general patterns of fish distribution. It is intended to be applied mostly at the family level, even though some species within each family may not fit the family category well. For example, the Galaxiidae, although containing a number of diadromous species, have a broad distribution pattern (Fig. 25.1) that seems to reflect the ancient connections of the southern continents to each other more than it does the ability of the diadromous species to disperse through the ocean (Campos 1984). However, on the southern continents, local distribution patterns of Galaxiidae may be explained at least partially by saltwater dispersal.

ZOOGEOGRAPHIC REGIONS

For the study of fish zoogeography, it is convenient to divide the world into six zoo-geographic regions (Darlington 1952): (1) the African Region, consisting of the African continent; (2) the Neotropical Region, consisting of South and Central America; (3) the Oriental Region, which includes the Indian subcontinent, Southeast Asia, most of Indonesia, and the Phillipines; (4) the Palaearctic Region, which includes Europe and Asia north of the Himalaya Mountains and the Yangtze River; (5) the Nearctic Region, which is North America down to central Mexico; and (6) the Australian Region, which consists of Australia, New Zealand, New Guinea, and the many smaller islands in the same region. Each of these regions has distinctive elements of its fish fauna that reflect its isolation from (as well as its connections to) the other regions.

AFRICAN REGION

The African Region possesses an extremely diverse fish fauna and is of special interest to students of fish evolution and zoogeography because of its wealth of ancient forms, such as lungfishes (Protopteridae), bichirs (Polypteridae), and osteoglossiforms (five families). The region contains at least 2500 species of freshwater fishes, belonging to about 280 genera and 47 families (Lowe-McConnell 1975; Roberts 1976). Over 95% of the species are freshwater dispersants. Over one-third of these belong to the Otophysi (about 300 cyprinid species, 180 characoid species, and 365 catfish species). The Otophysans belong to 15 families, which include seven endemic families and two families of marine catfishes. One or another of the remaining six families is also represeneted in other zoogeographic regions, except Australia.

The nonotophysan freshwater fishes belong to a variety of endemic and nonendemic families. One of the most numerous (190+ species) of the endemic families is the Mormyridae, a group related to the ancient Osteoglossidae but possessing many unusual adaptations, including electric organs, for living in muddy tropical waters. Another endemic family of interest is the Polypteridae (bichirs and reedfish, 11 species), lobe-finned fish that are now placed in with the ancient Chondrostei. The nonotophysan, nonendemic families are shared with a number of other zoogeographic regions. They include Osteoglossidae (bonytongues, shared with South America, Southeast Asia, and Australia), Anabantidae and Mastacembelidae (gouramis and spiny eels, respectively, both shared with the Oriental Region), and Cichlidae and Cyprinodontidae (cichlids and killifishes, respectively, shared with South America, North America, and the Oriental Region).

An interesting, if minor, component of the African freshwater fish fauna is the freshwater representatives of marine families, such as Tetraodontidae (puffer fishes), Syngnathidae (pipefishes), Mugilidae (mullets), Clupeidae (herrings) and Centropomidae (snooks). The latter family is important ecologically because the seven freshwater species in Africa, including the Nile perch *(Lates niloticus)*, are important predators in many lakes and rivers.

One of the curious aspects of the African freshwater fish fauna is that each of the dominant groups tends to be characteristic of a broad habitat type (Roberts 1976). Thus the cichlids (1000+ species) exist mostly as members of the spectacular species flocks that characterize the great rift lakes of East Africa. The characoid fishes (families Hepsetidae, Characidae, and Citharinidae) are found almost exclusively in sluggish lowland streams, as are most mormyrids. A number of minor families that have air-breathing abilities (e.g., Protopteridae, Polypteridae) are also confined to the lowland habitats. The cyprinids are most characteristic of flowing waters of middle to high elevations. The catfishes are found in most habitats, although with different types of specializations for the different environments. Their success is presumably due primarily to their nocturnal activity patterns, because most of the other large families (except the mormyrids) are diurnal.

Africa contains an extraordinary mixture of endemic and nonendemic families of different ages of origin because it has been a rather stable tropical land mass with at least intermittent connections with the other continents. These families have produced a large number of endemic species because Africa contains a number of ancient, isolated drainage basins. However, within those basins speciation may be extremely rapid, especially of the cichlid fishes (Owen et al. 1990). The region can thus be divided up into at least 11 ichthyological provinces, each with its characteristic fish fauna (Roberts 1976).

NEOTROPICAL REGION

The Neotropical Region has two distinct zoogeographic subregions, mainland South America and Central America. The fish faunas of the two subregions reflect the fact that South America was isolated from the other continents for a long period of time, while Central America is of geologically recent origin.

The diversity of South America's fish fauna is just beginning to be fully appreciated. It has the most species of obligatory freshwater fish of any continent (2600+), many of them undescribed. One of the most striking aspects of the South American fish fauna is the complete absence of the family Cyprinidae, which dominates the freshwater fish fauna in all other zoogeographic regions except the Australian region. Instead, the dominant fishes are characins (order Characiformes, eight families, seven of them endemic, with about 1200 species) and catfishes (order Siluriformes, 13 endemic families, with about 1300 species). The characins show an extraordinary variety of ecological and morphological adaptations, yet the basic similarities in the body plans of the many forms seem to reflect a common ancestry. Only the family Characidae occurs outside the Neotropical Region in Africa. The South American catfishes are as diverse as the characins and include the most ancestral family (Diplomystidae) of the order, as well as three families distinguished by the presence of bony plates on their bodies (Doradidae, Callichthyidae, and Loricariidae). Apparently sharing a common ancestry with the catfishes is the order Gymnotiformes. This order consists of six families of electric fishes that are strikingly convergent on the unrelated mormyrids of Africa.

In contrast to Africa, in South America the nonotophysan freshwater fishes are a relatively minor component (about 10%) of the fish fauna, although they often play important roles in South American lakes and streams. Cichlids (Cichlidae, ca. 150 species) are widespread in South American streams, while killifish (Cyprinodontidae, 80+ species) and poeciliids (Poeciliidae, 20+ species) are most abundant in habitats (such as stagnant backwaters) not utilized by larger fishes. In Lake Titicaca, a species flock of 23 endemic killifishes is present. The two most ancient families of freshwater fishes present in South America are the Lepidosirenidae (lungfishes, one species) and the Osteoglossidae (bonytongues, two species). Both families also have relatives in Africa, and osteoglossids occur in Australia as well.

The final elements of the South American fish fauna are fishes of marine origin and diadromous fishes. The lower Amazon alone has 20 to 30 endemic freshwater representatives of marine families and about an equal number of euryhaline marine species. Among the freshwater species are members of the families Dasyatidae (stingrays), Soleidae (soles), Clupeidae (herrings), Engraulidae (anchovies), and Sciaenidae (drums). The diadromous species (mainly galaxiids) are confined to coastal Chile, Patagonia, Tierra del Fuego, and the Falkland Islands.

South America can be divided into eight provinces characterized by distinctive fish faunas (Gery 1969). However, because many of the major geological features of South America are comparatively recent in origin (e.g., the Andes Mountains) and because connections between drainage systems are common, the regions share many species and genera.

Another portion of the Neotropical Region with a fish fauna resembling that of South America is Central America. The Central American fish fauna (which includes species in part of Cuba and other Antillean islands) also shows affinities to that of North America and has many unique characteristics of its own. The distributional history of the fishes of the region is confusing because the geological history of the region is extraordinarily complex (Rosen 1975b). Miller (1966) lists 456 species from the fresh waters of mainland Central America. Of these, 269 (59%) are freshwater dispersants, 57 (13%) are freshwater representatives of marine families, and the rest (28%) are euryhaline marine fishes. Most species in the latter group are only sporadic in their occurrence in the lower reaches of the streams. In contrast to both North and South America, only 38% of the freshwater dispersant species are otophysans. Most of these are found in the southernmost part of Central America and belong to families and species found otherwise only in South America. However, many species are endemic, with highly localized distribution patterns. In the northern part of Central America three of the otophysan species belong to the North American families Ictaluridae (catfishes) and Catostomidae (suckers), but even here most of the few otophysans present have South American affinities (e.g., Pimelodidae, Characidae). However, the otophysans do show a high degree of endemism, indicating long isolation from South America.

The most curious aspect of the Central American fish fauna is not the otophysan element but the fact that the most widely distributed, and often most abundant, fishes are cichlids (Cichlidae, 78+ species), livebearers (Poeciliidae, 60+ species), and killifishes (Cyprinodontidae, 23+ species). The success of these families is most likely related to adaptations that have enabled them to survive in an area that is geologically very unstable. These adaptations include an ability to live under fluctuating temperature and salinity regimes, viviparity (Poeciliidae), and small body sizes, which permit large populations to live in small, isolated streams and lakes. In addition, the success of the cichlids is at least partially related to their ability to do well in lakes. For example, the species "flocks" of the great lakes of Central America have many similarities to the species flocks of the great lakes of Africa, representing similar phenomena of speciation (Echelle and Kornfield 1984).

Bussing (1985) notes that the cyprinodonts, poeciliids, and cichlids, along with a few other fishes, may represent the original fish fauna of Gondwanaland (the great southern continent) that became isolated in Central America as early as the late Cretaceous period, when the region presumably became a series of large islands. Following the reconnection of North and South America during the Pliocene (or later), fish were able to invade from South America (various characins and catfish) and from North America (a gar, Lepisosteidae, three shads, Clupeidae, two suckers, Catostomidae, and a catfish, Ictaluridae). The invasions have been slow, however, so that South American forms for the most part have only penetrated as far north as mid-Central America.

ORIENTAL REGION

The Oriental Region has two subregions: the Peninsular India (including Sri Lanka); and the Southeast Asia, including Sumatra, Java, Borneo, and Mindanao. Although the subregions have distinctive aspects to their fish faunas, they have more in common than they have differences between them. In particular, they are all dominated by cyprinids and, to a lesser extent, by catfish, especially of the families Bagridae and Clariidae.

Peninsular India was an independent island continent for perhaps 100 million years before it collided with Asia, creating the Himalaya Mountains. It is somewhat surprising, therefore, to find that its freshwater fish fauna contains no truly ancient forms but is instead made up mostly of derived otophysans of Asiatic or recent African origin. Fossil evidence indicates that once invasion routes were open, the Asiatic otophysans must have overwhelmed the original fish fauna, a decline that may have been hastened by the climatic change that presumably took place as the Himalaya Mountains rose. There are over 700 species of freshwater dispersant fishes, from 27 families, known from Peninsular India (Jayaram 1974). Of these, 373 (53%) belong to the family Cyprinidae and 176 species (25%) belong to 12 families of catfishes. Since the presence of endemic genera is usually indicative of long isolation from surrounding areas, it is significant that there are no endemic genera of cyprinids or catfishes in Peninsular India. The genera present are found either in Southeast Asia, in Africa, or in both (Menon 1973). Those shared with Africa are also found in Southwest Asia (the Middle East). Other otophysan families found in India are the Cobitidae (loaches) and Baltoridae (river loaches), which are also found in the Palearctic Region. The nonotophysan freshwater fish families found here include the Channidae (snakeheads), Mastacembelidae (spiny eels), Anabantidae (climbing gouramis), Belontiidae (gouramis), Notopteridae (knifefishes), Cichlidae, Cyprinodontidae (killifishes), Nandidae (leaf-fishes), and Synbranchidae (synbranchid eels). All these families have representatives in Africa as well as elsewhere in the Oriental Region. The Notopteridae are particularly noteworthy because they are highly specialized members of the order Osteoglossiformes, members of which are usually regarded as relict species. Saltwater dispersant fishes play a relatively small role in the fresh waters of Peninsular India, presumably because of the dominance of the otophysans.

Southeast Asia contains over 1,000 species of fish but distribution patterns are not well known (Zakaria-Ismail 1994) . However, an idea of the composition of the fish fauna of this area can be gotten by analyzing the fish fauna of Thailand (Smith 1945). Of the 549 fish species listed for Thailand, from 48 families, 72% are from freshwater dispersant families, principally Cyprinidae (39%) and various catfish families (18%). The representatives of marine families found in Southeast Asia's fresh waters include representatives from at least 13 families such as stingrays (Dasyatidae), anchovies (Engraulidae), threadfins (Polynemidae), gobies (Gobiidae), and puffers (Tetraodontidae) (Roberts 1993). There are also a few representatives of ancient fish families (Notopteridae, Osteoglossidae). Zakaria-Ismail (1994) divides Southeast Asia into five zoogeographic regions:

1. Salween River Basin (Nyanmao), with close ties to the Indian Subcontinent and low endemism (ca. 3% of 150 species);
2. Indo-Chinese Peninsula (including the Mekong River), a high- diversity region (500+ species) with high endemism (48%);
3. Malay Peninsula, 260 species and low (ca. 2%) endemism;
4. Indo-Malayan Archipelago (including Sumatra, Borneo, and Java), with high diversity (400+ species) and many endemic species, especially gouramis (Belontiidae); and
5. The Phillipines, where freshwater dispersant fishes are found only on Mindanao. The Mindanao fauna is depauperate but contains an endemic flock (15 species) of cyprinids in Lake Lanao.

The fish fauna of the Indo-Malayan Archipelago is very similar to that of the mainland because the islands all protrude from a shallow continental shelf area that was dry during much of the Pleistocene, due to lower sea levels. At that time most of the river systems of the islands and those of the mainland drained into a large central system, giving the fishes ready access to all the areas (Myers 1951).

PALAEARCTIC REGION

The Palaearctic Region consists of all of Eurasia not included in the Oriental Region. Berg (1949) divides the area into six subregions, but a general idea of the composition of the fish fauna of this region can be obtained by examining the combined faunas of the Soviet Union and Europe (Berg 1949; Muus 1967). In this latter area 36 families of fish with at least 420 species are found in fresh water. Species from 12 families of freshwater dispersants make up 53% of the fauna, mostly Cyprinidae (minnows, 37%) and Cobitidae (loaches, 8%). The Otophysi are otherwise represented in the area by only 10 catfishes from three families (Siluridae, Bagridae, and Sisoridae) and one sucker (Catostomidae). The sucker is a recent invader from North America, although the loaches and silurid and sisorid catfishes apparently evolved in Asia. Other freshwater dispersants found in the area are the Percidae, Channidae, Cyprinodontidae, Esocidae, and Umbridae. All families except the Channidae are found in North America as well. Anadromous fishes make up 17% of the total fauna, representing six families (but principally the Salmonidae, 11%). However, anadromous species are most important in the arctic drainages, where they make up about 51% of the fishes, as opposed to 30% for freshwater dispersants. Freshwater representatives of eight marine families make up another 11% of the total fauna, if the endemic family of sculpins from Lake Baikal, the Cottocomephoridae (about 26 species), is counted here. The remaining 18% of the fish fauna of this region consists of euryhaline marine species, from 13 families but mostly from the Gobiidae (gobies, 11%).

A region with high fish endemism that was relatively unappreciated until recent times is the north Mediterranean region of Europe. At least 132 species are endemic to the fresh waters of this region, representing 13 families (Crivelli and Maitland 1995). Over 80% of the species are freshwater dispersants (mainly Cyprinidae and Cobitidae) and many are highly localized in their distribution. In Spain, for example, 86% of the 29 freshwater dispersant fishes are endemic species or subspecies (Elvira 1995). In Anatolia, Turkey, 24% of the 86 native species are endemic to the region and most of the others have limited distributions (Balik 1995).

NEARCTIC REGION

The Nearctic Region consists of North America down to the southern edge of the Mexican plateau (Fig. 25.2). It can be divided into three ichthyological subregions: (1) the Arctic-Atlantic Subregion, consisting of all drainages into the Arctic and Atlantic oceans, as well as the Gulf of Mexico down to the Rio Panuco; (2) the Pacific Subregion, consisting of all drainages along the Pacific coast down to the Mexican border (including Baja California, but excluding the Yukon River drainage in Alaska) and all interior drainages west of the Rocky Mountains; and (3) the Mexican Transition Subregion, consisting of most of Mexico except the upper Gulf of Mexico drainages, down to the imperceptible upper limits of Central America.

The zoogeography of North American fishes is the best documented of any continent thanks to two monumental works (Lee et al. 1980; Hocutt and Wiley 1986) and to the general fascination of North American ichthyologists with the subject. There are about 950 native species of fishes in the three subregions. If the Mexican Subregion is excluded because of its transitional nature, there are about 740 species in the two other subregions combined. Freshwater dispersant fishes make up about

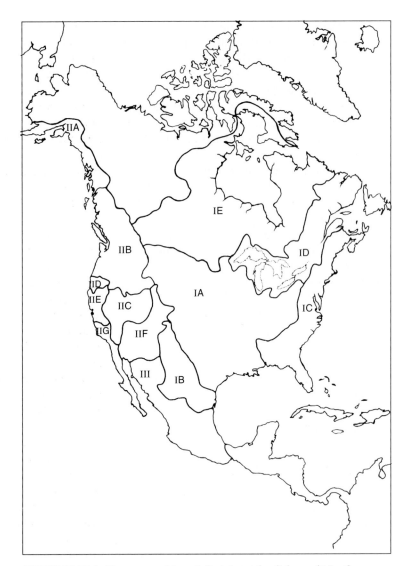

FIGURE 25.2 *Zoogeographic subdivisions, for fishes, of North America: (I) Arctic-Atlantic Subregion; (II) Pacific Subregion; (III) Mexican Transition Subregion; (IA) Mississippi Province; (IB) Rio Grande Province; (IC) Atlantic Coast Province; (ID) Great Lakes–St. Lawrence Province; (IE) Hudson Bay Province; (IF) Arctic Province; (IAA) Alaska Coastal Province; (IIB) Columbia Province; (IIC) Great Basin Province; (IID) Klamath Province; (IIE) Sacramento Province; (IIF) Colorado Province; (IIG) South Coastal Province.*

77% of the fauna of the two northern subregions. They represent 18 families, although most of the species are from the families Cyprinidae (minnows, 29%), Percidae (perches and darters, 17%), Catostomidae (suckers, 8%), Cyprinodontidae (6%), Ictaluridae (North American catfishes, 5%), and Centrarchidae (sunfishes, 4%). Another 11% of the fishes belong to diadromous families, principally the Salmonidae (salmon, trout, and whitefishes, 6%) and Petromyzontidae (lampreys, 3%). Freshwater representatives of marine families, including the Cottidae (sculpins, 4%), make up only 6% of this fauna, while an additional 6% is contributed by euryhaline marine species from 18 families.

The **Arctic-Atlantic Subregion** is the largest and most speciose of the Nearctic subregions. It can be divided into six ichthyological provinces that largely reflect the major drainage systems: (1) Mississippi, (2) Rio Grande, (3) Atlantic coast, (4) Great Lakes–St. Lawrence, (5) Hudson Bay, and (6) Arctic.

The **Mississippi Province** consists of all of the United States and Canada drained by the great Mississippi-Missouri River system, as well as many Gulf Coast drainages east of the Rio Grande. A number of tributary systems have large numbers of endemic forms (e.g., the Tennessee and Cumberland rivers) and so should, perhaps, be treated as separate provinces. The Mississippi Province, partly because of these partially isolated tributaries, is by far the richest in North America in obligatory freshwater species, with about 280 to 300. Freshwater dispersants make up about 88% of these species, predominantly Cyprinidae (30%), Percidae (26%), Centrarchidae (7%), Catostomidae (9%), and Ictaluridae (5%). Diadromous fishes (7%) and freshwater representatives of marine families (5%) are poorly represented. In addition, a small number of euryhaline marine forms occur in the Mississippi Delta area. As the high percentage of freshwater dispersant attests, the Mississippi-Missouri drainage system is an ancient one.

The Mississippi River is uniquely important in North America as a center of fish evolution. It was a refuge during times of glaciation where species have been able to reoccupy waters once covered by continental glaciers, and it is a refuge for representatives of past fish faunas. Its role in the development of the North American fish fauna is indicated by the fact that the families Centrarchidae, Percidae (Etheostominae), Ictaluridae, and Esocidae are most abundant and diverse in its waters, as are cyprinids of the large genus *Notropis*. Its role as a glacial refuge is indicated by the fact that most of the species found in the Great Lakes–St. Lawrence, Hudson Bay, and Arctic provinces, once largely covered by ice sheets, are also characteristic of the northern parts of the Mississippi Province. Its role as a refuge, however, has not been confined to just the Pleistocene period, because it still is a refuge for many relict Chondrostei and Neopterygii, including teleosts. The Chondrosteans consist of three species of sturgeons (Acipenseridae), including two species in the endemic genus *Scaphirhynchus*, and one species of paddlefish (Polyodontidae). Only one other species of paddlefish exists, in the Yangtze River of China, while the closest relatives of the *Scaphirhynchus* sturgeons live in the Palaearctic Region. Ancient neopterygians are represented by six species of gar (Lepisosteidae) and by bowfin (Amiidae). Aside from one additional species of gar found in Central America, these fishes are the only representatives on earth today of the fishes that were dominant during much of the Mesozoic period. Among the relict teleosts are the mooneye and goldeye (Hiodontidae, order Osteoglossiformes), a sucker (*Cycleptus,* which seems to be closest to the relict sucker *Myxocyprinus* of the Yangtze River in China), and the peculiar families Elassomatidae (pygmy sunfishes), Percopsidae (trout-perches), Amblyopsidae (cavefishes), and Aphredoderidae (pirate perch), which are confined to North America.

The **Rio Grande Province** is essentially the Rio Grande River and its tributaries in Texas, Mexico, and New Mexico, as well as nearby allied basins. One hundred fifty-four species are known from the region, but 22 are euryhaline marine species found in lower reaches of the main river or coastal streams (Smith and Miller 1986). One hundred twenty-five (81%) are members of freshwater dispersant families, mainly Cyprinidae (44 species), Cyprinodontidae (23), Poeciliidae (20), Catostomidae (11), Ictaluridae (9), and Percidae (6). Only 75 of these species are found in the main Rio Grande drainage itself. These 75 species belong mainly to species or genera that are also abundant in the Mississippi River drainage. The principal exceptions are a characin (Mexican tetra, *Astyanax mexicanus*) and a cichlid (Rio Grande perch, *Cichlasoma cyanoguttatum*), whose closest relatives are in the Mexican Transition Region. The remaining 50 freshwater dispersant species are mainly endemic inhabitants of numerous isolated basins affiliated with the drainage; most of these are cyprinodonts and poeciliids found in isolated springs. As a result, 55% (67) of the freshwater species in this province are endemics. Forty percent (48) of them are confined to just one drainage, including 10 found only in the Rio Grande itself.

The **Atlantic Coast Province** is an artificial assemblage of independent drainage systems that flow into the Atlantic Ocean or the Gulf of Mexico, from New Brunswick on the north to the gulf streams of Florida on the south. It should be subdivided into subprovinces, since the fish faunas at the two ends of the province bear little resemblance to each other (Hocutt and Wiley 1986). However, the changes in the fish fauna are gradual, so the faunas of adjacent streams are very similar to each other. Endemic forms exist in many streams, especially in those draining the southern Appalachians, but all the streams have faunas that show strong ties to that of the Mississippi River system. In the northern third of this province the streams are dominated by anadromous fishes and by minnows and suckers that can colonize new waters through headwater connections (e.g., blacknose dace, *Rhinichthys atratulus,* creek chub, *Semotilus atromaculatus,* and white sucker, *Catostomus commersoni*). This region was covered by glaciers during the Pleistocene. In the middle third there are many ancient drainage systems with former connections to the Mississippi drainage, through the low ridges of the Appalachian Mountains. The streams in this region often have endemic species among the many they contain. In the region bounded by the Potomac River on the north and Pee Dee River in the south, there are 94 species of fish spending at least part of their life cycle in fresh water, including 11 species endemic to just one drainage (Jenkins et al. 1972). Of the 94 species, six belong to diadromous families and five are freshwater representatives of marine families, leaving 87% of the fishes as freshwater dispersants. However, the marine element becomes more prevalent as one moves south and as the fauna becomes less rich.

The **Great Lakes–St. Lawrence Province** had major connections to the Mississippi River system in the late Pleistocene, so it is not surprising to find that its fauna is essentially that of the northern part of the Mississippi Province. Most of it was glaciated at one time or another during the Pleistocene. It is treated as a separate province here because it is a distinct large drainage system and because the Great Lakes do (or did) have a number of endemic forms, such as the members of the whitefish *(Coregonus)* species complex, the siscowet lake trout *(Salvelinus namaycush siscowet)*, and the blue walleye *(Stizostedion vitreum glaucum)*. Of the 173 native obligatory freshwater fishes listed for the province by Underhill (1986), 73% belong to freshwater dispersant families (28% Cyprinidae), 17% to diadromous families, and 10% to marine families.

The **Hudson Bay Province** includes most of central Canada and the portion of the United States drained by the Red River of the North. Although all its waters drain into Hudson Bay, its fish fauna shows strong affinities with that of the Mississippi Basin, particularly in its freshwater dispersants. Of the 101 native species listed for this drainage (Crossman and McAllister 1986), 73% belong to freshwater dispersant families (31% Cyprinidae), 21% to diadromous, and 6% to marine. These figures are deceptive, however, since most of the freshwater dispersant fishes occur in the southern edges of the basin. The more northern lakes and streams are dominated by salmonids, cottids, and a few cold-hardy cyprinids, catostomids, esocids, and percids.

The **Arctic Province** includes all those streams of Canada and Alaska that flow into the Arctic Ocean, up to and including the Yukon River drainage. There are 66 species of obligatory freshwater fish native to this region (Lindsey and McPhail 1986). Of these, 54% belong to diadromous families, 35% to freshwater dispersant families, and 11% to marine families. As in the Hudson Bay Province, most of the "true" freshwater fishes occur in the southern edge of the province. These species have invaded from both the Mississippi Province and the Pacific Subregion. The salmonids found in this province are also characteristic of both areas. There are no unique forms, although the Alaskan blackfish *(Dallia pectoralis)*, the inconnu *(Stenodus leucichthys)*, the Arctic cisco *(Coregonus autumnalis)*, the arctic lamprey *(Lampetra japonica)*, and the least cisco *(C. sardinella)* are otherwise found mainly in Siberia. This province should thus be regarded as a region transitional between the Palaearctic and Nearctic Regions, as well as between the Pacific and Arctic-Atlantic Subregions.

The **Pacific Subregion** contains many fewer species than the Arctic-Atlantic Subregion because it is smaller in size and, more importantly, because much of it is arid or semiarid. However, the fish faunas of its seven provinces are much more distinct from each other than are the faunas of the provinces of the Arctic-Atlantic Subregion. The presence of mountain ranges and deserts in the subregion has created many barriers to fish movements, resulting in many fish species that are endemic to small regions (Minckley et al. 1986). Many of these species appear to be relicts of the Nearctic fish fauna that partly gave rise to, and were displaced by, the dominant fishes of the Arctic-Atlantic Subregion. The zoogeographic provinces of the Pacific Subregion are (1) Alaska Coastal, (2) Columbia, (3) Great Basin, (4) Klamath, (5) Sacramento, (6) Colorado, and (7) South Coastal.

The **Alaska Coastal Province** consists of all the minor coastal drainages from the Aleutian peninsula down to the Canadian border of the Alaskan panhandle. Only 34 freshwater species are found in this province (excluding euryhaline marine forms): 79% of them in diadromous families, 12% in marine families, and 8% in freshwater dispersant families. The three freshwater dispersant species (*Esox lucius, Catostomus catostomus, Dallia pectoralis*) are also found in Siberia. This province could be regarded as part of the Arctic Province.

The **Columbia Province** includes the great Columbia River drainage, which penetrates into the interior as far as Montana and Idaho, and its associated coastal drainages of British Columbia, Washington, and Oregon. It contains the greatest number (61) of species of obligatory freshwater fishes of the provinces of the Pacific Subregion. Only 38% of these are freshwater dispersant fishes (21% Cyprinidae), but these are the most distinctive elements of the fauna, since 58% of these species are endemic to the province (Miller 1958). They include a relict mudminnow (Umbridae) and a trout-perch (Percopsidae). Of the remaining species, 41% are from diadromous families (23% from the Salmonidae alone) and the rest are freshwater representatives of marine families, especially the Cottidae (sculpins, 18%).

The **Great Basin Province,** the site of the classic studies of fish zoogeography and speciation by R. R. Miller and C. L. Hubbs, is a collection of 150 internal drainage systems roughly bounded by the Sierra Nevada on the west and south, by the Wasatch Mountains on the east, and by the Columbia plateau on the north. All the basins within the area are quite arid, although they were filled with large lakes during various periods of the Pleistocene. There is a high degree of endemism in the desert basins, but the species also tend to show a common faunal ancestry. The basins with the most fish species within the Great Basin are Death Valley (nine species); the Lahontan System, which includes Lakes Tahoe and Pyramid (13 species); and the Bonneville System, including Bear and Utah Lakes (20 species). The Great Basin Province contains a total of about 50 species. The exact number is uncertain, since there are a number of undescribed and/or controversial species present. Nearly 60% of the species are either cyprinids or catostomids, although six species of pupfish (Cyprinodontidae and Goodeidae) make up most of the Death Valley fish fauna and there are four species of whitefish (Salmonidae) in Bear Lake, Utah. About 80% of the species found in the Great Basin are endemic to it (Miller 1958).

The **Klamath Province,** consisting of the Klamath and Rogue drainages on the California-Oregon border, contains about 30 obligatory freshwater fishes, with only eight freshwater dispersant species (three cyprinids, five suckers). It is characterized instead by its representatives of diadromous families (53% of fishes, including four lampreys and eight salmonids) and its six species of sculpin (Cottidae). Thirty-seven percent of the species are endemic to the system, including all the suckers.

The **Sacramento Province** contains most of the water that flows in California, because it is dominated by the great Sacramento–San Joaquin drainage system. It also includes numerous coastal drainage systems from Monterey Bay north to the mouth of the Klamath River. It contains at least 43 native obligatory freshwater species, of which 42% are endemic (Moyle 1976a). Among the endemic forms are a unique complex of 10 minnow species and the Sacramento perch (*Archoplites inter-*

ruptus), the only centrarchid native west of the Rocky Mountains. Only 28% of its obligatory freshwater fishes are freshwater dispersant species, while 47% of the fishes belong to anadromous families and the rest are all freshwater representatives of marine families. Of particular interest is the tule perch *(Hysterocarpus traski)*, the only freshwater species in the marine family Embiotocidae (surf perches).

The **Colorado Province** is drained by the Colorado River system. This province is home mostly to freshwater dispersant fishes, which make up about 81% of its approximately 32 obligatory freshwater species. Among these fishes are six species of the endemic cyprinid group of spinedaces (Plagopterini), at least three species in a complex of the cyprinid genus *Gila* that live in the main Colorado River, and the Gila topminnow (Poeciliidae, *Poecilopsis occidentalis)*, which apparently entered the system from the Yaqui River of Mexico (Miller 1958). The rest are representatives of anadromous or marine families.

The **South Coastal Province** is an artificial collection of small coastal drainage systems that enter the ocean between Monterey Bay on the north and the tip of Baja California on the south. Only 12 species of obligatory freshwater fishes are found in this region, four of them freshwater dispersants. Minckley et al. (1986) show that at least one of these species, the arroyo chub *(Gila orcutti)*, arrived in the region "riding" on a piece of continental plate that shifted from its original position in Mexico.

The **Mexican Transition Subregion** has a fish fauna that is related to fishes in both the Arctic-Atlantic and Pacific subregions, as well as to Central American fishes. Seven families of North American fishes, for example, reach their southern limits in this region, while one family of South American catfishes (Pimelodidae) reaches its northern limits here (Miller and Smith 1986). Provinces are hard to define in this subregion because of its transitional nature and our incomplete knowledge of the fauna. However, three areas seem to be distinct: coastal drainages of northwestern Mexico, coastal drainages of central Mexico, and the central plateau region. The coastal drainages of northwestern Mexico (the largest being Rio Yaqui) contain about 26 obligatory freshwater species, all of them endemic and a number of them undescribed. The streams support such "western" fishes as minnows of the genus *Gila* and the Mexican golden trout *(Oncorhynchus chrysogaster),* and such "eastern" fishes as minnows of the genus *Notropis* and the Yaqui catfish *(Ictalurus pricei).* The lowlands of both coasts of Mexico seem to have been the dispersal route for fishes coming from both the north and the south. In the south, the most speciose groups are the characins, cichlids, and poeciliids, but in more northern drainages fishes with North American affinities become more common, especially minnows, suckers, and ictalurid catfishes. Marine fishes or fishes of marine families are common in the lower reaches of these streams. Altogether about 170 species have been recorded from the streams. The central plateau is an isolated region of high endemism. It contains, for example, 17 species of the odd viviparous family Goodeidae, which is largely confined to central Mexico, and at least 16 species of the endemic atherinid genus *Chirostoma.* Fishes of other families are scarce, although the northern drainages contain a few cyprinids, as well as a catfish, a sucker, and a centrarchid bass (now extinct).

AUSTRALIAN REGION

The Australian Region has long been cut off from the major evolutionary events taking place in the other continents. This is reflected dramatically in its fish fauna, which contains only three species from two families of ancient lineage that are exclusively freshwater dispersants: the Australian lungfish (*Neoceratodus forsteri*, Ceratodontidae) and the two species of saratoga (*Scleropages* spp., Osteoglossidae). The rest of its somewhat impoverished fish fauna is made up of representatives of diadromous or marine families. However, many of these species are from lineages that have been evolving in Australia's waters for millions of years and are now effectively freshwater dispersants. The Australian Region can be divided into three subregions in terms of its fish fauna: Australia (including Tasmania), New Zealand, and New Guinea, including nearby islands.

Australia contains at least 183 native species that spend all or most of their life cycles in fresh water, plus about 150 species of marine fishes found occasionally in fresh water or estuaries (Allen 1989). Many of the fishes characteristic of Australia's lakes and rivers are diadromous fishes or their freshwater derivatives including Petromyzontidae (lampreys, three species), Anguillidae (eels, four species), Galaxiidae (21 species), and Retropinnidae (New Zealand smelts, two species). There are also 33 families of marine fishes that have 146 freshwater representatives in Australia. Of particular interest are the marine catfishes (Ariidae and Plotosidae, 17 species), gudgeons (Eleotridae, 25 species), gobies (Gobiidae, 12 species), rainbow fishes (Melanotaeniidae, 13 species), hardyheads (Atherinidae, nine species), flagtails and pygmy perches (Kuhliidae, seven species), grunters (Terapontidae, 22 species), temperate perches (Percichthyidae, eight species, and glassfishes (Chanididae = Ambassidae, eight species). Members of the latter three families are the typical perciform predators of Australia's lakes and rivers, including the Murray cod (*Maccullochella peeli*), which reaches weights of over 110 kg.

The freshwater fish fauna shows a high degree of endemism: 127 of the 183 species are found only in Australia, while 37 are shared with New Guinea and four with New Zealand (Allen 1989). Based on patterns of endemism, Australia can be divided into 12 fish provinces. Fish species are most numerous, not surprisingly, in coastal areas where rainfall is highest and the most permanent water exists. It is interesting to note that 23 species manage to exist in the largely intermittent waters of the Lake Eyre Province of the interior (Glover 1982), but that only 25–30 freshwater or diadromous species inhabit the extensive Murray-Darling Province of southern Australia, with the 1900-km-long Murray-Darling River (Cadwallader 1986).

New Zealand has long been isolated from other land masses, even Australia, so its 27 recognized freshwater species are wholly of marine or diadromous origin (McDowall 1978). Most abundant are species from the diadromous families: Petromyzontidae (lampreys, one species), Retropinnidae (New Zealand smelts, two species), Galaxiidae (14 species), and Anguillidae (eels, two species). Despite their ability to enter salt water, it is quite possible that ancestral fishes in the four families were already present in New Zealand when it separated from Antarctica in the late Cretaceous period. Marine families with freshwater representatives are Pleuronectidae (flounders, one species), Eleotridae (gudgeons, six species), and Cheimarrichthyi-dae (freshwater sandperch, one species). All but four of the species found in New Zealand are endemic to it. The small number of species present is presumably due not only to the isolation of the islands, but to their geologic instability.

The fish fauna of New Guinea is very similar to that of Australia, reflecting a separation of the two land masses of less than 8,000 years. However, New Guinea is divided in half by a mountain range, and the fish fauna reflects this division. The fauna of the southern half is similar to that of northern Australia (32 of 130 species shared), while that of the northern half has a large number of species of its own. The two share just three native upland species (Allen and Coates 1990). Northern New Guinea has about 75 freshwater species, about 60% of them endemic. In both regions, however, most fishes are gobiies (Gobiidae), gudgeons (Eleotridae), rainbow fishes (Malanotaeniidae) or catfishes (Plotosidae, Ariidae) (Allen and Coates 1990).

CONTINENTAL DRIFT AND THE DISTRIBUTION OF FRESHWATER FISHES

The advances in geophysics that have led to the acceptance of the concepts of plate tectonics and continental drift have permitted the solution of many perplexing zoo-geographic problems. However, many of the families and species distribution patterns are still puzzling and await solution. Therefore, the following discussion, based in part on the papers of Cracraft (1974) and of Novacek and Marshall (1976), should be considered hypothetical.

About 200 million years ago, during the Triassic period, the continents were united as one land mass, Pangaea (Fig. 25.3). The freshwater fish fauna at this time was presumably made up of a mixture of chondrostean fishes (represented today by the paddlefishes and sturgeons), early neopterygian fishes (represented today by bowfin and gars), and lobed-finned fishes (e.g., lungfish). It is also possible that some early teleosts were present at this time, represented today by the osteoglos-sids, although teleost radiation is usually considered to have taken place in the Cretaceous. By the end of the Triassic (180 million years B.P.), Pangaea had split into two continents: Laurasia (the future North America and Eurasia), and Gondwana-land (the future South America, Africa, Antarctica, India, and Australia). In both areas the Pangaean fish fauna probably remained dominant until the Cretaceous period, when various modern freshwater fish groups started to develop. The modern descendants of the first of these groups to develop in Laurasia are the Esocidae (pikes), Umbridae (mudminnows), and Salmonidae (salmon and trout), as well as the exclusively North American families Percopsidae (trout-perches), Aphredo-deridae (pirate perch), and Amblyopsidae (cavefishes). However, most of whatever distinctive teleost fauna developed in Laurasia appears to have been swamped by the otophysans invading from Gondwanaland and by the perciform groups that evolved somewhat later.

The Otophysi (minnows, characins, catfish) seem to have developed in Gond-wanaland in the early Cretaceous period, when the African and South American

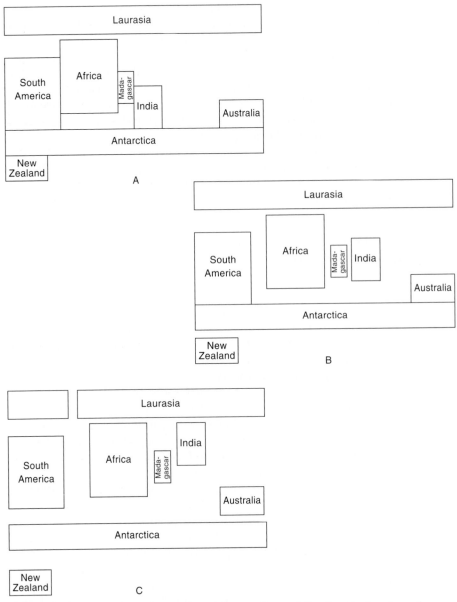

FIGURE 25.3 *Probable relationships of the continents following the breakup of Pangaea: (A) early Cretaceous (ca. 105 million years B.P.); (B) late Cretaceous (65 million to 70 million years B.P.); (C) middle Eocene (45 million to 50 million years B.P.). (Reproduced, with permission, from the* Annual Review of Ecology and Systematics, *Vol. 5, © 1974 by Annual Reviews, Inc.)*

plates were well on their way to separation. Antarctica, Australia, India, and Madagascar had separated from Gondwanaland soon after Laurasia split off and so played no role in the early development of the Otophysi. Because the most ancestor-like otophysans are known from South America, it is likely that the early stages of their evolution took place on the South American half of Gondwanaland (but see Briggs [1979] for an alternative point of view). Representatives managed to invade western Africa before the two continents finally separated, in the middle Cretaceous. South America then became an island continent, and its characoid fishes and catfishes diversified enormously into numerous endemic families. Africa, in contrast, made contact with the Eurasian portion of Laurasia at about the end of the Cretaceous period, permitting ostariophysans to enter Laurasia. Then, in the early Paleocene, the family Cyprinidae evolved either in North Africa or in Europe. This family, together with the catfishes, spread throughout Laurasia and most of Africa. However, the derived characins that had evolved in Africa managed to hold their own and diversify, as did the African catfishes, mormyrids, and other endemic groups.

During the early Cenozoic period, as the North American and Eurasian continents gradually separated from each other, the modern representatives of the holarctic fish fauna developed and spread: Cyprinidae, Catostomidae (suckers), and Percidae (perches). Following (and during) the final separation of North America and Eurasia, endemic groups of fishes developed on both continents. In North America, the sunfishes (Centrarchidae), the catfishes (Ictaluridae), and the darters (subfamily Etheostominae of the Percidae) evolved. In Asia the advanced subfamilies of cyprinids developed, probably in the Oriental Region, along with the Cobitidae (loaches), Siluridae, and other otophysan families with more restricted distributions. Many families of freshwater dispersants are endemic to the Oriental Region, which gradually became separated from the rest of Asia following the rise of the Himalaya Mountains, which in turn seems to have been related to the collision of India with Asia in the late Eocene. The Oriental fauna subsequently invaded India, replacing whatever indigenous families were present. There appear to have been some exchanges of fishes with Africa somewhat later, indicated by the broad distributional patterns of catfishes of the families Bagridae and Clariidae and perciform families such as the Channidae and Mastacembelidae.

PLEISTOCENE GLACIATION

While continental drift explains many of the broad patterns of fish distribution, explaining continental patterns requires an understanding of the events of the Pleistocene as well. This period began about 2.5 million years B.P. and ended (presumably) about 10,000 years B.P. During this time as much as a third of the land was covered with continental glaciers, which advanced (grew) and retreated (shrunk) at least four times during the period. As they advanced and as more and more of the earth's water became ice, sea level dropped, connecting many land areas currently separated by salt water. The ice wiped out all fishes in the land it covered and changed the water temperatures in nearby areas. As it advanced and retreated it scoured lakes out of bedrock or created them by damming streams with moraines or by leaving melting blocks of ice behind buried in the gravels. The melting ice created large rivers and enormous lakes behind ice dams that sometimes burst, resulting in catastrophic floods. The general climatic conditions that favored the buildup of glaciers in these areas also caused increased precipitation in other areas; in the intermountain basins of the American West this caused extensive lakes to develop, which have now dried up to small remnants, often too salty to support fish (e.g., The Great Salt Lake).

The Pleistocene events explain such things as the presence of freshwater dispersant fishes on many of the islands of Indonesia, which once were the uplands surrounding a large river system that existed when sea levels were lower. The paucity of native fishes in the western United States and Europe is at least partly due to the lack of refuges from Pleistocene events; while the richness of the fish fauna of glaciated areas of eastern North America is due to the ease with which the areas could be recolonized from the lower Mississippi River basin and other refuges (Moyle and Herbold 1987). Indeed, the last retreat of the glaciers was so recent that it is likely that many of the glaciated areas are still subject to natural invasions by fishes from unglaciated areas.

Supplemental Readings

Berg 1949; Berra 1981; Briggs 1979; Cracraft 1974; Darlington 1957; Greenwood 1976; Hocutt and Wiley 1986; Jayaram 1974; Kozhov 1963; Lake 1971; Lee et al. 1980; Lowe-McConnell 1975; McDowell 1978; Menon 1973; Miller 1958, 1966; Moyle 1976b; Muus 1967; Myers 1938, 1951; Novacek and Marshall 1976; Rosen 1974, 1975b.

CHAPTER **26**

Zoogeography of Marine Fishes

The zoogeography of marine fishes is much less well understood than that of freshwater fishes. Not only are there many more fishes spread over a much greater area, but there are fewer dramatic, seemingly permanent barriers to movement, such as mountain ranges, than are found on land. The distribution patterns of freshwater fishes can be broadly related to plate tectonics (continental drift) and drainage systems. For marine fishes, broad distribution patterns seem to be related to oceanographic features and to the positions of the continents. Because of the latter aspect (most marine fishes are shallow-water species), continental drift has undoubtedly played an important role in the distribution and evolution of marine fishes; however, this role is poorly understood and so is rarely considered in what analyses exist of their distribution patterns (but see Rosen 1975b and Springer 1982). Thus most discussions of marine zoogeography are largely descriptive in nature, dividing the marine world into zoogeographic regions whose boundaries are rather vague. Such boundaries are typically regions where oceanographic conditions, and consequently the fish fauna, change rapidly as the result of current patterns or the position of continental shelves and islands. Rarely are such boundaries complete barriers to fish movement, nor are they necessarily permanent features, so the designated zoogeographic regions are even more arbitrary than those found in fresh water. The two principal works in English on marine zoogeography are Ekman (1953) and Briggs (1974), and this chapter is based on these books. This chapter will

367

briefly describe the major zoogeographic regions of the world's oceans and discuss the kinds of fishes that occur in them. Following Briggs (1974), we will first discuss the fishes of the continental shelves and ocean reefs and then the fishes of the open sea and the deep sea.

CONTINENTAL SHELVES

The distribution of fishes on continental shelves can be related not only to the presence of continents and islands and the extent of the shelf surrounding them, but also to annual temperature regimes and oceanic currents (Fig. 26.1). On the basis of temperature regimes it is possible to divide the shelves into a wide tropical region around the equator, northern and southern temperate regions, and two polar regions. There are, of course, broad transition areas between adjacent regions, but particularly between the tropical and temperate waters (which, as a consequence, are frequently divided into warm temperate waters and cold temperate waters).

Tropical Regions

Nearly 40% of all known fish species occur in the shallow waters of the tropics. Most of these are associated with coral reefs (see Chapter 33). Largely on the basis of the reef fishes, the tropical oceans can be divided into four large regions: (1) the Indo-Pacific Region, (2) the Eastern Pacific Region, (3) the Western Atlantic Region, and (4) the Eastern Atlantic Region. The regions are separated from one another either by continents or by vast areas of open ocean. The northern and southern boundaries of these regions are roughly the 20°C isotherm for the coldest month of the year.

The **Indo-Pacific Region** contains by far the most diverse fish fauna of the four regions, presumably because the sheer size of the region has provided many opportunities for speciation. Most of the fishes belong to the same families that are characteristic of the other three regions as well, such as Muraenidae, Holocentridae, Scorpaenidae, Serranidae, Apogonidae, Carangidae, Lutjanidae, Mullidae, Chaetodontidae, Pomacentridae, Labridae, Scaridae, Blenniidae, Acanthuridae, and Tetraodontidae. However, a few small families are endemic to the region (Pegasidae, Sillaginidae, Kraemeriidae, Siganidae, Plesiopidae). Despite the size of the region, the presence of many wide-ranging species (most have pelagic larvae) makes it fairly homogeneous. Springer (1982) notes that the distribution of many species is coincident with an enormous piece of the earth's crust, the Pacific lithospheric plate, demonstrating the importance of continental drift to marine fish distribution. However, within the region there are areas with fish faunas distinctive enough so that Briggs (1974) has divided the region into provinces. Four of these provinces are associated with groups of isolated oceanic islands (Lord Howe-Norfork, Hawaiian, Easter, and Marquesas) that have a fairly high degree of endemism in the fishes (20% to 40%). Other provinces that have been designated are sections of the coastline containing endemic species; but because the continental shelf in this region is essentially continuous, from Australia to the Malay Peninsula, to India and down

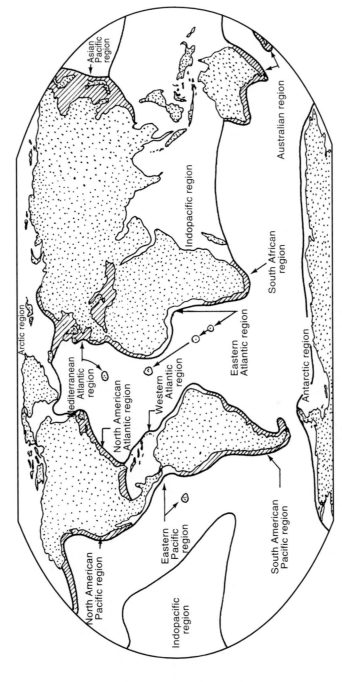

FIGURE 26.1 *Major zoogeographic regions associated with continental shelves and islands. Boundaries between regions are not firm but are wide, shift seasonally, and contain elements from both adjoining fauna.*

Arctic region

Asian Pacific region

Australian region

Indopacific region

South African region

Eastern Atlantic region

Antarctic region

Mediterranean Atlantic region

North American Atlantic region

Western Atlantic region

North American Pacific region

Eastern Pacific region

Indopacific region

South American Pacific region

along the east coast of Africa (including Madagascar and the Comoro Islands) to South Africa, much of the fish fauna is continuous as well. However, the fish fauna of the African coast is by no means identical with that of the Malay Peninsula, although there are no really abrupt breaks to separate one fauna from the other.

Despite the lack of distinctness, there are two areas along this vast stretch of coast that are worth mentioning separately: first, the triangle bounded by the Phillipines, the Malay Peninsula, and New Guinea; and second, the Red Sea.

The triangle was recognized by Ekman (1953) as the Indo-Malayan Region because of the extraordinary richness of its fauna. Although there are few species unique to this area, the total number of species is higher than in any similar-sized area of the world, and many families seem to have the most species here.

The Red Sea is of special interest partially because it is a semi-isolated part of the region without a particularly high number of endemics (10% to 15% of the fish fauna) and partially because it is a participant in a great zoogeographic experiment. The other participant is the Mediterranean Sea, which has been connected to the Red Sea by the Suez Canal since 1869. The high salinity of the Bitter Lakes area of the canal originally was a barrier to the movement of fish between the two basins, but at the present time the salinity of the entire canal is close to that of the water at both ends (about 41 ppt). It is thus possible for fish to move through the canal in either direction, although the length (160 km) of the canal, combined with its soft bottom and turbidity, undoubtedly have acted as a selective filter of species. The fish faunas of the two basins are quite distinct, that of the eastern Mediterranean being largely (250 of 290 species) the temperate fish fauna of the rest of the Mediterranean, while that of the Red Sea is the typical diverse Indo-Pacific fauna. As a result of the canal, at least 36 species of Red Sea fishes have immigrated to the Mediterranean Sea, where some of them have become established in very large numbers (Ben-Tuvia 1978). Only three fish species from the Mediterranean have managed to move into the Red Sea, although all three appear to be well established there. This mostly one-way dispersal seems to be related to the species-poor nature of the Mediterranean fauna as compared to that of the Red Sea, combined with the presumption that the temperate origin of the eastern Mediterranean fauna means they are less well adapted to tropical conditions and thus unable to compete successfully with Red Sea fishes (Ben-Tuvia 1978; Aron and Smith 1971).

The **Eastern Pacific Region** is often referred to as the Panamanian Region, because the Pacific coast of Panama is central to a region that extends from Bahia Magdalena near the tip of Baja California (but including the Gulf of California as well) down to the Gulf of Guayquil on the coast of South America. The southern boundary of this region is only about 3° of latitude from the equator because the cold Humboldt Current from the Antarctic keeps tropical conditions at bay (most of the time). The northern boundary is not very definite and there is considerable mixing of "temperate" and "tropical" species along the coasts of Baja California and Southern California and in the Gulf of California. The Eastern Pacific Region is separated from the Indo-Pacific Region by a wide stretch of deep water, and from the Western Atlantic Region by the isthmus of Panama. Most of the 800+ species therefore are confined to the region, although there are at least 62 species in common with the Indo-

Pacific Region and at least 12 in common with the Western Atlantic (Briggs 1974). Prior to the closing of the Panamanian isthmus in the Pliocene, the eastern Pacific and the western Atlantic presumably had a common fish fauna (Rosen 1975b, White 1986). There are few offshore islands in the Eastern Pacific Region, but they include the fascinating Galapagos. These islands' fish fauna is fairly rich (223 species according to Walker [1966]), with 23% of the species endemic, 54% shared with the coast of Central America, and 12% of Indo-Pacific origin.

The **Western Atlantic Region** includes the Caribbean and Gulf coasts of Central America and Mexico, the coast of South America to Cape Frio, the multitudinous islands of the West Indies, Bermuda, and the tip of Florida. Much of the fish fauna is associated with coral reefs and is similar to the fish faunas of coral reefs elsewhere, at least superficially. Many differences do exist, however. For example, in the Indo-Pacific Region the principal cleaner fishes are wrasses (Labridae), while in the Western Atlantic Region they are gobies (Gobiidae). Within the region, most species are mostly widely distributed, although there is enough endemism in some areas for Briggs (1974) to divide the region into provinces. However, two areas of particular interest to fish zoogeographers are not provinces as such: Bermuda and the Brazilian Coast.

Bermuda, which is a cluster of about 360 small islands, is of interest because it is the northernmost (32° latitude) bastion of tropical fishes. The tropical nature of its fauna is maintained by the warm Gulf Stream flowing up from Florida and the Gulf of Mexico. The Gulf Stream also helps to maintain a genetic connection of the fishes to their counterparts in the Caribbean, despite a separation of over 1400 km. Bermuda is a fairly ancient group of islands, but its fauna shows little sign of differentiation; this is presumably not only because of the present influence of the Gulf Stream but also because of its lack of influence during the Pleistocene (11,000 years B.P.), when it is believed that most of the tropical fauna of Bermuda disappeared as a result of lower water temperatures (Briggs 1974).

Along the coast of Brazil, the shallow-water coral reef fauna is sporadic for nearly 2900 km because of the influence of the Amazon, Orinoco, and other rivers, which decrease salinity, increase turbidity, and deposit large amounts of silt over a large area. Reef fishes are found primarily in association with sponges growing on hard bottoms in areas of oceanic salinity. Otherwise, in this stretch, typical reef fishes are replaced by fishes more characteristic of soft bottoms, such as sea catfishes (Ariidae) and croakers (Sciaenidae). The shallow-water reef fauna resumes as the influence of the rivers diminishes. This separation has resulted in a certain amount of endemism in the south Brazilian fauna, but the endemism seems to be most characteristic of shallow-water forms, since deep-water reefs are apparently still present along the entire coast. It is assumed that prior to the rise of the Andes, the influence of the rivers was not as strong in Atlantic coastal waters, so that shallow reefs could exist all along the coast (Briggs 1974).

The **Eastern Atlantic Region** consists of the continental shelf along the west coast of Africa from Cape Verde to central Angola in the south, plus three islands off the coast (Cape Verde, St. Helena, and Ascension). The northern boundary is rather arbitrary, but it does mark a region south of which temperate fishes are rare.

It is the smallest and most isolated of the tropical regions and contains the fewest fish species. Presumably, one of the reasons for its comparative lack of faunal richness is the near absence of coral reefs. Briggs (1974) lists 434 shore fishes from the region, compared with 900 on the opposite side of the Atlantic. The main affinities of the fishes are to those of the Western Atlantic Region. Not only are there about 120 species in common, but many of the genera are the same as well. About 40% of the species are endemic, however, reflecting the area's isolation. The Eastern and Western Atlantic regions presumably had a common fauna at the time Africa and South America were in the process of drifting apart and a much smaller Proto-Atlantic Ocean existed, which was less of a barrier to movement than the present ocean. However, one of the fascinating aspects of the Eastern Atlantic fish fauna is that it also includes about 32 species also found in the Indo-Pacific Region. Sixteen of these are found off the African coast as well the three islands; eight are also found in the western Atlantic; four are found only off West Africa, and four are found only around the island of St. Helena. Presumably, such fishes have made it around the Cape of Good Hope at one time or another; the presence of four such species at St. Helena is particularly indicative of this.

The fish fauna of St. Helena, although not rich (55 species), is curious for other reasons as well. It consists of a mixture of endemic species (18, including six shared with Ascension Island), circumtropical species, and species from all four major tropical regions (Briggs 1974). This fauna reflects the island's Miocene (?) origin as a volcano plus its strategic position in the central southern Atlantic, where it can intercept fishes (and emperors) coming from various directions. The fish fauna of St. Helena points out nicely the interconnectedness of the fauna of the four regions. They share most of their families, many of their genera, and even a few species. The similarities of the faunas reflects largely the closeness of the continents during the time the tropical fish fauna was evolving; the differences reflect the considerable isolation of the faunas that now exist and have for some time, as well as the limited dispersal abilities of most of the fishes.

North Temperate Regions

Although the North Temperate Regions of the Atlantic and Pacific oceans are marked on maps and generally broken up into a number of provinces or subregions, boundaries between them and the Arctic Region on the north and the Tropical Regions on the south are very hard to fix. The reason for this is that the change from one fauna to the next is rather gradual, and the ranges of many species fluctuate from year to year depending on the vagaries of coastal currents. Some coastal features, such as Point Conception of the California coast, do mark rather sharp changes in the fish fauna, yet even in such situations there are typically more similarities than differences on the two sides of the boundary. However, distinctive faunas of temperate-water fishes do exist along long stretches of coast on both sides of the Atlantic and both sides of the Pacific. These four areas will therefore be treated as separate zoogeographic regions: (1) the Mediterranean-Atlantic Region, (2) the

North American Atlantic Region, (3) the North American Pacific Region, and (4) the Asian-Pacific Region.

The **Mediterranean-Atlantic Region** consists of the Atlantic coast of Europe and North Africa, together with the Mediterranean, Black, and Caspian seas. In the north it merges with the Arctic Region, while in the south it merges with the tropical Eastern Atlantic Region. Because the Gulf Stream swings south along the coast of Europe, forming the North Atlantic Current, comparatively warm water is usually present as far north as the British Isles. As a result, representatives of "tropical" families such as the Gobiidae (gobies), Labridae (wrasses), Mugilidae (mullets), Sparidae (porgies), Mullidae (goatfishes), and Scaridae (parrotfishes) are common in the more southern portions of this region, including the Mediterranean Sea (Lythgoe and Lythgoe 1971). However, representatives of typically cold-water marine families, such as Gadidae (cods), Agonidae (poachers), Cottidae (sculpins), Pleuronectidae (righteye flounders), and Cyclopteridae (snailfishes), are common throughout much of the region. Although many of the fish species and genera found in this region are endemic, none of the families are. Many of the species characteristic of the more northern areas are shared with the Arctic Region and the North American Atlantic Region, while a number of the southern species occur in tropical areas on both sides of the Atlantic. Although the gradual faunal changes characteristic of this region make provinces difficult to establish firmly, it is worth examining some of the more isolated components of the region: the Mediterranean Sea, the Black Sea, and the Baltic Sea.

The *Mediterranean Sea,* despite its apparent isolation, contains a fauna of 540+ fish species that differs little from that of the Atlantic coasts of northern Africa and southern Europe. Indeed, 35% of the fish species found north of the Arctic Circle in Europe are also found in the Mediterranean (Lythgoe and Lythgoe 1971). However, the Mediterranean does possess a number of local endemic fishes, especially in the families Blenniidae, Gobiidae, and Labridae; it also possesses a distinctly tropical fauna in the eastern portion, a fauna currently being augmented by Red Sea fishes emigrating through the Suez Canal.

The *Black Sea* has a complex history of connections with the Mediterranean and Caspian seas, presumably with considerable fluctuations in salinity. At present its narrow connection with the Mediterranean, coupled with freshwater inflow from the Danube and other large rivers, gives it a salinity of 17 ppt to 18 ppt over much of its surface. This fish fauna (140 species) is mostly a depauperate Mediterranean fauna, with a few (33) endemic species and a few species (mostly gobies) shared with the Caspian Sea.

The *Baltic Sea* is the largest estuary in the world, with salinities that gradually increase from the upper to the lower end. The salinity gradient, the shallowness of the sea, and the extreme temperature fluctuations it experiences greatly limit the Baltic Sea's capacity to support a diverse fish fauna, although it does contain a mixture of freshwater and marine species. The marine fishes are the same as those found in the North Atlantic, although some (such as the cod [*Gadus morhua*]) are considered to have distinct Baltic "races."

The **North American Atlantic Region** consists of the Atlantic coast of North America (excluding the tip of Florida with its distinctly tropical fauna) and the northern Gulf of Mexico. Because of the presence of "tropical" fishes from the Caribbean along the Gulf and southern Atlantic coasts, there have been many attempts to subdivide this region (Briggs 1974); but general lack of agreement among people who work with different animal groups indicates the gradual nature of the change along the coasts. Usually, however, a boundary of some sort is made in the Cape Hatteras (North Carolina) area because the Gulf Stream tends to swing away from the coast in this area, permitting the cooler waters from the north to have greater influence. However, seasonal temperature fluctuations and vagaries in the flow of the Gulf Stream make even this boundary a tenuous one, especially for mobile fishes. Thus the region between Cape Hatteras and Cape Cod contains many typically "southern" species in the summer, when water temperatures are high, whereas in the winter the dominant species are typical fishes of northern waters. These northern fishes include representatives of the same families as are found off northern Europe, such as the Gadidae (cods), Pleuronectidae (right-eye flounders), Cottidae (sculpins), and Cyclopteridae (snail fishes), as well as diadromous members of the Anguillidae, Clupeidae, and Salmonidae. The fishes more characteristic of southern (warmer) waters include members of such families as Sciaenidae (croakers), Sparidae (porgies), Serranidae (sea basses), Haemulidae (grunts), and Labridae (wrasses). However, even these families are widely distributed up and down the Atlantic coast, with some species more characteristic of northern than southern faunas.

One of the factors complicating any discussion of the distribution patterns is the general decrease in the number of species toward the north. Thus there are about 375 to 400 species along the Gulf Coast of Texas, perhaps 350 along the coast of South Carolina, 200 to 250 in the area south of Cape Cod, about 225 (130 shore fishes) in the Gulf of Maine, 61 along the Labrador coast, and 34 from Greenland (Briggs 1974). The figures for Cape Cod and the Gulf of Maine are somewhat deceptive, because 50% to 60% of the species recorded are warm-water species of sporadic or rare occurrence.

The **North American Pacific Region** extends along the Pacific coast from Baja California north to the end of the Aleutian Island chain. As in the North American Atlantic Region, there is a very gradual change from a tropical fauna, to a mixed tropical-temperate fauna, to a largely temperate fauna, to a mixed temperate-arctic fauna. The region is extremely rich in fishes. At its southern end, most of the 800 or so species known from the Gulf of California (Thomson et al. 1979) can be expected at one time or another (although only about 220 have been recorded); this is especially the case in years when the California Current is not flowing strongly, so that the cool water from the Gulf of Alaska does not extend so far south. For the California coast, Miller and Lea (1972) list 554 species, of which 439 should perhaps be considered continental shelf species. Along the Pacific coast of Canada, 325 species are known, of which perhaps 40 species belong in deepsea or pelagic regions rather than inshore. Farther north the fauna merges with that of the Arctic Region and to the west with the Asian-Pacific Region.

There are many fascinating aspects of this fauna. It is extremely diverse, with 144 families represented off California alone. Several of these families are found only in this region and in the Asian-Pacific Region, most prominently the Embiotocidae (surfperches, 23 species), Hexagrammidae (greenlings, 11 species), and Anoplopomatidae (sablefish and skilfish). A number of other families have attained great diversity here, such as the Scorpaenidae, with over 60 species in the genus *Sebastes* alone; the Salmonidae, which includes seven species of Pacific salmon and trout *(Oncorhynchus);* the Cottidae, with about 60 species; the Pleuronectidae, with 20 to 25 species; the Agonidae, with 20 to 25 species; and numerous species in various blennioid families (Stichaeidae, Blenniidae, Clinidae, etc.).

The **Asian-Pacific Region** extends roughly from Hong Kong north past the Kamchatka Peninsula. These boundaries are very arbitrary since the warm Kuroshio Current brings a large number of Indo-Pacific Region species north to Japan, occasionally as far as the island of Hokkaido. Hong Kong marks the southern limit of many temperate species. However, the fishes of the coast of China (up to the Yellow Sea), of Formosa, and of southern Japan are predominantly tropical. For example, only 10% of the 924 species known from the southern Japanese island of Shikoku are also found in northern Japan, although another 29% are more or less endemic to the area and many of the tropical species do not occur on a regular basis (Kamohara 1964). The Yellow Sea, although at about the same latitude as Shikoku, contains a more characteristically cool-water fauna because the sea is not heavily influenced by the Kuroshio Current. Thus the main resident fishes are about 40 to 50 species of typical northern Pacific fishes (Cottidae, Hexagrammidae, Pleuronectidae, etc.), although at least 174 tropical species make sporadic appearances there (Briggs 1974). Farther to the north, the fauna of the Okhotsk Sea is very similar to that of Canada and Alaska in terms of families and genera present (Schmidt 1950). Only a few of the 300 or so species in the Okhotsk Sea are shared with the North American Pacific Region. The entire northern Pacific coast of Asia is also considered to have been an important center of salmonid evolution.

To the north, the fauna of this region merges with that of the Arctic Region in the Bering Sea. Presumably, the Bering Sea serves as something of a barrier for exchange of inshore species between North America and Asia because of its essentially arctic temperature regime, although it has also been dry when sea levels were lower during the Pleistocene.

Arctic Region

The Arctic Region includes all of the Arctic Ocean, the waters around Greenland, and the Bering Sea. Its fishes are discussed in some detail in Chapter 36 and so will be only briefly described here. There are probably fewer than 110 species that occur in the Arctic on a regular basis, most of them cold-tolerant species that also occur in the northern Atlantic or Pacific, in such families as the Cottidae, Cyclopteridae, Zoarcidae, and Pleuronectidae. About one-half of the arctic species are largely confined to the Arctic Region, and most of these species are circumpolar, providing connecting links to the faunas of the northern Atlantic and northern Pacific.

South Temperate Regions

Only three South Temperate Regions will be considered here: South American, South African, and Australian. Briggs (1974) and others tend to divide these regions into provinces, mostly on the basis of differences in the faunas of the coasts that border on different oceans and Antarctic waters. However, despite differences in the faunas of the various coasts of the three continents, there is a great deal of faunal interconnectedness on each continent, making it possible to treat each as a unit. There are also many similarities in the faunas of the three continents, presumably the result of their connections by ocean currents and by their ancient existence as just one continent.

The **South American Region** extends from the coast of Peru around the tip of South America to about Rio de Janeiro on the Brazilian coast. The northern ends of this region merge gradually with the tropical faunas of their respective coasts, while the fauna of the tip of South America shows strong affinities to that of the Antarctic. The strong prevailing winds along the west coast are responsible for the far northward extent of this region along the coast; they also create immense upwelling along the coasts of Peru and Chile, which once made the anchoveta (*Engraulis ringens*) the most abundant harvestable fish in the world (see Chapter 34). Although many purely tropical fish families are represented along the west coast of South America, especially in the more northern areas, families typical of the southern areas of the North Temperate Regions are also abundant here: Engraulidae (anchovies), Clupeidae (herrings), Serranidae (sea basses), Carangidae (jacks), Pomadasyidae (grunts), Sciaenidae (croakers), and Scorpaenidae (rockfishes). On the more southern portions of the coast, families such as the Gadidae (cods), Zoarcidae (eelpouts), Bovichthyidae, and Nototheniidae (plunderfishes) become well represented. There are a few small, peculiar families, such as the Normanichthyidae (with a single species apparently related to the Cottidae), the Aplodactylidae (otherwise found only in the Australian Region), the Psychrolutidae (cottidlike fishes with species in the North Temperate Regions as well as the South African Region), Cheilodactylidae (found in the three South Temperate Regions and in the Asian Pacific Region), Latridae (otherwise known only from the Australian Region), and Congiopodidae (scorpaeniform fishes confined to these three regions and the Antarctic). The fish fauna of the tip of South America contains many notothenioid fishes, many of them endemic, and so bears a great resemblance to that of the Antarctic Region.

The **South African Region,** because of the combination of its more northward location and the presence of warm currents (the South Equatorial Current on the Pacific side, the Agulhas Current around the Cape of Good Hope, and the Benguela Current on the Atlantic Coast), lacks most of the cold-water fish families characteristic of the South American Region, such as the Nototheniidae, Bovichthyidae (except one island species), Cyclopteridae, and Zoarcidae (Smith 1949). However, species in the latter two families do occur in deep water off the South African coast. Most of the region's fishes belong to widespread tropical families, although there are a number of endemic species, especially in the families Clinidae ("klipfishes," the most species-rich inshore family), Gobiidae, Blenniidae, Gobiesocidae, and Batrachoididae (Smith 1949). This region shares with the Australian Region a number of distinct families, such as the Pentacerotidae, Oplegnathidae (found also off Japan, Hawaii, and the Galapagos Islands!), Congiopodidae (racehorses), and Callorhynchidae (plownose chimaeras). The latter two families are also found in South America. However, many of the species and genera are endemic to the region, reflecting its long isolation.

The **Australian Region** is inhabited by a temperate fish fauna with a strong tropical element. This is because warm currents from the Indian and Pacific oceans moderate the water temperatures along the southern half of Australia, from Shark Bay on the west to about Hervy Bay on the east. Around Tasmania and the southern tip of Australia, as well as around much of New Zealand, the tropical element tends to drop out, and a more cold-water element comes in. Southern Australia, New Zealand, and small islands around New Zealand constitute the Australian Region. Along the coast of southern Australia, the pattern of fish distribution is indicated by the work of Scott (1962) on the fishes of the southern edge of the continent. He found that 101 of the 253 species discussed were characteristic of the entire Australian Region (and many lived in the Indo-Pacific Tropical Region as well). Another 114 species were endemic to the region between Shark Bay and Tasmania, although 72 of these species were not found in the colder waters around Tasmania. Thirty-eight species have a break in their distribution created by the cold water around the tip of Australia. This break has apparently also resulted in the evolution of a number of pairs of species, one on each side of the cold-water area. The exact composition of the fish fauna of Tasmania itself is poorly known, but besides the previously mentioned widely distributed species that occur here, there are a number of endemic forms, especially in the families Rajidae, Clinidae, Bovichthyidae, and Ostraciidae (Briggs 1974). Curiously enough, the fish fauna of Tasmania bears many resemblances to that of southern New Zealand, including the presence of the notothenioid fish family, Bovichthyidae. The fauna of northern New Zealand is more like that of southeastern Australia, with only about one-fourth of the species being endemic.

Antarctic Region

The Antarctic Region, thanks to the stability of the antarctic convergence, is one of the most isolated marine regions. Most of the species are endemic and belong to four families in the suborder Notothenioidei (see Chapter 36). The remaining fishes are divided up among five families, one of which (Muraenolepididae) is an Antarctic family with representation on the tip of South America and two of which (Cyclopteridae and Zoarcidae) are widely distributed cold-water families also present in the Arctic. Unlike the Arctic Region, however, the Antarctic Region does not connect the faunas of the surrounding continents and it shares few species with them. Nevertheless, the fact that the South Temperate Regions share most of their fish families, many of their genera, and even a few species is a strong indication of their past connection through the ancient continent of Gondwanaland. Presumably the more temperate elements died out in the Antarctic Region as the continent drifted into its present position, while the cold-adapted notothenioid fishes (represented in the South Temperate Regions by the Bovichthyidae) evolved into many species.

PELAGIC REGIONS

The Mesopelagic Zone and the offshore portions of the Epipelagic Zone (see Chapters 34 and 35) are inhabited by fishes that are, for the most part, not bound to the continents. Many of these species have a worldwide distribution while others are restricted in their distribution. Because the distribution patterns of species from many groups, vertebrate and invertebrate, that inhabit the open ocean often coincide, it is possible to divide the world ocean into pelagic regions. The boundaries between the regions are areas where oceanographic conditions, but particularly temperature, change more rapidly than elsewhere in the ocean. Such regions of change, while they tend to fluctuate seasonally, are often coincident with isotherms and thus have latitudinal limits. For mesopelagic fishes, temperature boundaries may be less important determinants of distribution patterns than the location of oxygen minimum layers or regions of low productivity (e.g., see Johnson and Glodek 1975). Even so, mesopelagic regions are usually largely coincident with epipelagic regions. Most of the regions used here are widely recognized (Parin 1968; McGowan 1974; Briggs 1974; Backus et al. 1977): Arctic, Subarctic, North Temperate, North Subtropical, Tropical, South Subtropical, South Temperate, and Antarctic (Fig. 26.2).

The **Arctic Region** seems to contain no true pelagic fishes, although the arctic cods *(Arctogadus, Boreogadus)* are associated with pack ice on a regular basis. Mesopelagic fishes are apparently of only irregular occurrence (Backus et al. 1977).

The **Subarctic Region** is, roughly, the area between the Arctic Region and the 8°C to 10°C isotherm. Its fish fauna differs considerably in the Atlantic and Pacific oceans. In the Pacific, the dominant epipelagic piscivores are Pacific salmon with a few odd forms such as pomfret (Bramidae: *Brama japonica*), skilfish (Anoplopomatidae: *Erilepis zonifer*), and ragfish (Icosteidae: *Icosteus aenigmaticus*) joining in. When temperatures warm up a bit in the summer, many large predatory fishes from the North Subtropical Region may move into this region. This movement is perhaps even more marked in the Atlantic than the Pacific because of the lack of a well-developed endemic epipelagic fish fauna, although Atlantic salmon *(Salmo salar)* and pomfret *(Brama brama)* are widely distributed in the region. Backus et al. (1977) note that the mesopelagic community in this region is dominated by just one species of myctophid.

The **North Temperate Region** is bordered on the south by the 14°C to 16°C isotherm. The dominant epipelagic fishes are such fishes as tuna (Scombridae), swordfish *(Xiphias gladius)*, basking shark *(Cetorhinus maximus)*, sauries (Scomberesocidae), and opah *(Lampris guttatus)*. They are joined in the summer months by many species, but especially other scombrids, from the North Subtropical Region.

The **North Subtropical Region** and its counterpart to the south, the **South Subtropical Region,** are bounded by the 14°C to 16°C isotherm on one side and the 18°C to 20°C isotherm on the other. These regions are characterized by tunas, sauries, fly-

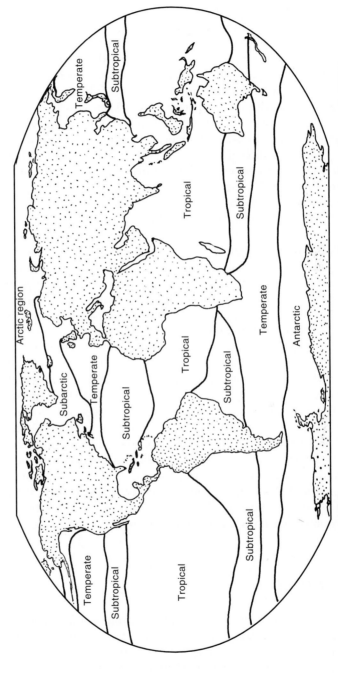

FIGURE 26.2 *Major zoogeographic regions for pelagic fishes. (Based on Briggs 1974 and Backus et al. 1977.)*

ing fish (Exocoetidae), louvar *(Luvarus imperialis),* and marlins *(Makaira* spp.). Backus et al. (1977) note that, in the Atlantic, 13 species of mesopelagic myctophids have their center of abundance in the two subtropical regions, and that 11 of these species are present in the two regions but missing from the Tropical Region in between. A similar **antitropical pattern** with many of the same species presumably exists in the Pacific as well. A unique feature of the North Subtropical Zone of the Atlantic is the Sargasso Sea, with its distinctive set of fishes associated with drifting sargassum weed (see Chapter 34). During the summer, virtually all the epipelagic fishes characteristic of the Tropical Region occur here as well, in both regions.

The **Tropical Region** consists of a broad, worldwide belt of equatorial water that rarely drops below 20°C. Its limits in the various oceans correspond roughly to the limits of the tropical shelf regions. Much of the epipelagic fish fauna of this region has a worldwide distribution, although distinct differences do exist between the faunas of the Atlantic and Pacific/Indian oceans. Since the epipelagic fishes do move into the subtropical regions during the summer, this region is perhaps better defined by the absence of many subtropical species of fishes than by its year-round residents. The characteristic species of the region are tropical flying fishes, scombrids, pelagic sharks, and billfishes (Xiphiidae). The mesopelagic fish fauna is most abundant and diverse in this region, especially in the Pacific and Indian oceans, although the distribution patterns of most species are not completely known.

The **South Temperate Region** is marked in the north by the 14°C to 15°C summer isotherm (subtropical convergence) and in the south by the 3°C to 5°C isotherm (Antarctic convergence). Its fish fauna is not as well studied as that of the other pelagic regions, but it shares many species and genera with the North Temperate Region. The lamnid sharks, the basking shark, and the sauries, pomfrets, and scombrids belong to the same or closely related species. This region is a relatively narrow one and so shares many fishes seasonally with the Subtropical Region.

The **Antarctic Region** consists of the shallow waters that circle the Antarctic continent. It is remarkable for its lack of true epipelagic fishes, except for a few coast-bound forms such as the antarctic herring (Nototheniidae: *Pleurogramma antarcticum*). The mesopelagic fauna is better developed, with a number of species in the families Myctophidae, Bathylagidae, Gonstomatidae, Paralepididae, and Scopelarchidae largely confined to the region (Andriashev 1962).

DEEPSEA REGIONS

In the deep sea there are two ecological groups of fishes that tend to be confined to zoogeographic regions: the bathypelagic fishes and the deepsea benthic fishes. For both groups, two factors of great importance in their distribution patterns are that the greatest number of individuals and species are located in tropical and subtropical areas, and that in all areas where they are found their abundance tends to be greatest near the continents. By and large, the bathypelagic fishes tend to be located in regions approximately equivalent to those described for epipelagic fishes.

However, there are relatively few species with worldwide distribution patterns; most tend to be associated with specific ocean basins or water masses with distinctive salinities, temperatures, and dissolved oxygen levels.

For the benthic species, those that inhabit the upper continental slope tend to fall into zoogeographic patterns like those for fishes of the continental shelf, although the greater uniformity of temperatures at great depths makes the fishes even less respectful of zoogeographic boundaries. In deeper water the dominant fish families are the Ophidiidae and Macrouridae, but in more polar waters the Zoarcidae and Cyclopteridae are usually more common. Despite their commonness, however, most species in these families are confined to single ocean basins; undersea mountain ranges and trenches seem to be barriers to dispersal. A few species do seem to have wide distributions, however. For example, the flatnose cod (*Antimora rostrata*) is found in deep water in the Atlantic, Pacific, and Indian oceans (although the populations are often listed as separate species). In the deep-water family Chlorophthalmidae there are 18 species of spiderfishes (*Bathypterois*). Most of the species have fairly restricted distributions, but one is found in the tropical and subtropical regions throughout the world, except for the northeastern Atlantic (Sulak 1977). Consequently the distribution patterns of deepsea fishes can either be related to those of the pelagic regions (by using distribution patterns of families and genera) or be divided up on a basin-by-basin basis, using the distribution patterns of species.

ANTITROPICAL DISTRIBUTION PATTERNS

One of the recurring patterns in marine zoogeography is the presence of species, genera, and families that are absent from the tropics but present in regions on both sides. These antitropical (or bipolar) patterns have been noted for entire families such as hagfishes (Myxinidae), eelpouts (Zoarcidae), snailfishes (Cyclopteridae), and cods (Gadidae); for genera within families such as Clupeidae (herrings), Engraulidae (anchovies), Merlucciidae (hakes), Rajidae (skates), and Squalidae (dogfish sharks); and for species such as Atlantic pomfret (*Brama brama*), flying fishes (*Hirundichthys speculiger, Exocoetus volitans*), basking shark (*Cetorhinus maximus*), and saury (*Scomberesox saurus*). Almost all species with antitropical distributions are pelagic, so it is likely that their distribution patterns are the result of movements across the tropical regions. However, many of the families or genera are bottom-oriented or shallow-water forms, which are not likely to move over long distances as pelagic forms. Further, the general lack of antitropical species of this sort indicates that the events leading to the present distribution pattern were fairly ancient.

Four theories have been advanced to explain the antitropical distribution patterns:

1. Lower sea temperatures in the tropics in the past may have permitted more continuous distributions of cool-water fishes.
2. Cool-water fishes may have moved through deep water of suitable temperatures, thus avoiding the warm surface waters.

3. The fishes with antitropical distributions may once have been present in the tropics as well but were displaced through competition with more advanced groups.
4. The distribution pattern may be the result of continental drift.

The first theory was proposed by Hubbs (1974) and is supported by White (1986), who provides evidence of climatic change in the Miocene that would have caused sea temperatures to rise at low latitudes, effectively eliminating cool-water species from the tropics. The second theory may explain the patterns of some antitropical genera of the subtropical and temperate regions, but it is applied with difficulty to explain the presence of families such as the Zoarcidae and Cyclopteridae at the two poles (Ekman 1953). The difficulty arises from the lack of family representatives in the deep waters of intermediate regions, since presumably, if such water was suitable for migration, it should also be suitable as a permanent place to live. The third theory is favored by Briggs (1974), although there is no evidence to support such drastic effects of competitive interactions among species that presumably coevolved (White 1986). If there were once species of eelpouts and snailfishes adapted to oceanographic conditions of the tropics, it is not unreasonable to expect relict populations in a few localities. In regard to the fourth theory, and as indicated at the beginning of this chapter, the role of continental drift in determining the present distribution of marine fishes is poorly understood. It seems very likely, however, given the fact that families such as the Zoarcidae and Cyclopteridae are closely tied to continents, that this theory will prove to be of major importance and help to explain many of the distribution anomalies that now exist. Applying what has been learned about plate tectonics and sea-floor spreading to the distribution of marine organisms is therefore one of the major challenges of the marine zoogeographer.

Supplemental Readings

Backus et al. 1977; Briggs 1974; Ekman 1953; McGowan 1974; Parin 1968; Schmidt 1950; Springer 1982; White 1986.

CHAPTER **27**

Introduction to Ecology

The study of fish ecology is one of the most dynamic areas of ichthyology. Understanding how environmental factors influence the distribution and abundance of fish is important for managing fisheries, protecting aquatic ecosystems, and setting water-quality standards. Increasingly, fish are being studied to answer fundamental questions of interest to all ecologists, such as how complex communities or food webs are structured. These studies have contributed to the "paradigm shift" that ecology has undergone in recent decades. In a clamshell, that shift has been away from the "balance of nature" paradigm and toward the paradigm that "the only constant is change." The change takes place not only on local and regional scales in response to environmental fluctuations, but on much broader scales in response to climate changes and evolutionary events. Today, of course, humans are often the main drivers of change, at least in the short term, and it has become increasingly important to understand how human perturbations to the biosphere interact with natural changes.

The dynamic nature of fish faunas can be revealed by thinking of each local assemblage of species as having passed through a series of filters to arrive at the particular assemblage observed (Smith and Powell 1971). In each marine or freshwater region, there is a large group of fishes that potentially could be part of local fish fauna. The first filter this broad fauna has to pass through is the response of individual species to Pleistocene events, 10,000 or more years ago (Fig. 27.1). The Earth's biota is still recovering from the massive glaciers that covered good chunks of North America and Eurasia, accompanied by lower sea levels worldwide and climate changes in nonglaciated areas. For example, the upper Mississippi River basin and many lakes and rivers in Canada may lack many species now present in areas that never were glaciated simply because the species have not have the time or opportunity to invade (or re-invade). Moyle and Herbold (1987) argue that the superficial resemblance between the freshwater fish faunas of Europe and of western North America (e.g., dominance by large cyprinids) is the result of Pleistocene events in those regions that selected for particular life history patterns.

The next filter is a zoogeographic filter, which sorts out fish of continental or oceanic faunas into sets of regional faunas due to the presence of natural barriers, such as mountain ranges, deserts, or ocean current systems. The importance of zoogeographic barriers in separating marine systems is indicated by the massive invasion of organisms into the Mediterranean Sea from the Red Sea after the Suez Canal was built. Once a fish species is in a body of water, its distribution is often restricted by its physiological tolerances of such factors as temperature, salinity, dissolved oxygen, and pH. A species will be "filtered out" of an area if the environment regularly exceeds its physiological limits for one or more of these factors. For example, codfish cannot move into water colder than 2°C in the North Sea because the cold water inhibits the chloride-secreting mechanism of their gills (Cushing 1968). These abiotic filters determine the **fundamental niche** of a species, a concept developed by G. E. Hutchinson to describe the potential range of environmental conditions a species can inhabit in the absence of predators and competitors.

The next filter is a biotic filter, representing interactions with other species. A species can be excluded from an area otherwise suitable for it by competitors, predators, parasites, or lack of suitable prey. When these factors are taken into consideration, the range of conditions in which a species lives is its **realized niche.** An assemblage of fishes found in a common set of environmental conditions or habitat is usually referred to as a **fish community,** implying that it is structured by the interlocking realized niches of the species.

The idea of predictable fish communities neatly assembled through biotic interactions has been assaulted by the development of an everything-is-change paradigm in ecology. Yet this idea is still remarkably true, at least for short periods of time, because fish have an astonishing ability to interact with other species and to establish what appear to be highly structured communities, even when some of the species are exotics introduced by humans. The flexibility of different fish species in their living arrangements with each other should not be surprising because even under natural conditions the environment is constantly changing through time, alternately favoring one species or group of species over another. For example, Strange et al. (1992) found that the fish community of a small alpine stream fluctuated between being dominated by non-native brown trout and by a cluster of native species. The driving force changing the composition of this community was the timing of flood

FIGURE 27.1 *Filters (dotted boxes) through which fishes must pass that result in local fish assemblages.*

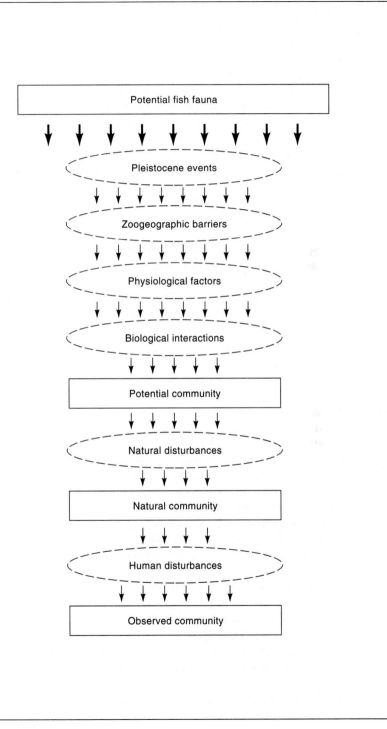

events. If these events occurred in the winter, they apparently scoured out the embryos of the brown trout that were incubating in the gravel. The native species are less affected by winter spates because they are all spring spawners; they need high-flow conditions at that time for successful spawning. If brown trout are abundant, they suppress the native fish populations through predation, regardless of the spawning success of the natives. During extended periods that favor brown trout, some native species of fish may be locally extirpated. Thus, understanding the composition of the local fish community often requires an understanding of the recent local environmental history, which is another filter (Figure 27.1).

The final filter that every community of fishes passes through is the one imposed by human activity. Humans have drastically altered most watersheds, even those that appear to be natural. In marine systems, fishing typically favors some species over others, with cascading effects throughout the ecosystem. These "filters" have increased the dynamism—and unpredictability—of local fish assemblages.

Despite the strong interaction between biotic and abiotic factors in fish ecology, the rest of this chapter will focus on the biological factors determining the realized niches of fishes. The influences of abiotic factors on fishes are explained in the chapters on physiology (Chapters 2 to 10) as well as in the subsequent chapters on ecology (Chapters 28 to 36). For convenience, biotic factors can be divided into interspecific and intraspecific interactions. The interspecific interactions in turn can be divided into (1) predation, (2) competition, (3) symbiosis, and (4) parasites and pathogens.

PREDATION

With few exceptions fish are simultaneously predator and prey, especially if humans are counted as predators. Relatively few species of fish are herbivores or detritivores, and even these species typically are predators on invertebrates during their early life history stages. As a result of their dual predator-prey role, fishes have evolved a wide array of feeding and defense mechanisms; these range from the strong beak and spiny covering of porcupinefishes (Tetraodontidae), to the sharp teeth and sleek bodies of barracudas (Sphyraenidae), to the pharyngeal teeth and fear scents of minnows (Cyprinidae), to the fine gill rakers and schooling behavior of herrings (Clupeidae). Such adaptations are a reflection of the coevolution of predators and prey through time. Defense mechanisms evolve presumably because they confer a reproductive advantage on the possessors, at least until their predators evolve the means to overcome the defense. While predators and prey obviously coexist, the predator-prey relationships are not necessarily stable, and even minor environmental changes (especially those created by humans) may result in gross imbalances. Thus, for example, squawfish (*Ptychocheilus* spp., large piscivorous cyprinids) have little impact on juvenile salmon populations in natural streams of the western United States, but can consume significant numbers of salmon in artifical circumstances below dams.

One of the major questions in ecology (and fisheries biology) is, Do predators control populations of their prey? The answer is often (but not always) yes. For example, Möller (1984) demonstrated that herring populations in a fjord off the Baltic Sea were regulated in good part by predation on their larvae by jellyfish. However, the most dramatic examples occur when planktivorous fishes are introduced into lakes that had previously lacked them. Often they will almost eliminate the larger species of zooplankton and cause small species to become dominant (Brooks and Dodson 1965). This in turn results in a **trophic cascade**, where change occurs at all levels of the ecosystem (Carpenter and Kitchill 1993). For example, the introduction of alewife *(Alosa pseudoharengus)* into Lake Michigan resulted in the near disappearance of two large species of zooplankton, the decline of five other species, and an increase in 10 species of small zooplankton (Wells 1970). When Pacific salmon were introduced into the lake, they greatly reduced the alewife populations through predation. As a result, large zooplankton species once again flourished in the lake. Because these species were more efficient grazers on phytoplankton than were the smaller species that could coexist with the alewife, phytoplankton densities decreased dramatically, causing the lake to become exceptionally clear (Scavia et al. 1986).

In some situations, a prey population may control that of a predator rather than the reverse. In a pond, for example, bluegill may limit the population of piscivorous largemouth bass by preempting limited nesting sites and by preying on the bass eggs in the nests. This situation is particularly likely to develop if fishermen have removed the largest bass, because such bass can keep bluegill numbers under control. Despite examples such as this, most predator populations seem to fluctuate independently of that of any single prey species, because they are usually capable of switching among prey species when the population of one gets too low.

A dramatic illustration of the importance of alternate prey is the recent collapse of cod *(Gadus morhua)* populations in the Berents Sea. The cod collapsed after gross overfishing reduced the population of herring, their favorite prey. The cod then starved because populations of alternative prey were also low, as the result of natural conditions (Hamre 1994). In most situations, however, alternate prey are available for predators but the decision of just when it is worthwhile to switch prey is a complex one. Under **optimal foraging theory,** it is assumed that maximizing the intake of energy is a major factor determining the choice. When it takes less effort for a bluegill to become satiated on zooplankton than to feed on invertebrates that live among aquatic plants, it will switch to feeding on zooplankton. However, the foraging strategy is tempered by other factors, such as the increased risk of predation by largemouth bass when bluegill feeds too far away from the cover provided by aquatic plants.

A similar problem exists for reproductive behavior. Male fish have to continually balance the need to attract females with the increased risked of predation that such behavior entails (Sih 1994). The commonness of red as a spawning color in sticklebacks, salmon, minnows, and other freshwater fish is presumably a reflection of this conflict. Red is conspicuous in shallow, well-lighted waters but is hard to see in deep cover or deep water.

COMPETITION

Competition is "the demand, typically at the same time, of more than one organism for the same resources of the environment in excess of immediate supply" (Larkin 1956). By definition, competition should not allow two species with identical ecological requirements to coexist if resources are limited. It works as a mechanism for structuring biotic communities because two species rarely have identical ecological requirements. Take, for example, two species that evolved in different regions and whose ecological requirements are similar but not identical. If these two species are brought together, the differences between them will presumably become emphasized through competitive interactions in such a way that the resources under dispute will be divided between them; that is, they will show **resource partitioning.** Selection pressure may eventually cause the species to diverge permanently from each other through behavioral, morphological, and physiological specializations **(character displacement).** An extreme result of this process is the many highly specialized fishes found in the ancient rift lakes of Africa (see Chapter 30). Character displacement can occur very rapidly. Crowder (1984) found that following the invasion of alewife into the Great Lakes, a native cisco shifted from plankton feeding to bottom feeding, with a concomitant reduction in the number of gill rakers in the ciscos.

At the opposite end of the spectrum are the species of trout characteristic of streams and lakes in recently glaciated areas. These trout have a behavioral plasticity that allows them to use interference competition to segregate quickly from other species of trout, as well as from other kinds of fishes with which they come in contact (Chapter 28). Because competition is such an ephemeral phenomenon, it is often difficult to demonstrate in natural situations (Fausch 1988). This does not prevent its frequently being invoked (usually without evidence) to explain the patterns of distribution and abundance of many fish species, particularly if the species are economically important and are declining in number while less valuable species are on the increase.

There are two general sources of evidence for competition between fish species: observational and experimental. Some of the best observational evidence is from studies of species segregation of salmonids in high mountain lakes. Nilsson (1963) found that Arctic char *(Salvelinus alpinus)* and brown trout in Swedish lakes will occupy both inshore and offshore habitats and feed on everything from zooplankton to benthic and terrestrial insects when either one of the species is the sole fish occupant of a lake. However, when the two species occur together, the trout concentrate close to shore and the bottom, where they feed on both benthic and terrestrial insects. The char, on the other hand, are almost entirely found out in the open waters of the lake, where they feed on zooplankton. In aquaria, trout have proven to be more aggressive than char and will consistently dominate them; in a lake this behavior presumably keeps char out of the inshore areas. The competition in this case is for the limited and productive inshore space, and segregation results directly from the behavioral interactions of the two morphologically similar salmonids. However, there *are* minor morphological differences between the species that also have some bearing on the results of their interactions. Arctic char, for example, have more and longer gill rakers than do brown trout, which should give them an advantage in feeding on zooplankton. Given enough time, the differences between the two species where they live together should become even greater, thereby increasing the efficiency of utilization of the limited resources present and reducing interactions between species.

Experimental demonstrations of competition are more difficult to obtain than observational ones, because they require controlled manipulations of fish populations or of the limiting resource, such as food or cover. For example, two species of surfperch (Embiotocidae) occur on rocky reefs off central California, but each occupies a different depth zone. The striped surfperch *(Embiotoca lateralis)* lives in food-rich shallow areas, while the black surfperch *(E. jacksoni)* lives in deeper areas where food is relatively scarce. Hixon (1980) found that black surfperch moved into shallow areas after he removed all the striped surfperch from a small reef, but that the striped surfperch would not move into deep water when he removed black surfperch from another reef. Further experiments showed that striped surfperch were aggressively dominant over black surfperch and forced them to live in the less productive areas.

As the preceding example indicates, a number of behavioral mechanisms may be acting simultaneously to enable fish to avoid competition by segregating them ecologically. Some of the most important of these mechanisms include differential exploitation, aggressive behavior, predation, and habitat imprinting. **Differential exploitation** of the resources available in a given environment (exploitation competition) occurs when one species is more efficient at using a limited resource than is its competitors (Nilsson 1967). Thus, when brown bullhead *(Ictalurus nebulosus)*, a bottom-adapted species, and the deep-bodied pumpkinseed *(Lepomis gibbosus)* are kept in separate aquaria, they both show a strong preference for benthic insect larvae over large zooplankton. However, when kept together in aquaria, the pumpkinseed switch to zooplankton, presumably because the bullhead is able to exploit the insects at a very rapid rate but is unable to feed effectively on the zooplankton (Ivlev 1961).

Interspecific **aggressive behavior,** especially when expressed as territoriality, may be one of the most important mechanisms that initially forces two similar species into different habitats or different diets (interference competition). This is demonstrated by the interactions described above for brown trout and arctic char, and those for striped and black surfperch.

Predation can reduce the numbers of potentially competing prey species in an area so that resources are not limiting for them. On the other hand, predators can also force species that might otherwise avoid competition into competitive situations. Thus largemouth bass apparently can keep juvenile bluegill and pumpkinseed sunfish confined to beds of vegetation, where they compete for limited supplies of invertebrates (Mittelbach 1984). Competition sometimes may be reduced when one species preys on the eggs and larvae of a potential competitor (**intraguild predation,** Polis and Holt 1992). Thus the rapid depletion of plankton-feeding whitefish in the Great Lakes following the invasion of alewife may have been as much the result of alewife predation on whitefish eggs and larvae as of direct competition.

Habitat imprinting is a poorly understood phenomenon that may permit species, or even morphs of the same species, to coexist with a minimum of interaction. The basic idea is that young fish become imprinted on the particular type of habitat with which they are first associated, and thereafter choose that habitat type over others that might be equally suitable. For example, juveniles of the reef damselfish, *Dascyllus aruanus,* will selectively choose, in an experimental situation, the type of coral from which they had originally been collected (Sale 1971). It has been hypothesized that one of the factors accounting for the extraordinary diversity of cichlid fishes in the rift lakes of Africa is that, because of the high degree of parental care, the juvenile cichlids become imprinted on the specific habitat of their parents, permitting divergence to occur over even minor habitat differences.

Although many mechanisms exist to reduce or avoid competition, coexistence of competitors is also often possible because the environment is so variable and resources are so "patchy" in their distribution. In general, potential competitors rarely reach population sizes at which resources become limiting. Some species have actually adopted life history strategies that allow them to take advantage of environmental variability, even though they are poor competitors. Thus the bay blenny *(Hypsoblennius gentilis)* manages to coexist with two similar species by having larvae that disperse quickly and early in the season to settle in newly disturbed areas before they are colonized by the other species (Stephens et al. 1970).

Of course, usually no single factor is responsible for the pattern of species segregation observed in any association of fishes (Ross 1986). This is well illustrated by the studies of P. A. Larkin and his students on Paul Lake, British Columbia, which show how competitive and predator-prey relationships interact to produce an observed community structure. Paul Lake was originally occupied only by rainbow trout, although redside shiner *(Richardsonius balteatus)* were introduced into the lake in 1945 (Johannes and Larkin 1961). Prior to the introduction of the shiner, the trout fry lived in the shallow waters of the lake where they fed primarily on small amphipods, crustaceans associated with beds of aquatic plants. The adult trout lived mostly in the open waters of the lake, feeding on surface insects and zooplankton, a diet that limited their ability to grow larger than 40 cm. Immediately following the introduction of the shiners (apparently by anglers) and their subsequent population explosion, it was found that both shiners and trout fry were feeding mostly on amphipods. However, the shiners were more efficient at capturing amphipods because they could penetrate the plant beds to get them, while the trout generally had to wait for the amphipods to emerge from the plants. In 15 years the amphipod population had become so depleted by the shiners that they were no longer a major item in the diet of either shiners or trout. Instead, the two species had become segregated, with the trout fry feeding mostly on aquatic and terrestrial insects and the shiners feeding mostly on zooplankton. Because the shiners had also moved out into the open waters of the lake, they came in contact with large rainbow trout. The trout avoided competing for zooplankton with the shiners by preying on the shiners themselves. As a result of these interactions, the overall biomass of fish in the lake was probably increased, although the biomass of rainbow trout was lower than previously. However, adult rainbow trout were able to grow to larger sizes because of the availability of shiners as prey.

SYMBIOSIS

Symbiosis means simply "living together," but is usually considered to include just three special types of interactions: mutualism, commensalism, and parasitism. Mimicry is another special type of symbiosis, but because examples in fishes come primarily from coral reefs, it will be discussed in Chapter 33.

Mutualism. Perhaps the most common instances of mutualism among fishes, where two or more species form a close association for their mutual benefit, are shoals involving more than one species. In streams and lakes of eastern North America, for example, it is common to find several species of minnows shoaling together. Presumably, such behavior confers on all the species the advantages of large shoals, which the species could not achieve individually (Morse 1977).

Another common mutualistic behavior is cleaning, where one species feeds on the external parasites and diseased tissues of other species. Both the cleaner and the fish being cleaned have special behavioral patterns that accompany the interactions. Cleaning behavior has been observed in many marine and freshwater fishes, but it has been most intensively studied in the cleaning wrasses (Labridae) of the Indo-Pacific Region, which make their living largely as cleaners. Typically, a cleaner wrasse has a station on a reef over which it displays its often brilliant color patterns. Large fish approaching the station to be cleaned assume a special relaxed posture and permit the cleaner wrasse to move over their bodies and even to enter their mouth cavities. Only rarely is a cleaner wrasse eaten. Although the advantages to both parties of cleaning behavior seem to be obvious, Losey (1978) points out that the relationship between the cleaner and the cleanee is not as clear-cut as once thought. When levels of parasitic infections are high, the fish being cleaned may gain from the cleaning, but usually their level of infection is low whether or not cleaner fish are available. Often the main food of cleaner fishes is mucus, pieces of fin, and other healthy tissues, as well as the eggs of reef fishes, making the cleaners more parasites or predators than mutualists. It appears that a fish being cleaned tolerates the attentions of the cleaner because it has a positive response to the tactile stimulation provided by the cleaner. This response appears to have evolved for other purposes and is taken advantage of by cleaners (Gorlick et al. 1978). In a sense, the cleaner is a vice of the cleanee! However, Foster (1985) provides evidence that wounded fish attended by cleaners have higher rates of recovery than might be expected.

Clearer examples (perhaps) of mutualism are the interactions between certain species of burrow-dwelling shrimp and small gobies (Gobiidae). The shrimp construct burrows inhabited by both species, so the goby gains a home by being associated with the shrimp. The shrimp benefits because the goby, with its superior vision, can warn the shrimp of approaching predators. The shrimp uses its long attenae to remain in physical contact with the goby when at the mouth of the burrow or when foraging nearby. A special series of signals between goby and shrimp have developed to enhance this relationship (Preston 1978).

Commensalism. While the goby-shrimp relationship is mutualistic, there are many other instances in which gobies use the burrows of invertebrates and the invertebrate gains nothing from the relationship (but is not harmed either). These are examples of commensalism. The remoras (Echeneidae) are a whole family of fish adapted for commensal living with large fish, particularly sharks. Each remora possesses a large sucker on top of its head with which it attaches to a host, who carries it to new sources of food. While the presence of remoras may have a negative impact on the hydrodynamics of their hosts, they may also benefit them by keeping them clear of parasites.

Parasitism. Clear examples of fishes acting as parasites are few. The pearlfishes (Carapidae) are one such example. These small, elongate fishes live in association with sea cucumbers (Holothuroidea) and actually enter the gut through the anus. Once inside, they penetrate into the body cavity of the host and feed on the gonads. The sea cucumbers usually survive the experience, although the activities of the pearlfishes may interfere with their reproduction (see Figure 20.5). Other examples are found in the South American catfish family Trichomycteridae. These catfish fish enter the gill cavities of large fish and feed on gill filaments and blood. One species, *Vandellia cirrhosa*, is renowned for entering, by mistake, the urogenital openings of bathing humans, with painful results for both species. While these examples fit most definitions of parasitism, there are many others that fall into the gray area between parasitism and predation, mostly because the predator (parasite) does not kill its larger prey (host). For example, there are the many species of fish that feed largely by removing scales from other species or by taking bites out of fins. Likewise, lampreys feed by attaching to the sides of fish and sucking out blood and other body fluids.

PARASITES AND PATHOGENS

The effects of parasites and pathogens on individual fish, on fish populations, and on fish communities is one of the least understood areas of aquatic ecology. All fish carry parasites and those parasites are carried at some cost to the fish. Fish that can minimize the effects of parasitism through biochemical or behavioral means will ultimately be at a reproductive advantage. Parasites (and pathogens) usually are under evolutionary constraints not to kill their hosts, at least until the time is right. Some tapeworms, for example, may change the behavior of their host, such as three-spine stickleback, in order to ensure the host's being eaten by a predatory bird that is host to the next stage of the parasite's life cycle (Milinski 1985). Occasionally, massive die-offs of fish are observed in response to parasites or pathogens. Wurtsbaugh and Tapia (1988) observed a major kill of fish in Lake Titicaca as the result of an infestation of a parasitic protozoan. Likewise, in 1973 a bacterial disease eliminated about 80% of the spawning run of steelhead rainbow trout in the Snake River (Oregon and Idaho). This disease is virulent mainly when water temperatures are warm, such as occurred in 1973, a drought year (Becker and Fugihara 1978). During most years, water temperatures during the time of steelhead runs are too cold for the disease to have an effect. The resident native cyprinids, which regularly experience warm temperatures in the river, are much more resistant to the disease. There is a growing realization that the absence of fish from some apparently suitable waters, which may be attributed to zoogeographic barriers, probably results from the presence of resident pathogens (Bayley and Li 1993).

INTRASPECIFIC INTERACTIONS

The interactions among members of the same species are similar in many respects to those among individuals of different species. Because most intraspecific interactions may alter the chances that particular combinations of genes will be passed on to the next generation, intense intraspecific interactions are more the rule than the exception. Thus the territorial behavior that causes salmon and trout species to segregate is even more important within each species as a way to divide up the limited space available for feeding and reproduction. In streams, trout that cannot find a suitable space to establish themselves must either colonize new areas or be eaten by predators.

In some species, **intraspecific competition** may be one of the main mechanisms regulating population size. In pelagic sardines and anchovies, high populations may reduce plankton densities, so growth rates of individual fish may be reduced. This in turn reduces the ability of individual fish to produce eggs or sperm, resulting in fewer young and a smaller population in the following years. In the absence of severe environmental fluctuations, intraspecific competition alone will produce regular population oscillations in such species.

Cannibalism is a form of predation that is surprisingly common in fish, presumably because the young are typically so small compared to the parents and because external fertilization provides plenty of opportunity for it. For example, both sticklebacks and sunfish regularly raid the nests of conspecifics to consume developing embryos. Males may raid neighboring nests, or schools of nonbreeding fish may overwhelm a guarding male to consume its young. In the case of bluegill sunfish, some females engage in "pseudocourtship" of males in order to gain access to a nest and consume its contents (Dominey and Blumer 1984). While cannibalism is common, the life history strategies of many fishes result in spatial segregation of adults and young, so that it is less likely to occur. Thus salmon and herring have breeding grounds that are far removed from the adult feeding areas. Many marine and lake-dwelling fish have planktonic larvae that spend the most vulnerable stage of their life history in a food-rich environment that is quite different from that of the adults.

Supplemental Readings

Diana 1995; Fausch 1988; Grossman et al. 1982; Ross 1986; Wooton 1990.

CHAPTER 28

Temperate Streams

Temperate streams are among the better-understood aquatic environments because of their accessibility and because they contain many species of sport fish. Unfortunately for the fish, however, these streams are also among the most manipulated of aquatic habitats, being dammed, diverted, polluted, channelized, or otherwise altered for the supposed good of humankind. Despite the radical changes in the amount and quality of water flowing through temperate streams, there have been few extinctions of temperate-stream fish species, although local faunal depletions are common. The reason for this is that most temperate-stream fishes are adapted for living in an environment that fluctuates, often considerably, on a daily and seasonal basis. Climatic changes also have created long-term environmental fluctuations that have had to be survived. Thus most temperate-stream fishes are able to maintain populations under a wide range of physical and chemical conditions; they are also capable of successfully interacting with many other fish species, and are quick to colonize new areas of suitable habitat. Usually, however, each species tends to be found in a rather predictable set of conditions, as part of a distinct faunal assemblage. The purpose of this chapter, therefore, is to describe how environmental factors affect the distribution and abundance of stream fish, and how interactions among the fish affect the composition of fish assemblages over broad geographic areas as well as in specific habitats.

FACTORS THAT AFFECT DISTRIBUTION

It is convenient to divide the factors that affect the distribution of stream fishes into four categories: physical, chemical, biological, and zoogeographic. Naturally, the distribution pattern of any one species is caused by an interaction of factors from all four categories.

Physical Factors

In the study of stream fish, four complex factors have proven most useful in predicting patterns of distribution and abundance: temperature regime, gradient, stream order, and flow regime. Fisheries managers have long recognized the importance of temperature in fish distribution and have divided the fluvial world into warm-water streams and cold-water streams. In North America, warm water-streams have temperatures that exceed 24°C to 26°C for extended periods of time and are characterized by species such as smallmouth bass, green sunfish, catfish, and a diversity of small fishes, especially cyprinids and darters (Percidae). In contrast, cold-water streams seldom exceed 24°C to 26°C and are characterized by trout and sculpins. Many of the "problem" streams of fishery managers are streams that do not easily fit into either category and consequently may not provide good fishing for any of the standard game fish. For example, when flows of a cold-water stream are reduced by a dam, suckers (Catostomidae) and minnows (Cyprinidae) may invade further upstream, even if the water temperatures are still suitable for trout. This is because the upstream limits of many "warm-water" fishes may be limited more by other factors than by temperature, particularly water velocity. Alternately, a slight upward shift in water temperature may make conditions more suitable for the suckers and minnows, resulting in a sudden increase in their abundance. Even in the face of presumed competition from such fishes, trout may still maintain the upper hand as long as the water temperatures remain fairly cold. At low temperatures, trout have comparatively high standard metabolic rates and are more active. They are therefore able to utilize the food resources more effectively than most other species.

Even in streams that fall clearly into the warm-water or cold-water catagories, there are considerable differences in the temperature tolerances and preferences of the species present. Brown trout, at least in Colorado, are usually found in streams that exceed 13°C for extended periods of time (Vincent and Miller 1969), while brook trout are rarely successful in such waters, especially when other species of trout are present. On the other hand, some warm-water species, such as the Rio Grande perch (*Cichlasoma cyanoguttatum*), cannot survive temperatures lower than 14°C to 18°C (Deacon and Minckley 1974). In some species the temperature tolerances of different life history stages may be different. In speckled dace (*Rhinichthys osculus*) the young can survive in water 2°C warmer than the maximum temperature adults can tolerate, which may permit them to survive periods of extreme low water in their streams (John 1964).

While temperature is of great importance in determining the broad distribution patterns of stream fishes, gradient (the number of meters of drop per kilometer of stream) is often of equal importance. This is because gradient has a profound influence on the water velocity and substrates and on the number, size, and depth of pools. Where gradients are high, the streams tend to have little slow water and their bottoms are predominantly bedrock, boulders, and cobbles, and there are few deep pools. More often than not, water temperatures are also cool, the water is saturated with oxygen, and the dominant fishes are trout and sculpins.

At the opposite end of the spectrum are the sluggish, muddy-bottomed reaches of low-gradient streams with a fish fauna characterized by deep-bodied forms; in big rivers, however, the water velocities are often high despite low gradients. In general, as the gradient increases, the diversity of habitat for fish decreases and fewer species of fish are present. For fish that feed on insects drifting in the water, there is an optimal range of velocity conditions for feeding associated with each species or size class within a species (Hill and Grossman 1993). Thus streams with moderate gradients are likely to have the highest number of drift-feeding species. The importance of habitat diversity is demonstrated by the effects of stream channelization. In a channelized section of stream, not only is the gradient increased (because the stream drops the same amount but over a shorter distance in the straightened channel), but habitat variety (e.g., large pools) is reduced. As a result, the species, numbers, and biomass of fish are also reduced. Thus when sections of a mountain stream in California were channelized, speckled dace and sculpin became dominant while populations of two species of trout decreased greatly, and the Modoc sucker (*Catostomus microps*, an endangered species) nearly disappeared altogether (Moyle 1976b).

Stream gradient and water temperature both contribute to the impact of the third factor, stream order, which is a means of classifying streams according to a complex of physical factors. Stream systems can be ordered according to their pattern of branching. The headwater streams are first-order streams and unite to form second-order streams, which in turn unite to form third-order streams, and so on until the main river is reached. In most systems first-order streams are the smallest, coldest, and highest-gradient streams, and they generally contain the fewest species of fish. As the stream order increases, habitat diversity, stream size, turbidity, and temperatures usually increase as well, while gradient and environmental fluctuations usually decrease. As a consequence, the number of species tends to increase with stream order. Thus in eastern Kentucky, Kuehne (1962) found that first-, second-, third-, and fourth-order streams contained, respectively, 1, 12, 20, and 27 species of fish. In most instances, as stream order increases, species are progressively added but few drop out. The ones that do drop out are either fishes adapted to cold water, such as brook trout and sculpins, or species that are adapted for surviving in intermittent headwater streams, such as the fathead minnow (*Pimephales promelas*) or green sunfish (*Lepomis cyanellus*). The latter species are capable of surviving under harsh physical and chemical conditions but tend to be eliminated from complex fish communities by predation or competition (although they may hang on in edge habitats). In some systems the number of species actually decreases in the highest-order streams, usually because of pollution, water removal by humans, or floods.

As might be expected, the trophic structure (food webs) of the fish community in a stream system changes with order. In first-order streams the dominant fishes usually feed largely either on insects that drop into the water from the overhanging vegetation (e.g., brook trout, creek chub), or on detritus (e.g., California roach, fathead minnow).

TABLE 28–1   OCCURRENCE (X) OF FISH SPECIES IN THE FIRST-, SECOND-, AND THIRD-ORDER STREAM PORTIONS OF CLEMONS FORK, KENTUCKY

Species	Food*	Order		
		First	Second	Third
Semotilus atrorgaculatus	T	X	X	X
Campostoma anomalum	A		X	X
Etheostoma sagitta	I		X	X
Etheostoma nigrum	I		X	X
Etheostoma flabellare	I		X	X
Etheostoma caeruleum	I		X	X
Hypentelium nigricans	I		X	X
Catostomus commersoni	A		X	X
Ericymba buccata	I			X
Notropis ardens	T			X
Notropis chrysocephalus	T			X
Pimephales notatus	D			X
Ambloplites rupestris	V			X
Lepomis megalotis	V			X
Micropterus dolomieui	V			X

Source: After Lotrich 1973.

*The principal food type of each species is indicated by the letters as follows: T—terrestrial insects; A—algae; I—aquatic invertebrates; D—detritus; V—vertebrates, principally fish.

In the downstream progression toward higher-order streams, predators on aquatic insects are added and then piscivores, herbivores, and other specialists (Table 28-1).

One factor that greatly modifies the usefulness of the preceding three factors as predictors of distribution patterns is fluctuation in flow, either annually or over a longer period. Severe floods or extreme low flows eliminate or reduce populations of some fishes from sections of stream where they would be expected to occur, while long periods of moderate fluctuations in flow may allow species normally found only in high-order streams to invade those of lower orders. The actual extirpation of a species from an area by a flood is a relatively rare event, because most adult fishes native to a stream system seem to be able to find refuge during floods. In California, streams that maintain a natural flow regime with frequent floods typically maintain their native fishes; regulated streams are susceptible to invasion by species imported from eastern North America (Baltz and Moyle 1993). Similarly, a tremendous flood in the Salt River, Arizona, virtually eliminated the exotic fishes present, while the native suckers survived (Deacon and Minckley 1974). Floods may also modify fish populations by washing away developing embryos or larvae. This is a common cause of missing year classes in stream fishes. Although floods have many negative effects on stream fishes, many species actually require them for reproduction, because they spawn on flooded vegetation and use flooded areas as nursery grounds for their young (Starrett 1951). Indeed, the loss of flood plains in large river systems is a major cause of the decline of riverine fishes because the forested areas that once flooded annually were major spawning and nursery areas for the fish (Bayley 1995).

Fish may also be eliminated from streams by low flows, whether caused by drought or by human diversion of water. P. W. Smith (1971) lists 12 species whose range in Illinois has been greatly reduced by long-term droughts. If a stream has not dried up completely, fishes may be eliminated by their inability to tolerate high temperatures, low oxygen levels, or even heavy growth of aquatic plants created by the low water. When more favorable conditions return to the stream, the "normal" fish fauna returns gradually. The order of appearance of the species depends on their relative abilities to colonize new waters or to withstand extreme conditions (Larimore et al. 1959). Examples of rapid colonizers are red shiner *(Cyprinella lutrensis)*, fathead minnow, Rio Grande killifish *(Fundulus zebrinus)*, mosquitofish, and green sunfish. In some desert streams in Arizona the dominant species may change depending on the amount of water flowing. During wet years the speckled dace and other species flourish, but during dry years the longfin dace *(Agosia chrysogaster)* may be the only fish found in abundance (Deacon and Minckley 1974). In general, the more variable the flows in a stream, the more variable the fish populations and the lower the number of species. For example, fish assemblages in the streams of Panama, with fairly constant flows, are richer and much more predictable than fish assemblages in Minnesota or Illinois streams that are of similar size but have much more variable flows (Angermeier and Schlosser 1989).

Chemical Factors

Because they flow over varied substrates, streams tend to be chemically well buffered and also well oxygenated. There are nevertheless broad relationships between fish distributions and the chemistry of the water. In Arkansas, for example, there are distinct clusters of species found along a gradient of water quality variables such as total dissolved solids, hardness, conductivity, and dissolved oxygen, although these variables are associated with different physical habitats as well (Matthews et al. 1992). Thus fish found in streams in the Ozark uplands are associated with high dissolved-oxygen levels, high alkalinities, low conductivities, and other factors that typify "clean" water. Under more extreme conditions, the ability of chemical factors to limit fish distribution becomes more apparent. Thus acid waters draining mines and roadfills are a major limiting factor of stream fish in parts of the southeastern United States (e.g., Huckabee et al. 1975), affecting fish through a combination of low pH and heavy metal and sulfide poisoning. In Pennsylvania, sculpins (Cottidae) are absent from streams subject to episodic acidification due to acid rain (Carline et al. 1994). In Oklahoma there is a definite group of fishes that is associated with moderately saline streams. This group increases in abundance in streams polluted by brine from oil-drilling operations (Stevenson et al. 1974). Many of the chemicals that may limit fish distribution in both acid and saline waters are present in sewage (e.g., heavy metals, chlorine), and as a result, many fish species may be absent from the immediate vicinity of sewage outfalls (Tsai 1973). Equally important, however, is the depletion of oxygen in the water caused by decay of the organic matter in sewage. This favors species such as common carp that are tolerant of low oxygen levels.

Biological Factors

Temperate-stream fish are, for the most part, members of complex communities. Yet because the physical environment fluctuates so much, the particular set of organisms with which any species interacts is likely to vary considerably from place to place, from year to year, and even from season to season. As a result, most species are quite flexible in their interactions with other organisms, particularly other fishes, although the morphological, physiological, and behavioral characteristics of each species place definite limits on these interactions. The ecology of species of minnows (Cyprinidae) in North American streams, for example, can be predicted to a certain extent from their morphology (Douglas and Matthews 1992). Often, however, the distribution of stream fish may be limited by predator-prey, competitive, and symbiotic interactions with other fish, including members of the same species (intraspecific interactions).

Predator-prey interactions. Predation is probably the ultimate cause of death of most stream fishes. Thus an increase in complex cover in a stream, such as fallen trees, undercut banks, and boulders, increases the numbers of fish as well as the complexity of the fish community. The presence of large woody debris (such as fallen trees) in the stream channel greatly increases the production of coho salmon from Pacific coast streams and is a strong argument for limits on the removal of streamside trees by logging (Fausch and Northcote 1992). The cover provided by the fallen trees helps small salmon to avoid predators such as larger fish, birds, and snakes. Often small fish seek shallow water in order to avoid predatory fish, but they must leave the shallow water when they become big enough to be sought after by predatory wading birds (Harvey and Stewart 1991). Likewise, the abundance of large fish in a stream depends on adequate cover, such as deep pools and deeply undercut banks, which the fish can use to avoid their own predators, such as herons, otters, and humans. In Brier Creek, Oklahoma, the abundance of stonerollers (*Campostoma anomalum*), a minnow that grazes on algae, is a favorite prey of largemouth bass (*Micropterus salmoides*). Therefore, in pools large enough to contain large bass, stonerollers are often rare; as a consequence, algae carpet the rocks much more thickly than in pools without bass (Power and Matthews 1983).

Not surprisingly, when piscivorous fish are introduced into a stream, it entire biota can sometimes be drastically altered, from algae to invertebrates to fish. For example, Lemly (1985) showed that when green sunfish were introduced into piedmont streams of North Carolina, they eliminated or greatly reduced populations of minnows that were formerly dominant species. Despite results like these, attempts to increase salmon and trout production through predator-control programs on streams generally have not worked well. The reason is that many other factors operate to counterbalance the reduced predation. Control of predatory birds, such as mergansers and kingfishers, on salmon streams may cause an increase in the numbers of young salmon. However, this results in an increase in competition for food among the juvenile salmon and consequently they are likely to go to sea at smaller sizes. This makes them more vulnerable to marine predators, and the increased predation at sea compensates for the decreased predation in the streams.

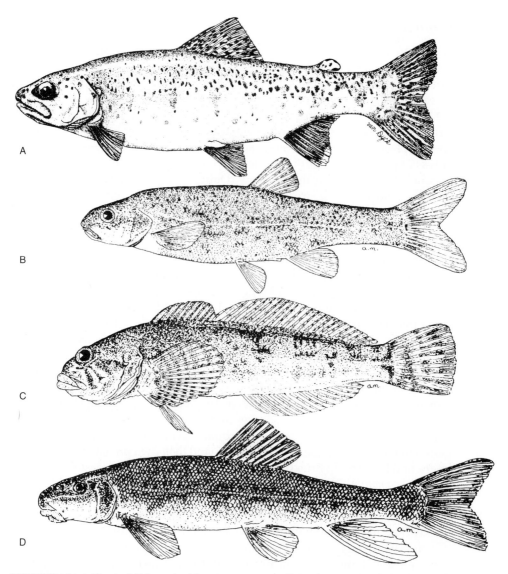

FIGURE 28.1 *Typical fishes of cold-water streams of North America: (A) trout*
(Oncorhynchus); *(B) dace* (Rhinichthys); *(C) sculpin* (Cottus); *and (D) sucker*
(Catostomus). *(From Moyle 1976a.)*

Competitive interactions. Most temperate-stream fishes have a considerable degree of behavioral plasticity that allows them to interact successfully with a variety
of other species, in a way that minimizes competition for food and space. The
plasticity of each species does have distinct limits that are imposed by its morphology, physiology, and total behavioral repertoire. Much of the ecological segregation observed among temperate-stream fishes results from differences in the morphology of the species. For example, a typical North American cold-water stream

may contain four species of fish: a trout (Salmonidae), a dace (Cyprinidae), a sculpin (Cottidae), and a sucker (Catostomidae) (Fig. 28.1). Body shape alone indicates that the trout is a fast-swimming predator, the sucker a bottom-oriented suction-feeder, the sculpin a bottom-dwelling ambusher of large invertebrates, and the dace an active, bottom-oriented browser on small organisms. In warm-water streams, such as those of the eastern United States, the number of species tends to be much higher and morphological differences among the species tend not to be as sharp, but such differences nevertheless can account for much of the segregation observed (Gatz 1979).

Although morphological differences among species can often explain habitat differences, behavioral differences that lead to differences in feeding habits and microhabitats are probably the most important mechanisms of segregation among species that regularly occur together. Such species may segregate according to where in the water column they take their food, the time of day they feed, the type of food eaten, and the size of food items taken. There may also be seasonal changes in distribution that reduce competition. Some of the best examples of these rather subtle kinds of segregation occur among the many species of small, silvery minnows referred to as "shiners." Many of the species are quite similar to one another, and typically two or more species are found together, in different combinations. In a Wisconsin stream, Mendelson (1975) found that four species of shiners minimized competition for food by feeding at different places in the water column, in slightly different microhabitats (e.g., head of pool vs. bottom of pool), on different types of food (drifting or bottom-dwelling organisms), and on different sizes of food. The difference between any two species in any one of the categories is not sharp, but the overall differences in all four categories result in apparent subdivision of the food and spatial resources.

Among the most interesting aspects of stream fish ecology are the behavioral mechanisms that result in the observed segregation. It appears that the two main mechanisms are aggressive behavior and differential exploitation (see Chapter 27). Among salmonids, aggressive behavior can determine hierarchies within species as well as between them. In streams of the Pacific Northwest, the use of different microhabitats by similar-sized juveniles of different species is often determined by the basic hierarchy: coho salmon > rainbow trout > cutthroat trout > chinook salmon (Bayley and Li 1992). Under this arrangement, coho salmon often occupy the best habitats for feeding and cover. Likewise, juvenile Atlantic salmon (*Salmo salar*) aggressively defend territories against minnows and suckers as well as other salmon (Symons 1976). Such aggressive interactions, although common in salmonids, are less frequent in other families of stream fishes, suggesting that differential exploitation is the main mechanism that segregates similar species in streams. Presumably the many species of shiners have broader feeding habits and occupy a wider range of microhabitats when by themselves than when they occur with similar species. Just how each species specializes in the presence of another depends on slight differences in body morphology (e.g., subterminal vs. terminal mouths) that give each species advantages in exploiting slightly different parts of the environment.

Despite the many demonstrations of ecological segregation among temperate-stream fishes, the frequent observation of large overlaps in the use of food and space indicates that such resources may not always be limiting fish populations. This is especially true in the complex fish assemblages of warm-water streams in eastern North America, particularly those heavily disturbed by humans or recovering from the effects of Pleistocene glaciation. In such cases, unpredictable fluctuations in the environment may reduce the ability of each species to reproduce successfully every year, or of their young to survive the first few months of life. Because such factors can affect each species differently, no one species can maintain dominance through competition indefinitely (Schlosser 1982; Grossman et al. 1982).

Symbiotic interactions. Clear examples of parasitism, commensalism, or mutualism affecting the distribution and abundance of stream fish are hard to find. In the western United States, infestations of exotic parasites brought in with exotic fishes have been given some blame for the decline of the native fish faunas (e.g., Vanicek and Kramer 1969). Under more natural conditions, stream fish that are confined to narrow habitats, such as riffles, may have fewer parasites than those found in broader or quieter habitats (Guegan et al. 1992). This may explain why the parasite load of fish sometimes increases when stream flow is reduced (Heckmann et al. 1986). In the Pit River system of California, the presence of *Ceratomyxa shasta*, an infectious protozoan to which the native trouts are resistant, has made the establishment of exotic trout strains difficult, indicating that disease does have some potential for limiting fish distribution. At the other end of the symbiotic spectrum, there is some evidence that the multispecies shoals of minnows frequently encountered in streams may function to give protection from predators for all species, while still permitting members to retain their feeding specializations (Mendelson 1975).

Intraspecific interactions. In streams it is common for young fish to be ecologically segregated from the adults. Many stream fishes make spawning migrations up small tributary streams, where the young may spend the first year or so of their lives without having to compete with the adults for food and space. In situations where the juveniles and the adults occur together there is frequently microhabitat segregation or segregation by feeding habits (Moyle and Vondracek 1985). Gee and Northcote (1963) found that the young of two species of dace shoaled together in shallow water, but as they matured the two species moved into different habitats, one into pools and one into riffles. Among trout, which consume a wide variety of organisms, the segregation among different-sized individuals of the same species is largely based on size of food items taken. Juvenile trout typically eat large numbers of small fly and mayfly larvae, while adults eat large stoneflies and caddisflies. Presumably this difference in food is why large trout typically tolerate small trout within their dominance hierarchies, even though one of the main functions of the hierarchies is to reduce competition for food among members of the same species.

Zoogeographic factors

One of the factors complicating any study of a local stream fauna is the presence of zoogeographic barriers that prevent fish from moving into habitats they presently do not occupy even though they are suitable for them. While sections of stream with different temperatures, salinities, or flow may act as barriers to some specialized species, zoogeographic barriers are usually waterfalls or at least high-gradient areas. For example, St. Anthony Falls in Minnesota has acted as a major barrier for fishes to the upper Mississippi River (Eddy et al. 1963). Likewise, Kanawha Falls in West Virginia, although only 7.3 m high, has been a major factor separating the fishes of the upper and lower Kanawha River. The upper river contains 49 species, including six endemic forms, while the river below the falls contains over 92 native species. Perhaps because of the "undersaturated" fauna (but also because of reservoirs and other habitat changes), the upper river now supports an additional 37 introduced species, while the lower river supports only about 12 introduced species (Hocutt et al. 1986).

ZONATION

Despite the fact that the distribution patterns of fish species are determined largely by interactions between the fish and various physical and chemical factors, in most regions there are groups of species that all respond to these factors in a similar fashion. Such species tend to occur together in particular stream environments, forming recognizable associations. Since such associations of species tend to replace one another as the stream environment changes from the high-gradient headwaters to the low-gradient river on the valley floor, they and the physical environment they typify are together called **fish zones.** Generally, the species found together in a fish zone complement one another ecologically, thereby minimizing competition and presumably maximizing the utilization of the resources present. However, fish zones are not sharply distinct from one another but rather blend together as the environment changes. Indeed, many fish species may typify several zones because, frequently, downstream zones are created mainly by the addition of species without any deletions. For example, in most temperate-stream systems the uppermost waters are dominated by trout and are referred to as the Trout Zone. However, trout typically also occur in one or more downstream zones, usually becoming less and less abundant relative to other species as one moves downstream. In some streams, the downstream change in the fish fauna is so gradual that clearly recognizable fish zones cannot be distinguished. In streams where zones can be recognized, to do so greatly facilitates the descriptions of regional and local fish faunas, and can even permit management of streams for assemblages of species rather than just for individual game-fish species. Examples of fish zones can be found in Europe (Huet 1959), central California (Moyle and Nichols 1974), and Oklahoma (Smith and Powell 1971).

Despite the fact that fish zones in different regions contain different species, the zones often have much in common in terms of environmental factors and fish morphology. Three general types of zones can therefore be recognized in most stream systems: an erosional zone, an intermediate zone, and a depositional zone (Cummins 1972). **Erosional zones** occur in high-gradient regions and are characterized by rocky bottoms and swift, usually cold water. Long riffles and small pools are the main habitat types. The fishes of the erosional zones tend to be streamlined, active forms such as trout, and small bottom-dwelling forms such as sculpins and dace. In regions where gradients in headwater streams are not very high, such as the central United States, the classic cold-water erosional zone may be replaced by zones dominated by warm-water fishes (e.g., fathead minnow, green sunfish) adapted for fluctuating or extreme conditions, such as are found in the headwaters of Oklahoma streams or in streams that drain swamps.

Intermediate zones characterize the long middle reaches of tributary streams. They typically have moderate gradients, warm water, and about equal amounts of shallow riffles, deep rock-bottomed or mud-bottomed pools, and runs that undercut the banks. They also merge imperceptibly with the erosional zones above and the depositional zones below and may be subdivided into two or more fish zones. In North America the typical fishes of the intermediate zones are minnows, suckers, sunfishes (Centrarchidae), darters (Etheostomatinae), and madtom catfishes *(Noturus)*. None of these forms is particularly deep bodied, and many specialize in particular habitats within the zone.

Depositional zones occur in the warm, turbid, and sluggish lower reaches of stream systems where bottoms are muddy and beds of aquatic plants common. A wide variety of fishes occur here, but most typical are deep-bodied forms such as those adapted for bottom feeding (e.g., carpsuckers, *Carpiodes*), picking up small invertebrates from plants (e.g., sunfish), plankton feeding (shads, *Dorosoma*), or predation (centrarchid basses). The assemblages of fishes are nearly the same as those found in lakes in the regions. Where a river runs into the sea, the depositional zone will merge gradually with an estuarine zone that contains a mixture of euryhaline freshwater and saltwater fishes (see Chapter 31).

Fish zones are as much descriptive tools of fish biologists as they are real entities. They typically merge into one another very gradually and in low-gradient areas one "zone" may occupy many miles of stream. In some streams no apparent zones exist because the distribution patterns of the fishes present do not coincide enough to form easily identified associations of species. It is also not uncommon for the sequence of zones described to be absent because the lower reaches of a stream have a higher gradient than the upper reaches (e.g., Hocutt and Stauffer 1975), or because high-gradient stretches are interspersed with low-gradient stretches (e.g., Barber and Minckley 1966).

CONCLUSIONS: FISH COMMUNITIES

The presence of fish zones indicates that distinct, recognizable assemblages of stream fishes exist. It is generally assumed that such assemblages are not just groups of fishes that co-occur because of common physiological responses to environmental conditions, but that they are coevolved assemblages that efficiently subdivide the resources available. While many stream communities clearly show such coevolved characteristics, others are more ambiguous (Moyle and Vondracek 1985). This ambiguity may be the result of inadequate study of complex stream fish assemblages; however, there are also many indications that environmental fluctuations often prevent fish populations from reaching high enough numbers so that resources are limiting and competitive segregation necessary (Angermeier and Schlosser 1989). For example, a severe summer freshet washed nearly all of one species of darter (*Etheostoma*) out of a Minnesota stream, apparently because they were spawning in riffles at the time. Despite the absence of this once-abundant species, Coon (1982) could detect no expansion of the niches of two other darter species that were present in the stream but were not affected by the flood. Such drastic changes in the species composition of fish communities as well as the lack of striking ecological segregation among similar species seem to be common in streams of northeastern North America. Differing interpretations of such information can lead to drastically different conclusions about the nature of stream fish communities (Grossman et al. 1982; Rahel et al. 1984; Yant et al. 1984; Herbold 1984). It is clear, however, that each stream fish community is the result of a unique combination of historical, zoogeographic, physical, chemical, and biological factors and that the structured systems so frequently observed are the result of the remarkable adaptability of most fish species.

Supplemental Readings

Bayley and Li 1993; Matthews and Heins 1987; Moyle and Li 1979; Whitton 1975.

CHAPTER 29

Temperate Lakes and  Reservoirs

Most lakes and reservoirs are ephemeral, with ages ranging from 50 to several thousand years. They disappear as they fill with sediment, or dry up in response to changes in climate, or are covered by advancing continental glaciers. They are also created rather easily, by water collecting in depressions and excavations left by various natural processes such as the scouring action of glaciers, or by the blockage of rivers by landslides, or from oxbows pinched off by meandering rivers. In recent years humans have been creating "lakes" by the thousands by impounding rivers. In North America alone, there are now over 1500 reservoirs with a surface area of 200 hectares or greater, and countless smaller ones. In view of the impermanence of lakes, it is not surprising to find that there are comparatively few species of fish in the North Temperate and Arctic regions that are adapted only for life in lakes. Instead, most lake fishes are the same as those found in nearby streams, especially large rivers. Many lake populations have made modest behavioral, physiological, and morphological adaptations to the lake environment, and a number of species are most abundant in lakes, yet most of them still must rely on streams for dispersal and long-term survival as species. The main exceptions to this rule are fishes that occur in very large lakes, such as the species complexes of salmonids found in the Great Lakes and the unique fish fauna of Lake Baikal in the Soviet Union. Baikal is not only one of the largest and deepest lakes in the world but is also one of the oldest (Kozhov 1963).

Despite the paucity of fish species that are highly specialized for lake living, lakes have many special characteristics that restrict the distribution of fish within and among them. The effects of physical, chemical, temporal, biological, and zoogeographical factors on fish result in distinctive regional fish faunas as well as partitioning by the fishes of the ecological resources of each lake.

PHYSICAL FACTORS

The principal physical factors that affect the distribution and abundance of fish in lakes are temperature, light, water movement, water-level fluctuations, size (surface area and depth), and substrate.

Temperature. Fisheries managers have long recognized that the basic fish fauna of a lake is determined in large part by temperature. As a consequence, they have tended to divide lakes into three basic types: (1) cold-water lakes, in which the dominant sport or commercial fishes are salmonids; (2) warm-water lakes, in which the dominant sport or commercial fishes are centrarchids (black basses and sunfishes), percids (perch and walleye), esocids (pike), and percichthyids (white, yellow, and striped basses); and (3) two-story lakes, with warm-water fishes in the warm upper layer (epilimnion) and cold-water fishes in the deep water (hypolimnion). There are, of course, many lakes that do not fit nicely into any of the three categories, but the system does demonstrate that in lakes, as in streams, temperature is a major determinant of distribution patterns. The presence of the two-story lake category indicates that temperature also is important in determining distribution patterns within lakes, at least during the summer months. When the thermocline forms during spring in such lakes, separating the epilimnion (warm surface waters) from the hypolimnion (cold deep waters), fish species quickly segregate by temperature preferences.

Even in lakes that are not easily categorized, temperature may be one of the main determinants of distribution. For example, in Lake Michigan the native fishes show fairly narrow ranges of preferred temperatures and seem to have segregated within the lake partly on the basis of these temperature preferences. One of the reasons why the introduction of the alewife *(Alosa pseudoharenqus)* has been so disruptive to the fish communities of the lake is that it occupies a broad range of temperatures and hence depletes zooplankton depended on by native fishes living both above and below the thermocline (Wells 1968).

Light. Light has many rather subtle effects on fish distribution patterns within and between lakes. Most warm-water lakes are rather turbid, so the typical deepwater fishes are species that do not have to rely on vision for prey capture, such as catfish, carp, and suckers. In such lakes, most aquatic plant growth is also in shallow water. Because beds of aquatic plants increase both habitat diversity and abundance of invertebrates, fish species and numbers tend to be highest in shallow water. Pelagic plankton-feeding fishes tend to concentrate in well-lighted waters, where their prey is most visible. For example, in highly turbid Clear Lake, California, the inland silverside *(Menidia beryllina)* is found almost exclusively in the upper meter of the water column. In contrast, in lakes that are fairly clear, including most cold-water lakes, vision-oriented predators such as lake trout *(Salvelinus namaycush)* are found at considerable depths. One predatory species that is successful in both turbid and clear lakes is the walleye *(Stizostedion vitreum),* which has exceptionally large eyes equipped with a light-gathering layer, the tapetum lucidum. In turbid lakes the walleye tends to feed during the day, while in clear lakes its feeding tends to be crepuscular (Ryder 1977).

Curiously, the clarity of lakes is often related to the abundance of plankton-feeding fish because of "top down" control of ecosystem structure. Where abundances of these fish are high, water clarity is often lowered because the fish feed on large zooplankton species which in turn graze on the algae. When zooplankton populations are reduced, the algae densities are higher so light does not penetrate as far into the lake. Thus, when there was a mass die-off of planktivores in Lake Mendota, Wisconsin, the lake became substantially clearer (Vanni et al. 1990). In small lakes, the reduced penetration of light resulting from fish predation can substantially change other lake characteristics as well, such as decreasing the depth of the thermocline (Mazumder 1990) and reducing the growth of beds of aquatic plants (McQueen 1990).

Water movements. Steady and predictable currents, such as those existing in the oceans, seldom occur in natural lakes, yet the movement of water by winds can have considerable impact on fish distribution within a lake. A series of days with wind blowing from one direction can cause zooplankton to concentrate along the lee shore. This may result in a concentration of zooplankton-feeding fishes as well. The distribution of larval fishes that drift in the surface waters of a lake may be quite patchy because of temporary gyres and currents created by winds, although these same currents also concentrate the zooplankton on which the larval fish feed. On the other hand, the discharge of water from reservoirs at critical times of the year may result in substantial losses of planktonic larvae, which in turn will greatly affect the number of adult fishes of certain species (Walburg 1971).

As these examples indicate, reservoirs frequently have conditions that are intermediate between those found in rivers and those in natural lakes, because the demand for the water they store is likely to cause detectable currents at both their upper and their lower ends. Consequently, the fish at the upper end of a reservoir may be somewhat different from those found in the more lake-like middle areas. In many North American reservoirs, smallmouth bass *(Micropterus dolomieui)* are most abundant at the upper ends of the reservoirs and largemouth bass *(M. salmoides)* most abundant in other areas. Although such current-related patterns of distribution are most characteristic of reservoirs, more subtle versions can be found in natural lakes. Most natural lakes have definite inlets and outlets, which create a general, if barely detectable, pattern of flow through the lake. Usually such patterns are too slight to affect fish distribution within the lake. However, in Lake Memphremagog, on the border of Quebec and Vermont, such flow results in graduallly decreasing amounts of nutrients from the inlet end of the lake to the outlet end and corresponding drops in the abundance and diversity of fish species (Gascon and Leggett 1977).

Water-level fluctuations. These are primarily a problem to fish in reservoirs and lakes with regulated water levels. Rapid drops in water level may expose the nests of spawning centrachids, especially largemouth bass; and rapid rises in water level may cover the nests with a depth of water intolerable to the spawning fish. Such fluctuations also prevent the establishment of plants such as cattails and willows along the reservoir edges. In natural lakes, flooded shoreline marshes are important spring spawning sites for fish such as northern pike *(Esox lucius)*. Later in the year, the emergent vegetation serves as cover for the young of many species, such as largemouth bass and carp. Drops in water level may also create barriers to migrations made by lake-dwelling species that spawn in streams. In Pyramid Lake, Nevada, the near extinction of the cui-ui *(Chasmistes cujus)* and the extinction of cutthroat trout *(Oncorhynchus clarki)* were largely caused by reduced flows into the lake from the Truckee River, which had been diverted for irrigation. The drop in lake level exposed an extensive, shallow delta that was impassable to the spawning fish.

Size. Three aspects of lake size particularly affect both the number of species and the total fish production in lakes: surface area, mean depth, and shoreline length. The relationship of surface area to number of species is not a strong one because so many other factors, especially zoogeographic factors, can affect the number of species. However, in general, the greater the surface area the more species are likely to be present (Barbour and Brown 1974). One factor that obscures the relationship between surface area and fish numbers is the negative relationship between mean depth and species number, as well as with standing crop (total fish biomass). Deep water in lakes is often cold, poorly lighted, and poorly oxygenated and hence supports few fish. The length of shoreline has the opposite effect of depth; usually, more shoreline means more species. All three of these size variables indicate one thing: Within a zoogeographic region, as habitat variety increases, so does the number of species and the standing crop of fishes. Overall, the greatest variety of habitat suitable for fish is likely to occur in a large, shallow lake with many bays and other irregularities in its shoreline.

Substrate. Although it is quite difficult to relate the overall distribution pattern of any lake-dwelling species to the presence of a particular kind of substrate, substrate nevertheless does have a strong influence on fish distribution within a lake, especially for spawning. For example, spawning sunfishes and black basses (Centrarchidae) require areas soft enough for digging a nest depression but firm enough so that the eggs will not be smothered in mud. Sculpins (Cottidae), darters (Percidae), and some minnows (Cyprinidae) lay eggs on the underside of overhanging rocks or logs. Perch *(Perca flavescens)* and many minnows scatter adhesive eggs over beds of aquatic plants. Lake trout *(Salvelinus namaycush)* lay their eggs in deep water among concentrations of boulders. The importance of substrate for lake trout spawning is well illustrated by the fact that in Cayuga Lake, New York, the trout populations have to be artificially maintained by planting because their main spawning ground was silted over by soil washed into the lake (Young and Oglesby 1972).

Even when they are not spawning, most lake fishes show some preference for a general type of substrate. Particularly attractive to many fishes are beds of aquatic plants, which contain abundant food and cover. Such beds are most often located on soft and usually muddy bottoms. Other species are associated mainly with rocky bottoms. Thus, in many lakes of eastern North America, sculpins and some darters are found mainly in rocky inshore areas. The cover provided by submerged objects, such as fallen trees and old boats, are also very attractive to fish, including many important game fish (catfish, bass, sunfish, etc.). This fact is being taken advantage of by fisheries managers who construct artificial reefs on sandy or muddy-bottomed areas with little natural relief in order to improve fishing (Johnson and Stein 1979). Another type of cover that is often attractive to lake fish is shade created by over-hanging trees, bushes, piers, and anchored boats. Although fish hovering in the shade may seem to be in a rather exposed position, they are less visible to preda-tors; at the same time it is easier for them to see predators approaching through sun-lit areas (Helfman 1981).

CHEMICAL FACTORS

Gases. The only gas dissolved in lake water that exerts a major direct effect on fish distribution is oxygen, although carbon dioxide is indirectly important to fish through the carbonate-bicarbonate cycle and the relationship of this cycle to pri-mary production (Wetzel 1975). Primary production is the main source of oxygen in lakes, although the action of wind and waves is an important secondary source. The absence of these two sources of oxygen, combined with the removal of oxygen through decay of organic matter, is the reason that major fish kills occur in shallow ice-covered lakes in the winter.

Because some species (e.g., common carp) have a much higher tolerance for low oxygen levels than other species (e.g., northern pike), the composition of the fish fauna of many lakes in the midwestern United States is in part determined by dis-solved oxygen levels in winter, when they are lowest (J. Moyle and Clothier 1959; Tonn et al. 1990). Similarly, the absence of trout from the deep water of many two-story lakes is due to low oxygen levels in the hypolimnion. Despite dramatic ex-amples such as these, the influence of oxygen on fish distribution in and between lakes is quite subtle and closely bound to temperature and ionic effects.

Ions. The influence of dissolved ions on the distribution of lake-dwelling fishes is complex because the concentrations of the various ions in a lake affect not only the fish but also every other organism present. Moreover, the chemistry of a lake's wa-ter is related to that of the surrounding rocks, soils, and plant communities, and so broad relationships between fish distribution and lake chemistry may be partly the result of zoogeographic coincidence. However, zoogeography usually does not go very far in explaining the high correlations often found between patterns of fish dis-

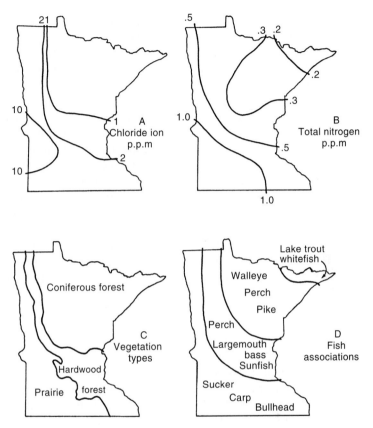

FIGURE 29.1 *Generalized clines of salinity (as measured by chlorinity), dissolved nutrients (as indicated by total nitrogen), and vegetation types in relation to major fish associations in Minnesota lakes. (From J. B. Moyle 1956.)*

tribution and production and the following factors: water chemistry patterns (expressed as pH); nutrient concentrations; and/or some measure of total dissolved inorganic and organic salts, such as salinity, total dissolved solids, conductivity, or alkalinity (see Fig. 29.1).

Lakes with pH values above 8.5 (alkaline) or below 5 (acid) support only a few rather tolerant fish species or, if the values are extreme, none at all. Thus one of the first signs that a region is being affected by acid rain is the disappearance of fish from its lakes. Within the normal pH range, alkaline lakes do have higher fish production than acidic lakes. Fish production in turn is determined through food chains by primary production, which is limited by the availability of nutrients, particularly phosphorus and nitrogen. Thus the fertilization of oligotrophic lakes in British Columbia and Alaska has been found to increase the growth and survival of juvenile sockeye salmon *(Oncorhynchus nerka)* by increasing the supply of zooplankton upon which the salmon feed (Hyatt and Stockner 1985). Unexploited oligotrophic lakes may support surprisingly high standing crops of fish (usually salmonids) despite low nutrient levels. Most of the fish biomass is tied up in large, old, slow-growing adults. Johnson (1976) compares such populations to "climax" communities of plants, since almost all the energy derived from primary production goes into maintenance and reproduction rather than growth.

The complexity of the interactions among dissolved salts, nutrients, and fish distribution and production are well illustrated by the broad distributional patterns of the four major fish associations found in Minnesota lakes (Fig. 29.1). Not only can presence or absence of the fish associations be related to water chemistry, but they can also be related to the surrounding plant communities and, to a lesser extent, climatic variables such as temperature. These same factors are related to the potential production of fish from lakes, a subject of great interest to fisheries managers. On a broad scale, fish production increases with increases in temperature, phosphorus concentration, phytoplankton production, and pH (Downing and Plante 1993). This suggests that total fish abundance is controlled by "bottom up" factors. Indeed, predatory and plankton-feeding fish ("top down" control) have much less effect on ecosystem structure in highly productive (eutrophic) lakes than they do in lakes of low productivity (oligotrophic) (Trippel and Beamish 1993).

TEMPORAL FACTORS

The composition of the fish fauna of most lakes is rarely constant. It is likely to change as a lake ages, as the climate fluctuates from year to year, as the abundance of species changes from season to season, and as fish engage in daily movements.

Long-term changes. Such changes in the fish faunas of lakes are poorly documented, although they are inevitable as the chemistry of lakes change with the accumulation of nutrients and other ions from the surrounding land and as the physical environment changes with the accumulation of sediments. A gradual addition of species is also likely as species enter lakes through outlets or inlets. Actually, the types of changes likely to occur naturally in lakes can be understood, more or less, through the study of lakes that have been strongly affected by humans through "cultural eutrophication" and the introduction of exotic species. For example, there are many lakes close to urban areas in North America and Europe that formerly were dominated by salmonids. Under the influence of increased nutrients, species introductions, and overexploitation, they have become dominated by cyprinids and perch, with an overall increase in fish biomass (Loftus and Regier 1972).

Reservoirs provide another general example of the changes that can take place in the fish fauna of a lake through time, although it seems unlikely that the typical sequence of events observed in reservoirs happens in many natural lakes, even on a more expanded time scale. For the first few years, fish populations and species numbers are high in reservoirs, because both the lacustrine species planted by humans and the riverine species already present grow rapidly in the new environment. Reproduction may also be good initially because spawning areas are not yet silted over and because water-level fluctuations are minor. But as the reservoir ages and extreme fluctuations become the rule, the total fish biomass declines, as does the number of abundant species, particularly riverine species. The species that remain abundant are those that (1) are long-lived, so that one successful spawn will sustain their populations over a long period (e.g., common carp); (2) migrate upstream to spawn (e.g., many suckers); (3) spawn pelagically (e.g., shad, *Dorosoma*); or (4) spawn in water deep enough not to be affected by the fluctuations (e.g., channel catfish, *Ictalurus punctatus*). The habitat of larval fish is also important because pelagic larvae may be washed downstream. Species that are most likely to decline from lack of reproductive success are piscivores, such as smallmouth bass. Angling pressure and lack of suitable prey may also contribute to the decline of these species.

Climatic fluctuations. Changes in climate are likely to cause fluctuations in the composition of a lake's fish fauna mainly as a result of their effect on water temperatures and lake levels. Most fish have a limited range of temperatures at which they will spawn. If these temperatures are not reached, spawning will not occur; or if they are reached late in the season, the eggs and larvae may have to face larger populations of small predatory fish. In either case reproductive failure is likely, and the species, or at least the year class, is likely to be less abundant in future years. Reproductive failure is also likely in drought years for species that require flooded vegetation for spawning, or emergent plants as cover for their young. The reproductive failure of one species may also affect the abundance of other species. In Oneida Lake, New York, young yellow perch are the principal prey of walleye. When the perch have poor reproductive success, walleye predation on their own young increases, resulting in a less abundant year class of walleye (Forney 1974). Such complex interactions among species and between species and their environments indicate that even minor long-term climate changes can create major changes in fish faunas (Schindler et al. 1990).

Seasonal changes. These changes in the fish fauna of lakes are related to a combination of reproductive and seasonal movements. The major fish species in lakes tend to reproduce at different times, and this results in a definite succession of planktonic larvae in the open waters of lakes in the summer (e.g., Amundsrud et al. 1974) as well as a succession of abundance of juvenile fishes in the inshore areas. Many adult and juvenile fish make seasonal migrations to different depths or parts of lakes, resulting in a seasonally changing species composition in some habitats, particularly inshore areas. The ability of alewife to move to different habitats as the seasons change has enabled it to disrupt the less migratory, more stationary inshore and deepwater populations of whitefish in Lake Michigan (Smith 1968).

Daily changes. The activity patterns of most lake fish are cued to light (Helfman 1981), so striking differences can be found in the distribution of fish within a lake according to time of day. Vision-oriented predators are most active during the day, often with peaks of feeding in the early morning and evening when invertebrates become more available: Zooplankton are moving upward, benthic insects start to become active, and flights of terrestrial and aquatic insect adults increase. Dawn and dusk are also the times when piscivorous fishes move into shallow water, attracted by the feeding activities of the smaller fishes. The predators are also less visible at low light intensities. After dark most day-active fishes lie quietly on the bottom, beneath submerged objects, or among aquatic plants, although some species such as the sunfishes may remain in slowly circling schools. Night-active fishes, particularly catfish and suckers, then move into shallow water to forage.

Daily movements in relation to temperature are also common, often for energetic reasons. In Bear Lake, Utah, larval sculpins *(Cottus extensus)* forage on the bottom during the day, where water temperatures are 4–5 C, but move up to the water column at night, where temperatures are 13–16 C (Wurtsbaugh and Neverman 1988). The vertical migrations take place because the fish digest their food faster at higher temperatures and grow three times faster. In contrast, kokanee salmon *(Oncorhynchus nerka)* apparently move up into warm water to forage on plankton at night and then move back into cold water to digest their prey in an energetically advantageous manner during the day (Bevelhimer and Adams 1993).

BIOLOGICAL FACTORS

Like the stream fish, lake fish are quite flexible in their living arrangements with other species of animals and plants, particularly other fish. These arrangements are best examined under the general headings of predation, competition, and symbiosis.

Predation. Predation by fish is a major factor influencing the composition of the biotic communities of lakes, from plants through invertebrates to fish. Grazing and rooting about by fish, particularly carp, can greatly influence the amount and species of aquatic plants growing on lake bottoms, as well as the species and numbers of invertebrates associated with the plants (Straskraba 1965). Most fish that browse on invertebrates associated with aquatic plants or the bottom are selective as to what species they prey on, and such selective predation will greatly affect the composition of the invertebrate community (Stein and Kitchell 1975). The impact of selective predation on the zooplankton community of lakes is even more pronounced, or at least better understood. In lakes without specialized planktivores, the dominant zooplankton species tend to be relatively large, effective grazers on phytoplankton. In lakes with specialized planktivores, the dominant zooplankton are much smaller, may have protective spines, or may have smaller eyes, making them less visible (Brooks 1968; Zaret 1972). The impact of fish on zooplankton has been demonstrated repeatedly when zooplanktivorous fish have been introduced into lakes. For example, the development of alewife populations in Lake Michigan resulted in declines in the populations of seven species of large zooplankton, including the near disappearance of two species, and increases in the numbers of 10 small species (Wells 1970).

Predation also has a major impact on the structure of fish communities and populations in lakes. Occasionally the introduction of a new predator into a lake can dras-

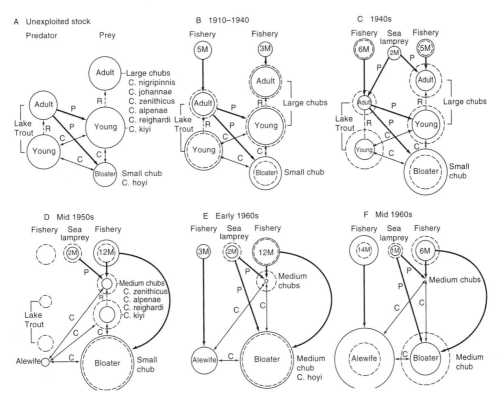

FIGURE 29.2 *Interrelations of major deepwater fishes of Lake Michigan: (A) before exploitation; (B) during moderate exploitation; (C) during the period of increasing sea lamprey abundance; (D) during the peak of sea lamprey abundance when large fish became rare and small chubs increased in numbers and in size; (E) during the period when bloaters were at their peak abundance and the alewife was just becoming established; (F) during the period of maximum abundance of the alewife. The nature of the interactions is indicated by P for predation, C for competition, and R for recruitment. (From Smith 1968.)*

tically reduce the populations of many of the fishes present, as the impact of the sea lamprey on the larger fish species of the Great Lakes so graphically illustrates. Interestingly enough, as the large predatory fishes of the Great Lakes declined, populations of fish species that were too small to be preyed on by lampreys increased greatly, presumably as a result of the absence of predation and competition from the larger fish (Smith 1968) (Fig. 29.2). The complexity of predator-prey interactions in lakes is well illustrated by the long-term studies of northern pike, perch *(Perca fluviatilus)*, and char *(Salvelinus alpinus)* in Lake Windermere, England (Le Cren et al. 1972). Prior to 1941, large pike apparently kept char numbers down by preying on the adults as they moved inshore to spawn. Although perch were the main food of the pike for the rest of the year, the number of adult pike was apparently too low to be able to limit the perch population size. Between 1941 and 1964, adult perch were removed from the lake by intensive fishing, but the perch populations failed to recover when the fishing was stopped. The reason for this apparently was that an experimental pike fishery had removed most pike larger than 55 cm from the lake from 1944 onward, resulting in optimum conditions for the growth and survival of small pike. The abundant small pike fed on small prey, particularly young perch, making it difficult for the perch populations to build up again to their former levels. Meanwhile, in the absence of predation from large pike, char numbers increased.

Obviously there are many ways in which predators and prey can affect each other's populations in lakes. Under more or less stable environmental conditions, self-regulating predator-prey systems can theoretically develop. Steady "cropping" of a prey species by a predator will reduce intraspecific competition and consequently increase growth rates of the prey. Such rapid growth may increase the reproductive potential of the prey by allowing the prey to mature at an earlier age and by increasing egg production, since the increase in fecundity of fishes tends to have an exponential relationship to length. If the increased reproduction by the prey results in a "surplus" of prey, two things may happen simultaneously: The predator population may increase, and intraspecific competition among the prey may increase, resulting in slower growth and lower reproduction. These two factors will then cause a rapid decline in the population of the prey, followed by a decline in the predator population to the former lower level of both species. The cycle then repeats itself. While this system may in fact operate in lakes, it is likely to be highly modified because predators will switch prey and because reproduction and growth are also likely to be affected by changing environmental conditions. For example, there is evidence that in some lakes used by sockeye salmon as nurseries, the feedback scheme described above plays a major role in determining the abundance of adult salmon (Hartman and Burgner 1972). However, in salmon nursery lakes in which there are a number of alternative prey species for the predators, the system may not work because the alternative prey either serve to maintain high populations of predators or, alternately, serve as buffer species that reduce predation on the young salmon.

Competitive interactions. Fish in lakes, like those in streams, show a considerable degree of ecological segregation. Although the segregation can be explained in part by differences in body morphology, the coexistence of similar, closely related species in lakes is common. Fish populations in lakes are probably more constant in general than those in streams, but there is nevertheless considerable year-to-year and season-to-season variation in species composition. In addition, food and habitat (e.g., aquatic plant beds) show considerable variation in availability from season to season. All these factors indicate that competitive interactions are likely to be important in the shaping of fish communities in lakes. As the studies of trout and char in Scandinavian lakes show, such interactions can be expressed as direct aggression of one species on another, resulting in the domination of the preferred habitat by the most aggressive species. However, differential exploitation of resources as a cause of observed ecological differences is probably more common. For example, when three species of sunfish (*Lepomis*) occur together, each is found in a different habitat and feeds on different invertebrates. However, in the absence of other species, any of the species will at least partially use the habitat and food that would otherwise be used by the other two species (Werner and Hall 1976). The least change in niche occurs with green sunfish *(L. cyanellus)*, which feeds on large invertebrates among aquatic plants. Green sunfish apparently protect these resources from the other species in part by aggressive behavior and in part by more efficient foraging for the prey. As a result of the interactions, bluegill *(L. macrochirus)* and pumpkinseed *(L. gibbosis)* prey on smaller organisms; pumpkinseed become more bottom oriented, favoring molluscs as food, and bluegill become more oriented toward the water column and zooplankton. In the spring, when food is most abundant and fish populations are lower, there is more overlap in food and habitat than in the fall, when resources are likely to be depleted (Seaburg and J. B. Moyle 1964).

Often the most dramatic effects of competition can been seen with introduced species. For example, a predatory mysid shrimp introduced into Flathead Lake, Montana, consumed most of the large zooplankton in the lake (Spencer et al. 1990). This resulted in a major decline in kokanee salmon which depended on the zooplankton (exploitation competition). Reduction in the spawning runs of kokanee salmon up tributary streams in turn affected black bears and bald eagles which came to the streams annually to forage on the salmon. In particular, several bald eagles apparently were killed by cars on local highways because they began feeding on road-killed animals in the absence of their usual salmon.

In reservoirs the effects of competitive interactions among species normally are minimized by the extreme fluctuations in the physical environment. The main exception to this occurs among the plankton-feeding fishes, in part because zooplankton populations are less likely to be affected by fluctuations in water level than are populations of benthic invertebrates. When a planktivore, such as threadfin shad *(Dorosoma petenense)*, is introduced into a reservoir that has lacked such a species, it will reduce the zooplankton populations and consequently the populations of bluegill, largemouth bass, and other fishes with early life history stages that depend on abundant zooplankton for survival (von Geldern and Mitchell 1975).

Symbiosis. Examples of symbiotic effects on fish communities in lakes are few, although this may be in part because they have not been looked for. It is common to find different species schooling with each other, presumably forming mutualistic or commensal associations. In Long Lake, Minnesota, small groups of bluntnose minnows *(Pimephales notatus)* were found in shallow water, outside weed beds, only when they were in association with large schools of mimic shiners *(Notropis volucellus)*. In the mixed schools the minnows were found below the main school of shiners, feeding on the bottom, while the shiners were feeding in midwater (Moyle 1973). Presumably, the minnows could take advantage of the protection from predators afforded by the large school of shiners to feed in a habitat otherwise too hazardous for them.

ZOOGEOGRAPHIC FACTORS

Barriers to fish dispersal are major determinants of the fish faunas of lakes (Tonn et al. 1990). The closer a lake is (or was) to a major river system, the more species are likely to be present. Lakes with long stretches of stream, especially high-gradient stretches, between them and a major river or other lakes are likely to contain only the same fishes found in headwater streams or derivatives of them, such as trout, suckers, dace, and chubs. Indeed, most of the lakes of the high mountains in the American West were without fish until trout and other species were introduced by humans. In remote lakes already containing fish, the fact that a number of new species can be added indicates the importance of barriers in limiting fish faunas. For example, Clear Lake, California, originally contained 11 native fish species. Between 1880 and the present, 16 exotic species were added to the fauna and six of the native species became extirpated, leaving a total of 21 species. Although it can be argued that the present fish fauna is unstable, with a number of further extinctions likely to occur, the ultimate fish fauna will undoubtedly contain more than 11 species (Moyle 1976a).

FISH ZONES

The designation of fish zones in lakes is even more arbitrary than in streams because lake fish are comparatively free to move from one zone to another. However, fish in lakes do tend to sort themselves out along environmental gradients during the summer months, when most individual and population growth occurs. As a result, distinct clusters of species tend to be associated with the broad habitat types within lakes, and these associations can be described as fish zones. Within each fish zone the species tend to segregate further by microhabitat and food preferences. As examples of these patterns, the zones in three types of lakes will be described here: (1) a small, two-story lake (Long Lake); (2) a large, cold-water lake (Lake Tahoe); and (3) warm-water reservoirs.

Long Lake. This lake, located in north central Minnesota, is somewhat unusual for its bathtublike morphology (deep and steep-sided) and for its clarity (Moyle 1969, 1973). However, these same factors result in sharp environmental gradients and easily observable fish zones. The 19 species of fish that are common in the lake are typical of small lakes in areas that were subjected to Pleistocene glaciation, and the patterns of segregation observed are also typical of such lakes (Keast 1965; Werner et al. 1977; Gascon and Leggett 1977). Four zones are recognizable in the lake: (1) shallow-water zone, (2) aquatic plant zone, (3) deepwater zone, and (4) open-water zone (Fig. 29.3).

The shallow-water zone occurs in water less than 1 m deep and is strongly influenced by wave action. Aquatic plants are thinly distributed, and cobbles are the main substrate close to shore. The most conspicuous fish in the zone are schools of mimic shiners, which feed in midwater and surface areas. Bluntnose minnows and common shiners are often associated with these schools as well. On the bottom are Iowa darters *(Etheostoma exile)* and, beneath the cobbles, mottled sculpin *(Cottus bairdi)*. The main resident predators are green sunfish, found associated with whatever cover (logs, etc.) the zone affords, although piscivorous largemouth bass and walleye move into the zone to forage at dusk.

The aquatic plant zone is characterized by dense beds of mixed species of aquatic plants, between 1 m and 9 m deep. The beds are thickest and most diverse at depths between 2 m and 3 m, and populations of the six most abundant species

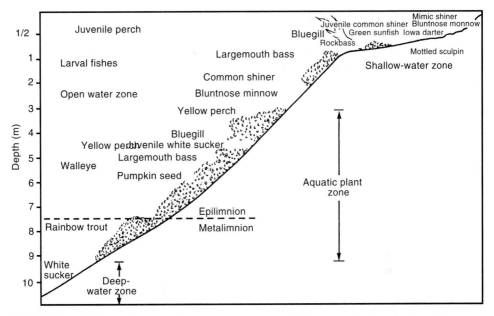

FIGURE 29.3 *Typical summer locations of common fish species during the day in Long Lake, Minnesota. (From Moyle 1969.)*

are also densest here. Bluntnose minnows are found in clearings among the plant beds, where they feed on detritus, diatoms, and small benthic invertebrates. In contrast, large common shiners and yellow perch are typically associated with clumps of aquatic plants that grow higher than the main mass of vegetation. Both species are opportunistic foragers, with the perch consuming large invertebrates and small fish. Rockbass (*Ambloplites rupestris*) are the main ambush predators on large prey in this zone and are consequently associated with logs, large rocks, and other cover in the shallower areas. Largemouth bass are roving predators on crayfish and fish. Bluegill and pumpkinseed are perhaps the most morphologically similar species in the zone, and both feed by picking invertebrates from the aquatic plants. However, pumpkinseed feed largely on snails, whereas bluegill feed on aquatic insects.

The deepwater zone is found below the lower limits of the aquatic plant beds and below the epilimnion. It is thus cold, dark, and silty-bottomed. Only two species, johnny darter (*E. nigrum*) and white sucker (*Catostomus commersoni*), are regularly found here. The darter feeds on small benthic invertebrates, while the sucker consumes detritus as well and may move into shallow water to forage at night.

The open-water zone, away from the influence of the bottom, is characterized by large schools of juvenile perch and by all size classes of walleye. The walleye generally move inshore to feed in the evening. During the summer there is undoubtedly also a succession of larval fishes, each species occupying the zone on a temporary basis.

Lake Tahoe. This lake is a large (surface area 304 km²), deep (mean depth 313 m), and clear (the bottom is visible at 20 m to 30 m) mountain lake on the California-

Nevada border. The six native fish species now characteristic of the lake are also found in the local streams. Originally the main piscivore in the lake was the cutthroat trout, but it has now been replaced by lake trout, rainbow trout, and brown trout. In addition, kokanee salmon have been added to the fauna. The lake can be divided into three broadly overlapping zones: (1) the shallow water zone, (2) the deepwater benthic zone, and (3) the midwater zone (Fig. 29.4).

Warm-water reservoirs. There are more surface acres of water in reservoirs in the United States than there are surface acres of natural lakes, excluding the Great Lakes (Hall 1971). Most of these reservoirs are dominated by fishes characteristic of warm-water lakes. They tend to be remarkably similar in their fish faunas because extreme fluctuations in water levels and other factors typical of reservoirs select for certain species, and because the reservoirs are always planted with a few preferred species of game fish. The main variations in the fish faunas of reservoirs are the result of the persistence of species native to the river impounded, although most such species are eliminated early in a reservoir's history through predation and competition by introduced species (Paller et al. 1992). The fluctuating conditions confer considerable instability on reservoir fish assemblages, but each species is generally most characteristic of one of three zones: (1) inshore zone, (2) open-water zone, and (3) deepwater benthic zone.

The **inshore zone** is associated with the sides of the reservoirs. Fish are most abundant where the bottoms are soft and the water is less than 3 m deep, but adults of the larger species are also commonly associated with steep, rocky areas. The typical species of this zone are sunfishes, black basses, catfish, crappie *(Pomoxis)*, common carp, carpsuckers *(Carpiodes)*, buffalofishes *(Ictiobus)*, minnows (Cyprinidae), and silversides (Atherinidae). The exact composition of the inshore fauna will depend on the particular reservoir, the location within the reservoir, and the time of day. Carp, carpsuckers, and buffalofishes are mobile bottom-feeding species that are most likely to be found close to shore at night. Predatory catfishes may move into shallow water at night to prey on the juvenile centrarchids and small minnows that are the most abundant fishes in the shallow areas. Fish assemblages in this zone show considerable variability, reflecting the fluctuating conditions of the reservoir (Gelwick and Matthews 1990).

The **open-water zone** is host to most reservoir species at some stage in their life cycle, but it is characterized consistently by plankton-feeding shad and predatory fishes that feed on the shad, typically white bass *(Morone chrysops)* but often striped bass *(M. saxatilis)*, or walleye. Large crappie may also be found in this zone, feeding on both zooplankton and shad. If a reservoir stratifies every summer, trout and/or kokanee salmon may be found in the hypolimnion. More often than not, the salmonid populations are not self-sustaining and must be supplemented each year by plants of fish.

The **deepwater benthic zone** contains mainly predatory catfish and fish that subsist on detritus or detritus-feeding insect larvae. The detritus-oriented species are typically suckers (Catostomidae) and common carp. In most reservoirs detri-

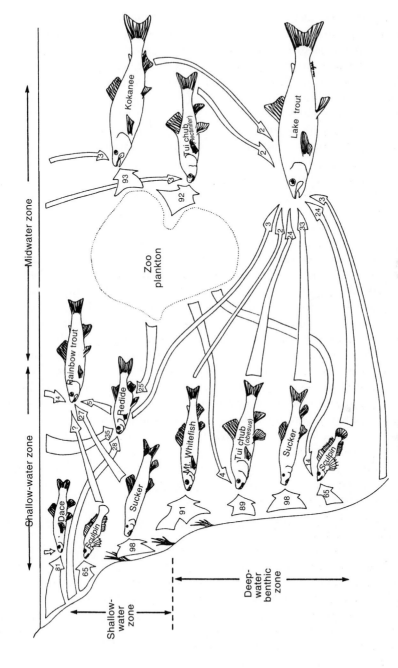

FIGURE 29.4 Zones and feeding relationships of Lake Tahoe fishes. The numbers represent the percentage of diet by volume of the most important food items for each species. The major food categories are benthic organisms, flying insects, zooplankton, and fish. Note that there are two forms of tui chub (Gila bicolor) in the lake, a bottom-feeding form (obesus) and a zooplankton-feeding form (pectinifer). The importance of zooplankton is now probably less than indicated because the introduction of a mysid shrimp into the lake has resulted in the near elimination of the larger species. (From Moyle 1976a, modified from Miller 1951.)

tus-oriented fishes, including bullheads and other species more characteristic of the inshore zone, make up a majority of the fish biomass (Cherry and Guthrie 1975).

The apparent structure of the fish assemblages of reservoirs reflects the adaptability of the fish more than the stability of the habitat. Although reservoirs are usually labeled "lakes" by their builders, they are very different in their physical and chemical characteristics from natural lakes; they are less predictable ecologically, and more ephemeral on the landscape. They are typically constructed for purposes other than maintaining fish populations. In the long run, therefore, reservoirs cannot be relied upon to provide reliable fish habitat and to support consistent fisheries.

CONCLUSIONS

With a few notable exceptions, temperate lakes are short-term features of the landscape, with expected life spans measured in a few hundred or thousand years. The original fish faunas of lakes were assemblages of regional stream fishes that had passed through major zoogeographic and physiological filters to become established. Introductions by humans have greatly increased the number of fish species in most lakes, even in regions in which the fishes are native. Despite the highly variable composition of lake fish communities, studies invariably find they have a high degree of organization. This structure is the result of complex biotic interactions playing on a constantly changing environmental stage. It is also apparent that fish predation is a major factor affecting the biotic and abiotic characteristics of lakes, although this top-down effect lessens as lake productivity increases. We probably have a better understanding of how temperate lakes "work" than we do of any other aquatic system; we therefore have, in relation to other systems, even fewer excuses to continue letting lake ecosystems deteriorate to conditions of poor water quality and few or no fish species.

Supplemental Readings

Carlander 1955; Carpenter 1988; Carpenter and Kitchill 1993; Kozhov 1963; Loftus and Regier 1972; Wetzel 1983.

CHAPTER 30

Tropical Freshwater Lakes and Streams

Fish in tropical fresh waters are affected by the same factors that affect fish in temperate waters, so patterns of distribution and abundance can often by explained by making comparisons to the much better-known temperate fish communities. On the other hand, the tropics contain an enormous number of fish species, often with extraordinary specializations for feeding and reproduction, and tropical lakes and streams have many distinctive characteristics. One of the generalities emerging from recent studies is that within lowland tropical lake or stream systems, biological factors are usually more important than physical and chemical factors in determining fish distribution and abundance. Physical and chemical factors retain their importance for explaining broad distribution patterns. The main reason for the importance of biological factors seems to be the general climatic constancy of tropical areas. Temperatures are warm all year round and food production, at least in rain forest areas, tends to be continuous. In many areas the alternation of wet and dry seasons produces considerable environmental fluctuation, although the fluctuations tend to be more regular in temperate areas. Coupled with the climatic stability is geological stability, so that many of the lakes and streams of the tropics are quite old; this gives plenty of opportunity for many highly specialized species to evolve to take advantage of localized physical, chemical, and trophic conditions (Lowe-McConnell 1975).

PHYSICAL FACTORS

The physical factors that seem to have the most noticeable impact on the distribution of tropical freshwater fishes are temperature, water-level fluctuations, gradient, stream order, and turbidity.

Temperature. The fish that live in large tropical lakes and rivers live in environments that are warm all year and have comparatively little temperature fluctuation. As a consequence, they tend to have rapid growth and short life cycles. Temperature is not a particularly important environmental cue for movements and reproduction. While seasonal low temperatures place broad distribution limits on tropical fishes (most do not seem to be able to survive temperatures below 15°C for extended periods of time), local distribution patterns are much more likely to be affected by high temperatures. In Lake Victoria (Africa), the young of two groups of cichlids sorted themselves out in shallow water on hot days according to their ability to tolerate high temperatures; tilapine cichlids were found in the hottest (to 38°C), shallowest water, while haplochromine cichlids were found in slightly cooler and deeper water (Welcomme 1964).

Water-level fluctuations. In contrast to temperature, annual fluctuations in water levels are extremely important cues to tropical fishes. With the advent of the rainy season, intermittent streams in the drier areas start flowing again, stagnant jungle pools and backwaters on the flood plains are flushed out, lake levels rise, and the flows of major rivers greatly increase. As a consequence of the flooding of land and the flushing of terrestrial nutrients into the rivers, habitats and food resources for fish expand greatly (Fig. 30.1). It is thus not surprising to find that reproduction and growth are often strongly related to rising water levels. Many tropical riverine fishes make extensive upstream spawning migrations at this time or move out into the flood plain to spawn. In either case, the young hatch rapidly and find abundant food for rapid growth. Adult fish also find food abundant and do most of their growing during this period. The seasonal differences in growth rates are often striking enough so that annual rings are deposited on scales and other bony structures, making it possible to determine the age of the fish (Lowe-McConnell 1975).

Tropical stream fish not only grow rapidly during the wet season, but many of the large species accumulate substantial fat reserves to last them through the dry season. In the Amazon River basin, fish that move into the flooded forests to feed show a considerable amount of specialization in their feeding habits, including feeding on fruits falling from trees. During the dry season, when food is less available, the fish become more omnivorous, and dietary overlap is common, with the larger species living in part on their stored fat.

Gradient and stream order. These two factors are usually strongly interrelated in their effects on fish distribution and seem to have the same general kind of effects on tropical fishes as they do on temperate fishes. In high-gradient headwater streams, the typical fishes are streamlined cyprinids (Africa and Asia), the highly specialized hillstream fishes (Balitoridae, Asia), and specialized catfishes (South

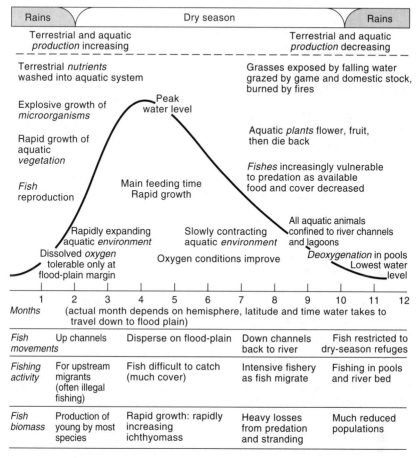

FIGURE 30.1 *The seasonal cycle of events in a tropical flood-plain river. (From Lowe-McConnell 1975.)*

America). As gradient decreases and stream order increases, the variety of body shapes increases, as do feeding specializations. In the headwater streams, most fishes feed either on terrestrial invertebrates or detritus. In higher-order streams, piscivorous forms become common and often seem to make up an extraordinarily large percentage of the fish biomass (Lowe-McConnell 1975).

Turbidity. While the lakes and most of the smaller streams of the tropics are usually quite clear, the large rivers are usually turbid with suspended or dissolved materials (or both). Often there is considerable seasonal variation in turbidity, with the clearest water flowing during the dry season. One impact of high turbidity has been the radiation of fish groups in rivers that do not rely primarily on vision for prey capture, particularly electric fishes (the gymnotid fishes of South America and the Mormyridae of Africa) and catfishes. These fishes also are mostly nocturnal in habit, which presumably reduces the amount of interaction with day-active cyprinids, characins, and other fishes. In clear water, bright colors seem to have an advantage for communication among the fish; most of the brightly colored "tropical" fishes favored by aquarists come from lakes and clear streams (Roberts 1972).

CHEMICAL FACTORS

Three chemical factors seem to have the most profound influence on fish distribution and abundance in tropical waters: dissolved oxygen, pH, and dissolved nutrients. These three factors interact with each other and with turbidity to produce three general types of stream environments: white waters, clear waters, and black waters (Roberts 1972; Sioli 1975).

White waters. These are characterized by high turbidity due to suspended material, pH values around neutrality (7), moderate levels of dissolved oxygen, and high nutrient levels. Because whitewater rivers tend to be the main rivers of most tropical systems, their flooding creates the flood-plain lakes and pools. When the rivers recede, these lakes and pools may become more transparent as the suspended material settles out. If the light is not blocked by trees, the high nutrient levels and clear water result in large blooms of plankton. However, the large amount of decaying organic matter can create low oxygen levels. In this situation, many of the fish are either air breathers or small fishes capable of utilizing the oxygen present in a thin band of water at the surface. In addition, the commonness of species that are livebearers, oral incubators, or nest builders in this type of habitat suggests that such methods may have developed to protect eggs and young from low oxygen levels. However, in the floodplain lakes of the Orinoco River of Venezuela, oxygen is not a limiting factor. Instead, the predictable shift in each lake's fish fauna following the recession of the river is related to strong predation by large piscivorous fishes on smaller fishes (Rodriguez and Lewis 1994).

Clear waters. These range in pH from 4.5 to 7.8 but typically are slightly acidic. They are transparent jungle streams with moderate to low gradients and usually flow into large whitewater rivers by way of a mouthbay. The current in mouthbays is usually so slow that they are more like lakes than rivers. Oxygen levels in clearwater streams are high enough to support abundant fish life, although the food chains are based primarily on organic matter of terrestrial origin. The frequent presence of abundant aquatic insect life in these streams increases the complexity of the food webs; and the variety of fishes, particularly small, brightly colored forms, is often considerable. Many of these streams may also be important as spawning streams for main-river and flood-plain fishes during the wet seasons. One of the more curious aspects of South American clear waters is that the mouthbays are now lower in dissolved nutrients and fish numbers than might be expected.

Black waters. These are transparent but dark brown in color (they appear black from a distance) because of dissolved organic humic matter. They are extremely acidic, with pH values often lower than 4.5, and contain almost no dissolved nutrients. The decay of organic matter present on the bottom of slow-moving stretches greatly reduces the amount of dissolved oxygen available. Such water is typically regarded as not conducive to the support of large numbers of fish. However, Henderson (1990) argues that in fact black waters can have quite high densities of fish, especially species that live among the leaf litter from surrounding forests, which supports large populations of invertebrates. Other species are concentrated around the edges, especially in flooded vegetation where terrestrial invertebrates are likely to be found. In the Amazon Basin there are a number of fishes that are largely confined to black waters and seem to be able to spawn only in waters with extremely low pH values (Roberts 1972).

BIOLOGICAL FACTORS

Because the number of fish species is so high in tropical environments, the interactions among them are complex. Predator-prey, competitive, and symbiotic interactions are often expressed in extraordinary morphological and behavioral specializations. These are most extreme in the cichlid fishes of the Great Lakes of eastern Africa, although the specializations of many stream fishes are almost as extreme.

Predator-prey relationships. Food webs in tropical fish assemblages tend to be more complex than those in temperate environments because detritus, algae, and plant matter are much more important in the diets of fish in tropical systems than in those of temperate fish (Winemiller 1990). In addition, predatory fish seem to exert a stronger influence on the community structure of tropical fishes. For example, fish were found to have had a strong effect on the abundance of invertebrates in a Venezuelan stream, both through direct predation and through altering the environment by foraging on algae and detritus (Flecker 1992). As in temperate systems, however, the most dramatic examples of predation affecting aquatic communities occur where humans have introduced new piscivores into a lake or stream. Thus the addition of peacock cichlids (*Cichla ocellaris*) and largemouth bass to Central American lakes has greatly altered their trophic structure by the elimination, through predation, of a number of small plankton-feeding fish species (Zaret and Paine 1973). In eastern Africa, introduction of piscivorous Nile perch (*Lates* sp.) into Lake Victoria resulted in the elimination of perhaps 200 species of native cichlids (Goldschmidt et al. 1993). On the other hand, reduction in the populations of piscivorous fishes in tropical lakes can cause a great increase in plankton-feeding fishes. This was illustrated by the increase in the biomass of native herrings (Clupeidae) in another east African lake, Lake Tanganyika, following the depletion, through fishing, of the populations of three species of predatory perch (Centropomidae); a heavy fishery for the herrings subsequently destabilized the entire pelagic fish community in the lake (Craig 1992).

In the absence of human disturbance, predator-prey relationships in tropical waters are presumably fairly stable. Nowhere, except on coral reefs, does one find fishes with more remarkable adaptations that reflect the coevolution of predators and prey. The abundant small catfishes of various families have a wide variety of antipredator features, including heavy bony armor, stout spines that lock in place, cryptic coloration, and nocturnal activity. Even these bony catfishes are not immune from bird predation, however. Power (1983) showed that algae grew thickly in the shallows of Central American streams because herons prevented grazing catfish from entering such areas. Other fishes seem to thrive by being small and living in environments too shallow, too low in oxygen, or too hot for large predators (e.g., Cyprinodontidae, small characins). The piscivorous predators have evolved many mechanisms to overcome the defenses of their prey, such as the cryptic coloration and behavior of the patient leaf-fishes (Nandidae), the stunning ability of the electric catfish *(Malapterurus electricus)* and electric eel *(Electrophorus electricus)*, and the formidable teeth and jaws of piranhas *(Serrasalmus)* and African tigerfish *(Hydrocynus)*.

In tropical waters, as in temperate waters, predation is probably the ultimate cause of death for most fish; this has led to the hypothesis that predation has been a major force in the creation of the large number of species in tropical waters, especially in lakes (Lowe-McConnell 1969). Predation could increase isolation by making it difficult for fish with specific habitat requirements to move from one patch of habitat to another and thus could promote speciation. The large number of piscivorous fishes that seems typical of tropical lakes and streams may also permit potentially competing species to coexist, by keeping the populations of the competitors low enough so that resources are never limiting. Another way predators may permit two competitors to coexist is to prey selectively on the form that has a competitive advantage over the other in a different environment. For example, bright gold males of the Midas cichlid *(Cichlasoma citrinellum)* in Lake Nicaragua are more successful at attracting females and defending nests, while dull-colored males are apparently more successful at avoiding predators. As a result, the gold males breed mainly in deeper water, where they are less visible to predators, while the dull-colored males occupy the prime breeding sites in shallow water (Barlow 1976).

Competition. As is true for predator-prey interactions, the most dramatic examples of competitive interactions in tropical fishes occur with introduced species. When redbelly tilapia *(Tilapia zilli)* were introduced into Lake Victoria their young displaced the young of a native tilapia species from crucial nursery areas, causing a severe decline in native species (Lowe-McConnell 1975). In undisturbed tropical streams and lakes it is usually assumed that direct competition is no longer of much importance because past competition has resulted in resource partitioning through morphological character displacement. The best evidence for this among tropical fishes is the extreme specializations in body shape and feeding habits often encountered, such as those found in the hundreds of coexisting cichlid species in the Great Lakes of Africa, discussed later in this chapter. Detailed studies of fish ecology in small tropical streams may show a high degree of species segregation on the basis of habitat, diet, and microhabitat (Moyle and Senanayake 1984; Bussing 1993). However, other studies frequently find just the opposite. For example, most of the 50 species of fish collected from some streams and small lakes of the upper

Amazon were feeding mainly on plant matter of terrestrial origin or on terrestrial insects, especially ants (Saul 1975). Even Goulding (1982), in his study of the extraordinary habits of the fishes that invade the flooded forests of the Amazon, noted that rarely was a food item used only by one species of fish. Most species occurred with several potential competitors. Possible explanations for these differing observations are many, and their variety reflects our general ignorance of the biology of tropical fishes: (1) the studies were done when certain kinds of food were superabundant, and segregation occurred at other seasons; (2) segregation occurred at other life history stages; and (3) the fish populations were regulated by random environmental fluctuations or by predation (Rodriguez and Lewis 1994), so they rarely reached a point at which there was likely to be competition and/or segregation.

Symbiosis. There are few examples of symbiotic interactions among tropical freshwater fishes, although this is not surprising when one considers how poorly known the habits of tropical fishes are in general. Mutualistic relationships among shoaling fishes are probably common, given the frequency with which small South American characins seem to be found together and the mixtures of cichlid species found in the Great Lakes of Africa. In Central America, cichlids guarding a school of their own young have been observed to "adopt" the young of other cichlid species in a manner that may reduce predation on their own young, while giving the foreign young some protection as well as the opportunity for more rapid growth (McKaye 1977). At the opposite extreme, a number of species of small South American catfishes enter the gill chambers of larger fish, where they feed on the gill filaments and blood (Baskin et al. 1980). At least one of these catfishes feeds mainly on the scales of other fishes, a feeding adaptation found as well in many South American characins and African cichlids. Still other cichlids and characins feed primarily by taking bites out of the fins of other fishes.

The diversity of symbiotic interactions possible among tropical fishes is illustrated by the interactions between various species of catfishes and cichlids in the Great Lakes of Africa. At the mutualistic end of the spectrum are the cichlids and catfish that brood their young together, with both species defending the nest (McKaye 1985). A more ambiguous example is that in which the cichlid cleans ectoparasites from the catfish but then takes advantage of the relationship to steal eggs from the catfish nests (Ribbink and Lewis 1982). At the parasitic end is the catfish that somehow gets its embryos into the oral cavity of a mouth-brooding cichlid. The developing catfish young then proceed to consume the young cichlids developing along with them, until the cichlids are gone (Sato 1986).

FISH COMMUNITIES

Because the fish species of tropical fresh waters are so numerous and diverse, it is difficult to find a body of water whose fish communities can be said to be typical of anything but itself. Three examples are presented here mostly to give an idea of the range of types of fish communities and interactions that are possible in tropical fresh waters: (1) rain forest streams of Sri Lanka, (2) Lake Malawi, and (3) Kainji Reservoir, Nigeria.

Sri Lanka streams. The rain forest streams in Sri Lanka contain few (between 10 and 20) species of fish compared to such streams elsewhere, but they have the advantage of having been well studied (Pethiyagoda 1991). The fishes show a remarkable degree of ecological segregation by habitat, microhabitat, and diet (Figure 30.2). For example, two species of cyprinids *(Puntius)* can be observed grazing on the same rock, yet one will be feeding mainly on filamentous algae and the other on diatoms. Likewise, when the two species of gobies (Gobiidae) are encountered in the same reach of stream, one species will be found clinging to boulders, while the other species will be found on patches of sand. There is a high diversity of body shapes and sizes and the most similar species usually occur in different habitats (Moyle and Senanayake 1984). When four specialized species were introduced into a stream that naturally contained only a small subset of the rain forest fish fauna, two of the introduced species retained their narrow niches, while the other two showed niche shifts (Wikramanayake and Moyle 1989). For example, the black ruby barb *(Puntius nigrofasciatus)* shifted from feeding primarily on diatoms to feeding on seeds and plant material. Species introduced into a stream with the fewest native species showed more rapid growth and larger sizes than they showed elsewhere. This suggests that despite the fact that the fishes have evolved morphological means to reduce competition, competition still plays a role in structuring the communities.

Another aspect of the Sri Lankan fish communities that seems fairly typical of tropical stream fish communities in general is the importance of algae and plant material in the diets of many fishes (e.g., Wootton and Oemke 1992).

Lake Malawi. This lake contains about 500 species of fish, all but four endemic to it. The large number of species is due both to the size of the lake (600 km long and up to 75 km wide, with a maximum depth of about 785 m) and to its long and complex geological history. While the traditional explanation for the high diversity of fishes has rested on the fact that the lake is very old (over two million years), recent work has indicated that its levels have fluctuated dramatically even in historic times and that most of the inshore species probably evolved within the last 200–300 years (Owens et al. 1990). Such rapid evolution is possible because most of the species are cichlids. The well-developed parental and territorial behavioral patterns of the cichlids seem to make them particularly subject to isolation and hence rapid speciation. Also, the highly developed pharyngeal "jaws" of cichlids have permitted extraordinary feeding specializations to evolve (Liem 1974). Lake Malawi can be divided into five broad habitat types, each with its characteristic fish community: (1) shallow bays and lagoons, (2) rocky-bottomed inshore areas of the main lake, (3) mud- or sand-bottomed shore areas of the main lake, (4) open water, and (5) deep-bottom water (Lowe-McConnell 1975).

The shallow bays and lagoons are a relatively small part of the lake, yet they are the most productive of food fish. They contain a complex of tilapia species (Cichlidae) that feed on small invertebrates. Associated with these interesting cichlid

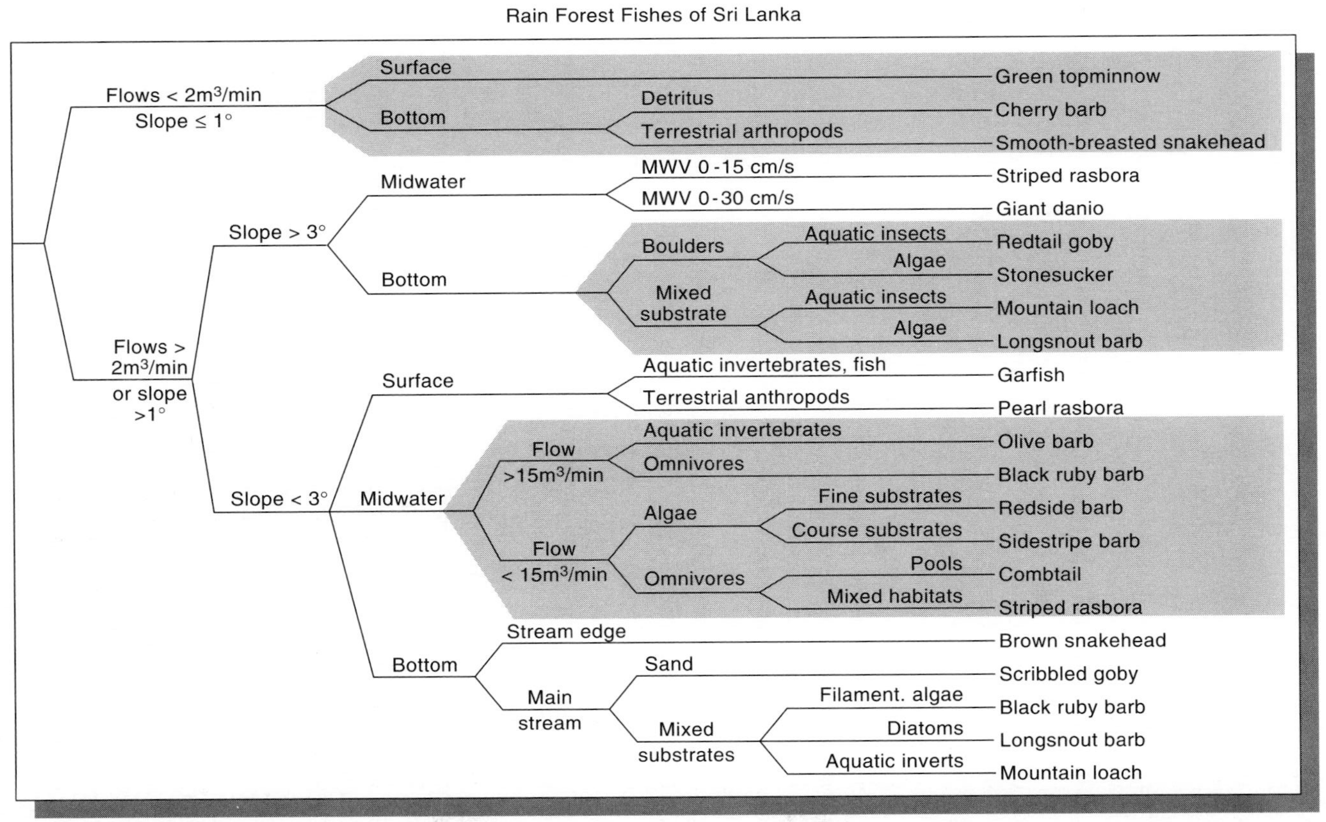

FIGURE 30.2 *Diagram showing the ecological segregation of 19 species of fishes in rain forest streams of Sri Lanka. MWV refers to mean water column velocity selected by the fishes. Categories such as "detritus" and "aquatic invertebrates" refer to principal foods, while categories such as "boulders" and "sand" refer to substrates selected. (Based on Moyle and Senanayake 1982.)*

species are two species of *Corematodus,* one of which mimics the tilapias so that it can feed on their scales, and the other of which mimics another inshore cichlid species, upon which it preys. Other species found in this habitat are large cyprinids and large predatory catfishes.

The rocky-bottomed inshore areas, which may have a steep profile, contain perhaps the most ecologically diverse group of fishes found anywhere in the world in such limited habitat. Most of the fishes are the "mbuna" cichlids. There actually seem to be more fish species present than there are basic types of resources to exploit, so species with similar feeding habits segregate by depth, size of food, method of feeding, and other subtle ways. Cichlids have also developed many ways to feed on other cichlid species. Among the basic feeding types listed by Fryer and Iles (1972) (Fig 30.3) are:

1. Epilithic algae feeders that live by scraping algae from the rocks. There are a number of different species in this group, with mouths modified variously for scraping diatoms, for combing filamentous algae, or for nipping off strands of algae.

2. Periphyton collectors that feed mostly on algae and invertebrates scraped from the leaves of higher plants. These species typically have a pointed snout with scraping teeth on the sides of the jaws. They feed by grabbing the leaf and then moving down it sideways, scraping as they go. Such activity does not harm the leaf.

3. Leaf choppers that feed by taking chunks out of leaves with their stout teeth.

4. Mollusc feeders of two types: shell crushers and foot grabbers. Shell crushers suck in small molluscs and crush them with their stout pharyngeal teeth. Foot grabbers grab the foot of a snail and somehow pull the snail out of its shell.

5. Invertebrate pickers that pick small invertebrates from algae beds with long, forceps-like teeth. These species also have the large eyes necessary for precision feeding. Other species are more generalized predators on large invertebrates, possessing protractile mouths and bands of inward-directed teeth inside their mouths.

6. Zooplankton feeders that consist of a number of species with sucking mouths and long gill rakers. While they feed in open water, they seldom venture far from rocky or sandy areas.

7. Scale eaters that have a scraping type of mouth similar to those of epilithic algae feeders, so they can scrape small scales (usually from the caudal peduncle region) of other cichlids and also of cyprinids. Each species typically seems to specialize in a particular type of host/prey. Other scale eaters devour large scales that they obtain by sliding their lower jaw under a scale, clamping down with the upper jaw, and then jerking out the scale. Stealing the scales from other species requires some highly specialized behavior just to get close enough to the prey to be able to grab the scales (Nshombo 1994).

8. Fin choppers that sneak up on their prey, presumably in part by mimicry, and take bites out of their fins.

9. Piscivorous cichlids that appear in a number of standard forms from rover-predator to pikelike lie-in-wait predator.

10. Egg, embryo, and larval fish eaters that seem to live mainly on the young of other species of cichlids, with different species apparently specialized for feed-

ing on different stages of development. Because most cichlids they prey on are mouth brooders, they get the brooding fish to jettison their young by ramming them (McKaye and Kocher 1983). It is possible that such predation is an important means of population control and that the susceptibility of adults to releasing their eggs or young might depend on the population density.

The muddy- and sandy-bottomed areas have their own highly specialized cichlids as well as various cyprinids and catfishes (Mochokidae). Among the cichlids are species with shovel-like lower jaws and stout gill rakers for digging in the sand and filtering out invertebrates. The different species feed on different sizes and types of prey. Other species of cichlids feed on organic deposits on the bottom, scrape periphyton from aquatic plants, or feed on the plants themselves. Piscivorous cichlids are also abundant.

The open waters of the lake are dominated by a species flock of zooplankton-feeding haplochromines (which tend to be localized in their distribution near shore or rocky reefs) and the small pelagic cyprinid *Engraulcypris sardella*. These fishes are preyed upon by a number of large cichlids, catfishes, and cyprinids.

The deep bottom water contains a poorly known group of fishes that live at depths as great as 100 m, below which the water is anoxic. The species are a mixture of catfishes, cyprinids, cichlids, and at least one electric fish (Mormyridae). Many of these species are piscivorous, and they may feed by moving into shallow water or moving up into the water column, perhaps after dark.

While the picture of Lake Malawi presented here, as an environment whose resources are extraordinarily finely subdivided among its fishes, has been widely accepted, it is mostly based on studies of cichlid morphology. Ongoing studies in the lake indicate that while cichlid fishes do indeed exhibit many amazing morphological and behavioral adaptations, their actual feeding is usually much less specialized than the morphology indicates. For example, the abundant zooplankton in the lake is an important food source for many of the cichlids, including the forms adapted for bottom feeding. It now seems likely that the extreme feeding specializations observed are an advantage mainly in times of food shortages, which, if they do not occur seasonally, may occur on an irregular basis over a longer time span.

Kainji Reservoir. In 1968, the closure of a dam turned 137 km of the Niger River into a 1280-km^2 reservoir (Lowe-McConnell 1975). Kainji Reservoir, like temperate reservoirs, seems to have three fish zones, although since 50 to 60 species occur in the reservoir, this may be a gross oversimplification. The inshore zone is shallow and contains considerable habitat diversity because of flooded trees and vegetation. It consequently contains most of the fish species and much of the fish production. The open-water zone is dominated by pelagic clupeids and characins, as well as their predators, particularly the tigerfish. The deepwater benthic zone is not well developed because of the shallowness of the reservoir but seems to contain mostly omnivorous characins, cyprinids, and catfishes. Despite this apparent general similarity of fish zones to those of temperate reservoirs, tropical reservoirs such as Kainji differ greatly from temperate reservoirs in that the number of species is much larger,

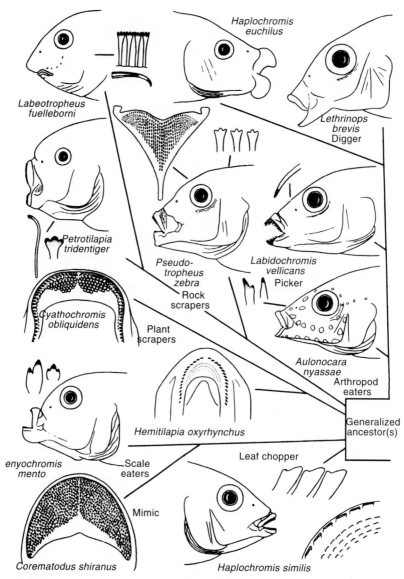

FIGURE 30.3 *Feeding mechanisms of "mbuni" cichlids from Lake Malawi, showing adaptive radiation from a generalized ancestor. (From Fryer and Iles 1972.)*

the environment is likely to be more constant in terms of both temperature regimes and water-level fluctuations, and there seems to be a greater predominance of piscivorous and omnivorous fish species.

One of the more interesting aspects of tropical reservoirs is the succession of fishes that takes place following the closure of the dams. The species that dominate

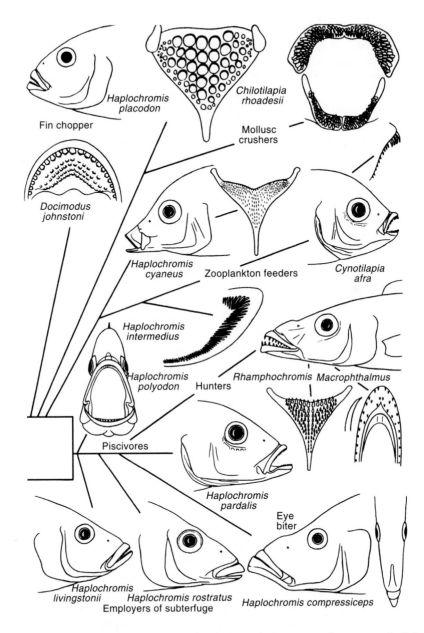

Fin chopper

Haplochromis placodon

Chilotilapia rhoadesii

Mollusc crushers

Docimodus johnstoni

Haplochromis cyaneus   Zooplankton feeders   *Cynotilapia afra*

Haplochromis intermedius

Haplochromis polyodon   Hunters   *Rhamphochromis Macrophthalmus*

Piscivores

Haplochromis pardalis

Eye biter

Haplochromis livingstonii   *Haplochromis rostratus*   *Haplochromis compressiceps*
Employers of subterfuge

such reservoirs are mostly native to the dammed rivers, yet the reservoir fish faunas are considerably different. The preimpoundment fish fauna of the Niger River was diverse but dominated by species typical of flowing water, mostly members of the families Mormyridae, Mochokidae (catfishes), and Citharinidae (moonfishes). As the reservoir filled up, there was initially a population explosion of one species of moonfish, followed by (1) increases in the predatory tigerfish and an omnivorous characin species; (2) increases in species of the catfish family Schilbeidae; (3)

a slight increase in members of the catfish family Mochokidae, but with a dramatic change in species composition; and (4) a decline in the Mormyridae. As the reservoir aged further, (1) the moonfishes declined; (2) the characins continued to be abundant; (3) herrings (Clupeidae) became abundant in the open waters of the lake; (4) introduced cichlids became abundant; and (5) the mormyrids increased in abundance again. In general, the species that became abundant in the reservoir were species that were relatively rare in the main river, being mostly characteristic of backwaters and swampy edges. The species that declined after the reservoir filled tended to be bottom feeders (on aquatic insects) or detritus feeders, while those that increased were piscivores, planktivores, and omnivores (Lelek 1973; Lewis 1974; Blake 1977).

One of the reasons that such changes are so fascinating is that most of them were unexpected, reflecting our lack of knowledge of tropical fish ecology, but especially that for large rivers. For example, in Kariba Reservoir, on the Zambezi River, a number of the dominant species are now fishes that were formerly known only from above Victoria Falls, 100 km upstream (Balon and Coche 1974, 1978). Previously, this falls was thought to be a barrier to fish movement, both upstream and downstream. As Balon (1978) points out, the changes brought about by the creation of such larger reservoirs as Kariba are more often than not more detrimental than beneficial, not only to the local fauna but to the local people as well. An increase in fish production may be balanced by a decrease in animal production from the terrestrial systems, as well as a decrease in agricultural production (from the flooding of vast valleys). Highly predictable systems become unpredictable, as species replace one another in response to new perturbations to the systems. Given the rapidity with which tropical rivers are now being "developed," it is likely that significant parts of the unique endemic fish faunas of these rivers may disappear in the near future.

CONCLUSIONS

The remarkable fish communities found in tropical waters are just beginning to be understood at a time when they are also being severely disrupted by human activities, such as dam building, introduction of exotic species, and commercial fishing. It is clear that many of the communities are highly structured, often containing species whose narrow specializations are rivaled only by those of coral reef fishes. The specializations and the intricate interactions among the fishes and between the fishes and their environments can only be called awesome. Until recently, we had no suspicion that:

- There might be a dependent relationship between fruit-eating fish and trees in the Amazonian floodplain forest.
- There are complex communities of fishes that communicate mainly with electric signals.
- There are communities of fishes that live in leaf litter in acid backwaters.

- The extraordinary assemblages of specialized fish in the Great Lakes of Africa may have evolved, at least in part, in less than 500 years.
- The single biggest human-caused extinction event in historic times was the elimination of hundreds of species of cichlids from Lake Victoria through the introduction of a predatory fish.

The last revelation indicates that tropical systems may be extremely fragile and need extraordinary conservation efforts to protect them.

Supplemental Readings

Echelle and Kornfield 1984; Goldschmidt et al. 1993; Goulding 1980; Lowe-McConnell 1975, 1987; Payne 1986; Roberts 1972; Thorson 1976; Welcomme 1985.

CHAPTER 31

Estuaries

Estuaries are transitional environments between fresh water and salt water. They are essentially bays whose waters are significantly diluted by water flowing in from rivers. Estuarine fish faunas are consequently a mixture of tolerant species from both marine and freshwater environments, species migrating from one environment to another, and a small number of resident species. While the fluctuating physical and chemical environment limits the number of species in estuaries, the abundance of nutrients allows estuaries to support large concentrations of individuals. These individuals often belong to economically important species or are major contributors to food webs that support such species. Unfortunately for fish, estuaries are also typically the focus of major urban areas and so are likely to be highly disturbed and polluted. Thus they are worth considering in some detail because they present many interesting challenges to the fish as well as to the biologists who study them. This chapter will consider (1) characteristics of estuaries, (2) types of estuarine fishes, (3) factors affecting the distribution and abundance of the fishes, (4) estuarine food webs, and (5) estuarine fish communities.

CHARACTERISTICS OF ESTUARIES

The characteristics of each estuary depend on its size, shape, geological history, location, amount and quality of the inflowing fresh water, and the nature of the surrounding land; yet all estuaries have two important characteristics in common: the harshness of the physical and chemical environment and high concentrations of nutrients.

The harshness of the estuarine environment is caused by the mixing of fresh and salt water. This creates not only salinity gradients but also simultaneous temperature gradients, because the salt water and fresh water are rarely of the same temperature. The gradients created by the mixing are not stable phenomena but move up and down the estuary on a daily basis according to tidal cycles. They are also affected seasonally by the amount of fresh water entering the estuary and by oceanic storms that may push in more salt water. The inflowing water carries suspended organic and inorganic matter, which may create gradients of turbidity and dissolved oxygen as well. Not only are there strong gradients from the head of the estuary to its mouth, but there are gradients in the water column as well because fresh water is less dense than salt water and tends to "float" on top.

The fluctuating nature of the estuarine environment means that estuarine fish must expend considerable amounts of energy adjusting to the changing conditions, either metabolically or by moving about in search of less stressful conditions. However, these energy costs are easily paid because the same factors that create the harsh environment also cause nutrients to become concentrated, and the nutrients support large populations of food organisms. The nutrients are mostly associated with detritus that is washed in with the fresh water or is created from the decay of plants in surrounding marshlands. Salt marshes (see Chapter 32) are particularly important as sources of nutrients in Atlantic and Gulf coast estuaries. Although the high turbidity of estuaries typically limits photosynthesis, phytoplankton may be another important source of energy input. Today, however, sewage is one of the most important sources. The constant mixing that occurs in estuaries assures that most of the nutrients are recycled in them and that major losses occur only during times of flood.

At least as important as the mixing processes in the retention of nutrients in estuaries are the activities of the invertebrates. Estuaries have large concentrations of filter-feeding zooplankton, particularly copepods, that feed on detritus and phytoplankton in the water column and are preyed on by fish. The fecal pellets from the zooplankton and fish drop to the bottom, where they form part of the organic ooze that serves as food for the abundant benthic invertebrates such as amphipods and nereid worms. Often even more abundant on the bottom are clams and oysters, which filter-feed from the water column. Because estuarine currents typically concentrate nutrients and zooplankton in the upper, low-salinity (2 ppt to 12 ppt) parts of the estuary, benthic invertebrates and fishes often show a peak of abundance in this region as well. The same processes that concentrate nutrients in estuaries also concentrate pollutants, including pesticides and heavy metals. This may not only have direct adverse effects on estuarine faunas (which are often naturally under stress) but may render the surviving organisms toxic to humans.

ESTUARINE FISHES

Fish found in estuaries are of five broad types: (1) freshwater, (2) diadromous, (3) true estuarine, (4) nondependent marine, and (5) dependent marine. Typically an estuary has representatives of all five types, although their relative abundance varies from season to season and locality to locality. On a worldwide scale, however, there may be major differences among estuaries. In South Africa and Australia, for example, freshwater and anadromous fish are insignificant parts of the estuarine fish faunas compared to the situation in North America (Potter et al. 1990).

Freshwater fish may complete their entire life cycle in the upper reaches of estuaries and invade lower reaches in response to decreasing salinities. Most "true" freshwater fishes will not be found at salinities higher than 3 ppt to 5 ppt and even the most tolerant species are not found where salinities are much higher than 10 ppt to 15 ppt. Examples of freshwater fishes that will live in the upper reaches of North American estuaries are white catfish *(Ictalurus catus),* mosquitofish, various sunfish species, and common carp.

Diadromous fish are found in estuaries in large numbers as they pass through on their way to either fresh or salt water. The estuaries frequently act as staging areas for anadromous fishes; for example, salmon and shad may remain in them for several days or weeks before finally moving upstream. For many anadromous species, estuaries also serve as nursery grounds for the young. American shad *(Alosa sapidissima)* typically spend the first few months to a year of life in estuaries. Some of the most important estuarine fishes might best be labeled **semianadromous,** because they spawn just above the head of the estuary, use the estuary as a nursery area, and may or may not go out to sea. Examples include striped bass and some sturgeons.

True estuarine fish, those that usually spend their entire life cycle in estuaries, are represented by a relatively small number of abundant species worldwide. Whitfield (1994) speculates that the temporary and fluctuating nature of estuarine environments mitigates against the evolution of true estuarine species. In the Sacramento–San Joaquin estuary of California, for example, only delta smelt *(Hypomesus transpacificus)* falls into this category. In East Coast estuaries, true estuarine fishes include white perch *(Morone americana)* and spotted seatrout *(Cynoscion nebulosus),* both of considerable importance to sport fishermen.

Nondependent marine fish are commonly found in the lower reaches of estuaries but do not depend upon them to complete their life cycles. These species may be important parts of estuarine ecosystems, but they are also important in shallowwater marine environments in general. On the Pacific coast of North America, two abundant estuarine species are in this category, staghorn sculpin *(Leptocottus armatus)* and shiner perch *(Cymatogaster aggregata).* On the southern Atlantic coast, typical species include pinfish *(Lagodon rhomboides),* weakfish *(C. regalis),* harvest *(Peprilus alepidotus),* and pigfish *(Orthopristis chrysoptera)* (Rulifson 1985; Peterson and Ross 1991). In Australian and South African estuaries, nondependent marine species make up about 70% of the estuarine fish fauna (Potter et al. 1990).

Dependent marine fish usually spend at least one stage of their life cycle in estuaries, using them as spawning grounds, nurseries for their young, or feeding grounds for the adults. Species such as the herrings that use the estuaries for spawning are relatively few and they tend to attach their eggs to submerged plants or objects. The turbulence of estuaries is likely to create problems for eggs that passively float in the water column. The main advantage of laying eggs in estuaries is that the young hatch close to abundant supplies of food. Most marine species whose young take advantage of estuaries spawn outside the estuaries and have the young migrate into them. Examples of this strategy are common in Atlantic and Gulf coast estuaries, with groups such as croakers (Sciaenidae) and menhadens (*Brevoortia* spp.). One of the few examples of this strategy on the Pacific coast seems to be the starry flounder *(Platichthys stellatus);* its abundance appears to be highest in years when there is high freshwater outflow through estuaries.

FACTORS THAT AFFECT DISTRIBUTION

The distribution and abundance of fish found in estuaries are determined primarily by physical and chemical factors and only secondarily by biological factors. One of the main reasons for this is that most estuarine fishes are only part-time residents of estuaries. They move in when conditions are favorable to take advantage of the abundance of food, either for themselves or their young, but move out when physical and chemical conditions become too severe. Dahlberg and Odum (1970) noted that only about half of the 70 fish species they collected from a Georgia estuary could be found there year-round. Results from other estuaries are similar (Fig. 31.1). The seasonality of estuarine fish populations seems to be created primarily by their responses to temperature and salinity, but oxygen levels, marsh vegetation, predation, and interspecific competition may also play a role.

Temperature is probably the single most important factor affecting fish distribution both between and within estuaries seasonally, although temperature effects are closely tied to the effects of other variables. The often striking differences between the summer and winter fish faunas of estuaries are probably due in large part to the temperature tolerances and preferences of the different species, as is the gradual change in the composition of estuarine faunas from north to south along the Atlantic coast of North America. For example, gulf menhaden *(B. patronus)* in Gulf Coast estuaries are most abundant at temperatures between 25° and 35°C. However, the distribution of menhaden is also strongly influenced by salinity and food supply; young menhaden seek out the upper reaches of estuaries, where salinities are low and detritus is abundant (Copeland and Bechtel 1974).

Salinity exercises a strong influence over the distribution of fish within estuaries (Table 31-1). The intermediate and fluctuating salinities typical of estuaries help to keep the number of species down because they prevent stenohaline marine and freshwater fishes from penetrating far into estuaries. Most estuarine fish are capable of living in a wide range of salinities, and the most tolerant species, such as striped bass, can survive abrupt transfers from fresh water to sea water. While some estuarine fish tolerate abrupt salinity changes caused by sudden increases in freshwater inflow and stay in one area, other species, such as the spotted seatrout, move

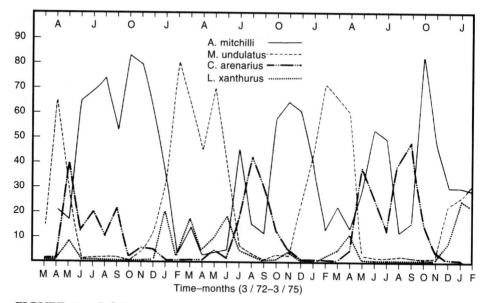

FIGURE 31.1 *Relative importance (percentage of total caught) of four species of estuarine fishes at different times of year in the Apalachicola Bay estuarine system, Florida. (From Livingston et al. 1975.)*

to more saline regions. The life history stages of a species may also differ in their ability to survive salinity changes. Young fish unable to avoid the low-salinity waters may, when confronted by sudden increases in freshwater inflow, suffer mass mortalities either by osmotic shock or by being flushed into less productive portions of the estuary where they may starve.

Oxygen levels are usually high in estuaries because of the constant inflow and mixing of both fresh and salt water, although the naturally high levels of organic matter may reduce oxygen levels during times of low flow. The modern practice of dumping sewage into estuaries increases the amount of organic matter in estuarine systems and may reduce oxygen levels to the point where fish will not enter them, or if they are already present, will be highly stressed or killed.

Marsh vegetation has long been recognized as an important source of organic matter to "power" estuarine ecosystems. However, it also plays a major role as cover for the larvae and juveniles of many fishes. In a Louisiana estuary, various species, such as gulf menhaden, spot, and spotted seatrout, appear to partially rely on vegetation as cover for their early life history stages (Baltz et al. 1993). In addition, naked goby (*Gobisoma bosci*), darter goby (*Gobionellus boleosoma*), and speckled worm eel (*Myrophis punctatus*) are species that appear to spend their entire life cycle in the vegetation. Submerged plants (e.g., eel grass) also are very important as cover for fish (Humphries et al. 1992).

Predation is an important process in estuaries, because a majority of the species are carnivores. The populations of the carnivorous fishes are large, and

TABLE 31–1   DISTRIBUTION OF COMMON FISHES IN THE NAVARRO RIVER AND ITS ESTUARY, CALIFORNIA, IN RELATION TO SALINITY

Species	Classification[a]	O[b]	O[c]	1	3	9 to 10	23 to 25	30+
		Salinity (ppt)						
Sacramento sucker	1	X[e]	X	X				
California roach	1	X	X	X	X			
Prickly sculpin	2	X	X	X	X	X	X	X
Rainbow trout	3	X	X	X	X	X	X	R
Threespine stickleback	2 and 3	X	X	X	X	X	X	X
Starry flounder	4		X*	X*	X*	X*	X	X
Shiner perch	4		R*	R*	X*	X	X	
Jacksmelt	4			R*	X*	X	X	
Bay pipefish	4				X	X	X	
Plainfin midshipman	4[d]				X	X	X	
Penpoint gunnel	4					X	X	
Pacific herring	4[d]					X	X	
Surf smelt	4					X*	X	
Northern anchovy	4					X	X	
Lingcod	5							X*

Source: From unpublished data of D. H. Varoujean and P. B. Moyle, 1973–1976.

[a]The species are classified according to their salinity tolerance as follows: 1–stenohaline, freshwater; 2–euryhaline, freshwater; 3–anadromous; 4–euryhaline, marine; 5–stenohaline, marine.

[b]More than 1 km upstream from first riffle.

[c]Just above first riffle.

[d]Spawning.

[e]X indicates that the fish were present and common, R that they were present but rare. An asterisk indicates predominantly young-of-year fish.

the impact of their predation on both invertebrates and fish populations seems to be considerable. Large concentrations of predators may also locally deplete prey populations. For example, spot (*L. xanthurus*) may severely limit the density of benthic invertebrates on soft bottoms of Atlantic coast estuaries (Virnstein 1977). Large schools of plankton-feeding menhaden may cause the water to be much clearer behind the school than ahead of it, presumably because the menhaden have filtered out most edible organisms (McHugh 1967). However, plankton production is often so high in estuaries that high densities are typically present despite intense predation. Benthic invertebrates similarly compensate for high losses due to predation through rapid growth and short generation times. Young fish also are subject to intense predation in estuaries, but their heavy mortality also appears to be offset in part by their rapid growth rates. Rapid growth enables them to more quickly reach sizes at which they are less vulnerable to predation, and to achieve adult (reproductive) status more quickly than they could in areas where food is less available. In general, the physical and chemical fluctuations of the estuarine environment seem to have a much greater influence on fish populations than does predation.

Competition, like predation, does not seem to be as important as environmental fluctuations in regulating the distribution and abundance of estuarine fishes. Most studies of the food habits of estuarine fishes show a high degree of overlap among all the species present. One reason for this is that the number of species of abundant invertebrates in an estuary is typically low. For example, the dominant detritus/phytoplankton filtering organism in the Sacramento–San Joaquin estuary is the opossum shrimp *(Neomysis mercedis).* This organism is important in the diet of almost all the fishes in the estuary at one life history stage or another. Nevertheless, it can be argued that the staggered use of estuaries by estuarine-dependent marine fishes may be at least partially a mechanism for the species to reduce interspecific competition for food by their young (Livingston 1976). In the York River estuary of Virginia, 10 species of croaker (Sciaenidae) manage to segregate partially on the basis of feeding habits (as reflected in body shape and mouth structure), and partially on the basis of differences in distribution within the estuary and timing of the use of the estuary (Chao and Musick 1977).

FOOD WEBS

Food, particularly in the form of detritus, detritus-feeding invertebrates, and small fishes, is abundant in estuaries, but the availability of any particular type of food is likely to show considerable fluctuation in even short periods of time. As a consequence, most estuarine fishes are not specialized feeders. Each species or life history stage shows a preference for some general type of food, such as small fish or benthic invertebrates, yet sooner or later almost every potential source of energy will appear in the diet. Thus Darnell (1961) found that, in a Louisiana estuary, detritus and detritus-feeding invertebrates were important in the diet of most fishes but that zooplankton and phytoplankton were relatively unimportant. Other studies have shown that even plankton may be important in the diets of estuarine fishes, particularly for planktonic juvenile fishes.

As a consequence of the flexibility of fish feeding habits, at any given time it is unlikely that any source of food will not be utilized. The simplicity of estuarine food webs, compared to other inshore marine systems, is caused not only by the lack of extreme specialization of many species but also by the small number of species that are abundant at any one time. For example, Dalhberg and Odum (1970) found that only 12 of 70 species in a Georgia estuary made up over 90% of the individuals and that at any given time only three to five of the common species were present in large numbers. In many estuaries the number of species increases in the summer, when conditions are most stable; but most of the additional species are relatively rare and probably do not have much impact on the structure of the food webs.

FISH COMMUNITIES

The species that make up estuarine fish communities change constantly, yet the basic structure of the communities is fairly stable, or at least predictable (Livingston 1976). This stability is the result of (1) the regular distribution of species along gradients of salinity, temperature, and other variables; (2) the predictable seasonal movements of fishes in and out of the estuaries; (3) the dominance of estuaries by a relatively few but interchangeable (in terms of trophic position) species; and (4) the robust food webs. These aspects of estuarine fish communities can be illustrated by the fishes found in estuaries along the coast of the Gulf of Mexico, which are among the best studied in North America.

Although the fishes of Gulf Coast estuaries have definite preferred temperature and salinity ranges, these ranges tend to be broad so that the alignment of species along environmental gradients is often hard to detect. Nevertheless, there are usually distinct differences between the fish communities at the upper ends of the estuaries and those of the more saline and less thermally fluctuating lower ends. The most numerous fishes at the upper ends are usually small planktivores, such as the bay anchovy (*Anchoa mitchilli*, a year-round resident) and juvenile gulf menhaden (an estuarine-dependent marine species). However, croakers, typically juveniles, are also abundant along with some "true" estuarine species such as the hogchoker (*Trinectes maculatus*). Freshwater fishes are often present in low numbers, as are anadromous species such as shad and Atlantic sturgeon (*Acipenser oxyrhynchus*). As the water becomes more saline, nondependent marine fishes dominate the species list, but each species is generally uncommon. In terms of numbers of individuals the dominant species are still true estuarine forms and estuarine-dependent marine species.

The exact composition of the fish community at any given place in a Gulf Coast estuary depends strongly on the season of year (Fig. 31.1). There is a tendency for the dominant species, particularly the various croakers, to peak in abundance at slightly different times of the year. The peaks are related mostly to the influx of young, although the exact timing and size of the peaks are also related to natural fluctuations in the estuarine environment as well as to human-caused disturbances. Both dependent and nondependent marine fishes show seasonal patterns of abundance in estuaries. In a Georgia estuary, sea catfish (Ariidae) were found almost exclusively in the summer, while hake (Gadidae, *Urophycis* spp.) were found only in the winter (Dahlberg and Odum 1970). The seasonal use of estuaries by fish species may show considerable variation from one estuary to another. For example, silver seatrout (*Cynoscion nothus*) are found in Georgia only in the summer but are most common in Texas estuaries in the winter.

The most numerous fishes in Gulf Coast estuaries are usually juveniles that are feeding on plankton, but the biomass is often dominated by larger individuals that are feeding on fish, benthic invertebrates, detritus, or all three. Despite seasonal changes in the fish fauna, no major source of food is neglected. In Apalachicola Bay, Florida, bay anchovy are usually the dominant planktivore in the summer, while juvenile Atlantic croaker *(Micropogon undulatus)* are dominant in the winter (Livingston et al. 1975). Similarly, Perret and Caillouet (1974) indicate that at least one species of benthic-feeding croaker is always present in a Louisiana estuary.

CONCLUSIONS

Despite the high natural variability of estuarine conditions, estuarine fishes have predictable patterns of distribution and abundance. Species succeed one another along the various environmental gradients within each estuary, as well as from season to season. Interactions among fish species typically seem less important in regulating fish numbers or assemblage composition than nonbiotic factors, although intereactions between fish and invertebrates (especially molluscs) may be more important than generally recognized. Estuarine fish populations can change dramatically (and permanently) in response to severe disturbances, particularly those that result from human activities. Although estuarine fish and food webs are very hardy and flexible, the low diversity of fishes found in many urban estuaries today attests to the fact that even estuarine fish have limits to their tolerance of extreme environmental conditions. To add insult to injury, new species of fish and invertebrates are being introduced into estuaries worldwide through the dumping of ballast water by ships (Carlton and Geller 1993). In the Sacramento–San Joaquin estuary of California, for example, the shimofuri goby *(Tridentiger bifasciatus)* from Japan had a population explosion at the same time that the estuary's resident fauna was declining (Meng et al. 1994). The biota of the world's estuaries is becoming increasingly cosmopolitan, as new, hardy species invade and native species disappear.

Supplemental Readings

Haedrich 1983; Livingston 1976; Livingston et al. 1975; McErlean et al. 1973; Meng et al. 1994; Moyle et al. 1985; Odum 1970; Potter et al. 1990; Wheeler 1979.

CHAPTER 32

Coastal Habitats

Most marine fish live on or near the edges of the continents, from the intertidal regions to the edge of the continental shelf. Within this region there are a wide variety of habitat types, each inhabited by a distinctive set of fishes. Because of the large numbers of individuals and species of fish, the variety of habitats, and the general difficulty of studying much of the inshore region, our knowledge of the ecological relationships of these fishes is not great. As this chapter should illustrate, the amount of information available on the fish communities increases in proportion to their closeness to shore, their closeness to institutions devoted to the study of marine biology, their attractiveness to divers, and their commercial value. In this chapter, the fish communities associated with the following habitat types will be briefly discussed: (1) rocky intertidal areas, (2) exposed beaches, (3) mudflats, (4) salt marshes, (5) mangrove swamps, (6) seagrass flats, (7) kelp beds, (8) near-shore rocky bottoms; (9) near-shore soft bottoms, and (10) hypersaline lagoons and salt ponds. The important inshore communities of tropical reefs and the polar regions are discussed in separate chapters. The various coastal habitats grade into one another, and many fishes are found in several different habitats or move between them. However, the categories do represent the most abundant and conspicuous habitat types found in coastal regions, and each does have distinct types of fishes associated with it.

ROCKY INTERTIDAL AREAS

Much of the coastline of the world is rocky and subject to the rise and fall of tides. The environment in these rocky areas is a harsh one, subject to crashing surf, strong currents, and daily exposure to the air; yet the faunas are quite diverse because the intertidal environment also has high biological productivity (Leigh et al. 1987). The faunal diversity, combined with the region's accessibility to observers, has made this perhaps the most studied of marine environments. The fish in particular present an interesting complex of adaptations to a harsh environment.

Intertidal rocky areas, as well as other intertidal environments, have four basic kinds of fish: true residents, partial residents, tidal visitors, and seasonal visitors. **True residents** are found in the intertidal zone throughout the entire year and have the greatest degree of specialization for living in this environment. Typical representatives of this group in temperate areas are members of the families Cottidae (sculpins), Blenniidae (blennies), Gobiesocidae (clingfishes), Gobiidae (gobies), Stichaeidae (pricklebacks), Tripterygiidae (triplefin blennies), Clinidae (clinids), and Pholidae (gunnels). These fishes are all small and have reduced or absent swimbladders, compressed or depressed bodies, and some means of clinging to the substrate (Gibson 1993). The wide, flattened head, large pectoral fins, and smooth body of sculpins serve them just as well for a bottom-hugging existence in intertidal areas as they do for a life in swift streams. The blennies tend to be laterally compressed and elongate, so that they can easily fit into crevices and holes. The gobies have their pelvic fins modified into a sucker for holding on to the rocks. The clingfishes also have a pelvic sucker and are extremely flattened dorsally, which allows them to live in areas of high turbulence. The gunnels and pricklebacks, in contrast, are eel-like fish that avoid turbulence by squeezing into narrow crevices and cracks or by living underneath the rocks. Among the eel-like fishes, there are distinct differences among species that live at different places in the intertidal zone. The species that live highest in the intertidal zone, and so are out of water for the longest periods, are more cylindrical in cross section than ones that live lower down. The reason for this is that the lower amount of surface area in comparison to body volume reduces the amount of water lost by evaporation (Fig. 32.1).

Partial residents are fish that are consistently found in the intertidal areas but are also found in deeper water. Typically these fish are juveniles of species with large adults, and they are often representative of the same families that make up the true residents (e.g., Cottidae, Pholidae). However, partial residents may also be small, deep-bodied forms (e.g., Embiotocidae, Labridae).

Tidal visitors are fish that move into the intertidal region to feed as the tide moves in. These fish can be almost any of the species that inhabit the more stable regions below the intertidal region. **Seasonal visitors** are often fish that use rocky intertidal areas for spawning, but the species that use them in this manner are few. Tidal visitors are often seasonal visitors as well, since the inshore fish fauna in general shows seasonal changes in composition.

The dominant fishes of the rocky intertidal areas are the residents and partial residents, and their distribution patterns strongly reflect the physical, chemical, and

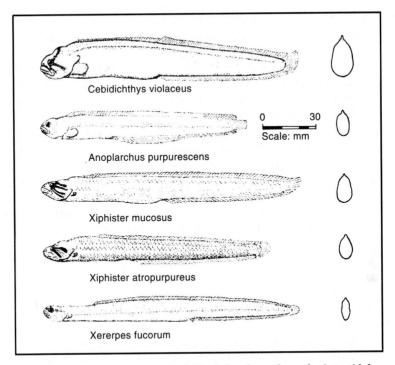

FIGURE 32.1 *Five species of eel-like fishes from the rocky intertidal zone of Southern California, with cross sections of their bodies. They are placed, from top to bottom, in order of their ability to resist drying out and surviving out of water. The top two species are most likely to be found under rocks in upper intertidal areas. (From Horn and Riegle 1981.)*

biological aspects of their environment. Because there are generally strong, fluctuating gradients of temperature and general environmental severity from the upper intertidal areas to the lower ones, the species distribution patterns tend to reflect their tolerance for these conditions. In the upper intertidal areas the species must have special adaptations to survive the harsh environment, such as a tolerance for fluctuating salinities and the ability to breathe air (Yoshiyama and Cech 1994). In the lower intertidal areas interactions among fish species may play an important role in determining distribution patterns, but usually similar coexisting species have strong preferences for particular environmental conditions that enable them to avoid competition. For example, the tidepool sculpin *(Oligocottus maculosus)* and the fluffy sculpin *(O. snyderi)* show segregation on the basis of habitat selection and temperature tolerances. The fluffy sculpin selects habitats with plenty of cover (eel grass) and low temperatures, while the tidepool sculpin shows a preference for shallow water and is more tolerant of a wide range of temperatures and salinities (Nakamura 1976). Because intertidal species often tend to align themselves along various environmental gradients, there is a succession of species from the upper to the lower intertidal regions (Yoshiyama 1981). However, the strong vertical zonation so often demonstrated by intertidal invertebrates is less apparent in fishes, probably because fish can move about more readily.

Although much of the ecological segregation among intertidal fishes is based on responses to the physical environment, fishes with overlapping distributions also tend to segregate on the basis of feeding habits. Most are carnivores, but herbivores and omnivores are not uncommon. One of the more remarkable omnivores is the amphibious pejesapo *(Sicyases sanquineus),* a clingfish of the rocky intertidal areas of the Pacific coast of South America. It lives where wave action is heavy, and it scrapes a wide variety of invertebrates and algae from the rocks, occupying a dominant grazer/predator role normally occupied by invertebrates in the upper intertidal zone (Paine and Palmer 1978).

Not only do intertidal fishes show a high degree of ecological segregation but local assemblages of fishes tend to be persistent through time (Grossman 1982). In a way this predictability is surprising because the assemblages of intertidal invertebrates and algae seem to be much less predictable. Constantly changing community organization might in fact be expected given the dynamic nature of the intertidal environment, which is constantly subjected to disturbances on various scales, ranging from logs being bashed onto shore, to heavy waves caused by storms, to major shifts in temperature caused by changing oceanographic conditions. Intertidal fish communities, however, show remarkable powers of recovery from disasters. Tide pools from which fish have been removed by collectors typically recover their faunas in a few months (Grossman 1982). Longer recovery times are experienced following larger-scale disasters, such as exceptionally cold winter temperatures in warm coastal areas. Usually, a core of tolerant species survive such conditions with few ill effects, and the less tolerant species return at various degrees of speed (e.g., Thomson and Lehner 1976). An important feature contributing to the recovery of intertidal communities is that most intertidal fishes have pelagic larvae with strong substrate preferences when they settle. Once established in an area, however, many intertidal fish become territorial, reducing the probability of additional colonization by larvae of their own and, perhaps, similar species. Such fish usually also have strong homing abilities and quickly return to their territories if displaced (Yoshiyama et al. 1992; Gibson 1993).

EXPOSED BEACHES

The fish associated with exposed coastal beaches live in the turbulent environment of the surf. The turbulence and currents would seem to require high energy expenditures by most of the fish that live there, just to maintain position. On the other hand, the turbulence also provides a constant source of small, disoriented invertebrates that are exceptionally vulnerable to capture by fish. Thus the surf zone is inhabited by a small but select group of fish, often in surprisingly large numbers, mostly of the following types: (1) small, active plankton-feeders; (2) roving substrate-feeders; (3) flatfishes; (4) migratory species; (5) beach spawners; and

(6) piscivores. Most species found in the surf are widely distributed in coastal habitats; few are found primarily in the surf.

Small, silvery, streamlined planktivores, such as silversides (Atherinidae), anchovies (Engraulidae), and herrings (Clupeidae), are often the most numerous fish in the surf. Along the Atlantic and Gulf coasts, fish species that are specialized for feeding on the peculiar invertebrates that live in sand may also be abundant. Examples of roving substrate-feeders are the Atlantic threadfin *(Polydactylus octonemus)* with its specialized pectoral fin rays used for poking into the sand to find prey, and the gulf kingfish *(Menticirrhus littoralis)*, a typical member of the bottom-feeding family Sciaenidae, with its sensitive barbels. The flatfishes in the surf zone also feed largely on benthic invertebrates. The flattened bodies of flounders and rays, particularly stingrays (Dasyatidae), enable them to avoid being swept about by the turbulence in the water column. Fishes that migrate along the coast in the surf zone and fishes that spawn on beaches typically do not feed in the surf, so their distinctive behavior patterns probably developed in large part to reduce their vulnerability to predation. The best-known examples of fish that migrate through the surf are mullets (Mugilidae), whose large schools can often be observed from shore. Fishes that spawn on beaches are few, but one of them, the California grunion *(Leuresthes tenuis)*, attracts hordes of people to witness the spawning and to collect the fish to eat. Their spawning is remarkably predictable because the fish move inshore on high tides that follow a new or full moon at certain times of the year. The grunion allow themselves to be washed ashore by the waves; between breakers the females wriggle tail first into the sand, lay their eggs, and have them fertilized by males lying close by. The eggs hatch on the next series of high tides, and the larvae are washed out to sea.

Considering the variety and abundance of fish found in the surf, it is not surprising to find that piscivorous fish make excursions into the region to feed. Typical examples are bluefish *(Pomatomus saltatrix)* and jacks (Carangidae). On the New England coast, one such predatory fish is the silver hake *(Merluccius bilinearis)*, which is found in the surf in the fall and winter. Since they frequently become stranded on beaches while pursuing their prey, they are known as "frost fish" to the people who go down to the beaches in season to pick them up. Occasionally, even large predators such as white sharks are present in the surf, in pursuit of other fish or marine mammals.

Fish abundance in the surf zone shows strong seasonal and diel patterns. In the Gulf of Mexico, fish are most abundant at night and in summer but the pattern is strongly influenced by the weather; fewer fish are present when the surf is low (Ross et al. 1987). Many beach areas are heavily fished and fishing can significantly reduce fish numbers and sizes. With protection, however, the fish communities can recover rapidly (Bennett and Attwood 1991).

MUDFLATS

Mudflats that are exposed by the falling tides are associated with backwaters, bays, or other features that allow sediment to accumulate. When exposed, they appear barren of life, yet they are extremely productive of polychaete worms, clams, and other burrowing invertebrates. Consequently, as the tide moves in to cover the flats, large numbers of fish move in to feed. The species are mobile forms that are typical of bays, estuaries, and other inshore environments: flounders from various families, skates and sharks, drums (Sciaenidae), and deep-bodied forms such as the surfperches (Embiotocidae).

These species find their prey with a variety of mechanisms. Rays often flap their "wings" rapidly to remove sediment that covers clams. Some sharks go about biting off the protruding siphons of tube-dwelling worms. Many bony fishes search the substrate carefully, either by sight or with barbels, to find individual prey. Although most mudflat fish are tidal visitors, there are a small number of species that are full-time residents of mudflats, aside from the few small tidal visitors that manage to survive in shallow drainage channels. These true tideflat residents are mostly small forms that can live in the burrows of marine invertebrates. Gobies (Gobiidae) are particularly well known for this trait. One species of goby, the longjaw mudsucker (*Gillichthys mirabilis*), has developed the ability to breathe air by having a highly vascularized buccal-pharyngeal chamber. If conditions in an invertebrate burrow or mudflat pool become too severe, the mudsucker is capable of "walking" with its pectoral fins across the muddy surface to a more favorable spot.

SALT MARSHES

When mudflats are present in sheltered coastal areas, particularly bays and estuaries, for long periods of time, they are invaded by salt-tolerant plants and become salt marshes. On the Atlantic and Gulf coasts, salt marshes and their associated networks of drainage channels and embayments are major coastal habitats. On the Pacific coast, thanks to its steepness and rockiness, such marshes are much less abundant, but those that exist appear to be ecologically similar to the marshes of the Atlantic coast. Like other intertidal environments, salt marshes are subject to extreme daily and seasonal changes of water levels, salinity, and temperature. They are nevertheless one of the most productive environments known, and estuarine salt marshes are important sources of nutrients for estuarine systems. Salt marshes also support large fish and invertebrate populations of their own, and the standing crops (grams per square meter) of these organisms may be among the highest of any coastal system.

As in other intertidal systems, the fish of salt marshes are a mixture of true residents, partial residents, tidal visitors, and seasonal visitors. At any given time the number of species present in a salt marsh is likely to be small, typically less than 15. The **true residents** of North American salt marshes, those fish that complete their entire life cycle in the marshes, are mostly killifish (*Fundulus, Cyprinodon*). Killifish can live at salinities ranging from nearly zero (fresh water) to several times that of sea water and at temperatures from near freezing to between 35° and 40°C. If stranded by the falling tide, individuals of some species such as the common mummichog (*F. heteroclitus*) will bury themselves in the mud or flop toward the receding water. As the tide rises, the killifish typically penetrate into the marsh as far as they can, in order to feed on the abundant invertebrates associated with the marsh vegetation.

The main **partial residents** of Atlantic and Gulf coast salt marshes are silversides *(Menidia)*. These fish are found associated with the marshes throughout the year as juveniles. However, the adults tend to school along sandy or gravelly beaches or among beds of eel grass. In Gulf Coast estuaries, juvenile spot and pinfish may also be present in salt marshes all year around.

Tidal visitors are typically larger fishes, such as adult sciaenids, flounders, and halfbeaks (Hemiramphidae), that move into the salt marshes at high tide to feed on the abundant juvenile fishes and invertebrates. The species that play this role vary from season to season (Table 32-1).

Seasonal visitors use the salt marshes as spawning or nursery areas or as seasonal refuges from predators. In both the Atlantic and Pacific coasts, the main salt marsh spawners are sticklebacks (Gasterosteidae). In the spring they build nests in the vegetation where the water is more or less permanent. The most important seasonal visitors to salt marshes of the southern Atlantic coast and the Gulf Coast are juvenile drum, anchovies, mullet, and mojarras (Gerreidae). They spend several months in the marshes, taking advantage of abundant food and warm temperatures that promote rapid growth. The nursery function of salt marshes appears to be less important in northern Atlantic marshes, although Nixon and Oviatt (1973) noted that juvenile menhaden concentrated in a New England salt marsh embayment in late summer, largely to avoid predators.

Although the fish communities of salt marshes are often dominated in terms of biomass by the true residents, they show considerable fluctuations in both species composition and numbers as well as in total numbers of individuals. The fluctuations are caused not only by fish movements that are related to reproduction and tides, but also by the differing responses of the fishes to changes in salinity and temperature and to the abundance of both predators and prey. For example, Subrahmanyam and Drake (1975) found that in a Florida salt marsh the abundance of killifish was related to warm temperatures while the abundance of pinfish was associated with high salinities; the abundance of spot was related to low temperatures and high salinities together. Although the fluctuating nature of the salt marsh environment undoubtedly exacts high energy costs from the fish that live there, the abundance of food usually more than makes up for these costs. Fish that can take advantage of the food supply are largely detritus feeders, small invertebrate-pickers (from the bottom or from plants), and piscivores (Table 32-1). The most abundant species are typically invertebrate-pickers, but the detritus they ingest while capturing their prey may also be a significant source of nutrition. Invertebrate-feeders such as the common mummichog may be so abundant and so efficient at utilizing the invertebrates associated with salt marshes that they can significantly affect the species abundance and size distributions of the invertebrate populations (Vince et al. 1976). At the same time they may achieve extremely high production of their own species. This high production of killifish in turn allows a large number of predators (birds and fish) to exist by feeding on them. Because the predatory

TABLE 32–1 ECOLOGICAL CHARACTERISTICS OF 16 COMMON FISHES IN NORTHERN FLORIDA SALT MARSHES

	Life history stage[a]	Main food[b]	Type[c]	Months											
				J	F	M	A	M	J	J	A	S	O	N	D
Longnose killifish	A, J	S, D	TR	X	X	X	X	X	X	X	X	X	X	X	X
Gulf killifish	A, J	S, M, D	TR		X	X	X	X	X	X	X	X	X	X	X
Sheepshead minnow	A, J	D	TR		X	X			X	X	X	X	X	X	X
Diamond killifish	A, J	?	TR		X			X	X	X	X		X	X	X
Sailfin molly	A, J	D, S	TR?					X	X	X	X	X	X	X	X
Rainwater killifish	A, J	S, D	TR?				X	X						X	X
Tidewater silverside	J	S, D	PR	X	X	X	X	X	X	X	X	X	X	X	X
Spot	J	D	PR	X	X	X	X	X	X	X	X	X	X	X	X
Pinfish	J	D, S	PR		X	X	X	X	X	X	X	X	X	X	X
Pinfish	A	S, M, D	TV					X			X		X	X	X
Spotfin mojarra	J	S	SV							X	X	X	X		
Bay anchovy	J	S	SV				X	X	X	X	X	X	X	X	X
Striped mullet	J	D	SV		X			X	X	X	X	X	X	X	X
Halfbeak	A	S, D	TV									X		X	
Atlantic needlefish	A	C, S	TV	X				X	X	X	X	X	X	X	
Sand seatrout	J	C, F	TV					X	X	X			X		
Atlantic threadfin	A, J	S	TV				X	X	X	X	X	X	X		X

Source: Information from Subrahmanyam and Drake 1975.

[a] A – adults; J – juveniles.

[b] S – small invertebrates; D – detritus; M – molluscs; C – crabs and other large invertebrates; F – fish.

[c] TR – true resident; PR – partial resident; SV – seasonal visitor; TV – tidal visitor

fish (e.g., bluefish, white perch) are important sport and commercial fish, the high productivity of salt marshes gives the marshes a high value to humans, even apart from their importance as nursery areas.

MANGROVE SWAMPS

On tropical coastlines the sea-land interface is often covered with dense thickets of mangroves. The mangroves create rich swamps that may extend for miles inland along estuaries or form narrow belts along coastlines. In subtropical regions, such as Florida, they may also be important, but their distribution is less extensive. The shallow water beneath the mangroves ranges from hypersaline to fresh and from moving (by tidal currents or freshwater outflow) to stagnant. Intersecting the mangroves are usually muddy drainage channels a meter or so deep. Mangrove swamps thus provide a wide variety of aquatic habitats. Although variations in salinity, temperature, and dissolved oxygen levels can make the environment a hostile one, fish, particularly juveniles of marine fishes, abound wherever there is much exchange of the water. There are two main reasons for this. First, mangrove swamps are among the most productive ecosystems in the world. Second, the interconnecting root systems and shallow water provide extensive cover. The mangroves support large populations of aquatic animals, mainly through a detrital food chain, because few of the invertebrates feed on the mangroves directly. Detritus-feeding invertebrates form the center of the food webs leading to fish. In Florida many game fishes have young that may spend part of their life cycle among the mangroves. Some of the more important species are tarpon (*Megalops atlanticus*), ladyfish (*Elops saurus*), snook (*Centropomus undecimalis*), and grey snapper (*Lutjanus griseus*).

Mangrove swamps frequently show zonation in the vegetation, based on the different tolerances of the various mangrove species to factors such as salinity and water depth. Not surprisingly, there often is a zonation of animals that follows that of the vegetation. The areas that are important as nurseries for marine fish are on the edges of the swamps or in the estuaries, where flow prevents stagnation and limits temperature extremes. The more severe interior environments of mangrove swamps are usually occupied by fishes such as the mollies (Poeciliidae), killifish, and, in tropical regions, by mudskippers (*Periopthalamus*). Mudskippers are often extremely abundant in mangroves, especially along muddy drainage channels, because they are capable of breathing air, of "walking" across exposed mud flats, and even of climbing the exposed roots of the mangroves.

SEAGRASS FLATS

The intertidal mud flats, salt marshes, and mangrove swamps of bays, estuaries, and other shallow coastal areas often grade into another habitat that is also extremely productive of fish: the subtidal, muddy-bottomed flats upon which grow beds of seagrass. There are 35 to 50 species of grass that can characterize these beds, but the dominant species in temperate regions is eelgrass *(Zostera marina)*. In tropical regions the dominant grass is usually turtlegrass *(Thalassia testudinum)*, which is often associated with flats around coral reefs (see Chapter 36). Seagrass beds are among the most productive plant communities in the world, comparing favorably with corn and other intensively cultivated crops and with plankton blooms in areas of upwelling. As a consequence of this high productivity, they support large populations of fish, which find both food and cover in the grass. These fish are principally either juveniles of large species or species with small (less than 200 mm) adult sizes. However, because seagrass beds are located in shallow coastal areas such as estuaries, the water is subject to both seasonal and daily changes in temperature and salinity, although the salinity changes are seldom as dramatic as the temperature changes. As a consequence of these environmental fluctuations, the number of species found in a bed is likely to be small and the species composition resembles that of nearby or associated estuaries and salt marshes. Adams (1976a) collected only 39 species of fish in two North Carolina eelgrass beds over a one-year period, and 15 of the species were collected only once. Of the biomass of the two beds, 45% and 67%, respectively, was from just one species, the pinfish. A similar pattern was found for New York eelgrass beds, except that there were two dominant species rather than one: Atlantic silverside *(Menidia menidia)* and fourspine stickleback *(Apeltes quadracus)* (Briggs and O'Connor 1971).

The number of fish in a seagrass bed fluctuates both diurnally and seasonally. Adams (1976a) found that densities of fish in eelgrass beds in the summer were highest at night, when temperatures were lowest. Because movement into the beds he studied was apparently not related to feeding, it may well have been to avoid nocturnal predators. The movement out of the beds in the morning permitted the fish, particularly larger individuals, to avoid potentially stressful temperatures. On a seasonal basis, densities of fish are highest in the summer, when the waters are warm and the eelgrass beds thickest. Again temperature seems to be the key factor regulating the movement of fish into and out of the beds. When the water cools down in the winter, many of the fish seek slightly warmer deep water away from the beds, just as in the summer they may seek cooler water when the water around the beds becomes excessively warm. Regardless of the temperature of the beds, however, there always seem to be at least some fish present. Usually they are members of the same four or five resident species, or of species using the beds as nursery grounds.

Seagrass beds are important as nursery areas because they are such a rich source of food for young fish. While the grass itself is rarely eaten, the detritus it produces is consumed by fish either directly or indirectly through detritus-feeding invertebrates. Given the abundance of food in eelgrass beds, it is not surprising to find that the diets of the various species overlap considerably. Nevertheless, there are four basic feeding types that can be found in the beds: detritivores, carnivores, planktivores, and omnivores. Usually, the most abundant fishes are **carnivores** which feed on the abundant invertebrates and small fishes associated with the grass, although omnivorous species such as pinfish may actually be the most numerous fishes, particularly in the more southern eelgrass beds (Adams 1976b). The **omnivores** include not only invertebrates, fish, and algae in their diets but also substantial amounts of detritus (organic matter). There are few complete **detritivores,** such as spot, but detritus is at times the dominant item in the diet of juveniles of many species. Such juveniles, particularly during their youngest stages, also are frequently **planktivores,** feeding on the zooplankton which thrives in the nutrient-rich waters around the eelgrass beds.

Overall, the structure of the fish communities of seagrass beds is very similar to that of salt marshes. Both environments are highly productive, and both are dominated by large populations of a few species of small, tolerant fishes capable of utilizing a wide spectrum of food resources. Like salt marshes, seagrass beds are frequently destroyed or altered by human activity. Fortunately, they can also become reestablished quickly on substrates such dredging spoils (Brown-Peterson et al. 1993).

KELP BEDS

Kelp beds are undersea forests of brown algae, typically found in temperate waters between 6 m and 30 m. The kelp are anchored to rocky or sandy bottoms with holdfasts and have fronds extending to the surface, forming a dense canopy. The kelp forests provide a variety of habitats for invertebrates and fish and are located in naturally productive waters, so they support an abundant and diverse fish fauna. However, relatively few species are exclusively kelp dwellers, although many are most abundant among the kelp. The most spectacular and most studied of the kelp bed fish communities are those found in the beds of giant kelp *(Macrocystis)* off the California coast. This section will consequently deal with the ecology of these beds (Ebeling et al. 1980; Foster and Scheil 1985).

Most fishes associated with kelp beds are acanthopterygians, particularly of the orders Perciformes and Scorpaeniformes, and the number of species can be quite high. Off California, probably most of the 150+ inshore subtidal species can be found in kelp beds at one time or another, but only 50 to 60 of these are common and only 15 to 20 are abundant and conspicuous enough so that they are easily observed by divers. The exact species composition of a kelp bed fish community will vary from place to place and time to time, depending on such factors as ambient water temperatures, depth of the beds, bottom type, season, water clarity, and the amount of turbulence created by wave action. At the same time, the variety of body shapes and sizes present in kelp bed fishes suggests that the species segregate on the basis of habitat preference and feeding habits. According to Ebeling et al. (1980) there are five main habitat groupings of the fishes: (1) a kelp-rock group, (2) a kelp-canopy group, (3) a bottom group, (4) an inner marginal group, and (5) a commuter group.

The **kelp-rock group** is the most diverse group of kelp fishes and is found where there are high-relief rocky reefs and/or dense beds of kelp. Some of the species are members of families that are also abundant on tropical reefs (Chapter 33): wrasses (Labridae), damselfishes (Pomacentridae), and rudderfishes (Kyphosidae). These fish are always found close to cover and show strong daily rhythms of behavior, much like their tropical relatives. They also have other complex behavior patterns usually associated with tropical reef fishes. For example, a large wrasse, the California sheepshead *(Semicossyphus pulcher)* has a complex reproductive behavior that includes the ability of females to change into males. Likewise, the bright orange garibaldi (a damselfish, *Hypsypops rubicundus*) gardens algae on rock surfaces as nest sites. Another damselfish, the blacksmith *(Chromis punctipinnis)*, forages on zooplankton above the reef during the day. It returns to the reefs to hide for the night and deposits there, as feces, large amounts of organic matter which is a significant source of nutrients for benthic organisms (Bray et al. 1981). This group of tropical derivatives is absent from the kelp forests north of Point Conception, where the California coast makes an abrupt bend. Hobson (1994) argues convincingly that the reason for this is these families all have an extended pelagic egg and larval stage. A lengthy pelagic stage is distinctively disadvantageous in the more northern coastal areas where more pronounced coastal upwelling tends to push the eggs and larvae off shore, away from shallow water. In contrast, the families that dominate the northern inshore areas are live bearers (Embiotocidae, Scorpaenidae) or engage in extended care of the eggs (Cottidae, Stichaeidae, etc.) so that the larval stage is short. On the Atlantic Coast, in contrast, fishes of tropical families can be found fairly far north.

The **kelp-canopy group** consists of species found largely beneath the canopy of kelp fronds. Two of this group, the señorita *(Oxyjulis californica)* and the kelp perch *(Brachyistius frenatus)* pick small invertebrates off the kelp plants, although some individuals specialize in picking ectoparasites off other fish (Bray and Ebeling 1975). Other abundant fishes in this group include juvenile rockfishes *(Sebastes* spp.).

The **bottom group** comprises fishes that live in continuous contact with the substrate, either the bottom or the kelp plant. Many of these species are small cryptic forms, such as blennies (Blenniidae), sculpins (Cottidae), kelpfish (Clinidae), clingfish (Gobiesocidae), and greenlings (Hexagrammidae), that feed on small invertebrates. Feeding on larger invertebrates and small fish are adult rockfishes and large ambush predators such as lingcod *(Ophiodon elongatus)*. In more southern kelp forests, California moray eels *(Gymnothorax mordax)* occupy crevices in the rocky bottom. Within this group there is considerable segregation by depth and feeding habits. For example, two similar species of rockfish *(S. chrysomelas, S. carnatus)* segregate by depth; the territorial behavior of one species excludes the other from the favored shallow-water habitat (Larsen 1980).

The **inner marginal group** consists primarily of adult surfperches (Embiotocidae) that inhabit the shoreward margin of the kelp beds, where the kelp forest thins and dense turfs of other algae often grow. These fishes segregate by depth and feeding methods; some species are adapted for winnowing invertebrates from the turf, while others pick individual invertebrates. Competition results in spatial segregation between at least two of the surfperch species (Hixon 1980).

The **commuter group** is a group of large, active fishes that move among habitats in search of prey. Most are surfperches and rockfishes again, but the piscivorous kelp bass *(Paralabrax clathratus)* is also part of the group. Within this group there is segregation by time of feeding and type of food. The pile perch *(Rhacochilus vacca)*, for example, feeds largely during the day on large hard-shelled molluscs, while the rubberlip perch *(R. toxotes)* feeds on smaller thin-shelled invertebrates that it finds at night with its thick, sensitive lips (Alevizon 1975).

Perhaps the most remarkable aspects of the biology of kelp forests are the complex biological interactions necessary to maintain the forests themselves. Occasionally a severe storm will destroy a kelp forest, and regeneration may be prevented by the grazing of fishes or sea urchins on new kelp plants. Regeneration can occur, however, if rapidly growing green algae colonize the area first, providing the new kelp plants with shelter from grazing fishes (Harris et al. 1984). One of these grazers is the señorita, which is actually after a small bryozoan that encrusts the blades of the plants. In order to eat the bryozoans, the señorita has to take bites from the blades; this can seriously weaken the plant if it is small, but has little effect when the plant is large. There is, however, another invertebrate, a herbivorous isopod, that can become so abundant it can destroy mature kelp plants. The señorita is the main predator on this isopod and keeps its populations small, maintaining the kelp beds in the process (Bernstein and Jung 1979).

NEAR-SHORE ROCKY BOTTOMS

Shallow (less than 50 m) rocky-bottomed areas, from cliff faces to flat shelves, have fish communities similar to those of kelp beds. The reason for this is partly that kelp beds grow mostly on rocky bottoms and partly that, to a fish, the two habitats have similar attributes. Both habitats contain a diversity of microhabitats where small fish can hide and large fish can forage; both provide substrate for the attachment of sessile invertebrates and cover for small, active forms, thus providing a diverse and abundant supply of food. The differences between the two habitats are mostly in the relative abundances of the different species. On the Pacific coast, kelp beds are likely to contain larger numbers of plankton-feeding fish, such as blacksmith, that use the beds for shelter between forays into the water column; while rocky areas on the Pacific coast are likely to have a higher density of crevice-dwelling forms, such as sculpins, blennies, gunnels, and pricklebacks. The most conspicuous fish in both habitats are invertebrate-pickers that roam over the substrate in schools or loose aggregations, feeding on small invertebrates. Such fish are mostly members of the Embiotocidae (surfperches), Scorpaenidae (mostly rockfishes), Labridae (wrasses), Sparidae (porgies), and Sciaenidae (drums). Similar complex communities exist on rocky areas of the Atlantic coast (Sedberry and Van Dolah 1984).

Most fish that favor rocky bottoms have pelagic larvae (as do the invertebrates). As a result, new areas can be rapidly colonized. Off Southern California, sewage outfall pipes that extend for several kilometers across muddy-bottomed areas have become spectacular, if narrow, reefs with large populations of fishes that otherwise would be rare in the area (Allen et al. 1976). It is now common practice to deliberately create artificial reefs from concrete, old tires, automobile bodies, and old ships to increase the fish populations in muddy-bottomed bays. This practice has met with mixed success.

The fish fauna of rocky areas deeper than 50 m is poorly known because of the difficulty of sampling the habitat and because of its inaccessibility to divers. It is likely that many species of fish now considered to be rare because of their infrequency in fish collections are actually abundant in such habitats, especially members of such families as the Cottidae (sculpins), Zoarcidae (eelpouts), and Ophidiidae (cusk-eels). Some of the better-known species that are associated with deep rocky-bottomed areas are various species of rockfish, which feed in the water column and so are taken by fishermen. Among these species are two of high commercial value that have (or had, prior to overexploitation) enormous populations: Pacific ocean perch *(Sebastes alutus)* and Atlantic redfish *(S. marinus)*. The Pacific ocean perch is typically associated with gullies and canyons at depths of 150 to 460 m. They generally stay on or close to the bottom during the day; it is at night, when they move up the water column to feed on large planktonic crustaceans, squid, and small fish, that they are caught by commercial fishermen. The standing crop of Pacific ocean perch in the Gulf of Alaska is estimated to have once been over a *billion* kg. In just six years (1963–1968) this stock was reduced by 60% due to commercial fishing.

NEAR-SHORE SOFT BOTTOMS

On the continental shelf and slope most of the sea bottom is soft and relatively featureless, covered with a layer of sand, silt, broken shells, and other fine materials in various proportions. The number of fish species found in a given soft-bottomed area is usually low; 40 to 60 species may be expected if the area is sampled for several years, with 15 to 20 occurring on a regular basis and only between two and five species making up most of the fish biomass. However, the most abundant species are often of major commercial importance. In particular, the trawl fisheries for various species of flatfish (Pleuronectiformes) and codfish (Gadidae) are largely associated with soft bottoms. Despite the importance of these fisheries, the actual standing crops of fish from these areas are not particularly high in comparison to such productive areas as salt marshes and estuaries. But the ease of fishing over soft bottoms, and the large size of the areas they cover, and the fact that many of the important species concentrate there at certain times of the year, combine to make up for the low overall productivity. Furthermore it is often possible to be fairly selective in a fishery over soft bottoms, because the different species show different patterns of distribution, depending on bottom type, depth, oceanographic conditions, pollution levels, and interactions with other fish species.

Bottom type. Commercial fishermen have long known that the presence of a particular species of fish in an area can often be predicted on the basis of bottom type. As Bigelow and Schroeder (1953, 184) note, the bottoms where cod *(Gadus morhua)* and hake *(Urophycis* spp.) are found "are so distinct that a long line set from a hard patch out over the soft surrounding ground will often catch cod at one end, hake at the other." Because most fish can readily move from one bottom type to the next, the consistent association of species with a particular bottom type (e.g., clay, silt, sand) is likely to be related to feeding habits. For example, bottoms with a high percentage of silt support a diverse "infauna" of benthic invertebrates, which in turn support fishes specialized for feeding on them. However, the association of species with bottom types may also be coincidental, the result of their responses to other factors such as depth or oceanographic conditions. Thus Day and Pearcy (1968) found that the associations of fishes found at different depths off the Oregon coast were also associated with distinct bottom types. Similar patterns have been found in areas as diverse as the coastal areas off South America and western Africa (Lowe-McConnell 1977).

Depth. Most species of bottom-oriented fishes have fairly narrow depth ranges (Fig. 32.2), and on the Atlantic, Pacific and Gulf coasts of North America distinct associations of fish found within depth intervals have been recognized. Usually on soft bottoms between depths of 50 m and 2000 m there is a gradual decrease in the number of fish species, in the overall abundance of fish, and in fish biomass, although the average size of the fish tends to increase. At depths less than 50 m trends are less predictable. The causes of the observed depth distributions of fishes are poorly known, but the fact that they frequently vary with season indicates that responses to oceanographic conditions play at least a partial role.

Oceanographic conditions. Perhaps the most famous example of a benthic fish species whose distribution is limited by oceanographic conditions (principally temperature) is the tilefish *(Lopholatilus chamaeleonticeps)* off the coast of New England, which is restricted to water with temperatures between 8° and 17°C and depths between 81 and 540 m; this species dies off in large numbers when conditions in its habitat change (Bigelow and Schroeder 1953). Off Southern California, upwelling, which brings close to shore deep water that is low in temperature and oxygen and high in salinity, causes dramatic changes in the distribution patterns of the inshore fishes (Fig. 32.3). Seasonal changes less dramatic than upwelling also have a profound effect on the soft-bottomed fish fauna. Tyler (1971) noted that in the shallow waters (< 55 m) of the Atlantic coast, there are four types of fishes in terms of their seasonal occurrences: year-round regulars, summer periodics, winter periodics, and occasionals. The latter group consists of species found in low numbers on an irregular basis. The relative proportions of these components in a local fish fauna seem to depend on the amount of annual temperature fluctuation. Where the temperature fluctuation is low, the regular component is more abundant than the seasonal component; where it is high, the seasonal component (and the occasional component) is much more important than the regular component (Fig. 32.4). Seasonal movements of fish, presumably in response to oceanographic conditions, have also been noted in deep water. For example, witch flounder *(Glyptocephalus cynoglossus)* off Newfoundland aggregate to spawn in waters 500 to 700 m deep in the spring (the young use the continental slope as a nursery area), but they move into the Gulf on St. Lawrence in the summer and back into deeper water in the winter (Bowering 1976).

Pollution. The effluent from cities is increasingly having a significant impact on the inshore fish communities. In the most extreme cases, such as areas where the wastes from New York City have been dumped repeatedly, anoxic or near-anoxic

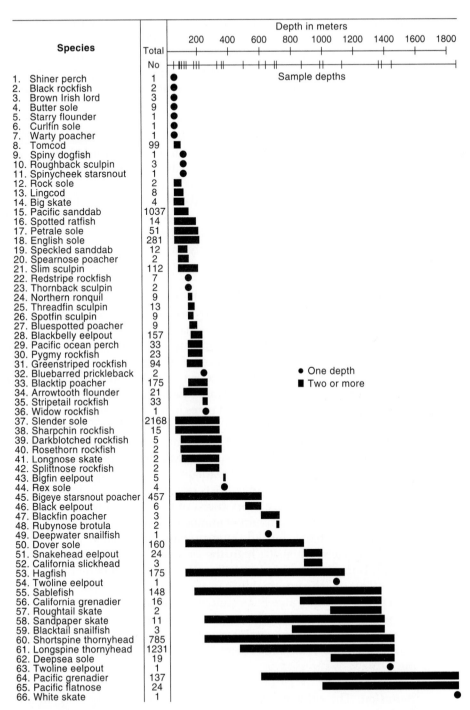

FIGURE 32.2 *Depth ranges of benthic fishes collected off the central coast of Oregon. (From Day and Percy 1968.)*

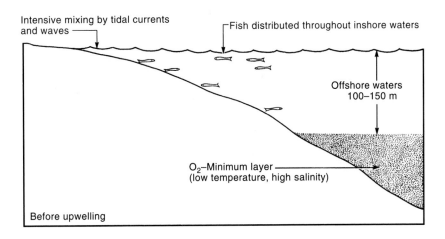

Intensive mixing by tidal currents and waves

Fish distributed throughout inshore waters

Offshore waters 100–150 m

O_2–Minimum layer (low temperature, high salinity)

Before upwelling

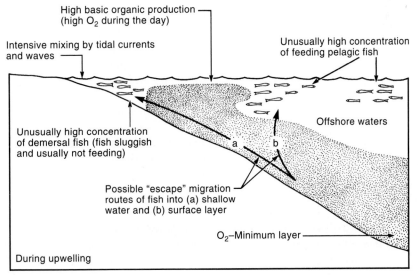

High basic organic production (high O_2 during the day)

Intensive mixing by tidal currents and waves

Unusually high concentration of feeding pelagic fish

Offshore waters

Unusually high concentration of demersal fish (fish sluggish and usually not feeding)

a   b

Possible "escape" migration routes of fish into (a) shallow water and (b) surface layer

O_2–Minimum layer

During upwelling

FIGURE 32.3 *Impact of upwelling on the distribution of benthic and epipelagic fishes along the coast of Southern California. (Used by permission of Southern California Water Research Project.)*

"wastelands" have been created. In less extreme situations the composition of the fish communities are changed, the abundance and diversity of fishes reduced, and the incidence of disease increased. For example, off Los Angeles the fish community appears to have shifted from one associated with sand bottoms to one associated with silt bottoms as a result (at least in part) of the deposition of sewage on the bottom. In the immediate vicinity of waste-water discharge sites, the diversity of fishes is low, even though some species, such as white croaker *(Genyonemus lineatus)* and Dover sole *(Microstomus pacificus)*, may actually be attracted to the dis-

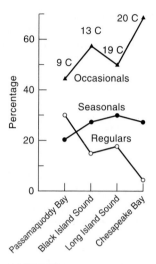

FIGURE 32.4
*Percentages of fish species
that are found on a year-
round basis (regulars),
seasonally, and irregularly
(occasionals), in coastal
waters at different
latitudes in eastern North
America. Annual
temperature ranges are
shown at top of graph.
(From Tyler 1971.)*

charges. In addition there is a high incidence of disease, particularly fin erosion disease and various tumors, in the benthic fishes of the area, apparently as a result of
contact by the fish with toxic materials on the bottom (Mearns 1973).

Species interactions. Competition and predation undoubtedly play an important
role in determining the structure of soft-bottomed fish communities, although there
is little direct evidence. However, the indirect evidence is compelling. The succession of similar species with depth would seem to indicate that some sort of competitive exclusion takes place, based in part on physiological specializations for different combinations of temperature and depth (pressure). Along the northern
portions of both coasts of North America, for example, flounders of the genus *Glyptocephalus* tend to replace other species of flounders in water deeper than 150 m.
The impact of overfishing on fish communities also indicates that the presence of
one species may result in the exclusion of others. On the Georges Bank overfishing
of the haddock *(Melanogrammus aeglefinus)* led to their replacement by the yellowtail flounder *(Limanda ferruginea).* Overfishing of the flounder in turn led to their

replacement by red hake *(Urophycis chuss)* (Rounselfell 1975). Before the fishery collapsed completely, the dominant fishes became spiny dogfish *(Squalus acanthias)* and skates. Another line of evidence indicating the importance of competitive exclusion, at least over long periods of time, is that studies of the feeding habits of coexisting fishes consistently show partitioning of the food resources available among the species (Tyler 1972). Overall, it appears that fishes on soft bottoms are specialized in terms of both habits and habitat requirements but that a number of them are flexible enough to take advantage of situations created when a normally dominant species is absent.

Zonation. Although the fishes of the continental shelf and slope may show seasonal patterns of movement, especially in relation to reproduction, it is usually possible to detect distinct fish zones in relation to depth. As in freshwater streams, these zones appear to be broad areas where the distributions of species with more or less similar habitat requirements overlap. Species frequently inhabit more than one zone (often at different times in their life cycles), but within zones segregation by feeding habits seems to be the rule. Off most coasts, five basic habitat zones can be recognized: (1) shallow-water, (2) inner continental shelf, (3) outer continental shelf, (4) upper continental slope, and (5) middle continental slope.

The **shallow-water zone** is typically found in water less than 50 m deep and includes bays and other sheltered areas. Within this zone, of course, are the other coastal ecosystems discussed previously. The **inner shelf zone** is typically found between 50 and 100 m up to 150 m. The bottom is often sand, or mixed sand, silt, and broken shells, and is flat and featureless, although interrupted by submarine canyons and islands or rocky reefs. The dominant fishes here are such forms as hagfish (Myxinidae), flounder, codfish (Gadidae), rockfish, and skates. The **outer shelf zone,** usually between 150 and 400 m in depth, is similar in many respects to the previous zone, although the bottom tends to contain more silt and clay. The fishes are also similar but are usually of different species. In addition, members of families such as the Ophidiidae (cusk-eels) and Zoarcidae (eelpouts) are more common. It is worth noting the species determined to be "dominant" are dominant in the catches of the sampling gear used and not necessarily dominant on the bottom itself. Photographs taken by cameras lowered to the bottom in such areas often reveal quite different patterns of species abundance than those determined from sampling programs.

The **upper slope zone** generally shows an increase in gradient from the previous zone, dropping from about 440 m to 1200 m. The bottom is mixed clay and silt. Along the Atlantic coast the fishes are mostly true deepwater forms that are rarely seen in shallower water: grenadiers (Macrouridae), longnose eel *(Synaphobranchus kaupi),* a small hake *(Phycis chesteri),* and eelpouts. Although species tend to be year-round residents in this zone, one other common species, the witch flounder, uses the zone as nursery grounds, so the young flounder eventually move up onto the continental shelf (Markle and Musick 1974; Haedrich et al. 1975). Off the Pacific coast many distinct deepwater forms are also present in this zone, but the dominant species seem to be some of the same species of rockfish, flounders, and hake abundant on the shelf. The **middle slope zone** is similar to the upper slope zone, but the number of species is much fewer and all are largely confined to the continental slope. The benthic fish fauna of this zone is remarkably similar in both the Atlantic and the Pacific, with the dominant fishes in trawl catches often being grenadiers (especially *Coryphaenoides*) and codlings (Moridae). The fishes of this zone and of the Upper Slope Zone are discussed in more detail in Chapter 34.

HYPERSALINE LAGOONS AND SALT PONDS

Hypersaline lagoons are shallow embayments in arid and semiarid regions in which the combination of high evaporation rates, poor oceanic circulation, and low freshwater inflow results in salinities frequently exceeding 40 ppt. The number of fish species in a hypersaline lagoon is typically low, but if the fluctuations in temperature and salinity are not too extreme, the fish populations can be quite large. The most abundant fishes are typically juveniles of the same species that characterize local estuaries and other shallow-water environments. In the Gulf of Mexico, where such lagoons are common, characteristic species are sea catfish, sheepshead minnow, tidewater silverside, striped mullet, pinfish, southern flounder *(Paralichthys lethostigma),* and various species of croakers (Sciaenidae). Most of the fishes are planktivores or predators on other fishes, although the sheepshead minnow, mullet, and some drum do browse on algae and detritus (Copeland and Nixon 1974).

Salt ponds, like hypersaline lagoons, are semi-isolated shallow embayments, but they are located in non-arid regions, so their salinities are seldom greater than that of the local sea water, and often less. The fishes are the same species found in local eelgrass beds and bays: silversides, pipefish, stickleback, killifish, and other small species, as well as the young of various larger species. Some salt ponds seem to be quite important locally as nursery grounds for inshore fishes. On the Hawaiian Islands there are numerous low-salinity ponds in old lava flows. These ponds are inhabited by a wide variety of euryhaline fishes that have accidentally been washed into them by storm waves or have moved into them through outlet streams. The ponds apparently are not used as nursery areas, but they are often good producers of fish for human consumption (Brock 1977).

CONCLUSIONS

Anyone who is even vaguely familiar with the fish and habitats of the continental shelves of temperate regions will know that this chapter has not done justice to their diversity. Ideally, each major habitat type deserves a separate chapter. Describing the kelp forest fish communities off California (as in this chapter), for example, provides only a general notion of the kelp bed communites off the Atlantic coast of North America or off Australia. Yet no matter where fish communities on the continental shelves are studied, they show a tremendous dynamism in response to constant changes in oceanic conditions, brought about by changes in ocean currents or in climate, or by local events such as major storms. However, we are also beginning to appreciate the fact that, while local fish faunas can show dramatic changes in abundance and composition, they also have a tendency to constantly readjust themselves into the fairly predictable patterns we recognize as fish communities. Even the recent shifts in many of these communities into new conditions caused by overfishing and pollution seem to be reversible, if the insults to the natural systems are taken away. Naturally, human endeavor constantly pushes the coastal marine environment into more extreme conditions to which the fishes have to adapt; but the limits of their ability to adapt are rapidly being discovered. Most marine fish, it turns out, are tied less to the vast open ocean than to the continents, the habitat of humans.

Supplemental Readings

Bigelow and Schroeder 1953; Culliney 1979; Foster and Schiel 1985; Gibson 1993; Hart 1973; Hobson 1994; Lugo and Snedaker 1974; Rounsefell 1975; Scott and Scott 1988; Thayer et al. 1975.

CHAPTER 33

Tropical Reefs

The diversity of fish life on tropical reefs can only be called astonishing. Somewhere between 30% and 40% of all fish species are associated with such reefs in one way or another, and anywhere from 250 to 2200 species are likely to be found in, on, or near a major complex of reefs. The number of species found in even one small area is often hard to comprehend; Smith and Tyler (1972) collected 75 species from an isolated coral dome that was only about 3 m in diameter and 1.6 m high. Most of the fishes found on reefs are acanthopterygians with an extraordinary array of adaptations for maintaining themselves in a crowded environment. Just as fascinating as the individual species are the complex evolutionary processes that have given rise to the complex structure of tropical reef ecosystems. Indeed, the reefs as we see them today are the product of millions of years of coevolution among fish, invertebrates, and algae. Arguably, fish are the movers and shakers of reef ecosystems; without them the reefs themselves would not exist.

While the diversity of reef fishes and the complexity of reef ecosystems has been appreciated for a long time, it is only recently that they have become the focus of ecological studies. Sale (1991) attributes this interest to three factors:

1. **Mobility and spatial scale.** The fishes of tropical reefs are small (mostly < 30 cm long) and sedentary, resulting in a wealth of species concentrated in areas that can be easily studied and manipulated.

2. **Accessibility.** The development of scuba gear, modern transportation systems, and a tourist industry on remote islands has made reefs readily accessible to biologists. Also, reefs are located in warm shallow water in which an observer can hover for hours, watching the activity below.

3. **Temporal scale.** Most reef fishes live 1–10 years and reproduce continually, so their pattern of life fits readily within the time scales of Ph.D. dissertation research projects and research grants.

This chapter will summarize some of the progress that has been made in the study of reef fish and their communities by describing (1) the reef habitat, (2) the types of reef fishes based on feeding habits, (3) life cycles of reef fishes, (4) species interactions, (5) activity patterns, and (6) community structure.

THE REEF ENVIRONMENT

Tropical reefs are found between latitudes 30° north and 30° south, in shallow water (usually less than 50 m deep) that is warm enough to support the growth of corals and clear enough to allow photosynthesis at moderate depths. This means that the water in reef areas rarely drops below 18°C (it is usually around 23°C to 25°C), and that underwater visibility usually extends to at least 10 m to 20 m. Although corals are typically associated with tropical reefs and are famous for their reef-building habits, many so-called coral reefs have largely been built up by calcareous algae. In addition, there are many rocky coastal areas and reefs that support a complex fish and invertebrate fauna similar to that of the coral and algal reefs. Most tropical reefs are surrounded by nutrient-poor oceanic waters, so their extremely high productivity is surprising. The productivity can be attributed to a combination of (1) a high degree of recycling of nutrients within the reefs; (2) the photosynthetic activity of attached algae under optimal light and temperature conditions; and (3) nitrogen fixation by blue-green algae on the reefs (Wiebe et al. 1975).

There are four major regions of the ocean that have tropical reefs: (1) the Indo-Pacific Region; (2) the Eastern Pacific Region; (3) the Western Atlantic (West Indian) Region; and (4) the Eastern Atlantic (West African) Region (see Chapter 26). While these regions have had long independent evolutionary histories, the processes that have formed the reef communities are very similar. Thus, each reef typically has a series of habitat zones with distinctive fish and invertebrate faunas. Six major zones can be recognized, although all are not present on every reef.

The **off-reef floor** is the shallow sea bottom around a reef. It is typically sandy and often supports beds of seagrass and thus may be an important foraging area for reef fish. Many reefs are not surrounded by a level sandy floor but drop off abruptly, often to great depths. The **reef drop-off** in its upper 50 to 60 m is favored by large numbers of fish, which can find shelter on the cliff face and abundant plankton in the water immediately off it. The **reef face** that is above either the floor or the drop-off is often the richest habitat for fish and invertebrates. Its complex growths of coral and calcareous algae provide innumerable cracks and crevices for protection, and the abundant invertebrates and epiphytic algae provide an ample source of food. The **reef surface** is also a rich habitat for life, but the organisms that live there must be able to withstand the constant surge of the waves and, in some areas, the rise and fall of tides. Behind the main reef, toward the shore, there is often a sandy-bottomed **reef flat** containing scattered chunks of coral. The reef flat may be a protected area bordering a lagoon or it may be a flat, rocky area between the reef and shore. In the former case the number of fish species living in the area is often the highest of any reef zone. Many coral reefs completely enclose an area, creating a quiet-water **lagoon** that usually contains small patches of reef.

Although the zones on a reef are fairly stable phenomena, the topography of a reef is constantly changing. Each reef is made up of irregular patches of algae, sessile invertebrates, and bare rock and sand. The size, shape, and relative abundance of these patches changes from year to year, in response to the various factors that favor one patch type over another. On a larger scale, tropical storms may knock out large sections of reef and cause boulders on sandy areas to move around. These changes, whether large or small, are essentially unpredictable and thus provide a habitat for reef fish that continually changes on a local scale, even if the overall environment seems quite benign and stable (Connell 1978).

TYPES OF REEF FISHES

There are many ways to classify reef fishes, but for understanding the structure of the fish communities, the clearest approach is to classify them by feeding habits. Following Hobson (1974) in good part, we place reef fishes into three general feeding categories: generalized carnivores, specialized carnivores, and herbivores.

Generalized Carnivores

These fish have the classic rover-predator body shape, with large, flexible mouths well suited for seizing large prey (Fig. 33.1). By and large, they prey on mobile fishes and invertebrates. The generalized carnivores are of three basic types: nocturnal, crepuscular, and diurnal.

The **nocturnal predators** are specialized to the extent that they have large eyes and typically feed on benthic crustaceans that move about the reef at night. The **crepuscular predators** are rover-predators, representing such families as the Serranidae, Carangidae, and Lutjanidae. These fishes become active during twilight because the low light levels offer a certain amount of concealment to the predators while still enabling them to see their prey, particularly schooling fishes. **Diurnal predators** are similar to crepuscular predators in their body shape and preferences for fish. They obtain their prey by slowly cruising over the reef or by lying in concealment. In either situation, they must wait until a nearby fish makes a defensive mistake, such as moving too far from cover or becoming separated from a school.

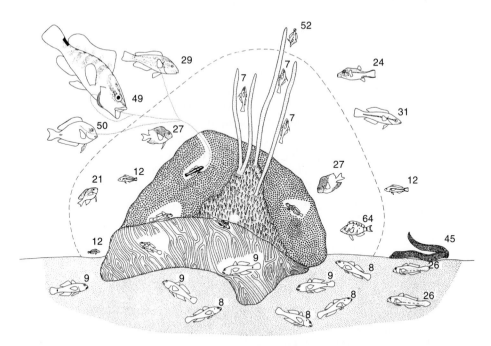

FIGURE 33.1 *Fishes associated with an isolated piece of West Indian reef, in which a cleaner goby (19,* Gobiosoma*) has a station. Waiting to be cleaned are herbivorous parrotfish (29,* Scarus*), a generalized carnivore (49, a grouper,* Epinephelus*), and a herbivorous surgeonfish (50,* Acanthurus*). Associated with the reef surface are diurnal planktivores (27, a damselfish,* Pomacentrus*; and 12, a wrasse,* Thalassoma*), a territorial herbivore (21, a damselfish,* Pomacentrus*), a herbivorous parrotfish (64,* Sparisoma*), small, plankton-feeding goby (7,* Coryphopterus*), and a small filefish (52,* Monacanthus*). Visiting the patch to feed on occasion are a diurnal feeder on hard-shelled invertebrates (24, a puffer,* Canthigaster*), a diurnal invertebrate-picker (31, a wrasse,* Halichoeres*), and a crevice-feeder (45, a moray eel,* Muraena*). Associated with the sand around the coral and the coral itself are a guild of gobies (8, 9, 25, 26, 28), feeding variously on algae, detritus, and small invertebrates, often at night. (From Smith and Tyler 1972.)*

Specialized Carnivores

A majority of reef fish species have highly specialized feeding habitats, reflecting the complexity of the evolutionary processes that characterize reef environments. Although many of the specializations are extraordinary, it is not unusual to find several species on the same reef with about the same specializations. These similar species form feeding guilds whose members may interact with each other through competition. On a broader basis, the specialized carnivores can be divided into eight types: (1) ambushers, (2) water-column stalkers, (3) crevice predators, (4) concealed-prey feeders, (5) diurnal predators on benthic invertebrates, (6)cleaners, (7) diurnal planktivores, and (8) nocturnal planktivores.

Ambushers. Ambush feeding is one of the principal methods of prey capture used by reef carnivores and there are many examples of extreme use of camouflage. Among these fish are lizardfish (Synodontidae), various scorpionfish (Scorpaenidae), and flounders (Bothidae). Such fishes match their backgrounds so well that they are frequently overlooked by prey (and divers). The scorpionfishes, including the deadly stonefish *(Synanceia),* are particularly famous for their ability to blend into the reef environment, looking more like corals than fish.

Water-column stalkers. This is another group of fishes that specialize in making themselves invisible to potential prey so they can ambush them. These fish are silvery, elongate forms, with long pointed snouts full of sharp teeth. A head-on view often belies their large size. They drift through the water column toward a small fish and then seize it with a sudden lunge, propelled by a fin structure typical of lie-in-wait predators. Examples of this group are cornetfish (Fistularidae) and trumpetfish (Aulostomidae).

Crevice predators. These fish actively seek their prey, which are mostly fish that hide in the numerous crevices and small caves characteristic of reefs. The main specializations of this group are elongate bodies and small heads that allow them to penetrate into crevices to find their prey. Examples are moray eels (Muraenidae) and reef brotulas (Ophidiidae).

Concealed-prey feeders. This group of fishes also actively seeks prey that are hidden on or about the reef, taking both active invertebrates and small fish. It consists mainly of the goatfishes (Mullidae), an abundant and conspicuous group of reef dwellers. Goatfish have long chin barbels which they use to probe the reef surface or sandy flats around a reef. Once a goatfish has located a prey organism with its barbels, it sucks it up with its flexible, slightly subterminal mouth. Depending on the species, goatfishes can be either nocturnal or diurnal.

Diurnal predators on benthic invertebrates. These are among the most colorful and peculiar-looking reef fishes. Most use vision to find their prey, which are typically the more conspicuous reef invertebrates such as sponges, corals, tunicates, sea urchins, and snails. These feeding relationships provide some of the more spectacular examples of coevolution of predators and prey. Over the course of several million years of predator pressure, the invertebrates have evolved a formidable array of defense mechanisms, mostly various combinations of spines, toxins, heavy armor, and adherence to the substrate. Simultaneously, the predatory fishes have evolved many mechanisms for overcoming the defenses of the invertebrates. One means of overcoming heavy armor is to have strong, hard jaws, such as the heavy beaks possessed by most members of the order Tetraodontiformes (puffers, boxfishes, etc.); another is to have strong pharyngeal teeth, such as those of many of the wrasses (Labridae). These fish crush various hard-shelled invertebrates. Other species circumvent the armed defenses of their prey by biting off exposed pieces of flesh, such as the polyps of coral and the "fans" of sessile polychaete worms. Many of the species that feed in this manner are the deep-bodied, brightly colored butterflyfishes (Chaetodontidae), which come equipped with elongate snouts tipped by small mouths containing tiny (but sharp) teeth, with which they can clip off pieces of invertebrates. Some butterflyfishes use the same type of feeding mechanism for seizing prey located deep in crevices, such as small crustaceans or even encrusting sponges. The depth to which a species can reach into a crevice is reflected in the length of its snout, which in some species may be over 25% of the body length. Yet another way some butterflyfishes feed is by scraping the surface of living coral, thereby obtaining mucus secreted by the coral along with small attached invertebrates and algae.

Diurnal predators also have a number of behavioral specializations. Some species of wrasse with small mouths feed by carefully searching the reef surface and then picking up invertebrates that are too small for most other species to feed upon. Other wrasses will use their snouts to overturn chunks of rock and coral on the reef edge and expose hidden invertebrates. Some tetraodontids obtain invertebrates in sandy-bottomed areas by uncovering them with a jet of water blown from their mouth. Fish that feed in such a manner are often followed around by other fish, who attempt to capture the exposed invertebrates first. "Following behavior" is also elicited by schools of herbivorous fishes which disturb the substrate or even by foraging octopuses and moray eels, whose activities may send small fish fleeing from cover and into the mouths of other predators (Diamant and Shpigel 1985).

Cleaners. These fishes utilize another specialized form of invertebrate feeding, picking ectoparasites and dead or diseased tissue from other fish. For some species, such as gobies of the genus *Gobiosoma* of western Atlantic reefs and wrasses of the genus *Labroides* of Indo-Pacific reefs, cleaning is the principal feeding specialization. The distinctive behavior and bright coloration of cleaner fish attract other fish to them. The client fish express their receptivity to cleaning by entering into a trancelike state, with fins held rigidly, opercula flared, and mouths open. Such fish often exhibit special contrasting color patterns as well. The cleaner then swims about the fish, picking off ectoparasites from the sides and, for larger fishes, often from within the mouth cavity as well. They will also pick dead or diseased tissue from wounds, eat loose scales, consume mucus, and nibble off pieces of healthy fin. Although the removal of healthy tissue is detrimental to the fish being cleaned, the cleaning of infected tissue from wounded fish may promote healing (Foster 1985). Cleaner fish either work from stations on the reef to which fish come to be cleaned, or move freely about the reef during the day, stopping to clean territorial fish. In the latter case they will apparently also steal eggs from nests being guarded by the territory holders (Losey 1978).

Diurnal planktivores. Rather than finding their food on the reef itself, diurnal planktivores use the reef mainly for shelter and hover above it in brilliant, shifting shoals, while feeding on zooplankton. These fish require specializations for (1) capturing prey that is either very small (copepods) or gelatinous (larvaceans, chaetognaths, fish eggs, etc.); and (2) escaping predators (Hobson 1991). These factors have caused fish from different families (e.g., Pomacentridae, Serranidae, Acanthuridae) to evolve quite similar morphologies: streamlined bodies, deeply forked or lunate tails, fine gill rakers, and small upturned mouths. The first two features enable fish to dive quickly into the cover of the reef at the approach of a predatory fish. However, their body shape, while streamlined, is more or less a compromise between the rover-predator shape and the deep-bodied shape, because a deep body is useful for hovering in the water column and picking out the plankton. Some planktivores have in fact opted for retaining a deep body and keeping stout spines to repel predators. Usually, the further a fish forages from the reef, the more streamlined the body (Hobson 1991). The flexible small mouth enables the fish to capture small prey by suction. It is upturned in order to shorten the snout, which gives the fish binocular vision at close range for pinpointing its small prey (Hobson 1974).

Nocturnal planktivores. These fishes have the moderately deep bodies, forked tails, and upturned mouths of the diurnal forms but they have a larger and less flexible mouth and large eyes. Typically their bodies are red. These species leave the reef at night to forage on large (2+ mm) zooplankton and invertebrates that also leave the reef to enter the water column at night.

Herbivores

Herbivores make up about 20% of all fish species that inhabit reefs (Sale 1977). What they may lack in variety, they make up for in numbers and conspicuousness as well as in their impact on the appearance of reefs (Horn 1989). Herbivores are often the most noticeable fish on reefs. Small, brightly colored damselfishes vigorously defend their territories, while schools of large parrotfishes (Scaridae) and surgeonfishes (Acanthuridae) browse over the reef surface. Other herbivores (or partial herbivores) are scattered through the various families of reef fishes, such as Kyphosidae, Chaetodontidae, Blenniidae, Pomacanthidae, and Siganidae. Their main sources of food are filamentous algae that coat a reef and, to a lesser extent, the seagrasses and algae that grow on reef flats. The herbivorous fishes (and invertebrates as well) keep the algae on the reef cropped down to a thin mat, only 1 mm to 2 mm thick, and can create a ring around reefs up to 10 m wide that is bare of vegetation (Randall 1965). Grazing by herbivores is important for the well-being of reef-building corals and algae because patches of reef from which herbivores are excluded quickly become covered with thick growths of filamentous and leafy algae, which may smother the corals (Lewis 1986).

The plants are eaten in various ways by the fish, such as scraping by parrotfish and plucking by damselfish. Nevertheless, the diets of the various herbivores seem to differ little from species to species although there may be major differences in their abilities to digest different kinds of algae. Smaller herbivores, such as damselfish, may protect their share of this food supply by defending sections of reef against their own kind as well as against other species of fish. This aggressive defense results in heavier growths of algae (and invertebrates) within the territories than outside them. In order to exploit these growths, some herbivores will move into a territory as a school, overwhelming the defender (Robertson et al. 1976). Some species of surgeonfish (Acanthuridae) that are regarded as herbivores actually feed on detritus, and they will therefore be tolerated in the territories of herbivorous surgeonfish species (Choat 1991).

LIFE CYCLES

For most of its life, a typical reef fish lives in a very restricted part of a reef. For some fish this resident period may last only a year, while for others it may last 10 or more. Divers commonly recognize individual fish for several years in the same place, so it is likely that most of the smaller reef fish live three to five years. Spawning takes place in this same general area, but embryos and larvae, with few exceptions, are planktonic. The length of the planktonic stage is highly variable, lasting from a few weeks to several months. The larval fish are dispersed widely by currents and they settle out on to reefs. Most are taken by predators, but a few survive to reproduce. Despite the risks involved, the larval stage in reef fishes seems to be necessary for dispersal of the young and to provide opportunities for colonization of new reefs or reefs devastated by storms.

Spawning may take place all year round in equatorial regions, but may last only four to six months in higher latitudes. During the spawning period the frequency of spawning ranges from daily to monthly, depending on the species. Most spawning takes place at dusk or at night, presumably to reduce predation on eggs by planktivores. Before spawning, many of the larger species migrate short distances to places where conditions are optimal for the newly fertilized eggs to be swept away by currents. Smaller fish cannot afford the risk of being eaten while migrating, so they spawn in place (Barlow 1981). Typically, they guard the developing embryos in hidden places until they hatch. Other species afford their embryos protection as bearers, such as the mouth brooding cardinalfishes (Apogonidae) and jawfishes (Opistognathidae), and a few species are livebearers. With few exceptions, the larvae of these species are planktonic although they do not seem to disperse as widely as the larvae of the larger, more fecund, pelagic spawners (Barlow 1981).

Regardless of the degree of parental care, spawning behavior among reef fishes is frequently complex (Thresher 1984). For example, parrotfishes (Scaridae) have elaborate mating systems that can involve the conversion of females to males, as needed (see Chapter 22). The presence of "converted" females is most common in situations where population densities are low (Warner 1982). While most reef fish are mass spawners or form only temporary pairs, a surprising number are monogamous. They include many butterflyfishes and angelfishes, and the anemonefishes (*Amphiprion*). The latter fishes lay their eggs under the protective tentacles of anemones. Among the more unusual pair-spawners are the harlequin bass (*Serranus* spp.) of the Caribbean, which are hermaphroditic and take turns being male or female during the spawning sequence with the same mate.

SPECIES INTERACTIONS

Because tropical reefs are both a physically benign and ancient environment, the fish fauna is complex and includes some of the most complex patterns of interactions among known species. These interactions are very important determinants of community structure, especially predation, competition, symbiosis, and mimicry.

Predation. The variety of ways in which reef fish act as predators has already been discussed. However, reef fish also serve as prey for each other and for certain reef invertebrates, so they consequently have many means, both morphological and behavioral, of protecting themselves. Most reef fishes possess a formidable array of spines, which often are venomous or can be rigidly locked in place. Many have cryptic or disruptive color patterns as well, to confuse predators. Behaviorally, small reef fish protect themselves from predators either by schooling or by hiding in reef crevices. Many reef fish spend most of their lives in one small area, so they have well-known hiding places instantly available. Others may roam the reef, typically in schools, but return to specific areas to hide during the times when they are not actively feeding. While resting, small fish are still vulnerable to crevice predators, so many fish cram themselves into the smallest possible hiding places and wedge themselves in with erect spines. Parrotfish can secrete a cocoon of mucus about themselves while resting, which seems to provide protection against predators that find hidden prey by smell or touch.

Predation is probably the most important cause of fish death on reefs, so it can have considerable effects, both direct and indirect, on the structure of fish communities (Hixon 1991). Predation may, for example, directly promote diversity by reducing populations of competitively superior species. Indirectly, predation may make shelters from piscivores a limiting resource and thereby cause interspecific competition for shelter (Shulman 1985). It may also be responsible for the general pattern of daily activity of reef fishes discussed in the next section. Curiously, the high level of piscivory on reefs also seems to enhance their productivity, because planktivores and other fishes deposit feces in their shelter areas, which are consumed by other fish and invertebrates (Robertson 1982). In fact, Meyer et al. (1983) have shown that coral heads that, during the day, shelter fishes that feed at night away from the reef grow faster than those without such fishes. Larger, more complex coral heads in turn support more fish.

Competition. Competition, like predation, has undoubtedly been an important process in shaping reef fish communities. Presumably the high degree of resource partitioning among reef fishes and the many morphological differences among related species, such as the different snout lengths of butterflyfishes, are the result of past competitive interactions that have led to coevolved divergence. Nevertheless, the importance of competition on reefs today is difficult to demonstrate because rarely can either shelter or food be shown to be limiting resources. For example, after a severe storm leveled much of a Hawaiian reef, there was little change in either its species composition or its population sizes (Walsh 1983). The resident fishes had moved into deeper water during the storm but then returned to occupy their greatly diminished habitat. Likewise, while ecological differences can be found among co-occurring species of butterflyfish, Findley and Findley (1985) could not find any evidence of competition among the species. Some species seem to have few ecological differences and form guilds that recognize each other's signals; the damselfish that "garden" algae defend their territories not only against conspecifics but against other damselfish species as well (Sale 1977).

Symbiosis. Of the types of symbiosis, only mutualism and commensalism are common among reef fishes. The classic example of mutualism among fishes is the interaction among cleaner fishes and the fishes being cleaned, although this relationship is more complex than once thought (see Chapter 27). Perhaps a better example is shoals made up of two or more species; such shoals confer on the cooperating species the advantages of large shoals. Mutualistic relationships may also form between invertebrates and fish, the classic example being anemone-fish and anemones (Fautin 1991). Anemonefish are protected from predators by the stings of anemones (from which the anemonefish are protected by a special mucus coating), while the anemones are protected from grazing predators by the aggressive actions of the anemonefish. The anemones may also benefit by being able to develop a more expansive shape, providing more surface area for the symbiotic algae that grow in the tentacles (Fautin 1991). Presumably the anemones also take advantage of waste products of the fish to improve growth, a factor demonstrated to be important in the growth of some corals that fish use as cover. Other fish-invertebrate interactions are commensal in nature, such as those exhibited by the fishes that hide among the spines of sea urchins and starfish or hide in the hollow tubes of sponges. An example of commensalism among fish species is the following behavior of fishes seeking prey stirred up by other fishes. A purely commensal relationship, however, is that of some cornetfish (Fistularidae) and parrotfishes. The long, narrow cornetfish "rides" on top of the parrotfish, essentially using the parrotfish as a mobile cover from which it can ambush small fish.

Mimicry. As reef fish become better known, more and more cases of mimicry among them are documented (Russell, Allen, and Lubbock 1976). Most of the examples known are either cases of **aggressive mimicry,** where a predator species mimics a harmless one for access to prey; or cases of **Batesian mimicry,** where a harmless species mimics a predatory species for its own protection. Often several species in one area resemble each other, forming a mimicry "ring" **(Mullerian mimicry).** Perhaps the most famous example of an aggressive mimic is the sabertooth blenny *(Aspidontus);* it mimics cleaner wrasses in morphology, color, and behavior, and then bites chunks out of hapless fish waiting to be cleaned. Usually only young or naive fish are fooled by the blenny, however. Examples of Batesian mimicry are found among reef fishes that have eye spots on the caudal peduncle. Such spots may be used to temporarily startle a predator by giving the impression that the pursued fish is much larger than it really is. An extreme development of this type of mimicry occurs in the plesiopid fish, *Calloplesiops altivelus*, which mimics the moray eel, *Gymnothorax melagris* (McCosker 1977). Both species have a similar color pattern, so when the fish dashes into the reef while fleeing a predator, it may leave its rear half exposed. The color pattern and eye spot combined give the impression of a moray eel in an aggressive posture.

ACTIVITY PATTERNS

One way that reef species avoid interactions with other species is to have periods of activity that do not overlap with those of potential competitors or predators. Indeed, one of the striking aspects of reef fish communities is the difference between night and day on a reef. During the day, the deeper cracks, crevices, and caves of a reef are filled with night-active fish, whereas at night they are filled with day-active fish (Fig. 33.2). The changeover from diurnal to nocturnal fish and then back again is a fascinating and complex phenomenon (Hobson 1975).

During the day the reef's surface is a busy place, because most of the brightly colored, specialized carnivores are active at this time, feeding, defending territories, and spawning. Immediately above the reef are schools of small plankton-feeding fish, which are under the surveillance of various piscivorous fish. Closer to the reef are large, relatively inactive schools of nocturnal planktivores and other nocturnal fish that do not feed on the reef. Deep within the reef are other nocturnal fish, often red in color with large eyes, such as squirrelfish (Holocentridae), cardinalfish (Apogonidae), and bigeyes (Priacanthidadae).

As twilight approaches, the transition between day and night fish faunas begins. The dominant behavior of the diurnal fishes is cover-seeking. As the light dims, the diurnal planktivores come closer to the reef, while the specialized carnivores become less active and seek out their nighttime hiding places. Fish that roam the reef during the day stream back to their regular resting places. Most of these fish are in place 15 to 20 minutes after sunset (Hobson 1975), and for the next 20 minutes or so the reef is remarkably quiet because the nocturnal fish have not yet emerged. One reason for this general hiatus in fish activity is presumably that during this time of low light intensity, piscivorous fish are most active and most effective at capturing prey. The quiet period ends when the nocturnal planktivores emerge in large numbers from their hiding places and swim up into the water column. By this time it is nearly dark. On the surface of the reef, small unspecialized predators begin to move about, feeding on small crustaceans that have also emerged from hiding. Nocturnal piscivores such as conger eels (Congridae) and some goatfish also become active at this time, seeking out hidden diurnal fish. Despite this activity, the number of active fish on the reef itself is smaller at night than during the day. As dawn approaches, the process observed in the evening reverses itself, and the diurnal fish once again resume their activities.

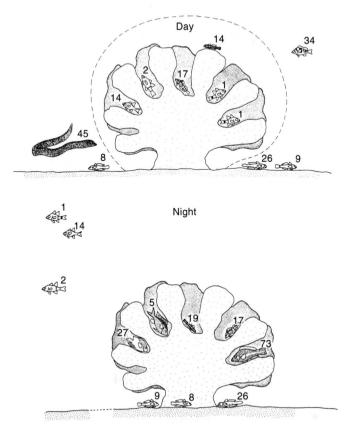

FIGURE 33.2 *Day and night residents of a West Indian coral head. Nocturnal planktivores (1, 2, 14, cardinalfishes, Apogonidae), a cleaner goby (19, Gobisoma), a predatory blenny (17, Labrisomus), a piscivore (34, Hypoplectrus), various gobies (8, 9, 26, Gobiidae), a crevice feeder (45, moray eel, Muraena), diurnal planktivores (5, 27, damselfishes, Pomacentridae) and a diurnal herbivore (73, a parrotfish, Sparisoma). (From Smith and Tyler 1972.)*

COMMUNITY STRUCTURE

The complexity of the interactions among fish of tropical reefs makes the overall structure of the fish communities very difficult to comprehend. The nature of reef fish communities is strongly influenced by three factors: (1) most reef fish are highly specialized, having developed complex adaptations to a complex environment; (2) the number of reef fish species is very large and their population densities are high; and (3) among spatially separated reef patches there is a great deal of variation in the composition of the fish fauna (Smith 1978). In addition, repeated surveys of coral reef areas often show considerable variation from one survey to the next, although on a large scale there is often repeatability in species composition between surveys. Such surveys have been used to support a range of concepts of how tropical reef fish communities are organized, from open, nonequilibrium systems that are almost chaotic in structure to highly organized, equilibrium systems. Hixon (1991) puts forth three general hypotheses that have been used to explain the structure of reef fish communities: (1) the competition hypothesis, (2) the recruitment limitation hypothesis, and (3) the predation hypothesis.

The **competition hypothesis** holds that the fish community is composed of specialized fishes that compete in a myriad of subtle ways to subdivide food and space. Much of the extreme specialization observed can be explained as the result of past competition, which has forced species into narrow niches. In this view the reef communities are in a state of equilibrium, so they should be predictable in composition and structure once the interactions among the species are understood. Under this hypothesis, reef resources must be limiting during some times for most species.

The **recruitment limitation hypothesis,** in contrast, argues that resources on reefs are rarely limiting. The reason for this is that mortality rates of the pelagic embryos and larvae of reef fish are so high that there are never enough recruits (newly settled fish) to saturate the environment. There should, in theory, be a steady rain of recruits onto the reefs because reef fish spawn over long periods of time and produce large numbers of larvae. However, the only successful recruits are those that happen to settle upon a vacant place on the reef. Because the vacancies are unpredictable and because the species of larvae likely to land in any given space is unpredictable, Sale (1980) likened the process to a "lottery" for living space. Thus the basic composition of a reef community is determined mainly by random processes. The randomness is driven not only by the "lottery" of reef fish recruitment but also by the constantly changing nature of the reef environment, through the growth of corals, damage by storms, and other factors.

The **predation hypothesis** argues that there are plenty of recruits arriving on the reefs to fill vacant spaces but that the intensity of predation on these small fish is so high that they rarely live very long. This intense level of piscivory (even on adult fish) prevents each reef from becoming saturated with fish and limits the role of competition in structuring the communities (Hixon 1991). Perhaps the most striking evidence for the predation hypothesis is (1) the large number of piscivores (or partial piscivores) on reefs, as much as 50% of the species in some areas; and (2) the many morphological and behavioral mechanisms fish possess to defend themselves against being eaten. Under this hypothesis, reef communities also tend to have a strong random component to their structure.

The three hypotheses presented above represent extreme perspectives. Presumably reef fish communities are actually assembled by a combination of ecological processes. However, Sale (1991) provides convincing arguments that reef fish assemblages show a high degree of variability at virtually any scale (from whole reefs to small reef sections), so that persistent structure is difficult to find. The assemblage of species found at any given location results from high variability in recruitment, combined with intense predation and competition among the resident fish in a habitat that shows a great deal of random variation in structure (patchiness). At the same time, each species has its own preferred habitat and food and is presumably able to interact flexibly with a large number of other fish species. These latter factors lend a certain amount of predictability to the busy chaos of the reef. Some of the evidence for this view includes:

- Almost all reef fishes have pelagic embryos and larvae; the larvae drift for 10–40 days, settling down in areas distant from the reef where they were spawned and making it difficult for one species to dominate a particular reef through local recruitment.
- Guilds of similar fish species are common, and evidence for direct competition is sparse.
- Many of the more visible reef fish have fairly long life spans and are very sedentary; thus they give the appearance of community constancy to human observers, while masking the variability in recruitment of small fish. Even so, reef fish assemblages are more variable through time than would be expected if there was a predictable structure (Sale and Guy 1993).
- Artificial reefs placed near natural reefs are quickly colonized by juvenile reef fish but in a highly variable fashion.

CONCLUSION

It is clear that we still have much to learn about the dynamic processes that result in the spectacular assemblages of fishes observed on tropical reefs. It is likely that the relative importance of factors affecting the distribution and abundance of reef fish vary from region to region, from locality to locality, and from time to time. Unfortunately, our opportunities to discover new interactions and to learn about and from tropical reefs are rapidly being diminished, as humans destroy reefs through pollution, sedimentation, mining of coral, and other activities (Richmond 1993). In some reefs, such as those around Jamaica, harvesting of fish of all kinds and sizes is so extensive that the coral reefs are dying because of the loss of the intense interactions with fish that they require for survival (Hughes 1994). If such trends continue, many areas where hundreds of species once coexisted in splendid complexity will soon be only simple systems with low productivity.

Supplemental Readings

Collette and Earle 1972; Hobson 1974; Sale 1980, 1991; Thresher 1984; Wilson and Wilson 1985.

CHAPTER 34

Epipelagic Zone

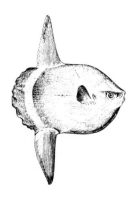

The surface waters of the oceans provide an enormous, if nearly featureless, habitat for fish. Lack of habitat diversity limits the number of species that occupy this region, the epipelagic zone, to less than 2% of all known fish species, and the region itself contains vast expanses of nutrient-poor water that can support few fish. As a consequence, epipelagic fish are concentrated in areas overlying continental shelves or in oceanic areas where upwelling increases the productivity of the water. They are also found almost entirely in the upper 100 m of the water column, where light can penetrate and permit phytoplankton to grow and where visual predators can see their prey. Despite the limited number of species, epipelagic fish are overall the most valuable group of fish to humans because they either occur in enormous numbers (herrings, anchovies) or are particularly favored as food fishes (tunas, salmon). As a direct consequence of their value, the biology of epipelagic fishes has been intensively studied, although the difficulty of such studies means that many basic questions about them are still unanswered. In this chapter, this information will be summarized by discussing (1) adaptations for pelagic life, (2) ecological types of epipelagic fishes, (3) factors affecting distribution and abundance, (4) migrations and movements, and (5) life history of a representative species, the Pacific sardine (*Sardinops sagax*).

ADAPTATIONS FOR PELAGIC LIFE

Most epipelagic fish have streamlined bodies that permit continuous, often rapid, swimming. Examples include (1) the galeomorph sharks (mackerel sharks, requiem sharks, whale sharks, etc.); (2) clupeiform teleosts (herrings, anchovies); (3) Salmonidae (salmon); (4) atheriniform teleosts (flying fishes, halfbeaks, sauries, etc.); and (5) perciform teleosts, most notably Carangidae (jacks), Coryphaenidae (dolphins), Bramidae (pomfrets), Sphyraenidae (barracudas), Scombridae (tunas), and Istiophoridae (billfish). Most of these fishes shoal; and most of them are visual predators on zooplankton or fish, although a number are filter-feeders on plankton. The predators typically have smooth, fusiform bodies, deeply forked tails, and large mouths. Both prey and predators reduce their visibility by being silvery in color, which scatters the incoming light, and by being countershaded.

Filter-feeding epipelagic fishes have the same general morphological features as the predatory fishes, and many of them are in fact facultative predators: They will pick individual invertebrates and small fish out of the water column or filter-feed on phytoplankton, depending on which mode is energetically most advantageous. However, all fishes capable of filter-feeding have a well-developed apparatus for straining small organisms from the water, usually long, fine gill rakers. Curiously, both the largest (whale sharks, basking sharks) and the smallest (anchovies) of adult epipelagic fishes are filter feeders.

ECOLOGICAL TYPES

Epipelagic fish can be divided, for convenience, into two basic ecological types: **oceanic forms,** those that spend all or part of their life cycle in ocean regions that are not above the continental shelves; and **neritic forms,** those that spend all or part of their life cycle living in the waters above the continental shelves. The two categories are not mutually exclusive because many epipelagic fish are both oceanic and neritic, often at different stages in their life cycle, and the two ecological regions have no firm boundaries.

Oceanic epipelagic fish can be divided into true, partial, and accidental residents of the open ocean. The **true residents** spend their entire life cycle there and are of two basic types, those that are free-swimming and those associated with drifting seaweed, jellyfish, and other objects. The number of species that are true residents is small, mainly a few species of shark, tuna, flying fishes, sauries, dolphins, swordfish, marlins, and ocean sunfish, plus the commensal remoras (Echeneidae) and pilotfish (Carangidae). Most of these fishes make extensive migrations across the open ocean and occasionally come close to the continents. Drifting seaweed, particularly pelagic *Sargassum,* provides abundant cover and food in some areas for epipelagic fish and even supports its own unique fish fauna, including the endemic sargassum fish *(Histrio histrio).*

The most abundant **partial residents** are typically the juveniles of neritic or benthic species that are associated with jellyfish and drifting seaweed. Such juvenile partial residents are also found free-swimming, although most partial residents are adult fish such as salmon, dolphin, flying fish, and whale sharks. These fish spawn in inshore areas (or in streams), and the young use similar areas as nursery grounds. Another group of partial residents are deepsea fish, such as the lanternfishes (Myctophidae), that often migrate up into the surface waters at night. Occasionally the true and partial residents of the zone are joined by adults and juveniles of species that are more properly associated with inshore and deepsea environments but that have been accidentally carried into the zone by currents.

Neritic fish are among the most abundant fish in the world, including herrings, sardines, anchovies, and menhaden, as well as the predators on them such as sharks, tunas, mackerel, jacks, billfish, and salmon. Such fish take advantage of the high productivity of inshore water caused by upwelling and shoreline productivity, and most can complete their entire life cycle in the region. However, some are partial residents that spawn in bays, estuaries, or streams, or on the bottom. It is also not unusual to find among these fishes species that are really characteristic of other inshore habitats but that have been carried into the open water by currents and storms.

FACTORS THAT AFFECT DISTRIBUTION AND ABUNDANCE

Physical Factors

Although the open ocean appears featureless, physical factors nevertheless are probably the most important determinants of fish distribution and abundance in the epipelagic zone. Important physical factors include temperature, light, flotsam, upwelling, currents, and islands and banks.

Temperature. This factor has a strong relationship to the distribution patterns of epipelagic fishes. The 8°C to 10°C isotherm, for example, loosely separates the cold ocean water dominated by salmon and the warm ocean water dominated by tunas and billfish. Many epipelagic fish, but particularly the tunas, move north as the water warms up and south as it cools, so that the arrival of commercially important species in some waters can be predicted on the basis of sea temperatures (Blackburn 1965). Similarly, changes in average sea temperatures of only 2°C to 3°C can cause dramatic changes in both fish species and fish abundance (Radovich 1961). In the Gulf of Alaska, for example, the catch of pink salmon by the commercial fishery is strongly correlated with sea surface temperature; an increase of 1°C to 2°C is associated with major increases in salmon abundance (Francis and Sibley 1991). As will be discussed later in this chapter, temperature is important because it interacts with other physical and chemical factors and can affect processes such as predation and competition. In discussions of global warming, changes in epipelagic fisheries are often used as indicators of climate change because the changes can be sudden and dramatic.

Light. Because most epipelagic fishes are visual feeders, light is an important factor. Tuna fishing is often best when the water transparency, as measured by a secchi disc, is 15 to 35 m (Blackburn 1965), but water that is too clear probably contains little food. On the other hand, some of the most productive waters are rather turbid from plankton blooms and consequently favor filter-feeding planktivores, as well as piscivores smaller than those found in clear water. Light is also important because vision is a principal cue that fishes use for shoaling, so that shoals tend to break up in the evening.

Flotsam. One of the more curious aspects of epipelagic fish is their tendency to associate with drifting objects (flotsam), jellyfish, floating seaweed, and other material. One reason for this association appears to be that flotsam serves as "a visual stimulus in an optical void" (Hunter and Mitchell 1966, 27). For juvenile fish, however, flotsam may be important in that it offers some protection from predators. The numbers and diversity of small fish hanging around such pelagic structures are little appreciated, and the abundance of jellyfish or drifting weeds in a region may have a significant positive impact on the year class strength of some species (Kingsford 1993). For example, Dooley (1972) found that 54 species from 23 families inhabited the pelagic *Sargassum* off Florida. Many of these fish were juveniles of neritic species that used seaweed for shelter and fed on the abundant fish and invertebrates associated with it. Likewise, juvenile fish may use jellyfish for shelter and food, even though the young fish may also serve as prey for the jellyfish as well. Even marine turtles can act as mobile cover for small fish, although occasionally the turtles become accidentally impaled by swordfish seeking to eat the fish being sheltered (Frazier et al. 1994).

Upwelling. Although light and temperature do have considerable independent influence on the ecology of epipelagic fish, they usually act in concert with oceanographic conditions, particularly those associated with upwelling and currents. Upwelling is a phenomenon found along coastlines and along midocean convergences of deep, strong currents where cold, nutrient-rich deep water is brought to the surface. This water supports large blooms of phytoplankton, which in turn support zooplankton and many of the world's most important fisheries. When the upwelling fails or is reduced in an area, the fisheries fail as well. This phenomenon is well illustrated by the Peruvian anchoveta *(Engraulis ringens)* fishery, once the largest fishery in the world. When oceanic conditions change and upwelling is reduced, the anchoveta populations decline precipitously, the fishery fails, and sea birds, which also depend on the anchoveta, die by the millions. Along the Pacific coast, Ware and Thomson (1991) hypothesize that there is roughly a 60-year cycle in wind-driven coastal upwelling and that epipelagic fish such as sardines become less abundant when upwelling is reduced.

Ocean currents. Ocean currents also play a major role in both concentrating and dispersing fish. Fish distributions may be bounded by current edges that form distinct, if fluctuating, boundaries to oceanic regions. At times these boundaries are even visible, but more typically they are detectable as rapid changes in temperature, salinity, and turbidity. For example, Nakamura (1969) indicates that albacore

(*Thunnus alalunga*) in the northern Pacific have a northern limit determined by the cold North Pacific Current and a southern limit determined by the North Equatorial Current and that, within the broad area between these two current systems, their distribution is determined by the Kuroshio Current, which flows at varying strengths according to the season. Many epipelagic fish also use currents for reproduction, spawning "upstream" so that the eggs and young will drift into suitable areas for feeding and eventually wind up in the adult feeding areas.

Islands and banks. Island and banks likely to concentrate epipelagic fish because of their interactions with currents and upwelling, which often make them areas of high ocean productivity. Large eddies may form on the downwind or down-current side of islands, concentrating plankton and consequently fish (Blackburn 1965). Such areas also contain concentrations of small fish and invertebrates that are associated with reefs and banks and thereby provide an additional source of food for pelagic predators.

Chemical Factors

The surface waters of the oceans are well mixed and well oxygenated, so it is seldom that salinity or oxygen have much effect on the distribution of epipelagic fish. Pollutants are chemical factors that may also be affecting populations of epipelagic fish in unknown ways. However, as Longhurst et al. (1972) pointed out, the effects of pollutants so far have been largely masked by natural fluctuations in fish populations in response to changing oceanic conditions, coupled with heavy exploitation by humans.

Biological Factors

Competition, predation, and symbiosis undoubtedly are all important in regulating the fish populations of the epipelagic zone, but their roles are poorly understood because of the difficulty of studying such processes in large, widespread fish populations and because the populations do respond so strongly to changes in oceanographic conditions and to the intense fishing efforts directed at them.

Competition among members of the same species appears to be one of the more important processes regulating the size of epipelagic fish populations, allowing each population to adapt to changing oceanographic conditions and exploitation (see the Pacific sardine example at the end of this chapter). Basically, intraspecific competition for limited food among adult fish leads to limited growth and smaller sizes and hence to decreased fecundity. Intraspecific competition for food among larval fish also leads to slower growth, which in turn results in increased mortality, particularly from predation.

The role of competition in interspecific interactions is less certain; the fact that many rather similar species coexist in the open oceans suggests that it may have an important function at times. For example, in the tropical and subtropical Pacific Ocean there are four species of tuna with wide, broadly overlapping ranges and ecological requirements. Often two species even school together. In the neritic epipelagic regions of the world, there are usually two or more species of clupeids present in each area. Each species appears to have a competitive advantage over the other(s) under appropriate oceanic conditions, so the dominant species may change with time. For example in the English Channel, herring *(Clupea harengus)* was replaced in the 1930s as the dominant planktivore by pilchard *(Sardinops pilchardus)*, but the situation was reversed in the 1970s (Cushing 1978). The change was accompanied by many other oceanic and biological changes. Similar shifts between clupeid species have been recorded in a number of other areas of the world. The actual mechanisms that allow one species to become dominant over the other are poorly understood, and are complicated in this case by the presence of large schools of other plankton-feeding fishes that may coexist with the clupeids while seeming to exploit the same food supply (Murphy 1977).

Predation has a powerful influence on epipelagic fish populations and interacts strongly with oceanic conditions and fisheries. Often the influence is very direct. On the Atlantic coast of North America, the seasonal arrival of large numbers of voracious bluefish results in a decline in the abundance of anchovies and sandlances on which they feed (Safina and Burger 1989). In the Bering Sea, cannibalism by adult walleye pollock *(Theragra chalcogramma)* on juveniles, combined with predation by marine birds and mammals, is a major factor regulating pollock numbers (Livingston 1993). On the other hand, because oceanic conditions exert a powerful influence on the populations of plankton-feeding fish, the populations of piscivores may be strongly affected by the environmentally induced fluctuations of their prey. Thus when upwelling is reduced off Peru and the anchoveta populations crash, millions of sea birds die of starvation. Off California, changes in the abundance of brown pelicans seem to show a direct relationship to the changes in local abundance of their main prey, the anchovy. On the other hand, the influences of predator and prey populations on each other are buffered somewhat by the fact that most predators are capable of preying on a wide range of organisms and will switch prey if the population of one prey species declines, unless a fishery reduces the abundance of alternate prey.

One of the strongest indications of the importance of predation to epipelagic fish is that shoaling is the dominant mode of behavior. Large shoals of small fish offer protection from predators and facilitate feeding, while schools of predatory fish presumably have an advantage in finding prey (see Chapter 9).

Examples of **symbiosis** are surprisingly common in the epipelagic zone, given the small number of species that inhabit it. Some examples include (1) multispecies shoaling, (2) tuna and porpoise, (3) remoras and large fishes, (4) pilotfish and sharks, and (5) fish that live in association with floating invertebrates (Parin 1968). Shoals of fish made up of more than one species are common, especially among the tunas and clupeids. Presumably much of the advantage of such relationships is an increase in shoal size, which results in increased protection from predators or increased probability of locating a patch of prey. These advantages would be particularly beneficial to a rare species that shoaled with an abundant one. Among the clupeids, the ability of one species to shoal with another may be one of the main methods by which a species that is at a competitive disadvantage can maintain small populations among the much larger ones of its competitor (Radovich 1979). The tuna-porpoise relationship is a special case of two species that school in close association. It seems to be a commensal relationship, with the schools of tuna following the schools of porpoise (or perhaps vice versa). The relationship is not obligatory for either species. How the two species benefit is not known, but the tuna may be taking advantage of the ability of the porpoise to find shoals of small fish through the use of this mammal's sonar. This relationship has been detrimental to both species, since tuna fishermen set nets around shoals of porpoise to capture the associated tuna and kill porpoises in the process.

In contrast to the first two examples, where animals of equal size (usually) are schooling together, remoras and pilotfish are small fish that live with large pelagic fish in relationships that have elements of both commensalism and parasitism. Remoras have a special suckerlike apparatus that they use to attach themselves to sharks and other large fish, turtles, and whales. The remora uses the host for transportation and protection, leaving it only for short pursuits of the small fish and invertebrates upon which it feeds. Remoras often act as cleaners, picking parasites off the host fish, but it is doubtful if this benefit compensates for the energy expended by the host in carrying the remora around. Pilotfish (Naucrates) have a relationship to their host similar to that of remoras, except that they swim in the friction layer of water around the host and are consequently pulled along by the host's swimming (Parin 1968).

Small epipelagic fishes are also commonly found in association with jellyfish, siphonophores, and pelagic tunicates, living in the body cavity or among the tentacles. The man-of-war fish (Nomeus) is always found among the tentacles of the man-of-war siphonophore. Presumably this fish has a mutualistic relationship with the man-of-war much like the one that anemone fish have with their hosts on coral reefs.

MIGRATIONS AND MOVEMENTS

Most epipelagic fish move freely from one area to another in search of food, or for spawning, or in response to changing oceanographic conditions. For large predators, such as tuna and salmon, these movements can cover thousands of kilometers, from one side of an ocean to the other and back (Fig. 34.1). For example, mako sharks (Isurus oxyrinchus) make long seasonal migrations apparently following temperature gradients; tagged individuals have been recorded as moving over 4500 km in one year (Casey and Kohler 1992). When spawning is involved, the overall migration pattern typically follows a triangular pattern (Harden-Jones 1968). The adults migrate in a direction opposite that of surface currents, toward areas suitable for spawning and close to waters that support the high concentrations of plankton needed by the larval fish. The adults then return to their feeding area, while the larvae drift in the surface currents to a nursery area. As they grow, the juvenile fish actively migrate to the adult areas. This pattern reduces competition for food

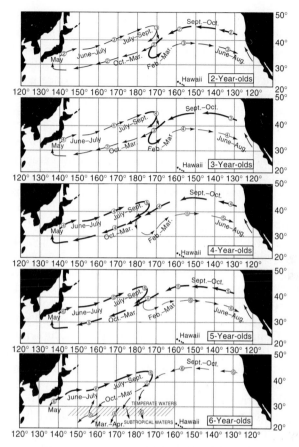

FIGURE 34.1 *Presumed albacore migration patterns in the northern Pacific Ocean, by age groups. (From Otsu and Uchida 1963.)*

among the different life history stages of a species and also reduces the incidence of cannibalism. A classic example of the triangular pattern is found in the herring of the North Sea. They migrate to spawning grounds off the coast of Great Britain, where the eggs are deposited on stones and gravel. The larvae hatch and drift over to the coast of Germany and Denmark, where shallow waters serve as nursery areas. After one or two years, at a length of 9 to 10 cm, they move off the coast toward the North Sea, where they eventually join the adults (Harden-Jones 1968).

PACIFIC SARDINE

As commercial fishermen are well aware, the local populations of epipelagic fish undergo considerable fluctuation from year to year, as well as over much longer periods of time. These fluctuations often seem to be unpredictable, but this is mainly because their causes are complex. Fish populations are simultaneously affected by oceanic conditions, interactions with other species, and fisheries. What is more, such factors may act in different ways and at different intensities on the various stages of a fish's life cycle. The factors may also act in concert, either in opposition to one another or synergistically. An idea of the complexity of the interactions can be obtained by examining the history of the Pacific sardine, one of the most studied of epipelagic fishes (Murphy 1966, 1977; Ahlstrom and Radovich 1970). The study was stimulated by the sudden collapse of the Pacific sardine fishery in the 1940s, a disaster caused by overfishing and unfavorable oceanic conditions acting together, compounded by apparent competition from the northern anchovy *(Engraulis mordax)*.

Sardines spawn off the coast of California and Baja California at temperatures between 13° and 19°C (mostly 15° to 18°C). The larvae hatch from the drifting, translucent eggs in two or three days. They then drift for another 40 to 45 days, absorbing the yolk sac and capturing organisms they bump into, until they develop the capability to swim actively. At this stage they begin to move inshore and grow rapidly on a diet of zooplankton and diatoms. By the end of the first year they typically reach lengths of 11 to 12 cm, the second year 17 to 18 cm, the third year 19 to 20 cm. They often live six to seven years and reach lengths of 25 cm. Prior to the collapse of the populations, the larger fish moved north in the summer, as far as British Columbia, and moved south again in the winter, although the timing and extent of these movements depended on oceanic conditions. The main oceanic feature that affected the sardines was the California Current, which flows southward along the coast, bringing with it cold water from the Gulf of Alaska. During years when the current flowed strongly, water temperatures were lower and the sardine did not move as far north, although increased upwelling presumably provided more food for the populations in the south. When the current was weak, water temperatures were warmer and the sardine was found farther to the north. It was also noted that the "warm" years were those in which the sardine had high reproductive success, while the opposite was true of the "cold" years. Despite the variations in reproductive success, prior to the heavy development of the fishery the sardine appeared to be able to maintain large populations off California, even through a series of unfavorable years. However, when a heavy fishery was coupled with a long series of such years (1944–1956), the populations collapsed.

The reasons for the collapse are not known for certain, but Murphy (1966) presents evidence that the key is in survival of the larvae. Each female sardine produces 100,000 to 200,000 eggs in a season, but less than 0.1% survive through the drifting larval stage. Murphy hypothesized that the main cause of death of the larval sardines was predation by invertebrates such as arrow worms and copepods. According to this hypothesis, despite the enormous numbers of larval sardines likely to be present in a spawning area, they are a relatively small part of the total plankton and consequently a small part of the total diet of the invertebrate predators. Therefore, the number of sardines that are eaten depends on the density of predators and on the length of time the larvae are exposed to predation. In years unfavorable for the sardine, productivity of the inshore areas increases, so that the zooplankton and invertebrate predator populations increase. At the same time, the sardine larvae take a few days longer to reach the point where they can actively avoid the invertebrate predators. These two factors result in much lower survival of the sardine larvae during the cold years. If the sardine population is large, so many eggs and larvae are produced that enough can probably survive to maintain the population or at least to keep the population decline minimal regardless of oceanographic conditions. If the sardine population is small, however, it will stay small and probably become even smaller, particularly if the cold years and fishing continue (which they did). Because of the high fecundity of the sardines and the high survival rates during warm years, a small adult population can lead to a large adult population again if there is no fishing and there is a series of years favorable to larval survival (Fig. 34.2).

While Murphy's predation hypothesis is an attractive one, another hypothesis, developed by Lasker (1978) to explain population fluctuations in the ecologically similar northern anchovy, may offer an even better explanation of the fluctuations of sardine populations in response to oceanic conditions. In this hypothesis, the critical factor for survival of the larvae is the availability of food of the proper size, abundance, and nutritional value during the first few days of feeding. Sardines (and anchovies) at this stage are weak swimmers, have high metabolic rates and small mouths, and feed only during the day. This means that small organisms (probably dinoflagellates) must be available in high densities if the larvae are going to be able to capture enough during the day not only to avoid starving to death at night, but also to grow quickly to a size at which a larger size range of prey is available. The best conditions for early larval survival therefore seem to be warm, stable oceanic conditions that produce blooms of organisms of the proper size and nutritional value. Storms or upwelling may disperse such organisms to a point where their density is too low for the larvae to survive on. Upwelling may greatly increase the total abundance of organisms, but the diatoms that result are too small, while the invertebrates are too large and active. However, upwelling may be beneficial for older larvae that are large enough to capture copepods and other invertebrates. Regardless of the mechanism, the amount of upwelling plays a crucial role in the abundance of sardines. Thus, Ware and Thomson (1991) suggest that optimal conditions for sardine larvae exist under moderate upwelling conditions produced by winds of 7–8 m/sec. for extended periods of time. A minor (so far) resurgence of sardine populations in recent years may therefore be related to changes in upwelling conditions.

Whether it was predation, starvation, a combination of both, or other factors coupled with overfishing that caused the decline of the sardine, competition from the northern anchovy may now be keeping the sardine populations at low levels. Following the decline of the sardine, the anchovy became the dominant planktivore, using a substantial part of the food and space resources once used by the sardine. Suppression of a once abundant species by a dominant species is apparently common in epipelagic fishes, and may be so strong that the population fluctuations of the suppressed species no longer track environmental fluctuations (Skud 1982). In the Atlantic Ocean the effect of dominance by one species is shown in the population fluctuations of the Atlantic herring and the Atlantic mackerel *(Scomber scombrus)*. When the mackerel is dominant, its populations fluctuate in response to tempera-

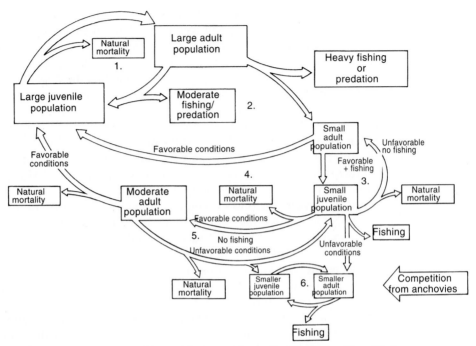

FIGURE 34.2 *Some possible population cycles in the Pacific sardine: (1) the no- or light-exploitation cycle, in which large populations maintain themselves regardless of fluctuations in oceanic conditions; (2) the heavy exploitation cycle, under favorable oceanic conditions; (3) the cycle for maintaining a small but significant population; (4) the cycle for restoration of large populations following overfishing, during years of favorable oceanic conditions; (5) the cycle resulting from unfavorable oceanic conditions following overfishing; and (6) the permanently small population cycle resulting initially from overfishing an already depleted population during unfavorable oceanic conditions, but maintained by competition from a large northern anchovy population and incidental capture of sardines in other fisheries. These cycles are only a few of the combinations possible, because the relationship between larval survival and adult populations is very complex and may be affected by several factors simultaneously. For example, Cycle 1 can revert directly to Cycle 6 even in the absence of fishing if the right combination of oceanic and biological conditions exists.*

ture conditions during the larval stage but those of the herring do not. The reverse is true when the herring is dominant.

CONCLUSIONS

The open ocean is full of biological surprises. Only recently, for example, have we begun to appreciate that drifting jellyfish can be a significant habitat for small fish. Considering that comparatively few species live in the open ocean environment, interactions among the species can be quite complex, including symbiotic interactions. The open ocean is also a place of extremes. In order to take advantage of regional concentrations of food or desirable conditions for spawning, larger epipelagic fish make some of the longest migrations of all vertebrates, often swimming from one side of an ocean to the other. Smaller inshore species develop some of the highest "standing crops" of any vertebrate. Such large populations depend on favorable local oceanic conditions, especially for their larval stages, and consequently show enormous fluctuations in numbers. While such species clearly depend on favorable environmental conditions for their persistence in large numbers, it is increasingly apparent that biotic interactions, especially predation, play a major role in determining abundance as well. For decades, the ultimate predators, commercial fishermen (abetted by fisheries managers), insisted that stocks of epipelagic fishes could not be overfished because when conditions are good, even a few fish can produce enough young to restock the environment. We know better now, but still overfish many stocks.

Supplemental Readings

Blackburn 1965; Blaxter and Holliday 1963; Cushing 1968, 1978; Harden-Jones 1968; Hart 1973; Murphy 1966; Parin 1968; Rounsefell 1975.

CHAPTER 35

Deepsea Habitats

In the surface waters of the ocean, the water is well lighted, well mixed, and capable of supporting actively photosynthesizing algae. Below this zone conditions change rapidly. Between 200 m and roughly 1000 m (the mesopelagic zone) the light gradually fades to extinction and temperatures fall through a more or less permanent thermocline to between 4°C and 8°C. Nutrient levels, dissolved oxygen, and rate of circulation also fall, while pressure increases. Below 1000 m (the bathypelagic zone) conditions are more uniform until the bottom (deepwater benthic zone) is reached, characterized by complete darkness, low temperatures, low nutrients, low dissolved oxygen levels, and great pressure. This environment is the most extensive aquatic habitat on the earth. With the mean depth of the oceans being about 4000 m, about 98% of their water is found below 100 m and 75% below 1000 m. The vastness of this environment, coupled with its probable stability through geological time, has led to the development of a diverse and often bizarre fish fauna, making up about 11% of all known fish species. Probably the most numerous fish in existence are the small (less than 10 cm) pelagic forms, particularly bristlemouths *(Cyclothone)*. These fish form much of the **deep-scattering** layer of the ocean, so called because the sonic pulses of sonar reflect off the millions of swimbladders, giving the impression of a false bottom.

The diversity and abundance of deepsea fishes is indicated by the results of midwater trawling. In a 12-km² area off Bermuda, 1500 trawl hauls produced 115,000 fish from 46 families and 220 species (Fitch and Lavenberg 1968). Similarly, Brewer (1973) reported catching 56,000 fish in 61 hauls in the eastern Pacific, representing 49 families and 113 species. In both studies, over 90% of the fishes belonged to two families, the Gonostomatidae (bristlemouths) and the Myctophidae (lanternfishes). Most of the species were quite rare, represented in the collections by one to 20 individuals. Large and diverse collections of deepsea fishes are made primarily in the tropical and subtropical regions of the oceans, particularly near continents. The bathypelagic fish fauna especially becomes depleted in high latitudes. It appears to be totally absent from the arctic region and represented by about only 30 species in the antarctic region. Regardless of where they are found, one of the more curious aspects of deepsea fishes is the scarcity of acanthopterygian species among them. Deepsea fishes are represented mostly by the orders Anguilliformes (eels), Notacanthiformes (spiny eels), Stomiiformes (bristlemouths, hatchet fishes, viperfishes, dragon fishes, etc.), Myctophiformes (lanternfishes, barracudinas, etc.), Gadiformes (grenadiers), and Lophiiformes (anglerfishes). The acanthopterygian forms are mainly in the orders Lampridiformes and Beryciformes.

By the standards of the lighted world, all the preceding fishes are very peculiar in appearance, and one of the challenges of deepsea ichthyology is to determine the uses of strange structural features. Inference is the main tool used in this endeavor, because trips to the deepsea habitat are extraordinarily difficult. Similar problems exist in attempting to study the distribution and ecology of deepsea fishes using trawls that are towed several kilometers beneath a ship. Nevertheless, these fishes are so fascinating that they are responsible for a large literature. Particularly important are the writings of N. B. Marshall (1954, 1960, 1966, 1971, 1984). These works are classics of clarity that have integrated the diverse information on deepsea fishes with many original insights and observations.

ADAPTATIONS

The fish that inhabit the mesopelagic, bathypelagic, and deepwater benthic zones are in many respects remarkably different from one another in structure, even though there are often closely related species in the different zones.

Mesopelagic fishes are adapted for an active life under low light conditions. Most of them make extensive vertical migrations, often moving at night into the epipelagic zone where they prey on plankton and each other, and then moving down several hundred meters during the day. These fishes have muscular bodies, well-ossified skeletons, scales, well-developed central nervous systems, well-developed gills (especially in forms that inhabit oceanic regions with low oxygen supplies), large hearts, large kidneys, and, usually, swimbladders. Because they are primarily visual predators, their eyes are large, often with high concentrations of photosensitive pigments in the rods of the retina, giving the fishes extreme sensitivity to light. Many mesopelagic fishes also have tubular eyes, typically pointing upward, with large lenses, which permit binocular vision. Such visual capabilities enable the fishes to pick out small planktonic organisms in dim light. Most mesopelagic fishes lack spines, so their main defense from predators is concealment. In color they are either black (lie-in-wait predators) or silvery, with countershading (migratory forms that encounter low light levels). In addition, many of them have rows of ventrally placed photophores, producing light that helps to break up the silhouette of the fish to predators peering up into the downward-streaming light. However, Muntz (1976) suggests that the special nature of bioluminescence has permitted some mesopelagic predators to overcome this camouflage by having yellow lenses that filter out the ambient light, leaving the bioluminescence visible. Because photophores are well developed in other locations on mesopelagic fishes, they may also serve other functions, particularly intraspecific signaling for shoaling and reproduction. Ecologically, mesopelagic fishes can be divided up into zooplankton feeders, which have small mouths and fine gill rakers, and piscivores, which have large mouths and coarse gill rakers.

Bathypelagic fishes, in contrast to mesopelagic fishes, are largely adapted for a sedentary existence in a habitat with low levels of food and no light other than bioluminescence. These fishes generally have poorly developed, flabby muscles, weak skeletons with minimal ossification, no scales, poorly developed central nervous systems (except those parts associated with the lateral line and olfactory systems), small gills, small kidneys, small hearts, and reduced or absent swimbladders. Marshall (1984) notes that these are also characteristics of fish larvae, indicating that these features have developed through the retention of larval characteristics in the adults. As they do in larvae, these features allow the fishes to remain suspended in the water column with almost no expenditure of energy, since they have achieved nearly neutral buoyancy without having to maintain a gas-filled swimbladder in a high-pressure environment. Their eyes are small and may be nonfunctional. The most important sensory system is usually the acoustico-lateralis system, although the olfactory system may also be well developed (especially in male anglerfish, which locate females by smell). Bathypelagic fish are uniformly black in color and have only a few small photophores. Among anglerfish, photophores are usually confined to the lures they use for attracting prey. Because of the scarcity of food, anglerfish and other bathypelagic predators consume whatever invertebrate or fish comes close enough to be grabbed. This means that the predator has to be able to capture a wide size range of prey, which is accomplished by having a large mouth with sharp teeth for the capture of large prey combined with well-developed, overlapping gill rakers to prevent the escape of small prey that have been swallowed.

Deepwater benthic fishes are similar to mesopelagic fishes in that they have muscular bodies and well-developed organ systems. However, they are more variable in many of their characteristics. Photophores may be present but are usually absent. Eyes range from being well developed to being absent, as do swimbladders. The fishes are also variable in size, with large species (in excess of 1 m) being fairly common. Curiously enough, many, if not most, deepsea benthic fishes are elongate, many of them being eels or at least eel-like. The most abundant forms, or at least the most conspicuous, seem to be rattails (Macrouridae) and brotulas (Ophidiidae); but a wide variety of other families such as the Myxinidae (hagfishes), Zoarcidae (eelpouts), Chloropthalmidae (greeneyes), eels (various families), Cyclopteridae

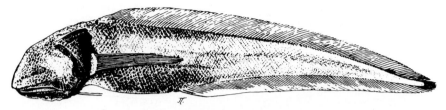

FIGURE 35.1 Abyssobrotula galatheae, *the deepest-living fish known. (From Nielson 1977, used by permission of Scandinavian Science Press Ltd.)*

(lumpfishes), and Ogcocephalidae (batfishes) are also well represented. The commonness of eel-like forms may be related to the importance of the lateral line as a sensory system, because an elongate body results in long lateral-line canals. The sense of smell is also important in many of these fishes, as indicated by the rapidity with which they find a trap baited with dead fish. Smell, combined with touch and well-developed cephalic lateral-line canals, may also be important for locating invertebrates of the deepsea benthos that, together with carrion, are the main items in their diets. The deepest-living fish known (Ophidiidae, *Abyssobrotula galatheae,* Fig. 35.1) is a blind, elongate fish that feeds on benthic invertebrates (Nielson 1977). However, members of the common and widely distributed genus *Bathypterois* (Chloropthalmidae, spider fishes), which also are nearly blind, feed on the community of zooplankton that lives within a meter or so of the bottom. These fishes have elongate rays on the caudal and pelvic fins that permit them to "stand" on the bottom, presumably facing into currents, and grab passing zooplankton (Fig. 35.2) (Sulak 1977).

Fish and their prey that live just above, but close to, the bottom are often labeled **benthopelagic.** Benthopelagic zooplankton are often important prey for the benthic fish (Mauchline and Gordon 1986). Some species of fish are adapted specifically for benthopelagic life, combining bathypelagic and benthic adaptations. One such predator is the cusk-eel *Acanthonus armatus,* which has an elongate body, large otoliths, and spiny operculi but also a body that is 90% water and a brain that is the smallest known in relation to body size for any vertebrate, located in a huge head (Fine et al. 1987).

REPRODUCTIVE STRATEGIES

Among the more remarkable adaptations of deepsea fishes are their methods of reproduction. Because population densities of many species are extremely low, just finding a mate is a major problem. As a consequence, many unconventional reproductive strategies have evolved. Most mesopelagic and bathypelagic predators have epipelagic larvae, which they can produce in large numbers. A female anglerfish, for example, may contain as many as 5 million eggs. The main problem is finding a mate to fertilize the eggs. To facilitate this process, female anglerfishes apparently release a species-specific pheromone into the water, which male anglerfish can detect and follow to the female. In many species, once the female is found,

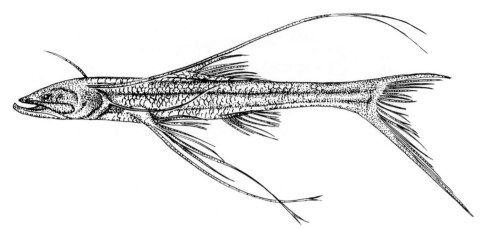

FIGURE 35.2 *The spiderfish,* Bathypterois oddi, *is a predator on benthopelagic organisms. (After Sulak 1977, used by permission of Scandinavian Science Press Ltd.)*

the male anglerfish attaches himself to her with specially equipped jaws and assumes a parasitic mode of existence. In species in which this strategy is best developed, the gonads of both sexes do not mature until the female has been parasitized by a male (Pietsch 1976). An additional advantage of this strategy is that the energy required for reproduction is reduced, but not at the expense of fecundity. Most species of mesopelagic and bathypelagic fishes have males that are smaller than females and have much larger olfactory organs, presumably also because of the energetic advantages. In some of these species (e.g., Idiacanthidae), the males do not feed, although they are free-living. Each male therefore has a limited time to find a female, which is enhanced by the male's extraordinary ability to detect female pheromones and by the behavior of the female (Jumper and Baird 1991). Another solution to the energy and mate-finding problems is to be hermaphroditic, ensuring that any individual can mate with any other individual of the same species. This is characteristic of a number of deepsea predators such as the lancetfishes (Alepisauridae) and the barracudinas (Paralepididae), although it is not known whether these fishes are capable of self-fertilization (Mead et al. 1964).

In deepsea benthic fishes, finding a mate seems to be less of a problem than assuring that the young will settle in suitable habitats. The grenadiers (Macrouridae) and brotulas (Ophidiidae) apparently can produce sounds with their swimbladders and thereby attract mates over some distance. In other deepsea benthic fishes, bioluminescence may also play a role in this regard. Deepsea eels, such as longnose eels *(Synaphobranchus),* may aggregate for spawning through the use of smell, or perhaps through homing to a hereditary spawning ground (Menzies et al. 1973). Although the eels all have pelagic leptocephalous larvae, most deepsea benthic fishes seem to have relatively short larval stages. Many species produce large, benthic eggs, resulting in large, active larvae, which settle out quickly. Some of these species, especially among the eelpouts (Zoarcidae), may have parental care as well. Other species are viviparous, most prominently chimaeras and other chondrichthyian fishes but also species of brotulas and eelpouts. Regardless of how the young are produced, they probably remain close to the spawning area. As a result, there is a much higher incidence of species that are confined to one ocean basin than is true for bathypelagic and mesopelagic fishes, many of which are nearly cosmopolitan in their distribution.

FACTORS THAT AFFECT DISTRIBUTION

Physical Factors

The main physical factors affecting the distribution of deepsea fishes are temperature, light, pressure, features of the ocean floor, and currents. **Temperatures** of the deep ocean are rather stable, between 4° and 8°C, so it seems unlikely that temperature has much of an impact on the local distribution patterns of deepsea fishes. However, the great reduction in diversity of bathypelagic and mesopelagic fishes at high latitudes may be partially a function of the slightly lower temperatures that exist there. Backus et al. (1977) were able to divide up the mesopelagic zone of the Atlantic Ocean into zoogeographic regions, noting that faunal changes coincided with changes in physical conditions, particularly temperatures at about 200 m. Many mesopelagic fishes nevertheless show a great tolerance for temperature changes and may migrate through the permanent thermocline on a daily basis, encountering temperature changes of 10°C to 20°C.

Light, in contrast to temperature, is extremely important in determining the local distributions of deepsea fish. Indeed, the distinction between mesopelagic and bathypelagic zones and the adaptations of the fish that live in the zones are directly or indirectly related in large part to light levels. In the mesopelagic zone the movements of fish that make vertical migrations are cued to light, the fish following the receding light levels up in the evening and then moving down in the early morning as light levels in the surface waters increase.

Pressure, like light, has a major impact on the vertical distributions of deepsea fishes, since it increases at the rate of 1 atm per 10 m. The absence or reduction of the swimbladder in so many deepsea fishes is undoubtedly related to the energy costs of filling the bladder at great depths. One indication of this is that the swimbladders of some deepsea fishes are functional when the fishes are juveniles living in the epipelagic zone, but they regress or become fat-filled when the fishes change to their adult habitat (Horn 1970). Mesopelagic fishes that make extensive vertical migrations apparently expend some energy deflating the swimbladder as they move up and inflating it as they move down. Even fishes that inhabit nearly anoxic waters at the bottom of the migratory cycle manage to reinflate their swimbladders with oxygen (Douglas et al. 1976). At great depths, pressure may be a limiting factor to fishes, although other factors, such as scarcity of food, are also important. Bathypelagic fishes are usually not found below 3000 m, and the greatest depth record for benthic fishes is about 8370 m (Nielson 1977).

Features of the ocean floor and **currents** often act together in determining both local and worldwide distribution patterns of deepsea fishes, particularly benthic fishes. Although much of the deep ocean floor is a featureless plain covered with sediment, many deepsea benthic fishes are associated with rock outcroppings or canyons, which have distinct invertebrate communities as well. On a broader scale, benthic fishes are also more diverse and numerous on the continental slope, presumably due to a combination of greater food supply and greater habitat diversity. On an even broader scale, undersea mountain ranges and ridges often form barriers to fish movement, as well as boundaries of distinct sets of oceanic conditions. Thus Brown (1974) found that each of three basins off Southern California separated by ridges had distinctive elements in its mesopelagic fish fauna that reflected in part the currents that flowed into the basins. There were enough differences that 11% to 16% of the fish Brown collected in each basin were not found in the other basins. When such patterns are examined for entire oceans, regions of endemism can be noted, particularly for benthic fishes, which do not disperse as easily over geologic barriers as do pelagic fishes.

Chemical Factors

Because the ocean is so well mixed chemically, salinity and oxygen levels are the main chemical factors likely to influence the distribution of deepsea fishes. Although the water masses with which distinct deepsea fish faunas are associated often differ slightly in their salinities, it seems unlikely, given the small differences that exist (1 to 2 ppt), that salinity by itself limits the distribution of any of the species. Oxygen, in contrast, is probably very important, because in many areas, often at depths between 100 and 1000 m, there is an oxygen minimum layer, where dissolved oxygen levels may be almost undetectable. While these layers undoubtedly act as barriers to movement of some fish, they are often inhabited by large numbers of mesopelagic fish for at least part of the day. Below the oxygen minimum layer, oxygen levels are typically low enough (5–6 mg\l) so that, in combination with the low temperatures, they greatly limit fish activity.

Biological Factors

Because the deepsea environment is so hard to study, predatory, competitive, and symbiotic interactions among species are poorly understood. **Predation** is presumably the most common type of interaction because all known deepsea fishes are carnivorous, and many of the behavioral and structural adaptations of the fish can best be explained as mechanisms either to help avoid being eaten or to increase the probability of capturing a suitable prey. In the bathypelagic zone most fish do not appear to be selective in their feeding habits, so who eats whom seems to depend largely on size. Even this rule does not always hold, because a number of anglerfishes, blackdragons (Idiacanthidae), and viperfishes (Chauliodontidae) are capable of swallowing fish considerably larger than themselves, through the use of distensible stomachs and "hinged" heads.

Competition, like predation, has presumably been an important force shaping the deepsea fish communities, as indicated by the surprisingly high diversity of the communities and the striking morphological differences among closely related species that occupy different habitat zones. On the other hand, within zones there are groups of coexisting species that all seem to do about the same thing, such as the small plankton feeders of the mesopelagic zone, the anglerfishes of the bathypelagic zone, and the various rattailed fishes of the deepwater benthic zone. Tyler and Pearcy (1975) noted that the diets of three species of mesopelagic lanternfish were broadly similar but indicated that, nevertheless, there was some segregation by food habits, perhaps related to slightly different depth distributions. Johnson and Glodek (1975) speculated that observed distribution differences among similar species of mesopelagic pearleyes (Scopelarchidae) is related to different tolerances to low oxygen levels, so that one species has a competitive superiority only when oxygen levels are low because of its longer gill filaments. In the bathypelagic zone there are about 100 widely distributed species of anglerfishes, many of which occur together. Although these species present an extraordinary series of morphological variations on the basic anglerfish theme, they all apparently consume whatever prey is available, including (presumably) each other. How these fishes manage to share the scarce food resources of the zone is not known, but it can be hypothesized that it is done through a combination of spatial (depth) preferences combined with the widespread dispersal of the epipelagic larvae. As Sale (1977) hypothesized for coral reef fishes, these larvae may be part of an anglerfish lottery, in which the winner is a larva that happens to settle out in an area not occupied by another anglerfish or predator (regardless of species) and so grows instead of being eaten. Given the apparent rarity of anglerfishes in general, long-term success of an individual would depend in large part on "winning" (i.e., consuming or avoiding) the rare encounters with other bathypelagic predators as well as encountering enough prey to avoid starvation.

The deepsea floor, like the bathypelagic zone, is a stable environment with scarce food and a wide array of ecologically similar species. Most of the fishes apparently roam the floor in search of food, mostly invertebrates (which are surprisingly diverse) or carrion that has dropped from the waters above. The latter food-falls are uncommon but important sources of energy for deepsea organisms (Stockton and DeLaca 1982). While it is likely that there is some segregation among the fishes based on depth and food preferences, there also appears to be a considerable amount of overlap among coexisting species. For example, photographs of areas baited with dead fish indicate that it is not unusual for five to six species of fish to be attracted to the bait in a few hours. However, the use of mucus secretions by hagfish to coat dead fish, thereby making them inedible to other species, indicates that there may be direct competition for this type of resource.

ECOLOGY

Mesopelagic Zone

The most conspicuous feature of the ecology of the Mesopelagic Zone is that many of the fishes make nightly vertical migrations into the Epipelagic Zone. This enables them to take advantage of the abundant zooplankton in this zone (which also often moves upward at night) and yet avoid full-time exposure to epipelagic predators. Where an oxygen minimum layer exists, migrating mesopelagic fish may further avoid large predators by seeking refuge in it. The result of these migrations seems to be a net export of energy downward. Much of this energy may be recycled in the Mesopelagic Zone through predaceous fish and through copepods that filter-feed in part on fecal material, although some is lost downward (and supports bathypelagic fish) and some is recycled upward, through squid and other epipelagic nocturnal predators that forage in the Mesopelagic Zone. The importance of energy recycling within this zone is indicated by the large populations of fish that do not make vertical migrations or that migrate on an irregular basis. Many of these species are predators that simply wait in the water column and prey upon passing migratory fish and zooplankton.

The pattern of energy flow through the Mesopelagic Zone combined with the abundance and diversity of fish found there indicate that the community structure is complex. Since little is known about annual fluctuations in abundance of the mesopelagic species, it is not known whether fish diversity is maintained through extremely complex specializations or through differential responses to environmental fluctuations, which prevent any one species in a group of potential competitors from becoming dominant. Although the evidence is scanty, it does seem to favor the latter hypothesis. Feeding and distribution studies of similar species generally do indicate some segregation by depth and food types, but a great deal of ecological overlap is also found (Dewitt and Cailliet 1972; Tyler and Percy 1975). The potential fluctuations in local mesopelagic fish populations are indicated by the study of Brewer (1973), who in his extensive sampling of the Mesopelagic Zone of the Gulf of California failed to capture a single specimen of bristlemouth, although they had been abundant there a few years earlier.

Bathypelagic Zone

If the most conspicuous feature of the mesopelagic zone is the movement of the fish, the most conspicuous feature of the bathypelagic zone is the sedentary nature of the fish. The dominant fish of this zone, anglerfish and bristlemouths, seem to spend most of their time suspended in the water column, waiting for prey organisms to pass by or to be lured to them by their photophores. Bathypelagic fish are extreme generalists in their feeding, which is necessary because of the scarcity of food. The limited energy available in this zone all comes from above, from fecal material, detritus, and an occasional mesopelagic fish or invertebrate. The scarcity of bathypelagic fish below 3000 m presumably reflects in part the small amount of food that filters through the upper regions of the water column. Considering the small amount of energy probably flowing through the zone, it is a wonder that bathypelagic fish exist at all, much less in such diversity.

Deepwater Benthic Zone

Compared with the fish of the bathypelagic zone, the fish of this zone are active and often quite abundant. Energy (in the form of organic matter) enters this zone through a number of pathways, originating either on the continents or in the water column (Sedberry and Musick 1978). Organic matter from the continents can move into the zone through migrations of fish and invertebrates, through the sinking of plant material such as eelgrass, and through currents that flow down and along the continental shelf and slope. That these are among the most important sources of energy for deepsea benthic organisms is indicated by the gradual decrease in fish and invertebrate numbers and biomass with distance from the continents. Organic matter from the water column enters in the form of (1) particulate matter raining from above, particularly where the deepwater benthic zone and the mesopelagic zone meet; (2) dead fish and other large "particles" that sink to the sea floor; and (3) mesopelagic fish that approach the bottom during their vertical migrations. The organic matter from these various sources is consumed, broken down, and recycled by both invertebrates and fish. Fish are considered to be especially important in this recycling process because they consume the dead material that falls to the bottom, crop the invertebrates, and then, through their feces, distribute the organic matter rather evenly over the ocean floor.

In order to play this role effectively, deepsea benthic fish should be relatively unspecialized, consuming whatever prey they can encounter. This seems to be largely the case, although the fishes do specialize to the extent that some species feed mostly on benthopelagic organisms, some on invertebrates that are on the surface of the bottom (epifauna), some on invertebrates that burrow into the substrate (infauna), and some on carrion (Sedberry and Musick 1978). On the upper continental slope, some of the more abundant fishes, such as longfinned hake and cutthroat eel, feed mostly on mesopelagic fish. What is surprising is that mesopelagic fish and invertebrates are also common in the stomachs of benthic fish that occur well below the intersection of the mesopelagic zone with the bottom. Because benthic fish are rarely captured more than a meter or so off the bottom it is likely that they are taking advantage of mesopelagic forms that become resident in deep water either seasonally or at certain stages of their life cycle.

Fish that feed on benthic invertebrates are usually the most abundant species in the deepwater benthic zone. As indicated previously, these fish consume whatever invertebrates they can capture. There is some specialization based on prey size (reflected in mouth size of the fish), depth distribution, and preference for epifauna or infauna. The infauna-feeders often have large amounts of sediment in their digestive tract as well as the small infaunal invertebrates they were presumably seeking. The nutritional value of the sediments to the fish is not known. The infauna is also important as a secondary food source for fish that are scavengers, such as hagfish and snubnose eels. When a dead fish is placed on the bottom with a camera suspended over it, the scavengers, both vertebrate and invertebrate, are seen to quickly congregate. If the dead fish is large, many of the scavengers will burrow into it and consume it from the inside out. Large numbers of other fish, such as grenadiers, are often also attracted to such bait stations, but they may be feeding primarily on scavenging amphipods and other invertebrates rather than on the bait itself.

CONCLUSIONS

The overall picture that develops from a study of the ecology of fish in the three deepsea zones is that the fish are part of complex and highly efficient systems that waste little of the energy available. Deepsea fish are also the links that connect the energy pathways (food webs) of the various zones. While our understanding of how these fish live is based largely on studies of mashed individuals brought up from great depths, they are so alien in appearance and ecology that they will continue to be favored for study and speculation.

Supplemental Readings

Dayton and Hessler 1972; Fitch and Lavenberg 1968; Grassle et al. 1975; Marshall 1954, 1971, 1984; Menzies et al. 1973; Pietsch 1976; Pietsch and Grobecker 1987.

CHAPTER 36

Polar Regions

The aquatic environments of the Arctic and Antarctic are often compared to those of the deep sea, in part because these environments are uniformly cold and in part because polar organisms have many of the same adaptations as deepsea benthic organisms. However, there are more differences than similarities because of the unique features of the polar environments, such as long summer days that make high levels of primary production possible and long winter nights that create and maintain the ice cover. Temperatures are also colder than those found in the deep sea, typically between +1.0°C and -1.9°C. The two polar regions also differ greatly from each other in their environmental characteristics, and this is reflected in the differences in their fish faunas. The Arctic consists largely of an ice-covered sea of low productivity; it is surrounded by land that greatly limits the exchange of water with the Atlantic and Pacific oceans. The Antarctic, in contrast, is a continent surrounded by highly productive seas that have "free" interchange with the world's oceans, although unique oceanographic conditions have effectively kept the fish fauna of the continental shelf of Antarctica isolated from other faunas. As a result, the Antarctic has a comparatively diverse fauna characterized by a high degree of endemism, while the Arctic shares much of its limited fauna with the northern Atlantic and Pacific oceans. Because of these differences, the Arctic will be treated only briefly in this chapter, but the Antarctic will be discussed in some detail.

ARCTIC FISHES

The Arctic is not rich in either species or numbers of fish. In arctic America there are less than 110 species (Legendre et al. 1975, plus records of D. E. McAllister, National Museum of Canada, 1979). The total for the entire Arctic is probably not much greater. Presumably because of the coldness and low productivity of the environment, a majority of the species belong to families of predominantly sluggish, bottom-dwelling fishes, such as the Cyclopteridae (lumpfishes and snailfishes, 15 species), Cottidae (sculpins, 14 species), Zoarcidae (eelpouts, 10 species), Gadidae (cods, eight species), Stichaeidae (pricklebacks, six species), Anarhichadidae (wolffishes, four species), Agonidae (poachers, four species), and Pleuronectidae (right-eye flounders, six species). Because of the grinding of arctic shores by sea ice, most of these fishes rarely venture into shallow water, and only sculpins (*Myoxocephalus*) occur on a regular basis in the intertidal or subtidal regions. However, there are 15 species of euryhaline or anadromous salmonids and three species of smelt (Osmeridae) known from the Arctic; these species, along with herring, may be of some importance in bays during the short summer months and in the midwaters above the shelf.

Perhaps the most distinctive and abundant arctic fish are two species of endemic codfish, the polar cod (*Arctogadus glacialis*) and the arctic cod (*Boreogadus saida*). These fish differ markedly from most other cods in that the mouth angles slightly upward, rather than being terminal or subterminal, and the barbels are much smaller in size. Such adaptations reflect the association of such cods with pack ice and the fact that they feed largely on the peculiar amphipods and diatoms found in or on the undersurface of the ice. The only other fish found on a regular basis in association with the ice are juvenile sandlances (*Ammodytes*), which may actually hide in holes in the ice (McAllister 1977). The community of organisms associated with the ice (which has its parallel in the Antarctic) is known as the **cryopelagic community** (Andriashev 1970). The cods are abundant enough so that flocks of kittiwakes will follow icebreakers to capture the fish thrown up in the wakes. They are also quite important in the diets of seals and whales that feed under the ice.

The presence of a cryopelagic community and the predominance of benthic fishes in the Arctic indicate the strong selective pressures the harsh environment must exert on the fishes. McAllister (1977) has observed that arctic fishes also tend to have larger eyes than equivalent species found farther south, presumably a response to the reduced light found under the ice, in deep water, and seasonally. One of the most interesting adaptations of benthic fishes of the Arctic, which links them with deepsea and Antarctic fishes, is their basic reproductive strategy. Most lay a small number of large eggs which are (presumably) cared for by one or both parents, until hatching or beyond. According to Marshall (1953) this strategy has the advantages of reducing competition among the larvae and of producing large, active young with a wide range of food items available to them. Such larvae are either pelagic or benthic, depending on the species.

ANTARCTIC FISHES

The Antarctic contains at least 274 species of fish from 49 families, of which 34% are from the suborder Nototheniodei (Eastman 1993). Depending on the taxonomic analysis that is accepted, and where the line separating the Antarctic from other regions is drawn, antarctic fish are 65% to 96% endemic. The best estimate of endemism seems to be that of DeWitt (1971), who found that 86% of the fishes (excluding deepsea forms) south of the Antarctic Convergence were found nowhere else. The Antarctic Convergence separates the "true" antarctic fauna (or at least the shallow-water fauna) from the fauna of the rest of the southern ocean because it is a remarkably stable oceanographic feature that surrounds the Antarctic continent. It is characterized by clockwise flows that tend to keep drifting organisms away from the continental area by spinning them off in a northward direction. In addition it presents a distinct temperature boundary, marking the region where the cold antarctic surface water sinks beneath the warmer subantarctic surface water. The convergence is strictly a surface phenomenon, so the deepwater fauna shows a much lower degree of endemism than the shallow-water fauna.

South of the Antarctic Convergence there are 90 to 100 species of fishes found at depths of less than 800 m, mostly close to the Antarctic continent. Most of these fishes, by both species and numbers, belong to four notothenioid families: Nototheniidae (antarctic cods), Harpagiferidae (plunder fishes), Bathydraconidae (antarctic dragonfishes), and Channichthyidae (icefishes). Other families represented in the shallower waters of the Antarctic are Rajidae (skates, 8 spp.), Muraenolepididae (eel cods, 4 spp.), Zoarcidae (eelpouts, 22 spp.), Liparidae (snail fishes, 31 spp.), and Achiropsettidae (southern flounders, 4 spp.). Most of these fishes show remarkable adaptations to the peculiar features of the antarctic environment. The rest of this chapter will therefore be devoted to a discussion of (1) morphological, physiological, and reproductive adaptations; (2) factors affecting distribution; and (3) fish communities.

Adaptations

Morphological adaptations. Most antarctic fish are bottom-oriented visual predators, and their basic external features reflect this. The dominant notothenioids have large, flattened heads with large mouths and large eyes, which are often located toward the top of the head. The bodies tend to be elongate, often tapering to a small tail, with large pectoral fins, small pelvic fins, and long dorsal and anal fins. The swimbladder is absent. With the conspicuous exception of the skates and flounders, other antarctic fishes deviate from this theme either by having more eel-like bodies, with continuous dorsal and anal fins, or by having more fusiform bodies, such as in the pelagic antarctic "herring" (Nototheniidae, *Pleuragramma antarcticum*). Despite the absence of a swimbladder, a number of antarctic fishes like the "herring" are neutrally buoyant, which enables them to feed on the abundant planktonic krill. Buoyancy is achieved through fat deposits beneath the skin and in the muscles and by reduced mineralization of scales and bone (Eastman and DeVries 1982).

Physiological adaptations. The remarkable nature of the physiological adaptations of antarctic fishes is indicated by two observations. First, many of the fishes have been observed to be active at temperatures very close to the freezing point of salt water (-1.9°C); some of these species are actually associated with ice on a regular basis, either resting on anchor ice or swimming among floating ice platelets. Second, the icefishes have no hemoglobin in their blood, so their gills are cream-colored rather than pink, while some other antarctic fishes have reduced amounts of hemoglobin.

Resistance to freezing seems to be accomplished either by living in deep water or by having "antifreeze" in the blood (Eastman 1993). Fish that live in water below 30 m actually have body fluids that will freeze at temperatures higher than the water in which they are living! These supercooled fish survive because of the absence of ice crystals in the water to "seed" body fluids and start ice forming internally. However, when such fish are caught in traps and brought up to the surface, they freeze just as soon as they enter the ice-laden surface waters (DeVries 1970). The notothenioid fishes that live in the shallow waters where ice crystals are present have glycoproteins in the blood that give the body fluids freezing points lower than that of the surrounding water (see Chapter 6). Further, some species have been shown to be extremely sensitive to minor temperature changes and to actively avoid "warm" temperatures (Crawshaw and Hammel 1971).

Reproductive adaptations. Antarctic fishes have large, yolky eggs, so Marshall (1953) predicted that the eggs would be laid on the bottom. In a study of a spiny plunderfish *(Harpagifer bispinis),* Daniels (1978) found that this was indeed the case and discovered further that this fish lays its eggs in a nest that is guarded for about four months. This is the longest period of nest guarding known for any species of fish; the behavior is probably common among antarctic fish, however, since such parental care is characteristic of many antarctic invertebrates as well. The eggs are laid during early winter, usually while there is still ice cover, and hatch when the ice breaks up and the spring plankton bloom begins. The larvae swim upward soon after hatching and join the plankton, upon which they feed. The planktonic stage may last as long as one year.

Factors that Affect Distribution

The known distribution limits of most antarctic species seem to be associated with physical factors, particularly temperature, currents, depth, and ice, although there are also some zoogeographic barriers as well, at least for the notothenioids (Eastman 1993). The annual range of temperatures in antarctic waters is usually less than 7° or 8°C, but the apparent sensitivity of the fishes to even small temperature changes means that temperature is an important environmental cue. The departure of many fishes from the food-rich inshore areas in the autumn may be largely a response to dropping temperatures (but perhaps cued by the changing light regime), and ensures avoidance of water containing ice crystals. On a broader scale, the restriction of most antarctic fishes to the polar region is probably a reflection of their stenothermy, with the Antarctic Convergence providing a particularly strong temperature barrier. The convergence is also a region of strong currents, which may limit the distribution of the fishes as well.

The depth distributions of the fish are tied to a number of factors, but principally temperature and substrate. Because of the presence of anchor ice in shallow water (less than 33 m) and the depth of the continental shelf around Antarctica (average depth 400–500 m), the greatest number of species occur between 300 and 600 m. In this region substrates are varied, benthic invertebrates are abundant, and temperatures are fairly constant. The antarctic fishes that are permanent residents of water less than 40 m deep are mostly species with antifreeze compounds in their blood.

Fish Communities

The fish of the Antarctic fall into three broad ecological groups: pelagic fish, benthic fish, and deepsea fish. The divisions between the groups are not sharp, however.

Pelagic fish. The open surface waters of the Antarctic are dominated by crustacean krill *(Euphausia superba)*, which support large populations of whales, seals, penguins, and other marine birds. Perhaps because of the presence of these large predators, there are few fish in the upper 200 m of the water column, but pelagic species are abundant in the mesopelagic region. Eastman (1993) indicates that there are several distinct ecological types of pelagic fish among the notothenioids, including mesopelagic predators, mesopelagic zooplanktivores, cryopelagic fish, and epibenthic fish. All of these fish have more fusiform bodies than those of bottom-dwelling species and have reduced hard parts and large fat deposits to increase buoyancy, yet they retain large fins and other "benthic" features. The species most specialized for pelagic life is the zooplanktivorous antarctic "herring," which is one of the few antarctic fishes with a forked tail and the only species regularly found in the epipelagic zone. Because this species is abundant, it is the principal prey of the large piscivorous fish *Dissostichus mawsoni*, which lives a permanently sluggish existence in the mesopelagic zone.

Perhaps the most unusual species among the pelagic forms are the cryopelagic fishes, which feed on invertebrates associated with the underside of the ice sheet or the sides of icebergs. The antarctic herring is a component of this community, which also includes two species of antarctic cod *(Pagothenia)* specifically adapted for cryopelagic life. These species live on the sides of icebergs by clinging to them with their pectoral fins or by resting in crevices, much as a benthic fish would use a rocky cliff. They are silvery white in color, with inconspicuous eyes and high levels of blood antifreeze (Eastman 1993).

Epibenthic species look like the pelagic forms but are not neutrally buoyant, although they are more buoyant than benthic species. They swim slowly above the bottom where they feed on a mixture of krill, benthic invertebrates, and mesopelagic fish (Eastman 1993).

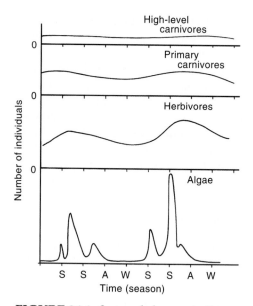

FIGURE 36.1 *Seasonal changes in the flora and fauna of the Antarctic. Most fishes are high-level carnivores. (Diagram by R. A. Daniels.)*

Benthic Fish. Most antarctic fish, including about half of the notothenioid species, live on the continental shelf. It is not unusual to find 10 to 20 species, many in quite large numbers, at one location. The reason for this is that the shelf is a very stable environment that supports large populations of invertebrates to serve as prey for the fish. This food supply is nearly constant all year around, in marked contrast to the strong seasonality exhibited by the availability of food in the pelagic regions (Fig. 36.1). As a result, the benthic communities are quite complex. The fish feed largely on invertebrates that are themselves largely carnivorous, and the fish in turn may be taken by seals, birds, and other fish. Thus food chains with seven or eight links are likely to be present. The energy for this system is derived from the plankton blooms and growths of benthic algae that occur during the austral summer, coupled with presumably efficient recycling of nutrients (ultimately through detritus) in the winter.

The efficiency of the system is indicated by the specializations of the fish. There is considerable segregation by depth preferences, most conspicuously the separation of fishes with high levels of antifreeze in the blood from those with low amounts. Among species coexisting at the same depth, there seems to be considerable specialization in type and size of prey consumed, as well as in method of feeding. Although some species are generalists, feeding on whatever prey is available, many specialize by feeding largely on just one or two taxa of invertebrates, such as amphipods or polychaete worms. The degree of specialization is illustrated by the feeding behavior of *Harpagifer bispinis*, which feeds mostly on amphipods and scaleworms. When feeding on scaleworms, the fish captures them by ambushing a passing individual. It removes the scales from each worm by spitting it out and sucking it in repeatedly, presumably scraping off the scales on its palatine teeth (R. A. Daniels, personal communication).

Deepsea fishes. The deepsea fishes of the antarctic region are poorly known, especially south of the convergence. The fish fauna of the continental slope and deeper areas, as well as of the mesopelagic one, is a mixture of notothenioid fishes and representatives of the typical deepsea fish families. A number of the non-notothenioid species are endemic, but many are more widely distributed. The bathypelagic and mesopelagic fish faunas are made up of about 80 species (Eastman 1993). Although many of the species are endemic, they all belong to widespread families. The mesopelagic lanternfishes (Myctophidae, 35 species) are particularly numerous, taking advantage of the abundant krill as a food source.

CONCLUSIONS

The polar regions both have distinctive fish faunas adapted to low temperatures and seasonally high productivity. Most remarkable, however, is the notothenioid fish fauna of the Antarctic which is the result of millions of years of adaptive radiation in an isolated, cold environment; this is also true of the other remarkable elements of the ecosystem, from krill to whales. The result is a system of highly structured, complex food webs with a great deal of biomass that is potentially harvestable by humans. Despite international agreements to protect biodiversity in the Antarctic, harvest of krill is taking place, with unknown effects on the ecosystem. Any harvest of fish would almost certainly be disastrous for the fish communities. The fishes are very slow growing (a 25-cm fish is likely to be 5 to 10 years old, with the largest individuals being from 25 to 30 years old or older), so replacement of harvested fish would be extremely slow. Although comparatively little is known about community structure of the continental shelf benthos where many of the harvestable fish occur, the complexity and apparent long-term stability of the communities may mean that a new stress (fishing) could severely disrupt them. In addition, because the method of fishing most likely to be used is bottom trawling, the physical damage caused by fishing could severely disturb the reproductive success of some species by destroying nests and removing parental guardians.

Supplemental Readings

Andriashev 1970; Daniels 1978, 1983; Eastman 1993; DeWitt 1971; Kock 1992; Walters 1955.

CHAPTER 37

Conservation

The fish faunas of the world are changing rapidly. In fresh water, extinction of endemic species is becoming increasingly common, while tolerant, aggressive species invade degraded ecosystems. In marine systems, fisheries are collapsing. In all aquatic environments, decreases in the abundance and diversity of fishes are being documented. Increasingly, aquaculture is being relied upon to provide fish for humanity. The direct cause of these dramatic changes is the exponential increase in human populations. Not only are we exploiting fish directly at unsustainable rates but we are competing directly with them for water, space, and food. Whether or not such changes are good, bad, or simply of no consequence depends on both one's value system and one's state of hunger; nevertheless the changes *are* taking place and the future of humankind is closely linked to that of fish (and the rest of Earth's biota). An earth turned into a wasteland for fish will equally be a wasteland for humans. On the other hand, wise treatment of the waters and the life within them can provide benefits for humankind for the indefinite future. It is therefore important to understand the changes that are taking place, to monitor them, and to regulate them. Thus this chapter will briefly discuss (1) the status of marine and freshwater fish faunas, (2) the causes of declines in fish diversity and abundance, (3) conservation biology as a new approach to fish conservation, and (4) values and fish conservation.

STATUS OF FISH FAUNAS

Fresh water. The vast majority of endangered fishes live in fresh water. Basically, the reason for this is the fact that freshwater environments are islands or ribbons of water surrounded by oceans of land filled with people. Not only do we confiscate the water flowing across the landscape for human use, but we pollute the water we do not directly use. Our streams and rivers are the ultimate recipients of the by-products of human activity, from sewage to sediment. While this means that endangered fishes can be found everywhere, they are most prevalent in regions with one or more of the following characteristics: (1) highly developed economies, (2) small isolated bodies of water, (3) high endemism, (4) arid or Mediterranean climates, (5) big rivers, and (6) big lakes.

For example, in the arid southwestern United States all of the fishes native to the lower Colorado River are endangered because the river has been dammed in many places, the water diverted, and exotic species introduced into the altered habitats. What water remains is full of salts and other pollutants (including exotic fish) because big rivers like the Colorado, and big lakes, are the ultimate sumps for vast regions. In the tiny springs and creeks of nearby desert regions, many of the endemic pupfishes and minnows are threatened by multiple factors, such as diversion of water for human use and the introduction of predatory fish. Even the desert fish that live in Death Valley National Park can be regarded as endangered because the city of Las Vegas (with one of the highest per capita water-consumption rates of any city in the world) is pumping ancient water from aquifers that may feed the spring systems upon which the fish depend. Tropical regions also increasingly qualify as areas with large numbers of endangered species, as third-world countries strive to dam, divert, and pollute their rivers following the model of the Western world (Dudgeon 1992). Because tropical waters have more species to lose, numbers of endangered species may be high although percentages are low.

These patterns are reflected in the numbers and percentages of species that are extinct or needing special protection (with the status of endangered, threatened, and special concern) in various parts of the United States and the world (Table 37-1). In North America, 40 fish taxa are extinct (Miller et al. 1989) and 364 need special protection (Williams et al. 1989); these comprise about one third of the region's entire fauna. These taxa are not evenly distributed over the continent, however. A much higher percentage of species are in trouble in states with arid or Mediterranean climates than in wetter regions. A similar pattern can be seen in Europe and other regions. Overall, a conservative estimate of the percentage of all freshwater fishes meriting special protection in order to prevent extinction in the next 25 to 50 years is 20% (about 2100 species), assuming present trends continue. As an indication of the conservative nature of this number, about 200 species of cichlids have been eradicated from Lake Victoria in East Africa since the introduction of the predatory Nile perch in the 1950s (Goldschmidt et al. 1993).

Estuaries and inland seas. Estuaries are naturally inhabited by ecologically resilient species of fish. However, estuaries are also the sites of major coastal cities, are subject

TABLE 37–1   PERCENTAGES OF SELECTED FRESHWATER FISH FAUNAS THAT ARE EX-
TINCT OR MAY NEED SPECIAL PROTECTION TO AVOID EXTINCTION IN THE NEXT
25–50 YEARS (CLASSIFIED AS THREATENED, ENDANGERED, VULNERABLE, OR SPECIAL
CONCERN). INFORMATION FROM MOYLE AND LEIDY (1992), ELVIRA (1995), JENKINS
AND BURKHEAD (1994), LARJE (1990), MAITLAND AND LYLE (1990), PETHIYAGODA (1994),
POLLARD ET AL. (1990).

Region	Total taxa	Percent needing protection
North America	1174	31
California	116	69
Arkansas	147	22
Wisconsin	200	29
Virginia	190	23
Europe		42
Sweden	58	28
Great Britain	55	18
Spain	27	67
Sri Lanka	88	18
Australia	192	34
South Africa	98	63
Costa Rica	156	9

to having their vital freshwater inflows diverted, and are the receiving waters for hundreds of exotic species brought in annually through the ballast water of ships. Thus most large estuaries are highly altered ecosystems. While this has resulted in the declines of many fish species (and their fisheries), surprisingly few estuarine species are endangered. A major exception to this observation are the native fishes of the upper Sacramento–San Joaquin estuary of California, where two fish species are already formally recognized as threatened species and a number of others have been proposed for such status. The resiliency of estuarine fishes is reflected in the ongoing recovery of striped bass populations in Chesapeake Bay following efforts to reduce fishing pressure and to clean up pollutants. There is much less hope, however, for recovery of fish populations in the Baltic Sea in northern Europe because of the accumulation of toxic chemicals, especially organochlorines, in the sediments. The fish that survive exposure to these chemicals are typically regarded as unsafe for human consumption because of the high levels of toxins in their tissues (Platt 1995). Among the most endangered aquatic ecosystems in the world are the Caspian and Black seas of Asia, which have suffered the cumulative insults of massive diversion of inflowing water coupled with unrestricted pollution. In the Caspian Sea, fisheries have collapsed and three species of sturgeon and the endemic "species flock" of shad *(Alosa)* species can be regarded as endangered (Rozengurt and Hedgpeth 1989).

Marine environments. There are few endangered marine fishes, but that situation may be changing rapidly. Marine fish are protected to some extent by the sheer volume of the oceans, which helps to shield them from pollution and other human insults. However, because the fish are concentrated on continental shelves and around islands, the negative influence of humans is gradually becoming more pervasive. Even tropical reefs have been severely degraded by sediments and pollutants washed onto them from nearby land or have been damaged by the mining of coral as a source of lime. Perhaps the most obvious manifestation of the problems marine fish face is the collapse of fisheries around the world as the result of overfishing, accompanied by major changes in marine ecosystems. For example, fisheries on the Georges Bank, off the northeastern United States, have been virtually shut down in hope of spurring a recovery of the once enormous populations of commerical "groundfish." Prior to the collapse of the fisheries, the major species in the catch switched from valuable codfish, haddock, and flounder to the much less valuable dogfish shark and skates (Sherman 1994). The total catch of fish also showed a steady decline during this period of change. One of the first species to be driven to near-endangered status by a fishery is the bluefin tuna *(Thunnus thynnus)* of the Atlantic Ocean. This species is so prized in Japan for its flesh that harvesting it is lucrative even when numbers are extremely low.

An additional but poorly understood threat to marine fish is the by-catch harvest. Fisheries are rarely entirely selective on the target species and many fish that are undersized or with no commerical value are caught. In shrimp fisheries, 50–90% of the catch by weight consists of small fish that are discarded. This amounts to between 8 and 16.5 million metric tons of fish per year, many of them juveniles of valuable commercial fish species (Norse 1993). Because shrimp fisheries are concentrated in some areas (e.g., Gulf of Mexico), their effects on nontarget species may be devastating. It is possible that some small benthic species may be endangered by such fisheries, but the information is lacking.

CAUSES OF CHANGE

The aquatic environment is changing constantly, even where it is not affected by humans. As the previous 10 chapters indicate, fish are often alternately abundant and rare, on an irregular basis, in response to natural environmental fluctuations. In a sense, therefore, the pressures humans put on fish populations are nothing new. On the other hand, humans are placing stress on fish populations to an extent the fish have never experienced before in such a short period of time. This stress, because it is in addition to the natural stresses that act on fish populations, results in greatly accelerated rates of extinction and other irreversible changes. For example, the rapid decline of coho salmon *(Oncorhynchus kisutch)* in California, Oregon, and Washington seems to be the result of accelerated human-caused stresses (stream alterations, etc.) during a period when coho populations would probably have been naturally low as the result of extended droughts and less productive conditions in the ocean (Brown et al. 1994).

The human-related stress can be divided into four components, which often act on fish populations simultaneously: (1) exploitation, (2) introduction of nonnative species, (3) habitat alterations, and (4) pollution.

Exploitation

Exploitation is a major cause of changes in fish populations and communities. There are few waters in the world today in which a fishery of some sort does not exist. The most dramatic changes are those brought about by overfishing, which may result in the elimination of fishable stocks of fish, such as codfish in the Georges Bank and sardines off California (see Chapter 34). Such disasters are best known for the economic hardships they bring to fishing communities, but comparatively little attention is paid to the impact they have on the biotic communities to which the overexploited species belong. The collapse of the anchoveta fishery off Peru, discussed in Chapter 34, was also accompanied by a permanent collapse of the huge populations of sea birds that depended on the anchoveta. Overexploitation of herring in the Norwegian–Berents Sea ecosystem ultimately resulted in large-scale starvation of predatory cod, sea birds, and seals that depended on the herring. There was also a great reduction in the abundance of other species of fish because the cod devoured whatever they could before the cod populations collapsed (Hamre 1994). Of course, the fisheries that depended on the cod and other species also suffered severely.

Species whose populations are fished to low levels are often replaced by other species that are ecologically similar although differing in their life history characteristics and desirability to humans. Thus California's sardines were replaced by anchovies. On the Georges Bank, codfish, haddock, and flounders were replaced by sharks and skates. These effects were recorded because of their spectacular nature, but they surely were accompanied by other, unrecorded effects, such as changes in the species composition of the zooplankton or benthos or changes in the abundance of unexploited species. These indirect effects are barely understood and we have little idea of their reversibility. However, overexploitation rarely leads to the extinction of a species or population of fish, because fishing usually becomes uneconomic when the populations get too low. Thus many of the changes wrought by overexploitation should in theory be reversible because the components of the original system are usually still present. The main exceptions to the "rule" that overexploitation of fish does not lead to extinction are with fishes of unusually high value that are unusually easy to catch, such as salmon and sturgeon.

Another possible exception to the above rule is the fishery for tropical fishes for the aquarium trade. Because of their cash value to poverty-stricken peoples, such fishes are being intensively collected in many parts of the tropics. Especially vulnerable to collection by nets are species that become confined to isolated pools during the dry season, so that few fish can escape a serious collecting effort. Even more damaging is the use of poisons to collect aquarium fish; here the basic technique is to pour some toxic substance into a stream and collect the largest and most valuable fishes as they appear at the surface in distress. Most will survive if placed immediately in fresh water. Such collecting, of course, kills nearly everything in the stream that is not collected, so it is not unusual to find streams, especially in Southeast Asia, with greatly depleted faunas as a result. Similar effects have been noted when coral reef fishes are collected for the saltwater aquarium trade, using sodium cyanide. Likewise, collection of reef fish by the use of dynamite kills many fish and destroys reef habitats. Because of depletion in the wild and high demand by aquarists, many species of aquarium fish are now raised in fish hatcheries. However, fish in such populations reflect selection processes aimed at producing fish capable of thriving under aquarium conditions, as well as fish that have color patterns favored by aquarists. Such fish may be poorly suited for returning to the wild, even if restoration programs for lost or damaged fish faunas ever become a reality.

The side effects of overexploitation can be as devastating as the direct harvest of the fish. Besides the by-catch problem mentioned above, fishing gear can alter habitats. In areas where bottom-trawl fisheries are active, the trawl boards plow up the bottom, destroying the burrows of invertebrates (important in food webs), killing small nontarget species, increasing suspended sediments, and generally reducing the productivity of the trawled areas (Norse 1993).

Introduction of Nonnative Species

Fish species are frequently introduced by humans, either deliberately or inadvertently, into waters to which they are not native. Deliberate introductions are typically made to "improve" local fish faunas. They often have the opposite effect, causing declines in fisheries, endangered species, and headaches for management agencies. This has been termed the "Frankenstein Effect" by Moyle et al. (1987). Harm can be done to local fish faunas by fish introduced from nearby waters, as well as by fish brought in from distant countries. The impact of introductions has been greatest in inland waters, but introductions of marine fishes are becoming increasingly common (Baltz 1991). The most pervasive marine invasions have been through the discharge of ballast water by ships, which has resulted in the establishment of hundreds of species of invertebrates and fish around the world (Carlton and Geller 1993). From a fish perspective, one of the most spectacular invasions has been that of the Mediterranean Sea, via the Suez Canal, by many species of Red Sea fishes (see Chapter 26).

Although virtually any aquatic environment that can support fish can be invaded by new species, introduced species are usually most successful in environments that have been altered by humans, where the native species are already stressed or reduced in numbers. Thus in the Central Valley of California, the streams with natural hydrologic regimes are still dominated by native species, while streams that have been dammed tend to be dominated by introduced species (Baltz and Moyle 1992). In the Laurentian Great Lakes, non-native fish invasions were facilitated by overexploitation of native fishes and by pollution. Nevertheless, native fish often persist and even thrive in altered environments if introduced fish are not present. This means that introduced species may be the direct cause of the disappearance of native forms through predation, competition, disease, and hybridization (Moyle 1986).

Predation can result in rapid and drastic changes in a fish fauna when an exotic piscivore is introduced into a community of fishes not adapted to its style of predation. Thus the sea lamprey was able to virtually wipe out the populations of large fishes in the upper Great Lakes in less than 20 years. Peacock bass (*Cichla ocellaris*) and largemouth bass have been able to eliminate most fish species from large lakes into which they have been introduced in Central America. Nile perch have been able to devour into extinction nearly 200 species of fish from Africa's Lake Victoria. Examples of predation eliminating species from streams are less well known, but introductions of piscivorous brown trout have been implicated in the decline of stream fishes worldwide, most notably in Australia and New Zealand (Crowl et al. 1992).

Competition from introduced fishes as a factor causing the decline of native fish populations is very difficult to demonstrate, yet it is undoubtedly important. For example, in the Great Lakes the decline of many of the plankton-feeding whitefish species *(Coregonus)* was related to the establishment of the alewife, which not only reduced the populations of large zooplankters in the lakes but crowded into whitefish "space" during critical times of the year (see Chapter 28). Often the competitive superiority of an introduced species over a native form is related to habitat change. Species that evolved in a stream environment typically decline in numbers if the stream is impounded and lake-adapted fishes are introduced. Some species may actually change the environment themselves. Thus in the Mississippi drainage, native bottom-feeding species, such as buffalofish *(Ictiobus* spp.), may disappear from shallow lakes once carp become established, root up the bottom, and decrease the water clarity.

Disease is a problem when pathogens and parasites carried by introduced species infect native species. It is a poorly understood factor but may be more important than generally realized. An introduced species may find invading easier if potential predators and competitors have been decimated by disease. For example, the invasion of red shiner *(Cyprinella lutrensis)* into the Virgin River, Utah, may have been facilitated by the negative effects on the native woundfin *(Plagopterus argentissimus)* of the Asian tapeworm carried by the invaders. The shiners had been infected with this tapeworm, carried by grass carp brought in from Asia for weed control (in Arkansas), and were apparently fairly resistant to its effects. The woundfin is now an endangered species.

Hybridization is a problem when an introduced species interbreeds with a closely related endemic form, producing hybrids that backcross with the parents. If the hybrid (intermediate) phenotypes then have some competitive or reproductive disadvantage compared with the phenotypes that most closely resemble the introduced form, the intermediate phenotypes will gradually be eliminated from the population. Gradually, the population will increasingly resemble the "pure" introduced species. This mechanism has apparently been responsible for the elimination of many interior cutthroat trout populations by rainbow trout. However, one of the best-documented cases is the virtual elimination of the Mojave tui chub *(Gila bicolor mohavensis)* from the Mojave River in California through hybridization with the arroyo chub *(G. orcutti)* (Hubbs and Miller 1942). The Mojave tui chub is now listed as an endangered species. A similar situation may exist in the Pecos River, Texas, where a single introduction of the sheepshead minnow *(Cyprinodon variegatus)* resulted in nearly complete hybridization with the endemic Pecos pupfish *(C. pecoensis)* in nearly 700 km of river in just a few years (Echelle and Connor 1989). It is expected that the hybrids will eventually take over the entire river system from the native form, except in isolated habitats.

Habitat Alterations

Habitat alteration by humans in inland waters (including estuaries) is the single biggest cause of faunal change and is increasingly becoming a major factor in the marine environment as well. Every time a stream is dammed, a stream bed channelized, a watershed logged or heavily grazed, or a lakeside marsh filled in, the fish fauna changes, often very subtly. Removing large trees that shade a salmon spawning stream may greatly increase salmon production, by increasing the amount of sunlight on the water and hence the stream's productivity. However, if such a logging operation causes the stream to become too warm or is accompanied by the silting in of the spawning gravels, minnows, suckers, and other species may increase in numbers instead. On a more extreme scale, most of our major river systems have been so altered by dams, locks, channelization, urbanization, deforestation, and wetland drainage that their fish faunas bear little resemblance to the ones that were present originally. Once common species have become rare and uncommon, but tolerant species become abundant, especially introduced species (e.g., Burr 1991, Edwards and Contreras-Balderas 1991). One of the most altered rivers in the United States is the upper Tennessee River in Virginia, North Carolina, and Tennessee (Neves and Angermeier 1990). Nearly 40% of the riverine habitat has been flooded by reservoirs or changed by discharges from 11 major dams. Reservoirs favor different species than those favored by riverine habitats and isolate populations of stream fishes so recolonization following local extinction events is no longer possible. In addition, domestic, agricultural, and industrial pollution are major problems, highlighted by a spill of fly ash into the Clinch River (a major tributary) in 1967 which killed nearly all the fish in 144 km of river. The upper Tennessee drainage has a rich fish fauna (224 taxa, including 25 endemic forms). 58 (26%) of these taxa are endangered or otherwise needing special protection. The fact that many river-dwelling fishes in North America are threatened species is a tip-of-the-iceberg indication of the extent to which the river fish communities have been changed.

In the oceans, shipwrecks and other debris of civilization have created numerous new reefs where none existed before, often greatly increasing the abundance and diversity of local fish faunas. In many coastal areas, such reefs are now being created deliberately. On the other hand, the destruction of intertidal habitats by the construction of breakwaters and marinas and the filling in of vital coastal habitats such as salt marshes, mangrove swamps, and estuaries is causing declines not only in the fishes unique to such areas but also in the populations of offshore fishes that require such areas as nurseries for their young. The filling of these areas can be deliberate, for land "reclamation" or the result of upstream erosion, which fills coastal lagoons with sediment. Often just as destructive is the creation of navigation channels through marshes, mangrove forests, and shallow areas of bays. The channels and the constant dredging needed to maintain them cause major disruptions of the local ecosystems, reducing biotic productivity and diversity (Norse 1993).

Pollution

Pollution is really a type of habitat alteration, but it nevertheless deserves separate consideration because of its extent and frequently subtle effects. Of course, the best-known effects of pollution are not subtle at all. Releases of toxic chemicals have caused massive kills in hundreds of miles of major river systems, as well as in lakes and estuaries. Many streams in mining areas are devoid of fish life because of acidic water draining from the mines; many mountain lakes are losing their fish faunas as they become acidic from material carried in the smoke of distant industries. Large amounts of sewage in lakes and streams cause depletion of the oxygen supply, killing all but the hardiest fish or forcing them to move elsewhere. Fortunately, fishes are by and large very adaptable and have the reproductive potential to quickly recolonize areas from which they have been eliminated, once the cause of their disappearance is eliminated. For example, Atlantic salmon returned to spawn in the Penobscot River in Maine, after a decade-long absence, following a successful effort to "clean up" polluting industries and towns. Permanent elimination of species by pollution occurs either where the populations are highly localized (endemic) or where the pollution is continual and severe.

While direct kills of fish by pollution are of obvious concern, in the long run the changes caused by the sublethal effects of pollution are equally significant. Power plants that use water for cooling may raise the temperatures of the stream, lake, or estuarine regions from which they draw and into which they discharge the water. While such thermal pollution may kill fish directly, more often it causes local shifts in the composition of the fish fauna. From a fisheries point of view, these shifts may even be desirable at times because during cool weather game fish (and hence fishermen) may be attracted to the warmer water associated with power plants. However, other fishes may avoid the warmer water, just as they may avoid water with reduced oxygen concentrations, increased turbidity, or gooey bottoms due to pollution. The overall effect in such situations is typically decreased numbers of species, accompanied by increases in tolerant species such as common carp. Similar effects may result from sublethal levels of toxic compounds such as pesticides, especially if the toxins accumulate in the flesh of the fish. In such cases, they may reduce temperature tolerances, change behavior patterns, increase vulnerability to disease, and generally reduce growth and survival rates. Since such toxins typically accumulate through food chains, predatory game fishes are especially likely to be affected. For example, mosquitofish (*Gambusia* spp.) living in waters adjacent to cotton fields may develop extraordinary tolerances to pesticides and so survive. However, predatory fish such as largemouth bass that would normally prey on the mosquitofish are now largely absent from such areas, presumably poisoned by their prey.

The interaction of mosquitofish, pesticides, and bass shows why the effects of pollution often take a long time to be noticed; the disappearance of the bass was a gradual process. Likewise, the disappearance of trout and other fish from mountain lakes in Europe and eastern North America took decades because the gradual increase in acidity due to atmospheric pollution affected the ability of fish to reproduce long before the water was actually toxic to adult fish. Such subtle environmental changes often interact with other factors as well. The extinction of the blue pike *(Stizostedion vitreum glaucum)* from Lake Erie was apparently largely the result of massive environmental changes due to pollution, but overfishing of the pike and other factors were also present (Miller et al. 1989).

CONSERVATION BIOLOGY

It should be clear that freshwater and other inland aquatic ecosystems are among the most endangered ecosystems in the world. They are being irreversibly altered at an accelerated pace, with marine systems following close behind. This is a tragedy not only because we are losing species but also because we are losing the enormous benefits that intact aquatic ecosystems provide to humans. The growing realization that ecosystem degradation is a worldwide problem that requires emergency measures to reverse has led to the emergence of the discipline of conservation biology, complete with academic programs at major universities, textbooks, scientific journals, and governmental funding initiatives. Conservation biology is a "new, synthetic field that applies the principles of ecology, biogeography, population genetics, economics, sociology, anthropology, philosophy, and other theoretically based disciplines to the maintenance of biological diversity throughout the world" (Meffe and Carroll 1994, 4). While the synthesis and synergism of the field are new, it has roots that are especially deep in theoretical ecology (the scientific basis), wildlife and fisheries management (the pragmatic tradition), and the environmental movement (the ethics and motivation). Because conservation biology is a "crisis discipline" (Soule 1985), it requires conservation biologists to make recommendations and to take actions based on inadequate knowledge, something that is very painful for inherently conservative scientists to do. Also implicit in the field is the understanding that most actions are short-term "holding" actions that will be effective in the long term only if we halt he human population explosion soon, and change the economic and philosophical value systems within which the world presently operates. The rest of this chapter therefore is devoted to value systems and how they apply to fish conservation.

VALUES AND FISH CONSERVATION

In a way, it is astonishing that fish conservation is so difficult to achieve because the overall value of fish is obvious. Most fish species have at least some direct market value, or are part of food webs that support economically important species, or live in environments whose good health is essential for the support of fisheries. Commercial and subsistence fisheries provide a good share of the protein needed by humans, yet they are in decline everywhere. It has been estimated that marine fisheries alone can yield, on a sustained basis, between 90 million and 100 million metric tons of fish per year (Rounsefell 1975). This figure was reached for a brief period, but present catches are now around 80 million metric tons per year (in-

cluding 15 million metric tons from fresh water) and the amount is declining
(O'Bannon 1994). Major fisheries around the world, such as the salmon fisheries of
the Pacific Northwest and the Atlantic cod fisheries, have collapsed. Other declining economic values of wild-caught fish include fish collected for the aquarium
trade and sport fisheries, both of which depend on large populations of healthy fish
in clean water. In most cases, the loss of fisheries and fish populations is predictable
and often it is blatantly obvious when the decline is taking place. Unfortunately,
corrective action is rarely taken in time, despite the economic, social, and ecological losses that can be seen looming on the horizon.

Economic Values

The basic problem is the economic system under which fisheries operate, in which
the value of short-term economic gains predominate over the value of more sus-
tainable long-term gains. "Wealth or the prospect of wealth generates political and
social power that is used to promote unlimited exploitation of resources" (Ludwig
et al. 1993, 17). Three alternative economic values that can be offered for fish are (1)
ecosystem values, (2) existence values, and (3) intergenerational values (Moyle and
Moyle 1995).

Ecosystem values. Functioning aquatic ecosystems provide many benefits to human society, even beyond edible fish. For example, aquatic systems have enormous
capacity to absorb and detoxify pollutants, a "free" service that has largely been
taken for granted until recently. As aquatic ecosystems become degraded, they lose
this capacity. The costs of purifying the water for drinking or other uses then becomes much higher, the quality of the water is reduced, and the likelihood of toxic
episodes through equipment failure increases. The value of healthy ecosystems can
often be measured in terms of human health and of the long-term economic health
of the human systems to which they are connected. Fish are an important component of ecosystem values because they are often the most sensitive and conspicuous indicators of ecosystem change, and so can give early warning if conditions
detrimental to human health are emerging.

   The problem with ecosystem values is that they are very difficult to quantify
except when disaster strikes as a result of their having been overlooked. For example, high levels of logging in the Pacific Northwest has resulted in widescale loss
of the ability of streams to sustain large salmon populations. If the many warnings
about the effects on salmon of clear-cutting and other logging practices had been
heeded, not only would there be harvestable, naturally produced populations of
salmon available for the indefinite future, but the forest ecosystems themselves
would have been able to produce a more constant income for local communities.

Existence values. The development of this concept is an effort by economists to put
a monetary value on what Norton (1987) calls amenity values: the recreational and
aethestic values derived from natural systems, the joy of learning from studying
the behavior of a fish, the appreciation of salmon for their cultural and historic sym-

bolism, the near-religious feelings anglers can experience when connecting with wild fish in a wild place. Such experiences can be highly valued even by individuals who never actively seek them, but who just like knowing that such an experience is available should they choose to seek it. The principal method for providing existence values is through surveys in which the public is asked, in regard to some natural feature, "How much would you be willing to pay to maintain this?" If the question is asked in terms of a few cents a month added to water or power bills (say to protect anadromous fish), the answer is often a strong yes; however, the probability of obtaining negative replies increases with the price. This implies, of course, that there *is* a price on species and habitats and that if the price is too high the species or habitats can be eliminated. Despite this serious weakness in the calculation of existence values, such calculations are increasingly common in decision-making with regard to management actions for endangered species.

One way around the high-price dilemma is to assume that the true existence value of species or habitats cannot be calculated and that, because species belong to the people as a whole, individual people who benefit economically from degrading a habitat or endangering a species should pay for the right to do so. In this case the public-value surveys, combined with estimates of direct economic losses, can indicate how much the payment should be. If the determined value of a species or habitat is high, actions severely damaging to it would presumably be altered or not allowed. For example, the introduction of aquatic organisms through the ballast water of ships has caused billions of dollars in damage to city water systems in the Great Lakes and disrupted estuarine ecosystems in many places. If ship owners were required to pay even a fraction of the damage, direct and indirect, caused by these expensive introductions, they would quickly become willing to adopt techniques to reduce them. Politically, of course, implementing such a value system for species in a market-oriented economy is nearly impossible, despite its obvious benefits.

Intergenerational values.   Existence values have received a great deal of attention from economists because in theory they can be fit into present economic systems. A basic problem is that most economists today treat resources, such as fish, as if they belonged *only* to the present generation, the present "owners." If there is no sense of these resources as also belonging to future generations, they can be spent, gambled, or traded in order to produce immediate wealth, until they are gone. The increasingly frequent collapse of major fisheries certainly demonstrates the prevalence of this lack of intergenerational values in the present economic system.

An opposite approach is to place a high value on **sustainability,** the equitable distribution of resources between generations, to make sure that future generations are no worse off than the present one (Daily and Ehrlich 1992; Norgaard 1994). Unfortunately it is difficult to place an economic value on sustainability, in part because it is impossible to know just what future generations will value. Desert pupfish are largely regarded as a scientific curiosity today but they might be regarded as a valuable and highly nutritional delicacy in the future (as they once were by the Panamint Indians). Thus, protective actions designed to make sure a species or habitat does not disappear may take many years to make a direct economic contribution, if ever. In contrast, development projects that might eliminate a species or a run of salmon may have an immediate economic and political payoff. This results in decisions such as the introduction of Nile perch into Lake Victoria, which is now the subject of a profitable export fishery. The cost of the introduction was the elimination of the small cichlids that were once the mainstays of subsistence fishery, as well as deforestation of the region around the lake to provide wood necessary for the kiln-drying of the large perch. The native cichlids had been sun-dried. Clearly, future generations of people around the lake will be worse off because of the introduction, which has resulted in a depletion of local non-cash resources.

The best way to demonstrate the need for intergenerational values is to look at how decisions made by past generations for short-term gain are now reaping enormous costs to present generations. The most obvious examples are the many dams installed on large rivers for diversion of water and generation of power. The effects of these dams on downstream ecosystems was usually not considered to be a cost when they were built. Yet these costs are very real today, as demonstrated by the disappearance of sturgeon fisheries in Russia, salmon fisheries in the Pacific Northwest, and sardine fisheries in the Mediterranean (from the construction of Aswan Dam on the Nile River). The substitutes for the loss of the wild fish have never really worked as promised (if they were promised at all), despite efforts to promote hatchery programs and reservoir fisheries. When dams were built on the Colorado River in the 1950s and early 1960s, who could have foreseen the passage of the federal Endangered Species Act which would ultimately mandate that large quantities of water should be devoted to saving obscure native fishes? These same fish were the target of a major poisoning program in 1962, for fear that they would compete with exotic game fish to be introduced into the newly built Flaming Gorge Reservoir.

Although the need for building intergenerational values into our economic system is clear, it is not clear how to do this. One approach is to use a **safe minimum standard,** which is based on the idea that if information on a species is limited and its potential for extinction is high, we should assume that it has, or will have, a high economic value. Another approach is to consider features of the environment, such as salmon runs, to be **natural capital,** the value of which should be placed on the same basis as monetary capital in investment funds. The idea here is that capital should be maintained in order to provide income for present and future generations. Endangered species or runs of salmon, under this scenario, are regarded as depleted natural capital that needs to be restored as an investment in the future (Moyle and Moyle 1995). A further extension of this idea is to protect natural diversity as **genetic capital** on the assumption that genetic diversity is needed to adapt valuable species to unpredictable climate change, or for use in selective breeding programs for aquaculture, especially through the use of genetic engineering (which can move genes among species).

Non-economic Values

The nontraditional economic values discussed above are often recognized as valid, but usually not by traditional market-oriented economists. These values are therefore having little impact on the decisions of businesses and governments today. An alternative approach waives economic arguments and presents various presumptive non-economic values as reasons for protecting fish and aquatic ecosystems. Examples of the kinds of values often put forth include aesthetic values, cultural values, scientific research values, and teaching values.

The **aesthetic values** of small obscure species have long been recognized by aquarists, and this very recognition has turned quite a number of small or unusually attractive fishes into resources with definite economic value. Although the demand by aquarists for exotic fishes seems to be insatiable, often to the detriment of wild populations, aquarists are rather selective in their tastes. Sterba (1959) lists over 1600 species that have been kept in aquaria in Europe at one time or another, and a generous estimate would put the worldwide total at perhaps double that number. Many of these species, of course, have been kept by a few individuals or public aquaria only for their curiosity value, and thus would be unlikely to have the steady market demand necessary for making them a true resource. Unfortunately, many fishes are not likely to have even fleeting value as curiosities (except to scientists). Examples might be the many rather similar species of minnows and darters in North American streams, the small benthic fishes of the Antarctic, or the numerous similar species of sculpins, blennies, and other forms found in tide pools.

In recent years the popularity of snorkeling and scuba diving, particularly on tropical reefs and in rocky coastal areas of temperate regions, has greatly increased public awareness and appreciation of fish (at least in Western countries). However, even in popular diving areas, the majority of species are rarely seen because they are either nocturnal, cryptically colored, or very small. In any case, often the most popular fishes for viewing are the large predatory fishes that also have commercial value. Overall, it appears that many fishes do have aesthetic value to people. Efforts are therefore made to attach dollar values to the aesthetic values in terms of money spent on recreation, travel, and equipment. However, such values are generally much less than other economic values (such as the value of a reef as the base for an oil refinery).

Because of their aesthetic and culinary properties, many fish have high **cultural value** as icons or symbols of tradition. In many cultures they are the frequent subject of art, often with considerable symbolic significance (Moyle and Moyle 1991). In the United States and Canada, the importance of some fish to Indian tribes has been a major force in conservation. In the Pacific Northwest, runs of salmon have been conserved or restored in order to provide traditional fishing opportunities. Flows in the lower Truckee River, Nevada, have been partially restored in order to save the cui-ui (*Chasmistes cujus*) from extinction; one of the most effective arguments in favor of doing this has been the importance of the fish in the culture of the Paiute Indians who still live in the area.

Currently, the cultural values of fish include **scientific research and educational values.** The scientific values of fish are obvious to ichthyologists, who find all fish intrinsically interesting. Fortunately for ichthyologists, who are relatively few in number (at least in their pure form), many other scientists find fish useful as well. Sticklebacks and poeciliids have proven to be invaluable for studies of evolution, behavior, and genetics that are of general interest. The study of reef fish ecology has provided considerable insight into the structure and function of complex ecosystems. Lampreys have proven to be invaluable for studies of neurophysiology. But important as fish already are in basic research, their potential for experimental and *in situ* studies is just beginning to be realized.

The educational values of fish are also obvious. They are the one group of vertebrates in which it is really possible to maintain large populations in the laboratory for observation and experimentation. Many varieties are readily available for dissection, giving an easy overview of the many types of adaptations possible in vertebrates. Most important of all, they can typically be found in large numbers and diversity in waters fairly close to most educational institutions, so that many types of ecological demonstrations can be made. Fish have the right combination of availability, size, and ease of handling to make them the most desirable group of vertebrates for comparative classroom studies of ecology, behavior, evolution, and anatomy, and to be very valuable in other areas such as genetics and physiology as well.

The problem with these "non-economic" arguments is that directly or indirectly they are an effort to turn non-economic values into economic values (Ehrenfeld 1976). Unfortunately, these values are so indirect or so tenuous that they will usually seem small when compared with the very real economic values that can be gained for the short-term exploitation of an environment or a species. A well-known confrontation between these values came with the efforts to stop the construction of Tellico Dam on the Little Tennessee River, in order to protect the endangered snail darter *(Percina tanasi)*. The Endangered Species Act of 1973 (ESA) was successfully invoked, passing all the way through to the U.S. Supreme Court to protect the species. Congress subsequently changed the law to make exemptions possible through the creation of a "God Committee." Even this committee was unwilling to condemn a species to apparent extinction and so a special exemption from the rules of ESA had to be obtained through congressional subterfuge. The dam was finally built. Subsequently, two rather ironic facts emerged: The snail darter existed in other streams and so was not condemned to extinction after all, and the dam has fallen far short of its projected economic value. If the darter had prevailed in this argument, a great deal of real money would have been saved.

Unfortunately, the political tide is currently (1995) running against the protection of obscure endangered species. The reason for this sea-change is easy to understand. The original ESA was passed after a majority of Congress was persuaded to save the more spectacular symbols of the disappearing American wilderness, such as bald eagles, wolves, and whooping cranes. Once the law passed, however, it quickly became evident that it had opened up a Pandora's box of problems for many elements of the ever-expanding U.S. economy; the list of endangered or threatened species is rapidly growing longer and longer as not only small, obscure fish but also invertebrates and plants are added. Thus it increasingly appears that while economic and some non-economic arguments can be used to save species and habitats, they can easily be overcome in a majority of cases. This means that the preservation of biotic diversity will ultimately depend on the development of arguments that appeal to a sense of morality or even to the feeling of religious awe that natural systems can invoke. One way such feelings can be expressed is in the basic idea that all species, and therefore the habitats in which they live, have a right to continued existence; that as humans we do not have the right to unthinkingly terminate evolutionary lines and wondrously complex natural systems.

Norton (1987) argues that this line of reasoning can be regarded as too extreme or dogmatic by many people and suggests that it is better to base the preservation of natural variety on the **transformative value** of natural systems. This argument maintains that interactions with natural systems have the potential to profoundly and positively transform our attitudes toward existence so that we can live on this planet in a less materialistic and more spiritual way; and that such a transformation provides the moral foundation for living on the earth as if it belonged to future generations.

It is possible to argue that a foundation for future-oriented conservation can be found in the tenets of the world's religions (Callicott 1994), even though such religious scruples seem to be lost in the rampant materialism of today. However, perhaps the fact that a plea for a kinder, more moral treatment of the natural (and human) world can be found at the end of a college science textbook is a hopeful sign that our value systems are being transformed. But even if this is so, the process is still too slow to save many species and ecosystems. Therefore political action is necessary today to protect enough pieces of our natural systems to ensure that widespread restoration will be possible when humanity finally realizes that its own welfare ultimately depends on environmental integrity. "Nature never did betray / The heart that loved her" (Wordsworth 1798).

Supplemental Readings

Ehrenfeld 1976; Moyle 1986; Moyle et al. 1987; Rolston 1985; Rounsefell 1975; Wilson 1985.

Bibliography

Adams, S. M. 1976a. Ecology of eelgrass, *Zostera marina* (L.) fish communities. I. Structural analysis. *J. Exp. Mar. Biol. Ecol.* 22:269–291.

Adams, S. M. 1976b. Feeding ecology of eelgrass fish communities. *Trans. Amer. Fish. Soc.* 105(4):514–519.

Ahlstrom, E. H., and Radovich, J. 1970. Management of the Pacific sardine. Pages 183–193 *in* N. C. Benson, ed. *A century of fisheries in North America.* Amer. Fish. Soc. Spec. Publ. 7.

Albers, C. 1970. Acid-base balance. Pages 173–208, *in* W. S. Hoar and D. J. Randall, eds. *Fish physiology.* Vol. IV. New York: Academic Press.

Aleev, Y. G. 1963. *Function and gross morphology in fish.* Jerusalem: Israel Prog. Scientific Trans.

Alevizon, W. S. 1975. Spatial overlap and competition in congeneric surfperches (Embiotocidae) off Santa Barbara, California. *Copeia* 1975:352–355.

Alexander, R. M. 1966a. Structure and function in catfishes. *J. Zool.* (London) 148:88–152.

Alexander, R. M. 1966b. Physical aspects of swimbladder function. *Biol. Rev.* 41:141–176.

Alexander, R. M. 1967. *Functional design in fishes.* London: Hutchinson Lib. 160 pp.

Alexander, R. M. 1970. Mechanics of the feeding action of various teleost fishes. *J. Zool.* (London) 162:145–156.

Allen, G. R. 1972. *The anemone fishes.* Neptune City, N.J.: TFH Publ. 288 pp.

Allen, G. R. 1989. Freshwater fishes of Australia. Neptune City, N.J.: TFH Publ. 240 pp.

Allen, G. R. and Coates, D. 1990. An ichthyological survey of the Sepik River, New Guinea. *Rec. West. Aust. Mus. Suppl.* 34:31–116.

Allen, M. J., Pecorelli, H., and Word, J. 1976. Marine organisms around outfall pipes in Santa Monica Bay. *J. Water Poll. Cont. Fed.* 48(8):1881–1893.

Alm, G. 1949. Influence of heredity and environment on various forms of trout. *Ann. Rpt. Inst. Freshw. Res.* (Drottningholm) 29:29–34.

Altringham, J. D., and Johnston, I. A. 1986. Energy cost of contraction in fast and slow muscle fibers isolated from an elasmobranch and an antarctic teleost fish. *J. Exp. Biol.* 121:239–250.

Amundsrud, J. R., Faber, D. J., and Keast, A. 1974. Seasonal succession of free-swimming perciform larvae in Lake Opinicon, Ontario, *J. Fish. Res. Bd. Canada* 31(10):1661–1665.

Andrews, J. W., and Stickney, R. R. 1972. Interactions of feeding rates and environmental temperature on growth, food conversion, and body composition of channel catfish. *Trans. Am. Fish. Soc.* 101:94–99.

Andriashev, A. P. 1970. Cryopelagic fishes of the Arctic and Antarctic and their significance in polar ecosystems. Pages 297–304 *in* M. W. Holdgate, ed. *Antarctic ecology.* New York: Academic Press.

Angermeier, P. L., and Schlosser, I. J. 1989. Species-area relationships for stream fishes. *Ecology* 70: 1450–1462.

Applegate, V. C. 1950. *Natural history of the sea lam-*

prey (*Petromyzon marinus*) in Michigan. U.S. Fish. Wildl. Serv. Spec. Sci. Rept. 555:1–237.

Aron, W. I., and Smith, S. H. 1971. Ship canals and ecosystems. *Science* 174 (4004):13–20.

Aspinwall, N. 1974. Genetic analysis of North American populations of the pink salmon, *Oncorhynchus gorbuscha:* possible evidence for the neutral mutation-random drift hypothesis. *Evolution* 28(2):295–305.

Atema, J. 1971. Structures and functions of the sense of taste in the catfish *(Ictalurus natalis). Brain, Behavior, and Evolution* 25(4):273–294.

Avise, J. C., Smith, J. J., and Ayala, F. J. 1975. Adaptive differentiation with little genic change between two native minnows. *Evolution* 29(3):411–476.

Backus, R. H. 1957. The fishes of Labrador. *Bull. Amer. Mus. Nat. Hist.* 113 (4):273–338.

Backus, R. H., Craddock, J. E., Haedrich, R. L., and Robison, B. H. 1977. Atlantic mesopelagic zoogeography. Pages 266–287 *in* B. F. Nafpaktitus et al., eds. *Fishes of the western North Atlantic, pt 7.* Mem. 1, Sears Found. Mar. Res.

Bagenal, T. B. 1978. Aspects of fish fecundity. Pages 75–101 *in* S. D. Gerking, ed. *Ecology of freshwater fish production.* New York: Wiley.

Bainbridge, R. 1958. The speed of swimming of fish as related to size and to the frequency and amplitude of the tail beat. *J. Exp. Biol.* 35:109–133.

Baines, G. W. 1975. Blood pH effects in eight fishes from the teleostean family Scorpaenidae. *Comp. Biochem. Physiol.* 51A:833–843.

Balik, S. 1995. Freshwater fish in Anatolia, Turkey. *Biol. Cons.* 72:213–223.

Balon, E. K. 1975a. Reproductive guilds in fishes: a proposal and definition. *J. Fish. Res. Bd. Canada* 32(6):821–864.

Balon, E. K. 1975b. Terminology of intervals in fish development. *J. Fish. Res. Bd. Canada* 32(9):1663–1670.

Balon, E. K. 1977. Fish gluttons: the natural ability of some fishes to become obese when food is in extreme abundance. *Hydrobiologia* 52:239–241.

Balon, E. K. 1978. Kariba: the dubious benefits of large dams. *Ambio* 7(2):40–48.

Balon, E. K. 1979. The theory of saltation and its application in the ontology of fishes: steps and thresholds. *Env. Biol. Fish* 4:97–101.

Balon, E. K. 1981a. Additions and amendments to the classification of reproductive styles in fishes. *Env. Biol. Fish.* 6:377–389.

Balon, E. K. 1981b. Saltatory processes and altricial to precocial forms in the ontogeny of fishes. *Amer. Zool.* 21:573–596.

Balon, E. K. 1984. Patterns in the evolution of reproductive styles in fishes. Pages 35–53 *in* G. W. Potts and R. J. Wootton, eds. *Fish reproduction: strategies and tactics.* London: Academic Press.

Balon, E. K., and Coche, A. G. 1974. *Lake Kariba: a man-made tropical ecosystem in Central Africa.* The Hague: W. Junk. 767 pp.

Balsano, J. S., Rasch, E. M., and Monaco, P. J. 1989. The evolutionary ecology of *Poecilia formosa* and its triploid associate. Pages 277–297 *in* G. K. Meffe and F. F. Snelson, Jr., eds. *Ecology and evolution of livebearing fishes (Poeciliidae).* Englewood Cliffs, N.J.: Prentice-Hall.

Baltz, D. M. 1984. Life history variation in female surfperches (Perciformes, Embiotocidae). *Env. Biol. Fish.* 10:159–171.

Baltz, D. M. 1991. Introduced fishes in marine systems and seas. *Biol. Cons.* 56: 151–178.

Baltz, D. M., and Moyle, P. B. 1982. Life history characteristics of tule perch *(Hysterocarpus traski)* populations in contrasting environments. *Env. Biol. Fish.* 7:229–242.

Baltz, D. M., and Moyle, P. B. 1993. Invasion resistance to introduced species by a native assemblage of stream fishes. *Ecol. Applic.* 3: 246–255.

Baltz, D. M., Rakocinski, C., and Fleeger, J. W. 1993. Microhabitat use by marsh-edge fishes in a Louisiana estuary. *Env. Biol. Fish.* 36:109–126.

Barber, W. E., and Minckley, W. L. 1966. Fishes of Aravaipa Creek, Graham and Pinal Counties, Arizona. *Southw. Nat.* 11(3):313–324.

Barbour, C. D., and Brown, J. H. 1974. Fish species diversity in lakes. *Amer. Nat.* 108(962):473–488.

Bardach, J. E., Johnson, G. H., and Todd, J. H. 1969. Orientation by bulk messenger sensors in aquatic vertebrates. *Ann. N.Y. Acad. Sci.* 163:227–235.

Bardach, J. E., Ryther, J. H., and McLarney, W. O. 1972. *Aquaculture.* New York: Wiley-Interscience. 868 pp.

Bardach, J. E., and Todd, J. H. 1970. Chemical communication in fish. Pages 205–240 *in* J. W. Johnson et al., eds. *Advances in chemoreception.* Vol. 1. New York: Appleton-Century-Crofts.

Barlow, G. W. 1961. Causes and significance of morphological variation in fishes. *Syst. Zool.* 10(1):105–117.

Barlow, G. W. 1972. The attitude of fish eye-lines in relation to body shape and to stripes and bars. *Copeia* 1972(1):5–12.

Barlow, G. W. 1973. Competition between color morphs of the polychromatic Midas cichlid *Cichlasoma citrinellum. Science* 179:806–807.

Barlow, G. W. 1974. Contrasts in social behavior between Central American cichlid fishes and coral-reef surgeon fishes. *Amer. Zool.* 14(1):9–34.

Barlow, G. W. 1976. The Midas cichlid in Nicaragua. Pages 333–358 *in* T. B. Thorson, ed. *Investigations of the ichthyofauna of Nicaraguan Lakes.* Lincoln: School of Life Sci., Univ. Nebraska.

Barlow, G. W. 1984. Patterns of monogamy among teleost fishes. *Arch. Fischwiss.* 35:75–123.

Barnes, R. D. 1974. *Invertebrate zoology.* Philadelphia: W.B. Saunders Co.

Barrett, B. A., and McKeown, B. A. 1988a. Sustained exercise increases plasma growth hormone concentration in two anadromous salmonids. *Can. J. Fish. Aquat. Sci.* 45:747–749.

Barrett, B. A., and McKeown, B. A. 1988b. Growth hormone response to sustained swimming in exercise-acclimated steelhead trout, *Salmo gairdneri. J. Fish. Biol.* 32:799–800.

Barrett, B. A., and McKeown, B. A. 1988c. Sustained exercise augments long-term starvation increases in plasma growth hormone in the steelhead trout, *Salmo gairdneri. Can. J. Zool.* 66:853–855.

Barrett, I., and Williams, A. A. 1965. Hemoglobin content of the blood of fifteen species of marine fishes. *Calif. Fish and Game* 51:216–281.

Barton, B. A. 1988. Endocrine and metabolic responses of fish to stress. *Proc. Int. Assoc. Aquat. An. Med.* 19:41–55.

Barton, B. A., and Iwama, G. K. 1991. Physiological changes in fish from stress in aquaculture with emphasis on the response and effects of corticosteroids. *Ann. Rev. Fish Diseases* 1:3–26.

Baskin, J. N., Zaret, T. M., and Mago-Leccia, F. 1980. Feeding of reportedly parasitic catfishes (Trichomycteridae and Cetopsidae) in the Rio Portuguesa basin, Venezuela. *Biotropica* 12:182–186.

Batty, R. S., and Wardle, C. S. 1979. Restoration of glycogen from lactic acid in the anaerobic muscle of plaice, *Pleuronectes platessa* L. *J. Fish Biol.* 15:509–519.

Bayley, P. B. 1995. Understanding larger river-flood plain ecosystems. *Bioscience* 45:153–158.

Bayley, P. B., and Li, H. W. 1993. Riverine fishes. Pages 251–281 *in* P. Calow and G. E. Petts, eds. *The rivers handbook.* Vol. 1. Oxford: Blackwell Scientific Pubs.

Beamish, F. W. H. 1964. Respiration of fishes with special emphasis on standard oxygen consumption. II. Influence of weight and temperature in respiration of several species. *Can. J. Zool.* 42:177–188.

Beamish, F. W. H. 1970. Oxygen consumption of largemouth bass, *Micropterus salmoides,* in relation to swimming speed and temperature. *Can. J. Zool.* 48:1221–1228.

Beamish, F. W. H., and Tandler, A. 1990. Ambient ammonia, diet and growth in lake trout. *Aquat. Toxicol.* 17:155–166.

Beamish, R. J. 1974. Loss of fish populations from unexploited remote lakes in Ontario, Canada, as a consequence of atmospheric fallout of acid. *Water. Res.* 8:85–95.

Beamish, R. J., and McFarlane, G. A. 1987. Current trends in age determination methodology. Pages 15–41 *in* R. C. Summerfelt and G. E. Hall, eds. *The age and growth of fish.* Ames, Ia.: Iowa State Univ. Press.

Becker, C. D., and Fugihara, F. G. 1978. The bacterial pathogen, *Flexibacter columnaris,* and its epizooiology among Columbia River fish: a review and synthesis. *Amer. Fish. Soc. Monogr.* 2.

Behnke, R. J. 1992. Native trout of western North America. *Amer. Fish. Soc. Monogr.* 6: 275 pp.

Bell, M. A. 1976a. Evolution of phenotypic diversity in *Gasterosteus aculeatus* superspecies on the Pacific coast of North America. *Syst. Zool.* 25(3):211–227.

Bell, M. A. 1976b. Reproductive character displacement in threespine sticklebacks. *Evolution* 30(4):847–850.

Bellamy, D., and Chester-Jones, I. 1961. Studies on *Myxine glutinosa*. I. The chemical composition of the tissues. *Comp. Biochem. Physiol.* 3:175–183.

Bemis, W. E., Burggren, W. W., and Kemp, N. E., eds. 1987. The biology and evolution of lungfishes. *J. Morphology Suppl.* 1:1–383.

Bennett, B. A., and Attwood, C. G. 1991. Evidence for recovery of a surf-zone fish assemblage following the establishment of a marine reserve on the southern coast of South Africa. *Mar. Ecol. Prog. Ser.* 75: 173–181.

Bennion, G. R. 1968. *The control of the function of the heart in teleost fish.* M.S. thesis, Univ. of British Columbia, Vancouver. 53 pp.

Ben-Tuvia, A. 1966. Red Sea fishes recently found in the Mediterranean. *Copeia* 1966(2):254–275.

Ben-Tuvia, A. 1978. Immigration of fishes through the Suez Canal. *NOAA Fish. Bull.* 76(1):249–255.

Ben-Yami, M., and Glaser, T. 1974. The invasion of *Saurida undosquamis* (Richardson) into the Levant Basin—an example of biological effects of interoceanic canals. *NOAA Fish. Bull.* 35:359–372.

Berg, L. S. 1940. *Classification of fishes both recent and fossil.* Ann Arbor, Mich.: J. W. Edwards. 517 pp.

Berg, L. S. 1949. *Freshwater fishes of the U.S.S.R. and adjacent countries.* Jerusalem: Israel Prog. Sci. Transl. 510 pp.

Berg, T., and Steen, J. B. 1965. Physiological mechanisms for aerial respiration in the eel. *Comp. Biochem. Physiol.* 15:469–484.

Bergman, E. N. 1990. Energy contributions of volatile fatty acids from the gastrointestinal tract in various species. *Physiol. Rev.* 70:567–590.

Bernstein, B. B., and Jung, N. 1979. Selective pressures and coevolution in a kelp-canopy community in Southern California. *Ecol. Mono.* 49:335–355.

Berra, T. M. 1981. *An atlas of distribution of the freshwater fish families of the world.* Lincoln: Univ. of Nebraska Press.

Berra, T. M., and Allen, G. R. 1989. Burrowing, emergence, behavior, and functional morphology of the Australian salamanderfish, *Lepidogalaxias salamandroides. Fisheries* (Bethesda) 14 (5):2–10.

Bevelhimer, M. S., and Adams, S. M. 1993. A bioenergetics analysis of diel vertical migration by kokanee salmon, *Oncorhynchus nerka. Can. J. Fish., Aquat. Sci.* 50: 2336–2349.

Beyenbach, K. W., and Kirschner, L. B. 1975. Kidney and urinary bladder functions of the rainbow trout in Mg and Na excretion. *Am. J. Physiol.* 229:389–393.

Bhattacharya, S. 1992. Endocrine control of fish reproduction. *Curr. Sci.* 63(3):135–141.

Bigelow, H. B., and Schroeder, W. C. 1948. Sharks. Pages 59–546 *in* J. Tee-Van et al., eds. *Fishes of the Western North Atlantic.* Mem. Sears Found. Mar. Res. 1.

Bigelow, H. B., and Schroeder, W. C. 1953. Fishes of the Gulf of Maine. *U.S. Fish. Wildl. Ser. Fish. Bull.* 74:1–577.

Binotti, I., Giovenco, S., Giardina, B., Antonini, E., Brunori, M., and Wyman, J. 1971. Studies on the functional properties of fish hemoglobins. II. The oxygen equilibrium of the isolated hemoglobin components from trout blood. *Arch. Biochem. Biophys.* 142:274–280.

Bjerring, H. C. 1985. Facts and thoughts on piscine phylogeny. Pages 31–58 *in* R. E. Foreman et al., eds. *Evolutionary biology of primitive fishes.* New York: Plenum Press.

Blackburn, M. 1965. Oceanography and the ecology of tunas. *Oceangr. Mar. Biol. Ann. Rev.* 3:299–322.

Blake, B. F. 1977. The effect of the impoundment of Lake Kainji, Nigeria, on the indigenous species of mormyrid fishes. *Freshw. Biol.* 7:37–42.

Blake, R. W. 1983. *Fish locomotion.* Cambridge: Cambridge Univ. Press.

Blaxhall, P. C., and Daisley, K. W. 1973. Routine

haematological methods for use with fish blood. *J. Fish Biol.* 5:771–782.

Blaxter, J. H. S. 1970. Light, fishes. Pages 213–320 in O. Kinne, ed. *Environmental factors 1, Marine ecology 1.* New York: Wiley-Interscience.

Blaxter, J. H. S. 1974. *The early life history of fish.* New York: Springer-Verlag. 765 pp.

Blaxter, J. H. S. 1985. The herring: a successful species? *Can. J. Fish., Aquatic Sci.* 42:21–30.

Blaxter, J. H. S., and Holliday, F. G. T. 1963. The behavior and physiology of herring and other clupeids. *Adv. Mar. Biol.* 2:261–393.

Block, B. A. 1994. Thermogenesis in muscle. *Annu. Rev. Physiol.* 56:535–577.

Blumer, L. S. 1979. Male parental care in the bony fishes. *Quart. Rev. Biol.* 54:149–161.

Bodznik, D. 1978. Calcium ion: an odorant for natural water discriminations and the migratory behavior of sockeye salmon. *J. Comp. Physiol.* 127:157–166.

Bonaventura, J., Bonaventura, C., and Sullivan, B. 1975. Hemoglobins and hemocyanins: comparative aspects of structure and function. *J. Exp. Zool.* 194(1):155–174.

Bone, Q. 1966. On the function of the two types of myotomal muscle fibre in elasmobranch fish. *Fish. J. Mar. Biol. Assoc. U.K.* 46:321–349.

Booth, J. H. 1978. The distribution of blood flow in the gills of fish: application of a new technique to rainbow trout. *J. Exp. Biol.* 73:119–129.

Booth, J. H. 1979. The effects of oxygen supply, epinephrine, and acetylcholine on the distribution of blood flow in trout gills. *J. Exp. Biol.* 83:31–39.

Bortone, S. A., and Davis, W. P. 1994. Fish intersexuality as indicator of environmental stress. *Bioscience* 44: 165–172.

Boulenger, G. A. 1907. *Zoology of Egypt: fishes of the Nile.* London: Hugh Rees. 578 pp.

Boulenger, G. A. 1910. Ichthyology. I. History of literature down to 1880. Pages 243–250 in *Encyclopedia Brittanica.* 11th ed. Vol. 14.

Bowering, W. R. 1976. Distribution, age and growth, and sexual maturity of witch flounder (*Glyptocephalus cynoglossus*). *J. Fish. Res. Bd. Canada* 33(7):1574–1584.

Braum, E. 1978. Ecological aspects of fish eggs, embryos, and larvae. Pages 102–136 in S. Gerking, ed. *Ecology of freshwater fish production.* New York: Wiley.

Bray, R. N., and Ebeling, A. W. 1975. Food activity, and habitat of three "picker-type" microcarnivorous fishes in the kelp forests off Santa Barbara, California. *NOAA Fish. Bull.* 73(4):815–829.

Bray, R. N., and Hixon, M. A. 1978. Nightshocker: predatory behavior of the Pacific electric ray (*Torpedo californica*). *Science* 200:333–334.

Bray, R. N., Miller, A. C., and Geesey, D. G. 1981. The fish connection: a trophic link between planktonic and rock reef communities. *Science* 214:204–205.

Breder, C. M., and Rosen, D. E. 1966. Modes of reproduction in fishes. Garden City, N.Y.: *Nat. Hist. Press.* 941 pp.

Brett, J. R. 1964. The respiratory metabolism and swimming performance of young sockeye salmon. *J. Fish. Res. Bd. Can.* 21:1183–1226.

Brett, J. R. 1971. Energetic responses of salmon to temperature. A study of some thermal relations in the physiology and freshwater ecology of sockeye salmon (*Oncorhynchus nerka*). *Am. Zool.* 11:99–113.

Brett, J. R. 1975. The swimming energetics of salmon. *Sci. Amer.* 212:80–85.

Brett, J. R. 1979. Environmental factors and growth. Pages 599–675 in W. S. Hoar, D. J. Randall, and J. R. Brett, eds. *Fish physiology,* Vol. 9. New York: Academic Press.

Brett, J. R., and Groves, T. D. 1979. Physiological energetics. Pages 279–352 in W. S. Hoar, D. J. Randall, and J. R. Brett, eds. *Fish physiology.* Vol. 9. New York: Academic Press.

Brett, J. R., Shelbourn, J. E., and Shoop, C. T. 1969. Growth rate and body composition of fingerling sockeye salmon, *Oncorhynchus nerka,* in relation to temperature and ration size. *J. Fish. Res. Bd. Canada* 26:2363–2394.

Brewer, G. D. 1973. Midwater fishes from the Gulf of California and the adjacent eastern tropical Pacific. *Los Angeles Co. Mus. Nat. Hist. Contrs. in Sci.* 242:1–47.

Bridges, W. W., Cech, J. J., Jr., and Pedro, D. N. 1976. Seasonal hematological changes in winter flounder, *Pseudopleuronectes americanus*. *Trans. Am. Fish. Soc.* 105:596–600.

Briggs, D. E. G. 1992. Conodonts: a major extinct group added to the vertebrates. *Science* 256: 1285–1286.

Briggs, J. C. 1974. *Marine zoogeography.* New York: McGraw-Hill. 475 pp.

Briggs, J. C. 1979. Ostariophysan zoogeography: an alternative hypothesis. *Copeia* 4:111–118.

Briggs, P. T., and O'Connor, J. S. 1971. Comparison of shore-zone fishes over naturally vegetated and sand-filled bottoms in Great South Bay. *N.Y. Fish. Game J.* 18(1):15–41.

Brill, R. W., Dewar, H., and Graham, J. B. 1994. Basic concenpts relevant to heat transfer in fishes, and their use in measuring physiological thermoregulatory abilities of tunas. *Env. Biol. Fishes* 40:109–124.

Brock, R. E. 1977. Occurrence and variety of fishes in mixohaline ponds of the Kona, Hawaii, coast. *Copeia* 1977(1):134–139.

Brocksen, R. W., and Cole, R. E. 1972. Physiological responses of three species of fishes to various salinities. *J. Fish. Res. Bd. Canada* 29:399–405.

Brodal, A., and Fänge, R., eds. 1963. *The biology of the myxine.* Oslo: Scand. Univ. Books. 588 pp.

Bromley, P. J. 1994. The role of gastric evacuation experiments in quantifying the feeding rates of predatory fish. *Rev. in Fish Biol. and Fisheries* 4:36–66.

Brooks, J. L. 1968. The effects of prey size selection by lake planktivores. *Syst. Zool.* 17(3):272–291.

Brooks, J. L., and Dodson, S. 1965. Predation, body size, and composition of plankton. *Science* 150:28–35.

Brothers, E. B., Mathews, C. P., and Lasker, R. 1976. Daily growth increments in otoliths from larval and adult fishes. *NOAA Fish. Bull.* 74:1–8.

Brown, C. R., and Cameron, J. N. 1991. The induction of specific dynamic action in channel catfish by infusion of essential amino acids. *Physiol. Zool.* 64(1):276–297.

Brown, D. W. 1974. Hydrography and midwater fishes of three contiguous oceanic areas off Santa Barbara California. *Los Angeles Co. Mus. Nat. Hist. Conts. Sci.* 261:1–30.

Brown, L. R. , Moyle, P. B., and Yoshiyama, R. M. 1994. Historical decline and current status of coho salmon in California. *North Amer. J. Fish. Mgmt.* 14:237–261.

Brown-Peterson, N. J. 1993. Fish assemblages in natural versus well-established recolonized seagrass meadows. *Estuaries* 16: 177–189.

Buckley, J. A. 1977. Heinz body hemolytic anemia in coho salmon (*Oncorhynchus kisutch*) exposed to chlorinated wastewater. *J. Fish Res. Bd. Canada* 34:215–224.

Buddington, R. K., and Doroshov, S. I. 1986. Development of digestive secretions in white sturgeon juveniles (*Acipenser transmontanus*). *Comp. Biochem. Physiol.* 83A:233–238.

Bullock, T. H. 1973. Seeing the world through a new sense; electroreception in fish. *Amer. Sci.* 61(3):316–325.

Bullock, T. H., Bodznick, D. A., and Northcutt, R. G. 1983. The phylogenetic distribution of electroreception: evidence for convergent evolution of a primitive vertebrate sense modality. *Brain Research Reviews* 6:25–46.

Bulow, F. J. 1970. RNA/DNA ratios as indicators of recent growth rates of a fish. *J. Fish. Res. Bd. Canada* 27:2343–2349.

Bulow, F. J. 1987. RNA/DNA ratios as indicators of growth in fish: a review. Pages 45–64. *in* R. C. Summerfelt and G. E. Hall, eds. *Age and growth of fish.* Ames: Iowa State Univ. Press.

Burger, J. W. 1962. Further studies on the function of the rectal gland in the spiny dogfish *Physiol. Zool.* 35:205–217.

Burger, J. W., and Hess, W. 1960. Function of the rectal gland in the spiny dogfish. *Science* 131:670–671.

Burgess, T. J. 1978. The comparative ecology of two sympatric polychromatic populations of *Xererpes fucorum* Jordan and Gilbert (Pisces, Pholididae) from the rocky intertidal zone of central California. *J. Exp. Mar. Biol. Ecol.* 35:43–58.

Burggren, W. W. 1978. Gill ventilation in the sturgeon, *Acipenser transmontanus:* Unusual adaptations for bottom dwelling. *Resp. Physiol.* 34:153–170.

Burggren, W. W., and Randall, D. J. 1978. Oxygen uptake and transport during hypoxic exposure in the sturgeon *Acipenser transmontanus. Resp. Physiol.* 34:171–183.

Burr, B. M. 1991. The fishes of Illinois: an overview of a dynamic fauna. *Bull. Ill. Nat. Hist. Surv.* 34:417–427.

Bussing, W. A. 1985. Patterns of distribution of the Central American ichthyofauna, Pages 453–473 *in* F. G. Stehli and S. D. Webb, eds. *The great American biotic interchange.* N. Y.: Plenum Pub.

Bussing, W. A. 1993. Fish communities and environmental characteristics of a tropical rain forest river in Costa Rica. *Rev. Trop. Biol.* 41: 791–809.

Butler, P. J., Taylor, E. W., Capra, M. F., and Davison, W. 1978. The effect of hypoxia on the levels of circulating catecholamines in the dogfish *Scyliorhinus canicula. J. Comp. Physiol.* B127:325–330.

Cadwallader, P. L. 1986. Fish of the Murray-Darling system. Pages 679–694 *in* B. R. Davies and K. F. Walker, eds. *The ecology of river systems.* Dordrecht: Dr. W. Junk.

Cailliet, G. M. 1992. Demography of the central California population of the leopard shark (*Triakis semifasciata*). *Aust. J. Mar. Freshwater Res.* 43: 183–193.

Cailliet, G. M., Love, M. S., and Ebeling, A. W. 1986. *Fishes: a field and laboratory manual on their structure, identification, and natural history.* Belmont, Calif.: Wadsworth Publishing Co.

Callicott, J. B. 1994. Conservation values and ethics. Pages 24–49 *in* G. K. Meffe and C. R. Carroll, eds. *Principles of conservation biology.* Sunderland, MA: Sinauer Associates.

Cameron, J. N. 1970a. Blood characteristics of some marine fishes of the Texas gulf coast. *Tex. J. Sci.* 21:275–283.

Cameron, J. N. 1970b. The influence of environmental variables on the hematology of pinfish (*Lagodon rhomboides*) and striped mullet (*Mugil cephalus*). *Comp. Biochem. Physiol.* 32:175–192.

Cameron, J. N. 1971a. Oxygen dissociation characteristics of the blood of rainbow trout, *Salmo gairdneri. Comp. Biochem. Physiol.* 38A:600–704.

Cameron, J. N. 1971b. Methemoglobin in erythrocytes of rainbow trout blood. *Comp. Biochem. Physiol.* 40A:743–749.

Cameron, J. N. 1975. Morphometric and flow indicator studies of the teleost heart. *Can. J. Zool.* 53:691–698.

Cameron, J. N. 1976. Branchial ion uptake in arctic grayling: resting values and effects of acid-base disturbance. *J. Exp. Biol.* 64:711–725.

Cameron, J. N. 1978. Chloride shift in fish blood. *J. Exp. Zool.* 206:289–295.

Cameron, J. N., and Davis, J. C. 1970. Gas exchange in rainbow trout (*Salmo gairdneri*) with varying blood oxygen capacity. *J. Fish Res. Bd. Canada* 27:1069–1085.

Cameron, J. N., Randall, D. J., and Davis, J. C. 1971. Regulation of the ventilation-perfusion ratio in the gills of *Dasyatis sabina* and *Squalus suckleyi. Comp. Biochem. Physiol.* 39A:505–519.

Campos, H. 1984. Gondwana and neotropical glaxioid fish zoogeography. Pages 113–125 *in* T. M. Zaret, ed. *Evolutionary ecology of tropical freshwater fishes.* The Hague: W. Junk.

Capra, M. F., and Satchell, G. H. 1977. The differential haemodynamic responses of the elasmobranch *Squalus acanthias* to the naturally occurring catecholamines adrenaline and noradrenaline. *Comp. Biochem. Physiol.* 58C: 41–47.

Carey, F. G. 1982a. Warm fish. Pages 216–233 *in* C. R. Taylor, K. Johansen, and L. Bolis, eds. *A companion to animal physiology.* Cambridge: Cambridge University Press.

Carey, F. G. 1982b. A brain heater in the swordfish. *Science* 216:1327–1329.

Carey, F. G., and Lawson, K. D. 1973. Temperature regulation in free-swimming bluefin tuna. *Comp. Biochem. Physiol.* 44A:375–392.

Carey, F. G., and Teal, J. M. 1966. Heat conservation in tuna fish muscle. *Proc. Nat. Acad. Sci. U.S.* 56:1461–1469.

Carey, F. G., Teal, J. M., Kanwisher, J. W., Lawson, K. D., and Beckett, J. S. 1971. Warm-bodied fish. *Am. Zool.* 11:137–145.

Carlander, K. D. 1955. The standing crop of fish in lakes. *J. Fish. Res. Bd. Canada* 12(4):543–569.

Carline. R. F., Gagen. C. J., and Sharpe, W. E. 1994. Brook trout (*Salvelinus fontinalis*) population dynamics and mottled sculpin (*Cottus bairdi*) occurrence in relation to acidic episodes in streams. *Ecol. Freshw. Fish* 3: 107–115.

Carlson, H. R., and Haight, R. E. 1972. Evidence for a home site and homing of adult yellowtail rockfish, *Sebastes flavidus. J. Fish. Res. Bd. Canada* 29:1011–1014.

Carlton, J. T., and Geller, J. 1993. Ecological roulette: the global transport and invasion of non-indigenous marine organisms. *Science* 261: 78–82.

Carmichael, G. J., Tomasso, J. R., Sinnco, B. A., and Davis, K. B. 1984. Characterization and alleviation of stress associated with hauling largemouth bass. *Trans. Amer. Fish. Soc.* 113:778–785.

Carpenter, S. R., and Kitchill, J. F. 1993. The trophic cascade in lakes. New York:Cambridge University Press. 385 pp.

Carrier, J. C., and Evans, D. H. 1976. The role of environmental calcium in freshwater survival of the marine teleost *Lagodon rhomboides. J. Exp. Biol.* 65:529–538.

Casey, J. G., and Kohler, N. E. 1992. Tagging studies on the shortfin mako shark (*Isurus oxyrinchus*) in the western Atlantic ocean. *Aust. J. Mar. Freshwater Res.* 43: 45–60.

Castro, J. I. 1983. *The sharks of North American waters*. College Station: Texas A&M Press. 180 pp.

Catlett, R. H., and Millich, D. R. 1976. Intracellular and extracellular osmoregulation of temperature-acclimated goldfish: *Carassius auratus* L. *Comp. Biochem. Physiol.* 55A:261–269.

Cech, J. J., Jr. 1988. Respirometry. *In* C. B. Schreck and P. B. Moyle, eds. *Methods in Fish Biology.* Bethesda, Md.: Amer. Fish. Soc. In press.

Cech, J. J., Jr., Bridges, D. W., Rowell, D. M., and Balzer, P. J. 1976. Cardiovascular responses of winter flounder, *Pseudopleuronectes americanus* (Walbaum), to acute temperature increase. *Can. J. Zool.* 54:1383–1388.

Cech, J. J., Jr., Laurs, R. M., and Graham, J. B. 1984. Temperature-induced changes in blood gas equilibria in the albacore, *Thunnus alalunga*, a warm-bodied tuna. *J. Exp. Biol.* 109:21–34.

Cech, J. J., Jr., and Massingill, M. J. 1995. Tradeoffs between respiration and feeding in

Sacramento blackfish, *Orthodon microlepidotus. Env. Biol. Fish.* In press.

Cech, J. J., Jr., Massingill, M. J., Vondracek, B., and Linden, A. L. 1985. Respiratory metabolism of mosquitofish, *Gambusia affinis:* effects of temperature, dissolved oxygen, and sex difference. *Env. Biol. Fish.* 13:297–307.

Cech, J. J., Jr., Mitchell, S. J., and Massingill, M. J. 1979. Respiratory adaptations of Sacramento blackfish, *Orthodon microlepidotus* (Ayres), for hypoxia. *Comp. Biochem. Physiol.* 63A:411–415.

Cech, J. J., Jr., and Wohlschlag, D. E. 1973. Respiratory responses of the striped mullet, *Mugil cephalus* L., to hypoxic conditions. *J. Fish Biol.* 5:421–428.

Cech, J. J., Jr., and Wohlschlag, D. E. 1975. Summer growth depression in the striped mullet, *Mugil cephalus* L. *Contr. Mar. Sci.* 19:91–100.

Cech, J. J., Jr. and Wohlschlag, D. E. 1982. Seasonal patterns of respiration, gill ventilation, and hematological characteristics in the striped mullet, *Mugil cephalus* L. *Bull. Mar. Sci.* 32:130–138.

Chan, S. T. H., and Yeung, W. S. B. 1983. Sex control and sex reversal in fish under natural conditions. Pages 171–222 *in* W. S. Hoar, D. J. Randall, and E. M. Donaldson, eds. *Fish physiology 9B: reproduction, behavior, and fertility control.* London: Academic Press.

Chance, R. E., Mertz, E. T., and Halver, J. E. 1964. Nutrition of salmonoid fishes, XII. Isoleucine, leucine, valine, and phenylalanine requirements of chinook salmon and interrelations between isoleucine and leucine for growth. *J. Nutr.* 83:177–185.

Chao, L. N., and Musick, J. A. 1977. Life history, feeding habits, and functional morphology of juvenile sciaenid fishes in the York River estuary, Virginia. *NOAA Fish. Bull.* 75(4):657–702.

Chen, L., and Martinich, R. L. 1975. Pheromonal stimulation and metabolite inhibition of ovulation in zebrafish, *Brachydanio rerio. NOAA Fish. Bull.* 73(4):889–894.

Cherry, D. S., and Guthrie, R. K. 1975. Significance of detritus or detritus-associated invertebrates to fish production in a new impoundment. *J. Fish. Res. Bd. Canada* 32(10):1799–1804.

Chesley, L. C. 1934. The concentrations of proteases, amylase, and lipase in certain marine fishes. *Biol. Bull.* 66:133–144.

Christiansen, J. S., and Jobling, M. 1990. The behavior and the relationship between food intake and growth of juvenile Arctic charr, *Salvelinus alpinus* L., subjected to sustained exercise. *Can. J. Zool.* 68:2185–2191.

Christiansen, J. S., Ringo, E., and Jobling. M. 1989. Effects of sustained exercise on growth and body composition of first-feeding fry of Arctic charr, *Salvelinus alpinus* (L.). *Aquaculture* 79:329–335.

Clark, E., and George, A. 1979. Toxic soles, *Pardachirus marmoratus*, from the Red Sea and *P. pavonius* from Japan, with notes on other species. *Env. Biol. Fish* 4(2):103–123.

Cohen, D. M. 1970. How many recent fishes are there? *Proc. Calif. Acad. Sci.* 37(17):341–346.

Cohen, D. M., and Nielsen, J. G. 1978. Guide to the identification of genera of the fish order Ophidiiformes with a tentative classification of the order. *NOAA Tech. Rept. NMFS Circ.* 417:1–72.

Cole, L. C. 1954. The population consequences of life history phenomena. *Q. Rev. Biol.* 29:103–137.

Collette, B. B., and Earle, S. A., eds. 1972. Results of the Tektite Program: ecology of coral reef fishes. *Bull. Los Angeles Co. Nat. Hist. Mus.* 14. 180 pp.

Colletti, A. E. and Olson, K. R. 1988. Catecholamine metabolism by the perfused rainbow trout gill. *J. Exp. Zool.* 248:177–184.

Colt, J., and Tchobanoglous, G. 1978. Chronic exposure of channel catfish, *Ictalurus punctatus*, to ammonia: effects on growth and survival. *Aquaculture* 15:353–372.

Compagno, L. J. V. 1973. Interrelationships of living elasmobranchs. Pages 15–62 in P. H. Greenwood, R. S. Miles, and C. Patterson, eds. *Interrelationships of fishes.* New York: Academic Press.

Compagno, L. J. V. 1977. Phyletic relationships of living sharks and rays. *Amer. Zool.* 17(2):303–322.

Compagno, L. J. V. 1979. Coelancanths: shark relatives or bony fishes? *Occ. Pap. Calif. Acad. Sci.* 134:45–52.

Compagno, L. J. V. 1990. Alternative life-history styles of cartilaginous fishes in time and space. *Env. Biol. Fish* 28: 33–76.

Connell, J. R. 1978. Diversity in tropical rain forests and coral reefs. *Science* 199:1302–1310.

Conover, D. O., and Kynard, B. E. 1981. Environmental sex determination: interaction of temperature and genotype in a fish. *Science* 213:577–579.

Coon, T. G. 1982. Coexistence in a guild of benthic stream fishes: the effects of disturbance. Ph.D. diss., Univ. of Calif., Davis.

Copeland, B. J., and Bechtel, T. J. 1974. Some environmental limits of six Gulf coast estuarine organisms. *Cont. Mar. Sci.* 18:169–204.

Copeland, B. J., and Nixon, S. W. 1974. Hypersaline lagoons. Pages 312–330 in H. T. Odum et al., eds. *Coastal ecological systems of the United States.* Washington, D.C.: The Conservation Foundation.

Copeland, B. J., and Bechtel, T. J. 1974. Some environmental limits of six Gulf coast estuarine organisms. *Cont. Mar. Sci.* 18:169–204.

Cortes, E. 1995. Demographic analysis of the Atlantic sharpnose shark, Rhizoprionon terraenovae, in the Gulf of Mexico. *NOAA Fish. Bull.* 93:57–66.

Cossins, A. R., and Kilby, R. V. 1989. The seasonal modulation of Na^+/H^+ exchanger activity in trout erythrocytes. *J. Exp. Biol.* 144:463–478.

Courtney, W. R., Sahlman, H. F., Miley, W. W., and Herrma, D. J. 1974. Exotic fishes in fresh and brackish waters of Florida, *Biol. Cons.* 6(4):292–302.

Cracraft, J. 1974. Continental drift and vertebrate distribution. *Ann. Rev. Ecol. Syst.* 5:215–261.

Craig, J. F. 1992. Human-induced changes in the composition of fish communities in the Africa Great Lakes. *Rev. Fish Bio., Fisheries* 2: 93–124.

Crawshaw, L. I., Wollmuth, L. P., and O'Connor, C. S. 1989. Intracranial ethanol and ambient anoxia elicit selection of cooler water by goldfish. *Amer. J. Physiol.* 256:R133–R137.

Crawshaw, L. I., and Hammel, H. T. 1971. Behavioral thermoregulation in two species of antarctic fish. *Life Sci.* 10(17):1009–1020.

Crivelli, A., and Maitland, P. S. 1995. Introduction: endemic freshwater fishes of the northern

Mediterranean region: *Biol. Cons.* 72:121–122.

Crossman, E. J., and McAllister, D. E. 1986. Zoogeography of freshwater fishes of the Hudson Bay drainage, Ungava Bay, and the Arctic archipelago. Pages 53–105 *in* C. H. Hocutt and E. O. Wiley, eds. *The zoogeography of North American freshwater fishes.* New York: Wiley.

Crowder, L. B. 1984. Character displacement and habitat shift in a native cisco in southeastern Lake Michigan: evidence for competition? *Copeia* 1984:878–883.

Crowl, T. A., Townsend, C. R., and McIntosh, A. R. 1992. The impact of introduced brown and rainbow trout on native fish: the case of Australasia. *Rev. Fish Biol., Fisheries* 2:217–241.

Culliney, J. L. 1979. *The forests of the sea.* Garden City, N.Y.: Doubleday.

Cushing, D. H. 1968. *Fisheries biology: a study in population dynamics.* Madison: Univ. of Wisconsin Press. 200 pp.

Cushing, D. H. 1978. Biology of fishes of the pelagic community. Pages 317–340 *in* D. H. Cushing and J. J. Walsh, eds. *The ecology of the seas.* Philadelphia: Saunders.

Cuthbert, A. W., and Maetz, J. 1972. The effects of calcium and magnesium on sodium fluxes through gills of *Carassius auratus. J. Physiol.* 221:633–643.

Dahlberg, M. D., and Odum, E. P. 1970. Annual cycles of species occurrence, abundance, and diversity in Georgia estuarine fish populations. *Amer. Midl. Nat.* 83(2):382–392.

Dailey, G. C., and Ehrlich, P. R. 1992. Population, sustainability, and the earth's carrying capacity. *Bioscience* 42:761–771.

D'Amico Martell, A. L., and Cech, J. J., Jr. 1978. Peripheral vascular resistance in the gills of the winter flounder, *Pseudopleuronectes americanus. Comp. Biochem. Physiol.* 59A:419–423.

Daniels, R. A. 1978. Nesting behavior of *Harpagifer bispinis* in Arthur Harbour, Antarctic Peninsula. *J. Fish Biol.* 12:465–474.

Daniels, R. A. 1983. Demographic characteristics of an Antarctic plunderfish, *Harpagifer bispinis antarcticus. Marine Ecol. Prog. Ser.* 13:181–187.

Darlington, P. J. 1957. *Zoogeography: the geographical distribution of animals.* New York: Wiley. 673 pp.

Darnell, R. M. 1961. Trophic spectrum of an estuarine community, based on studies of Lake Pontchartrain, Louisiana. *Ecology* 43(3):553–568.

Darnell, R. M., and Meierotto, R. R. 1962. Determination of feeding chronology in fishes. *Trans. Amer. Fish. Soc.* 92:313–320.

Davenport, J. 1994. How and why do flying fish fly? *Rev. Fish Biol., Fisheries* 4: 184–214.

Davie, P. S., Wells, R. M. G., and Tetens, V. 1986. Effects of sustained swimming on rainbow trout muscle structure, blood oxygen transport, and lactate dehydrogenase isozymes: evidence for increased aerobic capacity of white muscle. *J. Exp. Zool.* 237:159–171.

Davies, P. R., Hanyu, I., Furukawa, K., and Nomura, M. 1986. Effect of temperature and photoperiod on sexual maturation and spawning of the common carp. III. Induction of spawning by manipulating photoperiod and temperature. *Aquaculture* 52:137–144.

Davison, W., and Goldspink, G. 1984. The cost of swimming for two teleost fish. *N. Z. J. Zool.* 11:225–232.

Daxboeck, C., and Holeton, G. F. 1978. Oxygen receptors in the rainbow trout, *Salmo gairdneri. Can. J. Zool.* 56:1254–1259.

Day, D. S., and Pearcy, W. G. 1968. Species associations of benthic fishes on the continental shelf and slope off Oregon. *J. Fish. Res. Bd. Canada* 25(12):2665–2675.

Dayton, P. K., and Hessler, R. R. 1972. Role of biological disturbance in maintaining diversity in the deep sea. *Deep-sea Res.* 19:199–208.

Deacon, J. E., and Minckley, W. L. 1974. Desert fishes. Pages 385–488 *in* R. W. Brown, ed. *Desert biology.* Vol. 2. New York: Academic Press.

DeMartini, E. E. 1969. A correlative study of the ecology and comparative feeding mechanism morphology of the Embiotocidae (surfperches) as evidence of the family's adaptive radiation into available ecological niches. *Wassman J. Biol.* 27(2):177–247.

Demski, L. S., and Northcutt, R. G. 1983. The terminal nerve: a new chemosensory system in vertebrates? *Science* 220:435–437.

Denton, E. J., and Shaw, T. J. 1963. The visual pigments of some deep-sea elasmobranchs. *J. Mar. Biol. Assoc. U.K.* 43:65–70.

Denton, E. J., and Warren, F. J. 1956. Visual pigments of deep-sea fish. *Nature* 178:1059.

DeRenzis, G., and Maetz, J. 1973. Studies on the mechanism of chloride absorption by the goldfish gill: relation with acid-base regulation. *J. Exp. Biol.* 59:339–358.

DeVlaming, V. L. 1972a. The effects of temperature and photoperiod on reproductive cycling in the estuarine gobiid fish *Gillichthys mirabilis. NOAA Fish. Bull.* 70:1137–1152.

DeVlaming, V. L. 1972b. Reproductive cycling in the estuarine gobiid fish *Gillichthys mirabilis. Copeia* 1972 (2):278–291.

DeVlaming, V. L. 1972c. The role of the endocrine system in temperature-controlled reproductive cycling in the estuarine gobiid fish *Gillichthys mirabilis. Comp. Biochem. Physiol.* 41A:697–713.

DeVries, A. L. 1970. Freezing resistance in Antarctic fishes. Pages 320–328 *in* M. W. Holdgate, ed. *Antarctic ecology,* I. New York: Academic Press.

DeVries, A. L. 1984. Role of glycopeptides and peptides in inhibition of crystallization of water in polar fishes. *Phil. Trans. R. Soc. London B* 304:575–588.

DeVries, A. L., and Wohlschlag, D. E. 1969. Freezing resistance in some Antarctic fishes. *Science.* 163:1073–1075.

DeWilde, M. A., and Houston, A. H. 1967. Hematological aspects of the thermoacclimatory process in rainbow trout, *Salmo gairdneri. J. Fish. Res. Bd. Canada* 24:2267–2281.

DeWitt, F. A., and Cailliet, G. M. 1972. Feeding habits of two bristlemouth fishes, *Cyclothone acclinidens* and *C. signata* (Gonostomatidae). *Copeia* 1972 (4):868–871.

DeWitt, H. H. 1971. *Coastal and deep-water benthic fishes of the Antarctic.* Amer. Geogr. Soc. Antarctic Map Folio Series 15. 10 pp.

Diamant, A., and Shpigel, M. 1985. Interspecific feeding associations of groupers (Teleostei, Serranidae) with octopuses and moray eels in the Gulf of Eilat (Aqaba). *Env. Biol. Fish.* 13:153–159.

Diana, J. S. 1995. *Biology and ecology of fishes.* Carmel, Ind: Cooper Publishing Group. 441 pp.

Dickson, K. A. 1994. Tunas as small as 207 mm fork length can elevate muscle temperatures significantly above ambient water temperature. *J. Exp. Biol.* 190:79–93.

Dijkgraaf, S. 1962. The functioning and significance of the lateral-line organs. *Biol. Rev.* 38:51–105.

Dijkgraaf, S., and Kalmijn, A. J. 1963. Untersuchungen über die Funktion der Lorenzinischen Ampullen an Haifischen. *Z. Vgl. Physiol.* 47:438–456.

Dizon, A. E., Horrall, R. M., and Hasler, A. D. 1973. Long-term olfactory "memory" in coho salmon, *Oncorhynchus kisutch. NOAA Fish. Bull.* 71:315–317.

Dobbs, G. H., Lin, Y., and DeVries, A. L. 1974. Aglomerularism in Antarctic fish. *Science* 185:793–794.

Doherty, P. V. 1983. Tropical territorial damselfishes: is density limited by aggression or recruitment? *Ecology* 64:176–190.

Dominey, W. J., and Blumer, L. S. 1984. Cannibalism of early life stages in fishes. Pages 43–64 *in* G. Hausfater and S. Blaffer-Hrdy, eds. *Infanticide: comparative and evolutionary perspectives.* New York: Aldine.

Donald, J., and Campbell, G. 1982. A comparative study of the adrenergic innervation of the teleost heart. *J. Comp. Physiol.* 147:85–91.

Donaldson, E. M., Fagerlund, U. H. M., Higgs, D. A., and McBride, J. R. 1979. Hormonal enhancement of growth. Pages 455–597 *in* W. S. Hoar, D. J. Randall, and J. R. Brett. *Fish Physiology.* Vol. 9. New York: Academic Press.

Dooley, J. K. 1972. Fishes associated with the pelagic *Sargassum* complex, with a discussion of the *Sargassum* community. *Contr. Mar. Sci.* 16:1–32.

Douglas, E. L., Friedl, W. A., and Pickwell, G. V. 1976. Fishes in oxygen-minimum zones: blood oxygenation characteristics. *Science* 191:957–959.

Douglas, M. E., and Matthews, W. J. 1992. Does

morphology predict ecology? Hypothesis testing within a freshwater fish assemblage. *Oikos* 65:213–224.

Douglas, R. H. 1983. Spectral sensitivity of rainbow trout (*Salmo gairdneri*). *Rev. Can. Biol. Exptl.* 42:117–122.

Downing, J. A., and Plante, C. 1993. Production of fish populations in lakes. *Can. J. Fish. Aquat. Sci.* 50: 110–120.

Drummond, R. A., Spoor, W. A., and Olson, G. F. 1973. Some short-term indicators of sublethal effects of copper on brook trout, *Salvelinus fontinalis. J. Fish. Res. Bd. Canada* 30:698–701.

Dudgeon, D. 1992. Endangered ecosystems: a review of the conservation status of tropical Asian rivers. *Hydrobiologia* 248: 167–191.

Duman, J. G., and DeVries, A. L. 1974a. Freezing resistance in winter flounder, *Pseudopleuronectes americanus. Nature* 247:237–238.

Duman, J. G., and DeVries, A. L. 1974b. The effects of temperature and photoperiod on antifreeze production in cold-water fishes. *J. Exp. Zool.* 190:89–97.

Durbin, A. G., and Durbin, E. G. 1975. Grazing rates of the Atlantic menhaden *Brevoortia tyrannus* as a function of particle size and concentration. *Mar. Biol.* 33:265–277.

East, P., and Magnan, P. 1987. The effect of locomotor activity on the growth of brook charr, *Salvelinus fontinalis* Mitchell. *Can. J. Zool.* 65:843–846.

Eastman, J. T. 1993. *Antarctic fish biology: evolution in a unique environment.* San Diego: Academic Press. 322 pp.

Eastman, J. T., and DeVries, A. L. 1982. Buoyancy studies of notothenioid fishes in McMurdo Sound, Antarctica. *Copeia* 1982:385–393.

Eaton, J. W., Klopin, C. F., and Swofford, H. S. 1973. Chlorinated urban water: a cause of dialysis-induced hemolytic anemia. *Science* 181:463–464.

Ebeling, A. W., Larsen, R. J., and Alevizon, W. S. 1980. Habitat groups and island-mainland distribution of kelp-bed fishes off Santa Barbara, California. Pages 403–431 *in* D. M. Power, ed., *Multidisciplinary symposium on the California islands.* Santa Barbara Museum Nat. Hist.

Echelle, A. A., and Connor, P. J. 1989. Rapid, geographically extensive genetic introgression after secondary contact between two pupfish species (*Cyprinodon,* Cyprinodontidae). *Evolution* 43:717–727.

Echelle, A. A., and Kornfield, I., eds., 1984. *Evolution of fish species flocks.* Orono: University of Maine Press.

Echelle, A. A., and Mosier, D. T. 1982. *Menidia clarkhubbsi,* n. sp. (Pisces, Atherinidae) an all-female species. *Copeia* 1982:535–540.

Echelle, A. A., and Schnell, Gary D. 1976. Factor analysis of species associations among fishes of the Kiamichi River, Oklahoma. *Trans. Amer. Fish. Soc.* 105(2):17–31.

Eddy, F. B. 1971. Blood gas relationships in the rainbow trout, *Salmo gairdneri. J. Fish. Res. Bd. Canada* 24:2267–2281.

Eddy, F. B. 1973. Oxygen dissociation curves of the blood of the tench, *Tinca tinca. J. Exp. Biol.* 58:281–283.

Eddy, F. B. 1982. Osmotic and ionic regulation in captive fish with particular reference to salmonidae. *Comp. Biochem. Physiol.* 73B:125–141.

Eddy, S., Moyle, J. B., and Underhill, J. C. 1963. The fish fauna of the Mississippi River above St. Anthony Falls as related to the effectiveness of this falls as a migration barrier. *J. Minn. Acad. Sci.* 30(2):111–115.

Eddy, S., and Underhill, J. C. 1978. *How to know the freshwater fishes.* Dubuque: W. C. Brown. 215 pp.

Edwards, D. G., and Cech, J. J., Jr. 1990. Aquatic and aerial metabolism of juvenile monkey-face prickleback, *Cebidichthys violaceus,* an intertidal fish of California. *Comp. Biochem. Physiol.* 96A(1):61–65.

Edwards, R. J., and Contreras-Balderas, S. 1991. Historical changes in the ichthyofauna of the lower Rio Grande (Rio Bravo del Norte) Texas and Mexico. *Southwest. Nat.* 36: 201–212.

Egginton, S., and Sidell, B. D. 1989. Thermal acclimation induces adaptive changes in subcellular structure of fish skeletal muscle. *Am. J. Physiol.* 256 (*Regul., Integr., Comp. Physiol.* 25):R1–R9.

Ehrenfeld, D. W. 1976. The conservation of non-resources. *Amer. Sci.* 64:648–656.

Ehrenfeld, D. W. 1978. *The arrogance of humanism.* New York: Oxford.

Ehrlich, P. R., and Ehrlich, A. H. 1973. Coevolution; heterotypic schooling in Caribbean reef fishes. *Amer. Nat.* 107:157–160.

Ehrlich, P. R., Talbot, F. H., Russell, B. C., and Anderson, G. R. V. 1977. The behavior of chaetodontid fishes with special reference to Lorenz's "poster colouration" hypothesis. *J. Zool. Soc.* (London) 183:213–228.

Eisler, R. 1965. Erythrocyte counts and hemoglobin content in nine species of marine teleosts. *Chesapeake Sci.* 6:119–120.

Ekman, S. 1953. *Zoogeography of the sea.* London: Sedgewick and Jackson. 417 pp.

Ellis, A. E. 1977. The leucocytes of fish: a review. *J. Fish Biol.* 11:453–491.

Elton, C. S. 1958. *The ecology of invasions by animals and plants.* London: Methuen. 181 pp.

Elvira, B. 1995. Conservation status of endemic freshwater fish in Spain. *Biol. Cons.* 72:129–136.

Emery, A. R. 1973. Preliminary comparisons of day and night habits of freshwater fish in Ontario lakes. *J. Fish. Res. Bd. Canada* 30:761–774.

Emery, S. H. 1986. Hematological comparisons of endothermic vs. ectothermic elasmobranch fishes. *Copeia* 1986:700–705.

Endler, J. A. 1978. A predator's view of animal color patterns. Pages 319–364 *in* M. K. Hecht, W. C. Steere, and B. Wallace, eds. *Evolutionary biology.* Vol. 11. New York: Plenum Press.

Ensor, D. M., and Ball, J. N. 1972. Prolactin and osmoregulation in fishes. *Fed. Proc.* 31:1615–1623.

Evans, D. H. 1967a. Sodium, chloride, and water balance of the intertidal teleost *Xiphister atropurpureus.* 1. Regulation of plasma concentration and body water content. *J. Exp. Biol.* 47:513–518.

Evans, D. H. 1975. Ionic exchange mechanisms in fish gills. *Comp. Biochem. Physiol.* 51A:491–495.

Evans, D. H. 1977. Further evidence for Na/NH_4 exchange in marine teleost fish. *J. Exp. Biol.* 70:213–220.

Evans, D. H. 1979. Ionic and osmotic regulation in fish. Pages 305–390 *in* G. M. D. Maloiy, ed. *Osmotic and ionic regulation in animals.* New York: Academic Press.

Evans, D. H. 1984. The roles of gill permeability and transport merchanisms in euryhalinity. Pages 239–283 *in* W. S. Hoar and D. J. Randall, eds. *Fish physiology.* Vol. 10, Pt. B. New York: Academic Press.

Evans, D. H. 1993. Osmotic and ionic regulation. Pages 315–341 *in* D. H. Evans, ed. *The Physiology of Fishes.* Boca Raton: CRC Press.

Ezzat, A. A., Shabana, M. B., and Farghaly, A. M. 1973. Studies on the blood characteristics of *Tilapia zilli* (Gervais). 1. Blood cells. *J. Fish Biol.* 6:1–12.

Fänge, R. 1968. The formation of eosinophilic granulocytes in the esophageal lymphomyeloid tissue in the elasmobranchs. *Acta Zool. Stockh.* 49:155–161.

Fänge, R. 1976. Gas exchange in the swimbladder. Pages 189–211 *in* G. M. Hughes, ed. *Respiration of amphibious vertebrates.* London: Academic Press.

Fänge, R. 1982. Exogenous otoliths of elasmobranchs. *J. Mar. Biol. Ass. U.K.* 62:225.

Fänge, R. 1984. Lymphomyeloid tissues in fishes. *Vidensk. Meddr. dansk naturh. Foren.* 145:143–152.

Fänge, R., and Mattisson, A. 1981. The lymphomyeloid (hemopoietic) system of the Atlantic nurse shark, *Ginglymostoma cirratum.* *Biol. Bull.* 160:240–249.

Fänge, R., and Nilsson, S. 1985. The fish spleen: structure and function. *Experientia* 41:152–158.

Farlinger, S., and Beamish, F. W. H. 1978. Changes in blood chemistry and critical swimming speed of largemouth bass, *Micropterus salmoides,* with physical conditioning. *Trans. Am. Fish. Soc.* 107:523–527.

Farmer, G. J., and Beamish, F. W. H. 1969. Oxygen consumption of *Tilapia nilotica* in relation to swimming speed and salinity. *J. Fish. Res. Bd. Canada* 26:2807–2821.

Farrell, A. P. 1984. A review of cardiac performance in the teleost heart: intrinsic and humoral regulation. *Can. J. Zool.* 62:523–536.

Farrell, A. P., and Jones, D. R. 1992. The heart. Pages 1–88 in W. S. Hoar, D. J. Randall, and A. P. Farrell, eds. *Fish physiology*. Vol. 12, Pt. A. New York: Academic Press.

Fay, R. R., Kendall, J. I., Popper, A. N., and Tester, A. L. 1974. Vibration detection by the macula neglecta of sharks. *Comp. Biochem. Physiol.* 47A:1235–1240.

Fausch, K. D. 1984. Profitable stream positions for salmonids: relating specific growth rate to net energy gain. *Can. J. Zool.* 62:441–451.

Fausch, K. D. 1988. Competition between native and introduced salmonids in streams: what have we learned? *Can. J. Fish., Aquat. Sci.* 45:2238–2246.

Fausch, K. D., and Northcote, T. G. 1992. Large woody debris and salmonid habitat in a small coastal British Columbia stream. *Can. J. Fish. Aquat. Sci.* 49:682–693.

Fautin, D. G. 1991. The aneomonefish symbiosis: what is known and what is not. *Symbiosis* 10:23–46.

Feduccia, A., and Slaughter, B. H. 1974. Sexual dimorphism in skates (Rajidae) and its possible role in differential niche utilization. *Evolution* 28(4):164–168.

Feldmeth, C. R., and Jenkins, T. M., Jr. 1973. An estimate of the energy expenditure by rainbow trout *(Salmo gairdneri)* in a small mountain stream. *J. Fish. Res. Bd. Canada* 30: 1755–1759.

Ferguson, H. W. 1976. The ultrastructure of plaice leucocytes. *J. Fish Biol.* 8:139–142.

Findley, J. S., and Findley, M. T. 1985. A search for pattern in butterfly fish communities. *Amer. Nat.* 126:800–816.

Fine, M. L., Horn, M. H., and Cox, B. 1987. *Acanthonus armatus*, a deep-sea teleost with a minute brain and large ears. *Proc. R. Soc. Lond. B* 230: 257–265.

Fine, M. L., Winn, H. E., and Olla, B. L. 1977. Communication in fishes. Pages 472–518 in T. A. Sebeok, ed. *How animals communicate*. Terre Haute: Indiana University Press.

Fink, S. V., and Fink, W. L. 1981. Interrelationships of the ostariophysan fishes (Teleostei). *Zool. J. Linn. Soc.* 72:297–353.

Finn, J. P., and Nielson, N. O. 1971. Inflammatory response in rainbow trout. *J. Fish Biol.* 3:463–478.

Fischer, E. A., and Peterson, C. W. 1987. The evolution of sexual patterns in the seabasses. *Bioscience* 37: 482–489.

Fitch, J. E., and Lavenberg, R. J. 1968. *Deep-water fishes of California*. Berkeley: University of California Press. 155 pp.

Fitzsimmons, J. M. 1972. A revision of two genera of goodeid fishes (Cyprinodontiformes, Osteichthyes) from the Mexican Plateau. *Copeia* 1972(4):728–756.

Flecker, A. S. 1992. Fish trophic guilds and the structure of a tropical stream: weak direct vs. strong indirect effects. *Ecology* 73: 927–940.

Fletcher, G. L., King, M. J., and Hew, C. L. 1984. How does the brain control the pituitary's release of antifreeze synthesis inhibitor? *Can. J. Zool.* 62:839–844.

Forney, J. L. 1974. Interactions between yellow perch abundance, walleye predation, and survival of alternate prey in Oneida Lake, New York. *Trans. Amer. Fish. Soc.* 103(1):15–24.

Forrest, J. N., Jr., Mackay, W. C., Gallagher, B., and Epstein, F. H. 1973b. Plasma cortisol response to saltwater adaptation in the American eel *Anquilla rostrata*. *Am. J. Physiol.* 224:714–717.

Forrest, J. N., Silva, P., Epstein, A., and Epstein, F. H. 1973. Effect of rectal gland extirpation on plasma sodium in the spiny dogfish. *Bull. Mt. Des. Biol. Lab.* 13:41–42.

Forster, M. E., Axelsson, M., Farrell, A. P., and Nilsson, S. 1991. Cardiac function and circulation in hagfishes. *Can. J. Zool.* 69:1985–1992.

Forster, R. P., and Berglund, F. 1956. Osmotic diuresis and its effect on total electrolyte distribution in plasma and urine of the aglomerular teleost *Lophius americanus*. *J. Gen. Physiol.* 39:349–359.

Foreman, R. E., A. Gorbman, J. M. Dodd, and R. Olsson, eds. 1985. *Evolutionary biology of primitive fishes*. NATO ASI Series, Series A, Life Sciences 103. 463 pp.

Forey, P. and Janvier, P. 1993. Agnathans and the origin of jawed vertebrates. *Nature* 361: 129–134.

Forey, P. and Janvier, P. 1994. Evolution of the early vertebrates. *Amer. Scientist* 82:554–565.

Foskett, J. K., Logsdon, C. D., Turner, T., Machen, T. E., and Bern, H. A. 1981. Differentiation of the chloride extrusion mechanisms during seawater adaptation of a teleost fish, the cichlid *Sarotherodon mossambicus*. *J. Exp. Biol.* 93:-209–224.

Foster, M. S., and Schiel, D. R. 1985. The ecology of giant kelp forests in California: a community profile. *U.S. Fish Wildl. Serv. Biol. Rept.* 85(7.2).

Foster, S. A. 1985. Wound healing: a possible role of cleaning stations. *Copeia* 1985:875–880.

Fourie, F. LeR., and Hattingh, J. 1976. A seasonal study of the haematology of carp *(Cyprinus carpio)* from a locality in the Transvaal, South Africa. *Zool. Africana.* 11:75–80.

Fox, D. L. 1978. *Animal biochromes and structural colors.* Berkeley: Univ. of Calif. Press.

Francis, R. C., and Sibley, T. H. 1991. Climate change and fisheries: what are the real issues? *Northw. Env. J.* 7:295–307.

Freadman, M. A. 1979. Role partitioning of swimming musculature of striped bass, *Morone saxatilis* Walbaum, and bluefish, *Pomatomus saltatrix* L. *J. Fish Biol.* 15:417–423.

Frey, D. G. 1969. A limnological reconnaisance of Lake Lanao. *Verh. int. Verein. Limnol.* 17: 1090–1102.

Fricke, H. W. 1970. Ecological and ethological field observations on colonies of the garden eels *Gorgasia sillneri* and *Taenioconger hassi* (in German). *Zeit. Tierpysch.* 27(9):1076–1099.

Fricke, H. W., and Fricke, S. 1977. Monogamy and sex change by aggressive dominance in coral reef fish. *Nature* 266:830–832.

Fricke, H. W., Hissemann, K., Schauer, J., Reinicke, O., Kasang, L., and Armstrong, M. J. 1991. Habitat and population size of the coelacanth *Latimeria chalumnae* at Grand Comoro. *Env. Biol. Fish.* 32:287–300.

Fryer, G., and Iles, T. D. 1972. *The cichlid fishes of the Great Lakes of Africa.* Edinburgh: Oliver and Boyd. 641 pp.

Gannon, B. J., and Burnstock, G. 1969. Excitatory adrenergic innervation of the fish heart. *Comp. Biochem. Physiol.* 29:765–773.

Gardner, G. R., and Yevich, P. P. 1969. Studies on the blood morphology of three estuarine cyprinodontiform fishes. *J. Fish. Res. Bd. Canada* 26:433–447.

Garey, W. F. 1962. Cardiac response of fishes in asphyxic environments. *Biol. Bull.* 122: 362–368.

Gascon, D., and Leggett, W. C. 1977. Distribution, abundance, and resource utilization of littoral fishes in response to a nutrient/production gradient in Lake Memphremagog. *J. Fish. Res. Bd. Canada* 34(8):1105–1117.

Gatz, A. J., Jr. 1979. Community organization in fishes as indicated by morphological features. *Ecology* 60:711–718.

Gee, J. H. 1974. Behavioral and developmental plasticity in the longnose, *Rhinichthys cataractae*, and blacknose, *R. atratulus* (Cyprinidae) dace. *J. Fish. Res. Bd. Canada* 20:105–118.

Gee, J. H. 1980. Respiratory pattern and antipredator responses in the central mudminnow, *Umbra limi*, a continuous, facultative, air-breathing fish. *Can. J. Zool.* 58:819–827.

Gee, J. H. 1983. Ecologic implications of buoyancy control in fish. Pages 140–176 *in* P. W. Webb and D. Weihs, eds. *Fish biomechanics.* New York: Praeger.

Gee, J. H., and Northcote, T. G. 1963. Comparative ecology of two sympatric species of dace *(Rhinichthys)* in the Fraser River System, British Columbia. *J. Fish. Res. Bd. Canada* 20(1):105–118.

Gelwick, F. P., and Matthews, W. J. 1990. Temporal and spatial patterns in littoral-zone fish assemblages of a reservoir (Lake Texoma, Oklahoma-Texas, U.S.A.). *Env. Biol. Fish.* 27: 107–120

.Gerald, J. W. 1971. Sound production during courtship in six species of sunfish (Centrarchidae). *Evolution* 25:75–87.

Gerking, S. D. 1966. Annual growth cycle, growth potential, and growth compensation in the bluegill sunfish in northern Indiana lakes. *J. Fish. Res. Bd. Canada* 23:1923–1956.

Gery, J. 1969. The fresh-water fishes of South America. Pages 828–848 *in* E. Fittkau et al., eds. *Biogeography and ecology in South America.* Monogr. Biol. 19(2). The Hague: W. Junk.

Gesser, H., Anderson, P., Brams, P., and Sund-Laursen, N. 1982. Isotopic effects of adrenaline on the anoxic or hypercapnic myocardium of rainbow trout and eel. *J. Comp. Physiol.* 147:123–128.

Gibbs, A., and Somero, G. N. 1990. Na$^+$-K$^+$-adenosine triphosphatase activities in gills of marine teleost fishes: changes with depth, size and locomotory activity level. *Mar. Biol.* 106:315–321.

Gibson, R. N. 1993. Intertidal teleosts: life in a fluctuating environment. Pages 513–536 *in* T. J. Pitcher, ed. *Behaviour of teleost fishes.* 2nd ed. New York: Chapman and Hall.

Gilbert, C. R. 1977. Status of the western South Atlantic apogonid fish *Apogon americanus,* with remarks on other Brazilian Apogonidae. *Copeia* 1977(1):25–32.

Giles, M. A., and Vanstone, W. E. 1976. Ontogenetic variation in the multiple hemoglobin of coho salmon *(Oncorhynchus kisutch)* and the effect of environmental factors on their expression. *J. Fish. Res. Bd. Canada* 33:1144–1149.

Gillen, R. G., and Riggs, A. 1971. The hemoglobins of a fresh-water teleost, *Cichlasoma cyanoguttatum* (Baird and Girard). I. The effects of phosphorylated organic compounds upon the oxygen equilibria. *Comp. Biochem. Physiol.* 38B:585–595.

Gillespie, A. L. 1898. Changes in the digestive activity of the secretions of the alimentary canal of the salmon in different conditions. *Fish. Bd. Scotland Rep. of Investig. Life Hist. Salmon* 4:23–35.

Gilmore, R. G. 1993. Reproductive biology of lamnoid sharks. *Env. Biol. Fish.* 38:95–116.

Glebe, B. D., and Leggett, W. C. 1981. Latitudinal differences in energy allocation and use during the freshwater migrations of American shad *(Alosa sapidissima)* and their life history consequences. *Can. J. Fish. Aqu. Sci.* 38:806–820.

Glover, C. J. M. 1982. Adaptations of fishes in arid Australia. Pages 241–246 *in* W. R. Barker and P. J. M. Greenslade, eds. *Evolution of the flora and fauna of arid Australia.* Adelaide: Peacock Pubs.

Goldschmidt, T., Witte, F., and Wanink, J. 1993. Cascading effects of the introduced Nile perch on the detritivorous/phytoplanktivorous species in the sublittoral areas of Lake Victoria. *Cons. Biol.* 7:686–700.

Goldstein, L., Janssen, P. A., and Forster, R. P. 1967. Lungfish *Neoceratodus forsteri:* activities of ornithine-urea cycle and enzymes. *Science* 157:316–317.

Gonzalez, R. J., and McDonald, D. G. 1994. The relationship between oxygen uptake and ion loss in fish from diverse habitats. *J. Exp. Biol.* 190:95–108.

Goode, G. B., and Bean, T. M. 1895. *Oceanic ichthyology.* Smithson. Inst. Spec. Bull. 2. 540 pp.

Gordon, B. L. 1977. *The secret lives of fishes.* New York: Grosset & Dunlap. 305 pp.

Gorlick, D. L., Atkins, P. O., and Losey, G. S., Jr. 1978. Cleaning stations as water holes, garbage dumps, and sites for the evolution of reciprocal altruism. *Amer. Nat.* 112:341–353.

Gosline, W. A. 1966. The limits of the fish family Serranidae, with notes on other lower percoids. *Proc. Calif. Acad. Sci.* 33(6):91–112.

Gosline, W. A. 1971. *Functional morphology and classification of teleostean fishes.* Honolulu: Univ. of Hawaii Press. 208 pp.

Gosline, W. A. 1983. The relationships of the mastacembelid and synbranchid fishes. *Jap. J. Ichthy.* 29:323–328.

Goulding, M. 1980. *The fishes and the forest.* Berkeley: Univ. of Calif. Press.

Graham, J. B. 1971. Temperature tolerances of some closely related tropical Atlantic and Pacific fish species. *Science* 172:861–863.

Graham, J. B. 1983. Heat transfer. Pages 248–279 *in* P. W. Webb and D. Weihs, eds. *Fish biomechanics.* New York: Praeger Publ.

Grassle, J. F., Sanders, H. L., Hessler, R. R., Rowe, G. T., and McLellan, T. 1975. Pattern and zonation; a study of the bathylmegafauna using the research submersible *Alvin. Deep-sea Res.* 22:457–481.

Grau, E. G., Dickhoff, W. W., Nishioka, R. S., Bern, H. A., and Folmar, L. C. 1981. Lunar phasing of the thyroxine surge preparatory to seaward migration of salmonoid fish. *Science* 211:607–609.

Grayton, B. D., and Beamish, F. W. H. 1977. Effects of feeding frequency on food intake, growth and body composition of rainbow trout *(Salmo gairdneri). Aquaculture* 11:159–172.

Greaney, G. S., and Powers, D. A. 1978. Allosteric

modifiers of fish hemoglobin: in vitro and in vivo studies of the effect of ambient oxygen and pH on erythrocyte ATP concentrations. *J. Exp. Zool.* 203:339–349.

Greene, C. W. 1926. The physiology of the spawning salmon. *Physiol. Rev.* 6:201–241.

Greenwood, P. H. 1976. Fish fauna of the Nile. Pages 127–141 *in* J. Rzoska, ed. *The Nile, biology of an ancient river.* The Hague: W. Junk.

Greenwood, P. H. 1977. Notes on the anatomy and classification of elopomorph fishes. *Bull. Brit. Mus. (Nat. Hist.) Zool.* 32(4):65–102.

Greenwood, P. H., Miles, R. S., and Patterson, C., eds. 1973. *Interrelationships of fishes.* New York: Academic Press. 536 pp.

Greenwood, P. H., Rosen, D. E., Weitzman, S. H., and Myers, G. S. 1966. Phyletic studies on teleostean fishes, with a provisional classification of living forms. *Bull. Amer. Mus. Nat. Hist.* 131(4):341–455.

Gregory, W. K. 1933. Fish skulls. *Trans. Amer. Philosoph. Soc.* 23(2):75–481.

Griffith, R. W. 1994. The life of the first vertebrates. *Bioscience* 44:408–417.

Grigg, G. C. 1969. Temperature-induced changes in the oxygen equilibrium curve of the blood of the brown bullhead, *Ictalurus nebulosus. Comp. Biochem. Physiol.* 28:1203–1223.

Grigg, G. C. 1974. Respiratory function of blood of fishes. Pages 331–368 *in* N. Florkin and B. T. Scheer, eds. *Chemical zoology.* Vol. 8. New York: Academic Press.

Groot, C., Quinn, T. P., and Hara, T. J. 1986. Responses of migrating adult sockeye salmon (*Onchorhynchus nerka*) to population-specific odours. *Can. J. Zool.* 64:926–932.

Gross, M. R. 1982. Sneakers, satellites, and parentals: polymorphic mating strategies in North American sunfishes. *Z. Tierpsychol.* 60:1–26.

Gross, M. R. 1984. Sunfish, salmon, and the evolution of alternative reproductive strategies and tactics in fishes. Pages 55–75 *in* G. W. Potts and R. J. Wootton, eds. *Fish reproduction: strategies and tactics.* London: Academic Press.

Gross, M. R., Coleman, R. M., and McDowall, R. M. 1988. Aquatic productivity and the evolu-

tion of diadromous fish migration. *Science* 239:1291–1293.

Gross, M. R., and Sargent, R. C. 1985. The evolution of male and female parental care in fishes. *Amer. Zool.* 25:807–822.

Grossman, G. 1979. Demographic characteristics of an intertidal bay goby (*Lepidogobius lepidus*). *Environ. Biol. Fish* 4:207–218.

Grossman, G. 1980. Food, fights, and burrows: the adaptive significance of intraspecific aggression in the bay goby (Pisces, Gobiidae). *Oecologia* 45:261–266.

Grossman, G. D. 1982. Dynamics and organization of a rocky intertidal fish assemblage: the persistence and resilience of taxocene structure. *Amer. Nat.* 119:611–637.

Grossman, G., Coffin, R., and Moyle, P. 1980. Feeding ecology of the bay goby (Pisces, Gobiidae). Effect of behavioral, ontogenetic, and temporal variation on diet. *J. Exp. Mar. Biol. Ecol.* 44:47–59.

Grossman, G. D., Moyle, P. B., and Whitaker, J. O., Jr. 1982. Stochasticity in structural and functional characteristics of an Indiana stream fish assemblage: a test of community theory. *Amer. Nat.* 120:423–454.

Grothe, D. R., and Eaton, J. W. 1975. Chlorine-induced mortality in fish. *Trans. Am. Fish. Soc.* 104:800–802.

Gruber, S. H. 1977. The visual system of sharks: adaptations and capability. *Amer. Zool.* 17:453–470.

Gruber, S. H., and Cohen, J. L. 1978. Visual system of the elasmobranchs: state of the art 1960–1975. Pages 391–417 *in* E. S. Hodgson and R. F. Mathewson, eds. *Sensory biology of sharks, skakes, and rays.* Washington, D.C.: Off. Naval Res. Publ.

Gruber, S. H., Gulley, R. L., and Brandon, J. 1975a. Duplex retina in seven elasmobranch species. *Bull. Mar. Sci.* 25:353–358.

Gruber, S. H., Hamasaki, D. I., and Davis, B. L. 1975b. Window to the epiphysis in sharks. *Copeia* 1975 (2):378–380.

Guegan, J.-F., Labert, A., Leveque, C., Combes, C., and Euzet, L. 1992. Can host body size explain the parasite species richness in tropical freshwater fishes? *Oecologia* 90:197–204.

Gunter, G. 1957. Predominance of the young among marine fishes found in fresh water. *Copeia* 1957(1):13–16.

Guppy, M., and Hochachka, P. W. 1978. Skipjack tuna white muscle: a blueprint for the integration of aerobic and anaerobic carbohydrate metabolism. Pages 175–181 *in* G. D. Sharp and A. E. Dizon, eds. *The physiological ecology of tunas.* New York: Academic Press.

Haas, R. 1976a. Sexual selection in *Nothobranchius guentheri* (Pisces, Cyprinodontidae). *Evolution* 20:614–622.

Haas, R. 1976b. Behavioral biology of the annual killifish, *Nothobranchius guentheri. Copeia* 1976(1):80–91.

Haedrich R. L. 1983. Estuarine fishes. Pages 183–207 *in* B. H. Ketchum, ed., *Estuaries and enclosed seas.* New York: Elsevier.

Haedrich, R. L., Rowe, G. T., and Polloni, P. T. 1975. Zonation and faunal composition of epibenthic populations on the continental slope south of New England. *J. Mar. Res.* 33(3):191–212.

Haglund, T. R., Buth, D. G., and Lawson, R. 1992. Allozyme variation and phylogenetic relationships of Asian, North American, and European populations of the ninespine stickleback, *Pungitius pungitius.* Pages 438–452 *in* R. L. Mayden, ed. *Systematics, historical ecology, and North American freshwater fishes.* Stanford, Calif.: Stanford Univ. Press.

Hahn, G. 1960. Ferntastsinn and Stomungssinn beim augenlosen Hohlenfisch *Anoptichthys jordani* Hubbs and Innes im Vergleich zu einigen Teleosteern. *Naturwissenschaften.* 47:611.

Haines, T. A. 1980. Seasonal patterns of muscle RNA/DNA ratio and growth in black crappie, *Pomoxis nigromaculatus. Env. Biol. Fish* 5:67–70.

Hall, F. G. 1929. The influence of varying oxygen tensions upon the rate of oxygen consumption in marine fishes. *Amer. J. Physiol.* 88:212–218.

Hall, F. G., and McCutcheon, F. H. 1938. The affinity of hemoglobin for oxygen in marine fishes. *J. Cell. Comp. Physiol.* 11:205–212.

Halstead, B. W. 1967. *Poisonous and venomous marine animals of the world* Vols. 2, 3:

Vertebrates. Washington, D.C.: U.S. Govt. Printing Office.

Halstead, L. B. 1968. *The pattern of vertebrate evolution.* San Francisco: W. H. Freeman. 209 pp.

Halver, J. E. 1957. Nutrition of salmonoid fishes. IV. An amino acid test diet for chinook salmon. *J. Nutr.* 62:245–254.

Halver, J. E. 1972. The vitamins. Pages 29–103 *in* J. E. Halver, ed. *Fish nutrition.* New York: Academic Press.

Halver, J. E. 1976. Formulating practical diets for fish. *J. Fish. Res. Bd. Canada* 33:1032–1039.

Halver, J. E., DeLong, D. C., and Mertz, E. T. 1957. Nutrition of salmonoid fishes. V. Classification of essential amino acids for chinook salmon. *J. Nutr.* 63:95–105.

Halver, J. E., and Shanks, W. E. 1960. Nutrition and salmonoid fishes. VIII. Indispensable amino acids for sockeye salmon. *J. Nutr.* 72:340–346.

Hamasaki, D. I., and Streck, P. 1971. Properties of the epiphysis cerebri of the small spotted dogfish shark, *Scyliorhinus caniculus* L. *Vision Res.* 11:189–198.

Hamlett, W. C. 1993. Ontogeny of umbilical cord and placenta in the Atlantic sharpnose shark, *Rhizoprion terraenovae. Env. Biol. Fish.* 38:253–267.

Hamre, J. 1994. Biodiversity and exploitation of the main fish stocks in the Norwegian-Barents Sea ecosystem. *Biodivers. and Cons.*3:473–492.

Hankin, D. G. 1978. New fluorescent fish scale marker. *Prog. Fish. Cult.* 40:163–164.

Hansen, K., and Herring, P. J. 1977. Dual bioluminescent systems in the anglerfish genus *Linophryne* (Pisces, Ceratoidea). *J. Zool.* (London) 182:103–124.

Hanson, D. 1967. *Cardiovascular dynamics and aspects of gas exchange in Chondrichthyes.* Ph.D. diss. Univ. of Wash., Seattle.

Hara, T. J. 1986. Role of olfaction in fish behavior. Pages 152–176 *in* T. J. Pritcher, ed. *The behavior of teleost fishes.* Baltimore, Md.: Johns Hopkins Univ. Press.

Hara, T.J., Macdonald, S., Evans, R.E., Marui, T., Arai. S. 1984. Morpholine, bile acids, and skin mucus as possible chemical cues in salmonid homing: electrophysiological re-evaluation. Pages 363–378 in J.D. McCleave, G.P. Arnold, J.J. Dodson, and W.H. Neill, eds. *Mechanisms of migration in fishes*. New York: Plenum Press.

Harbison, G. R. 1987. Encounters with a swordfish *(Xiphias gladius)* and sharptail mola *(Masturus lanceolatus)* at depths greater than 600 meters. *Copeia* 1987:511–513.

Harden-Jones, F. R. 1968. *Fish migration*. London: E. Arnold Pub. 325 pp.

Harder, W. 1975. *Anatomy of fishes*. Pt. II. E. Schwelzerbart'sche Verlabsbuchhandling. Stuttgart. 132 pp.

Hardisty, M. W., and Potter, I. C., eds. 1971. *The biology of lampreys*. Vols. 1 and 2. New York: Academic Press.

Harrington, R. W. 1961. Oviparous hemaphroditic fish with internal self-fertilization. *Science* 134:1749–1750.

Harris, A. J. 1965. Eye movements of the dogfish, *Squalus acanthias* 1. *J. Exp. Biol.* 43:107–130.

Harris, L. G., Ebeling, A. W., Laur, D. R., and Rowley, R. J. 1984. Community recovery after storm damage: a case of facilitation in primary succession. *Science* 224:1336–1338.

Hart, J. L. 1973. *Pacific fishes of Canada*. Fish. Res. Bd. Canada Bull. 180. 740 pp.

Hartman, G. F., and Gill, C. A. 1968. Distributions of juvenile steelhead and cutthroat trout *(Salmo gairdneri* and *S. clarki clarki)* within streams in southwestern British Columbia. *J. Fish. Res. Bd. Canada* 25(1):33–48.

Hartman, W. L., and Burgner, R. L. 1972. Limnology and fish ecology of sockeye salmon nursery lakes of the world. *J. Fish. Res. Bd. Canada* 29(6):699–715.

Harvey, B. C. 1991. Interactions among stream fishes: predator induced habitat shifts and larval survival. *Oecologia* 87:29–36.

Harvey, B. C., and Stewart, A. J. 1991. Fish size and habitat depth relationships in headwater streams. *Oecologia* 87:336–342.

Hasler, A. D. 1966. *Underwater guideposts*. Madison: Univ of Wis. Press. 155 pp.

Hasler, A. D., Horrall, R. N., Wisby, W. J., and Braemer, W. 1958. Sun orientation and homing in fishes. *Limnol. Oceanogr.* 3(4):353–361.

Hasler, A. D., and Scholtz, A. T. 1978. Olfactory

imprinting in coho salmon *(Oncorhynchus kisutch)*. Pages 356–369 in K. Schmid-Koenig and W. T. Keeton, eds. *Animal migration, navigation, and homing*. Berlin: Springer-Verlag.

Hasler, A. D., and Scholtz, A. T. 1983. Olfactory imprinting and homing in salmon: investigations into the mechanism of the imprinting process. *Zoophysiology*. Vol. 14. Berlin: Springer-Verlag. 134 pp.

Hattingh, J., LeRoux Fourie, F., and Van Vuren, J. H. J. 1975. The transport of freshwater fish. *J. Fish Biol.* 7:447–449.

Hawkins, A. D. 1993. Underwater sound and fish behavior. Pages 129–170 in T. J. Pitcher, ed. *The behaviour of teleost fishes*. 2nd ed. New York: Chapman and Hall.

Hay, D. E., and McPhail, J. D. 1975. Mate selection in threespine sticklebacks *(Gasterosteus). Can. J. Zool.* 53:441–450.

Hayden, J. B., Cech, J. J., Jr., and Bridges, D. W. 1975. Blood oxygen dissociation characteristics of the winter flounder, *Pseudopleuronectes americanus* (Walbaum). *J. Fish. Res. Bd. Canada* 32:1539–1544.

Hazel, J. R. 1993. Thermal biology. Pages 427–467 in D.H. Evans, ed. *The Physiology of Fishes*. Boca Raton: CRC Press.

Heckmann, R. A., Deacon, J. E., and Greger, P. D. 1986. Parasites of the woundfin minnow, *Plagopterus argentissimus*, and other endemic fishes from the Virgin River, Utah. *Great Basin Nat.* 46:662–676.

Heisler, N. 1993. Acid-base regulation. Pages 343–378 in D. H. Evans, ed. *The Physiology of Fishes*. Boca Raton: CRC Press.

Heisler, N. 1988. Acid-base regulation. Pages 215–252 in T. J. Shuttleworth, ed. *Physiology of Elasmobranch Fishes*. Berlin: Springer-Verlag.

Helfman, G. S. 1981. The advantage to fishes of hovering in shade. *Copeia* 1981:392–399.

Helfman, G. S. 1981. Twilight activities and temporal structure in a freshwater fish community. *Can. J. Fish. Aq. Sci.* 38:1405–1420.

Helfman, G. S., and Clark, J. B. 1986. Rotational feeding: overcoming gape-limited foraging in anguillid eels. *Copeia* 1986:679–685.

Henderson, P. A. 1990. Fish of the Amazonian Igaop: stability and conservation in a high diversity–low biomass system. *J. Fish. Biol.* 37 (Suppl.A):61–66.

Hendrickson, W. A., Love, W. E., and Murray, G. C. 1968. Crystal forms of lamprey hemoglobin and crystalline transitions between lig- and states. *J. Mol. Biol.* 33:829–842.

Herald, E. S. 1961. *Living fishes of the world.* New York: Doubleday. 304 pp.

Herbold, B. 1984. Structure of an Indiana stream fish assemblage: choosing an appropriate model. *Amer. Nat.* 124:561–572.

Hevesy, G., Lockner, D., and Sletten, K. 1964. Iron metabolism and erythrocyte formation in fish. *Acta Physiol. Scand.* 60:256–266.

Hildebrand, M. 1974. *Analysis of vertebrate structure.* New York: John Wiley.

Hildemann, W. H. 1970. Transplantation immunity in fishes: Agnatha, Chondrichthyes, and Osteichthyes. *Transplant. Proc.* 2:253–259.

Hill, J., and Grossman, G. D. 1993. An energetic model of microhabitat use for rainbow trout and rosyside dace. *Ecology* 74:685–698.

Hill, L. G. 1969. Feeding and food habits of the spring cavefish, *Chologaster agassizi. Amer. Midl. Nat.* 82(1):110–116.

Hirano, T. 1986. The spectrum of prolactin action in teleosts. Pages 53–74 *in* C. L. Ralph, ed. *Comparative endocrinology: developments and directions.* New York: Alan R. Liso, Inc.

Hixon, M. A. 1980. Competitive interactions between California reef fishes of the genus *Embiotoca. Ecology* 61:918–931.

Hixon, M. A. 1986. Fish predation and local prey diversity. Pages 235–257 in C. A. Simenstad and G. M. Caillet, eds., *Contemporary studies on fish feeding.* The Hague: W. Junk.

Hixon, M. A. 1991. Predation as a process structuring coral reef fish communities. Pages 475–508 *in* P. F. Sale, ed. *The ecology of fishes on coral reefs.* San Diego: Academic Press.

Hoar, W. S. 1976. Smolt transformation: evolution, behavior, and physiology. *J. Fish. Res. Bd. Canada* 33(6):1234–1252.

Hoar, W. S., and Randall, D. J., eds. 1969. *Fish physiology.* Vol. 3. New York: Academic Press.

Hoar, W. S., and Randall, D. J., eds. 1984. *Fish physiology.* Vol. 10, Pt. A. New York: Academic Press. 456 pp.

Hobson, E. S. 1974. Feeding relationships of teleostean fishes on coral reefs in Kona, Hawaii. *NOAA Fish. Bull.* 72(4):915–1031.

Hobson, E. S. 1994. Ecological relations in the evolution of acanthopterygian fishes in warm-temperate communities of the northeastern Pacific. *Env. Biol. Fish.* 40:49–90.

Hochachka, P. W., and Somero, G. N. 1984. *Biochemical adaptation.* Princeton, N.J.: Princeton Univ. Press. 537 pp.

Hocutt, C. H., Jenkins, R. E., and Stauffer, J. R., Jr. 1986. Zoogeography of the fishes of the central Appalachians and central Atlantic coastal plain. Pages 161–211 *in* C. H. Hocutt and E. D. Wiley, eds. *The zoogeography of North American freshwater fishes.* New York: Wiley.

Hocutt, C. H., and Stauffer, J. R. 1975. Influence of gradient on the distribution of fishes in Conowingo Creek, Maryland and Pennsylvania. *Ches. Sci.* 16 (1):143–147.

Hocutt, C. H., and Wiley, E. O., eds. 1986. *The zoogeography of North American freshwater fishes.* New York: Wiley.

Hodgson, E. S., and Mathewson, R. F. 1978. Electrophysiological studies of chemoreception in elasmobranchs. Pages 227–267 *in* E. H. Hodgson and R. F. Mathewson, eds. *Sensory biology of sharks, skates, and rays.* Washington, D.C.: Naval Res. Publ.

Hogarth, P. J. 1973. Immune relations between mother and fetus in the viviparous poeciliid fish *Xiphophorus helleri* Haeckel. III. Survival of embryos after ectopic transplantation. *J. Fish Biol.* 5:109–113.

Hogman, W. J. 1968. Annulus formation of scales of four species of coregonids reared under artificial conditions. *J. Fish. Res. Bd. Canada* 25:2111–2112.

Holeton, G. F. 1970. Oxygen uptake and circulation by hemoglobinless Antarctic fish (*Chaenocephalus aceratus* Lonnberg) compared with three red-blooded Antarctic fish. *Comp. Biochem. Physiol.* 34:457–471.

Holland, K. N., and Sibert, J. R. 1994. Physiological thermoregulation in bigeye tuna, *Thunnus obesus. Env. Biol. Fishes* 40:319–327.

Holmes, W. N., and Donaldson, E. M. 1969. The

body compartments and the distribution of electrolytes. Pages 1–89 *in* W. S. Hoar and D. J. Randall, eds. *Fish physiology.* Vol. 1. New York: Academic Press.

Holmgren, S. 1977. Regulation of the heart of a teleost, *Gadus morhua,* by autonomic nerves and circulating catecholamines. *Acta Physiol. Scand.* 99:62–74.

Holmgren, S., Grove, D. J., and Fletcher, D. J. 1983. Digestion and the control of gastrointestinal motility. Pages 23–40 *in* J. C. Rankin, T. J. Pitcher, and R. Duggan, eds. *Control processes in fish physiology.* New York: Wiley-Interscience.

Hopkins, C. D. 1974. Electric communication in fish. *Amer. Sci.* 62(4):426–437.

Hopkins, T. E., and Larson, R. J. 1990. Gastric evacuation of three food types in the black and yellow rockfish *Sebastes chrysomelas* (Jordan and Gilbert). *J. Fish Biol.* 36:673–681.

Horn, M. H. 1970. The swimbladder as a juvenile organ in stomateiod fishes. *Breviora* 359:1–9.

Horn, M. H. 1972. The amount of space available for marine and freshwater fishes. *NOAA Fish. Bull.* 70(4):1295–1297.

Horn, M. H. 1975. Swimbladder state and structure in relation to behavior and mode of life in stromateoid fishes. *NOAA Fish. Bull.* 73(1):95–109.

Horn, M. H. 1984. Stromateoidei: development and relationships. Pages 620–628 *in* G. Moser et al., eds. *Ontogeny and systematics of fishes.* ASIH Spec. Publ. 1.

Horn, M. H. 1989. Biology of marine herbivorous fishes. *Oceanogr. Mar. Biol. Ann. Rev.* 27:167–272.

Horn, M. H., Grimes, P. W. Pfleger, C. F., and McClanahan, L. L. 1978. Buoyancy function of the enlarged fluid-filled cranium in the deep-sea ophidiid fish *Acanthonus armatus. Mar. Biol.* 46:335–339.

Horn, M. H., and Riegle, K. C. 1981. Evaporative water loss and intertidal vertical distribution in relation to body size and morphology of stichaeoid fishes from California. *J. Exp. Mar. Biol. Ecol.* 50:273–288.

Horn, M. H., and Riggs, C. D. 1973. Effects of temperature and light on the rate of air breathing of the bowfin, *Amia calva. Copeia* 1973(4): 653–657.

Houlihan, D. F., and Laurent, P. 1987. Effects of exercise training on the performance, growth, and protein turnover of rainbow trout *(Salmo gairdneri). Can. J. Fish. Aquat. Sci.* 44:1614–1621.

Houssay, S. F. 1912. *Forme, puissance, et stabilité des poissons.* Paris: Herman. 372 pp.

Houston, A. H., and Cyr, D. 1974. Thermo-acclimatory variation in the hemoglobin systems of goldfish *(Carassius auratus)* and rainbow trout *(Salmo gairdneri). J. Exp. Biol.* 61: 455–461.

Houston, A. H., and DeWilde, M. A. 1968. Thermacclimatory variations in the hematology of the common carp, *Cyprinus carpio. J. Exp. Biol.* 49:71–81.

Houston, A. H., and Rupert, R. 1976. Immediate response of the hemoglobin system of the goldfish, *Carassius auratus,* to temperature change. *Can. J. Zool.* 54:1737–1741.

Howell, J. B., Baumgardner, F. W., Bondi, K., and Rahn, H. 1970. Acid-base balance in cold-blooded vertebrates as a function of body temperature. *Amer. J. Physiol.* 218:600–605.

Hoy, J. B., Kaufman, E. E., and O'Berg, A. G. 1972. A large-scale field test of *Gambusia affinis* and Chlorpurifos for mosquito control. *Mosquito News* 32(2):163–171.

Hsiao, S., Greeley, M. S., Jr., and Wallace, R. A. 1994. Reproductive cycling in female *Fundulus heteroclitus. Biol. Bull.* 186:271–284.

Hubbs, C. L. 1955. Hybridization between fish species in nature. *Syst. Zool.* 4:1–20.

Hubbs, C. L. 1964. History of ichthyology in the United States after 1850. *Copeia* 1964(1):42–60.

Hubbs, C. L., and Hubbs, L. C. 1932. Apparent parthenogenesis in nature, in a form of fish of hybrid origin. *Science* 76:628–630.

Hubbs, C. L., and Lagler, K. F. 1964. *Fishes of the Great Lakes region.* Ann Arbor: Univ. of Mich. Press. 213 pp.

Hubbs, C. L., and Miller, R. R. 1942. Mass hybridization between two genera of cyprinid fishes in the Mohave Desert, California. *Papers Mich Acad. Sci. Arts, Letters.* 28:343–378.

Hubbs, C. L., and Potter, I. C. 1971. Distribution, phylogeny, and taxonomy. Pages 1–65 *in* M. W. Hardisty and I. C. Potter, eds. *The biology of lampreys.* Vol. 1. New York: Academic Press.

Huckabee, J. W., Goodyear, C. P., and Jones, R. D. 1975. Acid rock in the Great·Smokies: unanticipated impact on aquatic biota of road construction in regions of sulfide mineralization. *Trans. Amer. Fish. Soc.* 104(4):677–684.

Huet, M. 1959. Profiles and biology of Western European streams as related to fish management. *Trans. Amer. Fish. Soc.* 88:155–163.

Hughes, G. M. 1963. *Comparative physiology of vertebrate respiration.* Cambridge: Harvard Univ. Press. 146 pp.

Hughes, G. M., and Grimstone, A. V. 1965. The fine structure of the secondary lamellae of the gills of *Gadus pollachius. Quart. J. Micro. Sci.* 106:343–353.

Hughes, T. P. 1994. Catastrophes, phase shifts, and large-scale degradation of a Caribbean coral reef. *Science* 265:1547–1551.

Humphries, P., Potter, I. C., and Loneragan, N. R. 1992. The fish community in the shallows of a temperate Australian estuary: relationships with the aquatic macrophyte Ruppia megacarpa and environmental variables. *Est., Coast. Shelf Sci.*34:325–346.

Hunter, J. R., and Mitchell, C. T. 1966. Association of fishes with flotsam in the offshore waters of Central America. *NOAA Fish. Bull.* 66(1):13–30.

Hyatt, K. D., and Stockner, J. G. 1985. Responses of sockeye salmon *(Oncorhynchus nerka)* to fertilization of British Columbia coastal lakes. *Can. J. Fish. Aquat. Sci.* 42:320–331.

Idler, D. R., and Bitners, I. 1959. Biochemical studies on sockeye salmon during spawning migration. V. Cholesterol, fat, protein and water in the body of the standard fish. *J. Fish. Res. Bd. Canada* 16:235–241.

Jampol, I. M., and Epstein, F. H. 1970. Sodium-potassium-activated adenosine triphosphatase and osmotic regulation by fishes. *Am. J. Physiol.* 218:607–611.

Janssen, R. G., and Randall, D. J. 1975. The effects of changes in pH and P_{co2} in blood and water on breathing in rainbow trout, *Salmo gairdneri. Resp. Physiol.* 25:235–245.

Janssens, P. A., and Cohen, P. P. 1966. Ornithine-urea cycle enzymes in the African lungfish, *Protopterus aethiopicus. Science* 152:358–359.

Janvier, P. 1981. The phylogeny of the Craniata, with particular reference to the significance of fossil "agnathans." *J. Vert. Paleont.* 1(2):121–159.

Jara, Z. 1957. On the morphology and function of the so-called palatal organ in the carp (*Cyprinus carpio* L.). *Preeglad Zoologiczny* 1:110–112.

Jarvik, E. 1977. The systematic position of acanthodian fishes. Pages 199–225 *in* S. M. Andrews, R. S. Miles, and A. D. Walker, eds. *Problems in vertebrate evolution.* Linn. Soc. Lond. Symp. 4.

Jayaram, K. C. 1974. Ecology and distribution of fresh-water fishes, amphibia, and reptiles. Pages 517–584 *in* M. S. Mani, ed. *Ecology and biogeography of India.* The Hague: W. Junk.

Jenkins, R. E., and Burkhead, M. M. 1994. *Freshwater fishes of Virginia.* Bethesda, Md.: Amer. Fish. Soc. 1079 pp.

Jenkins, R. E., Lachner, E. A., and Schwartz F. J. 1972. Fishes of the central Appalachian drainages: their distribution and dispersal. Pages 43–117 *in* P. C. Holt, ed. *The distribution history of the biota of the southern Appalachians.* Virg. Poly. Inst. Res. Div. Mono 4.

Jenkins, R. M. 1975. Black bass crops and species associations in reservoirs. Pages 114–124 *in* H. Clepper, ed. *Black bass biology and management.* Washington, D.C.: Sport Fishing Inst.

Jenkins, T. M. 1969. Social structure, position choice, and distribution of two trout species (*Salmo trutta* and *Salmo gairdneri*) resident in mountain streams. *Anim. Behav. Monogr.* 2(2):57–123.

Jensen, A. C. 1966. Life history of the spiny dogfish. *NOAA Fish. Bull.* 65(3):527–554.

Jessen, H. L. 1973. Interrelationships of actinopterygians and brachiopterygians: evidence from pectoral anatomy. Pages 227–232 *in* P. H. Greenwood, R. S. Miles, and C. Patterson, eds. *Interrelationships of fishes.* London: Academic Press.

Jobling, M. 1981. Temperature tolerance and the final preferendum: rapid methods for the assessment of optimum growth temperatures. *J. Fish. Biol.* 19:439–455.

Johannes, R. E., and Larkin, P. A. 1961.

Competition for food between redside shiners *(Richardsonius balteatus)* and rainbow trout *(Salmo gairdneri)* in two British Columbia lakes. *J. Fish. Res. Bd. Canada* 18(2): 203–220.

Johansen, K. 1968. Air-breathing fishes. *Sci. Amer.* 219:102–111.

Johansen, K., and Hanson, D. 1967. Hepatic vein sphincters in elasmobranchs and their significance in controlling hepatic blood flow. *J. Exp. Biol.* 46:195–203.

Johansen, K., and Hanson, D. 1968. Functional anatomy of the hearts of lungfishes and amphibians. *Am. Zool.* 8:191–210.

Johansen, K., Lenfant, C., Schmidt-Nielsen, K., and Peterson, J. A. 1968. Gas exchange and control of breathing in the electric eel, *Electrophorus electricus Z. Vergl. Physiol.* 61:137–163.

Johanson-Sjobeck, M., and Stevens, J. D. 1976. Hematological studies on the blue shark, *Prionace glauca* L. *J. Mar. Biol. Assn. U.K.* 55:237–240.

John, K. R. 1964. Survival of fish in intermittent streams of the Chiricahua mountains, Arizona. *Ecology* 45(1):112–119.

Johnson, A. G., and Horton, H. F. 1972. Length-weight relationship, food, habits, parasites, and sex and age determination in the ratfish, *Hydrolagus colliei. NOAA Fish. Bull.* 70(2):421–430.

Johnson, D. L., and Stein, R. A. 1979. *Response of fish to habitat structure in standing water.* N. Cent. Div. Amer. Fish. Soc. Spec. Publ. 6.

Johnson, D. S. 1967. Distributional patterns in Malayan freshwater fish. *Ecology* 48:722–730.

Johnson, L. 1976. Ecology of arctic populations of lake trout *(Salvelinus namaycush),* lake whitefish *(Coregonus clupeaformis),* arctic char *(S. alpinus),* and associated species in unexploited lakes of the Canadian northwest territories. *J. Fish. Res. Bd. Canada* 33(11):2459–2488.

Johnson, R. H., and Nelson, D. R. 1973. Agonistic display of the gray reef shark, *Carcharhinus menisorrah,* and its relationship to attacks on man. *Copeia* 1973(1):76–83.

Johnson, R. K., and Barnett, M. A. 1975. An inverse correlation between meristic charac-

ters and food supply in mid-water fishes: evidence and possible explanations. *NOAA Fish. Bull.* 73(2):284–298.

Johnson, R. K., and Glodek, G. S. 1975. Two new species of *Evermanella* from the Pacific Ocean, with notes on other midwater species endemic to the Pacific Central or the Pacific Equatorial water masses. *Copeia* 1975(4):715–730.

Johnston, J. A., Davison, W., and Goldpink, G. 1977. Energy metabolism of carp swimming muscles. *J. Comp. Physiol.* 114:203–216.

Jonas, R. E. E., Sehdev, H. S., and Tonlinson, N. 1962. Blood pH and mortality in rainbow trout *(Salmo gairdneri)* and sockeye salmon *(Oncorhynchus nerka). J. Fish. Res. Bd. Canada* 19(4):619–624.

Jones, E. C. 1971. *Isistius brasiliensis,* a squaloid shark, the probable cause of crater wounds on fishes and cetaceans. *NOAA Fish. Bull.* 69(4):791–798.

Jonsson, N., Jonsson, B., and Hansen, L. P. 1991. Energetic cost of spawning in male and female Atlantic salmon *(Salmo salar* L.). *J. Fish Biol.* 39:739–744.

Jordan, D. S. 1895. The fishes of Sinaloa. *Proc. Calif. Acad. Sci.* 5:378–513.

Jordan, D. S. 1922. *The days of a man.* Vols. I, II. New York: World Book Co. 1616 pp.

Jordan, D. S., and Evermann, B. W. 1900. *The fishes of North and Middle America.* Bull. U.S. Nat. Mus. 47, pts. I–IV. 3313 pp. + 392 plates.

Jordan, D. S., and Evermann, B. W. 1903. The aquatic resources of the Hawaiian Islands. *Bull. U.S. Fish. Comm.* 23:1–765.

Jordan, D. S., and Starks, E. C. 1895. The fishes of Puget Sound. *Proc. Calif. Acad. Sci.* 5:785–855.

Jordan, H. E., and Speidel, C. C. 1930. Blood formation in cyclostomes. *Am. J. Anat.* 46:355–392.

Jordan, J. 1976. The influence of body weight on gas exchange in the airbreathing fish *Clarius batrachus. Comp. Biochem. Physiol.* 53A:305–310.

Jumper, G. Y., Jr., and Baird, R. C. 1991. Location by olfaction: a model and application to the mating problem in the deep-sea hatchetfish *Argyropelecus hemigymnus. Amer. Nat.* 138: 1431–1458.

Kalmijn, A. J. 1971. The electric sense of sharks and rays. *J. Exp. Biol.* 55:371–383.

Kalmijn, A. J. 1974. The detection of electric fields from inanimate and animate sources other than electric organs. Pages 147–200 *in* A. Fessard, ed. *Handbook of sensory physiology.* Vol. 3(3). Berlin: Springer-Verlag.

Kalmijn, A. J. 1977. The electric and magnetic sense of sharks, skates, and rays. *Oceanus* 20:45–52.

Kalmijn, A. J. 1978a. Electric and magnetic sensory world of sharks, skates, and rays. Pages 507–528 *in* E. S. Hodgson and R. F. Mathewson, eds. *Sensory biology of sharks, skates, and rays.* Washington, D.C.: Off. Naval Res. Publ.

Kalmijn, A. J. 1978b. Experimental evidence of geomagnetic orientation in elasmobranch fishes. Pages 347–353 *in* K. Schmidt-Koenig and W. T. Keeton, eds. *Animal migration, navigation, and homing.* Berlin: Springer-Verlag.

Kamohara, R. H. 1964. Revised catalog of fishes of Kochi Prefecture, Japan. *U.S. A. Mar. Biol. Stat.* 11(1):1–99.

Kandel, J. S., Horn, M. H., and Van Antwerp, W. 1994. Volatile fatty acids in the hindguts of herbivorous fishes from temperate and tropical marine waters. *J. Fish Biol.* 45:527–529.

Kapoor, B. G., Evans, H. E., and Pevzner, R. A. 1975. The gustatory system in fish. *Adv. Mar. Biol.* 13:53–108.

Kapoor, B. G., Smit, H., and Verighina, I. A. 1975. The alimentary canal and digestion in teleosts. *Adv. Mar. Biol.* 13:109–239.

Kavaliers, M. 1979. Pineal involvement in the control of circadian rhythmicity in the lake chub, *Couesius plumbeus. J. Exp. Zool.* 209:33–40.

Karnaky, K. J., Jr. 1986. Structure and function of the chloride cell of *Fundulus heteroclitus* and other teleosts. *Amer. Zool.* 26:209–224.

Keast, A. 1965. Resource subdivision amongst cohabiting fish species in a bay, Lake Opinicon, Ontario. *Univ. of Mich. Great Lakes Res. Div. Publ.* 13:106–132.

Keast, A., and Webb, D. 1966. Mouth and body form relative to feeding ecology in the fish fauna of a small lake, Lake Opinicon, Ontario. *J. Fish Res. Bd. Canada* 23(12):1845–1874.

Kerstetter, T. H., and Kirschner, L. B. 1972. Active chloride transport by the gills of rainbow trout, *S. gairdneri. J. Exp. Biol.* 56:263–272.

Keys, A. B. 1933. The mechanism of adaptation to varying salinity in the common eel and the general problem of osmotic regulation in fishes. *Proc. Roy. Soc. London B.* 112:184–199.

Khanna, S. S., and Singh, H. R. 1966. Morphology of the teleostean brain in relation to feeding habits. *Proc. Nat. Acad. Sci. India* 336:306–316.

Kiceniuk, J. W., and Jones, D. R. 1977. The oxygen transport system in trout (*Salmo gairdneri*) during sustained exercise. *J. Exp. Biol.* 69: 247–260.

Kinne, O. 1960. Growth, food intake, and food conversion in a euryplastic fish exposed to different temperatures and salinities. *Physiol. Zool.* 33:288–317.

Kisch, B. 1948. Electrocardiographic investigation of the heart of fish. *Expl. Med. Surg.* 6:31–62.

Kingsford, M. J. 1993. Biotic and abiotic structure in the pelagic environment: importance to small fishes. *Bull. Marine Sci.* 53:393–415.

Klimley, A. P. 1985. Schooling in *Sphyrna lewini,* a species with low risk of predation: a non-egalitarian state. *Z. Tierpsychol.* 70:297–319.

Klimley, A. P. 1994. The predatory behavior of the white shark. *Amer. Sci.* 82:122–133.

Kline, K. 1978. *Aspects of digestion in stomachless fishes.* Ph.D. diss., Univ. of Calif., Davis. 78 pp.

Klontz, G. W. 1972. Haematological techniques and immune response in rainbow trout. Pages 89–99 *in* L. E. Mawdesley-Thomas, ed. *Diseases of fish.* Symp. Zool. Soc. Lond. No. 30. London: Academic Press.

Kobayashi, H. 1990. CO_2 back-diffusion in the rete aids O_2 secretion in the swimbladder of the eel. *Resp. Physiol.* 79:231–242.

Kobayashi, S., Yamada, J., Maekawa, K., and Ouchi, K. 1972. Calcification and nucleation in fish scales. Pages 84–90 *in* H. K. Erban, ed. *Biomineralization research reports.* Stuttgart: Schattauer-Verlag.

Kock, K.-H. 1992. *Antarctic fish and fisheries.* Cambridge, England: Cambridge Univ. Press.

Kozhov, M. 1963. *Lake Baikal and its life.* Monogr. Biologicae 11. The Hague: W. Junk. 344 pp.

Kramer, D. L., and Graham, J. B. 1976.

Synchronous air breathing, a social component of respiration in fishes. *Copeia* 1976: 689–697.

Kramer, D. L., and McClure M. 1982. Aquatic surface respiration, a widespread adaptation to hypoxia in tropical freshwater fishes. *Env. Biol. Fish.* 7:47–55.

Krebs, J. R., and Davies, N. B., eds. 1978. *Behavioural ecology, an evolutionary approach.* Oxford: Blackwell. 494 pp.

Krough, A. 1939. *Osmotic regulation in aquatic animals.* London: Cambridge Univ. Press.

Kropf, A. 1972. The structure and reactions of visual pigments. *In* M. G. F. Fuortes, ed. *Handbook of sensory physiology.* 7(2), Physiology of photoreceptor organs. Berlin: Springer-Verlag.

Kuchnow, K. P. 1971. The elasmobranch pupillary response. *Vision Res.* 11:1395–1406.

Kuehne, R. A. 1962. A classification of streams illustrated by fish distribution in an eastern Kentucky creek. *Ecology* 43(4):608–614.

Kuhn, W., Ramel, A., Kuhn, H. J., and Marti, E. 1963. The filling mechanism of the swimbladder, generation of high gas pressures through hairpin countercurrent multiplication. *Experientia* 19:497–511.

LaBounty, J. F., and Deacon, J. E. 1972. *Cyprinodon milleri,* a new species of pupfish (family Cyprinodontidae) from Death Valley, California. *Copeia* 1972(4):769–780.

Lagler, K. F., Bardach, J. E., Miller, R. R., and Passino, D. R. M. 1977. *Ichthyology.* 2d ed. New York: Wiley. 506 pp.

Lanzing, W. J. R., and Bower, C. C. 1974. Development of colour patterns in relation to behaviour in *Tilapia mossambica* (Peters). *J. Fish Biol.* 6:29–41.

Larimore, R. W., Childers, W. F., and Hekcrotte, C. 1959. Destruction and reestablishment of stream fish and invertebrates affected by drought. *Trans. Amer. Fish. Soc.* 88:261–285.

Lapennas, G. N., and Schmidt-Nielsen, K. 1977. Swimbladder permeability to oxygen. *J. Exp. Biol.* 67:175–196.

Larje, R. 1990. Rare fish in Sweden—*Nemacheilus* survey and public reactions. *J. Fish Biol.* 37 (Suppl. A):219–221.

Larkin, P. A. 1956. Interspecific competition and population control in freshwater fish. *J. Fish. Res. Bd. Canada* 13(2):327–342.

Larsen, R. J. 1980. Competition, habitat selection, and the bathymetric distribution of two rockfish *(Sebastes)* species. *Ecol. Monogr.* 50: 221–239.

Lasker, R. 1978. The relation between oceanographic conditions and larval anchovy food in the California current: identification of factors contributing to recruitment failure. *Rapp. P.-v. Reun. Const. Int. Explor. Mer.* 173:212–230.

Lauder, G. V. 1983. Prey capture hydrodynamics in fishes: experimental tests of two models. *J. Exp. Biol.* 104:1–13.

Lauder, G. V. 1985. Aquatic feeding in lower vertebrates. Pages 210–229. *in* M. Hildebrand, D. Bramble, K. Liem, and D. Wake, eds. *Functional vertebrate morphology.* Cambridge: Harvard Univ. Press.

Lauder, G. V., and Liem, K. F. 1983. The evolution and interrelationships of the actinopterygian fishes. *Bull. Mus. Comp. Zool., Harvard* 150: 95–197.

Laurent, P., Hobe, H., and Dunel-Erb, S. 1985. The role of environmental sodium chloride relative to calcium in gill morphology of freshwater salmonid fish. *Cell Tissue Res.* 240: 675–692.

Laurent, P., Holmgren, S., and Nilsson, S. 1983. Nervous and humoral control of the fish heart: structure and function. *Comp. Biochem. Physiol.* 76A:525–542.

Leary, R. F., and Booke, H. E. 1990. Starch gel electrophoresis and species distinctions. Pages 141–170 *in* C. B. Schreck and P. B. Moyle, eds. *Methods for fish biology.* Bethesda, Md.: Amer. Fish. Soc.

LeCren, E. D., Kipling, C., and McCormack, J. C. 1972. Windemere: effects of exploitation and eutrophication of the salmonid community. *J. Fish. Res. Bd. Canada* 29(6):819–832.

Lee, D. S., Gilbert, C. R., Hocutt, C. H., Jenkins, R. E., McCallister, D. E., and Stauffer, J. R. 1980. *Atlas of North American freshwater fishes.* Raleigh, N.C.: State Mus. Nat. Hist.

Lee, R. F., Phleger, C. F., and Horn, M. H. 1975. Composition of oil in fish bones: possible function in neutral buoyancy. *Comp. Biochem. Physiol.* 50B:13–16.

Lee, R. M. 1920. A review of the methods of age and growth determination in fishes by means of scales. *Fish. Invest.*, Ser. II. 4(2):1–32.

Leggett, W. C. 1977. The ecology of fish migrations. *Ann. Rev. Ecol. Syst.* 8:285–308.

Leggett, W. C., and Carscadden, J. E. 1978. Latitudinal variation in reproductive characteristics of American shad (*Alosa sapidissima*): evidence for population specific life history strategies in fish. *J. Fish. Res. Bd. Canada* 35: 1469–1478.

Leggett, W. C., and Whitney, R. R. 1972. Water temperature and the migrations of American shad. *NOAA Fish. Bull.* 170(3):659–670.

Leigh, E. G., Jr., Paine, R. T., Quinn, J. F., and Suchanek, T. H. 1987. Wave energy and intertidal productivity. *Proc. Nat. Acad. Sci. USA* 84:1314–1318.

Leivestad, H., and Muniz, I. P. 1976. Fish kill at low pH in a Norwegian river. *Nature* 259:391–392.

Lelek, A. 1973. Sequence of changes in fish populations of the new tropical man-made lake, Kainji, Nigeria, West Africa. *Arch. Hydrobiol.* 71:381–420.

Lemly, A. D. 1985. Suppression of native fish populations by green sunfish in first-order streams of piedmont North Carolina. *Trans. Amer. Fish. Soc.* 114:705–712.

Lewis, D. S. 1974. The effects of the formation of Lake Kainji, Nigeria, upon the indigenous fish population. *Hydrobiologica* 45(1–3): 281–301.

Lewis, S. M. 1986. The role of herbivorous fishes in the organization of a Caribbean reef community. *Ecol. Mono.* 56:183–200.

Li, W., Sorensen, P. W., and Gallaher, D. D. 1995. The olfactory system of migratory adult sea lamprey (*Petromyzon marinus*) is specifically and acutely sensitive to unique bile acids released by conspecific larvae. *J. Gen. Physiol.* (in press).

Liem, K. F. 1963. *The comparative osteology and phylogeny of the Anabantoidei (Teleostei, Pisces).* Ill. Biol. Monogr. 30. 149 pp.

Liem, K. F. 1974. Evolutionary strategies and morphological innovations: cichlid pharyngeal jaws. *Syst. Zool.* 22:425–441.

Liem, K. F. 1981. Larvae of air-breathing fishes as countercurrent flow devices in hypoxic environments. *Science* 211:1177–1179.

Lighthill, M. J. 1969. Hydromechanics of aquatic animal propulsion. *Ann. Rev. Fluid Mech.* 1:413–446.

Lin, H., and Randall, D. J. 1991. Evidence for the presence of an electrogenic proton pump on the trout gill epithelium. *J. Exp. Biol.* 161: 119–134.

Lindberg, G. U. 1971. *Fishes of the world.* New York: Wiley. 545 pp.

Lindsey, C. C., and McPhail, J. D. 1986. Zoogeography of fishes of the Yukon and Mackenzie basins. Pages 639–674 *in* C. H. Hocutt and E. O. Wiley, eds. *The zoogeography of North American freshwater fishes.* New York: Wiley.

Lineaweaver, T. H., and Backus, R. H. 1969. *The natural history of sharks.* New York: Lippincott. 256 pp.

Livingston, P. A. 1993. Importance of predation by groundfish, marine mammals and birds on walleye pollock *Theragra chalcogramma* and Pacific herring *Clupea pallasi* in the eastern Bering Sea. *Marine Ecol. Prog. Ser.* 102:205–215.

Livingston, R. J. 1976. Diurnal and seasonal fluctuations of organisms in a north Florida estuary. *Est., Coast. Mar. Sci.* 4(3):373–400.

Livingston, R. J., Kobylinski, G. J., Lewis, F. G., and Sheridan, P. F. 1975. Long-term fluctuations of epibenthic fish and invertebrate populations in Apalachicola Bay, Florida. *NOAA Fish. Bull.* 74(2):311–321.

Loew, E. R., and Lythgoe, J. N. 1978. The ecology of cone pigments in teleost fishes. *Vision Res.* 18:715–722.

Loftus, K. H., and Regier, H. A., eds. 1972. Symposium of salmonid communities in oligotrophic lakes. *J. Fish. Res. Bd. Canada* 29(6):613–986.

Longurst, A., Coldbrook, M., LeBasseur, R., Lorenzen, C., and Smith, P. 1972. The instability of ocean populations. *New Sci.* 1972:1–5.

Loos, J. L., and Woolcott, W. S. 1969.

Hybridization and behavior in two species of *Percina* (Percidae). *Copeia* 1969(2):374–385.

Loretz, C. A., Collie, N. L., Richman, N. H. III, and Bern, H. A. 1982. Osmoregulatory changes accompanying smoltification in coho salmon. *Aquaculture* 28:67–74.

Losey, G. S., Jr. 1978. The symbiotic behavior of fishes. Pages 1–31 *in* D. I. Mostofsky, ed. *The behavior of fish and other aquatic animals.* New York: Academic Press.

Lotrich, V. A. 1973. Growth, production, and community composition of fishes inhabiting a first-, second-, and third-order stream of eastern Kentucky. *Ecol. Monogr.* 43(3):377–397.

Love, K. P., and Matty, A. J. 1982. The effect of feeding 11-ketotestosterone on the food conversion efficiency and tissue protein and nucleic acid contents of juvenile carp, *Cyprinus carpio. J. Fish Biol.* 20:93–104.

Love, M. S., and Caillet, G. M. 1979. *Readings in ichthyology.* Santa Monica: Goodyear 525 pp.

Love, R. M. 1970. *The chemical biology of fishes.* London: Academic Press. 547 pp.

Lowe-McConnell, R. H. 1975. *Fish communities in tropical freshwaters.* London: Longman. 337 pp.

Lowe-McConnell, R. H. 1987. *Ecological studies in tropical fish communities.* Cambridge, England: Cambridge Univ. Press.

Ludwig, D., Hilborn, R., and Walters, C. 1993. Uncertainty, resource exploitation, and conservation: lessons from history. *Science* 260:17, 36.

Lugo, A. E., and Snedaker, S. C. 1974. The ecology of mangroves. *Ann. Rev. Ecol. Syst.* 5:39–64.

Lundberg, J. G., and McDade, L. A. 1990. Systematics. Pages 65–108 *in* C. B. Schreck and P. B. Moyle, eds. *Methods for fish biology.* Bethesda, Md.: American Fisheries Soc.

Lurie, E. 1960. *Louis Agassiz: a life in science.* Chicago: Univ. of Chicago Press. 390 pp.

Lythgoe, J., and Lythgoe, G. 1971. *Fishes of the sea.* New York: Doubleday. 320 pp.

MacGintie, G. E. 1939. The natural history of the blind goby (*Typhlogobius californiensis* Steindachner). *Amer. Midl. Nat.* 21:489–508.

Madsen, S. S. 1990. The role of cortisol and growth hormone in seawater adaptation and development of hypoosmoregulatory mechanisms in sea trout parr *(Salmo trutta trutta). Gen. Comp. Endocr.* 79:1–11.

Maetz, J. 1974. Origine de la différence de potentiel électrique transbranchiale chez le poisson rouge *Carassius aurâtus.* Importance de l'ion Ca. *C. R. Hebd. Siance Acad. Sci. Paris.* 279:1277–1280.

Maetz, J., and Garcia Romeu, F. 1964. The mechanism of sodium and chloride uptake by the gills of a freshwater fish, *Carassius auratus.* II. Evidence of NH_4^+/Na^+ and HCO_3^-/CL^- exchanges. *J. Gen. Physiol.* 50:391–422.

Maetz, J., Sawyer, W. H., Dickford, G. E., and Mayer, N. 1967. Évolution de la balance minérale du sodium chez *Fundulus heteroclitus* au cours du transfert d'eau de mer en eau douce: effets de l'hypophysectomie et de la prolactine. *Gen. Comp. Endocrinol.* 8:163–176.

Maitland, P. S., and Lyle, A. A. 1990. Practical conservation of British fishes: current action on six declining species. *J. Fish Biol. (Suppl. A)*:255–256.

Major, P. F. 1978. Predator-prey interaction in two schooling fishes, *Caranx ignobilis* and *Stolephorus purpureus. Anim. Behav.* 26:760–777.

Mallatt, J. 1982. Pumping rates and particle retention efficiencies of the larval lamprey, an unusual suspension feeder. *Biol. Bull.* 163:197–210.

Mallatt, J. 1984. Feeding ecology of the earliest vertebrates. *Zool. J. Linn. Soc.* 82:261–272.

Mansueti, R. J. 1961. Effects of civilization on striped bass and other estuarine biota in Chesapeake Bay and tributaries. *Proc. Gulf. Carib. Fish. Inst.* 14:110–136.

Manwell, C. 1958. On the evolution of hemoglobin of the California hagfish, *Polistotrema stouti. Biol. Bull.* 115:227–238.

Manwell, C., Baker, C. M. A., and Childers, W. 1963. The genetics of hemoglobin in hybrid. I. A molecular basis for hybrid vigor. *Comp. Biochem. Physiol.* 10:103–120.

Markert, J. R., Higgs, D. A., Dye, H. M., and MacQuarrie, D. W. 1977. Influence of bovine growth hormone on growth rate, appetite, and food conversion of yearling coho salmon

(Oncorhynchus kisutch) fed two diets of different composition. *Can. J. Zool.* 55:74–83.

Markle, D. F. 1989. Aspects of the character homology and phylogeny of the Gadiformes. *Los Angeles Co. Mus. Nat. Hist. Sci. Ser.* 32:59–88.

Markle, D. F., and Musick, J. A. 1974. Benthic-slope fishes found at 900 m depth along a transect in the western North Atlantic ocean. *Mar. Biol.* 16:225–233.

Marshall, N. B. 1953. Egg size in arctic, antarctic, and deep-sea fishes. *Evolution* 7:328–341.

Marshall, N. B. 1954. Aspects of deepsea biology. London: Hutchinson's. 380 pp.

Marshall, N. B. 1960. Swimbladder structure of deep-sea fishes in relation to their systematics and biology. *Discovery Rept.* 31:1–122.

Marshall, N. B. 1962. Some convergences between the benthic fishes of polar seas. Pages 273–278 *in* R. Carrick, M. W. Holdgate, and J. Prost, eds. *Symposium on Antarctic biology.* Paris: Hermann.

Marshall, N. B. 1966. *The life of fishes.* New York: Universe Books. 402 pp.

Marshall, N. B. 1971. *Explorations in the life of fishes.* Cambridge: Harvard Univ. Press. 204 pp.

Marshall, N. B. 1979. *Developments in deep-sea biology.* Dorset: Blandford Press.

Marshall, N. B. 1984. Progenetic tendencies in deep-sea fishes. Pages 91–101. *in* G. W. Potts and R. J. Wooton, eds. *Fish reproduction: strategies and tactics.* New York: Academic Press.

Martin, L. K., and Cailliet, G. M. 1983. Age and growth determination of the bat ray, *Myliobatis californica* Gill, in central California. *Copeia* 1983:762–773.

Mattsoff, L., and Nikinmaa, M. 1988. Effects of external acidification on the blood acid-base status and ion concentrations of lamprey. *J. Exp. Biol.* 136:351–361.

Matthews, W. J., and Heins, D. C. 1987. *Community and evolutionary ecology of North American stream fishes.* Norman: Univ. of Okla. Press.

Matthews, W. J., Hough, D. J., and Robison, H. W. 1992. Similarities in fish distribution and water quality patterns in streams of Arkansas: congruence of multivariate analysis. *Copeia* 1992:296–305.

Mattisson, A., and Fänge, R. 1982. The cellular structure of the Leidig organ in the shark *Etmopterus spinax* (L.). *Biol. Bull.* 62:182–194.

Matty, A. J. 1985. *Fish endocrinology.* Portland, Ore.: Timber Press. 267 pp.

Matty, A. J. 1986. Nutrition, hormones, and growth. *Fish Physiol. Biochem.* 2:141–150.

Matty, A. J., and Cheema, I. R. 1978. The effect of some steroid hormones on the growth and protein metabolism of rainbow trout. *Aquaculture.* 14:163–178.

Mauchline, J., and Gordon, J. D. M. 1986. Foraging strategies of deep-sea fish. *Mar. Ecol. Prog. Ser.* 27:227–238.

Mayden, R. L. 1991. Cyprinids of the New World. Pages 240–263 *in* I. J. Winfield and J. S. Nelson, eds. *Cyprinid fishes: systematics, biology and exploitation.* New York: Chapman and Hall.

Mayden, R. L., ed. 1992. *Systematics, historical ecology, and North American freshwater fishes.* Stanford, Calif.: Stanford Univ. Press. 969 pp.

Mayden, R. L. 1992. Explorations of the past and the dawn of systematics and historical ecology. Pages 3–17 *in* R. L. Mayden, ed. *Systematics, historical ecology, and North American freshwater fishes.* Stanford, Calif.: Stanford Univ. Press.

Mayden, R. L., and Wiley, E. O. 1992. The fundamentals of phylogenetic systematics. Pages 114–185 *in* R. L. Mayden, ed. *Systematics, historical ecology, and North American freshwater fishes.* Stanford, Calif.: Stanford Univ. Press.

Mayr, E. 1963. *Animal species and evolution.* Cambridge, Mass.: Belknap Press. 797 pp.

Mazeaud, M., Mazeaud, R., and Donaldson, E. M. 1977. Primary and secondary effects of stress in fish. Some new data with a general review. *Trans. Amer. Fish. Soc.* 106:201–212.

Mazumder, A., Taylor, W. D., McQueen, D. J., and Lean, D. R. S. 1990. Effects of fish and plankton on lake temperature and mixing depth. *Science* 247:312–315.

McAllister, D. E. 1963. *A revision of the smelt family, Osmeridae.* Bull. Nat. Mus. Canada 91. 53 pp.

McAllister, D. E. 1977. Ecology of the marine fishes of arctic Canada. Pages 49–65 *in* Section II. *Marine ecology.* Ottawa: Proc. Circumpolar Conf. on Northern Ecology.

McCormick, S. D. 1990. Cortisol directly stimulates differentiation of chloride cells in tilapia opercular membrane. *Am. J. Physiol.* 259:R857–R863.

McCosker, J. 1977. Fright posture of the plesiopid fish *Calloplesiops altivelis:* an example of Batesian mimicry. *Science:* 197:400–401.

McCosker, J. E. 1979. Inferred natural history of the living coelacanth. *Occ. Pap. Calif. Acad. Sci.* 134:17–24.

McCosker, J. E., and Lagios, M. D., eds. 1979. The biology and physiology of the living coelacanth. *Occ. Pap. Calif. Acad. Sci.* 134. 175 pp.

McDowall, R. M. 1978. *New Zealand freshwater fishes.* Auckland, N.Z.: Heinemann.

McDowall, R. M. 1988. *Diadromy in fishes.* London: Croom Helm. 308 pp.

McDowall, R. M., and Robertson, D. A. 1975. Occurrence of galaxiid larvae and juveniles in the sea. *N. Z. J. Mar., Freshw Res.* 9(1):1–9.

McElman, J. F., and Balon, E. K. 1979. Early ontogeny of walleye, *Stizotedion vitreum,* with steps of saltatory development. *Env. Biol. Fish* 4:309–348.

McErlean, A. J., O'Connar, S. G., Mihursky, J. A., and Gibson, C. J. 1973. Abundance, diversity, and seasonal patterns of estuarine fish populations. *Est. Coast. Mar. Sci.* 1(1):19–36.

McFarland, W. N., and Munz, F. W. 1965. Regulation of body weight and serum composition by hagfish in various media. *Comp. Biochem. Physiol.* 14:383–398.

McGowan, J. A. 1974. The nature of oceanic ecosystems. Pages 9–28 *in* C. B. Miller, ed. *The biology of the oceanic Pacific.* Corvallis: Oregon St. Univ. Press.

McHugh, J. L. 1967. Estuarine nekton. Pages 581–620 *in* G. H. Lauff, ed. *Estuaries.* AAAS Publ. 83.

McKaye, K. R. 1977. Defense of a predator's young by herbivorous fish: an unusual strategy. *Amer. Nat.* 11(978):310–315.

McKaye, K. R. 1985. Cichlid-catfish mutualistic defense of young in Lake Malawi. *Oecologia* 66:358–363.

McKaye, K. R., and Barlow, G. W. 1976. Chemical recognition of young by the Midas cichlid, *Cichlasoma citrinellum. Copeia* 1976(2):276–282.

McKaye, K. R., and Kocher, T. 1983. Head-ramming behavior by three paedophageous cichlids in Lake Malawi, Africa. *Anim. Behav.* 31:206–210.

McKeown, B. A. 1984. *Fish migration.* London: Croom Helm. 224 pp.

McLaughlin, R. H., and O'Gower, A. K. 1971. Life history and underwater studies of a heterodont shark. *Ecol. Monogr.* 41:271–289.

McPhail, J. D. 1977a. A possible function of the caudal spot in characid fishes. *Can. J. Zool.* 55(7):1063–1066.

McPhail, J. D. 1977b. Sons and lovers: the functional significance of sexual dichromatism in a fish, *Neoheterandria tridentiger* (Garman). *Behaviour* 64:329–339.

McPhail, J. D., and Lindsey, C. C. 1970. *Freshwater fishes of northwestern Canada and Alaska.* Fish. Res. Bd. Canada Bull. 173. 379 pp.

McQueen, D. J. 1990. Manipulating lake community structure: where do we go from here? *Freshw. Biol.* 23:613–620.

Mead, G. W., Bertelsen, E., and Cohen, D. M. 1964. Reproduction among deep-sea fishes. *Deep-sea Res.* 11(4):569–596.

Meade, I. L., and Perrone, S. J. 1980. Selective haematological parameters in steelhead trout, *Salmo gairdneri* Richardson. *J. Fish. Biol.* 17:9–12.

Mearns, A. J. 1973. Southern California's inshore demersal fishes: diversity, distribution, and disease as responses to environmental quality. *CalCOFI Rpt.* 17:141–148.

Mearns, A. J., and Smith, L. 1975. Benthic oceanography and the distribution of bottom fish off Los Angeles. *CalCOFI Rpt.* 18:118–124.

Meffe, G. K., and Carroll, C. R. 1994. *Principles of conservation biology.* Sunderland, Mass.: Sinauer Associates. 600 pp.

Meffe, G. K., and Snelson, F. F., Jr., eds. 1989. *Ecology and evolution of livebearing fishes (Poeciliidae).* Englewood Cliffs, N.J.: Prentice-Hall. 453 pp.

Mendelson, J. 1975. Feeding relationships among species of *Notropis* (Pisces: Cyprinidae) in a Wisconsin stream. *Ecol. Monogr.* 45(3): 199–230.

Meng, L., Moyle, P. B., and Herbold, B. 1994. Changes in abundance and distribution of native and introduced fishes of Suisun Marsh. *Trans. Amer. Fish. Soc.* 123:498–507.

Menon, A. G. K. 1973. Origin of the freshwater fish fauna of India. *Curr. Sci.* 42(16):553–556.

Menzies, R. J., George, R. Y., and Rowe, G. T. 1973. Abyssal environment and ecology of the world oceans. New York: Wiley. 488 pp.

Meyer, J. L., Schultz, E. T., and Helfman, G. S. 1983. Fish schools: an asset to corals. *Science* 220:1047–1049.

Mihursky, J. A., and Kennedy, V. S. 1967. Water temperature criteria to protect aquatic life. Pages 20–32 *in* E. L. Cooper, ed. *A symposium on water quality criteria to protect aquatic life.* Amer. Fish. Soc. Spec. Publ. 4.

Miller, D. J., and Lea, R. N. 1972. *Guide to the coastal marine fishes of California.* Calif. Dept. Fish, Game Fish Bull. 157. 249 pp.

Miller, R. G. 1951. *The natural history of Tahoe fishes.* Ph.D. diss., Stanford University. 160 pp.

Miller, R. J. 1964. Behavior and ecology of some North American cyprinid fishes. *Amer. Midl. Nat.* 72(2):313–357.

Miller, R. J., and Evans, H. E. 1965. External morphology of the brain and lips in catostomid fishes. *Copeia* (4):467–487.

Miller, R. R. 1948. The cyprinodont fishes of the Death Valley System of eastern California and southwestern Nevada. *Mus. Vert. Zool., U. of Mich. Misc. Publ.* 68:1–155.

Miller, R. R. 1958. Origin and affinities of the freshwater fish fauna of western North America. Pages 187–222 *in* C. L. Hubbs, ed. *Zoogeography.* Washington, D.C.: AAAS.

Miller, R. R. 1966. Geographical distribution of Central America freshwater fishes. *Copeia* 1966(4):773–802.

Miller, R. R., and Smith, M. L. 1986. Origin and geography of the fishes of central Mexico. Pages 487–518 *in* C. H. Hocutt and E. O. Wiley, eds. *The zoogeography of North American fishes.* New York: Wiley.

Miller, R. R., Williams, J. D., and Williams, J. E. 1989. Extinctions of North American fishes during the past century. *Fisheries* 14:22–38.

Millikin, M. R. 1982. Qualitative and quantitative nutrient requirements of fishes: a review. *Fish. Bull.* 80:655–686.

Milinski, M. 1985. Risks of predation of parasitized sticklebacks *(Gasterosteus aculeatus)* under competition for food. *Behaviour* 93:203–216.

Milne, R. S., and Randall, D. J. 1976. Regulation of arterial pH during fresh water to sea water transfer in the rainbow trout *Salmo gairdneri. Comp. Biochem. Physiol.* 53A:157–160.

Minckley, W. K., and Deacon, J. 1968. Southwestern fishes and the enigma of "endangered species." *Science* 159:1424–1431.

Minckley, W. L., and Deacon, J. E. eds. 1991. *Battle against extinction: native fish management in the American West.* Tucson: Univ. Ariz. Press. 517 pp.

Minckley, W. L., Henrickson, D. A., and Bond, C. E. 1986. Geography of western North American freshwater fishes: description and relationships to intercontinental tectonism. Pages 519–614 *in* C. H. Hocutt and E. O. Wiley, eds. *The zoogeography of North American freshwater fishes.* New York: Wiley.

Mittlebach, G. G. 1984. Predation and resource partitioning in two sunfishes (Centrarchidae). *Ecology* 65:499–513.

Modde, T., and Ross, S. T. 1980. Seasonality of fishes occupying a surf zone habitat in the northern Gulf of Mexico. *NOAA Fish. Bull.* 78:911–922.

Moller, H. 1984. Reduction of a larval herring population by jellyfish predator. *Science* 224:621–622.

Mommsen, T. P., and Walsh, P. J. 1991. Urea synthesis in fishes: evolutionary and biochemical perspectives. Pages 137–163 *in* P. W. Hochachka and T. P. Mommsen, eds. *Biochemistry and molecular biology of fishes, Vol 1.* New York: Elsevier.

Montgomery, J. C., and MacDonald, J. A. 1987. Sensory tuning of lateral line receptors in antarctic fish to the movements of planktonic prey. *Science* 235:195–196.

Moodie, G. E. E., and Reimchen, T. E. 1976. Phenetic variation and habitat differences in *Gasterosteus* populations of the Queen Charlotte Islands. *Syst. Zool.* 25:49–61.

Morgan, M. D., Threlkeld, S. T., and Goldman, C. R. 1978. Impact of the introduction of kokanee (*Oncorhynchus nerka*) and opossum shrimp (*Mysis relicta*) on a subalpine lake. *J. Fish. Res. Bd. Canada* 35:1572–1579.

Morin, J. A., Harrington, A., Nealson, K., Krieger, N., Baldwin, T., and Hastings, J. 1975. Light for all reasons: versatility in the behavioral repertoire of the flashlight fish. *Science* 190: 74–76.

Morse, D. H. 1977. Feeding behavior and predator avoidance in heterospecific groups. *Biosci.* 27(5):332–339.

Moseley, F. N., and Copeland, B. J. 1969. A portable dropnet for representative sampling of nekton. *Contrib. Marine Sci. Univ. Texas* 14: 37–45.

Moss, S. A. 1984. Sharks: an introduction for the amateur naturalist. Englewood Cliffs, N.J.: Prentice-Hall, Inc. 246 pp.

Motta, P. J. 1985. Functional morphology of the head of Hawaiian and mid-Pacific butterfly-fishes (Perciformes, Chaetodontidae). *Env. Biol. Fish.* 13:253–276.

Moyle, J. B. 1956. Relationships between the chemistry of Minnesota surface waters and wildlife management. *J. Wildl. Mgmt.* 20(3): 303–320.

Moyle, J. B., and Clothier, W. D. 1959. Effects of management and winter oxygen levels on the fish population of a prairie lake. *Trans. Amer. Fish. Soc.* 88:178–185.

Moyle, P. B. 1969. *Ecology of the fishes of a Minnesota lake, with special reference to the Cyprinidae.* Ph.D. diss., Univ. of Minn., Minneapolis. 169 pp.

Moyle, P. B. 1973. Ecological segregation among three species of minnows (Cyprinidae) in a Minnesota lake. *Trans. Amer. Fish. Soc.* 102(4): 794–805.

Moyle, P. B. 1976a. *Inland fishes of California.* Berkeley: Univ. of Calif. Press. 405 pp.

Moyle, P. B. 1976b. Some effects of channelization on the fishes and invertebrates of Rush Creek, Modoc County, California. *Calif. Fish, Game* 62(3):179–186.

Moyle, P. B. 1977. In defense of sculpins. *Fisheries* 2(1):20–23.

Moyle, P. B. 1986. Fish introductions into North America: patterns and ecological impact.

Pages 27–43 *in* H. A. Mooney and J. A. Drake, eds. *Ecology of biological invasions of North America and Hawaii.* New York: Springer-Verlag.

Moyle, P. B., Daniels, R. A., Herbold, B., and Baltz, D. M. 1985. Patterns in distribution and abundance of a noncoevolved assemblage of estuarine fishes in California. *Fish. Bull.* 84: 105–117.

Moyle, P. B., and Herbold, B. 1987. Life history patterns and community structure in stream fishes of western North America: comparisons with eastern North America and Europe. Pages 25–32 *in* W. J. Matthews and D. C. Heins, eds. *Community and evolutionary ecology of North American stream fishes.* Norman: Univ. of Okla. Press.

Moyle, P. B., and Leidy, R. A. 1992. Loss of biodiversity in aquatic systems: evidence from fish faunas. Pages 128–169 *in* P. L. Fiedler and S. K. Jain, eds. *Conservation Biology.* New York: Chapman and Hall. 507 pp.

Moyle, P. B., and Li, H. W. 1979. Community ecology and predator-prey relationships in warmwater streams. Pages 171–180 *in* H. Clepper, ed. *Predator-prey systems in fisheries management.* Washington, D.C.: Sport Fish. Inst.

Moyle, P. B., Li, H. W., and Barton, B. 1987. The Frankenstein effect: impact of introduced fishes on native fishes of North America. Pages 415–426 *in* R. H. Stroud, ed. *The role of fish culture in fisheries management.* Bethesda, Md.: Amer. Fish. Soc.

Moyle, P. B., and Moyle, M. A. 1991. Introduction to fish imagery in art. *Env. Biol. Fish.* 31:5–23.

Moyle, P. B., and Moyle, P. R. 1995. Endangered fishes and economics: intergenerational obligations. *Env. Biol. Fish.* 42.

Moyle, P. B., and Nichols, R. 1973. Ecology of some native and introduced fishes of the Sierra-Nevada foothills in central California. *Copeia* 1073(3):478–490.

Moyle, P. B., and Nichols, R. 1974. Decline of the native fish fauna of the Sierra-Nevada foothills in central California. *Amer. Midl. Nat.* 92(1):72–83.

Moyle, P. B., and Senanayake, F. R. 1984. Resource

partitioning among the fishes of rainforest streams in Sri Lanka. *J. Zool. Lond.* 202:195–223.

Moyle, P. B., and Vondracek, B. 1985. Persistence and structure of the fish assemblage in a small California stream. *Ecology* 66:1–13.

Moy-Thomas, J., and Miles, W. S. 1971. *Paleozoic fishes.* New York: J. Saunders. London: Associated Book Publishers Ltd. 259 pp.

Muir, B. S., and Kendall, J. I. 1968. Structural modifications in the gills of tunas and other oceanic fishes. *Copeia* 1968 (2)388–398.

Muntz, W. R. A. 1976. On yellow lenses in mesopelagic animals. *J. Mar. Biol. Ass. U.K.* 56:963–976.

Munz, F. W. 1971. Vision: visual pigments. Pages 1–32 *in* W. S. Hoar and D. J. Randall, eds. *Fish physiology.* Vol. 5. New York: Academic Press.

Munz, F. W., and McFarland, W. 1964. Regulatory function of a primitive vertebrate kidney. *Comp. Biochem. Physiol.* 13:381–400.

Murdaugh, H. V., and Robin, E. D. 1967. Acid-base metabolism in the dogfish sharks. Pages 249–264 *in* P. W. Gilbert, R. F. Mathewson, and D. P. Rall, eds. *Sharks, skates, and rays.* Baltimore, Md.: Johns Hopkins Press.

Murphy, G. I. 1966. Population biology of the Pacific sardine (*Sardinops caerulea*). *Proc. Calif. Acad. Sci.* 34(1):1–84.

Murphy, G. I. 1968. Pattern in life history and the environment. *Amer. Nat.* 102:390–404.

Murphy, G. I. 1977. Clupeoids. Pages 283–308 *in* J. A. Gulland, ed. *Fish population dynamics.* New York: Wiley.

Murray, R. W. 1960. The response of the ampullae of Lorenzini of elasmobranchs to mechanical stimulation. *J. Exp. Biol.* 37:417–424.

Musick, J. A., Bruton, M. N., and Balon, E. K., eds. 1991. The biology of *Latimeria chalumnae* and evolution of coelacanths. *Env. Biol. Fish* 32: 436 pp.

Muus, B. J. 1967. *Freshwater fish of Britain and Europe.* London: Collins. 222 pp.

Muus, B. J., and P. Dahlstrom. 1974. *Collins guide to the sea fishes of Britain and North-western Europe.* London: Collins.

Myers, G. S. 1938. Fresh-water fishes and West Indian Zoogeography. *Smithson. Rpt.* 1937: 339–364.

Myers, G. S. 1951. Fresh-water fishes and East Indian zoogeography. *Stanf. Ichthy. Bull.* 4(1):11–21.

Myers, G. S. 1960. The endemic fauna of Lake Lanao and the evolution of higher taxonomic categories. *Evolution* 14:323–333.

Myers, G. S. 1964. A brief sketch of the history of ichthyology in America to the year 1850. *Copeia* 1964(1):33–41.

Myrberg, A. A., Jr. 1978. Underwater sound—its effect on the behavior of sharks. Pages 391–417 *in* E. S. Hodgson and R. F. Mathewson, eds. *Sensory biology of sharks, skates, and rays.* Washington, D.C.: Off. Naval Res. Publ.

Nafpaktitis, B. G. 1978. Systematics and distribution of lanternfishes of the genera *Lobianchia* and *Diaphus* (Myctophidae) in the Indian Ocean. *Los. Ang. Co. Nat. Hist. Mus. Sci. Bull.* 30:1–92.

Naiman, R. J. 1976. Productivity of a herbivorous pupfish population (*Cyprinodon nevadensis*) in a warm desert stream. *J. Fish Biol.* 9:125–137.

Naiman, R. J., and Soltz, D. L. 1981. *Fishes in North American deserts.* New York: Wiley.

Nakamura, H. 1969. *Tuna distribution and migration.* London: Fishing News Books. 76 pp.

Nakamura, R. 1976. Experimental assessment of factors influencing microhabitat selection by the two tidepool fishes *Oligocottus masculosus* and *O. snyderi. Marine Biol.* 37:97–104.

Nakano, T., and Tomlinson, N. 1967. Catecholamine and carbohydrate concentrations in rainbow trout (*Salmo gairdneri*) in relation to physical disturbance. *J. Fish. Res. Bd. Canada* 24:1701–1715.

Nakatsuru, K., and Kramer, D. L. 1982. Is sperm cheap? Limited male fertility and female choice in the lemon tetra (Pisces, Characidae). *Science* 216:753–755.

Neill, W. H., Chang, R. K. C., and Dizon, A. E. 1976. Magnitude and ecological implications of thermal inertia in skipjack tuna, *Katsuwonus pelamis* (Linnaeus). *Env. Biol. Fish* 1:61–80.

Neill, W. H., and Magnuson, J. J. 1974. Distributional ecology and behavioral thermoregulation of fishes in relation to heated effluent from a power plant at Lake Monona, Wisconsin. *Trans. Am. Fish. Soc.* 103:663–710.

Neill, W. H., Magnuson, J. J., and Chipman, G. G. 1972. Behavioral thermoregulation by fishes: a new experimental approach. *Science* 176: 1443–1455.

Nekvasil, N. P. and Olson, K. R. 1986a. Plasma clearance, metabolism, and tissue accumulation of ³H-labelled catecholamines in trout. *Am. J. Physiol.* 259:R519–R525.

Nekvasil, N. P. and Olson, K. R. 1986b. Extraction and metabolism of circulating catecholamines in the trout gill. *Am. J. Physiol.* 259: R526–R531.

Nelson, D. R., Johnson, R. R., McKibben, J. N., and Pittenger, G. G. 1986. Agonistic attacks on divers and submersibles by gray reef sharks, *Carcharhinus amblyrhynchos:* antipredatory or competitive. *Bull. Marine Sci.* 38:68–88.

Nelson, G. J. 1975. Anatomy of the male urogenital organs of *Goodea atripinnis* and *Characodon lateralis* (Atheriniformes, Cyprinodontoidei) and *G. atripinnis* courtship. *Copeia* 1975(3): 475–482.

Nelson, J. S. 1968. Hybridization and isolating mechanisms between *Catostomus commersoni* and *C. macrocheilus* (Pisces, Catostomidae). *J. Fish. Res. Bd. Canada* 25:101–150.

Nelson, J. S. 1984. *Fishes of the world.* 2nd ed. New York: Wiley-Interscience. 521 pp.

Nelson, J. S. 1994. *Fishes of the world.* 3rd ed. New York: John Wiley and Sons. 600 pp.

Neverman, D., and Wurtsbaugh, W. A. 1994. The thermoregulatory function of diel vertical migration for a juvenile fish, *Cottus extensus. Oecologia* 98:247–256.

Neville, C. M. 1979. Sublethal effects of environmental acidification on rainbow trout *(Salmo gairdneri). J. Fish. Res. Bd. Canada* 36:84–87.

Nichols, J. T. 1943. *The fresh-water fishes of China.* New York: Amer. Mus. Nat. Hist. 322 pp.

Nicol, J. A. C., and Zyznar, E. S. 1973. The tapetum lucidum in the eye of the big-eye, *Priacanthus arenatus* Cuvier. *J. Fish Biol.* 5:519–522.

Nielson, J. G. 1977. The deepest-living fish, *Abyssobrotula galatheae,* a new genus and species of oviparous ophidioids (Pisces, Brotulidae). *Galathea Rpt.* 14:41–48.

Nikinmaa, M. 1986. Control of red cell pH in teleost fishes. *Ann. Zool. Fennica* 23:223–235.

Nikinmaa, M., Cech, J. J., Jr., and McEnroe, M. 1984. Blood oxygen transport in stressed striped bass (*Morone saxatilis*): role of beta-adrenergic response. *J. Comp. Physiol. B* 154: 365–369.

Nikolsky, G. V. 1937. On the distribution of fishes according to the nature of their food in rivers flowing from the mountains of Asia. *Verh. Int. Verein. Theor. Angew. Limnol.* 8(2):169–176.

Nikolsky, G. V. 1954. *Special ichthyology.* Jerusalem (1961): Israel Prog. Sci. Trans. 538 pp.

Nilsson, N. A. 1963. Interaction between trout and char in Scandinavia. *Trans. Amer. Fish. Soc.* 92(3):276–285.

Nilsson, N. A. 1967. Interactive segregation between fish species. Pages 295–313 *in* S. D. Gerking, ed. *The biological basis of freshwater fish production.* New York: Wiley.

Nilsson, S., and Grove, D. J. 1974. Adrenergic and cholinergic innervation of the spleen of the cod *Gadus morhua, Eur. J. Pharmac.* 28:135–143.

Nixon, S. W., and Oviatt, C. A. 1973. Ecology of a New England salt marsh. *Ecol. Monogr.* 43(4): 463–498.

Nonnotte, G. 1981. Cutaneous respiration in six freshwater teleosts. *Comp. Biochem. Physiol.* 70A:541–543.

Norgaard, R. B. 1994. Ecology, politics, and economics: finding the common ground for decision making in economics. Pages 439–465 *in* G. K. Meffe and C. R. Carroll, eds. *Principles of conservation biology.* Sunderland, Mass.: Sinauer Associates.

Norse, E. A. 1993. *Global marine biological diversity: a strategy for building conservation into decision making.* Washington, D.C.: Island Press. 383 pp.

Northcote, T. G., ed. 1969. *Symposium on salmon and trout in streams.* H. R. MacMillan lectures in fisheries. Vancouver: Univ. of B. C.

Northcutt, R. G. 1978. Brain organization in the cartilaginous fishes. Pages 117–193 *in* E. S. Hodgson and R. F. Mathewson, eds. *Sensory biology of sharks, skates, and rays.* Washington, D.C.: Off. Naval Res. Publ.

Novacek, M. J., and Marshall, L. G. 1976. Early

biogeographic history of the ostariophysan fishes. *Copeia* 1976(1):1–12.

Nshombo, M. 1994. Foraging behavior of the scale-eater *Plecodus straeleni* (Cichlidae, Teleostei) in Lake Tanganyika, Africa. *Env. Bio. Fish.* 39:59–67.

Nursall, J. R. 1981. Behavior and habitat affecting the distribution of five species of sympatric mudskippers in Queensland. *Bull. Mar. Sci.* 31:730–735.

O'Day, W. T. 1974. Bacterial luminescence in the deepsea fish *Oneirodes acanthias* Gilbert (1915). *Los Ang. Nat. Hist. Mus. Contr. in Sci.* 255:1–12.

Odum, W. E. 1970. Insidious alteration of the estuarine environment. *Trans. Amer. Fish. Soc.* 99(4):836–847.

Oguri, M. 1964. Rectal glands of marine and freshwater sharks: comparative histology. *Science* 144:1151–1152.

Ohno, S. 1974. Protochordata, Cyclostomata, and Pisces. Pages 1–91 *in* B. John, ed. *Animal cytogenetics*. Vol. 4. Berlin: Bortraeger.

Olsen, P. E., and McCune, A. R. 1991. Morphology of the *Semionotus elegans* species group from the early Jurassic part of the Newark supergroup of eastern North America with comments on the family Semionotidae (Neopterygii). *J. Vert. Paleo.* 11.269–292.

Orvig, T., ed. 1968. *Current problems of lower vertebrate phylogeny.* New York: Wiley-Interscience. 539 pp.

Otsu, T., and Uchida, R. N. 1963. Model of the migration of albacore in the North Pacific Ocean. *NOAA Fish. Bull.* 63:33–44.

Ottaway, E. M., and Simkiss, K. 1977. "Instantaneous" growth rates of fish scales and their use in studies of fish populations. *J. Zool.* (London) 181:407–419.

Oviatt, C. A., Gall, A. L., and Nixon, S. W. 1972. Environmental effects of Atlantic menhaden on surrounding waters. *Chesapeake Sci.* 13:321–323.

Oviatt, C. A., and Nixon, S. W. 1973. The demersal fish of Narraganset Bay: an analysis of community structure, distribution, and abundance. *Est. Coast. Mar. Sci.* 1:361–378.

Owen, R. B., Crossley, R., Johnson, T. C., Tweddle,

D., Kornfield, I., Davison, S., Eccles, D. H., and Engstom, D. E. 1990. Major low levels of Lake Malawi and their implications for speciation rates in cichlid fishes. *Proc. R. Soc. Lond. B.* 240:519–553.

Paine, R. T., and Palmer, A. R. 1978. *Sicyases sanguineus:* a unique trophic generalist from the Chilean intertidal zone. *Copeia* 1978(1):75–81.

Paller, M. H., Gladden, J. B., and Heuer, J. H. 1992. Development of the fish community in a new South Carolina reservoir. *Am. Midl. Nat.* 128:95–114.

Panella, G. 1971. Fish otoliths: daily growth layers and periodical patterns. *Science* 173:1124–1127.

Parenti, L. R. 1981. A phylogenetic and biogeographic analysis of the cyprinodontiform fishes (Teleostei, Atherinomorpha). *Bull. Amer. Mus. Nat. Hist.* 168:335–557.

Parenti, L. R. 1984. A taxonomic revision of the Andean killifish genus *Orestias* (Cyprinodontiformes, Cyprinodontidae). *Bull. Amer. Mus. Nat. Hist.* 178:107–214.

Parenti, L. R. 1989. A revision of the phallostethid fishes (Atherinomorpha, Phallostethidae). *Proc. Calif. Acad. Sci.* 46: 243–277.

Parenti, L. R. 1993. Relationships of atherinomorph fishes (Teleostei). *Bull. Mar. Sci.* 52: 170–196.

Parin, N. V. 1968. *Ichthyofauna of the epipelagic zone.* Jerusalem: Israel Prog. Sci. Trans. 206 pp.

Parin, N. V. 1984. Oceanic ichthyologeography: an attempt to review the distribution and origin of pelagic and bottom fishes outside continental shelves and neritic zones. *Arch. Fischwiss.* 35:5–41.

Patten, B. C. 1964. The rational decision process in salmon migration. *J. Cons. Cons., Perma. Int. Explor. Mer.* 8:410–417.

Patterson, C. 1977. The contribution of paleontology to teleostean phylogeny. Pages 579–643 *in* M. K. Hecht, P. G. Goody, and B. M. Hecht. *Major patterns in vertebrate evolution.* New York: Plenum Press.

Patterson, C., and Rosen, D. E. 1977. Review of the ichthyodectiform and other mesozoic teleost fishes and the theory and practice of classifying fossils. *Bull. Amer. Mus. Nat. Hist.* 158:81–172.

Parrish, J. K. 1993. Comparison of hunting behavior of four piscine predators attacking schooling prey. *Ethology* 95:233–246.

Paul, A.J., Paul, J.M., and Smith, R.L. 1988. Respiratory energy requirements of the cod *Gadus macrocephalus* Tilesius relative to body size, food intake, and temperature. *J. Exp. Mar. Biol. Ecol.* 122:83–89.

Payne, A. I. 1986. *The ecology of tropical lakes and rivers.* New York: Wiley.

Pelster, B., and Scheid, P. 1992. Countercurrent concentration and gas secretion in the fish swim bladder. *Physiol. Zool.* 65(1):1–16.

Percy, L. R., and Potter, I. C. 1976. Blood cell formation in the river lamprey, *Lampetra fluviatilis. J. Zool.* (London) 178:319–340.

Perret, W. S., and Caillouet, C. W. 1974. Abundance and size of fishes taken by trawling in Vermilion Bay, Louisiana. *Bull. Mar. Sci.* 24(1):52–75.

Perutz, M. F. 1978. Electrostatic effects in proteins. *Sci.* 201:1187–1191.

Peterson, M. S., and Ross, S. T. 1991. Dynamics of littoral fishes and decapods along a coastal river-estuarine gradient. *Est., Coast, Shelf Sci.* 33:467–483.

Peterson, R. H., Coombs, K., Power, J., and Paim, U. 1989. Responses of several fish species to pH gradients. *Can. J. Zool.* 67:1566–1572.

Pethiyagoda, R. 1991. *Freshwater fishes of Sri Lanka.* Colombo, Sri Lanka: Wildlife Heritage Trust. 362 pp.

Pethiyagoda, R. 1994. Threats to the indigenous freshwater fishes of Sri Lanka and remarks on their conservation. *Hydrobiologia* 285: 189–201.

Pfeiler, E. 1986. Towards an explanation of the developmental strategy in leptocephalus larvae of marine teleost fishes. *Env. Biol. Fish.* 15:3–13.

Pflieger, W. L. 1975. *The fishes of Missouri.* Missouri Dept. Cons. 343 pp.

Pic, P., Mayer-Gostan, N., and Maetz, J. 1974. Branchial effects of epinephrine in the seawater-adapted mullet. I. Water permeability. *Am. J. Physiol.* 226:698–702.

Pietsch, T. W. 1974. Osteology and relationships of ceratioid anglerfishes of the family Oneirodidae, with a review of the genus *Oneirodes* Lutken. *L. A. Co. Nat. Hist. Mus. Sci. Bull.* 18: 1–113.

Pietsch, T. W. 1976. Dimorphism, parasitism, and sex: reproductive strategies among deepsea ceratoid anglerfishes. *Copeia* 1976(4):781–793.

Pietsch, T. W. 1978a. Evolutionary relationships of the seamoths (Teleostei, Pagasidae) with a classification of gasterosteiform families. *Copeia* 1978(3):517–529.

Pietsch, T. W. 1978b. The feeding mechanism of *Stylephorus chordatus* (Teleostei, Lampridiformes): functional and ecological implications. *Copeia* (2):255–262.

Pietsch, T. W., and Grobecker, D. B. 1978. The compleat angler: aggressive mimicry in an antennariid anglerfish. *Science* 201:369–370.

Pietsch, T. W., and Grobecker, D. B. 1987. *Frogfishes of the world: systematics, zoogeography, and behavioral ecology.* Stanford, Calif.: Stanford Univ. Press. 420 pp.

Piiper, J., Meyer, M., Worth, H., and Willmer H. 1977. Respiration and circulation during swimming activity in the digfish, *Scyliorhinus stellaris. Resp. Physiol.* 30:221–239.

Pisam, M., Caroff, A., and Rambourg, A. 1987. Two types of chloride cells in the epithelium of a freshwater-adapted fish: *Lebistes reticulatus*; their modifications during adaptations to salt water. *Amer. J. Anat.* 179:40–50.

Pitcher, T. J., ed. 1993. *The behaviour of teleost fishes.* 2nd ed. London: Chapman and Hall. 715 pp.

Pitcher, T. J., and Parrish, J. K. 1993. Functions of shoaling behavior in fishes. Pages 363–440 *in* T. J. Pitcher, ed. *The behaviour of teleost fishes.* 2nd ed. London: Chapman and Hall.

Pitcher, T. J., Partridge, B. L., and Wardle, C. S. 1976. A blind fish can school. *Science* 194: 963–65.

Platt, A. E. 1995. Dying seas. *World Watch* 8:10–19.

Polis, G. A., and Holt, R. D. 1992. Intraguild predation: the dynamics of complex trophic interactions. *TREE* 7:151–154.

Pollard, D. A., Ingram, B. A., Harris, J. H., and Reynolds, L. F. 1990. Threatened fishes in Australia—an overview. *J. Fish Biol.* 57 (Suppl. A):67–78.

Poluhowich, J. J. 1972. Adaptive significance of eel

multiple hemoglobins. *Physiol. Zool.* 45: 215–222.

Popper, A. N., and Fay, R. R. 1973. Sound detection and processing by teleost fishes: a critical review. *J. Acoust. Soc. Amer.* 53:1515–1529.

Popper, A. N., and Fay, R. R. 1977. Structure and function of the elasmobranch auditory system. *Amer. Zool.* 17:443–452.

Potter, I. C., Beckley, L. E., Whitfield, A. K., and Lenaton, R. C. J. 1990. Comparisons between the roles played by estuaries in the life cycles of fishes in temperate western Australia and Southern Africa. *Env. Biol. Fish.* 28:143–187.

Potts, W. T. W., and Fleming, W. R. 1971. The effect of environmental calcium and ovine prolactin on sodium balance in *Fundulus kansae. J. Exp. Biol.* 54:63–75.

Potts, G. W., and Wootton, R. J., eds., 1984. *Fish reproduction: strategies and tactics.* London: Academic Press.

Poulson, T. L., and White, W. B. 1969. The cave environment. *Science* 165:971–981.

Power, M. E. 1984. Depth distributions of armored catfish: predator-induced resource avoidance? *Ecology* 65:523–528.

Power, M. 1987. Predator avoidance by grazing fishes in temperate and tropical streams: importance of stream depth and prey size. Pages 333–353 *in* W. C. Kerfoot and A. Sih, eds. *Predation: direct and indirect effects on aquatic communities.* Hanover, N.H.: Univ. of New England Press.

Power, M., and Matthews, W. J. 1983. Algae-grazing minnows *(Campostoma anomalum)*, piscivorous bass *(Micropterus* spp.) and the distribution of attached algae in a small prairie margin stream. *Oecologia* 60: 328–332.

Powles, P. M., and Kohler, A. C. 1970. Depth distribution of various stages of the witch flounder *(Glyptocephalus cynoglossus)* off Nova Scotia and in the Gulf of Lawrence. *J. Fish. Res. Bd. Canada* 17:2053–2062.

Prejs, A., and Blaszczyk, M. 1977. Relationships between food and cellulase activity in freshwater fishes. *J. Fish Biol.* 11:447–452.

Preston, J. L. 1978. Communication systems and social interactions in a goby-shrimp symbiosis. *Anim. Behav.* 26:791–802.

Priede, I. G. 1976. Functional morphology of the bulbus arteriosus of rainbow trout *(Salmo gairdneri* Richardson). *J. Fish Biol.* 9:209–216.

Radakov, D. V. 1972. *Schooling in the ecology of fish.* New York: Wiley. 173 pp.

Radovich, J. 1959. Redistribution of fishes in the eastern North Pacific Ocean in 1957 and 1958. *CalCOFI Rpts.* 7:163–171.

Radovich, J. 1961. Relationships of some marine organisms of the northeast Pacific to water temperatures, particularly during 1957–1959. *Calif. Dept. Fish, Game Fish Bull.* 112:1–62.

Radovich, J. 1979. Managing pelagic schooling prey species. Pages 365–376 *in* H. Clepper, ed. *Predator-prey systems in fisheries management.* Washington, D.C.: Sport Fishing Inst.

Rahel, F. J., Lyons, J. D., and Cochran, P. A. 1984. Stochastic or deterministic regulation of assemblage structure: it may depend on how the assemblage is defined. *Amer. Nat.* 124:583–589.

Randall, D. J. 1968. Functional morphology of the heart in fishes. *Am. Zool.* 8:179–189.

Randall, D. J. 1970. The circulatory system. Pages 133–172 *in* W. S. Hoar and D. J. Randall, eds. *Fish physiology.* Vol. 4. New York: Academic Press.

Randall, D. J. 1982. The control of respiration and circulation in fish during exercise and hypoxia. *J. Exp. Biol.* 100:275–288.

Randall, D. J., and Cameron, J. N. 1973. Respiratory control of arterial pH as temperature changes in rainbow trout, *Salmo gairdneri. Amer. J. Physiol.* 225(4):997–1002.

Randall, D. J., Wood, C. M., Perry, S. F., Bergman, H., Maloiy, G. M. O., Mommsen, T. P., and Wright, P. A. 1989. Urea excretion as a strategy for survival in a fish living in a very alkaline environment. *Nature* 337(6203):165–166.

Randall, J. E. 1961. Overgrazing of algae by herbivorous reef fishes. *Ecology* 42(4):1–812.

Randall, J. E. 1965. Grazing effect on sea grasses by herbivorous reef fishes in the West Indies. *Ecology* 46(2):255–260.

Raven, P. H., Berlin, B., and Breedlove, D. E. 1971. The origins of taxonomy. *Science* 174:1210–1213.

Regan, C. T., and Trewavas, E. 1932. *Deep-sea angler fishes (Ceratoidea).* Dana Rpt. 2. 123 pp.

Reid, S. D., and Perry, S. F. 1991. The effects and

physiological consequences of raised levels of cortisol on rainbow trout *(Oncorhynchus mykiss)* erythrocyte beta-adrenoreceptors. *J. Exp. Biol.* 158:217–240.

Reid, S. D., Moon, T. W., and Perry, S. F. 1992. Rainbow trout hepatocyte beta-adrenoreceptors, catecholamine responsiveness, and effects of cortisol. *J. Exp. Biol.* 158:217–240.

Renfro, J. L., and Hill, L. G. 1970. Factors influencing the aerial breathing and metabolism of gars *(Lepisosteus). Southw. Nat.* 15(1):45–54.

Reynolds, W. W., and Casterlin, M. E. 1979. Behavioral thermoregulation and the "final preferendum" paradigm. *Amer. Zool.* 19: 211–224.

Ribbink, A. J. 1990. Alternative life styles of some African cichlid fishes. *Env. Biol. Fish.* 87–100.

Ribbink, A. J., and Lewis, D. S. C. 1982. *Melanochromis crabro* sp. nov.: a cichlid fish from Lake Malawi which feeds on ectoparasites and catfish eggs. *Neth. J. Zool.* 32:72–87.

Richards, S. W. 1963. The demersal fish population of Long Island South. *Bull. Bingham Ocean. Coll., Yale Univ.* 18(2):1–101.

Richmond, R. H. 1993. Coral reefs: present problems and future concerns resulting from anthropogenic disturbance. *Amer. Zool.* 33:524–536.

Ricker, W. E. 1979. Growth rates and models. Pages 677–743 *in* W. S. Hoar, D. J. Randall, and J. R. Brett, eds. *Fish physiology.* Vol. 8. New York: Academic Press.

Riggs, A. 1970. Properties of fish hemoglobins. Pages 209–252 *in* W. S. Hoar and D. J. Randall, eds. *Fish physiology.* Vol. 4. New York: Academic Press.

Rigley, L., and Marshall, J. A. 1973. Sound production by the elephant-nose fish *Gnathonemus petersii* (Pisces, Mormyridae). *Copeia* 1973(1):134–135.

Rimmer, D. W., and Wiebe, W. J. 1987. Fermentative microbial digestion in herbivorous fishes. *J. Fish Biol.* 31:229–236.

Ringler, N. H. 1979. Selective predation by drift-feeding brown trout *(Salmo trutta). J. Fish. Res. Bd. Canada* 46:392–403.

Roberts, J. L. 1975. Active branchial and ram gill ventilation in fishes. *Biol. Bull.* 148:85–105.

Roberts, J. L., and Graham, J. B. 1979. Effect of swimming speed on the excess temperatures and activities of heart and red and white muscles in the mackerel *Scomber japonicus. NOAA Fish. Bull.* 76:861–867.

Roberts, T. R. 1969. Osteology and relationships of characoid fishes, particularly in the genera *lepsetus, Salminus, Hoplias, Ctenolucius,* and *Acestrophynchus. Proc. Calif. Acad. Sci. Ser. 4* 36(15):391–500.

Roberts, T. R. 1971. Osteology of the Malaysian phallosteid fish, *Ceratostethus bicornis,* with a discussion of the evolution of remarkable structural novelties in its jaws and external genitalia. *Bull. Mus. Comp. Zool., Harvard* 142: 393–418.

Roberts, T. R. 1972. Ecology of fishes in the Amazon and Congo basins. *Bull. Mus. Comp. Zool., Harvard* 143(2):117–147.

Roberts, T. R. 1976. Geographic distribution of African freshwater fishes. *Zool. J. Linn. Soc.* 57:249–319.

Roberts, T. R. 1982. Unculi (horny projections rising from single cells), an adaptive feature of the epidermis of ostariophysan fishes. *Zool. Scripta* 11:55–76.

Roberts, T. R., 1984. Skeletal anatomy and classification of the neotenic Asian salmoniform superfamily Salangoidea (icefishes or noodlefishes). *Proc. Calif. Acad. Sci.* 43 (13): 179–220.

Roberts, T. R. 1986. *Danionella translucida,* a new genus and species cyprinid fish from Burma, one of the smallest living vertebrates. *Env. Biol. Fish.* 16:231–241.

Roberts, T. R. 1993. Artisanal fisheries and fish ecology below the great waterfalls of the Mekong River in southern Laos. *Nat. Hist. Bull. Siam* 41:31–62.

Robertson, D. R. 1982. Fish feces and fish food on a Pacific coral reef. *Marine Ecol. Prog. Ser.* 7: 253–265.

Robertson, D. R., and Hoffman, S. G. 1977. The roles of female mate choice and predation in the mating system of some tropical labroid fishes. *Zeit. fur Tierpsych.* 45:298–320.

Robertson, D. R., Sweatman, H. P. A., Fletcher, E. A., and Cleland, M. G. 1976. Schooling as a mechanism for circumventing the territoriality of competitors. *Ecology* 57:1208–1220.

Robertson, D. R., and Warner, R. R. 1978. Sexual patterns in the labroid fishes of the Western Caribbean. II: The parrotfishes (Scaridae). *Smithson. Contr. Zool.* 255:1–26.

Robertson, J. D. 1954. The chemical composition of the blood of some aquatic chordates including members of the Tunicata, Cyclostomata, and Osteichthyes. *J. Expt. Biol.* 31:424–442.

Robison, H. W., and Buchanan, T. M. 1988. *Fishes of Arkansas.* Fayetteville: Univ. of Ark. Press. 536 pp.

Robins, C. R., Bailey, R. M., Bond, C. E., Brooker, J. R., Lachner, E. A., Lea, R. N., and Scott, W. B. 1991. *Common and scientific names of fishes from the United States and Canada.* Amer. Fish. Soc. Spec. Publ. 20. 182 pp.

Rodriguez, M. A., and Lewis, W. M., Jr. 1994. Regulation and stability in fish assemblages of neotropical floodplain lakes. *Oecologia* 99: 166–180.

Rolston, H. 1985. Duties to endangered species. *Bioscience* 35:718–726.

Romer, A. S. 1966. *Vertebrate paleontology.* Chicago: Univ. of Chicago Press. 468 pp.

Rombough, P. J., and Moroz, B. M. 1990. The scaling and potential importance of cutaneous and branchial surfaces in respiratory gas exchange in young chinook salmon (*Oncorhynchus tshawytscha*). *J. Exp. Biol.* 154: 1–12.

Ronan, M., and Bodznick, D. 1991. Behavioral and neurophysiological demonstration of a lateralis skin photosensitivity in larval sea lampreys. *J. Exp. Biol.* 161:97–117.

Root, R. W. 1931. The respiratory function of the blood of marine fishes. *Biol. Bull.* 61:427–456.

Rosen, D. E. 1964. The relationships and taxonomic position of the halfbeaks, killifishes, silversides, and their relatives. *Bull. Amer. Mus. Nat. Hist.* 127(5):217–268.

Rosen, D. E. 1973. Interrelationships of higher euteleostean fishes. Pages 397–513 *in* P. H. Greenwood, R. S. Miles, and C. Patterson, eds. *Interrelationships of fishes.* New York: Academic Press.

Rosen, D. E. 1975a. Doctrinal biogeography, a review of *Marine zoogeography* by J. C. Briggs. *Quart. Rev. Biol.* 50(1):69–70.

Rosen, D. E. 1975b. A vicariance model of Caribbean biogeography. *Syst. Zool.* 24(4):437–464.

Rosen, D. E., Forey, P. L., Gardiner, B. G., and Patterson, C. 1981. Lungfishes, tetrapods, paleontology, and plesiomorphy. *Bull. Amer. Mus. Nat. Hist.* 167:159–276.

Rosen, D. E., and Greenwood, P. H. 1970. Origin of the Weberian apparatus and the relationships of ostariophysan and gonorynchiform fishes. *Amer. Mus. Novit.* 2428:1–25.

Rosen, M. W., and Cornford, N. E. 1971. Fluid friction of fish slimes. *Nature* 234:49–51.

Ross, S. T. 1986. Resource partitioning in fish assemblages: a review of field studies. *Copeia* 1986:353–388.

Ross, S. T., McMichael, R. H., and Ruple, D. L. 1987. Seasonal and diel variation in the standing crop of fishes and macroinvertebrates from a Gulf of Mexico surf zone. *Est., Coast. Shelf Sci.* 25:391–412.

Rossi-Fanelli, A., and Antonini, E. 1960. Oxygen equilibria of hemoglobin from *Thunnus thynnus. Nature* 186:895–896.

Rothschild, B. J. 1965. Hypotheses on the origin of exploited skipjack tuna (*Katsuwonus pelamis*) in the eastern and central Pacific Ocean. *U.S. Fish, Wildl. Serv. Spec. Sci. Rept. Fish.* 512:1–20.

Rounsefell, G. A. 1957. Fecundity of the North American Salmonidae. *U.S. Fish, Wildl. Serv. Fish. Bull.* 57:451–468.

Rounsefell, G. A. 1975. *Ecology, utilization, and management of marine fisheries.* St. Louis: C. V. Mosby. 516 pp.

Rovainen, C. M. 1979. Neurobiology of lampreys. *Physiol. Rev.* 59(4):1007–1077.

Rozengurt, M. A., and Hedgpeth, J. W. 1989. The impact of altered river flow on the ecosystem of the Caspian Sea. *Rev. Aquat. Sci.* 1:337–364.

Rulifson. R. A. 1985. Distribution and abundance of fishes in tributaries of South Creek Estuary, North Carolina. *J. Elisha Mitchill Soc.* 101: 160–176.

Russell, B. C., Allen, G. R., and Lubbock, H. R. 1976. New cases of mimicry in marine fishes. *J. Zool. London* 180:407–425.

Russell, F. S. 1976. *The eggs and planktonic stages of British marine fishes.* London: Academic Press. 524 pp.

Ryder, R. A. 1977. Effects of ambient light variations on behavior of yearling, subadult, and adult walleyes *(Stizostedion vitreum vitreum).* *J. Fish. Res. Bd. Canada* 34(10):1481–1491.

Safina, C., and Burger, J. 1989. Population interactions among free-living bluefish and prey fish in an ocean environment. *Oecologia* 79: 91–95.

Saila, S. B. 1961. A study of winter flounder movements. *Limnol., Oceanogr.* 6:292–298.

Sale, P. F. 1977. Maintenance of high diversity in coral reef fish communities. *Amer. Nat.* 111(978):337–359.

Sale, P. F. 1980. The ecology of fishes on coral reefs. *Oceanogr. Mar. Biol. Ann. Rev.* 18:367–421.

Sale, P. F., ed. 1991. *The ecology of fishes on coral reefs.* San Diego: Academic Press. 754 pp.

Sale, P. F., and Guy, J. A. 1992. Persistence of community structure: what happens when you change taxonomic scale? *Coral Reefs* 11: 147–154.

Sanderson, S. L., and Cech, J. J., Jr. 1992. Energetic cost of suspension feeding versus particulate feeding by juvenile Sacramento blackfish. *Trans. Am. Fish. Soc.* 121:149–157.

Sanderson, S. L., Cech, J. J., Jr., and Patterson, M. R. 1991. Fluid dynamics in suspension-feeding blackfish. *Science* 251:1346–1348.

Sansom, I. J., Smith, M. P., Armstrong, H. A., and Smith, M. M. 1992. Presence of the earliest vertebrate hard tissues in conodonts. *Science* 256:1308–1311.

Santer, R. M., and Greer Walker, M. 1980. Morphological studies on the ventricle of teleost and elasmobranch hearts. *J. Zool. London* 190: 259–272.

Sarawatari, T., and Okiyama, M. 1992. Life history of Salangichthys microdon, Salangidae, is a brackish lake, Lake Hinuma, Japan. *Nippon Suisan Gakkaishi* 58:235–248.

Satchell, G. H. 1965. Blood flow through the caudal vein of elasmobranch fish. *Aust. J. Sci.* 27: 241–242.

Satchell, G. H. 1971. *Circulation in fishes.* London: Cambridge Univ. Press. 131 pp.

Satchell, G. H. 1976. The circulatory system of air-breathing fish. Pages 105–123 *in* G. M. Hughes, ed. *Respiration of amphibious vertebrates.* London: Academic Press.

Sato, T. 1986. A brood parasitic catfish of mouth-brooding cichlid fishes in Lake Tanganyika. *Nature* 323:58–59.

Saul, W. G. 1975. An ecological study of fishes at a site in upper Amazonian Ecuador. *Proc. Phila. Acad. Sci.* 127(12):93–134.

Saunders, M. W., and McFarlane, G. A. 1993. Age and length of the female spiny dogfish, *Squalus acanthias,* in the Strait of Georgia, British Columbia, Canada. *Env. Biol. Fish.* 38: 49–58.

Savitz, J. 1971. Effects of starvation on body protein utilization of bluegill sunfish (*Lepomis macrochirus* Rafinesque), with a calculation of caloric requirements. *Trans. Amer. Fish. Soc.* 100:18–21.

Sawada, Y. 1982. Phylogeny and zoogeography of the superfamily Cobitoidea (Cyprinoidea, Cypriniformes). *Mem. Faculty of Fisheries, Hokkaido U.* 28:65–223.

Sawyer, W. H., Blair-West, J. R., Simpson, P. A., and Sawyer, M. K. 1976. Renal responses of Australian lungfish to vasotocin, angiotensin II, and NaCl infusion. *Amer. J. Physiol.* 231:593–602.

Scavia, D. et al. 1986. Influence of salmonid predation and weather on long-term water quality trends in Lake Michigan. *Can. J. Fish. Aquat. Sci.* 43:435–443.

Schaeffer, B. 1973. Interrelationships of chondrosteans. Pages 207–227 *in* P. G. Greenwood, R. S. Miles, and C. Patterson, eds. *Interrelationships of fishes.* London: Academic Press.

Schaeffer, B., and Rosen, D. 1961. Major adaptive levels in the evolution of the actinopterygian feeding mechanism. *Amer. Zool.* 1:187–204.

Schalles, J. F., and Wissing, T. E. 1976. Effects of dry pellet diets on the metabolic rates of bluegill (*Lepomis macrochirus*). *J. Fish. Res. Bd. Canada.* 33:2243–2249.

Schindler, D. W. et al. 1990. Effects of climatic warming on lakes of the central boreal forest. *Science* 250:967–970.

Schlosser, I. J. 1982. Fish community structure and function along two habitat gradients in the headwater stream. *Ecol. Mono.* 52:395–414.

Schmidt, J. 1922. The breeding places of the eel. *Phil. Trans. Roy. Soc. London,* Ser. B. 211:179–208.

Schmidt, P. Y. 1950. *Fishes of the Sea of Okhotsk.* Jerusalem: Prog. Sci. Trans. 392 pp.

Schmidt-Nielsen, K. 1975. *Animal physiology, adaptation, and environment.* London: Cambridge Univ. Press. 699 pp.

Schmitt, R. J., and Strand, S. W. 1982. Cooperative foraging by yellowtail, *Seriola lalandei* (Carangidae), on two species of fish prey. *Copeia* 1982:714–717.

Scholander, P. F. 1954. Secretion of gases against high pressures in the swimbladder of deep-sea fishes. II. The rete mirabile. *Biol. Bull.* 107:260–277.

Scholtz, A. T., Horrall, R. M., Cooper, J. C., and Hasler, A. D. 1976. Imprinting to chemical cues: the basis for home stream selection in salmon. *Science* 192:1247–1249.

Schreck, C. B. 1981. Stress and compensation in teleostean fishes: response to social and physical factors. Pages 295–321 in A. D. Pickering, ed. *Stress and Fish.* London: Academic Press.

Schultz, R. J. 1971. Special adaptive problems associated with unisexual fishes. *Amer. Zool.* 11:351–360.

Schultz, R. J. 1973. Unisexual fish: laboratory synthesis of a "species." *Science* 192:1247–1249.

Schultz, R. J. 1989. Origins and relationships of unisexual poeciliids. Pages 69–90 in G. K. Meffe and F. F. Snelson, Jr., eds. *Ecology and evolution of livebearing fishes (Poeciliidae).* Englewood Cliffs, N.J.: Prentice-Hall.

Schwartz, F. J. 1972. World literature on fish hybrids with an analysis by family, species, and hybrid. *Gulf Coast Mar. Lab. Mus.* 33:1–328.

Scott, T. D. 1962. *The marine and freshwater fishes of South Australia.* Adelaide: Govt. Printer. 338 pp.

Scott, W. B., and Crossman, E. J. 1973. Freshwater fishes of Canada. *Fish. Res. Bd. Canada Bull.* 184:1–966.

Scott, W. B., and Scott, M. G.. 1988. Atlantic fishes

of Canada. *Can. Bull. Fish., Aquat. Sci.* 219. 731 pp.

Sedberry, G. R., and Van Dolah, R. F. 1984. Demersal fish assemblages associated with hard bottom habitat in the South Atlantic bight of the U.S.A. *Env. Biol. Fish.* 251–258.

Sekhon, S. S., and Maxwell, D. S. 1970. Fine structure for developing hagfish erythrocytes, with particular reference to cytoplasmic organelles. *J. Morph.* 131:211–236.

Shapiro, D. Y. 1984. Sex reversal and sociodemographic processes in coral reef fishes. Pages 103–116 in G. W. Potts and R. J. Wootton, eds. *Fish reproduction: strategies and tactics.* London: Academic Press.

Sharp, G. D., and Dizon, A. E. 1978. *The physiological ecology of tunas.* New York: Academic Press. 485 pp.

Shaw, E. 1978. Schooling fishes. *Amer. Sci.* 66:166–175.

Shell, E. W. 1959. *Chemical composition of the blood of smallmouth bass.* Ph.D. diss., Cornell Univ.

Sherman, K. 1994. Sustainability, biomass yields, and health of coastal ecosystems: an ecological perspective. *Mar. Ecol. Prog. Ser.* 112:277–301.

Shoubridge, E. A., and Hochachlea, P. W. 1980. Ethanol: novel endproduct of vertebrate anaerobic metabolism. *Science* 209:308–309.

Shulman, M. J. 1985. Coral reef fish assemblages: intra- and interspecific competition for shelter sites. *Env. Biol. Fish.* 13:81–92.

Shuttleworth, T. J. 1988. Salt and water balance— extrarenal mechanisms. Pages 171–199 in T. J. Shuttleworth, ed. *Physiology of Elasmobranch Fishes.* Berlin: Springer-Verlag.

Sidell, B. D., and Driedzic, W. R. 1985. Relationship between cardiac energy metabolism and cardiac work demand in fishes. Pages 386–401 in R. Gilles, ed. *Circulation, respiration, and metabolism.* Berlin: Springer-Verlag.

Siebert, G., Schmitt, A., and Bottke, I. 1964. Enzymes of the amino acid metabolism in cod musculature. *Arch. Fisch. Wiss.* 15:233–244.

Sih, A. 1994. Predation risk and the evolutionary ecology of reproductive behavior. *J. Fish Biol.* 45 (Suppl. A):111–130.

Silva, P. et al. 1977a. Mechanism of active chloride secretion by shark rectal gland: role of Na-K-ATPase in chloride transport. *J. Physiol.* 233F: 298–306.

Silva, P., Solomon, R., Spokes, K., and Epstein, F.H. 1977b. Ouabain inhibition of gill Na⁺-K⁺-ATPase: relationship to active chloride transport. *J. Exp. Zool.* 199:419–426.

Singh, B. N. 1976. Balance between aquatic and aerial respiration. Pages 125–164 *in* G. M. Hughes, ed. *Respiration of amphibious vertebrates.* London: Academic Press.

Sinha, V. R. P., and Jones, J. W. 1975. *The European freshwater eel.* Liverpool: Liverpool Univ. Press. 146 pp.

Sioli, H. 1975. Tropical river: the Amazon. Pages 461–488 *in* B. A. Whitton, ed. *River ecology.* Berkeley: Univ. of Calif. Press.

Sire, J. 1990. From ganoid to elasmoid scales in the actinopterygian fishes. *Netherlands J. Zool.* 40: 75–92.

Skud, B. E. 1982. Dominance in fishes: the relation between environment and abundance. *Science* 216:144–149.

Smith, C. L., and Powell, C. R. 1971. The summer fish communities of Brier Creek, Marshall County, Oklahoma. *Amer. Mus. Nov.* 2458:1–30.

Smith, C. L., Smith, C. S., Schaeffer, B., and Atz, J. W. 1975. *Latimeria,* the living coelacanth, is ovoviviparous. *Science* 190:1105–1106.

Smith, C. L., and Tyler, J. C. 1972. Space sharing in a coral reef fish community. *Bull. L.A. Co. Mus. Nat. Hist.* 14:125–170.

Smith, C. L., Tyler, J. C., and Feinberg, M. N. 1981. Population ecology and biology of the pearl-fish *(Carapus bermudensis)* in the lagoon at Bimini, Bahamas. *Bull. Mar. Sci.* 31:876–902.

Smith, D. G. 1970. Notacanthiform leptocephali in the western North Atlantic. *Copeia* 1970(1): 1–9.

Smith, F. M., and Jones, D. R. 1978. Localization of receptors causing hypoxic bradycardia in trout *Salmo gairdneri. Can. J. Zool.* 56:1260–1265.

Smith, G. R., and Stearley, R. F. 1989. The classification and scientific names of rainbow and cutthroat trouts. *Fisheries* (Bethesda) 14(1): 4–10.

Smith, H. M. 1945. The freshwater fishes of Siam, or Thailand. *Bull. U.S. Nat. Mus.* 188:1–622.

Smith, H. W. 1929. The excretion of ammonia and urea by the gills of fish. *J. Biol. Chem.* 81:727–742.

Smith, H. W. 1961. *From fish to philosopher.* New York: Doubleday. 293 pp.

Smith, J. L. B. 1949. *The sea fishes of Southern Africa.* Capetown: Central News Agency. 580 pp.

Smith, J. L. B. 1956. *The search beneath the sea.* New York: H. Holt and Co. 260 pp.

Smith, L. S., and Bell, G. R. 1975. *A practical guide to the anatomy and physiology of Pacific salmon.* Ottowa: Fish. Mar. Serv. Misc. Spec. Publ. 27. 14 pp.

Smith, M. L., and Miller, R. R. 1986. The evolution of the Rio Grande Basin as inferred from its fish fauna. Pages 457–486 *in* C. H. Hocutt and E. O. Wiley, eds. *The zoogeography of North American freshwater fishes.* New York: Wiley.

Smith, P. W. 1971. Illinois streams: classification based on their fishes and an analysis of factors responsible for the disappearance of native species. *Ill. Nat. Hist. Surv. Biol. Note* 76:1–14.

Smith, R. J. F. 1982. The adaptive significance of the alarm substance-fright reaction system. Pages 327–342 *in* T. J. Hara, ed. *Chemoreception in fishes.* Amsterdam: Elsevier.

Smith, S. H. 1968. Species succession and fishery exploitation of the Great Lakes. *J. Fish. Res. Bd. Canada* 25(4):667–693.

Snedecor, G. W., and Cochran, W. G. 1967. *Statistical methods.* Ames: Iowa State Univ. Press. 593 pp.

Somero, G. N. 1986. Protons, osmolytes, and fitness of internal milieu for protein function. *Am. J. Physiol.* 251 (*Regulatory Integrative Comp. Physiol.* 20): R197–R213.

Sonnier, F., Teerling, J., and Hoese, H. D. 1976. Observations on the offshore reef and platform fish fauna of Louisiana. *Copeia* 1976(1):105–111.

Sorensen, P. W., and Scott, A. P. 1994. The evolution of hormonal sex pheromones in teleost fish: poor correlation between the pattern of steroid release by goldfish and olfactory sensitivity suggests that these cues evolved as a result of chemical spying rather than signal specialization. *Acta Physiol. Scand.* 152: 191–205.

Soule, M. E. 1985. What is conservation biology? *Bioscience* 35:727–734.

Southern California Coastal Water Research Project. 1973. *The ecology of the Southern California bight: implications for water quality management.* El Segundo, Calif.: SCCWRP TR 104. 531 pp.

Specker, J. L., and Schreck, C. B. 1982. Changes in plasma corticosteroids during smoltification of coho salmon, *Oncorhynchus kisutch. Gen. Comp. Endocr.* 46:53–58.

Springer, S. 1979. A revision of the catsharks, family Scyliorhinidae. *NOAA Tech Rpt. NMFS Cir.* 422:1–152.

Springer, V. G. 1982. Pacific plate biogeography, with special reference to fishes. *Smithson. Contrib. Zool.* 367:1–182.

Springer, V. G., and Gold, J. P. 1989. *Sharks in question.* Washington, D.C.: Smithsonian Inst. Press. 187 pp.

Stacey, N. E. 1984. Control and timing of ovulation by exogenous and endogenous factors. Pages 207–221 *in* G. W. Potts and R. J. Wootton, eds. *Fish reproduction: strategies and tactics.* London: Academic Press.

Starrett, W. 1951. Some factors affecting the abundance of minnows in the Des Moines River, Iowa. *Ecology* 32(1):13–27.

Stearns, S. C. 1976. Life history tactics: a review of the ideas. *Quart. Rev. Biol.* 51(1):3–47.

Steen, J.B. 1970. The swim bladder as a hydrostatic organ. Pages 413–443 *in* W. S. Hoar and D. J. Randall, eds. *Fish physiology.* Vol. 4. New York: Academic Press.

Steen, J. B. 1971. *Comparative physiology of respiratory mechanisms.* New York: Academic Press. 182 pp.

Steen, J. B., and Berg, T. 1966. The gills of two species of hemoglobin-free fishes compared to those of other teleosts, with a note on severe anaemia in an eel. *Comp. Biochem. Physiol.* 18:517–527.

Steffensen, J. F., and Lomholt, J. P. 1985. Cutaneous oxygen uptake and its relation to skin blood perfusion and ambient salinity in the plaice, *Pleuronectes platessa. Comp. Biochem. Physiol.* 81A:373–375.

Stein, R. A., and Kitchell, J. F. 1975. Selective predation by carp *Cyprinus carpio* (L.) on benthic molluscs in Skadar Lake, Yugoslavia. *J. Fish Biol.* 7(2):391–399.

Stein, R. A., Reimers, P. E., and Hall, J. D. 1972. Social interaction between juvenile coho (*Oncorhynchus kisutch*) and fall chinook salmon (*O. tshawytscha*) in Sixes River, Oregon. *J. Fish. Res. Bd. Canada* 29(12): 1737–1748.

Stephens, J. S., Johnson, R. K., Key, G. S., and McCosker, J. E. 1970. The comparative ecology of three sympatric species of California blennies of the genus (*Hypsoblennius*) Gill (Teleostomi, Blenniidae). *Ecol. Monogr.* 40: 213–233.

Sterba, G. 1959. *Freshwater fishes of the world.* London: Vista Books. 878 pp.

Stevens, E. D. 1968. The effect of exercise on the distribution of blood to various organs in rainbow trout. *Comp. Biochem., Physiol.* 25:615–625.

Stevens, E. D. 1979. The effect of temperature on tail beat frequency of fish swimming at constant velocity. *Can. J. Zool.* 57:1628–1635.

Stevens, E. D., Bennion, G. R., Randall, D. J., and Shelton, G. 1972. Factors affecting arterial pressures and blood flow from the heart in intact, unrestrained lingcod (*Ophiodon elongatus*). *Comp. Biochem., Physiol.* 43A:681–695.

Stevens, E. D., and Carey, F. G. 1981. One why of the warmth of warm-bodied fish. *Amer. J. Physiol.* 240 (*Regulatory Integrative Comp. Physiol* 9): R151–R155.

Stevens, E. D., and Randall, J. R. 1967. Changes in blood pressure, heart rate, and breathing rate during moderate swimming activity in rainbow trout. *J. Exp. Biol.* 46:307–315.

Stevens, E. D., and Sutterlin, A. M. 1976. Heat transfer between fish and ambient water. *J. Expt. Biol.* 65:131–145.

Stevenson, M. M., Schnell, G. D., and Black, R. 1974. Factor analysis of fish distribution patterns in western and central Oklahoma. *Syst. Zool.* 23(2):202–218.

Stewart, N. E., Shumway, D. L., and Doudoroff, P.

1967. Influence of oxygen concentration on the growth of juvenile largemouth bass. *J. Fish. Res. Bd. Canada* 24:475–494.

Stickney, R. R., and Shumway, S. E. 1974. Occurrence of cellulase activity in the stomachs of fishes. *J. Fish Biol.* 6:779–790.

Stockton, W. L., and DeLaca, T. E. 1982. Food falls in the deep sea: occurrence, quality, and significance. *Deep-sea Research* 29:157–169.

Strange, E. M., Moyle, P. B., and Foin, T. C. 1992. Interactions between stochastic and deterministic processes in stream fish community assembly. *Env. Biol. Fish.* 36:1–15.

Strauss, R. E., and Bond, C. E. 1990. Taxonomic methods: morphology. Pages 109–140 *in* C. B. Schreck and P. B. Moyle, eds. *Methods for fish biology.* Bethesda, Md.: Amer. Fish. Soc.

Strong, W. R., Snelson, F. F., and Gruber, S. H. 1990. Hammerhead shark predation on stingrays: an observation of prey handling by *Sphyrna mokarran. Copeia* 1990:836–840.

Subrahmanyam, C. B., and Drake, S. H. 1975. Studies of animal communities of two north Florida salt marshes. Part I. Fish communities. *Bull. Mar. Sci.* 25(4):445–465.

Sulak, K. J. 1977. The systematics and biology of *Bathypterois* (Pisces, Chloropthalmidae) with a revised classification of benthic myctophiform fishes. *Galathea Rpt.* 14:49–108.

Summerfelt, R. C., and Hall, G. E. 1987. *Age and growth in fish.* Ames: Iowa State Univ. Press. 544 pp.

Sutterlin, A. M. 1969. Effects of exercise on the cardiac and ventilation frequency in three species of freshwater teleosts. *Physiol. Zool.* 42:36–52.

Sutterlin, A. M. 1975. Chemical attraction of some marine fish in their natural habitat. *J. Fish. Res. Bd. Canada* 32:729–738.

Svardson, G. 1949. Natural selection and egg number in fish. *Ann. Rpt. Inst. Freshw. Res., Drottningholm* 29:115–122.

Symons, P. E. K. 1976. Behavior and growth of juvenile Atlantic salmon *(Salmo salar)* and three competitors at two stream velocities. *J. Fish. Res. Bd. Canada* 33(12):1766–2773.

Tavolga, W. A. 1956. Visual, chemical, and sound stimuli as cues in the sex discriminatory behavior of the gobiid fish, *Bathygobius soporator. Physiol. Zool.* 31:259–271.

Taylor, L. R., Compagno, L. J. V., and Struhsaker, P. J. 1983. Megamouth—a new shark species, genus, and family of lamnoid shark *(Megachasma pelagios,* Family Megachasmidae) from the Hawaiian Islands. *Proc. Calif. Acad. Sci.* 43:87–110.

Teichmann, H. 1962. Was leistet der Geruchssinn bei Fischen? *Umschau Wiss. Tech.* 62:588–591.

Templeman, W. 1976. Transatlantic migrations in spiny dogfish *(Squalus acanthias). J. Fish. Res. Bd. Canada* 33(11):2605–2609.

Tesch, F. W. 1977. *The eel: biology and management of anguillid eels.* London: Chapman and Hall. 434 pp.

Teylaud, A. R. 1971. Food habits of the goby *Ginsburgellus novemlinaetus* and the clingfish, *Acros rubiginosis,* associated with echinoids in the Virgin Islands. *Caribb. J. Sci.* 11:41–45.

Thayer, G. W., Wolfe, D. A., and Williams, R. B. 1975. The impact of man on seagrass systems. *Amer. Sci.* 63(3):288–296.

Thompson, W. F., and Van Cleve, R. 1936. Life history of the Pacific halibut. *Rpt. Int. Fish. Comm.* 9:1–184.

Thomson, D. A., Finley, L. T., and Kerstitch, A. N. 1987. *Reef fishes of the Sea of Cortez.* Tucson: University of Arizona Press.

Thomson, D. A., and Lehner, C. E. 1976. Resilience of a rocky intertidal fish community in a physically unstable environment. *J. Exp. Mar. Biol., Ecol.* 22(1):1–29.

Thomson, K. S. 1972. The adaptation and evolution of early fishes. *Quart. Rev. Biol.* 46(2):139–166.

Thomson, K. S. 1973. New observations on the coelacanth fish, *Latimeria chalumnae. Copeia* 1973(4):813–814.

Thomson, K. S. 1977. On the individual history of cosmine and a possible electroreceptive function of the pore-canal system in fossil fishes. Pages 247–269 *in* R. M. Andrews, R. S. Miles, and A. D. Walker, eds. *Problems in vertebrate evolution.* Linn. Soc. Lond. Symp. Series 4.

Thorson, T. B. 1958. Measurements of the fluid components of four species of marine chondrichthyes. *Physiol. Zool.* 31:16–23.

Thorson, T. B., ed. 1976. *Investigations of the ichthyofauna of Nicaraguan lakes.* Lincoln: School of Life Sci., Univ. of Nebraska. 663 pp.

Thorson, F. B., Cowan, C. M., and Watson, D. E. 1973. Body fluid solutes of juveniles and adults of the euryhaline bull shark *(Carcharinus leucas)* from freshwater and saline environments. *Physiol. Zool.* 46:29–42.

Thresher, R. E. 1977. Eye ornamentation of Caribbean reef fishes. *Z. Tierpsychol.* 43: 152–158.

Thresher, R. E. 1984. *Reproduction in reef fishes.* Neptune City, N.J.: TFH Publications.

Tilzey, R. D. J. 1976. Observations on interactions between indigenous Galaxiidae and introduced Salmonidae in the Lake Eucumbene catchment, New South Wales, Aust. *J. Mar. Freshw. Res.* 27:551–564.

Tippetts, W., and Moyle, P. 1978. Epibenthic feeding by rainbow trout *(Salmo gairdneri)* in the McCloud River, California. *J. Anim. Ecol.* 47: 549–559.

Todd, E. S. 1968. Terrestrial sojourns of the longjaw mudsucker, *Gillichthys mirabilis. Copeia* 1968(1):192–194.

Tonn, W. M., Magnuson, J. J. Rask, M., and Toivonen, J. 1990. Intercontinental comparison of small-lake fish assemblages: the balance between local and regional processes. *Amer. Nat.* 136:345–375.

Trippel, E. A., and Beamish, F. W. H. 1993. Multiple trophic level structuring in *Salvelinus-Coregonus* assemblages in boreal forest lakes. *Can. J. Fish. Aquat. Sci.* 1442–1455.

Trott, L. B. 1981. A general review of the pearlfishes (Pisces, Carapidae): *Bull. Mar. Sci.* 31: 623–629.

Tsai, C. 1973. Water quality and fish life below sewage outfalls. *Trans. Amer. Fish Soc.* 102(4):281–292.

Tsai, C., and Zeisel, R. B. 1969. Natural hybridization of cyprinid fishes in Little Patuxent River, Maryland. *Ches. Sci.* 102(2):69–74.

Turner, J. L. 1977. Changes in the size structure of cichlid populations of Lake Malawi resulting from bottom trawling. *J. Fish. Res. Bd. Canada* 34(2):232–238.

Tyler, A. V. 1971. Periodic and resident components in communities of Atlantic fishes. *J. Fish. Res. Bd. Canada* 28(7):935–946.

Tyler, A. V. 1972. Food resource division among northern marine demersal fishes. *J. Fish. Res. Bd. Canada* 29(7):997–1003.

Tyler, H. R., and Pearcy, W. G. 1975. The feeding habits of three species of lantern-fishes (Family Myctophidae) off Oregon, U.S.A. *Marine Biol.* 32:7–11.

Tzeng, W. N., and Tsai, Y. C. 1994. Changes in otolith microchemistry of the Japanese eel, *Anguilla japonica,* during its migration from the ocean to the rivers of Taiwan. *J. Fish. Biol.* 45:671–683.

Underhill, J. 1986. The fish fauna of the Laurentian Great Lakes, the St. Lawrence Highlands, Newfoundland, and Labrador. Pages 105–136 *in* C. H. Hocutt and E. O. Wiley, eds. *The zoogeography of North American freshwater fishes.* New York: Wiley.

Utida, S., and Hirano, T. 1973. Effects of changes in environmental salinity on salt and water movement in the intestine and gills of the eel *Anguilla japonica.* Pages 240–278 *in* W. Chavin, ed. *Responses of fish to environmental changes.* Springfield, Ill.: Chas. C Thomas.

Uyeno, T., and Smith, G. R. 1972. Tetraploid origin of the karyotype of catostomid fishes. *Science* 175:644–646.

Valerio, P. F., Kao, M. H., and Fletcher, G. L. 1992. Fish skin: an effective barrier to ice crystal propagation. *J. Exp. Biol.* 164:135–151.

van Dam, L. 1938. *On the utilization of oxygen and regulation of breathing in some aquatic animals.* Ph.D. diss., Univ. of Groningen, Netherlands.

Vanicek, C. D., and Kramer, R. H. 1969. Life history of the Colorado squawfish, *Ptychocheilus lucius,* and the Colorado chub, *Gila robusta,* in the Green River in Dinosaur National Monument, 1964–1966. *Trans. Amer. Fish. Soc.* 98(2):193–208.

Vanni, M. J., Luecke, C., Kitchell, J. F., and Magnuson, J. J. 1990. Effects of planktivorous fish mass mortality on the plankton community of Lake Mendota, Wisconsin: implications for biomanipulation. *Hydrobiologia* 200/201:329–336.

Victor, B. C. 1983. Recruitment and population

dynamics of a coral reef fish. *Science* 219: 419–420.

Vince, S., Valiela, I., Backus, N., and Teal, J. M. 1976. Predation by the salt-marsh killifish *Fundulus heteroclitus* (L.) in relation to prey size and habitat structure: consequences for prey distribution and abundance. *J. Exp. Mar. Biol. Ecol.* 23:255–266.

Vincent, R. E., and Miller, W. H. 1969. Altitudinal distribution of brown trout and other fishes in a headwater tributary of the South Platte River. *Ecology* 50(3):464–466.

Virnstein, R. W. 1977. The importance of predation by crabs and fishes on benthic infauna in Chesapeake Bay. *Ecology* 58(6):1199–1217.

Vladykov, V. D., and Kott, E. 1977. Satellite species among the holarctic lampreys (Petromyzonidae). *Can. J. Zool.* 57(4):860–867.

Volya, G. 1966. Some data on digestive enzymes in some Black Sea fishes and a micromodification of a method for the identification of a trypsin, amylase, and lypase. In "Fisiologia morskikhyzhitvotnykh." *Nauka.* (In Russian).

von Arx, W. S. 1962. *An introduction to physical oceanography.* Reading, Mass.: Addison-Wesley. 422 pp.

von Geldern, C., and Mitchell, D. F. 1975. Largemouth bass and threadfin shad in California. Pages 436–449 *in* H. Clepper, ed. *Black bass biology and management.* Washington, D.C.: Sport Fish. Inst.

Vrijenhoek, R. C. 1978. Coexistence of clones in the heterogeneous environment. *Science* 199: 549–552.

Vrijenhoek, R. C. 1994. Unisexual fish: model systems for studying ecology and evolution. *Ann. Rev. Ecol. Syst.* 25:71–96

Walburg, C. H. 1971. Loss of young fish in reservoir discharge and year-class survival, Lewis and Clark Lake, Missouri River. Pages 441–448 *in* G. E. Hall, ed. *Reservoir fisheries and limnology.* Amer. Fish. Soc. Spec. Publ. 8.

Walker, B. W. 1960. The distribution and affinities of the marine fish fauna of the Gulf of California. *Syst. Zool.* 9(3–4):123–133.

Walker, B. W. 1966. The origins and affinities of the Galapagos shore fishes. Pages 172–174 *in*

R. I. Bowman, ed. *The Galapagos.* Berkeley: Univ. of Calif. Press.

Walker, M. W., Kirschvinke, J. L., Chang, S. R., and Dizon, A. E. 1984. A candidate magnetic sense organ in the yellowfin tuna, *Thunnus albacares. Science* 224:751–753.

Walls, G. L. 1942. *The vertebrate eye and its adaptive radiation.* Bloomfield Hills, Mich.: Cranbrook Inst. Sci.

Walsh, W. J. 1983. Stability of a coral reef fish community following a catastrophic storm. *Coral Reefs* 2:49–63.

Walters, V. 1955. Fishes of western arctic America and eastern arctic Siberia. *Bull. Amer. Mus. Nat. Hist.* 106(5):255–368.

Wardle, C. S. 1971. New observations on the lymph system of the plaice *Pleuronectes platessa* and other teleosts. *J. Mar. Biol. Ass. U.K.* 51: 977–990.

Wardle, C. S. 1975. Limits of fish swimming. *Nature* 255:725–727.

Wardle, C. S., and Reid, A. 1977. The application of large-amplitude elongated body theory to measure swimming power in fish. Pages 171–191 *in* J. H. Steel, ed. *Fisheries mathematics.* London: Academic Press.

Ware, D. M., and Thomson, R. E. 1991. Link between long-term variability in upwelling and fish production in the northeast Pacific ocean. *Can. J. Fish. Aquat. Sci.* 48:2296–2306.

Warner, R. R. 1982. Mating systems, sex change, and sexual demography in the rainbow wrasse, *Thalassoma lucasanum. Copeia* 1982: 653–661.

Warner, R. R., and Robertson, D. R. 1978. Sexual patterns in the labroid fishes of the western Caribbean. I. The wrasses (Labridae). *Smithson. Contrib. Zool.* 254:1–27.

Watson, L. J., Schechmeister, I. L., and Jackson, L. L. 1963. The hematology of goldfish (*Carassius auratus). Cytologia* 28:118–130.

Webb, P. W. 1971. The swimming energetics of trout. I. Thrust and power at cruising speeds. *J. Exp. Biol.* 55:489–500.

Webb, P. W. 1975a. Hydrodynamics and energetics of fish propulsion. *Bull. Fish. Res. Bd. Canada* 190:1–159.

Webb, P. W. 1975b. Acceleration performance of

rainbow trout *(Salmo gairdneri)* and green sunfish *(Lepomis cyanellus). J. Exp. Biol.* 63:451–465.

Webb, P. W. 1978a. Fast-start performance and body form in seven species of teleost fish. *J. Exp. Biol.* 74:211–226.

Webb, P. W. 1978b. Temperature effects on acceleration of rainbow trout, *Salmo gairdneri. J. Fish. Res. Bd. Can.* 35:1417–1422.

Webb, P. W., and Brett, J. R. 1972. The effects of sublethal concentration of whole bleached kraftmill effluent on the growth and food conversion efficiency of underyearling sockeye salmon *(Onchorhynchus nerka). J. Fish. Res. Bd. Canada* 29:1555–1563.

Webb, P. W., and Weihs, D. 1983. *Fish biomechanics.* New York: Praeger Publ. 398 pp.

Webber, R. E., Wells, R. M. G., and Rossetti, J. E. 1983. Allosteric interactions governing oxygen equilibria in the haemoglobin system of the spring dogfish, *Squalus acanthias. J. Exp. Biol.* 103:109–120.

Weber, D. D., and Ridgway, G. J. 1962. The deposition of tetracycline drugs on bones and scales of fish and its possible use for marking. *Prog. Fish. Cult.* 24:150–155.

Weber, D. D., and DeWilde, J. A. M. 1975. Oxygenation properties of haemoglobins from the flatfish plaice *(Pleuronectes platessa)* and flounder *(Platichthys flesus). J. Comp. Physiol.* 128:127–137.

Weber, R. E. 1990. Functional significance and structural basis of multiple hemoglobins with special reference to exothermic vertebrates. *Comp. Physiol.* 6:58–75.

Weber, R. E., and Lykkeboe, G. 1978. Respiratory adaptations in carp blood: influences of hypoxia, red blood cell organic phosphates, divalent cations, and CO_2 on hemoglobin-oxygen affinity. *J. Comp. Physiol.* 128:127–137.

Weihs, D. 1973. Hydromechanics of fish schooling. *Nature* 24(5387):290–291.

Weihs, D. 1974. Energetic advantages of burst swimming of fish. *J. Theoret. Biol.* 48:215–229.

Weiner, G. S., Shreck, C. R., and Li, H. W. 1986. Effects of low pH on reproduction in rainbow trout. *Trans. Amer. Fish. Soc.* 115:75–82.

Weinreb, E. L. 1958. Studies on the histology and

histopathology of the rainbow trout, *Salmo gairdneri iridius.* I. Haematology under normal and experimental conditions of inflammation. *Zoologica* 43:145–154.

Weinreb, E. L., and Weinreb, S. 1969. A study of experimentally induced endocytosis in a teleost. I. Light microscopy of peripheral blood cell response. *Zoologica* 54:25–34.

Welcomme, R. L. 1967. The relationship between fecundity and fertility in the mouthbrooding cichlid, *Tilapia leucosticta. J. Zool. Lond.* 151:453–468.

Welcomme, R. L. 1985. River fisheries. *FAO Fish. Tech. Pap.* 262: 330 pp.

Wells, L. 1968. Seasonal depth distribution of fish in southeastern Lake Michigan. *NOAA Fish. Bull.* 67(1):1–15.

Wells, L. 1970. Effects of alewife predation on zooplankton populations in Lake Michigan. *Limnol. Oceanogr.* 15(4):556–565.

Wendt, C. A. G., and Saunders, R. L. 1973. Changes in carbohydrate metabolism in young Atlantic salmon in response to various forms of stress. Pages 55–82 *in* M.W. Smith and W.M. Carter, ed. *Proceedings of the International Symposium on the Atlantic Salmon: management, biology and survival of the species.* Frederiction, N.B.: Unipress.

Wendelaar Bonga, S. E., Flik, G., Löwik, C. W. G. M., and Van Eyes, G. J. J. M. 1985. Environmental control of prolactin synthesis in the teleost fish *Oreochromis* (formerly *Sarotherodon) mossambicus. Gen. Comp. Endocr.* 57:352–359.

Werner, E. E., and Hall, D. J. 1974. Optimal foraging and the size selection of prey by the bluegill sunfish *(Lepomis macrochirus). Ecology* 55:1042–1052.

Werner, E. E., and Hall, D. J. 1976. Niche shifts in sunfishes: experimental evidence and significance. *Science* 191:404–406.

Werner, E. E., Hall, D. J., Laughlin, D. R., Wagner, D. J., Wilsmann, L. A., and Funk, F. C. 1977. Habitat partitioning in a freshwater fish community. *J. Fish. Res. Bd. Canada* 34(3):360–370.

Werns, S., and Howland, H. C. 1976. Size and allometry of the saccular air bladder of *Gnathonemus petersi* (Pisces, Mormyridae):

implications for hearing. *Copeia* 1976(1): 200–202.

Westby. G. W. M. 1988. The ecology, discharge activity, and predatory behavior of gymnotiform electric fish in the coastal streams of French Guiana. *Behav. Ecol. Sociobiol.* 22:341–354.

Westoll, T. S. 1949. On the evolution of the Dipnoi. Pages 121–184 *in* G. L. Jepsen et al. *Genetics, paleontology, and evolution*, Princeton: Princeton Univ. Press.

Wheeler, A. 1979. *The tidal Thames: a history of a river and its fishes.* London: Routledge and Kegan Paul.

White, B. N. 1986. The isthmian line, antitropicality and American biogeography: distributional history of the Atherinopsinae (Pisces: Atherinidae). *Syst. Zool.* 35:176–194

Whitfield, A. K. 1994. Fish species diversity in southern African estuaries: an evolutionary perspective. *Env. Biol. Fish.* 40:37–90.

Wickler, W. 1968. *Mimicry in plants and animals.* New York: McGraw-Hill. 255 pp.

Wiebe, W. J., Johannes, R. E., and Webb, K. L. 1975. Nitrogen fixation in a coral reef community. *Science* 188:257–259.

Wikramanayake, E. D., and Moyle, P. B. 1989. Ecological structure of tropical fish assemblages in wet-zone streams of Sri Lanka. *J. Zool. London* 218:503–526.

Wiley, B., and Collette, B. 1970. Breeding tubercles and contact organs in fishes: their occurrence, structure, and significance. *Bull. Amer. Mus. Nat. Hist.* 143(3):145–216.

Wiley, E. O. 1978. The evolutionary species concept reconsidered. *Syst. Zool.* 27:17–26.

Williams, G. C. 1966. *Adaptation and natural selection.* Princeton: Princeton Univ. Press. 307 pp.

Williams, G. C. 1975. *Sex and evolution.* Monogr. Pop. Biol. 8, Princeton Univ. 200 pp.

Williams, J. E. et al. 1989. Fishes of North America: endangered, threatened, or of special concern, 1989. *Fisheries* 14:2–20.

Wilson, E. O. 1975. *Sociobiology.* Cambridge: Harvard Univ. Press.

Wilson, M. H. V., and Caldwell, M. D.. 1993. New Silurian and Devonian fork-tailed "thelodonts" are jawless vertebrates with stomachs and deep bodies. *Nature* 361:442–444.

Wilson, R., and Wilson, J. Q. 1985. *Watching fishes: life and behavior on coral reefs.* New York: Harper and Row.

Winemiller, K. O. 1990. Spatial and temporal variation in tropical fish trophic networks. *Ecol. Monogr.* 60:331–367.

Winfield, I. J., and Nelson, J. S. 1991. *Cyprinid fishes: systematics, biology, and exploitation.* New York: Chapman and Hall. 667 pp.

Winterbottom, R., and Emery, A. R. 1981. A new genus and two new species of gobiid fishes (Perciformes) from the Chagos Archipelago, central Indian Ocean. *Env. Biol. Fish.* 6: 139–149.

Wintrobe, M. M. 1934. Variations in the size and hemoglobin content of erythrocytes in the blood of various vertebrates. *Folia Heamat., Lpz.* 51:32–49.

Wirgin, I. I., and Waldman, J. R.. 1994. What DNA can do for you. *Fisheries* (Bethesda) 19 (7):16–27.

Wittenberg, J. B., and Haedrich, R. L. 1974. The choroid rete mirabile of the fish eye. II. Distribution and relation to the pseudobranch and to the swimbladder rete mirabile. *Biol. Bull.* 145:137–156.

Wittenberg, J. B., and Wittenberg, V. A. 1962. Active secretion of oxygen into the eye of the fish. *Nature* 194:106–107.

Wohlschlag, D. E. 1960. Metabolism of the antarctic fish and the phenomenon of cold adaptation. *Ecology* 41:287–292.

Wohlschlag, D. E. 1961. Growth in antarctic fish at freezing temperatures. *Copeia* 1961 (1):11–18.

Wohlschlag, D. E., Cameron, J. N., and Cech, J. J., Jr. 1968. Seasonal changes in the respiratory metabolism of the pinfish (*Lagodon rhomboides*). *Contr. Mar. Sci.* 13:89–104.

Wohlschlag, D. E., and Wakeman, J. M. 1978. Salinity stresses, metabolic responses, and distribution of the coastal spotted seatrout, *Cynoscion nebulosus. Contr. Mar. Sci.* 21:173–185.

Wood, C. M. 1993. Ammonia and urea metabolism and excretion. Pages 379–425 *in* D.H. Evans, ed. *The physiology of fishes.* Boca Raton: CRC Press.

Wood, C. M., and Marshall, W. S. 1994. Ion balance, acid-base regulation, and chloride cell function in the common killifish, *Fundulus heteroclitus*—a euryhaline estuarine teleost. *Estuaries* 17(1A):34–52.

Wood, C. M., Perry, S. F., Wright, P. A., Bergman, H. L., and Randall, D. J. 1989. Ammonia and urea dynamics in the Lake Magadi tilapia, a ureotelic teleost fish adapted to an extremely alkaline environment. *Resp. Physiol.* 77:1–20.

Wood, C. M., and Shelton, G. 1975. Physical and adrenergic factors affecting systemic vascular resistance in the rainbow trout: a comparison with branchial vascular resistance. *J. Exp. Biol.* 63:505–523.

Wood, S. C., Johansen, K., and Weber, R. E. 1972. Haemoglobin of the coelacanth. *Nature* 239: 283–285.

Woodward, J. J., and Smith, I. S. 1985. Exercise training and the stress response in rainbow trout, *Salmo gairdneri* Richardson. *J. Fish Biol.* 26:435–447.

Wootton, J. T., and Oemke, M. P. 1992. Latitudinal differences in fish community trophic structure and the role of herbivory in a Costa Rican stream. *Env. Biol. Fish.* 35:311–319.

Wooten, R. J. 1973. The effect of size of food ration on egg production in the female threespined stickleback. *J. Fish Biol.* 5:89–96.

Wooten, R. J. 1977. *The biology of sticklebacks.* New York: Academic Press. 388 pp.

Wooton, R. J. 1984. *A functional biology of sticklebacks.* London: Croom Helm.

Wooton, R. J. 1990. Ecology of teleost fishes. Chapman and Hall, London. 404 pp.

Wourms, J. P. 1977. Reproduction and development in chondrichthyan fishes. *Amer. Zool.* 17(2):379–410.

Wourms, J. P. 1981. Viviparity: the maternal-fetal relationship in fishes. *Amer. Zool.* 21:473–515.

Wourms, J. P, 1993. Maximization of evolutionary trends for placental viviparity in the Atlantic sharpnose shark, *Scolidon laticaudus*. *Env. Biol. Fish.* 38:269–294.

Wourms, J. P., and Demski, L. S., eds. 1993. The reproduction and development of sharks, skates, rays, and ratfishes. *Env. Biol. Fish.* 38. 294 pp.

Wurtsbaugh, W. A., and Cech, J. J., Jr. 1983.

Growth and activity of juvenile mosquitofish: temperature and ration effects. *Trans. Am. Fish. Soc.* 112:653–660.

Wurtsbaugh, W. A., and Neverman, D. 1988. Postfeeding thermotaxis and daily vertical migration in a larval fish. *Nature* 333:846–848.

Wurtsbaugh, W. A., and Tapia, R. A. 1988. Mass mortality of fishes in Lake Titicaca (Peru-Bolivia) associated with the protozoan parasite *Ichthyophthirius multifilis*. *Trans. Amer. Fish. Soc.* 117:213–17.

Wu, T. Y., and Yates, G. T. 1978. A comparative mechanophysiological study of fish locomotion with implications for tuna-like swimming mode. Pages 313–337 *in* G. Sharp and A. E. Dizon, eds. *The physiological ecology of tunas.* New York: Academic Press.

Yancey, P. H., and Somero, G. N. 1980. Methylamine osmoregulatory solutes of elasmobranch fishes counteract urea inhibition of enzymes. *J. Exp. Zool.* 212:205–213.

Yant, P. R., Karr, J. R., and Angermeier, P. L. 1984. Stochasticity in stream fish communities: an alternative interpretation. *Amer. Nat.* 124: 573–582.

Yoshiyama, R. M. 1981. Distribution and abundance patterns of rocky intertidal fishes in central California. *Env. Biol.Fish.* 6:315–332.

Yoshiyama, R. M., and Cech, J. J, Jr. 1994. Aerial respiration by rocky intertidal fishes of California and Oregon. *Copeia* 1994(1): 153–158.

Young, G. C. 1986. The relationships of placoderm fishes. *Zool. J. Linn Soc.* 88:1–57.

Young, P. S., and Cech, J. J., Jr. 1993a. Improved growth, swimming performance, and muscular development in exercise-conditioned young-of-the-year striped bass (*Morone saxatilis*). *Can. J. Fish. Aquat. Sci.* 50:703–707.

Young, P. S., and Cech, J. J., Jr. 1993b. Effects of exercise conditioning on stress responses and recovery in cultured and wild young-of-the-year striped bass, *Morone saxatilis*. *Can. J. Fish. Aquat. Sci.* 50:2094–2099.

Young, P. S., and Cech, J. J., Jr. 1994. Optimum exercise conditioning velocity for growth, muscular development, and swimming performance in young-of-the-year striped bass,

(Morone saxatilis). Can. J. Fish. Aquat. Sci. 51:1519–1527.

Young, W. D., and Oglesby, R. T. 1972. Cayuga Lake: effects of exploitation and introductions on the salmonid community. *J. Fish. Res. Bd. Canada* 29(6):787–794.

Zakaria-Ismail, M. 1994. Zoogeography and biodiversity of the freshwater fishes of Southeast Asia. *Hydrobiologia* 285:41–48.

Zaret, T. M. 1972. Predators, invisible prey, and the nature of polymorphism in the Cladocera (Class Crustacea). *Limnol. Oceanog.* 17(2): 171–184.

Zaret, T. M. 1977. Inhibition of cannibalism in *Cichla ocellaris* and hypothesis of predator mimicry among South American fishes. *Evolution* 31(2):421–437.

Zaret, T. M., and Paine, R. T. 1973. Species introduction in a tropical lake. *Science* 182: 421–437.

Zhadin, V. I., and Gerd, S. V. 1961. *Fauna and flora of the lakes and reservoirs of the U.S.S.R.* Jerusalem: Israel Prog. Sci. Trans. 626 pp.

Zyznar, E. S., and Nicol, J. A. C. 1973. Reflecting materials in the eyes of three teleosts, *Orthopristes chrysopterus, Dorosoma cepedianum,* and *Anchoa mitchilli. Proc. Royal Soc. London B.* 184:15–27.

Index